MOVER AND SHAKER

MOVER AND SHAKER

Walter O'Malley, the Dodgers,
& Baseball's Westward Expansion

Andy McCue

University of Nebraska Press | Lincoln and London

Acknowledgments for the use of
copyrighted material appear on page
359, which constitutes an extension
of the copyright page. All rights
reserved. Manufactured in the
United States of America

⊗

Library of Congress Cataloging-in-
Publication Data

McCue, Andy.
Mover and shaker: Walter O'Malley,
the Dodgers, and baseball's
westward expansion / Andy McCue.
pages   cm
Includes bibliographical references
and index.
ISBN 978-0-8032-4508-2 (cloth: alk.
paper)
— ISBN 978-0-8032-5506-7 (epub)
— ISBN 978-0-8032-5507-4 (mobi)
— ISBN 978-0-8032-5505-0 (pdf)
1. O'Malley, Walter F. (Walter
Frank), 1903–1979. 2. Baseball
team owners—United States—
Biography. 3. Brooklyn Dodgers
(Baseball team) 4. Los Angeles
Dodgers (Baseball team) I. Title.

GV865.O63M44 2014
796.357092—dc23
[B]   2013046057

Set in Ehrhardt by Renni Johnson.
Designed by A. Shahan.

To Bernadette Kenney McCue and Seanacchie Kenney Jackie Robinson McCue, because I promised them after the first book. And to Mary Colleen Kenney, for always and everything.

Contents

ILLUSTRATIONS

Acknowledgments

In twenty years of research and writing, you can run up a lot of debts to a lot of people. I hope I remember them all. Some of these people have moved on, but I'll describe them as they were when they helped me.

Librarians and archivists, whose professionalism, knowledge of their holdings, and insistence on my being precise were of immeasurable help.

Tom Heitz, Tim Wiles, and the staff of the National Baseball Hall of Fame Library in Cooperstown.

Steve Gietschier of the *Sporting News*.

Wayne Wilson, Shirley Ito, Michael Salmon, and the staff at the LA84 Foundation Library in Los Angeles.

Dave Kelly and the staff of the Manuscripts Division at the Library of Congress.

Jim Thompson and the staff at the Tomas Rivera Library at the University of California, Riverside.

Bob Timmermann and staff at the Los Angeles Public Library.

Judith Walsh in the History Division of the Brooklyn Public Library.

The interlibrary loan staff at Riverside City and County Library's main branch.

Staff, especially in the History and Genealogy Room, at the Indian River County Public Library, Vero Beach, Florida.

Bill Marshall, archivist of the Happy Chandler Papers at the University of Kentucky Library, Lexington.

Ryan Janda and the folks at the University of Pennsylvania Archives.

Allen Loehr at the Culver Academy Alumni Office.

My colleagues at the Society for American Baseball Research (SABR), who have been generous with their time, help, opinions, fact-checking, and tips. In roughly chronological order they are: Matt Kachur, Bob Bluthardt,

Bobby Plapinger, Dick Beverage, Joe Murphy, Steve Milman, Greg King, Jim Kreuz, Allan Roth and the SABR members (David Stephan, Chuck Carey, Sam James, et al.) who worked so hard to save his papers, Mark Armour, John Pastier, Peter Morris, Gary Gillette, Dan Levitt, Anthony Giacalone, Eric Thompson, and Jim Gordon.

Other authors who have trod, or are treading, the same or similar ground. Their published work and subsequent conversations have been invaluable whether we agreed or not: Neil Sullivan (who also provided a free bed for a week's worth of New York research), Lee Lowenfish, Chuck Korr, Bob McGee, Michael Shapiro, and Rob Garratt. Also, to Henry Fetter, whom I've never met, but whose *Taking on the Yankees* provided excellent analysis.

Professionals met along the way included Tony Biesada of Pfizer, Inc.; Shirley Jobe of the *Boston Globe*; Dr. Francis Carney; Larry Reisman, editor of the *Vero Beach (FL) Press-Journal*; architect and stadium critic Phil Bess; and journalists Leonard Koppett and Jerome Holtzman.

Friends (also chronological): Marty Beiser (including another week of free bed), Michael Hazen, Mel Opotowsky, Rosalind Smith, George Valencia, Roger Repohl, and Jean Ardell.

Blessings be upon Retrosheet.org (Dave Smith, Tom Ruane, Dave Vincent, et al.) and Baseballreference.com (Sean Forman and staff), who have made so much fact-checking an absolute breeze.

Gabriella Salvatore and Debra Fram, who gave permission for the use of Boris Chaliapin's portrait of O'Malley that appears on the dust jacket.

Rob Taylor, Courtney Ochsner, Ann Baker, Annette Wenda, Acacia Gentrup, and all at the University of Nebraska Press.

My family, above all the beautiful and talented Mary Colleen Kenney, for patience and support. My mother who, despite living nine decades in New York and Los Angeles and having never attended a game, or caring about one, still asked every week how the book was coming.

And all of you people I forgot but should have mentioned.

Introduction | Hitler, Stalin, Walter O'Malley

Jack Newfield told of the time he was having dinner with Pete Hamill, another Brooklyn-born luminary of the New York literary scene. "We began to joke about collaborating on an article called, 'The Ten Worst Human Beings Who Ever Lived.' And I said to Pete, 'Let's try an experiment. You write on your napkin the names of the three worst human beings who ever lived, and I will write the three worst, and we'll compare.' Each of us wrote down the same three names in the same order: Hitler, Stalin, Walter O'Malley."[1] It was a tale often repeated down the years, eliciting gleeful approval from diehard Brooklyn fans and an uneasy feeling about perspective from others. By the most recent accounting, Adolf Hitler killed 11 million people and Joseph Stalin murdered 6 million.[2] O'Malley moved a baseball team.

Walter O'Malley has been defined in great part by a group with large reason to hate him—the fans of the baseball team he moved from Brooklyn to Los Angeles and the newspaper reporters who covered that team. Given the number of Brooklynites in the 1950s, it was inevitable that some of them became very talented polemicists. As new generations of reporters and fans came along, the caricature had been defined.

Through the early 1950s Walter O'Malley would generally be presented positively by New York writers, who found him refreshing after Branch Rickey. But with his decision to transplant the Brooklyn Dodgers to Los Angeles, all that changed. More than twenty years later, he was "a political wheeler-dealer, a smoker of big, long cigars, a man who had greased the way for the exile of Branch Rickey to Pittsburgh. A roly-poly type, his thick eyebrows and accentuated speech pattern suggested the kind of person who would foreclose mortgage payments on a widow and four children."[3]

"Greedy" would almost become part of his name for the New York partisans. It was not only journalists such as Dick Young of the *Daily News*. It was professors writing for an academic audience.[4] In articles and books, the caricature would be reaffirmed.

It was in part the tyranny of "the clips." News organizations all keep records of what they have reported. In Walter O'Malley's day, news organizations meant newspapers, and their librarians clipped out copies of all the day's stories and sorted them by topic into manila folders. The manila folders were known as "the clips." If something was in there, you could trust it, because it had been printed and had not drawn a squawk big enough to cause a correction. Otherwise, the correction would be in the manila folder as well.

To Walter O'Malley, correcting a reporter's facts was less important than keeping a good relationship with the team's major source of free publicity. Reporters who covered the Dodgers said he would argue with them about the tone or thrust of a story, especially in the early years, but rarely disputed factual inaccuracies, unless they touched on some hot button such as profits. Keeping reporters in the proper frame of mind was more important than a misunderstood anecdote. Fred Claire, a Dodgers public relations type in the 1960s and 1970s, recalled taking what he thought was an unfair newspaper portrayal to O'Malley's office. "Fred," he recalled the owner saying, "never stop to get into a tiff. Keep the big picture in mind."[5]

Thus, many "facts" about Walter O'Malley were reported again and again. Even the most respected newspapers in the business would repeat incorrect information. The *Los Angeles Times*, *New York Times*, *New York Daily News*, and *Sporting News* all had mistakes in their obituaries, either from "the clips" or from Walter O'Malley's entry in *Who's Who in America*.[6] Subsequent descriptions of O'Malley would pick up information from these stories, and new links in the chain of "facts" would be forged.

It is not like O'Malley was blameless in this process. "Remember," Walter O'Malley said to Roger Kahn, "only half the lies the Irish tell are true."[7] Like his entry in *Who's Who*, a good deal of the erroneous information about O'Malley came from himself. Maybe he was blatantly gilding things, or maybe he implied something and let the reporter gild it for him.

For that reason this book has a lot of endnotes. I believe everything in this book is either a fact, or, if it isn't, you can figure out where I found it. If it is an opinion, you will know where I found that. The book is also full of endnotes because people I wished to interview deferred to the O'Malley family's desires. I spoke with Walter's children, Peter O'Malley and his sister, Terry Seidler, near the beginning of my research and asked for their cooperation. They declined, which is their privilege. But, I discovered, quite a number of people with ties to Walter O'Malley's story remain connected to the Dodgers or the family. When I called for an interview, they checked with Peter, and, according to several, Peter asked them not to talk to me. Most did not. The book is poorer for that.

To the outside world Walter O'Malley remained opaque. Roger Kahn described him as "an earth force lightly filtered through a personality."[8] In public he could be a backslapper. He loved a drink and a party but he never seemed to get drunk, and many who worked for and against him could not figure out what made him tick. His personal papers have never been fully made public, and the one author who has seen more than anyone else also remarked on how few things in the papers revealed the inner man.[9]

Even in baseball circles he was not the typical executive. He was a businessman, not someone who had grown up in the game or migrated from the field to the front office. He had barely played, even as a boy. He had become a season ticket holder only when it made business sense. He came to baseball as a lawyer with experience resurrecting troubled businesses.

Why a biography of O'Malley? Because he changed the game, from a parochial midsize business anchored in the Northeast United States to a national, and then an international, game earning and spending billions. In December 1999, as news organizations looked back on the twentieth century, the *Sporting News* named him the eleventh most powerful person in sports for the era. ABC Sports said he was the eighth most powerful off-the-field sports figure of the century. Marvin Miller, his intellectual opponent and sometime friend, called him "the most rational businessman I know."[10]

By 1957, when the Dodgers moved west, the Boston Braves (to Milwaukee), the St. Louis Browns (to Baltimore), and the Philadelphia Athletics (to Kansas City) had already moved. Horace Stoneham took his New York Giants to San Francisco the same time O'Malley moved the Dodgers. In the next few years, the Braves moved again, this time to Atlanta. The expansion Seattle Pilots traveled to Milwaukee after one year of incompetence on and off the field, in part to resolve a lawsuit caused by the Braves' departure for Atlanta. The Kansas City Athletics went to Oakland. The Washington Senators moved to Minneapolis–St. Paul. The team that replaced them, also called the Washington Senators, moved to Dallas–Fort Worth.

Only the most dedicated baseball fans could name the owners of these teams. But you have heard of Walter O'Malley. Books have been written condemning him. His name is a curse on the lips of many New Yorkers. Even people in Los Angeles view him with cynicism as the man who opened a brand-new stadium without drinking fountains to encourage sales of beer and soft drinks.

Why the difference? Why are Lou Perini, Bob Short, and William Daley known only to a small baseball-saturated audience, while Walter O'Malley can cause lips to curl and fingers to point on both coasts? Unlike the others Walter O'Malley was making a lot of money when he moved. He played his cards close to the vest and left many in New York believing he had no real intention of staying in Brooklyn. His professed desire to remain in New York, they say, was no more than a man attempting to up the ante from Los Angeles.

Perhaps more important, O'Malley's move was a sign that New York's reign as the unchallenged first city of the country, indeed of the world, might be in doubt. The team was lost from a satellite part of the city, but it was lost to a city challenging New York in size and importance to the country. The team was lost, in major part, because the byzantine politics of New York City could not broker an issue that was of paramount importance to one geographical subunit and of minimal interest to the others.

Although the move from New York is the ball bearing on which most people's knowledge of Walter O'Malley's life turns, there was much more to the man. He was a major force in moving Major League Baseball (MLB) from a group of sixteen teams clustered in the Northeast and encrusted in the business practices of the turn of the century to an international grouping of twenty-six franchises, competing fiercely for entertainment dollars and constantly searching for new ways to sell the product. He was a hard-headed businessman in a world of economic playboys more interested in baubles or ways to get their very rich names into the papers.

For almost three decades he was the most influential man in the game, although he did not always get his way. As such he was the man who sat at the table while television began to dictate to the game, from longer breaks between innings for more commercials to night games at the World Series. He was there for three rounds of expansion, the institution of the amateur draft, the split into divisions, and the creation of multiple rounds of playoffs.

When he entered the game teams controlled players' contracts like so many medieval serfs, whose average salary was about $13,000 a year. When he died players were much closer to freedom, and the enormous increase in their salaries reflected that; the average salary was now around $180,000. Walter O'Malley's organization was the one that handed Miller the chisel he used to pry open the vault of free agency.

All this became part of the collective portrait of a man who is often caricatured as a greedy, fat, grinning, cigar-twirling Scrooge McDuck. He was occasionally all of those things, but he was never that caricature. A more sympathetic cartoonist would have painted a generous, benevolent, charming, thoughtful man who was above all concerned about his family, for, at times, he was all of those as well.

He was a man whose hard-hearted ways were a byword. He was a man who ignored his father's orders not to marry the girl next door after cancer forced the removal of her larynx, and thus her voice. He was a man who traded Maury Wills for defying an order. He was a man who employed Roy Campanella for life after the veteran catcher was crippled in an auto accident. He was a man who knew everybody who counted in New York and couldn't get what he wanted. He was a man who complained he couldn't figure out who the boss was in Los Angeles and got everything he dreamed of.

MOVER AND SHAKER

1

From County Mayo to Montague Street

The O'Malley family in America is a chronicle of the American dream—following a distinctly Irish path from potato famine to immigrant laborer to middling civil servant to political power and then business success over four generations. But with a spotty group of public documents and a collection of suspect reminiscences, reconstructing the details of O'Malley's family and early career is problematic.

In Walter O'Malley's telling, family history started with his paternal grandfather, Thomas. Walter O'Malley told many a reporter that Thomas had been born in Ireland and immigrated to the United States.[1] But Thomas told census takers in 1880 and 1900 that he was born in New York in 1854. Thomas's father, John, was the real immigrant. He apparently immigrated about the time of the great Irish potato famine of the late 1840s. Born in 1835, he first appeared as a laborer in the 1860 census in Brooklyn, married to Margaret, a dressmaker, and father to seven-year-old Thomas.

Both John and Margaret had been born in Ireland, but exactly when they came and whether they married before or after they immigrated remains unclear.[2] The O'Malleys came from County Mayo, pronounced "may-YO!" by the Irish. County Mayo is in the far northwest corner of Ireland, part of Connaught, the poorest of Ireland's four great divisions. In the mid-nineteenth century, it was the poorest, most backward area of a poor, backward English colony. Substantial numbers of Mayo people had not forsaken Irish for English, and the potato provided almost the entire diet of an estimated 90 percent of the people.[3] There are a lot of O'Malleys in Connaught, and during the decade that covered the potato famine, County Mayo's population fell 29 percent.

It was Thomas who began to establish a trail that can be followed. He fathered more than a dozen children with one wife who outlived him. He worked his way up the postal service, despite some apparent trouble over union organizing, and died when his grandson was fourteen. Thomas first surfaced in the New York City directories of 1876, which listed him living at 49 Gouverneur in Lower Manhattan and working as a carrier with the post office. His wife, Georgiana, also born in 1854, first appears in the 1880 census, and they had moved a couple of blocks away to 382 Madison with their oldest son, Frank, then four.

Georgiana's background is about as obscure as Thomas's. Her maiden name was Reynolds, and although she told census takers her mother was born in Ireland, she told them her father was born in either Vermont (1880 census) or Maine (1900 census). Her death certificate would list her father's birthplace as New York City.

Wherever her father was born, it was an anomaly for the neighborhood around Madison Street. This is not the glamorous Madison Avenue of twentieth-century Manhattan, but a six-block side street on the Lower East Side. There are fifty people listed on the 1880 census page, which includes Thomas, Georgiana, and Frank O'Malley. Forty-eight of those people said both of their parents were born in Ireland. Only Georgiana and Frank could not make that claim.

It was the same neighborhood that would produce future New York governor and presidential candidate Al Smith, before becoming a Jewish enclave after the turn of the twentieth century. Near the docks, the area had been a first stop for immigrants for as long as they had been coming to New York. The neighborhood survived on two institutions—the Catholic church and Tammany Hall. The church, generally staffed by fellow Irish immigrants, provided the new Americans with education, social structure, and some connection with the lives they had left behind. Tammany Hall offered financial aid, mediation with the strange authorities of the New World, and help in finding work, all for just the price of a vote or three on election day.

Tammany Hall had been founded as a patriotic and social club in 1788. Its early membership leaned to artisans and other small businesspeople. These groups tended to be in political opposition to the wealthier classes, who clustered around Alexander Hamilton, John Adams, and others of the Federalist Party. As such, Tammany members migrated toward the supporters of Thomas Jefferson, and thus to the Democratic Party. By the 1870s, when Thomas O'Malley was reaching adulthood, Tammany Hall dominated the Democratic Party in New York City. In 1871 "Honest"

John Kelly, the first Irish American head of Tammany, had taken office in the wake of the scandals brought on by William "Boss" Tweed, the last of the non-Irish bosses.

In Kelly's system, each of Manhattan's wards had its boss, supported by squads of lieutenants down to the block level who provided help when it was deemed needed. The system was designed to make the bosses rich, and it usually did, but it also eased the transition for immigrants often living on the financial edge. If a fire burned out a tenement, the boss was expected to be on the scene as soon as the fire engines, dispensing blankets, finding shelter, and organizing donations to replace the personal property lost to the fire. The boss was expected to toss a big annual picnic, providing all the food anybody could want plus plenty of liquor for the men, candy for the children, and gifts for the women.[4]

The biggest carrot the bosses offered, however, was jobs. The ward boss had both jobs in his own ward and portions of those allotted to his bosses higher up the Tammany chain. The city was growing rapidly all through the nineteenth and early twentieth centuries. A rapidly growing city needed sewers, bridges, roads, firehouses, and other public buildings. A boss would ensure that a crony got the construction contract in return for a kickback. Boss and crony would ensure that the construction jobs went to men of the proper political loyalties. The boss also had government jobs to hand out, in his ward, in citywide institutions such as the police and fire departments, and in some federal jobs, such as the postal service.

Still, the Fourth Ward was not an easy place to get out of. Maybe it was the babies. At the 1900 census, when she was forty-six, Georgiana said she had had nineteen children, eleven of whom were still alive, a not unusual mortality rate for that time, that neighborhood, and that poverty level.[5] After Frank's birth in 1876 there had not been another survivor until Grace in 1881. Thereafter, they came more regularly. Edwin, Walter's father, was next, followed by Mabel in 1885, Leonard in 1886, and Arthur in 1889. Postal carriers such as Thomas made between $800 and $1,000 a year, a middle-class wage in this period, but Arthur made eight mouths to feed and more on the way.[6]

Walter O'Malley told two different versions of what got Thomas off Madison Street. In one Thomas was transferred to San Francisco in 1890 to be postmaster of a world exposition.[7] In another he was exiled from New York for trying to organize a union among postal workers in Brooklyn.[8] Another telling of the tale mentioned both reasons for the move.[9]

The 1900 census records narrow the story a bit. They show Thomas and Georgiana's daughter Agnes was born in New York in September 1891, while their son Joseph was born in California in October 1893.[10] Another daughter, Estella, was born fifteen months later back in New York. These dates jibe with the California Midwinter International Exposition, held in San Francisco's Golden Gate Park during the first half of 1894. The exposition, which 2.5 million people paid to see, would have generated a significant amount of mail traffic from the tourists and locals viewing its 138 buildings, Japanese Tea Garden, and other attractions.[11] (When he got to California Walter would use Thomas's exile to establish the O'Malleys as fifth-generation Californians, stretching from Thomas's short sojourn and Uncle Joseph's birth to Walter's grandchildren.)[12] Thomas also disappeared from the 1893 New York City directory, covering mid-1893 to mid-1894.[13]

It was a time when the postal service, and the country, was undergoing a considerable amount of labor agitation. Up until 1883 postal jobs were completely political patronage. In a heavily Democratic city such as New York, Thomas's job was safe with Tammany patronage. But in 1883 the Pendleton Act made the post office subject to civil service reforms. Thomas's place was not affected, as only future employees would be subject to entrance examinations, but civil service reform had the immediate effect of eliminating politicians' interest in postal service jobs. That indifference came at a time when railroads were increasing the mail system's efficiency and Congress was lowering postal rates, leading to a boom in volume that was not balanced by a matching increase in staff or pay. Working conditions began to deteriorate. Even a decade or so after Thomas's exile, the post office continued to experience twelve-hour days six days a week, poor ventilation that bred tuberculosis, and exposed toilet facilities. Turnover was 12 percent in 1906 and 20 percent a year later.[14]

If Thomas was not a labor organizer, other people were. The National Association of Letter Carriers was founded in 1889 and the National Association of Post Office Clerks in 1890. Clerks' union organizers were suspended and fired in this period, so disciplinary action on Thomas certainly seems possible.[15]

Thomas's status is also unclear. City directories listed him as a letter carrier until 1897, when he was first listed as a clerk. Carriers delivered the letters. Clerks worked in a variety of inside jobs at the post office, from unloading bags of mail to serving customers at windows. Most supervisors, such as postmasters in San Francisco, were drawn from the ranks of clerks, and it seems unlikely the postal service would transfer someone across the country to walk a route.

Indeed, there are signs that perhaps Thomas's period in San Francisco was a promotion rather than an exile. Most notably, when he returned the O'Malleys moved off Madison Street, first to East 106th Street and then to the South Bronx in 1899, when Walter's father, Edwin, would have turned sixteen. Beginning in 1900 Thomas appeared consistently as a clerk in city directories, and the move to the Bronx was a sign of firm establishment in the middle class.

Thomas settled Georgiana and the eleven children in a rented house at 21 Ritter Place in St. Augustine's Parish. The South Bronx was then a burgeoning bedroom community on the outskirts of the city. Streetcars had reached the area by the 1890s, and the subway was on the way.[16] Thomas was making at least $1,200 s a year as a carrier, and perhaps more as he became a supervisor. The 1900 census listed him as a marine agent for the post office.

The paper trail of Edwin, Walter's father, is as spotty as Thomas's. The 1900 census said Edwin was born in July 1883, but two obituaries listed his birth date as August 23, 1883, the date the family used for a number of years.[17] There is a New York birth certificate that appears to be Edwin's. It lists an unnamed child born to Thomas and Georgiana (Reynolds) O'Malley on July 4, 1883, at 169 Madison Street. However, it lists Thomas's age as thirty-three (he, like the correctly listed Georgiana, was twenty-nine), and it lists the baby as a female.[18] Edwin muddied the waters further by listing his birth date as August 23, 1881, on his World War I military registration card and August 23, 1882, when he registered for the World War II draft, the date now used by the family's website.[19] That date does match up with calculations based on the 1920 and 1930 censuses. Walter said his father attended school in San Francisco, which is likely, as he would have been about ten at the time.[20] But by sixteen he was out in the working world, a not unusual situation for a lower-middle-class child at the turn of the twentieth century.

St. Augustine's Parish was a new world for the O'Malleys, if for no other reason than not everybody was Irish. There were German families in the neighborhood, people who had also moved to the Bronx to take advantage of the cleaner air and suburban atmosphere. One family was named Feltner. George and Dorothy (Schmaus) Feltner had been born in Germany, he in 1851, she a year later. She immigrated in 1872 and he in 1875. A year later they were married, and by 1877 George was appearing in New York

City directories as a tailor living on East Fourth Street in what is now called the East Village. He and Dorothy learned to speak, read, and write English.

Through the 1880s his address changes document a move up Manhattan Island and a move to solid middle-class status. By 1883 he was working as a tailor in what was then called Longacre Square and is now called Times Square or the Theater District. The city directories began to list him as a "merchant tailor," a man who ran his own shop and perhaps employed other tailors. He would move through three shops over the next thirty years, all of them clustered within a block of the corner of Forty-Fifth Street and Eighth Avenue. For much of the 1880s the growing Feltner family lived near his tailor shop. But by 1890 the Feltners were living on Fulton Street in St. Augustine's Parish. By 1893 they were established at 1423 Franklin Place, just across from the south side of Crotona Park and a couple of blocks from 21 Ritter Place.

The Feltners were somewhat better off than the O'Malleys. They were buying the Franklin Place house, according to the 1900 census, while the O'Malleys were renting on Ritter Place. Whereas Thomas O'Malley had a solid civil service job, George Feltner owned his own business. The Feltners had eight children, all of whom lived. In 1900 two of the Feltner boys were listed as being at "college," although one of these boys was fifteen and probably in some kind of prep school. The older Feltner girls were employed as a bookkeeper, a dressmaker, and a stenographer. Frank O'Malley, by then almost twenty-four and living at home, was working as a bookkeeper for a rubber company, and Edwin, almost seventeen, was working as a clerk in a dry goods concern. The oldest O'Malley girl, Grace, eighteen, was helping her mother at home.

The youngest of the working Feltner girls, the stenographer, was Alma, who had caught Edwin's eye. She had been born in the Longacre Square area in April 1883, a few months before Edwin. In later years Walter O'Malley would make little public mention of his mother, and there is little information to go on. Clearly, sometime around 1900 Edwin O'Malley and Alma Feltner met, although neither the city nor the parish has any record of a marriage between the two. Walter's October 9, 1903, birth date would indicate Alma became pregnant early in 1903, when she was nineteen and Edwin either nineteen or twenty. The only document that survives is an intriguing but inconclusive note in the St. Augustine's Parish register that Alma Mary O'Malley, daughter of George Feltner and Dorothy Schmaus, was given a conditional baptism on June 8, 1905.

Usually, a conditional baptism is given when there is no record of a baptism in infancy. And it is usually given because the Catholic Church needs to be sure a person is baptized before a subsequent sacrament, such as a marriage, can be performed. Interestingly, Alma's older sister Rose, by then with the Irish surname Donovan, was also given a conditional baptism on the same date by the same priest.[21] Perhaps the Feltners had not had their daughters baptized, or perhaps the records had been lost. Walter told a later interviewer that his mother came from a South German Catholic family.[22] But the conditional baptism also raises the possibility that the Feltners were originally non-Catholic and the baptism was part of a conversion process. The later baptism also raises speculation about an earlier marriage in a civil ceremony that would only later be affirmed with a church wedding.[23]

To support his young family—there would be no more children after Walter—Edwin stayed with dry goods. His business was listed as "merchant" or "cotton goods" or "salesman" over the next few years, working out of office buildings in Lower Manhattan that were full of others in the textile trades. He moved his family to a series of apartments in the South Bronx.

Sometime around 1910 he moved his family to Queens, which was replacing the Bronx as the semirural growth borough in the city.[24] They moved to a community called Hollis, almost at the edge of New York City. It was beyond Flushing Meadows and the mudflats that are now La Guardia Airport and the lowlands that housed Shea Stadium and now Citi Field. It was beyond St. John's University, another distant place that has been absorbed by the city. It was near Belmont Park Race Track, which had opened in 1903. It was the suburbs. People took the Long Island Rail Road into "the City." New streets and single-family homes sprawled across land that had recently been the cow pastures of the Skidmore farm.[25]

As a new man in a new suburb, Edwin O'Malley began to spread his wings a bit. He was a family man, nearing thirty, getting established. He began to get involved. He was a founding member and director of the Grand Street Boys Club, several times the elected chief of the Hollis Volunteer Fire Department, a member of the Woodhaven Volunteer Exempt Firemen's Association, a life member of Elks Lodge No. 878, and president of the Hollis Civic Association, which acted as a chamber of commerce and promotional group for the neighborhood.[26] He even got involved in community theatricals. At a July 4 celebration "thousands" witnessed Edwin play a Dutch farmer in a pageant portraying the purchase of the area from the Canarsie Indians. Alma was listed among those playing the "squaws."[27]

For an Irish Catholic whose father held a government job, Edwin's big commitment was as natural as breathing. He got involved in Democratic politics. In the early years of the century, lightly populated Queens was an appendage of Brooklyn, and the local party operation was called the Brooklyn Democracy. Edwin hooked up with a group of men surrounding a Brooklyn judge named John Francis Hylan.

"Red Mike" Hylan had the kind of story that appealed to voters. He had been born in upstate New York in 1868, son of an Irish immigrant who had fought in the Civil War. It was a hardscrabble life, with limited education and a lot of work around the family's heavily mortgaged farm. At fourteen he went to work on the Stony Cove, Catskill Mountain, and Kaaterskill Railroad. At nineteen he decided to try the big city, arriving in New York with $1.50 and ambition. He parlayed his railroad experience into a job with the new elevated railroad in Brooklyn and rose from track layer to fireman to engineer. But he still had the itch, and with prodding from his wife he went to a business college to make himself eligible to "read law" in the offices of a practicing attorney, the path many nineteenth-century lawyers took to the bar.

By his thirtieth birthday Hylan had begun a modest practice in Bushwick in the northern part of Brooklyn, near Queens. For twenty years he retained his modest practice and received modest returns on his interest in politics, speaking to a great many small businessmen's and taxpayers' groups, but getting no further than a judgeship. Then he made a friend of William Randolph Hearst, onetime New York congressman, publisher of the *New York Journal*, and a political manipulator with municipal and national aspirations.

Hylan and Hearst came together over the issue of public mass transit. Hylan carried a grudge from his days with the Brooklyn Rapid Transit Company and was always ready to attack the "traction interests." Hearst had taken the nickel subway fare as yet another populist issue and recognized in Hylan a highly plastic front man.[28] Hylan was a man of "marvelous mental density," note Alfred Connable and Edward Silberfarb in their history of Tammany Hall.[29]

The Brooklyn Democracy and Manhattan's Tammany Hall were uncomfortable partners in New York City Democratic politics. Brooklyn was the most populous and Manhattan the most powerful of the five boroughs that had been melded into the unified New York City in 1898. In real (i.e., political) terms, the Bronx, Queens, and Staten Island counted for little.

Tammany had its well-developed organization, the brains of Charles Francis Murphy, its current sachem, and the financial resources of being in the nation's business capital and at the center of citywide building contracts. Brooklyn had more voters, especially more Democratic voters. Hearst, a man who could finance a great number of Democratic campaigns and had his own rivalries with Murphy, and Murphy's protégé Al Smith, liked that flexible man Hylan and his attitude about transit companies.

Murphy needed a win in 1917, for New York's current mayor was of the reformist persuasion. John Purroy Mitchel, though an Irish Catholic, had embraced the ideas of the city's Protestant establishment. That had helped get him elected as a reformer, but his outspoken views that the United States should help Britain (archvillain to the city's Irish) and oppose Germany in the current Great War had alienated the two biggest ethnic voting blocs in the city. Murphy also needed to cement Tammany influence in the New York–wide Democratic Party by backing a Brooklyn candidate for mayor. Thus, Hylan rose quickly from obscurity, helped by a campaign organization that rarely let him deviate from a prepared script for fear he would say something embarrassing.[30]

Taking office in early 1918, Hylan helped those who had helped him. "His appointees, often obscure persons who had befriended him during his youth, were not well received by the press," notes the *Dictionary of American Biography*.[31] However, surrounded by enemies and opportunistic allies, Hylan felt he needed friends whose loyalty was guaranteed. Among those newly elevated to municipal office was Edwin O'Malley, who became a deputy commissioner of public markets in March 1918. He was thirty-four, and even in the context of Tammany politics, the Department of Public Markets was recognized as "a dumping ground for Tammany heelers."[32]

Edwin O'Malley and John Hylan would show a lot of mutual loyalty over the next eight years, and each would need that loyalty. Hylan's years were full of scandals, investigations of scandals, and political mudslinging. Much of this was part of the standard political calculus of New York. The state legislature generally was controlled by upstate Republicans, who ruled over their fiefdoms in much the same way their Democratic rivals did in New York City. Albany Republicans were always ready to investigate a New York City scandal for political profit. The major investigation that touched on O'Malley's office just happened to be grabbing headlines during Hylan's 1921 reelection campaign. And New York newspapers were often ready to support the investigations. Some, such as the *New York Times*, believed in the need for municipal reform. Others, such as Hearst's papers, saw it as so much wonderful theater that could be packaged for the entertainment of their readers. And if it advanced their publishers' agendas, so much the better.

The voting public, especially the Irish, knew how to read all the subtexts. Upstate Republicans' distaste for New York City was, in their eyes, a thinly disguised dislike for Catholics in general and the Irish in particular. The Irish knew the city's government was corrupt. But it was a corruption that delivered jobs and other services they needed. An honest administration was a thinly disguised Old Yankee administration, where the contractors would be driven by a desire to keep costs, and therefore wages, down. Hylan, O'Malley, and other successful New York City politicians knew to keep repeating that they were merely the champions of the poor workingman, hounded by the rich and their newspapers, and all the code words would be understood.

There were other currents within the New York City Democratic Party, however. Murphy, with Al Smith in the governor's office, had realized the possibilities of tying progressive legislation at the state level with traditional back-scratching practices within the city. He had even begun to think that maybe an urban Irish Catholic could be elected president. The Hearst–Hylan–Brooklyn Democracy faction comprised those who still believed in the old methods and could prove an embarrassment to an urban Irish Catholic looking to enter the national stage. Hylan and his supporters would not only have to watch their traditional Republican rivals, but also have to realize that support from Tammany was not automatic.[33]

The tests of loyalty started early. Eighteen months after his appointment as deputy, Edwin O'Malley's boss, Dr. Jonathan Day, a Protestant minister and reformer, fired him, charging corruption.[34] Hylan salted O'Malley away in the Department of Charities for a couple of months, then dumped the minister and brought O'Malley back as commissioner of public markets in December 1919.[35] He would stay in that office until Hylan stepped down in 1925. Commissioners, in New York City's system, were the executive officers of various city departments. O'Malley's job paid $7,500 annually, an upper-middle-class salary for the time, and made him part of the mayor's cabinet. He oversaw the various market areas, mostly wholesale markets, that funneled food and other necessities into the city. He would spend a good deal of his tenure trying to establish more efficient, cleaner markets to serve a growing city more and more dependent on motor transportation. The Bronx Terminal Market still stands from his tenure. But he also had to administer the existing public markets and their intricate, traditionally bribery-prone, system of licenses, rental spaces, and preferences.

There were at least four major investigations of the Public Markets Department during O'Malley's tenure, three by New York City grand juries and one by a Republican-led committee from the state legislature. All would find that a great deal of smoke surrounded Edwin O'Malley, but nobody found the fire. Subordinates would be sacrificed and responsibilities shuffled, but O'Malley survived until the Murphy forces recaptured the mayor's office with Jimmy Walker in 1925.

Not that survival was always easy. The state legislative committee's investigation found that the Public Markets Department had been "perverted into a vehicle for the levy of 'graft' and the play of political favoritism" and charged that "Commissioner O'Malley must have been incredibly stupid and incompetent if he did not know and approve" of the actions of various subordinates.[36] Even the Democrats' dissent from the report did not bother to defend the department.[37]

For the newspapers who saw these investigations as theater, O'Malley was perfect. When two witnesses testified they had had to make payoffs to obtain permits to transfer leases, O'Malley immediately had their permits revoked for paying bribes.[38] When the city's board of aldermen sought department records in an investigation triggered by Dr. Day, O'Malley said his old boss had sold the papers to junk dealers.[39] When the state legislature's committee started in, O'Malley revealed its chairman was employing an ex-convict.[40] On another occasion O'Malley stalked off the witness stand after a lawyer claiming to represent him stood up and told him to walk away. The audience cheered.[41]

While maintaining his defiant stance in public, Edwin O'Malley had his private crises. At the height of the state legislative investigations, the *New York Times* reported Hylan was considering dumping him.[42] At the first whiff of public scandal in 1919, Edwin's reaction led to a big change in Walter O'Malley's life.

When Jonathan Day fired Edwin O'Malley in October 1919, Walter O'Malley had passed his sixteenth birthday just a few days earlier. Up to that point his life seems to have been that of a pretty normal suburban boy. He told a Catholic newspaper he had been baptized and attended kindergarten in the Bronx, but took his first Holy Communion (normally at about age seven) and his confirmation (normally about age twelve) in Queens. At his confirmation, he said, he had taken the additional name of Francis out of admiration for Francis of Assisi.[43]

Some of his earliest memories touched on baseball. He recalled walking across the railroad trestle from the Bronx to Manhattan with his mother's brother Clarence to watch the New York Giants play at the Polo Grounds.[44] He said his first "business deal" was to trade ten of the baseball cards that came with cigarette packs in those days for one of Giants star Christy Mathewson.[45] He remained a Giants fan well into adulthood.[46] While keeping up with the Catholic sacraments, he went to public schools, first PS 35 in Hollis and then Jamaica High School.[47] He was active in Boy Scouts, where he had risen to assistant scout master and Star rank.[48] He went to camp in the summer.[49] His father had gotten him involved in the volunteer fire department, and when the men returned from practicing, Walter and other boys had to lay out the hoses to dry, a job for which they were not paid.[50]

So when a reporter from the *Brooklyn Eagle* knocked on his door on the night of October 18, 1919, it is doubtful Walter O'Malley was prepared to deal with the adult world. There he was, a skinny youth of five feet, nine inches and 145 pounds, wearing glasses, speaking to a reporter who wanted to know if his father wanted to comment on accusations he was a crook. It was not Edwin defending himself, or even Walter's mother, responding adult to adult. It was sixteen-year-old Walter entering the public arena by saying, "I don't know where he is and I don't know when he will be home."[51] The paper reported Edwin's friends were saying they had not seen him for several days. Soon afterward Edwin decided it was time to get Walter away from a city awash with newspapers filled with Day's charges that Edwin was skimming profits off the sale of Navy surplus goods from World War I. He also evidently was concerned about Walter's preparation for college.

In July 1920 Edwin O'Malley contacted Culver Military Academy in Indiana. Culver was a twenty-six-year-old preparatory school run on military lines and catering to the fairly wealthy. Edwin had heard about the school from a neighbor named Asche, who had a son at Culver. Edwin said Walter had passed all the necessary New York Regents Exams but would benefit from "the Culver training."[52] What kind of student Walter O'Malley was is not clear. Passing the Regents Exams, showing mastery of high school subjects, at sixteen was good, but not unusual. In a referral letter to Culver, Jamaica high school principal Charles Vosburgh described Walter as industrious but an "average" student. Referral letters from Edwin's friends tabbed him as "bright" or "extremely bright."[53] Asche's letter contained a marginal note to his friends in the Culver administration: "well connected." A public political role could cut both ways.

Walter, despite his father's political troubles, did not want to go. He said he just did not like to be told what to do.[54] But when he got to Culver he settled in fairly quickly. He did well in most of his classes, except for economics, and managed a couple of appearances on the honor roll. He participated in the Hospital Visitation Committee, the Plebe Battery, and the Young Men's Christian Association (YMCA). In later years he often would tell a self-deprecating story of the day he gave up baseball. He was playing first base on the varsity team when a ball hit him in the nose, he would say.[55] But the Culver records do not show O'Malley participating on the varsity baseball teams, just the company teams.[56] By the end of his first year at Culver, he was the manager of the varsity team.[57]

Like many high school seniors, O'Malley blossomed in his final year. In the fall he joined the *Vedette*, Culver's weekly campus newspaper, as a reporter and by February had become one of the five-member executive staff. By graduation time the school yearbook was predicting he would be a newspaper reporter within a year. He continued on the Hospital Visitation Committee and took up debating and Bible discussion. He played soccer and tennis, although not on the varsity level. All this affected his grades. By April of his senior year, the assistant headmaster was writing to Edwin that Walter's grades had fallen below passing in physics and French. "This does not look favorable for successful work in college when he slumps immediately upon the granting of more liberal privileges to first classmen."[58] Walter was definitely enjoying himself. He was the subject of inside humor in the paper. "O'Malley accompanied the rifle team to Chicago. At least we know that he accompanied it as far as Chicago—but the Irish are a restless race." O'Malley's dispatch from Chicago told of losing the rifle match, but also of visits to the theater, a vaudeville house, a dance, and a dinner party at the home of one cadet's parents. "A good match, a good bunch, a good time, and a good pillow fight," he wrote.[59]

His yearbook picture bears a strong resemblance to his son, Peter. At eighteen and a half years, he has a high forehead, with his medium-length hair combed straight back. His long face is dominated by glasses with round lenses. The nose is slightly large and the mouth small. His gaze is direct. There are no signs of the jowls that would dominate his face by the time he entered the public eye in his midforties.

College, however, was becoming a bit of a quandary. Walter O'Malley's sights were first set on Princeton. But his lackluster grades and the lack of enough language credits forced him to abandon that idea.[60] In June, soon after graduation, Edwin and Alma pushed him to take a trip to Cornell University in Ithaca, New York. "Since my return from Culver, family sentiment is strongly bent towards Cornell—so there I went to 'inspect' the college. I am really disappointed! Cornell is too large!" It also wasn't too impressed with Walter's academic record or the fact that he did not have a transcript with him. His lack of enough French credits arose again. He might be able to gain conditional admission, but that was all. "This college business is an awful bother! A fellow can't seem to decide where to go and when he does, they can't take him. I wish I had all the languages and everything else in the academic curriculum so that I could go anywhere!!"[61] Eventually, he was rescued from his plight by the University of Pennsylvania, "a dandy bit of news," he wrote to a Culver mentor, especially since Penn said he did not need to take any qualifying exams.[62]

If Walter O'Malley had been a late bloomer in high school, he was a wire-to-wire phenomenon in the political and social life of the University of Pennsylvania. About forty of Walter's Culver classmates attended Penn. They organized a Culver club, and O'Malley used it as a political base. He was elected president of his class for both junior and senior years.[63] "Walter built the strongest political machine in campus history," a classmate recalled.[64]

In the fall of 1922, as O'Malley and seventeen hundred or so other freshmen arrived on campus, O'Malley and his Culver classmates decided not to run a candidate for freshman president.[65] Instead, O'Malley took on class leadership for the Penniman Bowl, a contest between the freshman and sophomore classes designed to stimulate class pride and togetherness.[66] The Penniman Bowl covered seventeen contests, mostly in sports, from baseball to a three-legged race. But the big tests were the "poster fight" and the "pants fight." Both "fights" featured scrums of young men pushing, shoving, and grabbing. In the poster fight the sophomores defended fifteen posters prominently placed in the central quad. In the pants fight they tried to keep their pants on. No particular skill was involved, although the possibility of bruises, scratches, and perhaps something worse was always present.[67] In O'Malley's senior year, when his class was no longer involved, a student died from injuries suffered in the pants fight.[68] Violence was part of the campus scene. Overton Tremper, a Penn undergraduate a year behind O'Malley and later an outfielder for the Dodgers, described O'Malley gleefully dispensing swats with a large paddle because Tremper had neglected to wear his mandatory freshman beanie.[69] That was when O'Malley was chairman of the Vigilance Committee, a group of sophomores charged with keeping freshmen in their place.[70]

Winning the fights involved getting as many people as possible to turn out and participate enthusiastically. It also involved preventing kidnapping by the other class to reduce the number of participants. Walter O'Malley proved to be a very good organizer. His class (motto "Hard as nails, full of tricks, Pennsylvania, twenty-six") won the bowl as both freshmen and sophomores, an unprecedented feat.[71] O'Malley was designated the class's permanent custodian for the trophy.[72]

Despite the freshman Penniman Bowl triumph, O'Malley's crowd could not win the class presidency for sophomore year. But the sophomore Penniman victory cemented the machine. The class of '26 history in their senior yearbook praised O'Malley's committee, which had "led us to victory in the greatest attainment which we as underclassmen could achieve."[73] But it was not just exhortations to class glory that moved O'Malley to the top of Penn's political pyramid, but also the skills learned in the household of a Tammany political operative. "We realized we had to work with certain fraternity groups and the Independents and what not. It paid off," O'Malley said.[74]

As a campus wheel O'Malley was at the heart of social activities. He organized the dances and the smokers and other class activities. He did not dance, but he made sure the dances made a profit.[75] He even checked himself into the Rittenhouse Hotel for the Ivy Bowl at the end of his senior year because he wanted to be sure things went well, even though he was bedridden with appendicitis.[76] He was a member of the Theta Delta Chi fraternity. He was chairman of the Undergraduate Council, a member of the Councils on Athletics and Welfare. He was on the Soccer Committee and the Track Committee and, briefly, a member of the Polo Club. He was salutatorian of his class and elected "Spoon Man."[77] The "Spoon Man" award had been started in the 1860s as a derisory salute to the lowest-ranking freshman among scholastic leaders, supposedly because he was the furthest from the head of the table.[78] It had evolved into an election indicating the senior class's general regard for one of their own.

Perhaps many of his classmates knew of the Spoon Man's origins. Despite telling one newspaper reporter he had graduated first in his class, O'Malley had a mixed academic career.[79] By November of his freshman year he was on probation in psychology, his transcript shows. He soon added math and English to his probation lists and by the end of his freshman year had made it to general academic probation. He cleared up those problems over the summer and managed to overcome another bout with probation, in philosophy, during his junior year. Overall, he mostly got "pass" grades, the equivalent of Cs in Pennsylvania's system then. Of the 72.5 units O'Malley took at Penn, only 9 rated the grade of "distinguished," the equivalent of today's As.[80]

Undoubtedly, the most interesting thing about Walter O'Malley's college transcript is what it does not show. Over the years O'Malley would many times tell of studying engineering at Pennsylvania, occasionally describing it as his major.[81] His transcript contains no engineering courses. It contains no science courses, and it shows two of his three mathematics courses were cause for probation. What Walter O'Malley concentrated on was psychology, a relatively new and highly trendy discipline in the 1920s, when the theories of Freud and Jung were first being spread to a popular audience.[82] His colleagues and competitors in later years would argue he certainly absorbed something, for his ability to bring people to his point of view was legendary.

Walter O'Malley must have felt he was graduating into the best of all possible worlds. He had been a social and political success on campus. He was well off. He would tell one interviewer that his family was of "average circumstances" when he entered Penn and another that he "was an Irish hod carrier with a wheelbarrow," but after eight years in public office, Edwin had clearly left that status behind.[83] "I was an only child. My father had great love for his son. He spoiled me. When I graduated from college, he gave me a 42-foot cabin cruiser. And automobiles and things. He was a pretty swell guy."[84] He influenced Walter's habits of a lifetime. "My father was against cigarettes, so I took up cigars and pipes. I guess that was in college."[85]

Walter's pictures of this era show a somewhat more mature version of the Culver graduate. He looks less like Peter. He tops out just under six feet in height, with hazel eyes. He appears to have weighed about 160 or 170 pounds. The slick-backed brown hair still rises from a high forehead. The lenses of his glasses are still round and steel framed. The nose is more prominent and looks flatter and wider, as if he had gone out for the boxing team rather than polo and soccer. He favors three-piece suits. He is known as the "Turk" and "Walt." His class prophecy for 1946 says, "'Walt'

O'Malley is now District Attorney of New York City and is also a leader of Tammany Hall."[86]

By then his classmates knew O'Malley was heading off to law school at Columbia University in New York. He clearly had been thinking of the law for some time. He said he had taken four years of Latin at Penn because he knew it was a requirement for admission to Ivy League law schools.[87] He had seen his father's colleagues and knew how many were lawyers and judges. And he was the first of his family to attend college and surely carried the inherited desire for professional status. O'Malley entered Columbia's law school in the fall of 1926, continuing his undergraduate lifestyle and living on Waverly Place in Greenwich Village.[88] It lasted about a year, for Edwin O'Malley evidently went broke.

The trajectory of Edwin's business career is not at all clear. He was successful enough in the dry goods business to move his family to the suburbs by his late twenties. Walter told one interviewer that Edwin had been promoted to sales manager.[89] Edwin is listed as a salesman in cotton goods in city directories up through 1909, about the time he moved his family to Hollis. After that he disappears. It is clear that at some point he switched to the real estate business and that he had a severe reduction in income around the spring of 1927. But beyond that nothing is very clear.

Walter mentioned several times that Edwin's fortunes failed when petticoats went out of style.[90] Maybe that was a turn of phrase to catch reporters' ears, for Edwin's company also made suit and trouser linings. Petticoats disappeared during World War I, a decade before Edwin's fortunes caused Walter to change course abruptly.[91] Certainly, Walter's years at Culver and Penn, and the lifestyle he lived in Philadelphia, were costly and borne without apparent strain. Perhaps the death of petticoats was the first blow to a business that failed a decade later. More likely, Edwin turned to real estate soon after he moved to the suburbs and came to an appreciation of the profits to be made in getting others to move there. Certainly, Edwin's wide range of civic activities in Hollis was more in keeping with someone promoting a local community and its real estate rather than working in an office in Manhattan's garment district. By the 1930 census Edwin was listing his business as real estate. Others have tied Edwin's financial straits to the stock market crash that precipitated the Great Depression, but Walter dropped out of Columbia two years before Black Thursday.[92]

It also seems significant that Edwin's financial straits hit just over a year after he left public office. The opportunities of running the Public Markets Department were no longer available, and perhaps some investments went bad. Whatever happened, Walter O'Malley withdrew from Columbia's law school in June 1927.[93]

Even if Edwin lacked financial resources, he did not lack friends. By the end of the month Walter had a job paying $130 a month working for the city's Board of Transportation. The secretary of the board was Francis J. Sinnott, a Brooklyn politician whose younger brother was the secretary and son-in-law of Edwin's patron, former mayor John Hylan.[94] That fall Walter O'Malley began taking law classes at night at Fordham. He had fallen from the well-tended path of the Ivy League to walk among the other Catholic strivers.

This probably is also the period when O'Malley's spurious engineering background came into being, for he was hired as a temporary engineering assistant in the board's Transportation Department, which was building the Eighth Avenue subway line. O'Malley worked at the board for just over two years, resigning on September 14, 1929, just about the time his last year at Fordham was beginning.[95]

At about that time O'Malley went to work for the Riley Drilling Company, which, six weeks after O'Malley joined, was part of a group that won a $2 million contract for geologic and other preliminary work on the Queens Midtown Tunnel. The contract was overseen by the Board of Transportation and its secretary, Francis Sinnott.[96] The firm also reportedly did drilling work for the Board of Education, the New York Telephone Company, a Wall Street building, and the Triborough Bridge.[97]

Meanwhile, working away at nights, O'Malley completed his Fordham law studies in June 1930. And he left Riley to go out on his own. O'Malley later placed the founding of the W. F. O'Malley Engineering Company in 1930, but it makes no appearance in New York City phone books until the second half of 1931.[98] O'Malley said he and Riley had been going strong until they had to choose between jobs drilling artesian wells or working on a tunnel to bring upstate New York water to the city. Riley thought the wells would be unprofitable and the water-system work lucrative. O'Malley thought the opposite. So they split, and each took the work they wanted.[99] O'Malley said he got a $15,000 loan to help start the business, but did not say who the lender was.[100] The wells were to number fifty, but as the Depression deepened the well contracts dried up.

O'Malley tried publishing a legal guide to the city's building code and the *Sub-contractors Register and Bulletin*, which listed contract opportunities with the city. The reports of those years are decidedly mixed. He said he did $1 million of drilling work while still a law student.[101] He said he sold ten thousand copies of the legal guide to the city's building code for $5 apiece.[102] But others report that the contractor guides were a flop.[103]

What is clear is that when Walter O'Malley finally passed the bar, W. F. O'Malley Engineering disappeared quickly. He received notice he had passed the bar exam in May 1931.[104] Within a year the engineering company listing disappeared from the phone book, to be replaced at the same address and the same phone number with Walter F. O'Malley, lawyer. Part of that year was spent doing a clerkship, in which young lawyers were supposed to complete their training by working under an experienced lawyer for at least six months. But that was not Walter O'Malley's way. Instead, he gave an experienced but officeless lawyer space in the engineering firm and used this as his clerkship.[105] O'Malley was not fully credentialed until 1933, when he was approved by a New York Bar Association committee on character and fitness.[106]

In the meantime O'Malley was making at least enough money that he felt he could marry. Although he was a sparkling political success at Penn, his coed social life was evidently limited. Culver had been an all-boys school, and Penn was close to it. Years later he told an interviewer there had been no campus romances and he had spent most of his undergraduate career hanging around with a group of male friends.[107] Perhaps Walter was shy, or maybe he was just loyal to the girl next door.

As Walter was entering Penn in September 1922, Edwin had bought a second home at 318 Ocean Avenue in Amityville, on the south shore of Long Island. The house backed onto Amityville Creek and gave easy access to the Great South Bay and, through breaks in the sand dunes, to the Atlantic Ocean. Edwin, Alma, and Walter would use the house for weekends and summers. Two months later Peter B. Hanson bought the house at 314 Ocean Avenue, bringing with him his daughters, Katharina Elizabeth, known as Kay, fifteen, and Helen, ten.[108]

Peter B. Hanson had been born in Sweden in 1877 and immigrated to New York with his parents in 1883.[109] He graduated from New York Law School in 1900 and practiced in his own firm and as counsel to both the sheriff and the public administrator of Kings County (Brooklyn).[110] He was proud of his Swedish heritage and active in many Swedish community organizations, as well as Democratic Party politics. He was leader of the Democratic Party in Brooklyn's Seventeenth Assembly District and familiar with all the political leaders from the Brooklyn area, presumably including Edwin O'Malley. In 1927 Hanson was named a judge of the Children's Court in Brooklyn, overseeing cases of child custody, juvenile delinquency, and similar matters.

Inevitably, as Walter O'Malley came home for weekends, holidays, and the summer, he met the Hanson girls and took a shine to Kay, a shy, pretty young woman who was deeply Catholic. By the time Walter graduated from Penn, Kay was about to enter her last year at the College of New Rochelle, a Catholic women's college a few miles north of New York City. After graduating she took some law school classes at St. John's University, but never finished.[111] In her senior year at New Rochelle, growing hoarseness in her throat sent Kay to the doctor. He diagnosed her with throat cancer, and she had one of the earliest operations to replace her larynx with a "voice box." For the rest of her life she would rely a great deal on gestures and smiles, for her voice was reduced to a difficult whisper.[112]

Walter O'Malley said his father had forbidden him to marry Kay, whom Edwin considered damaged goods. Walter quoted himself telling his father, "She's the same girl I fell in love with."[113] By November 1930 he was taking a cruise to Bermuda with Kay and her parents.[114] They were married September 5, 1931, at St. Malachy's, the actors' church. They moved into an apartment at 2 Beekman Place in Manhattan. A daughter, Therese, known to all as Terry, would be born in 1933 and a son, Peter, in 1937.

Walter O'Malley was beginning to spread his legal wings. The story, O'Malley said, stretched from his roots to his recent past. He told the story often, and well, as in this early rendering to Roger Kahn:

> I remember realizing that as long as I was a lawyer, I ought to practice law. I set up an office, got a listing in the phone book and the day the book came out I got a call. It was from a man who said his name was Barrett and I asked Mr. Barrett what I could do for him. He told me it was Father Barrett, and he wanted something that sounded like a cross between a well and a will. He had such a strong brogue, I couldn't tell what he meant. I had been doing wells. I wanted to do wills. Either way, I was safe, so I told him to come to my office. He said he couldn't because the church was in mourning and I realized he didn't want a well.

I went to a little church in Manhattan, found another priest gravely ill and took the will. What I couldn't understand was how, with all the established lawyers listed in the telephone book, Father Barrett had happened to choose me. I asked him.

"I just went through the phone book," he answered, "and yours was the first County Mayo name I could find."[115]

Father Barrett had started Walter O'Malley down the trail that would lead him first to Ebbets Field and then across the country to build his dream stadium.

The dying priest's estate contained some mortgage bonds, which before the Depression had been the kind of conservative investment recommended to widows, orphans, and Catholic priests.[116] But with the Depression many people and companies had found it hard to make their payments, and the bonds had gone into default. It was a nasty political mess because it basically pitted home buyers who could not pay their bills against retired people who counted on the income to live.

O'Malley would later say he worked with George Brower, a superior court judge and the state superintendent of insurance, on legislation to create nonprofit trust corporations that could hold the mortgage bonds, continue to make payments to bondholders, and work with the home owners.[117] O'Malley said he perceived an opportunity for legal work in these instruments and began to pursue it. There is little evidence to back up O'Malley's claim of participation. The crisis emerged in the period between his graduation from law school and his full acceptance at the bar. In fact, passage of the key legislation came within a month of his concluding appearance before the bar association's character and fitness committee. Although he certainly had strong political connections with a Democratic administration in Albany, he was a partially fledged lawyer who was running his own small firm, while major Manhattan law firms with large real estate practices were interested in the legislation.[118]

Whether Walter O'Malley participated in framing the legislation or not, he certainly saw how to take advantage of it. Sometime in 1933, he recalled, he was making the rounds of the bank and trust companies that had handled the bonds and could organize and administer (for fees) the nonprofit corporations that would handle the repayments. He was in the office of George V. McLaughlin, president of the Brooklyn Trust Company, the biggest financial institution in Brooklyn and, as a trust company, the executor for many estates and trust funds.

As O'Malley told it, McLaughlin at first was not interested. It was something for Brooklyn Trust's lawyers to work out, he said. As a discouraged O'Malley rose to leave, McLaughlin threw out one last question: "How much business could this mean for the bank?" O'Malley said he reacted calmly and quoted a figure of $50 million. McLaughlin offered O'Malley a seat and a cigar, and one of the most important relationships in Walter O'Malley's life began.[119]

George V. McLaughlin would prove to be the mentor Walter O'Malley needed to go from struggling young lawyer to Brooklyn pillar and financial success. McLaughlin was of Edwin O'Malley's generation, born in 1887 in Brooklyn, the son of a tugboat captain. At fifteen he got a part-time job as a bank messenger and, after high school, became a bank clerk while continuing his education at night. He eventually became both a lawyer and a certified public accountant. In 1910 he had taken a civil service examination to become a state bank examiner. He had worked his way up to deputy state superintendent of banks when he was recognized by Governor Al Smith and made the state's banking superintendent.[120] McLaughlin served under both Democratic and Republican governors.

In 1925 Smith helped engineer the election of one of his protégés, Jimmy Walker, as New York mayor to replace John Hylan. He also urged Walker to make McLaughlin, another of his protégés, police commissioner. As Edwin O'Malley was leaving the mayor's cabinet, McLaughlin was coming in. Although a Democrat, McLaughlin was not a Tammany man or any kind of machine politician. In Albany he had worked with the group of reformers of both parties who clustered around Al Smith—people such as Belle Moskowitz and Robert Moses. Thus, he was uncertain about joining a Tammany administration in New York City and extracted promises from Walker that he would be allowed a free hand to run an honest police force.[121]

It lasted fifteen months. He not only reduced crime but also raided Tammany district clubs because there was gambling going on.[122] Eventually, under pressure from Walker, who was in turn under tremendous pressure from Tammany leadership, he resigned to take a job with a large telegraph and cable company.[123] Eight months later, in November 1927, he returned to banking as president of the Brooklyn Trust Company.[124]

McLaughlin's fifteen months as police commissioner had made a strong impression on many in the political world. When Smith announced he was stepping down as governor, McLaughlin's name was raised as a possible candidate as early as 1926.[125] And in 1933, the year O'Malley paid his mortgage-reorganization call at Brooklyn Trust, McLaughlin was offered the post of mayor on the reform Fusion ticket. He turned Fusion down, and they turned to their next choice, Fiorello La Guardia.[126]

George McLaughlin was often described as "strapping"—six feet tall, solidly built, with a strong jaw. He was a demon handball player and kept neat stacks of $1, $5, and $10 bills in separate pockets of the stylish vests he liked to wear. He also liked a drink. George V. became George the Fifth, not merely for his dominating presence, but also for his fondness for alcohol.[127] He had known O'Malley, presumably through Edwin and his Democratic Party connections, since Walter's college days and had attended baseball games with him while Walter was at Penn, which probably explains how a fledgling lawyer got in to see him in the first place.[128]

O'Malley soon became McLaughlin's protégé. He specialized in bankruptcy work, a lucrative choice during the Depression, and McLaughlin steered financially troubled clients his way. McLaughlin was on the Advisory Board for the Reconstruction Finance Corporation, a New Deal creation that loaned money to Depression-damaged companies to help them get back on their feet. Such companies had an RFC nominee added to their boards, and O'Malley took on this role to his profit. O'Malley's contacts expanded from Brooklyn's political leadership into the business community. He wound up on the board of Trommer's Brewery and the Brooklyn Borough Gas Company.[129] In some cases he took stock in companies instead of his lawyer's fees and wound up as an owner of the Hotel Lexington, J. P. Duffy & Company, a Bronx building contractor, and a concrete-block company out on Long Island.[130] He retained the companies that produced the *Sub-contractors Register.*

The relationship with McLaughlin became social as well. O'Malley began accompanying McLaughlin to games of the Bushwicks, a premier semipro baseball team in Brooklyn.[131] When McLaughlin had too many orange-blossom cocktails (gin and orange juice) at the New York Athletic Club, it was O'Malley who took him home and poured him into bed.[132]

O'Malley would later throw out some impressive figures for his work during this era. He said he did $100 million in real estate legal work from 1933 to 1943. Another time it was eight hundred thousand. He told reporters he could get $100,000 for a single case and represented nine large banks.[133] By the early 1940s the law firm of O'Malley & Wilson was up to twenty lawyers, with O'Malley as senior partner.[134] Buzzie Bavasi, O'Malley's longtime general manager with the Dodgers, relayed a story O'Malley told him about this period that illuminates his knack for doing business. O'Malley had done some work for a wealthy man who people had warned him did not like to pay his bills. O'Malley thought the work was worth $500, but sent the man a bill for five thousand. The man called enraged. O'Malley apologized profusely for the clerical error, said the bill was $500, and got his money from the man, who thought he had won the argument.[135]

But others had a different view. Roger Kahn, who wrote often of O'Malley in his books on the Dodgers and other baseball topics, had an ambivalent view of the man over the years. It was he who reported the figure of $100 million in 1954 in the *New York Herald-Tribune*. It also was he who characterized O'Malley as just "a lawyer for a bank" in a later book.[136] He also quoted William Shea, another young lawyer who did work for George McLaughlin. "He was one lousy lawyer. O'Malley was the most brilliant businessman I've ever met, but we were talking about law here, weren't we?" Shea asked rhetorically. "I wouldn't have let O'Malley plead a parking ticket for me."[137]

O'Malley undoubtedly contributed to the confusion with his habit of improving on the facts. His listing in *Who's Who*, listings that are almost always created with facts supplied by the subject, contains a number of errors. It says he was admitted to the bar in 1930. It says he served on the Brooklyn Borough Gas Company board beginning in 1932. The company's annual reports first list him on the board a dozen years later. In later years, when O'Malley came to control the Dodgers and writers started profiling him, he would mention he owned 6 percent of the Long Island Rail Road, which reporters interpreted as a sign of his wealth.[138] In fact, the Long Island Rail Road was in bankruptcy, which is why O'Malley was involved at all. And the company had provided him the stock to avoid taxes.[139] That did not faze "The O'Malley." Nearly two decades later he enlarged his role yet again. Describing his decision to focus on the Dodgers rather than his other businesses, he said, "I sold MY railroad."[140]

The *Who's Who* listing was probably also the source of the oft-repeated "fact" that O'Malley joined the Brooklyn Dodgers board of directors in 1932. In 1932 he had not even been fully certified to the bar and had no connection to the team. Listings of Dodger executives in baseball guides through the 1930s make no mention of him, nor does correspondence in the Branch Rickey Papers over Rickey's recruitment refer to O'Malley's presence on the board, although representatives for the Brooklyn Trust Company, the Mulveys, and the Ebbets and Edward McKeever estates are clearly listed. The minutes of the corporation show him joining the board only after he gained an ownership stake in 1944 and 1945.

The United States' involvement in World War II triggered a patriotic urge in O'Malley. His military exposure at Culver had led him into the Reserve Officers' Training Corps while at Penn, and he had kept up a connection by serving in the Chemical Warfare Reserve Corps until at least 1936.[141] After World War II broke out, O'Malley evidently sought a commission, as he contacted both Penn and Culver for copies of his transcripts to submit with an application for a commission.[142] Whatever the military's response, O'Malley did not go in. He was, after all, a man pushing forty with two small children and little in the way of specific military skills.

He did turn his legal expertise to the war effort. Todd & Brown was a major engineering contractor for whom O'Malley had done some legal work. In 1940 they commissioned O'Malley to do the legal work on a government contract to build the Kingsbury Ordnance Plant near La Porte, Indiana. O'Malley worked on writing the contract, buying the land, and the other issues. The plant rose on 13,454 acres of farmland and produced $500 million worth of ammunition over the course of the war.[143] It employed as many as 20,785 workers from nearby farms and from the African American migrants moving up from the South.[144] The plant's most famous employee would prove to be another Irishman, one Charles O. Finley, who would later join O'Malley in the ranks of baseball ownership.[145]

Although he may not have been quite the business baron he painted, O'Malley was certainly a financial success by late 1942. He was extremely well connected in Brooklyn, both politically and in the business community. He was president of the Brooklyn Club, where the borough's business and political elite met, and a member of the even more exclusive "Coal-Holers," a group set up by Charles Ebbets to enjoy a lavish dinner commemorating Ebbets each year.[146] In October of that year, when Branch Rickey arrived to take over the Dodgers, George McLaughlin took him to a luncheon at the Brooklyn Club, where he met O'Malley for the first time. Rickey subsequently asked George Barnewall, one of McLaughlin's top assistants, for a rundown on the men at McLaughlin's table. Barnewall described O'Malley as "a lawyer and very close to Mr. McLaughlin and myself. Very well connected about town."[147] Maybe that was why, a little while later, Walter O'Malley got a call from Branch Rickey.

2

From Gowanus to
Montague Street

In the spring of 1883 there were other births in New York and Brooklyn besides Edwin O'Malley's, and two of them would affect his son greatly. About five blocks southwest of Thomas and Georgiana O'Malley's rented rooms on Madison Street, workers were putting the finishing touches on the Brooklyn Bridge. About three miles to the southeast, across the future bridge in the Gowanus section of Brooklyn, near a smelly industrial canal, carpenters were throwing up a grandstand for a new baseball team.

As with much of nineteenth-century professional baseball, the birth and childhood of the Dodgers were a bit haphazard. They began 1883 in the Inter-state Association, then a minor league. By the next year they were in the majors, in what was called the American Association. As ownership upgraded the players, the Dodgers moved to the top of the association and then made the jump to the National League (NL) in 1890.[1] They did it with a changing cast of owners, more and more dominated by a young man named Charles Ebbets, who started with the team as ticket taker and general office help and then became the day-to-day business manager of the team and eventually majority owner by the first decade of the twentieth century.[2] By 1911 Ebbets's control of the team and the general growth of baseball led him to set out to build a modern steel and concrete stadium.

Ebbets was born in Manhattan's Greenwich Village on October 29, 1859, of an old Dutch family. His father had been a bank president and an associate of Alexander Cartwright, whose Knickerbocker Baseball Club had played an important role in codifying baseball's early rules.[3] Ebbets had left school early, joining an architectural firm where he worked as a draftsman on the Metropolitan Hotel and Niblo's Garden, a famous amusement center. He later went to work for publishing houses, selling cheap fiction and doing the accounting. All these skills were to stand him in good stead when he ran the Dodgers.[4]

Ebbets was a marketing campaign all by himself. He was a joiner, founding the Old Nassau Athletic Club among others. He was active in the Masons, Democratic Party politics, and bicycling and bowling clubs. He participated in at least four bowling clubs and many secret societies. He had been elected a state assemblyman and an alderman and lost an 1897 race for city councilman by literally the narrowest of margins, 23,183 votes to 23,182. He also lost a 1904 race for the state senate when Democrats were buried in the Theodore Roosevelt landslide.

Over the years Ebbets developed a baseball reputation as a man who could put together a league schedule that would cause the minimum level of complaints.[5] He also developed a reputation as cheap. Perhaps this was simply because he was among the first baseball team owners to build up a considerable fortune solely through the game and without having been a player. But it is also because he was cheap. One day a reporter wandered into Ebbets's office and found him arguing with the woman who washed the Dodgers' uniforms. "You want to make a living. If I pay what you want for washing these uniforms, I can't possibly make a living," Ebbets was yelling.[6]

During games Ebbets's customary perch was on a high-backed accountant's stool behind home plate. He was accessible to the fans, and his reputation for cheapness, emphasized by the newspapers, was a constant source of comment. During one high-volume conversation, Ebbets felt compelled to point out to his debating partner that he was the only Major League owner who did not have a car.

He did have an appetite. Abe Yager, sports editor of the *Brooklyn Eagle*, told of attending a thirteen-course World Series banquet one evening at the Waldorf with Ebbets and some other writers. After the banquet Ebbets and his party went downstairs to the hotel's bar, and Ebbets washed down a plate of hors d'oeuvres with beer. Then they decided to walk down to Nick Engel's bar, a favorite with the sports crowd. Engel's bar was about twenty blocks south of the hotel, and every block, it seemed, had a tavern. Ebbets led Yager and the other sportswriters into each tavern, where he sampled the free, usually salty, food traditional at bars of the period. When they finally made it to Engel's, Ebbets polished off a couple dozen raw oysters.[7]

Ebbets's reputation was not all negative. Baseball was his business, unlike owners who could be distracted by producing musicals or running breweries or ice-making companies.

Ebbets had to choose his ballpark site carefully. He had put much of the blame for the Dodgers' bad decade in the 1890s on their move to Eastern Park—too far from the center of downtown Brooklyn. But now it was almost twenty years later, and the city had grown enormously. The 1890 census, taken the year the Dodgers won their first National League pennant, showed 806,343 people in the city of Brooklyn. By the time of their sixth-place finish in 1910, the population had doubled.

He targeted Brooklyn's Pigtown section, relatively cheap because of its population of squatters, but along the path of rapid growth. It was in a district known as Flatbush, a corrupted version of the Dutch for "wooded flatland." His site, as Ebbets noted excitedly in a letter to August Herrmann, chairman of the National Commission, the three-man body that oversaw baseball before the commissioner system, was served by nine mass-transit lines. "Between 3,000,000 and 4,000,000 people can reach the new site by surface, subway or elevated in thirty to forty five minutes," Ebbets wrote.[8]

In January 1912 Ebbets announced he had put together the parcel and intended the Dodgers to have a modern ballpark on the site. It was to feature a terrazzo-floored rotunda under the stands behind home plate eighty feet in diameter, with ticket windows and entrance tunnels dotted around the marble walls.

Construction began in March 1912. The eighteen-thousand-seat stadium was supposed to be finished by June, or maybe August, 1912.[9] It wasn't. Excuses were given about undelivered materials and labor troubles. Apparently, though, the real trouble was money. In late August Ebbets announced he had taken new partners. They were two politically well-connected brothers, Ed and Steve McKeever, who were in the construction business.[10] Each had received 25 percent for their investment. The breakdown of stock blocs created by this transaction was to persist for almost fifty years.

The brothers McKeever had textbook careers on how the nineteenth-century Irish got ahead. Steve was born in 1854 and Ed in 1859, both in Brooklyn, sons of a cobbler. Both received minimal education, Steve's being interrupted when he ran away in an unsuccessful attempt to join the Union army as a Civil War drummer boy. He went to work as a horse boy for a trolley line down near the Fulton Street Ferry and was eventually apprenticed to a plumber. One of Steve's first contracts was for plumbing work on the Brooklyn Bridge. Ed also left school at fourteen, first working for a brass wholesaler and then joining with Michael J. Daly to form the Hudson River Broken Stone Company.[11]

Within a few years the brothers combined their expertise in plumbing and stone work to form the E. J. & S. W. McKeever Contracting Company. They had also learned well from Daly, who got government contracts through his excellent (Republican) political contacts. When Steve McKeever married in 1892, one of his ushers was Hugh McLaughlin, boss of the Brooklyn Democracy. The McKeevers built their company with lucrative government contracts to construct sewers and water mains and pave streets. Steve, the more gregarious of the two, was a former city alderman. Ed was more the businessman. With New York's growth, winning government construction contracts was an excellent business. In the early twentieth century, the brothers moved into house construction. And they had a lucrative city contract to take Brooklyn's garbage out to sea and dump it. When the McKeevers' identity was revealed, sportswriters outdid each other suggesting which of the Dodgers should be given one-way rides on the brothers' fleet of scows.[12] The sale of the garbage contract, for more than $1 million, provided the brothers with the cash to buy into the Dodgers.

The stadium was done in time for the 1913 season. At least it was finished in a fashion that came to epitomize the Brooklyn franchise in people's minds. On opening day the gatekeeper forgot to bring the keys.[13] Once everybody got inside, sportswriters discovered there was no press box, despite Ebbets's conferring with their editors about one the previous year.[14] A couple of rows of seats had to be cleared for reporters. (A real press box would not be built until 1929.) With everyone inside the park and the press seated, a party of dignitaries led by Ebbets's daughter Genevieve marched to center field to raise the flag. They arrived, looked around, and realized none of them had brought a flag.[15]

The 1916 pennant-winning season portended a prosperous era, which would leave Charles Ebbets with an estate worth more than $1 million. The improvement started with the quality of the team. A second pennant was added in 1920, and an unexpectedly fine team in 1924 led to a tight pennant race and another attendance record. It was helped by the new stadium, which was expanded to twenty-two thousand seats for the 1917 season.

Ebbets died near the peak of his success as an owner. He fell ill early in 1925 and died of heart failure in April in his suite at the Waldorf-Astoria Hotel. His funeral was held on a raw day, and when the cortege got to Greenwood Cemetery, it was discovered the grave had been dug too small for the oversize casket. The funeral party, including Ed McKeever, stood in the rain for an hour while gravediggers widened the muddy hole. McKeever caught a cold, which turned into pneumonia and killed him only eleven days later.

The team's ownership was thrown into turmoil, and a pattern was set that was to last for thirteen years. Management was weak, and when the Depression hit the losses mounted, putting the team effectively in control of its lenders.

Ebbets had had a somewhat involved family life and left multiple heirs. His estate was divided into fifteenths. Joseph Gilleaudeau, husband of Ebbets's daughter Genevieve, served on the Dodgers' board, but with a fragmented family behind him, he could offer little direction.[16]

Ed McKeever's heirs were also divided. Although he was childless, his estate was broken into eighteenths, as he provided for several nieces and other relatives. Steve McKeever took up a more active role, but his baseball experience was limited. He was soon at loggerheads with Wilbert Robinson, who had been named the team's president with the support of the Ebbets family. The two men literally snarled epithets such as "rat" at each other across their small offices above the rotunda at Ebbets Field.[17]

The matter went beyond personalities. The Ebbets heirs thought the McKeevers had taken advantage of Charles Ebbets when he needed the funds to complete Ebbets Field. Soon after the McKeevers took over half the team as collateral for their $150,000 loan, the team received a purchase offer of $3.2 million for the whole team, the family said. "They stole $1,000,000 from my father," Charles Ebbets Jr. told Branch Rickey.[18] For their part the McKeevers, conservative, lace-curtain Irish, were horrified at Charles Ebbets's divorce and refused to socialize with him.[19]

It was just the beginning of a precipitous decline in the franchise. In a review of the team's status soon after the deaths, the *New York Times* described the Dodgers as "one of the soundest organizations financially in professional baseball."[20] It was a team that sparked buyer demand. Former Yankees owner Tillinghast Huston was reported interested, as was former Boston Braves owner James Gaffney.[21] Song-and-dance man George M. Cohan was also mentioned. In 1928 there was a brief stir when it was reported Mayor Jimmy Walker, with the financial backing of publisher Paul Block, would make a bid.[22] A month later the rumored bidder was former Pittsburgh Pirates great Honus Wagner.[23] But it turned out Ebbets's will had prevented his heirs from selling his Dodger shares for ten years, and the buying interest soon drifted away as the management fell behind on the mortgage and turned the team into the joke of the league.

The team was known as the "Daffiness Boys," a tag hung on them by Westbrook Pegler, then a young sportswriter. It was epitomized by the incident when three men arrived on third base at the same moment. Typically, that play went down in Dodger lore as the time Babe Herman tripled into a triple play. Actually, he only doubled into a double play. There was the time Wilbert Robinson created a Bonehead Club to punish mental mistakes with fines. The club lasted one day, a day on which Robinson gave the wrong lineup card to the umpire.[24]

The anecdotes came from the playing field, but the problem started at the top, emanating from the snarling of Robinson and Steve McKeever. The problem was that the ownership breakdown of the team lent itself to division and stalemate. The McKeever and Ebbets families each owned exactly 50 percent. Any disagreement and the board's vote split.

Two of the stronger personalities were Gilleaudeau and James Mulvey, who had married Steve McKeever's only daughter, Dearie. But Gilleaudeau was a senior sales executive for the Stetson Hat Company, and Mulvey was movie mogul Samuel Goldwyn's top man on the East Coast. They gave counsel when they could, but their other business interests had to take the vast majority of their attention. Robinson blew up one winter when he saw a deal to purchase future Hall of Famer Paul Waner fall apart because he could not find the directors to get approval.[25]

Eventually, the National League stepped in, naming a president to arbitrate between the two factions. Robinson was eased out, first as president and then as manager. But the unity among management had come too late. When John Quinn, an experienced baseball executive, was brought in to run the team, he was struck by the utter listlessness of the front office.[26] Managers were fired in the desperate hope of sparking fan interest, because the players were not going to get any better. Thus, with a team losing money, the club's directors were paying two managers in both 1934 and 1937.

Mismanagement was widespread. After a big season in 1930, the directors decided to expand the stadium by replacing the wooden bleachers behind left field with concrete stands. They borrowed $600,000 from the bank. When the stands were completed the directors found to their horror that there were not any additional seats. The case wound up in court. And the consequent appearance of anxious bankers on the club's board did little good. One supposedly protested the purchase of a player for a Dodger farm team because, he said, the team did not need any farmers. In the 1930s manager Casey Stengel was still complaining he could not even claim a player on waivers without getting the board's permission.[27]

And then there was the Depression. Team attendance peaked in 1930, when they drew just over 1 million fans for the first time. The number of paying fans had dropped to 434,188 by 1934 and had stayed at that level. The team even began to look like the most disadvantaged of its fans. During spring training in the mid-1930s, the wonderfully named clubhouse man Babe Hamberger set up a sewing machine outside the dressing room to fix rents in the already patched team uniforms.[28]

It was in this period that the bond between the Dodgers and their fans was forged so tightly. Perhaps it was the intimacy of the ballpark with those small crowds. Perhaps it was the Dodgers as symbol of Americanization for Brooklyn's immigrant hordes. Perhaps it was a fan's ability to find white-haired Steve McKeever in a chair in back of the last row of the grandstands behind home plate, a glass of milk perched on the stanchion next to him. McKeever, like Babe Ruth, had trouble with names, so he called everybody Judge. So everybody called him Judge. Grasping his blackthorn cane, McKeever habitually muttered to himself, but was always willing to engage in conversation with others. Perhaps the conversation would turn to the glass-doored cabinet just behind him. It was filled with old baseballs dating back to Brooklyn's great club teams in the years just after the Civil War.[29]

Even with their fans, who were more vociferous than numerous, the Dodgers had fallen on exceedingly hard times by the end of the 1937 season. Phone service had been cut off because the bills were not being paid. The team's office was crowded with process servers seeking payment.[30] Ebbets Field was a mass of broken seats, begging for a paint job. Charles Ebbets's pride, the beautiful rotunda, was covered with mildew.[31] The heirs had borrowed heavily against the value of their Dodger stock, and the stock was worth less and less. The team's officials had begun to seek the solace of banks, owing more than $500,000. Its office address became 215 Montague Street, in the Brooklyn Trust Company building.[32]

From time to time stories that the club was about to be sold would make the papers, only to have Jim Mulvey or some other club official say the current owners were dedicated to rebuilding the team. Left unsaid was that the club's debt level was so high that the heirs could expect little cash from any sale, and cash was their main interest.[33]

The Brooklyn Trust Company was the team's bank and also represented the estates of Ebbets and Ed McKeever. Its president was Walter O'Malley's sponsor, George V. McLaughlin, a man to continue the Dodgers' history of intimate connections with New York politics.

Brooklyn continued to grow in population through the 1930s, but there were troubling signs of economic change. In 1939 *Fortune* did a special edition on New York City, including a long article detailing the important economic role played by Brooklyn and Queens, Manhattan's workshops as well as its bedrooms. There had been significant economic decline for the city in the decade between 1927 and 1937, even more than the effects of the Depression would lead one to anticipate, *Fortune* editors wrote. The value of Brooklyn's manufacturing production was off 29 percent, led by declines in clothing and shoes, while the nation's manufacturing production had fallen barely 3 percent. The number of factories had dropped to 4,100 from 5,300, and eleven thousand manufacturing jobs had disappeared.[34] The character of what was left was interesting. Only 8 of the combined 5,460 factories in Brooklyn and Queens employed more than a thousand people. Most employed fewer than ten. That pointed to lightly capitalized businesses, sensitive to costs and capable of being moved easily.

By late 1937 the Dodgers owed $700,000 to the Brooklyn Trust Company, $470,000 on a refinanced mortgage for Ebbets Field.[35] It had lost $129,140 in 1937 and had not turned a profit since 1930.[36] New York bank examiners were pressuring McLaughlin about overdue loans to the team.[37] National League president Ford Frick was threatening to take the franchise back for unpaid bills.[38] It was not a unique situation. The Depression had hit many Major League teams. Sidney Weil had lost the Cincinnati Reds to his bank in 1933. In Philadelphia the Phillies and Athletics spent the decade keeping their heads above water by selling their players at the first sign of competence.

The board remained divided, with the Ebbets and McKeever blocs unable to reach agreement. McLaughlin, anxious to get repaid, cut off any future advances to the team unless the board found a strong executive. Thrashing around for a solution, Jim Mulvey approached Frick. Frick suggested Cardinals vice president Branch Rickey might be interested. Rickey said no, but suggested he might have someone who wanted the job, Leland Stanford "Larry" MacPhail. McLaughlin consulted Frick and got the go-ahead.[39]

When he came to Brooklyn the forty-seven-year-old MacPhail carried a large and speckled reputation.[40] Born in Michigan, MacPhail had gotten his law degree and made a success of retailing in Nashville. During World War I he had joined a Tennessee regiment. He was nicked by shrapnel and caught a whiff of poison gas, but the war story he loved to tell happened after the cease-fire. MacPhail joined a scheme to kidnap the German kaiser, in retirement in Holland after the war. The harebrained escapade was unsuccessful, although MacPhail forever after kept a bronze ashtray embossed with "W I" (Wilhelm Imperator) on his desk. MacPhail said he had stolen it from the kaiser's desk while waiting (unsuccessfully) to be shown into Wilhelm's presence.

In Columbus, Ohio, after the war, MacPhail was refereeing college football games while moving from glass manufacturing to car sales to construction. His inventive mind led him to develop the system of hand signals for penalties still used by football referees today. He was making money, but remained restless. He formed a group to buy the town's Minor League team after the 1930 season. He ran the team for three seasons, making it profitable and selling it to the Cardinals as a farm club. He had impressed Rickey despite a clash that got MacPhail fired. In late 1933, when the National League was casting around for someone to run the struggling Cincinnati Reds for the team's bankers, Rickey had suggested MacPhail.

In three years with the Reds, he turned the team into a profitable franchise. He was one of the game's first marketing innovators, from such seemingly obvious things as keeping the ballpark nicely painted and the seats in good repair to touches such as spiffy uniforms for ushers and pretty young women wandering the stands selling cigarettes. There were fireworks and bands.

But MacPhail also broke new ground. Years before Charlie Finley he tried colored baseballs. He greatly expanded the reach of the Reds' radio network. Many baseball owners had believed free broadcasts would give people little reason to come to the ballpark. MacPhail saw radio as a way to build interest and excitement. Not the least of the reasons for radio's success in Cincinnati was MacPhail's use of a young announcer from Florida named Walter "Red" Barber.

His most spectacular promotion was night baseball. Although night games had been used in exhibitions as far back as 1883, it had not caught on, even in the Minors, until owners tried every possible way to sell a ticket during the Depression. Baseball, as conservative as ever, was considered an afternoon game. But nobody had done it in the Majors until MacPhail's Reds hosted the league-doormat Phillies on May 24, 1935, in front of 20,422 fans.

But he also wore out his welcome. "There is no question in my mind but that Larry MacPhail was a genius," said Leo Durocher, who managed the Dodgers for him. But "there is that thin line between genius and insanity, and in Larry's case it was sometimes so thin you could see him drifting back and forth." MacPhail was an abrasive man whose abrasiveness was made worse by a drinking problem. "Cold sober he was brilliant. One drink and he was even more brilliant. Two drinks—that's another story," said Durocher.[41] He would look for scapegoats on his staff, get into fights with one and all, and offend many. By the end of the 1936 season, Cincinnati owner Powel Crosley had had enough, and MacPhail spent 1937 with a family business in Michigan.

MacPhail was a florid man in hair, complexion, dress, and manner. He gave interviews slumped in his office chair, scrunching down so much one interviewer said he eventually could see nothing but the soles of the shoes MacPhail propped on his desk.[42] He was verbally aggressive, belittling employees and raging when things did not go his way. He could fire people numerous times, or only once, depending on his mood. One secretary got her job, and kept it for years, after a confrontation with MacPhail in her first hours.[43] But others were not so fortunate. While in Brooklyn MacPhail's marriage with his first wife was falling apart as he took up with his secretary. When the distraught Mrs. MacPhail decided she had to get away, she went to stay with the fiancée of the couple's oldest son, future Major League general manager and American League (AL) president Lee MacPhail. When the enraged MacPhail found where his wife was, he fired his son's fiancée, who had been working in the Dodgers' office.[44]

MacPhail began the first steps toward creating the solid franchise the Dodgers are today. Some of those changes were cosmetic, but others were fundamental. The cosmetics began with $200,000 McLaughlin had agreed to provide before MacPhail would take the job. Ebbets Field, a monument to peeling paint and mildew, was cleaned and painted turquoise. Its many broken seats were repaired. The infamous corps of usher-thugs was weeded out and retrained. One afternoon in MacPhail's first year, the unemployed Babe Ruth walked into the ballpark. MacPhail noticed that far more people watched Ruth in the stands than the hapless Dodgers on the field. The next day Ruth was hired as a coach. Ruth was hopeful the coach's berth would turn into a managing job. But it was clear MacPhail wanted him to take his daily round of batting practice for the fans and coach a little first base.

MacPhail, in fact, already had his eye on his manager, a loud-mouthed, light-hitting clotheshorse who was playing shortstop for the team. Leo Durocher was one of MacPhail's noncosmetic moves. Another was using an additional $50,000 from McLaughlin to buy first baseman Dolph Camilli from the even more hapless Phillies.

He began to spend money on other players. With Durocher as manager in 1939, the team moved into a competitive third-place finish, and the fans started to come back. He scheduled Brooklyn's first night game and was rewarded when the fates tossed up Cincinnati lefthander Johnny Vander Meer as the opposing pitcher. Vander Meer's last outing had been a no-hitter, and under the lights that night he became the only pitcher every to throw consecutive no-hitters.

MacPhail also broke the gentlemen's agreement among New York teams not to broadcast their games on radio. He imported Barber from Cincinnati and locked up a powerful channel and a strong sponsor before the Yankees or the Giants moved. It took Brooklyn fans a while to get used to Barber's southernisms such as "the catbird seat" and "the rhubarb patch," but once they did he became a valuable tool for building interest in the improving product on the field.

With the ballpark fixed up, the team improving, and the Depression finally being dispersed by the onset of World War II, the results quickly showed at the box office and in the team's books. Attendance was up 37 percent in 1938, despite a drop in the standings from sixth to seventh place. By 1940 the Dodgers led the National League in attendance for the first time. The next year, with a pennant-winning team, attendance hit a franchise record 1.2 million.

After the team's steep losses from 1931 through 1937, MacPhail cut the team's loss to a paltry $3,751 in 1938 and began making profits the next year. And all that financial improvement came despite MacPhail's buying ballplayers left and right. The club owed Brooklyn Trust $230,000 when MacPhail arrived, with another $470,000 owed on the Ebbets Field mortgage. Spending money on players and paint, he ran the club's debt to $501,000 by early 1939. By mid-July 1941 the deficit was gone, as attendance turned into profits.[45] The mortgage remained, but was down to $300,000, and the team had $300,000 in the bank, MacPhail told reporters.[46] The team's book-keeper would tell MacPhail's replacement that there was $143,768.99 in the bank and $358,000 still owed on the mortgage.[47]

There was not as much money as the board thought there should be, however. When Mulvey had sought Rickey's advice on hiring MacPhail, Rickey had warned that MacPhail would not pay the heirs dividends. In fact, MacPhail's whole record was a long rap sheet of welcomes worn out. The erratic behavior and drinking eventually overcame extraordinary per-formance. Despite the profits the Ebbets and Ed McKeever estates and the

Mulveys had not received a dividend since 1932.[48] And they had begun to hear stories. MacPhail was known to dip into the cash drawer before going to the racetrack.[49] They were outraged when, in August 1942, MacPhail called the whole team to a meeting, included all the newspaper reporters, and then predicted the Dodgers would lose the pennant race, where they had taken an eight-game lead.[50] That he was right only made it worse.

Although MacPhail had proved himself a great promoter, he was a disaster as an administrator. Dodger scout Ted McGrew told of being ordered to fly from Seattle to Memphis to check out a player with whom MacPhail had become fascinated. McGrew had seen the player many times before and judged him unsuitable. When he got to Memphis he found MacPhail had sent the Dodgers' other scout as well. McGrew then had to return to the West Coast, the whole journey adding $500 to the scouting budget to deal with one of MacPhail's passing enthusiasms.[51] With MacPhail's departure a state banking examiner ordered McLaughlin to find out "what the hell is going on with the Dodgers' books." McLaughlin's investigator found the team was grossing somewhere between $2.5 million and $4 million, but not all of it was making its way to the bank.[52] This had to be stopped.

Whether MacPhail quit or was fired is a matter of dispute. MacPhail said he had been talking about going back into the Army beginning in March 1942. The *Sporting News* printed a rumor to that effect in August. After that rumor surfaced MacPhail reportedly irritated the board yet again by disobeying specific orders and paying $40,000 for pitcher Bobo Newsom.[53] In September MacPhail announced he was going into the service.

Mulvey turned once again to Branch Rickey. Rickey, wrote the *New York Times*'s John Drebinger, was "a man of strange complexities, not to mention downright contradictions."[54] The great decision to break baseball's policy of excluding blacks, for which he is justly praised, has, in recent decades, tended to overwhelm the highly negative image he had earned before that decision. He went from "El Cheapo" to moral beacon in just a few years, and richly deserved each characterization.

He was deeply religious, sowing biblical quotations and religious axioms like Johnny Appleseed.[55] He was a tightwad. "Rickey believes in economy in everything except his own salary," wrote the *New York Daily Mirror*'s Dan Parker.[56] *Daily News* columnist Jimmy Powers tagged him "El Cheapo" after Rickey dumped a number of the Dodgers' older, and better-known, players soon after taking over. Ralph Kiner, who engaged in some slashing salary battles with Rickey in Pittsburgh, said, "Rickey had all the money and all the players. He just didn't believe in letting the two mix."[57] He was politically and socially conservative. He preached on the temperance circuit as a young man and, as an older man, would regularly attack communism, communists, and liberal politicians.[58] He was devious. Bob Broeg of the *St. Louis Post-Dispatch* dubbed him "Branch Richelieu."[59] Rickey could "think up many a little scheme that, while not dishonest, still will not leave Rickey & Co. holding the sack on the snipe hunt," wrote Bill Corum in the *New York Journal-American*.[60] In later life he could write a letter to Jackie Robinson congratulating Robinson on his public support of liberal Republican presidential candidate Nelson Rockefeller. "I deeply opposed Mr. Goldwater," the letter swears. At the same time Rickey was contributing $200 to the conservative Goldwater's presidential campaign.[61]

He could bring Robinson to the Majors and tell stories of being deeply moved when an African American player he coached in college sought to rub off his skin color to escape the prejudices of white America, but he could also relate dialect jokes.[62] He made anti-Catholic remarks at the dinner table and characterized a potential Dodger purchaser as "of Jewish extraction and characteristics."[63] He also reneged on a contract offer when he found the player was Jewish.[64] He was idealistic, regularly giving talks suggesting wars should be replaced by athletic contests.[65] He was articulate, if inclined to overdo the rhetoric and the vocabulary. "Rickey's natural element is the pulpit," wrote Red Smith.[66] "He talks with such pontifical oratory that he could and would make a reading of batting averages sound as impressive and as stirring as Lincoln's Gettysburg Address," said the *New York Times*'s Arthur Daley.[67]

He was absent-minded, often tossing lighted matches into trash cans filled with paper and acknowledging defeat when his five daughters all wound up with fingers next to their noses, the family code that somebody was talking too much. Jane Moulton Rickey, whom he had met at twelve, proposed to a hundred times, and married at twenty-four, could note, "Mr. Rickey is not, and never has been, one of the ten best-groomed men in America."[68] He was fearsomely intelligent, well read, and thoughtful.

Wesley Branch Rickey had been born November 20, 1881, in Scioto County, Ohio, to a poor farming family. He finished grade school, but then farm labor called. With help from a sympathetic retired educator, he read as widely as the resources of Scioto County allowed in the 1890s. He educated himself enough to become the teacher at the local grade school, saving money for college. Eventually, he went off to Ohio Wesleyan University.

For the next decade Rickey's life was a welter of sporadic academics, sports, and, eventually, coaching. He played baseball and football at Wesleyan and realized he could make money to pay for his studies. He spent part of several seasons in the Majors, getting himself a reputation as a marginal catcher, a poor hitter, and an odd duck for honoring a vow to his deeply religious mother never to play baseball on Sundays.

He had married Jane in 1906, just before getting his BA from Ohio Wesleyan. Her family gave him leave to continue playing professional baseball for two more seasons. But they wanted him to become a professional man. After a bout with tuberculosis he managed to convince the University of Michigan to admit him to its law school and to make him the baseball coach to support his family.

In 1911, on the verge of thirty, Branch Rickey graduated from law school and chose Boise, Idaho, as the site of his law office. He was, by his own account, a miserable failure. The impressions he had made as a baseball player and coach came to his rescue. Even while in Boise, he had spent his summers scouting for Robert Hedges, owner of the American League's St. Louis Browns. After his second unsuccessful winter in Boise, Rickey was only too happy to respond to Hedges's request for a meeting in Salt Lake City to discuss a full-time job with the Browns. He borrowed the train fare from Hedges and began a half century of life in professional baseball.[69]

By mid-1913 Rickey was the manager of the Browns. In 1916 a new Browns owner made him business manager, and a year later he moved to St. Louis's National League entry, the Cardinals, in that role. He was soon off to the Army, joining the chemical-warfare branch for the remainder of World War I and returning as field manager of the Cardinals until 1925. His record was mediocre, and he gained a label as too much of a theorist, inclined to lecture his players on how to do things, but unable to motivate them. The proof they pointed to was that in 1926, with the players Rickey had chosen and trained, but with Rogers Hornsby as manager, the Cardinals won their first pennant.

His bosses and his rivals all recognized his brilliance as a baseball man, but thought he was too otherworldly for the tobacco-stained game on the field. Baseball simply did not know what to do with him. In those days baseball was a game of entrepreneurial owners, who functioned in the roles twenty-first-century teams split among a general manager, a business manager, a scouting director, and a president. It was only when Rickey was kicked upstairs from the Cardinals' dugout that he found his true role. "Rickey practically created the office of business manager as it is understood today," wrote the *New York Times*'s John Drebinger in 1943.[70]

Rickey's first great innovation was the farm system. "When the Cardinals were fighting for their life in the National League, I found that we were at a disadvantage in obtaining players of merit from the minors," Rickey said.

> Other clubs could outbid. They had money. They had superior scouting machinery. In short, we had to take what was left or nothing at all. The New York Giants, a wealthy club, became the worst thorn in the side of our open negotiations for players. We simply could not compete with the inducements they offered minor clubs for players. Thus it was that we took over the Houston Club for a Class A proving ground in 1924. . . . Still, I do not feel that the farming system we have established is the result of any inventive genius—it is the result of stark necessity. We did it to meet a question of supply and demand of young ball players.[71]

The Cardinals eventually created a chain of Minor League teams where they could sign players cheaply, winnow the good from the great, win pennants, and make money. Rickey would sell the good to others and keep the great for the Cardinals.

Rickey proved a cold-blooded judge of talent and a man with the knack of nurturing what talent he had. He was not the sentimentalist to hang on to an aging player who had contributed greatly to the team's past success. It is better to trade a man a year too early than a year too late, he preached. He created the concept of the "anesthetic ballplayer," the one who is good enough to be a Major Leaguer, but not good enough to help win a pennant or a World Series.[72] Trading the anesthetics and the fading stars filled holes the farm system could not. And in the Minors Rickey was an innovator not just in creating, but also in teaching.

He came up with sand pits to teach players to slide, a set of strings to define the strike zone and help pitchers with control, the batting tee to help hitters hone their swings, and evening chalk talks.[73] He was the first baseball executive to hire a club statistician and to use him to help improve the team. Allan Roth charted where Dodger batters' hits fell, noted that more and more of Dixie Walker's were going to the opposite field rather than being pulled, and gave Rickey the tip to trade the former National League batting champion a year too soon.[74] Rickey was observant in a way that amazed other baseball men. There was the story of one pitch—a foul ball—while Rickey was sitting behind the plate one day. After the pitch he turned to an aide and dictated the following notes: the center fielder had failed to get a jump on the ball, the pitcher had an unbalanced motion and would not be able to field his position, and the catcher had blinked as the batter swung, causing him to miss the foul tip.[75]

Rickey was asked to speak often and was never afraid to tie his conservative religious and political beliefs with his baseball success. He befriended political figures, usually conservative Republicans. He was approached to run for governor of Missouri.[76] He was described as one of Republican presidential candidate Thomas Dewey's closest friends and supporters and touted as New York governor if Dewey was elected president.[77] His political convictions were highly colored. In late 1945 he wrote a letter to another conservative friend and ally, Ohio Republican senator John Bricker, extolling the legal and personal talents of Rickey's son-in-law John Eckler, pushing him to be hired by Bricker's law firm. After the praise Rickey wrote, "Now, the bad part. John is a Democrat. He's a Jeffersonian Democrat, thank heaven—not too much a New Dealer. . . . But you're probably made up pretty strong Republican—as a firm, a cordial Democrat might not hurt—one with sense and good breeding—and there's not too many."[78]

By late 1942 Rickey's relations with Cardinal owner Sam Breadon could best be described as rocky. Beginning in 1926 the Cardinals had won a third of the National League's pennants plus four World Series. The team Rickey had constructed would win three more pennants and two World Series in the four years immediately after he left. Yet Sam Breadon was unhappy. He said Rickey earned more money than he did.[79] The two were fighting over Rickey's bonus payments and Breadon's dismissal of Rickey protégés in the farm system.[80] Rickey reportedly was upset at Breadon's refusal to back him in a dispute with baseball commissioner Kenesaw Mountain Landis and with Breadon paying a large bonus to himself while cutting Rickey's budget for salaries.[81] Rickey was considering a top executive post with a large insurance company.[82]

In 1937, when Mulvey first approached Rickey, he had reportedly been authorized to offer an ownership stake.[83] Rickey had quietly made inquiries about buying the Dodgers.[84] Now, after five years of MacPhail, the team's finances had improved. With Rickey's reputation, and the Dodgers' financial improvement, it would be easier for the Brooklyn Trust Company to fulfill its responsibilities to the Ebbets and McKeever estates. A sale in which

Branch Rickey gained some ownership and remained to run the team would be attractive to many potential buyers. For Rickey, ownership was a positive inducement to complement his desire to escape Breadon.

The wooing was relatively quick. The *New York Times* first reported Brooklyn-Rickey talks October 4, 1942. The move was announced on October 29, a day when Rickey was introduced as the new general manager at a lunch at the Brooklyn Club. At that lunch Rickey was also introduced to a thirty-eight-year-old lawyer who shared the Brooklyn Trust table with him. The lawyer's name was Walter O'Malley.

3

Under New Management

Walter O'Malley's appearance at Branch Rickey's table was no coincidence. George V. McLaughlin needed an exit strategy for Brooklyn Trust's entanglement with the Dodgers, and he was lining up the dominoes.

McLaughlin had multiple, at times conflicting, obligations centered on the Dodgers. The bank was a trustee of both the Charles Ebbets and the Edward McKeever estates and thus bound to protect the heirs' interests, getting them the greatest return possible on their Dodger stock. And because much of the stock had been used as collateral for loans from the bank, a higher price for the stock would make it more likely those loans would be repaid. Like the shareholders, the team still owed money to Brooklyn Trust, and he had to make sure his bank was repaid. The Dodgers were the most visible symbol of Brooklyn, and any misstep could be a public relations boondoggle for the borough's biggest bank. In early 1942 he had attempted to end the bank's role as trustee for the Ebbets heirs in part because of the bad publicity the bank was receiving for the perceived conflict of interest.[1] He needed to sell the team to a person or a group who could satisfy the heirs, the bank, and the borough's fans.

Branch Rickey was the first piece of the puzzle. For the team to pay off the debts, it would have to be successful and well managed. Who better to do that than Rickey? Success would be necessary to provide Rickey with the money he would need to buy a share of the team, and McLaughlin was in a position to make sure Rickey had the opportunity to buy. But there would have to be other pieces of the puzzle. Rickey would need partners with their own substantial funds. And McLaughlin would like to keep his own man around to make sure things continued to run well, someone who had both McLaughlin's confidence and the skills to watch the business end of the team while Rickey concentrated on the baseball end.

Rickey had his own motivations. The Dodgers' legal business had been handled by a large Wall Street firm that also represented the National League. Rickey recognized those relationships might create a conflict of interest.[2] He also wanted to cut costs and consulted George Barnewall, who represented Brooklyn Trust on the Dodgers' Board of Directors. Barnewall, not surprisingly, recommended O'Malley, and Rickey soon recognized that O'Malley was "the personal representative, in all legal matters, of Mr. George V. Mclaughlin."[3] Soon O'Malley was the Dodgers' legal representative and getting his hands into the business aspects of the team.

To all appearances, Walter O'Malley was a casual fan at that point. His boyhood interest in the Giants had evolved into a more practical relationship with the game. He recalled seeing his first Ebbets Field game about 1935, as his relationship with McLaughlin was flowering, and he became a boxseat holder because he could get better seats for entertaining clients there than he could at Yankee Stadium.[4] Working with Brooklyn Trust's financially troubled customers was the core of Walter O'Malley's law practice, and adding a high-profile client such as the Dodgers could only enhance his law firm's reputation. "I never realized O'Malley would be this interested in baseball," Rickey said later, but Rickey was impressed by how quickly O'Malley got a property near Ebbets Field condemned by city authorities so the Dodgers could use it.[5]

Unlike many owners O'Malley was entering the ranks as an investment proposition. He was not a "sportsman," a rich man such as Tom Yawkey of the Red Sox or Dan Topping of the Yankees, who wanted a fun business to give them a higher profile. He was not a baseball lifer such as Rickey, who expected to spend his life with the game and was therefore emotionally committed to it. O'Malley saw opportunity for profits. Although his fandom would grow, he remained a businessman and not a "baseball man."

Rickey and O'Malley settled into their roles. Rickey began to remake the Dodgers' roster and build up the farm system. O'Malley began learning the world of marketing, broadcasting contracts, ticket sales, and stadium operations. The team's on-field operations stumbled as players left for the military, but the business operations improved, and others noticed.

The first offer to buy the team had actually come before Rickey and O'Malley arrived. MacPhail's boasted progress and the increasing attendance brought out a syndicate headed by boxing promoter Mike Jacobs in August 1940. Jacobs said his bid was more than $2 million, but was contingent on getting full control of the team. McLaughlin reacted negatively, and Dearie Mulvey said there was no way she would sell her 25 percent of the team. The bid died quickly.[6]

As the effects of the Rickey-O'Malley management became clearer, and the end of World War II began to appear on the horizon, other bidders emerged. Max Meyer, a Brooklyn jeweler and former part owner of the Boston Braves, revealed in early 1944 that he had obtained an option to purchase the 25 percent owned by the Ed McKeever estate and was negotiating to buy the 50 percent owned by the Ebbets heirs.[7] This bid fell apart, too, with Meyer claiming he had been confronted by "additional financial burdens" necessary to conclude the deal and McLaughlin claiming Meyer could not come up with the money. While McLaughlin and bank officials were dismissive of Meyer's offer in public, Rickey said in a private letter that Meyer was almost successful.[8] Another rumored sale floated to the surface in early March, but never amounted to anything.[9]

The abortive sales highlighted another complication for McLaughlin. For the smooth future operations of the club, an ownership group that could exercise full control was necessary, and, since the Mulvey quarter ownership was clearly not available, that meant obtaining both the Ed McKeever and the Ebbets shares. As the team's banker McLaughlin had watched throughout the 1930s as the team's management stagnated while the fifty-fifty stock split of the McKeever and Ebbets blocs strangled daily operations, much less attempts to deal with long-term problems. Rickey noted the bank had found it impossible to get an offer for the Ebbets shares throughout that decade because potential buyers knew their investment would bring them not control, but a few seats on the board of directors with the necessity of sitting through rancorous, often unproductive meetings. In fact, when James Mulvey offered to buy the McKeever shares after the Meyer offer fell through, McLaughlin would not agree to sell the shares to him for fear of the fifty-fifty split that would make the Ebbets shares all but impossible to sell.[10]

Nevertheless, it was clear to all concerned that pressure for a sale was building. As the option Meyer had obtained showed, the Ed McKeever shares were available. Rickey and O'Malley, who had been discussing the potential problems that could be produced by new ownership, began exploring. They clearly had the inside edge with the bank, but they had to raise the money, which they knew would be $240,000. "Mr. O'Malley took hold of things at this point," wrote Rickey. O'Malley put down $25,000 of his own money to get an option on the Ed McKeever heirs' shares.[11]

Rickey was a man who constantly lived at the edge of his income. O'Malley could come up with his share and put down the option money, but they needed partners with serious money. By March 1944 Rickey was soliciting old acquaintances, but did not want to get too many more people involved.[12] By the fall another social and business acquaintance of McLaughlin and O'Malley entered the fold. He was Andrew Schmitz, a highly successful insurance executive with Brooklyn ties. Rickey borrowed $20,000 from Brooklyn Trust in September, and the deal was closed October 27.[13]

The newspaper accounts focused on Rickey's move into ownership, with lesser attention paid to Schmitz and O'Malley. But several of the stories noted that this was only a preliminary to gaining the Ebbets shares and full control of the team.[14] The Ebbets shares would be harder, as the Ebbets family was divided, hocked to the hilt on their shares, and fully lawyered up. Many rested their hopes for the future on the sale of their Dodger stock. Ebbets had divided his estate among his second wife, four children by his first wife, plus various grandchildren. The will was also encumbered by promised annuity payments to his first wife and son and by a bequest to fund the "Coal-Holers" annual banquet group that O'Malley attended. By 1944 the Surrogates Court handling the case had fifty-nine separate claimants or litigants, many of whom had borrowed money from Brooklyn Trust using the team's stock as collateral. The file contained claims from twenty-five law firms totaling $150,000 in fees.[15] O'Malley would have to guide an offer through the Surrogates Court that satisfied all parties.

While O'Malley worked behind the scenes, other potential buyers clouded the public picture. Early in 1945 the Brooklyn American Legion announced it was interested in buying the team.[16] Rickey and his partners said little in public and did not respond to the legion's request to see the books.[17] The legion's offer dribbled into silence. At the same time another potential buyer, future Broadway producer Lester Osterman, approached Rickey about a purchase of the Ebbets shares. He provided documentation of his ability to pay and was sent off to talk to Brooklyn Trust.[18]

For the partners, anxious to strike a deal with both Brooklyn Trust and the Surrogates Court for the Ebbets shares, the problem these offers presented was the price they were willing to pay. The legion said it would pay $2 million for all the shares. (The Yankees had recently sold for $2.8 million.) Osterman said he would pay $1 million for the Ebbets shares alone. Both of these offers ran up against the problem that had dogged the club since Ebbets's death. For Osterman, $1 million would not buy him control, but only get him a chance for head-butting. For the legion, the Mulvey share, and presumably the Rickey-O'Malley partners share, was not for sale at all, leaving their bid in limbo. And if they accepted the possibility of buying just the Ebbets shares, they would be in the same position as Osterman. Nevertheless, the price that was being put on half the franchise was $1 million, more than the $650,000 the partners hoped to pay or the $750,000 they were willing to pay.[19] Brooklyn Trust, with its fiduciary duty to the trustees, had seen both offers.

By early-May 1945 the partners were making their first formal offer for the Ebbets shares and examining how they could finance it out of team revenues.[20] In June the Surrogates Court refused the $650,000 offer at the behest of the Ebbets heirs. In July, with the bid raised to $800,000, the court approved the sale. It was announced in mid-August. In all the newspapers it was Rickey who had bought the team, with his partners relegated to the lower paragraphs. In the *Brooklyn Eagle* Harold C. Burr confidently reported that the sale gave Rickey "absolute control of the Dodgers, to run as he pleases."[21]

In the background that control was not so clear, as events were to prove over the next five years. The partnership had changed in important ways. When the sale of the Ed McKeever estate's shares had been announced the previous year, the buyers had been presented as Rickey, O'Malley, and Schmitz. Silent in the background was a fourth partner, John L. Smith, president of Brooklyn-based Pfizer Chemical. In May, while they were making their first formal offer, the group had approached James Mulvey about buying 5 percentage points of his family's 25 percent share of the team. This 5 percent was to be split among Rickey and his three partners, giving each of the five shareholders 20 percent of the team, assuming the partners bought the Ebbets shares. Such a distribution would prevent fifty-fifty standoffs in the boardroom.[22] Mulvey was not interested.

The failure of this gambit led Schmitz to drop out of the partnership.[23] And it led McLaughlin to require a partnership agreement among Rickey, O'Malley, and Smith to prevent boardroom stalemates. This agreement was to set the stage for governing the team over the next five years and set the ground rules that led to O'Malley's final control. In the agreement Rickey, O'Malley, and Smith stipulated that they would each own 25 percent of the team separately, but that they would pool their shares for purposes of voting in the boardroom.[24] Thus, if there was a disagreement between, say, Rickey and O'Malley, whoever could swing Smith to their point of view would control how the 75 percent share of the stock was voted.

Smith's role was also enhanced because he had the money to make the deal go smoothly. Brooklyn Trust had agreed to finance the triumvirate's purchase. The $240,000 to purchase the Ed McKeever shares was turned over into a new financial package totaling $1,046,000, a sum that also included buying out Schmitz. The bank loaned the triumvirate $650,000 against the value of the Dodgers stock. O'Malley and Smith financed the remainder of their shares out of their own pockets. Rickey borrowed $99,500 from the bank using stock and life insurance policies as collateral. With Rickey's personal assets used up, the bank loaned him another $72,000 based on guarantees from Smith and O'Malley.[25] Smith could have handled his share of the $650,000 with a check, but chose to go along with his partners in the overall financial agreement.

When he died in 1950, John Lawrence Smith's *New York Times* obituary called him a "noted chemist," a label the unassuming executive would have appreciated.[26] It was not until later that the story mentioned he was a part owner of the Brooklyn Dodgers. To the nonbaseball world Smith had made his name as an executive of Charles Pfizer & Company, and especially for his role in leading the Brooklyn company's pioneering effort in the mass production of penicillin. His leadership was critical in moving Pfizer from a chemical supplier into an international pharmaceuticals giant.[27]

But to the baseball world of the late 1940s, he was the pivot on which the ownership of the Dodgers balanced. His financial resources and his relationship with McLaughlin made him a useful partner, and he soon struck up a relationship with Rickey based on their parallel rags-to-riches stories and their religious sympathies. With O'Malley the tie was less significant, but older. As a young man Smith had worked with Edwin O'Malley on the Hollis Volunteer Fire Company. After a fire Smith would slip Walter and his friends a few dollars for sodas when they did the dirty work of rolling up the wet hoses.[28]

Smith was born in Krefeld, Germany, on February 10, 1889, as Johann Schmitz, the son of Gottfried and Johanna Schmitz.[29] Krefeld was a center of the German velvet industry, and Gottfried moved his family to Stonington, Connecticut, in 1892 to pursue opportunities in Stonington's velvet mills. Although they spoke German at home, the family formally changed its name to Smith in 1918, presumably as the result of anti-German agitation during World War I. John, who was naturalized in 1908, used the Anglicized version from the time he entered the working world.

That was at seventeen. Gottfried and his four other children remained in Stonington, mostly working in the mills, but John had larger ambitions. In 1906 he moved to New York City, looking for work as a chemist. He found a job as a laboratory assistant with Pfizer in Brooklyn and began to take classes at Cooper Union. While working and studying Smith found time for baseball, which he said he played poorly, and track, where he did rather better. It was the sign of a lifelong interest in sports.

In 1914 he got his degree in chemistry, married Mary Louise Becker, and moved to E. R. Squibb, where he oversaw the development of a large-scale ether-making facility at their Brooklyn plant. By 1919 he returned to Pfizer, becoming plant superintendent. He would remain at Pfizer the rest of his life.

The Pfizer Smith rejoined specialized in producing chemical ingredients used by food and beverage manufacturers as well as druggists, as it had since its founding in 1849. Smith would push Pfizer to a much stronger emphasis on research into both chemistry and production methods, hiring the company's first director of research in 1920. Pfizer moved from being an industrial chemical supplier to a consumer pharmaceuticals producer. In the 1920s John McKeen, who would succeed Smith as Pfizer's president, described the man who had recently hired him:

> [Smith was] neat, orderly and impeccably dressed. Seated at his desk, his daily attire was an immaculate high-starched collar and a four-in-hand necktie in the fashion of the day. In his daily visits through the plant, Mr. Smith appeared with sleeves rolled up, no collar or tie, and delved into the operations, moving into all areas, including those that were hot and humid as well. He was personally on hand for the start-up of any operation and kept an eye on any new construction in progress. He worked long hours, nights and Saturdays, was acquainted with all details of the operations, and was a thoroughly competent scientist.

The first major fruit of Smith's work was a revolutionary process to manufacture citric acid. Traditionally, citric acid had been made using lemons and limes from Mediterranean countries. When World War I severely curtailed the availability of citrus from Italy, manufacturers such as Pfizer turned to a process that produced citric acid from sugar. Through the 1920s and up to 1933, Smith led the company's efforts to perfect the process of fermentation in large tanks and then extend that process to other chemicals.

By 1929 Smith was a vice president of the firm and living a upper-middle-class life. The census of 1930 found him on East Eighteenth Street in Brooklyn, living in a fully paid-for house valued at $28,000. For comparison, only 10.5 percent of New York City home owners had homes valued at more than $20,000, and that figure fell to 3.4 percent nationwide. Smith owned a radio, and he and Mary Louise had daughters aged eight and twelve.

As his responsibilities grew Smith showed an eye for people as well as research and management. In 1934 an attempt at unionization in one part of Pfizer's operations left two other Pfizer departments with little to do during a strike. They challenged each other to a baseball game. When the word got to Smith he encouraged them to keep playing after hours and on weekends. He paid for sandwiches and beer for the after-game refreshments. The Pfizer team moved on to challenge other companies, and when they suffered some serious defeats, Smith suggested to other company managers that they hire people who were also good ballplayers. Bowling, basketball, golf, and softball teams for both men and women followed as the company sports program expanded.

Smith's benevolence with the employees was balanced by a driving desire for results. In the staff dining room he instituted a system where every manager was assigned a number, which was then embossed onto a napkin ring. Most of the napkin rings were distributed randomly by the dining staff so that people who would not otherwise talk would share a table and be led into exchanging experiences and ideas. But many days Smith would call down to the dining room before lunch and ask that certain napkin rings be assigned to his table. The manager of some department Smith was interested in or concerned about would be grilled over the roast chicken. He was focused on results, but also keeping costs down. In the 1920s the people overseeing the citric-acid fermentation process were often his luncheon companions. By the 1940s the people subjected to the lunchtime interrogation were working on a revolutionary product and process, one that would cement Smith's, and Pfizer's, place in the world of pharmaceuticals.

In 1928 Scottish physician Alexander Fleming noticed a mold in his laboratory that destroyed bacteria. He sought funding from the British government for further research, but was denied. After World War II began in late 1939, the government began to reexamine research proposals to identify those that might help win the war. Suddenly, there was money to continue Fleming's research, which soon confirmed the antibiotic properties of penicillin. But manufacturing the drug in any but the smallest amounts proved impossible.

With many pressures on their own economy, the British turned the possibilities of penicillin over to the United States in early 1941. Washington sought the help of American chemical companies. Some companies, such as Merck and Squibb, decided to focus on breaking down the basic chemistry of penicillin with an eye to producing a synthetic drug. Pfizer wanted to explore adapting the deep-tank fermentation process they had developed for citric acid. But the risks were high. In late 1942 yields were still very low, and the capital costs were high. That fall Smith called a meeting of the company's managers and shareholders, laying out the risks as well as the possibilities. The meeting agreed they would bet the company's future on its ability to solve the production problems. Smith's lunchtime question sessions intensified.

There was pressure not only to produce it, but to produce it in useful quantities. Several early trials of the drug failed because physicians were not using large enough doses. The government clamped down on usage to ensure that virtually all the available supply went to wounded servicemen. Pfizer took some of its small allotment for research purposes and turned it over to Dr. Leo Loewe at Brooklyn Jewish Hospital. The critical case came with a young girl stricken with subacute bacterial endocarditis, an infection of the inner lining of the heart. She was not responding to the penicillin, and Smith and McKeen spent hours sitting by her bed trying to coax her through. Eventually, Loewe upped the dosage far beyond recommendations, and the color began to return to her cheeks as Smith and McKeen watched.

Eventually, after much trial and error, the deep-tank fermentation process began to produce in quantity. In the first half of 1943 enough penicillin was produced to treat about 180 severe cases. In the last half enough was produced to handle more than 9,000 cases. By D day, it was just under 40,000 cases worth of production per month. Half of the world's penicillin was coming from Pfizer's Brooklyn plants, and the price per dose had dropped from $20 in early 1943 to $1. The company's first public stock offering was oversubscribed, and the share's value soared on Wall Street.[30] Smith's reward was Pfizer's presidency in 1945.

By then Smith had embarked on his baseball career. He was fifty-six by the time of this promotion, and his days of baseball playing and track were behind him. But, as with the employee sports program, his interest had never left him. One of his favorite ways to relax was to go to Ebbets Field for an afternoon to watch the Dodgers. He was encouraged in this relaxation by McLaughlin, whose Brooklyn Trust Company served as the bank for Pfizer.

McLaughlin must have seen Smith as a possible solution to one of the team's problems. The afternoons at Ebbets introduced him to Rickey, who had the brains and experience to run the baseball operation, and to O'Malley, who had the business acumen. The problem was that Rickey had no capital and O'Malley only a modest amount. With the explosive growth of Pfizer, Smith had plenty.

For Smith, the Dodgers were a hobby, a chance to relax. He thoroughly enjoyed his spring training trips, going swimming or piloting a wheeled buggy powered by a sail around the nearby beaches. He accompanied the team to Havana, Venezuela, and Panama. At times he sailed a boat from New York to Vero Beach, Florida, for spring training. After the Dodgers clinched the 1949 pennant, he invited all the reporters traveling with the team plus Brooklyn borough president John Cashmore to dinner at a fancy Italian restaurant in St. Louis.

Smith would invite colleagues, customers, and others to his Ebbets Field box for a little relaxation. One frequent guest was Alexander Fleming himself. When civilian travel resumed after World War II, Pfizer brought Fleming to their Brooklyn plant at least once a year. Smith, ever the good host, took him to Ebbets Field. Fleming was intrigued by the game and wound up with quite a collection of Dodger-autographed balls, pennants, caps, and other paraphernalia.

At Pfizer Smith was fending off an attempt at unionization and presiding over the transition of a chemical company selling to other firms into a pharmaceuticals manufacturer selling consumer products. The basis for the transition was the development of a research capability under Smith's leadership and the profits generated from penicillin. The research already was bearing fruit. In 1948 a Pfizer chemist invented tetracycline, the first of the broad-spectrum antibiotics. As the registered trademark Terramycin, it become the first drug to be marketed to the public under the Pfizer name. In later decades Pfizer would turn out such breakthrough drugs as Lipitor, Zoloft, and Viagra. Smith would move from Pfizer's president to chairmanship of the board in 1949. He would also become deeply involved in the struggles within the Dodgers' boardroom.

4

Learning the Business

As the Brooklyn Dodgers entered the postwar world, each of the partners assumed the role that everyone assumed they would. Branch Rickey ran the baseball team, scouted for players, made the trades, set the salaries, and dealt with the other owners, the press, and the baseball establishment. John Smith kept his eye on the financial side. Walter O'Malley did the legal work and thus began the process of educating himself about the business of baseball.

Much of the legal work was fairly standard: a worker's compensation suit at the Olean, New York, farm team; buying the Texas League franchise in Fort Worth; negotiations with contractors doing improvements on Ebbets Field; handling tax matters and union issues.[1] He also took the team into new areas, putting together a royalty deal with the country's largest retailer, Sears, Roebuck & Company, and a clothing company to produce and sell apparel featuring Dodger logos and trademarks.[2]

The Dodgers were a growing organization. When Branch Rickey joined the Dodgers in late 1942, staff memos reported the company had barely twenty full-time front-office employees.[3] By late 1946 that number had risen to seventy-five people, as attendance rebounded, Rickey expanded the scouting department, and ballpark maintenance was increased.[4] By 1950 O'Malley would be wrapping up negotiations on a larger team headquarters building on Pierrepont Street in downtown Brooklyn.[5]

It was also a more profitable organization. Rickey's baseball operations acumen was making the team successful on the field. With the outbreak of World War II, other teams had cut back on scouting and signing amateur players, citing the uncertainties of the war and the fate of young men subject to the draft. Rickey had made the simple calculation that the war would end, and the vast majority of the young men would return. Bucking the conventional wisdom, he expanded the scouting effort, signing promising players even when he knew they were about to disappear into the military. In the postwar years that calculation had blossomed into pennant winners in 1947 and 1949 and near misses in 1946 and 1950. Anyone interested in buying the team could assume, correctly as it turned out, that the success on the field was translating into income, with profits rising every year from 1945 through 1949.

Arthur Mann, who came on board as Rickey's assistant in 1946, said requests for meetings with Rickey to talk about purchasing his stock were so common that Mann did not even report them all to his boss.[6] Rickey turned over the ones Mann did report to O'Malley. There was a broker from Pennsylvania named Michael Yurkovsky who approached the Dodgers in 1948 on behalf of Anthony Margiotti, a former Pennsylvania attorney general and minority owner of the Pittsburgh Pirates.[7] There were other offers that surfaced briefly. The *Sporting News* reported a rumor that an upstate New York group fronted by Larry MacPhail would buy the club.[8] Leo Durocher represented Brooklyn jeweler Roy Marcher who was interested.[9] A movie actor named Sonny Tufts was reported to be making an offer.[10]

The "graveyard [for these offers] was Mr. O'Malley's office on 42nd Street," said Mann, despite his admission that he did not take some offers to Rickey.[11] And it seems clear O'Malley was not a unilateral undertaker. Asked about one bid, Branch Rickey told an inquiring reporter, "I have no such offer. You may say, however, that the Dodgers are for sale for 25 million dollars."[12]

The most intriguing offer would not surface for more than a decade, when one of the principals had become the U.S. president. O'Malley said Joseph Kennedy had approached the team about buying the Dodgers for his son John to run. In the first telling the approach was made in 1947.[13] Subsequent versions put the offer in 1950.[14] The details varied, but O'Malley said he had made it very clear he was not interested in selling his share, and Kennedy wanted full control. These buyers' interest could only reinforce O'Malley and Rickey in their sense of the value of their holdings.

Amid his other legal and management work, O'Malley was moving into two areas that would affect the franchise years into the future. Television was a fledgling technology as the partners took over. The Dodgers, and announcer Red Barber, had participated in the first televised Major League game back in 1939, but that had been seen only on the estimated four hundred television sets in the Greater New York area.[15] Television's development was suspended during World War II, and the business was just emerging as the postwar era dawned. In 1946 there were nine commercial television stations in the United States, serving a total audience of six thousand people.[16] CBS televised eighteen Dodger home games on an experimental basis.[17] In November of that year, the Dodgers agreed with CBS to broadcast their entire home schedule for the 1947 season, the first Major League team off the mark.[18] It was also the first to tie up major sponsorships, with Ford Motor Company and General Foods sharing the contract.[19] For 1948 the CBS contract would add $125,000 to the team's income, about half what they had received for the World Series the year before.[20]

Both Rickey and O'Malley worked on the television contracts. Rickey talked with Barber, the sponsors, and the networks on the broad structure of the deal, while O'Malley negotiated the details of the contracts.[21] When the Dodgers and Cardinals finished the 1946 season in a first-place tie, and Rickey was out of town, O'Malley negotiated with the National Broadcasting Corporation (NBC) for the rights to televise the National League's first postseason playoff series.[22]

Like many businesses, the Dodger leadership struggled to understand the implications of television. "The diversity of opinion on video is startling. There is scarcely a ball club on which any two officials agree on this subject," Rickey said.[23] Just days after the Dodgers signed the contract with CBS for the 1947 season, Rickey's assistant Mann warned that television stations would be filming the Dodger games and playing them as reruns whenever they needed programming, undercutting the value of future games played live at the same time as the filmed telecasts.[24] While Mann's concern seemed far-fetched, O'Malley and Rickey, at first, did not seem to realize the implications of televising home games. After the 1947 season the minutes of the board meeting record: "The board was unanimous that television has not adversely affected attendance and it has reason to believe that the additional publicity is a proper promotion for greater attendance."[25] In public both men retained that attitude.[26] Both would change their minds within a few years.

O'Malley also showed a strong interest in learning more about communications technology. He took Smith to a demonstration of color television, then just a preview of a coming attraction.[27] A related media initiative, driven by O'Malley, was a desire to gain an FM radio channel for the Dodgers. Rickey said the team was concerned that "present radio facilities" would not be available after 1948, as WHN had begun cutting off game broadcasts at

5:30 p.m.[28] Because of its higher sound quality FM radio was seen as a promising advance, and the Federal Communications Commission was dividing
up the band wave. The Dodgers felt an FM station would allow them to fully
control broadcasts of their games, one of the team's major means of publicity.[29] O'Malley was delegated to put together the application to the FCC, and
the board began to plan for providing the $150,000 that would be needed to
equip the station. But O'Malley's further suggestion that the board instead
purchase an existing FM station was ignored.[30] The Dodgers eventually won
the FM license in 1950, but, by that time, television had surpassed radio as
the preeminent technology and the license was never used.[31]

The issue Walter O'Malley committed the most effort to was the team's
ballpark. The idea of replacing Ebbets Field would not surface into the public's vision in New York City until 1953, but O'Malley was raising questions
about the stadium from his earliest meetings on the board of directors.[32]

Despite Larry MacPhail's maintenance efforts, Ebbets Field was showing its age. When Charles Ebbets opened the stadium, he boasted it would
last thirty years.[33] By the end of World War II, it was thirty-three. Age
meant upkeep. In 1946 the tab for park maintenance and improvements was
$238,276.23, equivalent to more than half of the team's net profit.[34] By the
end of 1948 the total capital outlay for Ebbets Field since 1944 had come
to $673,144.63.[35] There were questions in the boardroom about inadequate
toilet facilities, and $50,000 was committed to improvements for 1946 and
another $100,000 for 1947.[36] Even with all these expenditures, Rickey was
telling the board in 1949 that "a substantial sum of money would have to
be spent to maintain the Ebbets Field Stadium."[37]

Ebbets was looking smaller in the postwar attendance boom. The capacity was somewhere over 32,000, which was adequate for all but the biggest
games.[38] For those the lost income could be substantial. After the 1947
World Series Rickey said it was "pitiful" the team had to return $3 million
to ticket buyers because there were not enough seats.[39] And that was in a
year the stadium's assessed valuation for city taxes had been raised almost 6
percent.[40] Adding seats could prove problematic. Over the winter of 1945–
46 additional field box seats were constructed, but the project had come
in well over budget because "unforeseeable defects in the old structure
demanded immediate correction," Rickey told the board.[41]

The park's condition also affected how much money could be made by
renting the stadium for things other than Dodger games. In looking for

extra income from the stadium, the team had turned to hosting championship boxing. But that provoked a confrontation with Brooklyn building commissioner Benjamin Saltzman over the park's facilities. The aisles were dangerously narrow, and the exits were insufficient, the city said.[42] The Building Commission's refusal to authorize boxing led to a lawsuit from the promoter.[43] Eventually, a new exit from the main stands had to be constructed.[44]

By October 1946, barely a year into his ownership, Walter O'Malley was talking to the board about "the possibility of moving to a new site and erecting thereon a modern sports stadium."[45] He contacted Emil Praeger, an eminent civil engineer, for a preliminary design and cost estimate.[46] A year later he told the team's annual meeting, "There is a possibility future requirements will call for a stadium at a different location and of greater capacity."[47] He took Rickey and Smith on a tour of two sites, but the other partners were cautious about attendance and team resources. O'Malley wrote to Praeger about "enlarging or replacing our present stadium."[48] Others had noticed the Dodgers' plight. Renowned architect Norman Bel Geddes approached the board about increasing the capacity of Ebbets Field, and O'Malley was delegated to talk to him.[49] Bel Geddes's firm was put on retainer to see whether it was practical to rebuild at the Ebbets Field site.[50] His report, which estimated a new stadium would cost $6 million, went into a file, but O'Malley was authorized to look into the possibility of buying land in the Boro Hall area.[51]

O'Malley was peripheral to the issue that would echo for decades, Rickey's signing of Jackie Robinson to break baseball's color barrier. Rickey had begun to lay the groundwork for signing Robinson soon after taking over as general manager. He ran the idea past George McLaughlin in his early months on the job.[52] He talked about it with the board of directors. He told John Smith and O'Malley about it.[53] He told his Mississippi-born radio voice, Red Barber.[54] He met silence from Barber, but acceptance from the others. O'Malley could have objected, but did not, at a time when Rickey felt everybody had to be on board for such a revolutionary move. However, according to Red Barber, Rickey was willing to sign more African American players but feared resistance from his board, specifically O'Malley, who would just as soon have "skipped the whole integration problem.[55] There is also the text of a Rickey speech in the Arthur Mann Papers that says "ownership thought there was surfeit of colored boys on the Brooklyn club," but it is not clear when or if that speech was delivered. The *Sporting News* reported in 1949 that the Dodgers had a self-imposed limit of three black players, a charge the team denied.[56]

In later years O'Malley would try to award himself a larger and more active role at the expense of Rickey, telling of a trip to Cuba to sign a black short-stop named Silvio Garcia for $25,000.[57] In O'Malley's version he was sent by Rickey but found Garcia had been drafted into the Cuban Army. Not wishing to buck the Cuban Army, O'Malley said, he took the check back to Brooklyn.

Actually, Rickey had sent scout Tom Greenwade to look over Garcia within a few months of joining the Dodgers and a year earlier than O'Malley's tale. At that point, May 1943, Garcia was playing in Mexico, and O'Malley arranged to get Greenwade a line of credit in Mexico to cover his expenses. Greenwade, however, concluded that the twenty-eight-year-old Garcia was not worth signing.[58] Thus, it seems unlikely Rickey would have sent O'Malley with a $25,000 check a year later.[59]

O'Malley also would be called on to defend the team when Negro League owners tried to extract some compensation after Rickey signed their players.[60] In most cases they were unsuccessful.

O'Malley's legal skills would come into play on some highly public issues for the team, and for Rickey. The issues would take him into baseball's peculiar legal position, into dealing with the commissioner, and into the role of the press and public opinion on the sport.

Major League Baseball's duel with the Mexican League would provide the beginning of Walter O'Malley's education in the reserve clause. The Mexican League, which had existed outside the arc of organized baseball since the 1920s, had been energized by the Pasquel brothers, who decided to turn their multimillion-dollar fortune into making the Mexican League the equal of the Major Leagues. In 1946 they began offering contracts to National and American League players at salaries far higher than what they were earning. A number, including such name players as Mickey Owen, Luis Olmo, and Max Lanier, took the money, or "jumped" in the jargon of the day.

Although the St. Louis Cardinals probably suffered the biggest losses, the Pasquels also struck at the New York teams. And the New York teams struck back. In May 1946 the Yankees won an order from the New York Supreme Court enjoining the Mexican League from tampering with their players, but that order applied only in New York.[61] On May 6 the Dodgers went a step further, winning a temporary injunction from a federal judge in Missouri that applied throughout the country. O'Malley confessed that Major League teams were powerless to bring a player back once he had crossed the border, but they hoped the injunction would stop a player from going.[62] It did not. The judge rescinded the injunction on technical grounds on May 31 without getting into the validity of the players' Mexican League contracts or the validity of the reserve clause.

The reserve clause would be a constant of O'Malley's life for the next three decades, until one of his own players helped break the clause and start the free-agent era. The standard Major League contract was for one year, plus a "reserve" year. If a player did not sign his next contract by spring training of the "reserve" year, the team could renew the contract. According to baseball's legal theory, the renewal covered the entire contract, including the reserve clause, effectively giving the team eternal control of the player. The players who took the Pasquels' money had played out the first year of the contracts, but not the "reserve" year.

It was not a clause the powers of baseball wanted tested in court, and there were rumblings the Yankees and Dodgers were playing with fire. Leslie O'Connor, who had been Kenesaw Mountain Landis's right-hand man, said the Commissioner's Office had spent all those years trying to keep the contract wording out of court.[63] Any challenge to the Pasquels' contracts invited a Mexican League counterattack on the validity of the contracts that tied Owen, Olmo, Sal Maglie, and the others to their Major League teams. And the Pasquels had hired a major New York law firm to represent their interests.[64]

While the Dodgers and O'Malley were getting their wrists slapped for exposing the crown jewel, the Mexican League threat faded as the Pasquels lost money and, eventually, interest. The players lured south began to trickle back, dismayed by living and playing conditions and broken promises. Further raids were not successful. The focus turned to when and how the players who had left would be reinstated. After much blustering, the Commissioner's Office allowed the players back in 1949, in large part because the New York Giants' Danny Gardella and others had filed suit for reinstatement and brought up the reserve clause.[65]

Other legal work was leading O'Malley into the arcane realm of baseball politics. The collision of Leo Durocher, Branch Rickey, and Larry MacPhail in the spring of 1947 was an *Alice in Wonderland* introduction to the commissioner's arbitrary powers and flexible grasp of due process.

It started with the Dodgers' manager, Leo Durocher. Leo had friend-ships with gangsters both real and Hollywood. In the winter of 1946–47, he was living in actor George Raft's house in California and wooing recently divorced actress Laraine Day.[66] Durocher, a lapsed Catholic, was divorced himself, and the marriage to Day ignited the church. In March 1947 the Catholic Youth Organization (CYO) and the National Catholic Welfare Con-ference withdrew their representatives from the Dodgers' Knothole Gang program, which provided youth organizations with cheap tickets to games.[67] The reason they gave was Durocher.

As the Catholic in the triumvirate, O'Malley was designated to smooth over the situation. He did, with the CYO rejoining the Knothole Gang by late April, after Durocher had been suspended by MLB commissioner Happy Chandler.[68] Harold Parrott, then the Dodgers' traveling secretary, asserted years later that O'Malley had orchestrated the CYO withdrawal to embarrass Durocher and, ultimately, Rickey himself.[69] It was a sentiment echoed only by Leo Durocher, for whom Parrott was ghostwriting a column.[70] Parrott offered only his opinion, no evidence of collusion with the organization.

Durocher's situation was about to get infinitely more complicated. Whereas the Catholic Church might be concerned with his marital state, Rickey and others in the baseball establishment were more concerned with his associations with gangsters and gamblers. Late in 1946, after threats by right-wing muckraking columnist Westbrook Pegler to expose Durocher's Mob ties, Rickey had sent Arthur Mann, armed with background informa-tion, to Chandler's Cincinnati office. Rickey wanted the commissioner to warn Durocher.[71] Rickey biographer Lee Lowenfish believes the Brooklyn president knew he was too soft on Durocher, whom Rickey saw as a prodi-gal son eternally on the verge of reform.[72] Chandler, he hoped, would play the Dutch uncle. Chandler was obliging and, on a trip to California, sum-moned Durocher to a golf course, asked him about his relationships with Bugsy Siegel, Joe Adonis, Connie Immerman, and Memphis Engelberg and told him to break them off. He also ordered Durocher to move out of George Raft's house.[73] Durocher complied.

It should have been an enjoyable spring for O'Malley in 1947. The team was touring the Caribbean, giving him a chance to see Panama and the Dominican Republic. Dominican dictator Rafael Trujillo invited Leo Duro-cher, Laraine Day, Rickey, and O'Malley to a sumptuous lunch with a tour of the presidential palace. When they were leaving Trujillo presented them with personally signed baseballs. In the middle of the night each was awakened by a Dominican soldier who asked for the balls back. No reason was given, but the Dodger officials asked no questions.[74]

Then, on March 8, the Dodgers were playing an exhibition game in Havana against the Yankees. Sharing Yankee president Larry MacPhail's box seats were Immerman and Engelberg. Rickey, apparently forgetting who had set the commissioner onto Durocher, complained to several sportswriters about the apparent double standard of whom baseball people could associate with.[75] A few days earlier Harold Parrott, Durocher's ghostwriter, had irritated MacPhail with a "Durocher Says" column in the *Brooklyn Eagle*, complaining that MacPhail had pirated Dodger coaches Charlie Dressen and Red Corriden over the winter.[76] MacPhail exploded, demanding a hearing before Chandler to clear his name about both the gambling connections and the coach pirating. MacPhail expanded the latter issue by alleging O'Malley and John Smith had told him he could recruit Durocher to be his manager if he wished.[77]

The pressures on Chandler were various. The New York reporters portrayed him as a hick, forever given to singing "My Old Kentucky Home."[78] He was being painted as passive, with his lack of movement on gambling charges a particular source of comment.[79] He later revealed he was receiving notes from Frank Murphy, a former governor of Michigan who was now sitting on the Supreme Court. Murphy was one of the leading Catholic laymen in the country and was echoing the CYO's demands that Chandler "do something" about Durocher.[80] MacPhail, everyone said, had been the major force in persuading Major League owners to make Chandler the commissioner.[81]

It was a difficult time in the Dodger camp. Rickey was focused on easing Jackie Robinson into the Major Leagues, hoping to be able to portray it as a demand from Dodger players rather than an assertion of front-office authority. Durocher was a strong partisan of Robinson's, but some team members were resisting.[82] Dodger officials viewed the Parrott-Durocher column as a mere piece of publicity in the buildup to the regular season.[83] At first they thought MacPhail's response was the traditional counterstroke and were surprised at his vehemence and the consequent involvement of the commissioner. O'Malley, as the team's lawyer, was denying MacPhail's contention that he and John Smith had said the Yankees could hire Durocher while also trying to convince Laraine Day not to attend the hearings. The Dodgers feared the beautiful Hollywood star would become the focus of coverage, while they wished the failed publicity gambit would simply go away. Day wanted to stand by her man, broke down in tears, and shattered O'Malley's resistance.[84]

On March 24 Chandler convened a hearing, but it turned out it was not the hearing MacPhail had asked for, nor one that the Dodgers expected. The hearing was closed to all the newspapermen, and Chandler forbade the participants to speak about it. But Arthur Mann was in the room the entire time, knew shorthand, and kept a record, which was the basis of a book he wrote a few years later.

Even as the principals collected at the hearing room's door, O'Malley had a sharp exchange with MacPhail, denying he had ever told the Yankee executive he could hire Durocher.[85] Under Chandler's questioning, the first two witnesses rambled around the edges of the question of whether MacPhail had tampered with Dodger employees. At least that testimony was on a topic raised by MacPhail in his demand for a hearing. Chandler's questions to MacPhail were perfunctory. The third witness was former Dodger outfielder Augie Galan, and Chandler began to grill him remorselessly about clubhouse gambling on the wartime Dodgers and Durocher's role in that gambling. Galan whitewashed Durocher.[86]

The next witness was Harold Parrott, testifying because of the "Durocher Says" column chastising MacPhail for recruiting Durocher's coaches. Mann says that neither Chandler nor MacPhail questioned the basic truth of the allegation. Instead, Chandler quickly let Parrott know he could be either a baseball executive or a newspaperman, but not both.[87] Dressen was up next, and Mann says Dressen substantiated the Dodgers' position that Dressen had broken his word to sign with the Yankees.[88]

Durocher's turn on the stand was a mixture of the *Brooklyn Eagle* column and a return to Chandler's questions about Durocher's gambling habits. Durocher also acknowledged he had raised pointed questions about the way his association with Immerman and Engelberg, as opposed to MacPhail's, was handled. But Chandler did not ask Durocher any questions about whether MacPhail had offered to make him the Yankee manager the previous year, an allegation Durocher had made in public several times. When Chandler asked MacPhail the question, MacPhail was allowed to avoid a direct answer.[89]

O'Malley mostly kept his mouth shut. Mann, a strong Rickey partisan ever suspicious of O'Malley, reported: "It was impossible for any of us three at the Dodger table to overlook the fact that O'Malley had not yet found it necessary to cross-examine or check statements or turn the questioning into a sharper scrutiny of information. It was also impossible to overlook the fact that no witness thus far had injured the Dodgers. The case seemed to be going along very well and it was possible, even to the lay mind, to sense that perhaps O'Malley's approach in the defense, a watchful-waiting policy, was best after all."[90]

Later that week the hearing resumed. Rickey, who had missed the first session to attend a family funeral, took the stand and sparred over exactly what he had said and what had been attributed to him by the reporters. While quibbling over wording, he stood by the general thrust of the reporting of the double standard he perceived. The last witness was Yankee traveling secretary Arthur "Red" Patterson, who tried to dance around the issue of how Immerman and Engelberg had wound up in MacPhail's box. "I can't recall," he said of the game three weeks earlier, but admitted it was conceivable he could have given the gamblers the tickets.[91]

According to Mann, the hearings were clearly not what they, or MacPhail, expected. Durocher and MacPhail threw compliments at each other. O'Malley praised Charlie Dressen. Then, after Patterson's testimony, Chandler asked everyone except Rickey, O'Malley, and Mann to leave the room. Chandler walked over to the Dodger table, looked at Rickey, and asked, "How much would it hurt you folks to have your fellow out of baseball?"

"Happy, what on earth is the matter with you?" Rickey said in what Mann described as a "quavering, half-sobbing voice." O'Malley joined in the protests.[92] Chandler pulled out a letter from someone he would identify then only as a "big man" and said this person wanted Durocher expelled. He later revealed that the "big man" was Frank Murphy.[93] He listened to some more protests, claimed he was just sounding them out, and left the room.[94]

Two weeks later Chandler's decision came in. Parrott was fined $500. The Dodgers and Yankees were each fined $2,000. Durocher was banned from baseball. "For what?" asked Durocher, and Rickey could not answer.[95]

It was a pivotal learning experience for Walter O'Malley. MacPhail had basically demanded his name be cleared of a relationship with the gamblers in his box and of tampering with Dodger employees. Chandler had failed to pursue fully either question with the witnesses. MacPhail was fined instead of absolved. Durocher, a "defendant" because of his ghostwritten column, was punished harshly for gambling and gambling associations, something that was not on the hearing's formal agenda. As a lawyer O'Malley had expected to defend his clients against specific charges, which were ignored. The commissioner had powers and processes that had nothing to do with the courtroom procedures O'Malley had learned in law school and fifteen years of practice.

Another lesson had to sink in as well. Rickey had managed the Durocher situation badly. Instead of dealing with Durocher's issues himself, he had tried to manipulate the commissioner into doing it for him. That tactic had backfired to a major degree. Chandler had taken the information supplied by Rickey through Mann and used it as part of the case against Durocher.

The hearing worked well for Chandler. Press reaction, especially in the New York papers, focused on a new, tougher commissioner.[96] The *New York Times* referred to his "firm hand."[97] Other writers, while often arguing the Durocher penalty was too drastic, noted the toughness with approval.[98]

In early 1949 further fallout from the Mexican League situation brought O'Malley the lawyer back to work. Speaking to the Baltimore Chamber of Commerce, Rickey returned to his deep-seated conservatism with typical rhetoric. "Those people who oppose the reserve system have avowed Communistic tendencies," he railed. The people in question were Danny Gardella, Fred Martin, and Max Lanier, players who had jumped to the Mexican League in 1946. They had come back but faced a five-year ban by Commissioner Chandler. They were suing to overturn the ban and cited the reserve clause in the suit.[99] Earlier that spring Rickey had discussed a similar suit by former Dodger players and expressed the hope that the matter could be concluded "without too much unfortunate publicity."[100]

He got what he did not want. Lanier and Martin were represented by John L. Flynn, a Wall Street lawyer who recognized an opportunity when he saw one. He wrote O'Malley, demanding an explanation absolving him and his clients of the "communistic" charges. If it was not forthcoming, Flynn said, he would regard Rickey's "vicious slander as maliciously intended" and pursue legal action to recover "substantial punitive damages."[101] O'Malley fired back, denying any slander, but noting the team felt that the "vicious slander" passage was libelous.[102] Flynn dropped his threat. Rickey biographer Murray Polner reports that while O'Malley's public conduct was supportive, soothing Flynn and denying any negative intention, he privately agreed that the attack was libelous and that Flynn's "vicious slander" charge was accurate. Polner says Rickey was forced to thank O'Malley, which pleased O'Malley greatly. "Rickey lost his cool and I showed how I could act in a bad situation," Polner quotes O'Malley as saying.[103]

While all the work was legal, O'Malley seemed only too happy with the greater public exposure. In fact, he pushed for more. Often at Rickey's invitation he attended baseball events, such as the Junior World Series, the championship of the upper Minor Leagues, which in 1948 featured two Dodger farm teams.[104] He and John Smith threw a cocktail party for the Dodger press corps in Santo Domingo, as he and Smith joined the team for spring training most years.[105] He was also using the Dodgers for his political and business contacts. At the annual New York Baseball Writers Association dinner in 1949, Walter and his father hosted George McLaughlin, Brooklyn borough president John Cashmore, and other borough notables.[106]

While O'Malley seemed only too happy in his greater public role, it was clear the team needed to divert some of the pressure on Rickey from New York reporters, notably Jimmy Powers, sports columnist of the *Daily News*, the most widely circulated paper in the city. In late 1946 Rickey had ordered his staff, probably Arthur Mann, to put together what proved to be a thirty-seven-page diatribe titled "The Case against Jimmy Powers (by the Brooklyn Baseball Club)." The "case" noted Powers's consistent portrayal of Rickey as a "hypocritical penny-pinching businessman who had attached his tentacles to the historic Dodger franchise for the purpose of bleeding it dry."[107] O'Malley and Smith talked Rickey out of confronting, and perhaps suing, Jimmy Powers at that time.[108] But the image remained. The long-term importance of the Jackie Robinson decision had not really sunk in, and the stereotypes Rickey had allowed to develop still prevailed.[109] "I don't think he would lie," said Red Smith of Rickey, "but he was so good at evasion, at circumlocution, that he didn't have to lie."[110] After an unexpected World Series appearance in 1947, the 1948 team was floundering. Attendance was dropping, and there was a growing drumbeat of press criticism of Rickey, both personal and professional. "President Rickey is being exposed to broadsides instead of the cursory sniping which has been his lot since he came here from Missouri," wrote Tom Meany.[111] One aspect was Rickey's trades. Always an advocate of youth, daring, and speed, Rickey had traded away team and fan favorites Dixie Walker and Eddie Stanky over the winter. The players blamed the trades for their performance, and reporters dredged up earlier unpopular trades of veterans Dolph Camilli and Billy Herman.[112]

There was fan unhappiness over higher prices for some seats and the transfer of many seats into higher-priced categories.[113] One Dodger fan amended a sign posted by the New York Fire Department at Ebbets Field.

The sign warned that occupancy by "more than 33,000 is unlawful." The fan added "and unlikely."[114] After leading the league in attendance in 1946 and 1947, the Dodgers fell to fourth in 1948.

By June it was agreed that O'Malley would host an evening of dinner and a game for the reporters who covered the team regularly and their sports editors. O'Malley would make the invitations personally, but Rickey suggested John Smith should be invited as well, and the meeting would be off the record. There was one overwhelming worry Rickey expressed to O'Malley:

> Frankly, it involves your complete approval of me and the policies of the Club and the deals that have been made. There must be an all-outness on this. Otherwise, I would most earnestly oppose any conference whatever. I know full well it is your purpose to indicate that sort of support and, that being true, I mention it in the way I have because there must be no lingering about it. . . . Above all I do not wish a result to indicate that I have sought, or that I am in need of an official expression of confidence on the part of a member of the Board or anyone else.[115]

Despite his growing commitment to the Dodgers, Walter O'Malley was still doing other things. His law practice took time and effort. He had hobbies and contacts that spanned both his public and his private lives. He became president of the board of trustees of the Froebel Academy, a private school in Brooklyn that his son, Peter, attended.[116] Through his wife's family he became involved in the Brooklyn Swedish Hospital and eventually joined the board. He was a member of the New York Athletic Club and on the board of the Brooklyn Club, the center for the business and political elite of the borough.

O'Malley had become quite close with Henry Ughetta, the first Italian American on the New York State Supreme Court and a high-ranking Catholic layman. Throughout the early 1950s Ughetta's name would surface in speculation about running for mayor of New York or lieutenant governor of the state.[117] His legal expertise was in real estate law, and he was often assigned cases involving the condemnation of property in Brooklyn, which is probably where O'Malley, with his bankruptcy practice, first came in contact with him.[118] By 1947 O'Malley had brought Ughetta onto the Dodgers' board of directors.[119] Their wives also socialized and would bring John

Smith's wife into the circle as well.[120] Ughetta gave O'Malley the nicknames "the Big Oom" or "Oom the Omnipotent," and they lunched regularly at the Hotel Bossert, three blocks from the Dodgers' offices, as part of a circle around George McLaughlin.[121]

Walter's family had become the major tenant of the Amityville house, and its access to the Atlantic led to O'Malley's involvement in deep-sea fishing. He became chairman of the annual Atlantic Tuna Tournament as a representative of his home Freeport Tuna Club.[122] He invited friends such as Ughetta and colleagues such as Rickey and Smith to join him for fishing trips. He won awards for his prowess.[123]

O'Malley was settling into middle age. The hair was still dark and slicked back. The glasses were still wire rimmed. But the jowls that would dominate his face as he got older were starting to appear. Terry, born in 1933, and Peter, born four years later, were growing up and devoting much of their time to sailing in the waters of the Great South Bay and off the south coast of Long Island.[124] Terry, a student at St. Saviour Academy in Brooklyn, described a house where her father nurtured an Irish heritage, with Irish books around the house. Many years later she still cherished a novel called *Charles O'Malley, the Irish Dragoon*. It had her father's business card stapled to the flyleaf, and on the back he had written, "Your O'Malley heritage makes this a must read. It is an old classic (college English IV) and very funny. Pop."[125] Kay had settled into the life of mother and wife. Accepting the limits imposed by her missing voice box, she was still very active in alumni events for the College of New Rochelle.[126] Although many in the coming years would criticize her husband for one thing or another, there was never a negative word about Kay around the Dodger family. Red Barber's wife, Lylah, for example, often shared the owners' box with Mrs. O'Malley and recalled that she "spoke in almost a whisper. It was difficult to understand her, but we both tried, and with the help of some sign language and a bit of writing we grew to be friends. She was one of the bravest and gentlest people I have ever known."[127]

Reading the minutes of the board meetings during the years of the triumvirate, it is easy to see each member constantly returning to his major concern. With Rickey the emphasis is on acquiring and nurturing talented players. With Smith it is about economy and using money wisely. With O'Malley it is about renovating or replacing Ebbets Field. Within the context of their ownership agreement, it was always a triangular discussion, as each partner sought the ally he needed to carry his position. Smith had no ambitions to run the Dodgers. He was highly successful as a chemist and a businessman, and being on the board of the Dodgers was a duty, albeit a pleasant one. His partners, however, were men of ambition and confidence, and each knew Smith was the key ally.

Murray Polner, a sympathetic Rickey biographer who was the first to have access to Rickey's papers, argues that Rickey and Smith admired each other as self-made men and devout Christians. But "eventually, when Smith lay dying of cancer, O'Malley would wean him away and turn him against Rickey."[128] However, the minutes of the board of directors meetings and the press reports of the time paint a picture of Smith considering a host of issues over several years before he counseled his wife to vote with O'Malley in the partnership agreement after his death.

Two years before Smith's death, John Drebinger was writing in the *New York Times* that "the majority stockholders, represented by Walter O'Malley and John L. Smith, were not seeing eye-to-eye with Brother Rickey on a number of things."[129] That same year Jimmy Powers, forever a Rickey critic, wrote, "The rumor mill is working overtime these days producing hints that Branch may not be as firmly anchored in his Brooklyn post as he used to be."[130]

The reasons for Smith's decision are found in a host of issues, in which he allied himself at various times with both of his partners. But they are rooted in his own path to success, investing for the future while keeping costs down.

The Dodgers were profitable throughout the late 1940s, but John Smith saw economies that could have made them even more profitable. As a young Pfizer executive, Smith had required his people to justify a request for a new pencil by producing the stub of the old one. If you wanted something as small as a Pyrex container, you had to convince him it was absolutely necessary.[131] When Rickey gave his first major interview as an owner, the reporter's questions are all framed in the environment set by Jimmy Powers—Rickey as a "cheapo." Eventually, Smith counterattacked. "I have read that Rickey is cheap. As treasurer of the Brooklyn club, I think he is extravagant. He makes financial gambles you wouldn't dare make in any other business."[132] Coupled with Rickey's handling of Durocher's gambling and underworld connections, you can see questions about Rickey's management arising in Smith's mind. By 1949 the board granted Smith's request to go deeply into the company's books.[133]

Most historians and biographers of the period have approached the story of Rickey, O'Malley, and the Dodgers through the lens of Jackie Robinson or the team's Rickey-created successes on the field. It is clear, however, that not only O'Malley but also Smith, the experienced businessmen on the board, used an additional lens. In March 1949 the board minutes reported, "Mr. Rickey was authorized, as usual, to use his best judgment in the baseball department of the corporation's activities."[134] Although the "as usual" affirmed and limited Rickey's primacy to one area, the whole of the sentence clearly implied O'Malley's and Smith's determination to get involved in the business end.

Some of the early disagreements were indicative. Rickey, on moral grounds, was opposed to beer sponsorships for the radio broadcasts, even when he was having trouble finding sponsors.[135] O'Malley and Smith saw no problems, and eventually Brooklyn's Schaefer Brewing became a major sponsor.[136] Rickey saw it as a defining moment. He said, "I'm doomed. He [O'Malley] will force me out," daughter Elizabeth Rickey told Polner.[137]

There were regular disagreements over the farm system, where Rickey's focus on producing future talent collided with O'Malley's desire to save money to refurbish Ebbets or build a new stadium. Although the farm teams were generally profitable in this period, there were significant costs in scouting and acquiring players.[138] By the late summer of 1949 Rickey was writing to the heads of his Minor League department about cutting the 1950 scouting budget from $44,900 to $25,000. He asked, if "you were compelled, either by financial necessity or by compunction from the Board of Directors, how would you do it?"[139]

There had been earlier pressures. When Rickey moved to buy the St. Paul franchise in the American Association in 1947, he won Smith's approval only by promising economies elsewhere.[140] The differences between O'Malley and Rickey became clearest in 1949, when fire destroyed the main grandstands at the farm club in Fort Worth of the Texas League.[141] Rickey argued strongly to rebuild, citing attendance in Fort Worth and the likely return on the $450,000 investment. O'Malley argued forcefully that the seats in Brooklyn could be sold for a much higher price than anywhere else and that the money should be put aside for improvements there. Board member Hector Racine, president of the Dodgers' top Minor League club in Montreal, drew on his knowledge of the International League, and thus of the Minors, to caution about future attendance. Judge Ughetta picked up that theme and noted that Fort Worth's attendance would be based on performance, which could not be guaranteed. Smith came down with Rickey, arguing that the investment was small compared to the return. The board eventually deferred to Rickey and his promise of performance.[142] In the event Racine's and Ughetta's warnings proved prophetic, as attendance throughout the Minors, including Fort Worth, fell to about half the level of the immediate postwar years.

Smith did not move firmly into O'Malley's camp immediately. There were important issues where they disagreed or that aroused Smith's tightfisted ways. The costs of spring training were a constant source of concern. Rickey was trying to balance two main issues. One was finding a place where all of the Dodgers' seven hundred or so Minor Leaguers could receive consistent instruction and evaluation by team staff. The second was to find a way around the Jim Crow regime in Florida to bring along Jackie Robinson and the team's other African American players. In 1946 the Minor Leaguers had trained in Sanford, Florida, and moved to Pensacola in 1947. But that year for the Dodgers and their top farm club, Montreal, the teams toured the Caribbean, winding up with the Yankee series in Havana that had touched off the MacPhail-Durocher-Rickey-Chandler debacle. The lack of quality opponents early in the trip hindered preparation for the season, and the bills for airplanes, hotel rooms, and meals wound up costing the team $100,000.[143] Pensacola had cost another $127,000.[144]

In 1947 Rickey had been introduced to Bud L. Holman, a man who had parlayed his skills as a mechanic into a seat on Eastern Airlines' board of directors.[145] Holman lived in Vero Beach, Florida, and was concerned the Navy was abandoning a pilot-training base it had built for use during World War II. The base was beginning to deteriorate, and Holman was looking for an economic stimulus for the town. In the early fall of 1947 Rickey sent Buzzie Bavasi from his Minor League department to make an estimate of what it would cost to convert the Navy base into a spring training site.[146] Rickey appreciated the value of former military bases because they were designed to house and feed large numbers of young men. They had also been designed to last only the length of the war, but that was a problem that would not become clear for a number of years. Rickey told the board he was leaning toward Vero Beach for 1948 in October 1947 and presented them with the lease in December.[147]

The lease from the city cost only $1 a year, but made the team responsible for building its own training facilities and maintaining the barracks and feeding facilities. That was the point that stuck with Walter O'Malley.[148] Rickey's plan called for the building of extensive facilities and the housing of the Minor Leaguers plus a staff that included fifteen umpires, seventeen groundskeepers, two doctors, seven trainers, and three people just to keep track of all the bats, balls, and uniforms. The cost was $200,000 a year, although this could be partially offset by gate receipts for exhibition games.[149] Smith saw it as a necessary investment in both preparing the current year's team and developing players who could either help the Dodgers or be sold for cash, and Rickey went ahead in creating what would become Dodgertown, a place O'Malley came to treasure.

Another point of disagreement between O'Malley and Smith was a contract the team signed with a company called Allied Maintenance for the operation of Ebbets Field. The issue first surfaced in September 1946, when O'Malley informed the board the employees at Ebbets Field were being organized by either the American Federation of Labor (AFL) or the Congress of Industrial Organizations (CIO). The same thing was happening at Yankee Stadium. O'Malley suggested that hiring an outside contractor would smooth union-related issues.[150] Rickey and Smith both had doubts, though, and when the contract was approved, it was described as "an experiment" and would run only one year.[151] In December 1947, when O'Malley pressed for extension of the contract, Rickey and Smith argued it was too high, and any action was delayed while Smith studied the contract. After study Smith allowed the contract to be renewed for another year, but insisted on a meeting between Rickey, himself, and Allied representatives to go over their costs.[152] When it came up again in 1949, Smith insisted that he, rather than O'Malley, negotiate the contract.[153]

There were other issues where O'Malley and Smith came to the same conclusions. Leo Durocher was one. Although O'Malley and Smith may not have told Larry MacPhail in late 1946 that Leo was available, there were other indications they were not happy with his performance. Despite Durocher's reputation the Dodgers would not win a pennant under his direction after 1941. Others, however, did feel that O'Malley and Smith were not happy with keeping Durocher as the manager.[154] At the same time O'Malley, despite fears a Durocher return would hurt attendance, had not used his influence within the Catholic Church to block Durocher, as the Catholic Youth Organization indicated they would not boycott the team if he returned.[155] In informing the board of his intention to rehire Durocher for 1948, Rickey acknowledged "frank opposition" to the idea, although it was not clear if that was from the board or Commissioner Chandler.[156] In public O'Malley and Smith kept their mouths shut about Durocher. After all, the practice was that they might offer advice to Rickey about what were considered to be "baseball matters," but the decisions were always Rickey's.

It is also clear Rickey was becoming disenchanted with Durocher. Near the end of spring training in 1948, Rickey dictated a memo about his unhappiness. It cited Durocher's continued gambling; his refusal to attend some exhibition games; his allowing nonuniformed people to sit on the bench; his refusal to honor an agreement to live at the Vero Beach camp; his denigration of Coach Ray Blades, a Rickey appointee; and his recommendations on player moves, which Rickey said would cost the team $250,000. There were other complaints as well.[157] Rickey had confronted Durocher over several of these issues, so the manager knew of his boss's unhappiness. Later, he would claim that Rickey was setting him up for failure by not giving him the players he wanted, notably Roy Campanella.[158] In early July Rickey shocked the baseball world by conniving with New York Giants owner Horace Stoneham to take Durocher, while he brought back Burt Shotton, who had managed the team during Durocher's 1947 suspension.

For experienced businesspeople such as Smith and O'Malley, the twists and turns of the Durocher saga could have only reinforced concerns about Rickey's management acumen. He successfully courted problems with Chandler and the Catholic organizations. He risked attendance losses in a year that was down already and further damage with a concerted campaign to retain and then reinstate Durocher. Then, just six months later, he dumped him. O'Malley and Smith constantly deferred to Rickey in baseball matters, but they would use their experience to judge his performance as a businessman.[159]

Rickey's biggest management blunder, however, came in football. He was first approached in late 1945 by promoters looking for a place to field a team in the fledgling All-American Football Conference.[160] Rickey was amenable, and although the AAFC did not get off the ground in 1946, the team popularly called the Brooklyn Football Dodgers was renting Ebbets Field by the fall of 1947. It was not successful, and Dan Topping, an owner of both the baseball and the AAFC football Yankees, asked for a meeting with the Dodgers. He wanted Rickey to take over the AAFC team. As Rickey was out of town, Topping had lunch with O'Malley. "I told him that my personal preference was against the Brooklyn Baseball Club going into the football business," O'Malley wrote in a memo to Rickey about the lunch conversation. Topping argued that the National Football League (NFL) Giants were weak, and there was a strong market for pro football in the city. He also said that combining administrative functions for both the football and the baseball Yankees had saved money. O'Malley reiterated his opposition, but said he would pass on the information to Rickey.[161]

When he did Rickey, the old football coach, was interested. He reminisced about his days coaching Ohio Wesleyan. "I never wanted to manage a ball club," he told one interviewer. "I would have coached football for nothing, if I had other means of support."[162] The board was considerably less interested. The first takeover proposal was quickly rejected.[163] The split became even clearer two days later at an extraordinary Sunday meeting of the board when Rickey, O'Malley, and Smith each proposed a solution and none could get a second to his motion.[164] Eventually, Rickey and O'Malley reached a compromise in agreeing to pay no more than $1 for the entire assets of the football team. John Smith would not support even that.[165] The deal was consummated on the last day of 1947. Rickey put his assistant Arthur Mann in charge of the team's business affairs and publicity.

It still did not work. After a poor 1948 season, the football Dodgers and Yankees merged for 1949, despite Smith's calling attention to poor attendance at football Yankees games.[166] That did not work, either. The AAFC's San Francisco 49ers and Cleveland Browns would move into the NFL that winter, but the rest of the league dissolved. For the baseball Dodgers, it led to sales of top prospects such as Irv Noren and Sam Jethroe to balance the books.[167] Smith began to talk of taking a more active role in managing the team's business, as he moved from president to the less time-consuming job of chairman at Pfizer in the late summer of 1949. After an interview, Gus Steiger of the *New York Mirror* paraphrased Smith's thinking as correcting business-management practices that were "offensive to him as an executive."[168]

Exactly how much the team lost is not clear. Mann said it was $400,000 in 1948 and half that much in 1949 plus another $75,000 for contract payments still to come.[169] The board was told the 1949 loss was going to be closer to $350,000.[170] The financial records in the Rickey Papers are incomplete. They show losses totaling at least $560,244.94, and maybe closer to $700,000.[171] Given that the team's consolidated profit for 1948 was $543,201 and $642,614 for 1949, the professional football losses represented somewhere near the team's normal annual profit.[172] Rickey recognized the failure. At the beginning, he said, he was "greatly hopeful of nationalizing Brooklyn in football. We felt that Brooklyn would respond to football much as it has to baseball. My subsequent view is changed. It was regrettable."[173]

5

Buying Out Rickey

It was more than regrettable. Whether it was the kind of player-development commitment desired by Rickey or the new or refurbished stadium O'Malley was fighting for, a year's profit was a tremendous loss. The three partners had spent five years arguing over where to put their limited resources, and Rickey's decisions were narrowing their choices by taking money off the table.

The issue that lurked behind all the questions about beer sponsorships and communistic tendencies and Leo Durocher and football was the future of Rickey's contract. When he signed with the Dodgers in late 1942, Rickey had agreed to a base salary of $25,000 until World War II ended and then $50,000 annually for the rest of a five-year contract.[1] He would also receive a bonus of 15 percent of the team's pretax net profit during the war and 10 percent thereafter. In 1945 the board agreed to add a $5,000 annual expense budget for which Rickey did not have to account.[2] In November 1945, after the end of the war but two years before the original contract would expire, the board gave Rickey a new five-year contract at the postwar terms, pushing his guaranteed employment out to October 28, 1950.[3]

For its time it was a very lucrative contract. In the five years of the extended contract, Rickey would earn just over $500,000 in salary, expense accounts, and bonuses. Then there was $43,312.50 in his share of the stockholder dividends declared by the board. Over the same period, the highest-paid Dodger player would earn less than $120,000.[4] O'Malley constantly complained about the size of the contract, even though he had voted for its extension. In O'Malley's mind the bonuses eventually amounted to $750,000.[5] A look at the reported pretax profits for the period would indicate his bonuses amounted to at least $237,000.[6] Although this was well below O'Malley's memory, it was still substantial. For comparison, both O'Malley and Smith received annual salaries of $2,000, half from the team and half from the Ebbets-McKeever Exhibition Company, which owned the stadium and surrounding real estate.[7]

Rickey began to fish for more certainty at least three years before the contract was due to run out. He consulted Louis Carroll, a lawyer who did a lot of work for baseball leagues, teams, and executives. The board resolution approving extension had never been translated into a contract, and Rickey had never formally accepted the offer.[8] Rickey continued to raise the issue, and the board asked him for his ideas. In September 1948 he outlined the terms he was looking for. He wanted a five-year commitment to running the team and a further five-year contract as an adviser. He mentioned no salary terms, but did say he thought a straight salary and no bonus would be a better arrangement.[9] The board took no action.

Ultimately, it was a game of king of the mountain, with Smith serving as the referee. Branch Rickey had been trying to get into ownership since his earliest days with the St. Louis Browns, and he was not about to give up easily now.[10] "Rickey wanted a one-man operation, which he hadn't been able to get in St. Louis," said New York newspaperman Leonard Koppett, who covered baseball beginning in the late 1940s.[11] Bill Veeck would later slap at O'Malley for his determination to get his way, but he also said, "Papa Branch is incapable of moving into any kind of any organization without maneuvering to establish himself as the dominant force."[12] Or, as Jane Rickey said of her husband, "No one could make friends easier than Branch. But he can't take a back seat."[13] Nor could anyone accuse Walter O'Malley of being less than ambitious.

There were also different styles. Branch Rickey was a midwestern Methodist Victorian and proud of it. He counseled all his players to marry. He wanted nothing to do with alcohol or Democrats. Rickey saw his business as a family and paid wages as if all his employees had an equity stake in the firm. Even with all his innovations in baseball, he was a man whose concept of marketing was to put a talented, interesting team on the field and let the fans flock to it. The reporters were a necessary evil. Marketing was not even considered.

O'Malley, like Smith, was a product of the corporate world. Owners owned. Managers managed. Players (employees) played. It was to be a joint effort aimed at maximizing profits, but it was not a cooperative. You needed to market your product and innovate off the field as well as on. You needed to coddle the reporters, who were your best source of free publicity. You would certainly help employees, but you would not step outside of the basic role of the corporation. In 1949 Red Barber approached the team for a loan, and Rickey advocated for him. O'Malley took the more corporate approach. The team would be happy to introduce Barber to some local banks (with the introduction implying their support), but O'Malley did not want to get into a lender-borrower relationship, even with a valued employee.[14]

And there were differences in style. Both men could be charmers, but O'Malley was more apt to slap your back, buy you a drink, and tell some jokes, many with a little sting at the end. Rickey retained a lot of the farm boy, and O'Malley was New York City born and bred. Both were masters at parsing their sentences, their meanings, and their implications like surgeons. They could dodge a question or cover it with ambiguity as they felt the situation demanded. As *Newsweek* columnist John Lardner encapsulated two men he did not like: "They do the same things, but O'Malley won't admit it."[15]

As their differences over issues unfolded in the late 1940s, the rhetoric and the sarcasm flourished. In Room 40 at the Hotel Bossert, O'Malley's circle ridiculed Rickey as a "psalm-singing faker" and went so far as to play pin the tail on the donkey using Rickey's picture in a row with the other Dodger directors.[16] Harold Rosenthal of the *New York Herald-Tribune* said O'Malley wooed Mrs. Smith by constantly painting Rickey as a "midwestern farmer."[17] Rickey was not far behind, telling Barber that O'Malley was "the most devious man I ever met" and telling Dodger scout Rex Bowen that "we have a man trying to take over the organization."[18]

O'Malley did have a tendency to prefer the complicated over the straightforward. "Between the devious and the direct, he vastly preferred the devious—and baseball was the perfect spot for it," said longtime *Los Angeles Times* sports columnist Jim Murray.[19] O'Malley himself acknowledged he liked a multisided complication. "I like a challenge," he said as the Los Angeles situation got muddled soon after the Dodgers' arrival. "I think things out here are going to work out well and then I'll be able to relax—at least until I find some other mess to get into."[20] Said future Dodger broadcaster Vin Scully, "I think he'd be very happy if you'd give him a long piece of string, all tangled up in knots, so he could have fun untangling it."[21]

Despite the growing tensions, it is interesting to see that both Rickey and O'Malley were professional enough, concerned enough about their investment, that much of the routine business of running the team went smoothly despite the growing tension about Rickey's contract and his fate with the team. Rickey's appointment book for 1950 shows regular meetings with O'Malley.[22] Although unrealized at the time, John Smith's last board meeting had been January 24, and they had a team to run.

By June the board agenda included a tax situation with the Montreal farm team, a report on progress on rebuilding in Fort Worth, questions about selling a searchlight and generator set, discussions about a new New York state disability insurance law, a Florida Tax Commission ruling that would add to the costs of spring training, the creation of a supplemental radio network outside New York City, updates on whether to move the St. Paul team to Omaha, the scouting program, attendance, and the Dodger team plane. Some of these are delegated to Rickey, some to O'Malley. In early 1950 the New York Legislature was considering a bill that would ban the Dodgers' practice of split doubleheaders, charging separate admissions for each game. Rickey and O'Malley acted in tandem, successfully opposing the bill.[23]

Branch Rickey began searching for maneuverability in 1948, when a hint appeared in the *Sporting News* that Rickey's shares could be purchased for $1 million.[24] The next year Arthur Mann, Rickey's assistant, entertained Michael Yurkovsky, one of the dismissed bidders from a couple of years earlier, at a ball game. He sent him detailed financial information about the team and promised that 25 percent of the team's stock was available for $1 million. If Yurkovsky could up with $100,000 now, he promised the "quickest possible action toward consumation."[25] No names are mentioned, but of the four owners of Dodger stock, Mann could act for only one man, and Rickey had paid for a financial background check on Yurkovsky.[26] Rickey had set his price.

On January 24, 1950, attending what turns out to be his last board meeting, John Smith learned the football loss for the 1949 season was going to be close to $350,000. It was his last direct impression of Rickey's management.

The board did not meet again until June, when O'Malley suggested they postpone discussion of Rickey's contract until the next board meeting. Apparently, Rickey had gotten wind of some criticism from Smith. A choppy transcript of the meeting indicates O'Malley offered Rickey a blank check to stay and reports him saying: "Mr. Smith may have appeared to be critical, but that was not the fact."[27] Just over two weeks later Rickey and O'Malley rushed back from the Major League meeting at the All-Star Game in Chicago to attend Smith's funeral.

Rickey, at this point with Smith's criticism hanging in the background, had clearly moved beyond any thought of staying with the Dodgers. The terms of the partnership agreement began to exercise their control. Any partner wishing to sell must offer the others the chance to buy his shares. When Rickey approached O'Malley, he was offered $346,666.66 for his shares, the price he, O'Malley, and Smith had paid in 1944 and 1945. This was not the $1 million price tag Rickey had established in his own mind, a price that was far closer to the real value of the franchise.[28]

O'Malley was clearly low-balling Rickey. Apparently, he calculated that no one would pay much for a nonmajority interest in a team where O'Malley's influence over the Smith bloc would leave him in control. He would also say he was concerned for Mrs. Smith, as a sale at $1 million would raise the taxes on her husband's already substantial estate.[29] It was a sentimental argument that he knew buttressed his desire to pay less, but it was also an argument that knitted Mrs. Smith closer to O'Malley.[30]

In addition, O'Malley knew Rickey was, as usual, hocked to his substantial eyebrows.[31] O'Malley evidently had not paid attention to a situation a year earlier when one owner of the St. Louis Cardinals had leveraged a similar agreement and an outside offer from Joseph Kennedy to gain a higher price from his partner.[32] The partnership agreement gave Rickey a similar right to find an outside buyer whose presumably higher offer would have to be matched. Walter O'Malley had miscalculated.

Rickey had a fraternity brother named William Galbreath, a highly successful real estate developer based in Columbus, Ohio. Galbreath was a part owner of the Pittsburgh Pirates who had substantially raised his stake that summer and assumed the team's presidency.[33] Galbreath was looking for a baseball man to run the team. Rickey was looking for a buyer willing to pay $1 million for his shares. Who approached whom is not clear, but Galbreath eventually referred Rickey to a New York real estate man named William Zeckendorf.

September 1, 1950, was a pleasant Friday in Brooklyn, with temperatures in the seventies and a bit of rain. The Dodgers were six games behind the Phillies and ready to open a weekend series at Ebbets Field against the Giants. The duel scripted from the partnership agreement was about to get serious.

Walter O'Malley did not necessarily want Branch Rickey out of Brooklyn. He valued Rickey's expertise in choosing, training, and evaluating players. He just wanted to run the show, but knew that probably meant Rickey was gone. Still, he had prepared a new contract for Rickey, which he offered that day. It was very similar to what Rickey had proposed to the board back in 1948—a straight salary for five years as president, then five as an adviser. O'Malley did supply the numbers Rickey had not, $100,000 annually as president and half that for his advisory role.[34]

Late in the afternoon O'Malley went to the Lower Manhattan offices of Louis Carroll, who was acting as Rickey's personal attorney, to present the contract terms. Carroll was waiting for him with a different story. He told O'Malley that Rickey had told him to prepare a formal notice that he intended to sell his shares outside the partnership agreement. O'Malley rushed back to his office and dictated an agitated telegram to Rickey in Fort Worth, asking what was going on.[35]

The next day Rickey calmly replied from California, where he was conferring with the Hollywood Stars about the Dodgers' relationship with the Pacific Coast League (PCL) team. The telegram's bland wording could only have agitated O'Malley more. "Will be glad to discuss anything and everything with you upon my return," Rickey wrote.[36]

O'Malley's talk with Carroll was ominous because Rickey's lawyer had referred to a conversation with the Mulveys.[37] It raised the specter of a split board. If Rickey sold to an outside investor, maybe even to the Mulveys, Rickey's bloc of stock would leave the partnership agreement. O'Malley might be able to vote Mrs. Smith's stock, but his will could be blocked by either the Mulveys with 50 percent or Rickey's outside buyer plus the Mulveys. The team would be back in the days of the Ebbets-McKeever management disaster.

Rickey was back in Brooklyn by the middle of September, but he was keeping his face blank. A September 19 board meeting was postponed at his request, and his president's report to the Ebbets-McKeever Exhibition Company was unusually short.[38] The next two days Rickey spent meeting with Zeckendorf and his associates. Arthur Mann reported that Zeckendorf was at first resistant to Galbreath's overtures. Playing to Galbreath's love of horse racing, Zeckendorf asked, "Would you buy a racing stable, if they retired the best horse [meaning Rickey]?"[39] Assured Rickey would stay if he bought in, Zeckendorf began to listen. He did not balk at the $1 million price tag, but was taken aback when Rickey told him the partnership agreement would force Rickey to allow O'Malley to counteroffer. "You're using me to force a price. I can't tie up capital" for that, Mann quoted Zeckendorf as saying. Rickey agreed to a $50,000 fee for Zeckendorf if O'Malley bought the stock.[40]

On Friday, September 22, Rickey presented the offer to O'Malley and Mrs. Smith. *Brooklyn Eagle* sports editor Lou Niss broke the story on page

1 the next day. O'Malley said immediately he would match the offer.[41] He told Dick Young of the *Daily News* that he had not known until the evening of the twenty-second that Rickey was planning to sell his stock. Young described O'Malley as "stunned" and "peeved."[42] For years O'Malley would complain that Zeckendorf was not a real buyer, simply doing Galbreath a favor and pocketing $50,000 in the process.[43] Zeckendorf, on the other hand, described himself as a real baseball fan. He had made an earlier attempt to buy the St. Louis Browns.[44]

The newspapers were most concerned with whether Rickey was moving to Pittsburgh, whom O'Malley might name as general manager, and whether Burt Shotton would return as the manager for 1951. Two New York papers reported that Mrs. Smith's shares were for sale, an unlikely event, as her husband's estate was deep in probate court.[45]

Rickey dodged and danced around the Pittsburgh question. He left open the possibility of staying with the Dodgers. On Monday, the twenty-fifth, the *New York Times* reported that Rickey was definitely going to Pittsburgh, and the *New York Post* reported that O'Malley hoped to change Rickey's mind. Rickey said he was not going, but then had Harold Parrott issue a press release, noting that he did not say he would "never" go to Pittsburgh.[46] After the doubleheader split with the Giants that evening, Rickey started a press conference at 11:45 p.m. It ran until 12:30 a.m. Rickey again diverted all the questions about his future. O'Malley, in the room, decided to become reporter and undermine some of the newspaper stories he did not like. He asked Rickey if he or Smith had ever criticized him for the football losses or pressured him to fire Durocher or Shotton. Entering into the sham, Rickey responded, "No pressure was ever brought on me by any of my associates on any of those questions." Assured they were operating from the same script, O'Malley pressed in again: "Have there ever been sharp words between you, me and the board member?" Rickey said, "By and large, our relations have always been most pleasant." Then there was a pause, a puff on his cigar, and a look toward the ceiling. "We've had differences," Rickey added. When a real reporter then asked him why, given this atmosphere of sweetness and light in the Brooklyn offices, he was selling his stock, he chose humorous evasion. "When did you stop shooting your wife?" he asked.[47]

O'Malley was most concerned with where he was going to raise $1 million. He said he intended to take full advantage of the sixty-day window to come up with the money.[48] But it was obviously a strain. The next Sunday,

October 1, the Dodgers and the Phillies played the last game of the regular season. If the Dodgers won, they would force a playoff for the pennant. Ebbets Field was full, 35,073 fans screaming for the home team. In the radio booth Red Barber said he had to reposition his mike because the noise of Rickey and O'Malley yelling at each other in the adjacent owners' box was filtering into the broadcast.[49]

Three weeks later O'Malley started to show his hand. He announced that he and Mrs. Smith would buy out Rickey, and each would own 37.5 percent of the team.[50] Two days later Rickey resigned. In early November few were surprised to learn he had joined the Pirates as executive vice president and general manager.[51] His contract was virtually identical to the contract O'Malley had offered Rickey two months earlier.[52]

Harold Rosenthal of the *New York Herald-Tribune* described Rickey's mood at his resignation press conference as ranging from "the facetious to the sentimental."[53] The sentimental was when he touched on his relationship with the sportswriters. The facetious was everything else. He entered the press conference asking the reporters if they had come to see "the reed driven by the wind." He described O'Malley as having youth, courage, enterprise, and desire. "And double chins," added O'Malley.[54]

O'Malley's response was even more aimed at public consumption. "I am terribly sorry and hurt personally that we now have to face this resignation," he said.[55] Rickey said he was going to his Maryland farm to check out a prize bull, then raised his eyebrows, moved his cigar around his mouth, and said, "I contemplate studying a new tangent in handling the bull."[56]

O'Malley was still struggling to raise the money. He formally accepted the $1,025,000 price on November 1.[57] Mrs. Smith dropped out of her agreement to participate in buying the Rickey stock on November 20.[58] Whether this had been contemplated all along is not clear. Rickey's success in winning his price was certainly an additional financial burden for her husband's estate.[59] O'Malley now had come up with the full price by himself. He was helped by the terms Rickey had negotiated with Zeckendorf, which called for a ten-year payoff. On November 24 he wrote Rickey that he had matched those terms, paying $175,000 down on December 5 and another $125,000 by March 1, 1951. The remaining $750,000 would be paid in ten annual installments beginning in 1952.[60]

O'Malley would later say he "liquidated everything" to make the initial payments.[61] Clearly, that was not true. He held on to the New York Subways Advertising Company stock, for example. But he did sell his interests in J. P. Duffy & Company, a Long Island building contractor, and the Long Island Rail Road. He had picked up both of those companies in his bankruptcy practice. The payments over the next decade could be financed out of the Dodgers' earnings.[62] The sale was complicated by a baseball rule that precluded a club executive from having a financial interest in another team. O'Malley's promissory note to Rickey was backed by the shares in the Dodgers. If O'Malley had defaulted, the shares would have gone back to Rickey, but Commissioner Chandler ruled there was enough of a remove that Rickey's interest would be tolerated.[63]

There remains the intriguing question of whether a true Rickey-O'Malley partnership could have been worked out. Given the personal tensions generated between the two men during the late 1940s, it seems highly unlikely. People as diverse as Bill Veeck and Jane Rickey affirmed that both men wanted to be the alpha dog. Rickey had chafed under Sam Breadon in St. Louis and found his experience in Brooklyn was evolving toward a similar subordination. For O'Malley, there was the personal drive to be the unquestioned leader, not just the businessman, and his knowledge that his desire to build a new stadium would clash continually with Rickey's concerns for player development.

As much as O'Malley had carped, and Smith had worried, about Rickey's management, the Dodger organization Rickey took over had been improved substantially during his eight years. Because of the football fiasco, Rickey had not put as much in the bank as the team could have, but consistent success on the field had been transformed into a healthier balance sheet. The mortgage on Ebbets Field had finally been retired, and the team had no debts except the mortgage on a recently purchased office building.[64] The team had been able to absorb the football losses and the cost of rebuilding in Fort Worth without borrowing.[65] The book value of the team's capital stock had more than doubled.[66] There was $283,000 in the bank and another $473,000 awaiting transfer from Minor League clubs.[67]

The team reflected Rickey's focus on the players. The "boys of summer," as Roger Kahn would later label them, would win four of the next six National League pennants, narrowly miss another, and bring Brooklyn its first World Series victory.[68] The aura of being the franchise that had signed Jackie Robinson would stay with the team for decades after Rickey left it and would be used as a marketing tool by O'Malley, future Dodger owners, and, ultimately, Major League Baseball. The executives whom Rickey had trained and left behind would ensure that the Dodgers continued the highly effective use of Rickey's methods of selecting and training ballplayers. Nearly four decades after Rickey's departure, and nearly a decade after O'Malley's death, the Dodgers' vice president of player personnel would be Al Campanis, spotted by Rickey as a player with management potential and brought along by the man he would always call "Mr. Rickey." But Campanis would have to say that quietly because there was a new man in charge, and the new man instituted a $1 fine for anyone who mentioned Rickey's name.[69]

6

Running the Team

Walter O'Malley was a new kind of team owner. He had not played the game or built a career in the front office. He was not a "sportsman" or a corporate scion. He was a forty-seven-year-old lawyer who had sat at Branch Rickey's elbow for eight years. That was a great education for how to do things the traditional way. But Walter O'Malley had some new ideas as well.

Except for Bill Veeck, who would not be back as an owner until the middle of 1951, the baseball owners of the 1950s believed that marketing was giving the newspapers their schedules, finding the best possible players, and, in a big innovation, broadcasting the games on radio. In those days even the National League pennant-winning Phillies closed their offices over the winter.[1]

Walter O'Malley knew his own skills, and over his next three decades as the Dodgers' owner, he would rarely interfere with the executives he hired to sign, develop, trade, and manage players. Instead, he would focus on the business operations, especially marketing. For Rickey's baseball role he split the job between Emil J. Bavasi, the Montreal Royals' general manager nobody ever called anything except "Buzzie," and Lafayette Fresco Thompson, the Dodgers' director of Minor League operations. Bavasi would handle the Major League club and the farm teams in Montreal and St. Paul, the direct feeders into the Brooklyn roster. Thompson would handle all the lower Minor League teams, some seventeen in 1951, and oversee scouting. These duties, though handled differently in some cases, existed at every Major League team.

Off the field O'Malley created new positions, a real estate manager and a director of special events and extra revenue.[2] The real estate man would oversee Ebbets Field, various Minor League properties, the growing list of parcels used for parking near Ebbets Fields, and maybe the property

O'Malley envisioned for a new stadium. The special events and extra revenue job encompassed nonbaseball uses of Ebbets Field as well as radio, television, and concessions.

Some of the front-office changes were cosmetic. Rickey's fish tank and elk head disappeared from the president's office. The midwesterner's portrait of Abraham Lincoln was replaced by one of George V. McLaughlin of the Brooklyn Trust Company.[3] The color scheme of "County Mayo" green honored the O'Malley family's ancestral home amid $13,000 in renovations to the team's offices.[4] O'Malley instituted a fine of $1 every time someone mentioned Rickey's name. That was petty, but it also served the management function of reminding everyone the team was taking a new approach. O'Malley publicly criticized Rickey for taking too much money from the team and not being concerned with the fans. The Dodgers would no longer sell players for profit, but would be focused on making the World Series, he said.[5]

O'Malley did seek to keep some Rickey men, including Branch Rickey Jr.[6] Bavasi along with Bob Clements, John Reeves, and Mel Jones had been offered jobs by Rickey.[7] Bavasi stayed, and Reeves delayed joining Rickey for a couple of years. The others, plus George Sisler, Rex Bowen, Harold Roettger, Milt Stock, and Howie Haak, went to Pittsburgh immediately, despite O'Malley's efforts to dissuade Haak.[8] Bavasi later told author Joshua Praeger that O'Malley had wanted to get rid of traveling secretary Harold Parrott and statistician Allan Roth because they were Rickey men, but both stayed for more than a decade, through the move to Los Angeles.[9] Although Parrott would become quite critical of O'Malley, at the time columnist Dan Parker of the *New York Mirror* indicated Parrott was happy with the new regime because under Rickey he had been "kept in the background."[10]

Overwhelmingly, perhaps indicative of underlying cultural patterns in the office, the Protestants went to Pittsburgh while the Catholics stayed in Brooklyn.[11] Admittedly, the Catholics, especially people like Bavasi and Parrott, were New Yorkers to the bone with a great liking for company, liquor, conversation, and telling baseball stories, all characteristics they shared with O'Malley. Some felt there was an undercurrent. Roger Kahn noted O'Malley was very conscious of people's ethnicity, although not bigoted.[12] "The goyim did okay. Very true. They were tolerant, but it helped if you were Irish," said Irving Rudd. "In hindsight, I wonder if being Jewish didn't hurt me."[13] As Rudd acknowledged, O'Malley made an effort to recruit Jewish executives to bond with the fan base of Brooklyn, about half the borough's population in that era. When O'Malley took over the team, statistician Allan Roth was the only Jew prominently placed in the front office. The team hired former Brooklyn newspaperman Frank Scott as part of its public relations staff. Everyone, including evidently O'Malley, thought he was Jewish until the Ash Wednesday he walked into the office with a smear on his forehead. Scott, it turned out, had been shortened from Scotto, Italian and Catholic.[14]

There were petty undercurrents fed by O'Malley's mistrust of personal and professional loyalties. In late-January 1951 O'Malley called auditor Don Beech into his office. He asked if Beech had spent time over the weekend with Rickey, Beech's college fraternity brother and so long a friend he actually called him "Branch." When Beech said he had, O'Malley then said he trusted Rickey had not tried to "pump" Beech and that Beech would not have responded had Rickey done so. Still, though, the possibilities had O'Malley worried, and so he was going to let Beech go.[15] He offered Beech two months with pay to look around for another job. The next morning Beech mentioned the conversation to Bavasi, who had assured Beech the new management wanted him to stay. Bavasi relayed the complaint to O'Malley, who quickly changed the time table. Beech was to turn over his work to another employee immediately. He would still be paid through March 31, but was out of a job.[16] O'Malley would not have to pay Beech for the full two months. By March he was working for the Pirates.[17]

But distancing the Dodgers from the Rickey name was not all spite. It contained a good measure of calculated marketing. O'Malley felt the team needed a new image after attendance fell by 447,851, or 27 percent, in 1950. He felt Rickey's image, especially with the press, was a hindrance. The main driver, noted Joe King of the *New York World-Telegram and Sun*, was "the urgent need of the club to regain the good-will of the fans who deserted by the thousands during the past season."[18] The split doubleheaders O'Malley had defended during his partnership with Rickey were banned, and other policies were changed to make it easier for fans to buy tickets on game day.[19]

The lesser and greater motives were on display in O'Malley's decision on the team's manager for 1951. Rickey's close friend Burt Shotton had guided the team for much of the last four seasons, winning two pennants and narrowly losing another. Dodger executives took more shots at Rickey by implying Shotton's efforts had been frustrated by front-office interference.[20] Still, Shotton had been hammered in the press, and many fans had picked up on the criticisms there.[21]

From a marketing perspective, fan unhappiness was magnified by what O'Malley perceived as Shotton's dullness. Shotton, who turned sixty-six that fall, managed in street clothes. Baseball rules said only uniformed personnel could go onto the field during games. "Fans like to see a manager," O'Malley said. "They like to cheer him and jeer him, and suffer with him. They can't see him if he isn't in uniform."[22] The decision went to Charlie Dressen, a short, cocky man who was always available to give a newspaper reporter a quote or an umpire an argument.

The Dressen decision reflected another part of the front-office calculation. "The fans quit on us. It is my job to win them back," O'Malley said. "It has not seemed like a Brooklyn operation recently because it has not been neighborly or friendly."[23] Although O'Malley was only too happy to blame Rickey for that image problem, he knew a large part of the cause was New York's biggest newspaper, the *Daily News*. The *New York Times* might have dominated national discourse, but the *Daily News* had the most popular, and probably the best, sports section in the city. The *Daily News'* sports editor, Jimmy Powers, had hung the "El Cheapo" tag that bothered Rickey so much. Its Dodger beat writer was Dick Young, a particularly aggressive reporter with a barbed typewriter. In a more distanced interview several years later, Young summed up his perception:

> Much of the adverse comment written about Rickey resulted from his condescending approach to the press. Writers not so much resented his evasiveness, but rather his insufferable belief he was getting away with it. Rickey, while talking to newsmen, would create the impression in his audience that he was thinking: "I can wrap these lame-brains around my little finger with my rhetoric." Few men have the nimble brain of Branch Rickey, including the newsmen whom he tried to deceive, but baseball writers are proud of the trust which is often placed in them. Rickey, inordinately suspicious, failed to project this feeling of trust. He substituted arrogance and scorn, and as a result received the "bad press" he could not understand.[24]

Young had come up with the acronym KOBS (kindly old Burt Shotton) for the Dodgers' manager and played remorselessly on his supposed incompetence. In 1950 it had become "a virtual campaign by New York's largest newspaper to drive Shotton out of town," wrote Joe King. "This was a bitter and remorseless drive."[25]

Replacing Shotton would remove the immediate cause for the *Daily News'* attitude, but O'Malley knew longer-term measures were necessary. One of the specific charges he gave Buzzie Bavasi was managing the *Daily News* relationship. Other reporters snidely began calling Bavasi the "Vice President in charge of Dick Young." They suggested he and O'Malley were slipping Young tidbits before telling the other reporters.[26] It worked, wrote Roger Kahn, neatly conflating an old Young nickname with a new one. "Young also demanded special treatment, in the form of exclusive interviews and tips from the people he covered. When he got that, as he did classically from the Brooklyn Dodgers of the 1950s, Ol' Poison Pen turned into Master Lionel Lollipop."[27]

Managing difficult personalities was a role for which Bavasi was eminently suited. There is a long tradition in baseball of storytelling, often lubricated by liquor. All baseball executives and managers, some more consciously than others, realize they are in the entertainment business, and telling stories to media people that might get passed on to the customers is extremely good business. And, like Hollywood movies, the impact of the story, usually humorous and self-deprecating, is more important than a strict adherence to the facts. Bavasi, balding and bow-tied, was a master at mixing a reporter a cocktail and telling tales of past and present that would liven up a reporter's copy. Over time details would change, and thus certain aspects of his own life are hard to pin down.

Bavasi was born in 1914 to a wealthy family who lived in the plush New York suburb of Scarsdale. His father had emigrated from Marseilles, France, at the age of seven and eventually built up the Union News Company, which distributed all of New York's newspapers except the *Daily News*.[28] When Bavasi moved into the general manager's role, his family still owned the real estate under several of New York's major hotels.[29] Throughout his nearly fifty years in baseball, Bavasi could look at his paycheck as a way of judging how his employers valued him rather than as a means of sustaining his lifestyle.

Bavasi's father died when he was sixteen, and he developed a close bond with the father of his best friend, Frederick Frick. Ford Frick was then a reporter and sportscaster in the Hearst media empire. "Ford had been like a father to me since my father died," Bavasi said.[30] Frick soon moved to the National League as its public relations director, and in 1934, when the younger Frick and Bavasi were at DePauw University in Indiana, the elder Frick became president of the National League.

At DePauw Bavasi was the baseball team's catcher for three years and said he was offered $1,500 to sign with the Giants, but turned it down because he did not think he had Major League talent.[31] After his graduation in 1938, the details of Bavasi's life scatter. He either went to work in circulation for the *New York Times* or did nothing. Either that fall or the following spring, he asked Frick Sr. to ask Larry MacPhail if there was a job for him in Brooklyn.[32] MacPhail made one, and Bavasi helped around the Montague Street office until early 1940, when MacPhail shipped him off to be the business manager, and bus driver, for the Americus Pioneers of the Georgia-Florida League. With all of MacPhail's personnel maneuvers, Bavasi said the team had only eight players late in the year, so he signed himself to a contract and batted .333 over a four-game series, but gave up a home run to the first batter when he put himself in to pitch.[33] He married Evit Rice, his Scarsdale fiancée and neighbor, in Americus that summer, moving on to Valdosta, Georgia, in 1941 and Durham, North Carolina, in 1943 while enduring the *Sporting News*' inability to get his name straight. He went from Bauasi in Valdosta to Bervasi in Durham before a Harold Parrott freelance piece got it straight in late 1943. That was just as Bavasi was disappearing into the Army, where he served in a machine gun unit that fought the Germans from Naples to the Austrian border.[34]

When he got out in late 1945, the family money allowed him, Evit, and three-year-old Peter, later an executive with several Major League teams, to spend three months at Sea Island, Georgia, recuperating.[35] The Dodgers were only too happy to have him back, sending him to Nashua, New Hampshire, for the 1946 season. There he was presented with what other Dodger Minor League executives felt was a hot potato. Jackie Robinson was joining the Montreal Royals that spring, but the Dodgers had other African American players—Roy Campanella and Don Newcombe. Other Dodger farm clubs had refused to take them due to fears of the local reaction. Bavasi did not hesitate a moment and forged another link in what Jules Tygiel calls the Great Experiment.[36] The two players' bonds with Bavasi would remain strong for the rest of their lives.

It was not just his personality. Bavasi challenged the manager of the Lynn Red Sox to a fight over race-baiting and foul language.[37] When manager Walter Alston was kicked out of a game for arguing balls and strikes, Alston named Campanella rather than one of the white players as his replacement.[38] Bavasi backed Alston up.

After two years in Nashua, Bavasi was promoted to the Dodgers' top farm club, the Montreal Royals, where he was general manager when Walter O'Malley called in October 1950. Rickey had tried to hire him away already, and he had a growing reputation in baseball. Cautiously, O'Malley chose not to call Bavasi the team's general manager. Instead, he was given the mushy title of vice president, a title that gave O'Malley flexibility. If Bavasi did not work out, he could move Thompson or another executive into the role more easily. Bavasi would not be given the formal title of executive vice president and general manager until the team moved to Los Angeles, but he got the duties immediately.[39]

He quickly earned the informal title. Barely six months into the job, Bavasi shored up what was considered the only weakness in the Dodgers' starting eight—left field. He obtained Andy Pafko from the Cubs for a collection of Minor Leaguers and bench players. The *Sporting News* called it "the big steal of 1951" and said it meant the pennant for the Dodgers.[40] It did not, but the trade still brought heartfelt comparisons of Bavasi to his mentor, Branch Rickey.

For the next two decades Bavasi would be acknowledged as one of the game's sharpest operators. He would maintain the Dodgers' power-oriented team that Rickey had built in Ebbets Field and build a pitching and speed team in Dodger Stadium. His baseball acumen would allow O'Malley to concentrate on the business aspects of the team. Four decades later Bavasi would say that O'Malley never interfered in his baseball decisions, and the *never* was only a bit of an overstatement.[41] O'Malley was making noises that his law practice would remain his major focus, but the Dodgers beckoned, and Bavasi's charm, storytelling ability, and media savvy made him an invaluable piece of the new emphasis on marketing.[42]

At his first spring training as owner in 1951, O'Malley started his tradition of a big party on St. Patrick's Day. Players were not invited. It was for press, team executives, other baseball people, and whoever important happened to be around. "Those St. Patty's Day parties cost a fortune," Bavasi said later. "He would spare no expense." There were music, green caps, or other paraphernalia and a lot of liquor and a menu spiced with O'Malley's often ethnic blend of humor.[43] One year the menu included "Bacon Pitler," in honor of Jake Pitler, the Dodgers' Jewish coach.

Another new tradition that spring was an all-expense-paid junket for the reporters. The first year they went to Key West for a cocktail party and fish fry.[44] In subsequent years the junket would go to Havana, Jamaica, the Bahamas, or other hot spots. On the road during the season, he would cultivate the reporters at lavish dinners.[45] It worked. Writers caught the contrast with Rickey. "Throwing the bull? O'Malley can do that, too, in a happy, optimistic way, and not in a devious manner intended to mislead. He is a facile speaker and arrives quickly at a judicious appraisal of a problem. He is also a formidable antagonist in the barb and wit department, as Rickey found out first."[46]

There were also changes that directly helped the newspapers. A darkroom was installed at Ebbets Field so photographers could do their own developing and editing before sending pictures to their papers.[47] Allan Roth had been hired by Rickey as a statistician, and Roth had pioneered many techniques that would be the foundation of SABRmetrics three decades later.[48] But Charlie Dressen managed by the seat of his pants, and Walter O'Malley did not catch on to the significance of what Roth offered. He made Roth part of the public relations department and had him feed his statistical nuggets to the broadcasters and use them to expand the nightly notes sheets handed out in the press box. Roth compiled the notes sheet, and his papers contain full sets of a number of years in the late 1940s and early 1950s.[49] The tidbits no doubt helped the writers, but they also reveal O'Malley's innovations on the marketing side. Rickey's famous innovations—pitching strings, sliding pits, the farm system, the signing of Jackie Robinson, and the unified training camp—were all centered on the game on the field. O'Malley's were on the business side, seeing the game from the fans' point of view in the stands.

What the press box notes of 1951 reveal was a huge surge in community nights—Levittown Night, Republic Aircraft Night, Valley Stream Night. There had been none in 1950. There were several dozen in 1951 and more on the way. It was an O'Malley brainstorm. The team *yearbook* was revamped, substituting pictures for statistics and adding features to make it chattier. Yearbook sales more than doubled. Happy Felton's kid-oriented television show was introduced, and the Knothole Gang program was expanded.[50]

O'Malley and the marketing people remained light on their feet. When twenty thousand women turned out for a Ladies' Night and many had to be turned away, O'Malley apologized and immediately made the next game free for women as well. When a successful Father-Son Day event brought squawks from the mothers, a Mother-Child Day was quickly scheduled.

The liveliest promotion came from turning a problem into a positive. For years a group of enthusiastic fans had come to games with a motley collection of musical instruments and a motlier collection of musical talents. They played "Three Blind Mice" for the umpires and similar ditties for other occasions. They called themselves, with proper modesty, the "Dodger Sym-phony."

In mid-July 1951 Local 802 of the American Federation of Musicians, American Federation of Labor, announced that the Sym-phony must be paid and paid at union scale. If the Dodgers did not comply, the union said, ushers, park police, groundskeepers, and even Red Barber, Vin Scully, and the other announcers would have to go out on strike. Walter O'Malley said the band members were not musicians performing; they were fans blowing off steam. Two band members actually were union members. O'Malley met with the local's officials, who were chagrined at the negative reaction flowing around town, and reached a compromise. The two union members of the band would have to quit, but the amateurs could keep playing.[51]

O'Malley then took it a step further, scheduling a special night on August 13 called variously Music Appreciation or Music Depreciation Night. Anybody who showed up with any kind of an instrument, or sometimes just the case, could get into the upper left-field stands for free. The real "Dodger Sym-phony" played. The musical guests played. The presidents of the city's five boroughs played harmonicas and sang "Take Me Out to the Ball Game." The *Daily News* sent its "music critic pro tem" and gave his dateline as the Musical Black Hole of Calcutta. Nobody appreciated the music; everybody (26,450, 50 percent more than average, and on a Monday night) had a good time.[52]

A month later a committee headed by Judge Samuel Leibowitz presented each member of the Sym-phony with a television and a new instrument.[53] Even with the greater excitement at the ballpark, 1951's attendance rebounded barely 8 percent, still below every postwar year except 1950. It was a sign of things to come. Noted Joe King of the *New York World Telegram*, "It is becoming clear that the O'Malleys have the best product in this business, but have not yet discovered how to merchandise it."[54]

Walter O'Malley's relationship with Jackie Robinson was off to a rocky start. Robinson, understandably, had a strong personal relationship with Rickey, the man who had given him his chance. With the Rickey-O'Malley battle to control the Dodgers brewing in early 1950, Robinson heaped praise on Rickey.[55] Years later he would tell Jimmy Cannon, "It all boils down to I'm a very good Branch Rickey man, and always will be."[56]

There was a widely held perception that O'Malley, other Dodger executives, and many reporters favored the amiable, nonconfrontational

Roy Campanella over Robinson. As Robinson himself said, "I was not O'Malley's kind of black. Campanella was."[57] That characterization of Campanella undoubtedly downplayed Campanella's commitment to racial change, but there is no question the catcher was not as confrontational as Robinson.[58] And Robinson's willingness to butt heads was not appreciated by the image-conscious O'Malley. Through the 1940s and early 1950s, the Dodgers stayed at the Netherlands Plaza Hotel in Cincinnati, a city conscious of its closeness to the segregated South. The hotel's dining room was closed to blacks. Robinson consistently presented himself at the dining room and forced them to turn him away. O'Malley told Robinson he was "causing a scene" and asked him to back off. Robinson did not. Sportswriter Sam Lacy wrote, "From that day forward, Walter O'Malley hated his guts."[59] It seems more of a clash of personalities than anything rational. Confronted with similar counseling by Rickey, or racially touchy situations with people he liked, Robinson had backed down.[60] If Walter O'Malley hated Robinson's guts, the player reciprocated. Robinson "felt that O'Malley patronized him and treated him unfairly, and Jackie could not abide the sight of him."[61]

Whatever he thought at this point, O'Malley did not want his relationship with Robinson to be a public issue. So he tried to say the politic thing. Asked about Robinson's potential as a manager, O'Malley dodged.[62] When National League president Ford Frick singled out Robinson after the Dodgers swept a series from the Giants marked by bean balls and even more bench jockeying than usual, O'Malley leaped to Robinson's defense.[63] When Robinson told a radio audience that he thought the Yankees were a racist organization, O'Malley defended Robinson's right to say what he believed.[64] But not all was sweetness and light. When Robinson was fined for criticizing an umpire, O'Malley asked him to keep quiet about it while he talked with the league president. Robinson, who said he assumed everybody knew about the fine, discussed it in the presence of a reporter, who printed the story. Robinson said O'Malley accused him of "seeking publicity."[65] According to Roger Kahn, O'Malley would regularly paint Robinson as a "shameless publicity seeker."[66]

O'Malley's standing in Robinson's eyes could not have been helped by the persistent rumors that Dodger management was concerned the team had "too many" black players. O'Malley's name was never specifically put on the table, but the years the issue was raised pointed right at him. It was an issue Robinson raised himself, which O'Malley denied had any bearing on management's thinking.[67] Rickey, after leaving the Dodgers, would say that the sale of Sam Jethroe in late 1949 was due to "ownership" being concerned the team had reached a saturation point.[68] Others, as related earlier, tied the sale of Jethroe and Irv Noren to the financial losses occasioned by the football fiasco.

By late 1956 it was obvious to both the Dodger brass and Robinson that his career was winding down. He would be thirty-eight when the 1957 season began. His performance had faded from star to journeyman. Robinson began to make plans. On December 10 he accepted a vice president's position with Chock Full o' Nuts, a New York coffee-shop company. He had an obligation to tell the Dodgers he would not be back for 1957, but was inhibited by a contract he had signed with *Look* in 1954. That contract had guaranteed him $50,000 for a couple of articles in that year and an exclusive right to the story of his retirement. *Look*, a weekly, could not publish the retirement story before January 8, so Robinson kept his mouth shut. On December 11 Bavasi contacted him to tell him he had been traded to the Giants.[69]

Robinson's best biographer, Arnold Rampersad, says Robinson heard Bavasi's news "with a widening smile."[70] It confirmed his feelings that it was time to retire. There was also regret, for his image and that of the Dodgers were closely tied. The idea that he had been traded to the hated Giants stung many Dodger fans deeply.

O'Malley's role in this is unclear. He had returned from a two-month round-the-world trip just days before Bavasi made the trade, but many assumed he was behind it. Dick Young, in listing reasons for the trade, wrote, "There was no love lost between Robinson and prexy Walter O'Malley."[71] Bavasi said an exasperated O'Malley had discussed trading Robinson many times over the years, but had never ordered him to do so.[72] O'Malley wrote Jackie and Rachel Robinson a smoothly worded letter, noting that their paths might cross again. "If it makes him so sad, why did he trade me to the Giants?" Robinson asked rhetorically.[73]

Because of the silence Robinson felt the *Look* contract imposed, Bavasi and O'Malley were left to fend off both the normally curious and those fans with diehard attachments to the Robinson-Dodgers relationship. Robinson quibbled by saying he was not sure whether he would report to the Giants or retire.[74] When *Look* finally began promoting their exclusive January 5, 1957, the relationship worsened. Bavasi blasted Robinson for not being up front about his retirement. Informed Robinson planned to write Giants general manager Chub Feeney a note of apology, Bavasi said, "That's typical of Jackie. Now he'll write a letter of apology to Chubby. He has been writing letters of apology all his life." Robinson fired back, "After what Bavasi said, I wouldn't play ball again for a million dollars."[75]

There was continued sniping. When the Urban League of Los Angeles gave O'Malley a plaque honoring his "enlightened leadership" in integration, Robinson called it "preposterous" and gave full credit to Rickey.[76] When the National Association of Colored People's Pasadena chapter honored Robinson in 1959, O'Malley did not attend.[77] When Robinson and Carl Rowan published *Wait till Next Year* in 1960, Robinson revisited the stories of O'Malley's treatment of him and his contention that O'Malley had no commitment to racial equality.[78]

O'Malley, however, did keep a channel open to Rachel Robinson, who had a much more positive view of the owner and the organization than Jackie. And, over time, the relationship improved. By 1964, when Robinson and Charles Dexter wrote *Baseball Has Done It*, Robinson was writing, "I personally did not think Mr. O'Malley was as liberal in his thinking on integration as Mr. Rickey. I have grown to respect him a great deal in recent years and my wife has a sincere affection for him and Mrs. O'Malley."[79] Soon afterward he told *Los Angeles Times* columnist Sid Ziff, "I shall never forget what Mr. Rickey did for me. I feel Mr. Rickey is one of the great human beings. It was because of my love and admiration for him that I had my difficulty with Mr. O'Malley. That is the only thing that caused the resentment. I'm glad our relations have been ironed out."[80]

Despite this resolution some of the feelings clearly remained. Robinson's public reconciliation of the Dodgers would have to wait until 1972, when a dying Robinson joined Sandy Koufax and Roy Campanella as the Dodgers retired their uniform numbers, the first time the team had given that honor.[81] Significantly, it was not Walter but Peter O'Malley, by now the president of the team, who reached out to both Jackie and Rachel and convinced them of the organization's commitment to racial equality and to repairing their relationship with Jackie.[82]

With full ownership of the Dodgers, O'Malley now moved into the politics of the game. Although O'Malley had brushed against baseball's internal workings with the Durocher-MacPhail-Rickey hearings in 1947, Rickey had been the one who sat in the regular meetings of baseball's owners. Barely two weeks into his new role, O'Malley's first owners meeting was like being thrown into an ice-filled swimming pool. In a rump session on December 10, 1950, by an evenly split vote, the owners declined to meet Commissioner Happy Chandler's request for an extension of his contract beyond May 1952.[83] The vote was reaffirmed the following March, and in June Chandler assented to a separation agreement.[84]

O'Malley's role in this is murky.[85] The *Sporting News* reported he was expected to vote for Chandler at the December meeting and again at another meeting the following March.[86] The paper also noted that the voting method, anonymous scraps of paper dropped into a hat, made it hard for anyone to figure out who voted which way.[87] The *New York Times* reported he voted against Chandler at the March meeting, but the *Sporting News* reported he made the motion to retain Chandler.[88] In his "Old Scout" column, Herb Goren hinted at one reason O'Malley might have been unhappy with Chandler, writing that the Dodger owner felt Chandler needed to do a better job of public relations and that "Chandler's public relations activity was too self-centered."[89] William DeWitt, who represented the St. Louis Browns at the meetings, said O'Malley swung back and forth.[90]

If O'Malley remained in the background while Chandler was fired, he began to emerge in baseball's leadership with the search for a new commissioner. He moved into the public arena with both his list of qualifications and the name of the man he thought filled them—Ford Frick.[91] To O'Malley baseball faced too many issues to leave its head office vacant for long. He cited the hearings in Washington where the Celler Committee was examining baseball's antitrust exemption and the reserve clause. Without being specific he noted "litigation of various sorts."

For the new commissioner O'Malley suggested he needed "a judicial temperament, administrative ability, an awareness of public relations and a firm belief baseball is the national sport and must be sustained as such."[92] Frick, O'Malley said, had shown the necessary qualities as National League president and a member of the sport's executive council, which would act as the commissioner until Chandler's successor was found.[93]

Others had different ideas. Del Webb of the Yankees wanted a major industrialist. Lou Perini of the Braves wanted General Douglas MacArthur. The names of Ohio senator Fred Lausche; Supreme Court justice Fred Vinson; George Trautman, head of the Minor Leagues; and former postmaster general James Farley were batted around. Clark Griffith of the Senators wanted a baseball man, but not Frick.[94] Frick was clearly a National League man in an era when the leagues were much more distinct rivals than they are today. O'Malley undoubtedly thought Frick would be sympathetic to the Dodgers. They had worked on various issues since O'Malley became the team's lawyer, and Bavasi's personal relationship with Frick could only help.

As the summer progressed the owners met to reduce the candidate list and then to add more names to the pot. Air Force general Emmett O'Donnell, Army general Maxwell Taylor, and Warren Giles of the Cincinnati Reds were touted. Finally, on September 20, O'Malley's candidate emerged the winner. It took fifty ballots and Giles's withdrawal after a series of inconclusive votes.[95]

The Frick vote put the stamp on Walter O'Malley's ascendancy into the upper reaches of baseball management. With Frick's promotion Warren Giles of the Cincinnati Reds was named National League president. Giles, who had represented National League owners on the game's executive council, was replaced by O'Malley. The executive council, the first line of advice for a commissioner, was composed of the commissioner, the two league presidents, and an owner representative from each league.

A few months later Joe King would write, "In his second year as president of a big league club, O'Malley is increasingly recognized by his colleagues as a man of good balance, who thinks clearly, and who acts with dignity and fairness." King quoted one owner saying, "Maybe O'Malley is no Rickey, but he is not a fathead, either. He's a comer."[96]

For lifetime baseball executives such as Buzzie Bavasi, Walter O'Malley was always a "businessman," not a "baseball man," the label they cherished for themselves. Still, O'Malley was becoming more of a fan—in fact, a bit of a screamer. The National League pennant race that year was a made-for-TV movie, featuring the scrappy little guy rallying to tumble the favored colossus at the last moment. Unfortunately for O'Malley, the Dodgers were the favored colossus.

The Dodgers started the season well, and with Bavasi's Pafko trade in June the *Sporting News* was conceding them the pennant. In July they won three-quarters of their games and then swept the second-place Giants in a three-game series early in August. On August 11 they stood thirteen games ahead of the Giants, and everyone except the Giants thought it was over.

It is commonly heard that the Dodgers collapsed. That is not true. From August 11 onward the team went a pedestrian 26-22, still winning more than half their games. What is true is that the Giants ascended to another plane, winning thirty-seven of their last forty-four games and tying the Dodgers on the last day of the season.

The Dodgers' last seven games were on the road in Boston and Philadelphia. In February O'Malley said the press of business had kept him from the opening of spring training, but now he was traveling to every game.[97] On the season's last day the Giants played a quick game in Boston, while the Dodgers' contest in Philadelphia dragged on into extra innings. Kay O'Malley was with her husband, seated with Buzzie and Evit Bavasi as Jackie Robinson saved the day with a diving catch and a fourteenth-inning home run. O'Malley jumped to his feet, screaming like many another Dodger fan.[98]

The joy would not continue. The Dodgers lost the third game of the playoff series on Bobby Thomson's dramatic home run. Walter O'Malley was the first visitor to enter the Giants clubhouse and offer his congratulations. "I told Leo that his team had played the greatest baseball ever heard of and that I wanted to congratulate him in all sincerity."[99] In the Dodger dressing room O'Malley tried to offer a little humor with his condolences and encouragement for next year. Noting third baseman Billy Cox's black shorts, O'Malley asked him, "How did you know to plan for the mourning?"[100]

Kay O'Malley drove daughter Terry back to New Rochelle College after the game and then proceeded home to Amityville, wrote Tom Meany. There, she became alarmed when she found the house fully lighted, with police cars in front. She feared the Thomson homer had caused Walter to commit suicide. Inside, she found her husband and the cops trying to evict two Dodger fans who had been drinking at a local bar. They were very persistent in their questions about why Dressen had brought Ralph Branca in to face Thomson. They escalated to what O'Malley should have done and then to what they might do to O'Malley. It was then he called the police.[101]

Fresco Thompson told a story set a while after the game. O'Malley was riding an elevator when a disgruntled Brooklyn fan complained to the operator that the Dodgers had cost him $50 on the game. "A terrible thing," says O'Malley. "You're complaining," the guy responds. "How much did you lose?" At this point the elevator stopped, and as O'Malley got out, he said, "I figure it cost me between two hundred fifty and three hundred thousand dollars."[102]

Jack Collins had started as a Dodgers office boy in 1913 when Ebbets Field opened. He had been an usher and a telephone operator, sold tickets, and took them.[103] By 1942, when Rickey took over the team, he was called business manager and had his finger in many Dodger pots. He ran both Ebbets Field and the ticket operation as well as performing lesser duties.[104]

In November 1951 Arthur Young and Company, the Dodgers' accountants, discovered a $24,486 shortfall in the ticketing department. The Dodgers were covered by insurance through Lloyd's, and the Dodgers, Lloyd's, and Arthur Young began a two-month investigation. On January 29, 1951, O'Malley went to the Brooklyn district attorney's office with their complaint. The next day Collins resigned, saying he had long been intending to go into business in Florida.[105]

Rumblings of money disappearing from the ticket department could hardly have been news to O'Malley. In 1947 the Dodgers had hired the Pinkerton Detective Agency to investigate scalping of their tickets. At Branch Rickey's request Commissioner Happy Chandler then arranged for a North Carolina lawyer named A. P. Kitchin to look into the situation. Kitchin traveled to New York City, talked to Arthur Mann, and raised some pointed questions about Collins. Mann quickly backed off, saying the team did not want to do anything that would "embarrass" Collins. Kitchin described Mann's reaction as "fear."[106]

That fear was clearly still present in 1952. Collins rescinded his resignation, despite O'Malley's announcement of a management shuffle to succeed him. O'Malley let him back and gave him office space, supposedly to work with the district attorney's office on the investigation. Collins said he regretted the shortfall, blaming it on temporary workers and the confusion attendant to having to return $8 million in payments for World Series tickets after the playoff collapse against the Giants. The grand-jury process went nowhere, and no indictments against Collins were returned, although one lower-level ticket department employee was arrested.[107] The district attorney said there was enough evidence to indict, but not to convict. The Dodgers received $100,000 from Lloyd's, indicating Collins raids were more costly than first revealed.[108] Collins moved to Clearwater, Florida, and bought himself a hotel.[109]

It is possible O'Malley had been setting a trap for Collins. Rickey said team assistant treasurer William Gibson exposed Collins, "a careful man who covered his tracks almost beyond proof of deceptive conduct."[110] Certainly, O'Malley avoided mentioning Collins's name in later years, although he did describe the situation. The outcome was messy, but O'Malley had moved to solve a problem that had plagued the team at least back as far as the Rickey years.

O'Malley was also beginning to work on the problem of spring training. He had not yet become reconciled to its costs and still had not fallen in love with Vero Beach. The costs were escalating. By 1953 O'Malley would present a detailed budget showing more than $400,000 in expenses.[111] In those years, before the coming of the interstate highway system, Vero Beach was very isolated from other spring training sites, which clustered around the Tampa–St. Petersburg area in west-central Florida. The closest facility was the Athletics' in West Palm Beach, seventy miles down U.S. 1.[112] But other teams could be persuaded to leave central Florida for the larger potential payout of Miami.

To offset the costs the team began the practice of early training in Vero Beach, with the Major League team then moving to Miami for exhibition games before barnstorming home and ending with a weekend against the Yankees. This pattern would continue until the team moved to Los Angeles. It cost more to house the varsity in Miami, but attendance would average around seven thousand a game during the 1950s. Bavasi, despite O'Malley's promises that the practice would stop, was able to continue selling players.[113] O'Malley also noted the team's peak time for season ticket sales, worth around $500,000, was in late February, when spring training publicity was blossoming.[114]

O'Malley also began to turn his thoughts to other ways to make money from the Vero Beach facility. In 1954 he initiated the Dodgertown Boys Camp, where boys from ten to sixteen could spend July and August with instruction in baseball and other sports. The camp, which cost $500, took in 150 to 200 boys a year.[115] Peter O'Malley started his baseball management career as a sixteen-year-old counselor at the camp.

More money could also be made if the expenses of Miami could be avoided or lowered. O'Malley, ever the builder, began to think of constructing an appropriate stadium at Dodgertown. But first he needed assurance the team would be there long enough to justify the cost, estimated at $5,000. The original 1948 agreement with Vero Beach was due to run out in 1953, although it had a five-year renewal clause. On March 26, 1951, O'Malley spoke at the annual Vero Beach banquet honoring the Dodgers. He suggested the team would like a longer, firmer relationship with the city. The city council quickly asked the city attorney to put together a contract for its approval.[116] It took until January 1952 to work out the lease, but it was set to run for twenty-one years, with the Dodgers getting an option to renew for an additional twenty-one years.[117] Rent was set at $1 a year plus the proceeds of one exhibition game. O'Malley plowed through two pages of legalese about what would happen if the Dodgers missed a payment and then reached for his wallet, peeled off $21, and handed them to a Vero Beach official.[118]

The contract gave O'Malley the confidence to hire Norman Bel Geddes as the architect and Emil Praeger as the construction boss for what would be called Holman Stadium, after the Vero Beach businessman who had brought the Dodgers to the city. The stadium would have more than four thousand seats and a berm around the outfield that could provide flexible capacity.[119] Ground was broken in the late summer of 1952, with the goal of being open for spring training the next year.[120] Fifty-one days later, it was done.[121] O'Malley made a flying trip to Vero Beach in October when a hurricane threatened South Florida. He was worried the newly created outfield berm, which had not fully settled, might be washed away. It held.[122]

O'Malley was not done. The berm had been built with dirt removed from an adjacent lot. O'Malley, the avid fisherman, filled the hole with water and stocked it with bass. When the pond began emitting a sulfurous odor, he named it Lake Gowanus, after the sewer-like canal near the Dodgers' old Washington Park in West Brooklyn.[123] Soon, he and Mrs. Smith surrounded the stadium and lake with palm trees, an early example of his landscaping fetish.[124]

As Vero Beach became more his project than Branch Rickey's, O'Malley began to enjoy it more and make it reflect his personality. He was meeting visitors and proudly giving personal tours of the facility.[125] The sportswriters noted the greatly improved food, the open bar, and the high-stakes card games.[126] Children of players, executives, and reporters were welcome, although O'Malley at one point became concerned with the food the children were wasting and banned the younger ones from the dining room.[127] He installed a pitch-and-putt golf course near Lake Gowanus, but then had to redo it after heavy rains.[128] He finally learned to drive, and although he retained a chauffeur as long as the team remained in New York, he drove himself around Florida and later California.[129]

He brought his own family, and the players, reporters, executives, and their families mixed together in the activities. There were tennis matches featuring Terry O'Malley partnering with publicity man Red Patterson against Bavasi and Thompson and Peter O'Malley joining Jack Lang of the *Long Island Press*, broadcaster Vin Scully, and others in half-court basketball.[130] He began to enjoy the perks of ownership a bit more. A winter trip to Vero and the Caribbean could be explained by a scouting expedition to see Brooklyn players in winter leagues.[131]

Lang said the atmosphere O'Malley created, especially in Vero Beach, made covering the Dodgers the best beat for a New York sportswriter. The Yankees' George Weiss was "on his throne—inaccessible," said Lang. The Giants' Horace Stoneham was "half of the time drunk and the rest you weren't sure." On the Dodgers, "We had an owner who played cards with the boys." That made it "easy to lean in their favor." [132]

In 1952 the Dodgers reversed the debacle of 1951 and made the World Series against the Yankees. O'Malley proved a variable host. There was a lavish spread of chicken, ham, and prime rib, plus four open bars and a carton of Camel cigarettes at each table at a Hotel Bossert reception the eve of the Series.[133] During the games at Ebbets Field, however, reporters complained that the level of hospitality did not measure up to World Series standards, and Bavasi had to rustle up lunch in the press room.[134] In contrast, when the Dodgers clinched the pennant in mid-September, O'Malley had thrown an impromptu dinner for the team, reporters, team executives, and their wives at a Boston hotel.[135]

Another team party tradition was started that December, when team members, press, all employees, and their wives were invited to a Christmas party at Ebbets Field's press room. O'Malley bought the liquor from Roy Campanella's store, hired the musicians, and put out the spread. Al Campanis and his wife showed off their ballroom dancing skills. The party started at 3:30 in the afternoon on December 23 and was still going at 8:30 that evening.[136]

O'Malley was also making the effort to repair relationships among the Dodgers' ownership groups. Mae Smith was included in spring training invitations and other social occasions. But deep wounds still lingered with Dearie and Jim Mulvey.

The Mulveys had emerged from the triumvirates' purchase of the majority shares bruised and unhappy. Given their senior position as shareholders and the unpaid work and effort Jim had put into the team's board over the years, they felt they deserved a greater share in the team, and all they had been offered was a reduction of their holdings from 25 percent to 20 percent.

Marie McKeever was Steven McKeever's much-beloved only child. Dearie, his affectionate nickname for her, had been taken up by everyone she knew. Fred Lieb, a reporter who covered baseball for more than a half century, described her as "tall and good-looking, full of fun and with a flair for excitement. She drove her own automobile at a time when nicely raised girls still were letting their daddies or older brothers tend to the wheel . . . and how she loved to step on the gas!"[137] Dearie was a record-setting horsewoman and even after a marriage and three children would slip away to racetracks near Dodger spring training sites to exercise horses.[138]

Her marriage, in 1924, was to "round-faced" James A. Mulvey.[139] That year Mulvey had moved from an accountant's position at Price, Waterhouse & Company to an association with movie producer Samuel Goldwyn that would last until Mulvey's retirement in 1960. For much of that period he would be Goldwyn's business representative on the East Coast, working with distributors, government bodies, and foreign governments.[140]

By 1932 his father-in-law had him on the Dodgers' board of directors. For periods of time in the 1930s, Mulvey was the de facto general manager, approving trades and disciplining the errant Van Lingle Mungo.[141] His most important role had been executive recruiter, bringing in MacPhail and then Rickey. Given the parlous state of the team, Mulvey deferred his $5,000 annual salary.[142]

At times his real job and his Dodger role overlapped, as when he helped persuade Goldwyn there really was a movie in Lou Gehrig's story and Dearie helped persuade Eleanor Gehrig to sell the rights to the story.[143] *Pride of the Yankees* appeared in 1942. He staged an annual outing to Ebbets Field for friends and colleagues in the movie business.[144]

Mulvey's prominence in the sports pages disappeared with MacPhail's arrival, resurfaced briefly during the Rickey recruitment, and then faded. But he remained on the board and fully in the councils of the team. For Mulvey the first problem surfaced with the heirs of Ed McKeever. Mulvey had always thought of the "McKeever interests" as being one bloc with common goals.[145] When Max Meyer announced he had an option to buy the Ed McKeever heirs' 25 percent in 1944, Mulvey learned that was not the case.

When the Mulveys' own offer to buy the Ed McKeever shares was turned down by McLaughlin, Mulvey moved to block any sale. He brought up the matter of his unpaid director and executive fees, and those of Joseph Gilleaudeau, who represented the Ebbets' heirs on the board. This issue, amounting to at least $100,000 and possibly twice that, was the "additional financial burdens" that had caused Max Meyer to back out of his option on the Ed McKeever shares.[146] When the sales to the Rickey, O'Malley, and

Smith partnership went ahead, the Mulveys were incensed, and the board-room fireworks started immediately.

In the first board meeting after the conclusion of the new partners' purchase, Mulvey restated his claim to unpaid salary, and he began to vote against the majority on routine matters.[147] In public the partners were forced to deny Mulvey-inspired reports that O'Malley was nothing but a stalking horse for McLaughlin, who wanted to participate in ownership.[148] Matters came to a head at the annual shareholders meeting of 1946. After Mulvey asked to be recorded as "not voting" for approval of some standard items, O'Malley asked him for his reasons. Mulvey said he had "no comment." O'Malley responded that as a result, he could not vote for Mulvey's continued service on the board. The other partners agreed.[149]

His dismissal did not stop Mulvey from escalating the conflict. He retained a lawyer to represent his and Dearie's interests with the board.[150] At the 1947 annual meetings he began questioning many details of the officers' reports and brought a professional stenographer to record the proceedings word for word.[151] By the 1948 meeting Mulvey was asserting his right to the full financial records of the corporation and not just a summary. The partners were willing to have their accountant answer any and all questions, but not turn over the books. They wanted a copy of the stenographer's transcript in return.[152] Mulvey also told his story to certain favored columnists, who posed the question of why someone who owned a quarter of the company was not represented on the board.[153] After all, the McKeever-Mulveys had a much longer connection to the team than Rickey, O'Malley, or Smith.

It was a question that resonated with Happy Chandler. By mid-1947 the commissioner was telling Rickey he had talked with Mulvey and wanted to speak with Rickey and the other partners.[154] Mulvey had presented his complaints about back pay, lack of dividends, and a lack of representation and had threatened to sue, something the commissioner wished to avoid.[155] In June Rickey traveled to Versailles, Kentucky, to discuss several matters and presented the partners' point of view. For Mulvey to rejoin the board, Rickey said, he would have to drop all complaints that he had not been able to buy additional stock, quit saying that McLaughlin wanted to buy the team and that O'Malley was nothing but a horse holder, agree to stop opposing routine matters in board meetings, accept a settlement of the back-pay claims, and cease complaining in public. Chandler, according to Rickey, told Rickey to send a letter along these lines and said he would talk to Mulvey.

If Chandler did so, it had less effect than desired. O'Malley, negotiating with Mulvey's lawyer, reached an agreement that paid Mulvey, Joseph Gilleaudeau of the Ebbets estate, and some other officers $140,554.56 in back pay.[156] Dividends were resumed in 1948, but Mulvey and his resentment simmered in the background when O'Malley took over the team.[157]

Harold Parrott, the Dodgers' traveling secretary at the time, maintained that O'Malley was the heavy who "bumped off" Mulvey from the Dodgers' board.[158] The minutes of board meetings and annual meetings and other items in Branch Rickey's papers, however, paint the disputes with Mulvey as a joint concern of all three partners, with O'Malley delegated to doing the legal work.[159] Certainly, the early news stories of the time ascribed Mulvey's ejection from the board as caused by objections to Rickey policies.[160] Tom Meany, the longtime New York writer who always seemed to have a pipeline into Mulvey's office, said, "It was Rickey who put Mulvey in the deep freeze."[161]

With Rickey gone, O'Malley moved to repair the relationship. It was not hard. The Mulveys had remained fervent fans and used their box seats regularly.[162] Social occasions, such as the engagement and marriage of their daughter Ann to Dodger pitcher Ralph Branca, offered opportunities for quiet talk of reconciliation.[163] Jim Mulvey was back on the board of directors by late 1952.[164] The family, as with Mrs. Smith, was included in all organization activities. After Dearie died in 1968, the team began a rookie-of-the-year award in spring training and named it after her.

Matters were not going as smoothly with some members of the Dodgers' front office. Harold Parrott had not been happy to be moved to business manager from traveling secretary after John Collins's resignation. Parrott liked the travel and the financial opportunities the traveling secretary's post gave him. He knew the traveling secretary was awarded a share of the World Series money and figured those Dodgers of the early 1950s would give him several of those shares.

Parrott at first declined, even with the offer of a yearly raise of $2,500. Then O'Malley called Parrott's wife, Josephine, and leaned heavily on her, noting the four young Parrott boys and her husband's life on the road. He won her over with what Parrott later called a "line of palaver" that reminded Parrott of George Bernard Shaw's Hungarian diplomat who "oiled his way around the floor, oozing charm from every pore."[165] Parrott says O'Malley also agreed to match his World Series share ($4,200 for 1952), and with pressure from Josephine, Parrott capitulated.

Parrott's family, and providing for them, occupied a good deal of his thoughts. He and his wife deeply appreciated the way players such as Hodges and Reese would take time on road trips to help the boys with their homework.[166] Parrott had continued to take advantage of outside income sources. It was Parrott's ghosted Leo Durocher column that helped get Durocher suspended for the 1947 season. There was also an autobiography he ghosted for Durocher, and he later wrote Jackie Robinson's national radio program. At times, even while working for the Dodgers, he would crank out articles that appeared under the bylines of columnists such as J. G. Taylor Spink of the *Sporting News* and Jimmy Powers of the *New York Daily News*.[167] All these activities were generating about $10,000 a year by the early 1950s, and much of it was lost in the ticket manager's job.[168]

Parrott became even more alienated when O'Malley did not meet Parrott's interpretation of the World Series bonus pledge. After the 1952 Series O'Malley dutifully paid Parrott a bonus equal to the World Series share he would have gotten as traveling secretary. But after the 1953 Series O'Malley refused, and refused nastily, according to Parrott. "How long did you think a giveaway like that was going to continue?" Parrott quotes O'Malley as saying.[169] Parrott interpreted O'Malley's actions as reneging on an agreement, but Parrott's rendering of O'Malley's reasoning leaves open the possibility that O'Malley considered the offer to be only a one-year deal.

Others were unhappy with their salaries as well. Irving Rudd, hired to pump the gate in Miami during spring training and then moved to promotions in Brooklyn, shared a love of promotional ideas with O'Malley, and they often brainstormed together.[170] But, Rudd said, he also worried about O'Malley's attitude toward him. After O'Malley sent him a congratulatory note about plumping attendance, Rudd reminded him of a memo requesting a raise. "Irving . . . . I *don't* like to be pushed," Rudd recounted O'Malley as saying.[171] Rudd went back to boxing promotion soon afterward.

Even Buzzie Bavasi could feel short-changed. One time in Brooklyn, Bavasi said, O'Malley promised to transfer one of the plots that the Dodgers owned around Ebbets Field to Bavasi. O'Malley called it "something that will stick to your ribs," Bavasi said. When O'Malley died, though, nothing came to Bavasi. When he asked Peter about it, Peter said his father had never said anything to him about it.[172]

Red Barber had a complicated relationship with O'Malley. He was very clearly a Rickey man, but his wide popularity with Dodger fans and his undoubted skills kept him aboard. The friction started with small things.

Barber described Dodger outfielder Carl Furillo as slow, which he saw as accurate reporting to give fans a clear picture. O'Malley, with a joking edge, suggested Barber was trying to denigrate the players. Barber felt pressure to be positive.[173] Another time Barber returned from a trip wearing a Spanish-style beret, and O'Malley tried to get him to discard it. Barber got his back up and kept the hat on. "O'Malley and I never had an argument. We never had anything open. It was just a combination of small things that kept growing and growing," Barber said.[174] Barber reached his own conclusion. "O'Malley is a devious man, about the most devious man I ever met."[175]

The broadcaster could also be positive, noting the multiple chances O'Malley gave Connie Desmond, Barber's broadcasting partner, who had a drinking problem. Lylah Barber, Red's wife, was even more positive, especially about O'Malley's relationship with Kay. "I found much to admire and respect and, yes, like in Walter O'Malley," she wrote, using words such as "gentle, soft-spoken, and attentive" and "pleasant, always gracious and polite."[176]

Barber's relationship with the team ended after the 1953 season. In 1952 Gillette, the razor-blade company sponsoring the telecast, had paid Barber a flat fee for doing the first national broadcast of the World Series. Barber was incensed that the company had not told him what he would be paid, but simply presented a check afterward. For 1953, he vowed, things would be different. They were. Gillette announced that Barber and Mel Allen of the Yankees would be broadcasting the Series without asking Barber, much less telling him his fee. Barber referred them to his agent and then rejected the offer, the same he had been paid for 1952. He felt obliged to tell O'Malley that his lead broadcaster would not be working the Series. O'Malley, according to Barber, snapped, "That's your problem." At that point Barber hung up the phone and decided to resign.[177]

O'Malley's sense of humor could often be a problem. Barber described it as "heavily arch."[178] And it often came out worst when O'Malley was talking about money. Frank Graham, the Dodgers' publicity director in the early 1950s, described him as a "portly, jowly, florid man, with a raspy voice, and he circulated with a kind of bonhomie that no one ever confused with charm. Socially, he had a tin ear. Complimented sincerely by Pee Wee Reese after an agreeable but hardly sumptuous victory celebration, he could only reply, 'Well, it *should* have been nice. It cost me an arm and a leg!'"[179] It could also be perceived as downright mean. One night at Ebbets Field, a ricocheting foul ball hit Roger Kahn's wife, Joan, in the nose while she was sitting in the photographers' booth. The nose was broken. O'Malley sent a note to Kahn in the press box: "Don't bother to sue. Courts have held we don't have to protect that location. If you sue me, you will lose."[180]

In later years O'Malley decided to decorate new quarters at Dodgertown with reproductions of Dodger World Series programs. For manager Walter Alston's room he chose a program the team had created for the 1962 World Series, which the Dodgers missed after a late-season collapse some attributed to Alston's decisions.[181] The owner's sense of humor was a combination that "disconcerts friends with a Groucho Marxist air of insincerity," noted *Los Angeles Times* columnist Jim Murray. O'Malley was "half-oaf, half-elf," Murray wrote.[182]

He loved boys' club humor, such as producing a pad of gin-rummy scoring sheets for use at Vero Beach during spring training. Every score sheet included a preprinted, perforated check made out to O'Malley.[183] Or it would be taking Jocko Conlan on the Dodgers' 1956 trip to Japan, waiting until they were on the twenty-three-hundred-mile stretch from Honolulu to Wake Island, and then telling the umpire that Japanese custom prevented him from paying Conlan as much as the players were making on the trip. When Conlan started sputtering, and demanding to be put off the plane at Wake, O'Malley produced the check made out to Conlan and equal to the players' payments.[184]

As with many eastern urbanites of his generation, there was also a significant ethnic component to his humor. He was a bit of a stage Irishman, rarely mentioning his half-German ancestry. He and Bavasi (half-French, half-Italian) would joke about whose heritage was better. O'Malley and his father-in-law (full Swedish) would do the same. As O'Malley told the tale: "The Judge would wait until a later hour at the [St. Patrick's Day] party and then contend St. Patrick was a Swede. He said that's where the Irish got their good looks, from the Swedes. The fight usually broke out right after that." The St. Patrick's Day party menu, as with "Bacon Pitler," also usually featured ethnic references, with Al Campanis (Greek) becoming McCampanis and Coach Danny Ozark (Polish, born Orzechowski) becoming O'Zark.

Partially, the reaction to O'Malley's pointed humor was a reflection of the confidence of the recipient. "He's a pretty good needler," one front-office executive acknowledged without umbrage.[185] People in marketing and promotions seemed to take the remarks more to heart than other employees. "It doesn't do harm to needle with sound criticism," O'Malley philosophized.[186] Roger Kahn, who talked with O'Malley regularly over the years, thought he used humor to confuse issues.[187]

People such as Bavasi and Alston let the needles slide off their backs. And Graham noted that he felt guilty about writing the description above because O'Malley had never been anything but nice to him.[188] There was also a certain camaraderie in the office. O'Malley, for all his needles, did not separate himself from the staff. He was willing, for example, to enter a weight-loss competition with statistician Allan Roth. After two weeks of what he described as "spinach and eggs, spinach and eggs," he had lost 14 pounds to get down to 206. He won. Roth lost only 8 pounds.[189]

John Burton was a college student whose father audited the Dodgers for Arthur Young & Company. That led to a job helping Allan Roth, a job he kept for the first half of the 1950s. He felt the office staff had liked Rickey better than O'Malley. "He was respected. He was disliked," Burton said. "He never much communicated warmth."[190]

O'Malley was approaching fifty. His marriage was solid. Terry was finishing college. Peter was in high school and aiming to follow his father to Penn. Walter's weight was up, as he enjoyed restaurants such as Gage and Tollner, a downtown Brooklyn steak-and-chop house, and Lundy's, a seafood institution in Sheepshead Bay, Brooklyn. When he got up each morning, he lit a cigarette and then dropped to his knees to say his prayers. After prayers he made breakfast for Kay and the children. An only child, he could not understand why siblings fight, and he would deliver a lecture in which the world escalated from brother-sister squabbling to world wars, a lecture that left Terry and Peter feeling guilty. He went to Peter's athletic contests and joined Kay in chaperoning Terry's dances.[191]

He still dressed conservatively. "He didn't buy suits from the tailor Leo Durocher used," said Jack Lang, a sports reporter for the *Long Island Press* and, later, the *Daily News*. "His clothes weren't expensive or flashy, but solid, very very banker type, except every once in a while he'd wear a gag tie somebody from Room 40 had given him."[192] The energy that was not devoted to the Dodgers went into his hobbies.

In Amityville he had built a hothouse and, with Kay, developed a serious interest in growing orchids, another side of the landscaping focus he would show in Vero Beach. He rose at six each morning and puttered in the greenhouse and visited again each evening when he got home. He said their orchids had won first prize at a Brooklyn flower show.[193]

He continued his interest in fishing, both at Lake Gowanus and in the oceans. On a trip to Acapulco, he was photographed with a 125-pound sail-fish. Dodger board member Judge Henry Ughetta claimed that he had actually caught the fish, and the rest of the Dodger party delighted in spreading contradictory stories about who had caught what.[194] O'Malley was also elected a member of the "Society for the Protection and Preservation of Little Fishes," protection to be provided by catching the big fishes before they ate the little ones.[195] It was the kind of man-to-man humor O'Malley enjoyed.

O'Malley very much lived in a man's world. In March 1958, preparing for a cover story on the Dodger owner that *Time* would run the next month, a reporter visited O'Malley's Brooklyn office. He asked O'Malley who his closest friends were. He got the names of bankers, board chairmen, factory owners, and company presidents. After fifteen years in the game, O'Malley had to be pressed for names from the baseball world and could come up with only a few. Asked about women he looked puzzled and then mentioned his wife and, after some thought, Mae Smith, his partner in Dodger ownership.

The Dodgers won the pennant again in 1953, easily outdistancing the newly relocated Milwaukee Braves. But in six games they once again lost the World Series to the New York Yankees. O'Malley was publicly gracious.[196]

In private rumors had surfaced after each season that O'Malley was not all that happy with his manager.[197] Dressen, however, never lacked confidence and was reportedly being heavily nagged by his wife, who saw Leo Durocher, still managing the Giants, with a long-term contract. A week after the World Series, Dressen requested a three-year contract, despite earlier public statements from O'Malley that he was not giving more than one year.[198]

O'Malley blandly wished Dressen good luck finding a three-year contract, which he quickly did with the Minor League Oakland Oaks.[199] Parrott, always critical, described Dressen as trying to provide for a sickly wife and O'Malley as callously rejecting him.[200] Roger Kahn suggested O'Malley could not stand a manager who had a higher profile than the owner.[201] Graham, then the Dodgers' publicity director, noted that O'Malley, at the press conference and with Dressen present, offered a one-year contract should Dressen reconsider. However, when Dressen called back to take the offer, O'Malley could not be found. After Dressen signed for his new job, O'Malley archly said, "I'm sure Mrs. Dressen will be very happy in Oakland."[202]

Significantly, Bavasi raised no objections and passed over Dressen's departure in his autobiography.[203] That is because he had another candidate. The public discussion was all about Pee Wee Reese, but Bavasi had asked the Dodgers' captain and he had declined.[204] Instead, Bavasi was pushing Walter Alston, his manager at Nashua in 1946 and leader of the Dodgers' top farm club in Montreal for the last four seasons. O'Malley, Bavasi acknowledged, was not too sure about Alston, but, as in most cases, he relied on Bavasi's judgment in baseball matters.[205] He also may have been influenced by a phone call he had received the previous spring from Branch Rickey, who had swallowed his pride to ask for permission to talk to Alston about the Pirates' managing job.[206] It was denied.

In the spring of 1953, baseball made its first move to reflect the changing demographics of the country. Given baseball's conservative nature, it was not much of a move. The Boston Braves moved to Milwaukee, a shift that was more about Boston's inability to support two teams than an acknowledgment of the population growth of the West and South.

As a member of the executive council, O'Malley was in the middle of the discussions. At first, he said, he opposed the move because the Braves had sought approval only well into spring training of 1953. For a National League team to move, the team had to secure a unanimous vote of the league's owners, and O'Malley's objections had to be overcome. Boston owner Lou Perini was able to do that, O'Malley said, and O'Malley even made the motion approving the move.[207] Some suggested O'Malley was thinking ahead. Irving Rudd recalled overhearing a phone conversation in which O'Malley stroked Perini and later concluded the Dodger owner was laying the groundwork for his own move, but that was clearly a conclusion reached years later.[208]

The 1954 season was a down year for the Dodgers, the first time since 1948 the season had not featured a championship or a race down to the wire. The season did produce two player moves that would resonate down through the years.

One was a handshake with Irving Koufax, stepfather of a young left-hander named Sandy whom the Dodgers wanted to sign. The young Koufax was such a talent that the Dodgers and other clubs were willing to make him a "bonus" player under contemporary rules. That meant they would have to keep him on their Major League roster for two years, even though he probably did not yet have the skills to be a Major Leaguer. That summer the Dodgers did not have the roster space to accommodate him, so their offer was basically a promise to sign him later that year. Sandy was willing to take the offer, but Irving, a lawyer, noted that accepting the Dodgers' offer would bind Koufax morally to follow through even if higher offers surfaced. The Dodgers, noted Irving, might not produce on their promise of a roster spot. Irving requested a meeting with Walter O'Malley. The lawyers agreed on Irving's analysis of the offer. Irving offered to agree to the verbal deal based solely on Walter O'Malley's handshake. O'Malley shook, and in December the Dodgers cleared the roster space and announced Sandy's signing.[209]

The other player was another Hall of Famer, Roberto Clemente, and, again, roster limits played a role. Clemente signed in February 1954 for $15,000.[210] Because that was over $4,000, the bonus rule mandated the Dodgers put him on their roster or risk having him drafted by another team the next winter. Bavasi felt the Dodger roster was full and decided to take the risk.[211] It did not work. That December Rickey and the Pirates drafted Clemente.[212]

In more than three decades of talent evaluation, Buzzie Bavasi made few mistakes. Clemente was clearly one of them, and an unnecessarily defensive Bavasi told many stories over the years about how it happened, some involving Walter O'Malley.

In the earliest rendering Bavasi gave the loss the "irrelevant" label by saying the Dodgers had signed the Puerto Rican outfielder only to keep him away from the Giants.[213] A few years later he was resigned. "That was probably my biggest mistake," he told Charles Maher of the Los Angeles Times. "We can blame the rules for part of it, but part of it was our judgment."[214]

Later still, his version began to have scapegoats. The first was O'Malley. Bavasi said he was fully aware of Clemente's talent and knew Branch Rickey and the Pirates were convinced of it, too. Bavasi said he went to Rickey, his old mentor, and called on his friendship. Rickey agreed not to take Clemente. But, Bavasi said, Rickey and O'Malley got into a shouting match over some unrelated issue at an owners meeting. O'Malley cursed Rickey and Rickey changed his mind.[215]

In later renderings a racial issue was added. Bavasi told author Thomas Oliphant both the O'Malley cursing tale and that O'Malley ordered him to limit the number of blacks on the team because he was fearful of fan and team reaction.[216] Clemente was a very dark-skinned Latino, and in Bavasi's final version it was now O'Malley's partners who had vetoed the idea of more blacks, an angle he also told Oliphant. He cited the partners as Jim Mulvey and John Smith.[217] Mulvey was back on the board of directors in 1954, but O'Malley had full control. Bavasi evidently forgot Smith had been dead nearly four years by the time the Dodgers even signed Clemente.

Sometimes O'Malley's needling could get him in trouble. In 1954 an injury to Roy Campanella's left hand had required surgery, and the All-Star catcher had a miserable season. That fall the hand was still not improving, and Campanella had a second operation by Dr. Samuel Shenkman that October.[218] That operation proved to be a success, and Campanella won the National League's Most Valuable Player (MVP) award again in 1955.

Meanwhile, Dr. Shenkman presented a bill for $9,500, which O'Malley thought was too high. Unable to resist, he borrowed a quip from Fresco Thompson: "It appears that Dr. Shenkman thought he was operating on Roy's bankroll, not his hand."[219] Shenkman sued Campanella for his bill and O'Malley $500,000 for slander. The bill was settled for $5,000.[220] O'Malley wound up paying $15,000 in the slander settlement.[221]

As the 1955 season progressed, O'Malley moved deeper into fan mode. The team, with Campanella healthy, had exploded out of the box, winning ten straight to start the season and twenty-two of their first twenty-four. They clinched the National League pennant in Milwaukee on September 8, the earliest date ever.

O'Malley was in the County Stadium clubhouse, shaking hands, slapping backs, and hoping (not vowing, as he had in previous years) that the Dodgers could beat the Yankees in the World Series.[222] He threw the team and the traveling group a party at the expensive Mader's Restaurant and kept the celebration going on the bus the team took to Chicago for its next series.[223] There was another party in New York when the team got home from the road trip. "Everybody danced except The O'Malley, who doesn't," wrote the *New York Times*'s Roscoe McGowen, "but Mrs. O'M. displayed skill and grace on the floor with other partners."[224]

The World Series was made for manic-depressives. The Yankees took the first two games in the Bronx. The Dodgers rebounded to sweep three at Ebbets Field. Whitey Ford beat the Dodgers again at the stadium in Game Six. Then, in Game Seven, behind the pitching of Johnny Podres, the catch of Sandy Amorós, and Gil Hodges's two runs batted in (RBIs), it finally happened. The Dodgers had won their first and only World Series in Brooklyn. "Who's a Bum!" screamed the *Daily News* headline.

O'Malley suffered through the game's bad moments and exulted at the good. The party moved from a beer- and champagne-soaked clubhouse at Yankee Stadium to the Hotel Bossert.[225] O'Malley had planned for six hundred people at the hotel. Twice that number showed up.[226] "There were no speeches. There probably was no need for the stimulating beverages that flowed so freely, because no group of people ever was so hilariously happy about a baseball club's success," McGowen wrote. "The O'Malley's smile was beaming for hours."[227]

His fifty-second birthday arrived the following Sunday, and he celebrated at home with "World Series cake" and French wine.[228] More private celebrating was coming. Although he would not say anything about it publicly, he had paid off Branch Rickey that fall. He had been reducing the original $750,000 note steadily, paying nearly $300,000 in 1953 alone. That was mostly done with a loan from the Brooklyn Trust Company, as O'Malley later acknowledged financial problems earlier in the year. He had been tempted by an offer from the Philadelphia Phillies of $650,000 for any two of Campanella, Duke Snider, or Gil Hodges.[229] In addition, he had gone to the commissioner to complain that Bill Veeck had not paid him the $90,000 sale price for shortstop Billy Hunter.[230] Now, with the World Series income, he was in a position to pay the rest, exchanging the documents and checks on December 14.[231]

It was a very good winter for Walter O'Malley as 1955 became 1956. The *Sporting News* named him Major League Executive of the Year, with Alston as the Manager of the Year and Duke Snider as the Player of the Year, a sweep of top honors for the Dodgers. "No executive ever attained a position of leadership in a game in so short a time as has O'Malley. He is often called the 'bell cow' of the league. When a progressive idea is suggested, it often comes from Walter," the paper said.[232]

The marketing innovations continued. O'Malley worked with Brooklyn's largest department store, Abraham & Straus, to stage a series of Saturday clinics aimed at teaching women about the game—so they could keep up with husbands and boyfriends.[233] He ordered that the Dodgers' uniform numbers be repeated, in red, on the front of uniforms so that someone who could not see the player's back could still get the right information off the scorecard.[234] On Father's Day in 1952 O'Malley instituted Autograph Day and installed a booth near the players' dressing room. The players moved into the booth in shifts of three, and it was reported at least half the youngsters in attendance got a signature during the hour.[235] There were traditional Father-Son Days, but Mother-Daughter Days were coming, too.[236]

Conscious that his Brooklyn constituency was moving to the suburbs, O'Malley opened a commuter ticket office. The office was open during the morning and afternoon hours that commuters passed through the Flatbush Avenue terminal of the Long Island Rail Road.[237] O'Malley also bought into an idea that came from Red Patterson and Parrott. The Dodgers would print tickets much earlier than normal and sell them during the Christmas and Hanukkah season. The tickets would come in booklets of ten or twenty-five tickets, with free tickets to opening day in both denominations and the right to purchase World Series tickets with the twenty-five-ticket booklet.[238]

In one ambitious effort O'Malley proposed a National Baseball Day, in which Major League rosters would be reshuffled into twenty teams that would then play existing Minor League teams in their home parks. Proceeds (O'Malley estimated $500,000) would go to the Minor League teams. The Commissioner's Office farmed out the idea to the public relations firm of Stephen Fitzgerald and Company, which endorsed the idea but suggested a reduction to twelve games because of the limited number of Minor League parks capable of holding a crowd large enough to justify the expense and disruption.[239]

O'Malley, noted *Newsweek* in an article on the changing business of baseball, was "probably the most promotion-minded man in the game."[240] Others were not as positive. John Burton, Allan Roth's aide during Burton's college years, went on to become the chief accountant at the Securities and Exchange Commission and the dean of the business school at Columbia University.[241] Looking back, Burton said, O'Malley "was not a managerial genius in my opinion." He showed no interest in the mechanics of ticketing or the possibilities of computers. When Burton suggested a system of pricing differentiated by opponent, time of day, day of week, and other variables, O'Malley brushed it off.[242] Such systems would not catch on in Major League Baseball for a half century.

Not all the innovations were in marketing. The Dodgers added an official team physician.[243] Heating panels were added to the dugouts for cold nights in the spring.[244] O'Malley ordered the players to take the new Salk polio vaccine.[245]

The 1956 World Series had its own thrills, but nothing to match the Dodgers' victory of 1955. O'Malley shared his box with President Dwight Eisenhower and asked Don Larsen for an autograph after the Yankee pitcher threw a perfect game against the Dodgers in Game Five.[246] The Dodgers' owner slipped and fell on steps at the Hotel Bossert after the Series ended and spent the night in the hospital.[247] World Series income was the frosting on a good year, and the Dodgers finished with net income of $487,462.[248]

Soon after the Series ended, O'Malley set out on a trip that would begin his commitment to international baseball. The Dodgers played nineteen games in Japan, winning fourteen and tying one. They played before 591,000 people, including 60,000 for a game in Osaka.[249] The trip was sponsored by the *Yomiuri Shimbun*, Japan's largest daily newspaper.

In 1952 the Dodgers and Cleveland Indians announced a tour to be promoted by Abe Saperstein. O'Malley was enthusiastic, but so many Indians players did not want to go that the tour fell apart.[250] The New York Giants had toured Japan after the 1953 season and the New York Yankees after 1955, but both delegations had been led by their teams' managers.[251] O'Malley was the first owner to accompany his team, and he made contact with Japanese officials that laid a foundation for future trips and exchanges.[252] After the games in Japan O'Malley and his family completed a round-the-world journey, accompanied by Vin Scully, then dating Terry O'Malley, and Ann and Ralph Branca. The group arrived home on the *Queen Mary* in early December.[253]

O'Malley's preferred mode of travel was airplanes. He had been exposed to plane ownership during the Rickey years and became more and more involved. Driving past the Vero Beach airport one day, he told the team pilot, Harry R. "Bump" Holman, "I don't need these things, but I love to drive by and say, 'they're mine.'"[254]

In the Rickey era the Dodgers' plane was a small craft useful for junketing top executives. But in 1950 Bud Holman, Bump's father, won a DC-3 in a crap game with Eddie Rickenbacker, while both were on the board of directors of Eastern Airlines. Holman, soon to be on the Dodgers' board, donated the plane to the team. The plane was used for spring training trips, but its twenty-seat capacity made it impractical for moving the Dodgers. After watching it sit for much of the year, O'Malley hit on the idea of using it to transport the Dodgers' Minor League clubs, with their smaller rosters, and from 1954 to 1956 Bump Holman flew St. Paul and later Fort Worth on their road trips.[255] The Dodgers flew commercial or rode trains.

In late 1956 O'Malley moved to find a bigger aircraft. Bud Holman knew Eastern Airlines was about to buy twenty Convair 440s, a two-engine plane with forty-four seats. He suggested they make the order twenty-one, with the Dodgers taking the extra plane. Bump Holman said the plane cost $690,000. The purchase caused reporters to ask if this indicated the club might move to the West Coast. O'Malley acknowledged any team moving to the West Coast would have to fly and, he felt, would need to own its own plane. But, he said, the Dodgers' future was in Brooklyn.[256] Bump Holman said the Convair 440 did not have the range for nonstop transcontinental flights, and after the Dodgers had moved they used it only for flights around the East, using commercial flights for the longer legs.[257]

Sometime in 1957, Walter O'Malley became the unchallengeable majority owner of the Dodgers. Nothing was said publicly at the time. The only acknowledgment came in 1961, when Mae Smith, widow of John, died. A paragraph in the press-box notes for April 25 said she had "sold her stock in the company when the Dodgers moved from Brooklyn to Los Angeles."[258] Bavasi said Mrs. Smith's shares cost O'Malley $360,000, although this seems ridiculously low in light of the $1 million Rickey received.[259] Although Mrs. Smith had allowed O'Malley to exercise full control, the partnership agreement under which they had pooled their stock and which allowed O'Malley to control the team, had expired in September 1955. Theoretically, if Mrs. Smith had sold after the partnership agreement expired, that buyer could have teamed with the Mulveys and re-created the fifty-fifty split management that had plagued the Dodgers from the mid-1920s into the 1940s. Instead, O'Malley worked with the Mulveys, and they took a portion of the Smith holdings. O'Malley now owned two-thirds of the stock and the Mulveys the rest.[260]

It is possible O'Malley had to pay Mrs. Smith even more than he had paid Rickey. In 1954 he received an offer of $5 million or $6 million from Dorothy Killiam for his and Smith's shares.[261] Even the lower number would have valued Smith's shares at just under $1.7 million. O'Malley and Smith said no, and Killiam went on to become one of the original partners of the New York Mets.

7

A New Stadium—Economics

Walter O'Malley's dedication to finding a new home for his baseball team was growing and evolving. And, as usual with O'Malley, economics trumped all. There was the push of changes in New York—sagging attendance, his crumbling ballpark, and the changing demographics and faltering economy of Brooklyn. There was the heightened competition within the league. And, eventually, there was the pull of the promise of Los Angeles and pay television.

The dominant issue was attendance. Despite the legend of legions of vocal, supportive, and, above all, devoted Brooklyn fans, the evidence is that not enough of them were buying tickets to Ebbets Field at the rate the legend would have predicted. Dodger attendance had drifted down steadily since the record 1947 season, when the team drew 1.8 million.

TABLE 1. Dodger attendance in the Walter O'Malley years

Year	Dodger Attendance
1943	661,739
1944	605,905
1945	1,059,220
1946	1,796,824,[a] breaking 1929 Cubs
1947	1,807,526,[a] breaking 1946 Dodgers
1948	1,398,967
1949	1,633,747
1950	1,185,896
1951	1,282,628
1952	1,088,704
1953	1,163,419

1954	1,020,531
1955	1,033,589
1956	1,213,562
1957	1,028,258
1958	1,845,556,[b] breaking 1947 Dodgers
1959	2,071,045,[b] breaking 1958 Dodgers
1960	2,253,887,[a] breaking 1957 Braves
1961	1,804,250
1962	2,755,184,[c] breaking 1948 Indians
1963	2,538,602
1964	2,228,751
1965	2,553,577
1966	2,617,029
1967	1,664,362
1968	1,581,093
1969	1,784,527
1970	1,697,142
1971	2,064,594
1972	1,860,858
1973	2,136,192
1974	2,632,474
1975	2,539,349
1976	2,386,301
1977	2,955,087,[c] breaking 1962 Dodgers
1978	3,347,845,[c] breaking 1977 Dodgers
1979	2,860,954

[a] New National League record.

[b] New franchise record.

[c] New Major League record.

Source: baseball-reference.com

In 1951 O'Malley's early post-Rickey marketing measures pushed ticket sales back to nearly 1.3 million, but the downward drift resumed, despite pennant wins in 1952 and 1953. The *Sporting News* editorialized with the question, "Has Dodger fan lost his zip?"[1] Tommy Holmes, the *New York Herald-Tribune*'s lead Dodger reporter, cast a jaundiced eye at the already building legend in the early 1950s. "Just as the speech of the Brooklyn fans has been exaggerated, so the patriotic zeal of the community toward its ball club has been distorted by fanciful legend. Dodger defeat is something less than a civic calamity, and Dodger victory is not regarded as the superlative cultural achievement. . . . The communities that go to make up this immense sprawling borough of New York City include the homes of almost three million people. It may be hard to believe, but many of these do not give a hoot about the Dodgers . . . or baseball."[2] The 1955 world championship team drew barely 1 million, and the traditional postchampionship attendance rebound nudged it to slightly more than 1.2 million in 1956.[3] By that point, the Dodgers had not led the league in attendance for five years. "We have given the fans the finest baseball possible in the last nine years—four pennants and never worse than third—and still our attendance declines," O'Malley said after 1954. "I don't know what the solution is. It's just up to us to put on the best possible show."[4]

To be sure, attendance was falling across baseball. A national survey funded by Commissioner Ford Frick found fans around the country echoed the Brooklyn concerns, citing parking and the availability of television as the main reasons for not attending.[5] Major League attendance dropped from 16.9 million in 1947 to 13.2 million in 1956, a decline of 22 percent. Dodgers attendance fell 33 percent over the same period. The team's share of National League attendance, a mark of its ability to keep up with the competition, dropped from more than 20 percent in 1946 to 14 percent in 1956. The team was selling tickets in the biggest market in the country, but it could barely outpace the 12.5 percent share of a middling team.

FIGURE 1. Declining attendance as a percentage of league totals

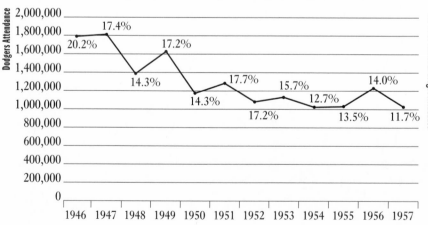

Source: baseball-reference.com

Out-of-town fans seemed to be more appreciative, as the Dodgers led the league in road attendance every year of the decade after World War II.[6] It was not just baseball's attendance that was falling. Movie patronage declined and other forms of entertainment suffered as television came to dominate the living room.

Even more troubling to both the myth of the Brooklyn fan and the team's profit picture was that some big games were not selling out. You could have walked up and bought a ticket for the first game of the Dodgers-Giants playoff in 1951, the single game played at Ebbets Field.[7] The sixth and seventh games of the 1952 World Series at Ebbets Field were not sellouts. In 1956, as the Dodgers battled the Braves down to the wire, only 7,847 turned out for a game against the Phillies. "The turnout of the Flatbush Faithful was not in keeping with the occasion," *New York Times* columnist Arthur Daley wrote with capitalized sarcasm the next day.[8] Sportswriter Harold Rosenthal noted that season ticket holders had trouble giving away their tickets in the mid-1950s.[9]

And on the occasions when the fans would turn out, Ebbets Field's official 31,902 capacity looked small. The stadium's capacity was only slightly under average by National League standards of the mid-1950s, but it seemed smaller when compared to the Giants' Polo Grounds at 54,000 and Yankee Stadium at 70,000 for the potential of the largest market in the country. As far back as Larry MacPhail in 1941 and Branch Rickey in 1947, Dodger executives had discussed the possibility of playing all their World Series games at Yankee Stadium to take advantage of the extra capacity.[10] With the frequency with which the Dodgers were making the World Series in that era, Walter O'Malley could see money circling the drain.

There were also things that were driving fans away. As with childhoods, old relationships, and past houses, we tend to remember the good. There is enormous nostalgia for Ebbets Field, for its intimacy, for the relationships among the fans, and, most of all, for the charismatic team that played there. The defects were a small price to pay for the dedicated fan, but for the less committed Ebbets Field had problems. As Dodger fan and author Wilfrid Sheed notes of O'Malley's immediate postwar efforts at refurbishing Ebbets Field, "The overall effect was simply to underline how hopeless it was and how incorrigibly old-shoe, unstreamlined and honest our little playground was."[11] Even the most romantic of fan memoirs would note that the bathrooms "stank" or that the urinals were "fetid troughs."[12] Red Barber called it a "dirty, stinking old ball park" with rusting girders.[13] The stands were dotted with posts that restricted views.

And then there was the changing neighborhood. The *New York Herald-Tribune*'s Harold Rosenthal said O'Malley showed him letters from season ticket holders canceling their purchases because they were afraid to go to Ebbets Field at night.[14] O'Malley said there were mounting complaints about vandalism to automobiles and that his wife and mother-in-law would not come to night games unescorted. Women, he noted, made up 30 percent of the Dodgers' audience.[15] Others noted tensions between black and white fans in the stands, mirroring what was happening in Brooklyn neighborhoods.[16]

Flatbush was directly in the path of African American expansion in Brooklyn and was becoming more Puerto Rican.[17] O'Malley noticed, and people have parsed that different ways. Dick Young said O'Malley told him he wanted to leave Ebbets Field "because the area is getting full of blacks and spics."[18] Bavasi told a story of O'Malley calling him to a window to note Puerto Ricans lined up for their checks at a welfare office across the street. O'Malley's concern, says Bavasi, was not their color, but their poverty.[19] People on welfare did not make likely customers. Between 1950 and 1957 Brooklyn lost 235,000 Caucasians and added 100,000 nonwhites.[20] In fact, O'Malley's favored site for a new park, at Flatbush and Atlantic Avenues less than a mile and a half from his current site, was in a neighborhood racially similar to the Ebbets Field area.

There were signs of the economic decline of Brooklyn. The Brooklyn Navy Yard, the borough's largest employer, had started the shrinking that would end with its closure in 1966. George McLaughlin, O'Malley's mentor, sold the Brooklyn Trust Company, the borough's largest bank, to the Manhattan Trust Company in 1950. The *Brooklyn Eagle*, the borough's only remaining daily paper and a dedicated supporter of O'Malley both in print and behind the scenes, closed in January 1955. "The *Eagle* thrived during Brooklyn's century of growth and died when the community it served was likewise in an unexpected and almost traumatic period of decline," wrote the paper's biographer.[21] Of the four major tony department stores that advertised in the *Eagle*, three had closed.[22] Manufacturing was fleeing. In 1947 13.1 percent of the factory employees in the Greater New York area worked in Brooklyn. In the next five years the borough received only 5.7 percent of new factories. Only one of them cost $500,000 or more.[23]

There was also new competition arising in the Midwest. The Boston Braves, one of the league's perennial weaklings, moved to Milwaukee in 1953, just as young stars such as Eddie Mathews and Henry Aaron were joining the team. Attendance leaped from 281,000 to 1.8 million, passed 2 million in 1954, and stayed there for the rest of the Dodgers' stay in Brooklyn. Suddenly, the Dodgers were neither the most popular nor the most profitable team in the league. To O'Malley that was another reason for a new park. With the Braves' extra revenue, they would be able to spend more on scouting and developing young players, absorb more farm-club losses, hire better off-field personnel, and force the Dodgers to compete from a disadvantageous position.[24] Although the Braves did roughly double the Dodgers' attendance, the profit picture was not so absolute. For the years 1952 through 1957, where figures are available, the Dodgers' profits barely surpassed the Braves'. And if the Braves' last year in Boston is removed, they actually were more profitable, although not by a huge margin.

TABLE 2. Dodgers versus Braves

Year	Dodgers Attendance	NL Rank	% of NL Attendance	Dodgers Profits	NL Rank
1951	1,282,628	1	17.7	n/a	
1952	1,088,704	1	17.2	$446,102	1
1953	1,163,419	2	15.7	$290,006	2
1954	1,020,531	4	12.7	$209,979	4
1955	1,033,589	2	13.5	$427,195	2
1956	1,213,562	2	14.0	$487,462	1
1957	1,028,258	5	11.7	n/a	
Year	**Braves Attendance**	**NL Rank**	**% of NL Attendance**	**Braves Profits**	**NL Rank**
1951	487,475	8	6.7	n/a	
1952	281,278	8	4.4	-$459,099	7
1953	1,826,397	1	24.6	$637,798	1
1954	2,131,388	1	26.6	$457,110	1
1955	2,005,836	1	26.1	$807,396	1
1956	2,046,331	1	23.7	$414,398	2
1957	2,215,404	1	25.1	n/a	

Note: Profits, when available, are from the Celler Hearings of 1951 and 1957.
The Braves moved from Boston to Milwaukee for the 1953 season.
Source: baseball-reference.com; Celler hearings.

There are those who point to Fenway Park in Boston and Wrigley Field in Chicago and argue that Ebbets Field could have been refurbished and served for decades more.[25] But neither Chicago's North Side nor Boston's Fens suffered the neighborhood decline Flatbush did. Fenway had been completely rebuilt in 1934 and refurbished again in 1940, to deal with structural issues and add seating.[26] Both Tom Yawkey in Boston and Phil Wrigley in Chicago had the financial wherewithal to keep maintaining their parks. By contrast the Dodgers' financial troubles in the Depression years had shortcircuited maintenance. In 1942, when the team's stadium manager reported to Rickey on the state of the structure, he said nothing but the botched expansion of the stands in 1930 had been done to upgrade the facility.[27] After twenty-five years of neglect, the maintenance and improvements the board of directors had started in the postwar years were barely keeping up.

There was also the parking problem at Ebbets. O'Malley maintained there were only seven hundred parking spaces available near the ballpark. He never mentioned it, but another drawback to a refurbished Ebbets Field was that there were no major arterial highways existing or planned near Ebbets Field, another discouragement to suburban drivers.

Brooklyn's residents were already voting with their feet and speeding the borough's decline in the process. Pete Hamill, the native Brooklyn writer who hated O'Malley, recalled the early 1950s mantra "'We gotta get outta Brooklyn.' You heard it over and over in those days. . . . [I]t was out 'to the island,' or to California or Rockland County. The idea was to get out."[28] William Levitt began building his archetypal Nassau County, Long Island, suburb in 1947. Other developers followed, and so did Brooklyn residents. With them they took the job skills that had made Brooklyn a manufacturing center. Many employers followed their workforce.[29] In the decade of the 1950s Nassau County's population grew 93 percent to 1.3 million, and Walter O'Malley was creating the community-day promotions to acknowledge where his customers lived.

And then there was television. For the casual fan, who no longer came to Ebbets in postwar numbers, Jackie Gleason was more entertaining than Jackie Robinson. If he or she wanted a ball game, the Giants and Yankees televised all their home games, too. For the diehard Dodger fan the home games, and beginning in 1955 a third of the road schedule, were on television.[30] It was more significant for the Dodgers, as they were "far and away the top television attraction of the three New York clubs," one market researcher said, drawing twice as many viewers as the Giants and half again as many as the Yankees.[31]

With television the fan did not have to get off his couch or fight the traffic or search for a parking spot. "With TV, people can see a ball game at home. If it's a bother to get out to the park—why bother," said Bill Veeck, another club owner. "The single most important improvement that can be made in baseball today is improved parking."[32] And every fan who stayed home to watch the game on television did not pay the Dodgers for their minimal number of parking spaces or buy their beer and peanuts from Walter O'Malley.

Demographic shifts and the rise of television were offering O'Malley opportunities as well as problems, even if he was not focused on them yet. People had started moving west in large numbers, especially to California, and the developments in long-distance air travel force-fed by World War II had made a baseball schedule including the West Coast practical.

Los Angeles had become the nation's fifth-largest city by 1930, the fourth largest by 1950, just a tick behind Philadelphia in third. San Francisco ranked twelfth in 1950. Of the ten largest U.S. cities in the 1950 census, only two have grown since then—Los Angeles and New York. Baseball's adjustments to the changing demographics might charitably be described as unimaginative. The Braves had moved west to Milwaukee in 1953. But the Browns went the other direction, east to Baltimore, the next year. The Philadelphia Athletics' jump to Kansas City in 1955 was farther west, but Kansas City is closer to Boston than it is to the West Coast.

Everybody recognized the potential of Los Angeles and San Francisco. They were regularly mentioned in discussions of franchise moves and expansion in the postwar years. O'Malley had first gotten acquainted with Los Angeles in the late 1940s, when the Dodgers had a working agreement for player development with the Pacific Coast League Hollywood Stars, and Rickey had talked enthusiastically about the potential.[33]

He had also become acquainted with the idea of pay television. O'Malley was changing his attitude toward television. Publicly, the Dodgers continued to describe television as a stimulant to attendance. Vice president and public relations director Arthur "Red" Patterson described the Dodgers' position: "We must learn to live with TV. More people are talking about baseball—know about baseball—more than ever before thanks to this added medium. Now we must find a way to use TV to bring people to the ball park."[34] Privately, O'Malley was looking for a way out. A little more than a year later, freed from the expectations of Brooklyn fans, O'Malley was making it clear there would be no television in Los Angeles.[35] O'Malley's public statements in Brooklyn (though not his actions in Los Angeles) were at odds with the views shared by other baseball executives who felt television was hurting attendance.[36] Although he was concerned when telecasts threatened his revenue, he continued to recognize the value of television exposure on the national level, pushing the idea of the national baseball "Game of the Week."[37]

Quietly, he began to explore other ways to make Dodger games available without undercutting attendance and, hopefully, without cutting his lucrative television income, which led the Majors from 1952 through 1956, topping out at $888,270 in the latter year.[38] His first exploration was the idea of showing Dodger games in movie theaters. Motion pictures were another casualty of consumers' move to television. In March 1952 O'Malley announced that Loews Theatres and the movie studio MGM would sponsor the Dodgers' television pregame show, *Happy Felton's Knothole Gang*. It was an experiment, O'Malley said, that might well lead to baseball games on theater screens.[39]

That idea did not come to fruition, but that did not stop the Dodger owner's exploration of the possibilities. In early 1953, in a talk with Joe King of the *New York World-Telegram and Sun*, O'Malley suggested that some kind of pay television would work in some of the smaller baseball markets, where the local teams did not televise their games.[40] The article triggered a letter from Zenith Radio, which had a pay-per-view system it called Phon-eVision and whose chief executive, Eugene McDonald, was trying to push the idea.[41] In later years O'Malley would tell the story of watching a Dodger game with a "radio-wise" executive. The Ebbets Field crowd numbered 15,700 that night, and O'Malley asked the executive how many televisions were tuned to the game. The executive made some checks and came back with the figure of 2.4 million television sets in the Greater New York area tuned to the game. "That made me a convert right away," O'Malley said.[42] O'Malley said he tried to talk to RCA president David Sarnoff about a pay-TV program, but could not get a meeting.[43]

Pay-TV was an idea being pursued by several companies, but it was stalled while the Federal Communications Commission decided whether it should be allocated part of the broadcast frequency band. O'Malley wrote the FCC, urging its approval of the technology. He said the Dodgers were very interested in starting such a program, which he thought would be priced around 50 cents a game, roughly the price of a bleacher seat at Ebbets Field.[44] A television official estimated this could earn $50,000 a game for the team, or about 100,000 households using the system.

O'Malley also became enamored of a pay-television company called Ski-atron, founded by Matty Fox, a whirlwind of a salesman from Racine, Wisconsin, who parlayed his skills into the ownership of the RKO movie library and Skiatron. Fox needed more programming than old movies and thought baseball was the answer. He approached O'Malley with the offer of Ski-atron shares. O'Malley passed on that but began meeting Fox regularly at the Hotel Bossert.[45]

By early 1957 reports of a Skiatron-Dodgers deal and its impact on a possible move to the West Coast were rampant. San Francisco mayor George Christopher told papers there that Skiatron had already paid the Dodgers $2 million for closed-circuit rights in Los Angeles.[46] The next day Skiatron stock jumped nearly 15 percent on Wall Street.[47] Fox said his company had been talking to both the Dodgers and the Giants, but nothing was signed.[48] O'Malley denied there was a firm contract and that he had taken an ownership position in Skiatron. But he also sang its praises and suggested his thinking on pricing was up to $1 a game.[49] The Associated Press (AP) reported that a Skiatron rival had offered both the Dodgers and the Giants $2.5 million apiece for the New York rights.[50] In fact, Skiatron was a much more interesting proposition on the West Coast than it was in New York. Skiatron's system required that a wire be laid to each subscriber's house. In New York, where phone lines were buried, that would require streets be torn up at immense cost. In Los Angeles and San Francisco only the small downtown cores had buried telephone wires. In most areas the wires ran on telephone poles, and an additional wire could be added at much lower cost.[51]

Although pay-TV was clearly a factor in making Los Angeles more attractive to O'Malley, it was only some potential frosting. O'Malley was a cautious businessman, and a move to the West Coast was a big-enough risk without the additional gamble of counting on large doses of pay-television money. The technology had not been widely tested, the FCC had been dithering for years about approving its use, and Congress, prodded by the television networks claiming to represent consumers and voters, was eyeing the possibility of stepping in with its own legislation. People were used to free television.

O'Malley's goal remained his new stadium with the amenities he thought would be needed to attract more fans, whether in Brooklyn or elsewhere. If pay television came about, he would welcome it with open arms, but he knew he could not count on it.

8

A New Stadium—Politics

The economics of Ebbets Field were pressing Walter O'Malley to find a solution, but the barriers were daunting. The Ebbets Field site was too small to support a larger structure, and the possibility of closing McKeever Place behind third base, or some other bordering street, was deemed impractical.[1] The projected cost figure he had for a new stadium was $6 million, and O'Malley's team did not have that kind of money, especially with the added burden of paying Rickey for his share of the team.[2]

The publicity-conscious architect Norman Bel Geddes contacted O'Malley in 1948 and offered a design for a new stadium he said would seat 80,400 people. He invited reporters to his Park Avenue apartment and told them the Dodgers were planning a new stadium, which was vaguely true, and implied that his was the design.[3] O'Malley, with Rickey at spring training, quickly tried to put Bel Geddes's tale in perspective, calling his study "interesting" and saying the Brooklyn fans deserved better than the current Ebbets Field, but "it just does not seem possible in the near future."[4] O'Malley was very willing to listen to people with new ideas, and Bel Geddes had plenty of those. He had designed a teardrop-shaped car and a nine-deck amphibian airliner with the pool, deck-games area, and other amenities of a cruise ship. It would sleep 606 people.[5]

Imaginative ideas would not solve the location or the cost issues. By 1952 O'Malley was moaning that the Dodgers' struggling attendance was hurting the effort for a new stadium. Construction would require bank financing, and banks would not loan the team the amounts needed, given the flat attendance.[6]

That did not stop Bel Geddes. In the spring of 1952 he was at Vero Beach at O'Malley's invitation to help design Holman Stadium. But he was not talking about a spring training park for 5,000. He was talking about a downtown-Brooklyn retractable-roof stadium of the future. It would include foam-rubber seats, with heating elements for cold weather, a seven-thousand-car garage, hot dogs from vending machines (mustard included), and "a synthetic substance to replace grass on the entire field and which can be painted any color."[7]

In the fall of that year he expanded the idea across *Collier's*. There was a thirteen-by-sixteen-inch artist's rendering that showed the separate approaches for pedestrians, taxis, buses, and individual cars. The parking areas would provide maintenance services. There would be a supermarket, a movie theater, secure storage areas, playgrounds, and offices for doctors and dentists, giving the structure uses beyond baseball. O'Malley was quoted only at the very end of the story with cautious enthusiasm. "I'm not saying, of course, that we're going to go out and break ground for the new stadium next week. I'm merely saying it will be built someday."[8]

O'Malley was cautious because he recognized the difficulties of finding a site and financing construction, but he was interested in convincing both fans and the decision makers that the Dodgers needed and deserved a new facility. Roger Kahn was in just his second year on the Dodger beat in 1953 when O'Malley began to talk of the new stadium as if he were letting Kahn in on a great secret. He pointed out the drawbacks of Ebbets Field and then outlined his view of 70,000 domed seats, no upper-deck supports, and plenty of parking. "Just thought this might make a story for you sometime," he told Kahn. Kahn tried his editor, who was not interested.[9] O'Malley was also trying to interest other newspaper people in his project, such as *Brooklyn Eagle* publisher Frank Schroth.[10]

In June 1953 O'Malley finally directly approached Robert Moses, the man everybody was telling him was key to his plans.[11] O'Malley had clearly discussed these plans with George V. McLaughlin, his old mentor and a man who served with Moses on multiple municipal boards, including Moses's core agency—the Triborough Bridge Authority.[12]

O'Malley had come to the conclusion that he could solve both the site and the financing problems of a new stadium by linking his quest with the city's programs to redevelop distressed areas. That meant Moses, whose titles covered a wide range of agencies charged with building and rebuilding the city's infrastructure and neighborhoods. In the words of Moses' biographer Robert Caro, "He held power, a power so substantial that in the fields he chose to exercise it, it was not challenged seriously by any Governor of

New York State or, during a thirty-four year period, 1934 to 1968, in which it extended over city as well as state, by any Mayor of New York City."[13]

Born in 1888, Moses came from a wealthy German Jewish family and was raised in the privileged path of tutors, prep school, Yale, and Oxford. Back at Columbia University, he earned a PhD in political science with a dissertation on civil service reform. His classmates were in awe of his memory, intellect, and relentless search for knowledge. Full of idealism and with his family ready to support him, Moses embarked on a career of public service.

Civil service reform, making government jobs available to the qualified rather than the politically connected, was his first crusade. He went to work for the Bureau of Municipal Research, a privately funded good-government group interested in civil service reform. Bursting with idealism, impatience, and arrogance, Moses spent his late twenties trying to bring reform to New York's patronage system. His initial efforts, vaguely supported by Mayor John Purroy Mitchel, came up against Tammany Hall, whose lifeblood was patronage. For four years he drew up forms to objectively measure performance, lobbied editorial writers, and visited bureau heads. Tammany operatives organized the employees, argued about technicalities, and lobbied the mayor, who was up for reelection in 1917. They could do better than lobbying the mayor. They ran their own candidate and won. "Red Mike" Hylan took office and dismantled all of Moses's reforms. "The net result of all his work was nothing," Caro wrote.[14] The humiliation sent him off to work briefly at a World War I shipyard, but he soon tried to return to government work, standing in line at Cleveland OH City Hall, seeking a minor municipal post. He did not get it and returned to an "insultingly small" job at the Bureau of Municipal Research.[15]

Moses was rescued by a remarkable woman named Belle Moskowitz. She was a leading player in New York reform politics, and her husband had been Moses's boss in the civil service efforts. She had been impressed with him in that role, and when newly elected governor Alfred E. Smith put her in charge of a commission to reorganize the state's administrative machinery in 1918, she hired Moses as her chief of staff. In that position Moses impressed Smith, who regularly sought his advice and gave him more responsibility. When Smith lost a reelection bid in 1920, Moses went to work for the New York State Association, another good-government group. He turned the association into an anti-Hylan lobby and headed a campaign committee to stop the man who had undone his civil service work.[16]

Hylan was reelected, but in 1922 so was Smith, and Moses was back advising the governor. One of his reports put forward an ambitious plan for improving New York's state park system, especially on Long Island. In 1924 a park-system bond issue designed by Moses was passed, and Smith named him president of the Long Island State Park Commission.

Moses was a dynamo, building parkways out onto the island, going into immense detail in designing parks along the barrier islands on the south shore. When the New Deal programs to counter the Depression arrived, Moses was the one man in the state with the plans in place to immediately take advantage of the federal funds. Invited by new mayor Fiorello La Guardia, Moses added the New York City Parks Department to his responsibilities in 1934, a job that gave him access to the steady revenue from tolls of the city's bridges and parkways through the Triborough Bridge Authority. In 1946 Mayor William O'Dwyer made him the city's construction coordinator, a vaguely defined job that Moses quickly turned into control of building throughout the city. He soon added the post of slum-clearance coordinator.

Moses's power was built on several factors. One, as Caro notes, was his ability to draft bills in the state legislature that gave him extensive control over his fiefdoms and allowed him to escape pressure from elected officials. When his various agencies issued bonds, he ensured they were written such that banks could back out if Moses's power was circumscribed. Another factor was Moses's combination of effectiveness and personal honesty. Unlike earlier generations of good-government advocates fighting Tammany and its imitators, Moses delivered the goods. Under his administration parks, highways, swimming pools, public housing, bridges, tunnels, and all manner of things were built, and they were built without Bob Moses getting rich. As a result the newspapers and good-government advocates loved him. He courted them assiduously and could count on their support, especially that of the quality papers such as the *Times* and the *Herald-Tribune*. Mayors and governors deferred to him with a combination of fear and relief they could leave knotty problems in the hands of someone financially honest and competent.

Warren Moscow, a longtime *New York Times* reporter on city politics and later an aide to Mayor Robert Wagner Jr., told an anecdote that illustrated the power relationship between Moses and mayors. When Wagner took office in early 1954, his supporters had urged him not to reappoint Moses to the City Planning Commission, a post that allowed Moses to vote to approve projects proposed by Moses's agencies. When Moses came to take the pro forma oaths of office, he noticed Wagner had not presented the one for the Planning Commission. When he demanded to know where it was,

Wagner said an underling had not prepared it properly. Moses marched into the city clerk's office, grabbed a blank form, rolled it into a typewriter, filled it out, and plunked it down in front of Wagner. Resolutions forgotten, Wagner signed.[17]

In O'Malley's case, Moses responded promptly to the overture. Within four days he sent the Dodgers' president a letter outlining the arguments Moses would return to again and again over the next four years. A stadium for a baseball team could not use public funds set aside for slum clearance, even if it was part of a larger project that did involve improving a neighborhood and creating public housing. "Our Slum Clearance Committee cannot be used to encourage speculation in baseball enterprises," he wrote.[18] O'Malley's actions over the next four years were all part of an unsuccessful attempt to overturn or circumvent this decision.

His first step was to get a face-to-face meeting with Moses, and by September 1953 he had lured him to the Coal Hole at the Hotel Brooklyn. O'Malley knew he was facing a major task, but it is not clear he knew he entered the game with two strikes against him. Robert Moses had a phenomenal memory, a memory strong enough to remember that it was "Red Mike" Hylan who had presided over the destruction of Moses's dreams of civil service reform—and that it was Hylan who had appointed Edwin J. O'Malley to his cabinet. In the early 1920s, as Edwin suffered and grandstanded through his investigations by committees of the legislature, Moses would have been reading the papers and making notes about the things he had not been able to clean up. Now, his son, Irish name and Democratic connections fully on the record, approached. Moses was also no fan of professional sports. A swimmer at Yale and a water polo player at Oxford, Moses believed strongly in amateur sports and disparaged the professionals.[19] Moses also did not like the Coal Hole, which was clearly O'Malley's territory, with the Brooklyn club a hive for the borough politicos and business leaders O'Malley socialized with and Moses abhorred.[20]

O'Malley was undoubtedly counting on his own connections, and not merely to the political leaders in Brooklyn. McLaughlin, his old mentor, sat at Moses's right hand on numerous agency boards and always had access. Emil Praeger, O'Malley's choice for engineering and architectural work, had done many projects for Moses and was a man Moses turned to for advice on design and construction issues.[21] Frank Schroth of the *Brooklyn Eagle* was reflexively supportive of Brooklyn institutions and, with the newspaper behind him, could always get the ear of Moses.

At this first formal meeting O'Malley presented his basic idea, phrased in enormous deference to Moses. Moses was looking to build parking structures around the city. O'Malley's ballpark needed such parking. If Moses could help put together the land for a stadium, the attendant parking structure, built and paid for by the Dodgers, would justify the use of federal funds to buy up the land.[22] O'Malley had concluded that putting together at least fifteen acres in downtown Brooklyn would simply cost too much. And doing it with a dummy corporation and keeping the multiple necessary purchases quiet to prevent owners from raising their prices, as Charles Ebbets had, was impossible.

Moses sarcastically described O'Malley's presentation—"a wonderful spiel"—but thought the idea might work within the context of his plans for a massive Brooklyn Civic Center. He thought it might work if the Dodgers would throw in the Ebbets Field property, which could then be used for public housing.[23] A few days later, after an inspection of the Brooklyn Civic Center site, he decided the idea was "impractical." Moses had another idea instead; maybe a site on Atlantic Avenue, which had been a Catholic school for wayward girls, could be used.[24] He sent the suggestion to O'Malley and said they would get together after the World Series.

In letters to public officials Moses was already referring to work on the stadium proposal as a "chore."[25] He could not resist forwarding O'Malley a postcard he had received showing a natural rock amphitheater near Denver. "Here's the way to build a stadium," he wrote.[26]

After the (losing) World Series, O'Malley was back. He was working through intermediaries, asking Schroth to set up the meeting. Presumably, O'Malley was counting on Moses's willingness to please the people who owned printing presses.[27] The meeting was set for October 21, back at the Coal Hole Moses disliked.[28]

But five days before the meeting, Moses drew the line. "We obviously cannot select areas to be cleared for the primary purpose of providing a fifteen acre location for a new privately owned baseball stadium," Moses wrote Schroth. "It has been difficult to make Mr. O'Malley understand these distinctions and the principles which must control our committee. . . . [W]e will give no further consideration whatever to the use of Title One as suggested by Mr. O'Malley." He suggested O'Malley buy the land he needed without the use of the government's power of eminent domain.[29] Moses would not attend the meeting.

O'Malley responded with continued deference. Ignoring the substance of Moses's arguments, he said, "Any disposition you make of the matter will have my understanding. In all of this I have really wanted your personal advice and guidance."[30] He enclosed some suggestions he and Praeger had devised for possible locations for a joint project that ran directly contrary to the arguments Moses had put forward.

Moses was losing patience. "You and your advisers have not grasped the restrictions under which we work," he said. He advised O'Malley that the House of Good Shepherd site (the former school for wayward girls) was his best bet and suggested the city and the borough (but not Moses's agencies) could help with street work and perhaps a school or playground to help advance the stadium project.[31]

The House of the Good Shepherd site, at Atlantic and Hopkinson Avenues, had a number of drawbacks from O'Malley's point of view. It was too small for both a stadium and parking. It was served by only one subway line, and even that would require a walk of several blocks through a neighborhood that was even poorer and more heavily African American than Ebbets Field's. It was miles from any large motorway and a half-mile walk from the nearest Long Island Rail Road station. And, as Moses agreed, there was no real need for a public parking garage in that neighborhood.

A few days later Moses was telling a subordinate to "wind up the new Dodger Ebbets Field Stadium rhubarb. Let's see if O is serious. Pin it down to the purchase by him of the old institution on Atlantic Ave. If he won't do this, he is kidding us."[32]

By now Moses's and O'Malley's letters are talking past each other. Moses is curt. O'Malley is chummy, anxious to establish a friendly relationship and keep the doors open. He writes that Moses's dismissive letter suggesting he look at the Good Shepherd property leaves him "with the hope that when we get together after the election a way will be found for a new Dodger stadium."[33] He is also looking to show Moses that he has alternatives, as when he coyly sends him a copy of a report favorable to the possibilities of Major League Baseball in Los Angeles.[34] This was not the kind of pressure to which Moses responded.

Moses remained firm with his argument that federal money could not be used to help private enterprise, although he certainly worked with private developers on other projects, notably the Lincoln Center district redevelopment in Manhattan. On the Upper West Side of Manhattan, Moses had used his powers to clear six blocks for a private developer and been applauded by the *New York Times* for doing so.[35] Ironically, one of the private-sector developers Moses felt comfortable with was William Zeckendorf, the putative buyer of Rickey's Dodger stake.[36] Perhaps aware of the history, O'Malley ignored Moses's argument and tried to show Moses how their goals could work together. Clearly, neither is really listening, and the flow of letters passing in the night slows.

Early the next year the Dodgers were approached about a site over the rail yards in Long Island City, in Queens, just across Newtown Creek from Brooklyn. Moving out of Brooklyn is "a shocking thought," O'Malley said. "A move to Long Island City, however, would be preferred to a move to Los Angeles."[37] O'Malley's approach was to Frank Schroth, who shared with him the desire to keep the Dodgers in downtown Brooklyn, and it had the effect of bringing Moses back to the table at Schroth's behest.

In March Schroth hosted another meeting—Moses, three of his aides, Brooklyn borough president John Cashmore, three of his aides, O'Malley, and Praeger. Moses's reaction could not have been more definitive. "I think yesterday's meeting was a dud and as far as I am concerned I am attending no more sessions with Walter O'Malley," he wrote Schroth. "He bores everyone to death by his endless monologue, says the same things, but shows no grasp of the Constitution, legal, public and practical aspects of the problem and keeps threatening in a rather snide way to quit Brooklyn and go to Los Angeles or Long Island City."[38]

Hope, however, was arising from another O'Malley ally. The week after the meeting where O'Malley bored Moses, the Dodger owner received a letter from Cashmore. The borough president was forwarding a letter he had received in January from Joseph Kaufman, president of the New York Council of Wholesale Meat Dealers. The Fort Greene Meat Market, located across the street from the Long Island Rail Road depot at Flatbush and Atlantic Avenues, was "deteriorating very rapidly," Kaufman had written. Kaufman wanted Cashmore to find a place to move the market. Cashmore saw the old meat-market site as a possibility for a new Dodger stadium.[39]

O'Malley immediately recognized the site's potential. The Long Island Rail Road was a blessing. Nine subway lines used the adjacent IRT, BMT, and IND Atlantic Avenue stations. It was less than a mile from the planned route of the Brooklyn-Queens Expressway. The suburbanites could return by car or train, while the subways brought the city people.

As a major redevelopment project in the city, O'Malley was once again in Robert Moses's backyard. By August he was writing Moses about a new stadium, suggesting the city would benefit from a new terminal for the railroad, plus the parking spots. As usual he couched the letter in terms of asking Moses for his advice.[40] Instead, he got another primer on Moses's view of public policy. "I must say to you that we don't speak the same language," Moses wrote. The redevelopment funds were to build housing and for neighborhood redevelopment, not stadiums. "The tail can't wag the dog," and a stadium for the Dodgers "by itself is no public purpose."[41]

O'Malley finally conceded he was getting rejected. He realized he needed to take another tack, and he thought he had the political and public relations connections to make it work. From the beginning he had marshaled his Brooklyn connections—Cashmore; Schroth; Walter Rothschild and Robert Blum of Abraham & Straus, the borough's largest department store; and Manhattan real estate mogul Charles Noyes.[42] His most direct line to Moses remained McLaughlin.

He had been willing to talk to reporters about the stadium for several years, and he had acquiesced in Bel Geddes's publicizing the architect's ideas about a new stadium. But he had not made it the focus of his interactions with the press and public. Now, he began to step up the public profile of the stadium project. First, he tried to make clear exactly what he was asking for and what he was not. He was asking the city to assemble a parcel of land and sell it to the Dodgers at what O'Malley considered a reasonable price. O'Malley would then use his own money to build a stadium, and perhaps a parking structure, making it private property and subject to property taxes. That the difference between the likely price of putting together the parcel and what O'Malley considered a reasonable price would be large, he lightly skipped over.

In early 1953 he had veiled a pitch to Roger Kahn to write about his stadium plan. Now, the veil disappeared. In December 1953, no doubt with Frank Schroth's help, he got a front-page story in the *Brooklyn Eagle* about his plans and a strongly supportive editorial as well. He pegged the stadium at fifty-two thousand seats and a $7.2 million price tag. He said it would be operating within five years, faster if one of three proposed sites in Brooklyn was approved within the next six months. He declined to name the sites, but said talk of Queens or Montreal or Los Angeles was "silly." Neither the story nor the editorial mentioned Robert Moses or any specific roadblocks to the project.[43] O'Malley wanted to promote his project but did not want to get into a public struggle with Moses.

He talked regularly about the issue to newsmen, either because he was asked or because he tied his stadium concerns into other issues the sports reporters were interested in—attendance, Major League expansion, trades, or television. There were few major headline stories like the *Eagle*'s, but his arguments appeared regularly in the sports pages and in the *Sporting News*.[44]

O'Malley went public with his Moses problem in August 1955 as the Dodgers were coasting to their fifth pennant in the past nine years. He could not get Moses on board by going through the front door, so he started what would become a series of flanking maneuvers in which he tried to increase the political pressure on Moses to make some accommodation.

To get everyone's attention, he announced late on Monday, August 15, that the Dodgers would play seven games of their regular-season schedule for 1956 in Roosevelt Stadium in Jersey City, New Jersey. The announcement gave him the excuse to discuss poor attendance in Brooklyn and better parking facilities in Jersey City. O'Malley said the plan was preparation "for the day when Ebbets Field will have to be sold" and subsequently indicated the team would use the facility for only two more years. He raised the possibility of leaving New York. He referred to Moses elliptically and said, "We will consider other locations only if the club is unsuccessful in building a new ball park in Brooklyn."[45]

Fan sentiment, as collected by New York newspapers, was predictably concerned, ranging from "They shouldn't move, even to Jersey City," to "It's a bad thing but they do need a new park."[46] O'Malley went public with the Flatbush and Atlantic Avenues site and took advantage of the sudden interest to repeat his arguments about the need for the new stadium and the features that would be included. By Thursday Mayor Robert Wagner was announcing a Friday-morning meeting at his Gracie Mansion residence. It would include O'Malley; Cashmore; Schroth, who was now working for the *Daily News* in the wake of the *Eagle*'s closure; and, maybe, Moses. Asked if he would go along with O'Malley's plan, Moses said, "Talk to the mayor."[47]

They met on a windy porch facing the East River and reiterated their positions. Cashmore, seconded by Schroth, pushed for the Fort Greene site. Moses, who did show up, said there was no legal way for the city to aid the team. The mayor said he would take it under study and support Cashmore's plea to fund a survey of the site proposed by Cashmore and

Brooklyn leadership. "Moses Puts Chill on City Help for Dodger Ball-park," headlined the *Daily News*.[48]

Cashmore asked the city's Board of Estimate, which controlled the city's purse strings, for $278,000 for the study. Moses quietly opposed. The board voted $125,000, of which only $25,000 was to be spent on the stadium site. The rest would be used for a study on redeveloping the wider area surrounding the site as part of a downtown Brooklyn project, which Moses desired.[49]

O'Malley had taken his drive for a new stadium public, but with decidedly modest results. His longtime supporters remained, but Wagner's response was tepid and the Board of Estimate's funding for the site study was perfunctory. Essentially, he had not raised enough concern among either the political and business elites or the average Dodger fans. And the sports reporters, even more insulated in the baseball world than O'Malley, simply did not understand Robert Moses. Five weeks after the Board of Estimate's vote, the Dodgers won the 1955 World Series, their first. Wrote the *New York World-Telegram and Sun*'s Dan Daniel, "I dare say Bob Moses is not likely, now, to oppose the wishes of the people of Brooklyn as regards that new ball park Walter O'Malley wants to build at Flatbush and Atlantic avenues."[50]

The public airing of O'Malley's plans had at least stirred up other possibilities. There was the site of the Jamaica racetrack in the far end of Queens, scheduled for redevelopment after its sister Aqueduct track was refurbished.[51] Officials from Edison, New Jersey, Queens, Sheepshead Bay and Bay Ridge in Brooklyn, and Nassau and Suffolk Counties on Long Island all offered sites.[52] Queens real estate agent Charles M. Richardson wrote Moses suggesting the site of the Flushing Airport. Moses curtly passed him on to Cashmore.[53] Even Moses returned to thinking about it, writing Cashmore to suggest that a program of street widening and rerouting might provide enough additional land near Ebbets to allow expansion.[54]

In February 1956 there finally seemed to be some movement. Wagner and Cashmore sponsored a bill in the state legislature to create a Brooklyn Sports Center Authority with the specific goal of facilitating a new stadium for the Dodgers within the larger downtown area that the Board of Estimate had voted to study the previous August. The mayor and the borough president both cautioned this did not mean a new stadium would necessarily be approved. Wagner further covered his rear by having aides leak doubts about the bill's chances of passage, constitutionality, and ability to raise funds. Walter O'Malley was complimentary, ignoring that the bill contemplated a city-owned facility rather than the private property the

Dodger owner wanted.[55] The next day he pledged the Dodgers would buy $4 million of the $30 million in bonds the authority would be authorized to issue. Clearly, staying in Brooklyn had a higher priority than owning the stadium. The New York Civic League opposed the idea as an inappropriate use of the power of eminent domain.[56] Moses agreed.

Wagner knew the political arena. At that time a bill in the state legislature from an individual city required a two-thirds vote of support from that city's governing body. Manhattan and Queens city councilmen did not think any civic sports authority should be exclusively for Brooklyn.[57] They were overruled.[58] In Albany the cautioning notes from Wagner's aides began to come true quickly. Albany legislators wondered if another authority was a good idea.[59] They heard complaints about more property being taken off the tax rolls.[60] The legislature eventually passed the bill, and Governor Averell Harriman signed it in late April.[61]

Though encouraged, O'Malley was keeping his options open and trying to keep the pressure on. The Jersey City games, which began April 19, gave him an excuse to trot out his arguments. He was now consistently raising the possibility of New York becoming a one-team town, with the Giants leaving as well, and he was adamant that the 1957 season would be the Dodgers' last at Ebbets Field.[62]

The process was not moving as O'Malley hoped. It took Wagner three months to name the three members of the authority's unpaid board.[63] The mayor's papers are full of nominations from various interested parties and he had multiple viewpoints to consider, but Wagner's clock was clearly not ticking at the same speed as O'Malley's. He was also careful to keep his options open, telling a state assemblyman that the creation of the authority was not a commitment to build the Dodgers a stadium. That would happen only if it was "feasible."[64]

O'Malley found another way to reiterate how serious he was. On October 30 he announced he had sold the Ebbets Field property to Marvin Kratter, a developer who said he would be building housing on the site. The agreement said the Dodgers could keep playing in the park through at least the 1961 season, although the rent would go up after 1959.[65] O'Malley would later say he did this in a burst of optimism over the Brooklyn Sports Authority, but it clearly also worked well as an implied threat.[66]

In late November the engineering, legal, and real estate consultants hired by Cashmore with the original $100,000 from the city all presented favorable reports on the potential for a Dodger stadium in the area surrounding

Flatbush and Atlantic Avenues.[67] The authority asked the Board of Estimate for $274,000 to fund its activities and a more detailed study of the ballpark site.[68] Moses, noting that the whole project was bogging down, recommended to Wagner that the authority be given $40,000. It was evidence of a split between Moses's people, focused on the full 110-block area covered by the redevelopment study, and the authority, which was intent on the ballpark.[69] If there had to be a ballpark, Moses wanted it on the north side of Atlantic Avenue, where O'Malley had first proposed it, while the authority wanted it across the street.

The Board of Estimate gave O'Malley a bitter Christmas present. On December 23 it approved $25,000 for the authority's budget, even less than Moses had recommended.[70] The Brooklyn Sports Center Authority was destined for irrelevance.

As 1957 began O'Malley started to look for more ways to make his point without making any commitments. He started with what Joe King of the *New York World-Telegram and Sun* characterized as his "first downright threat to move the Dodgers."[71] "There is still a short time before we could be forced to take an irrevocable step to commit the Dodgers elsewhere," O'Malley said, adding that he was leaving immediately for Los Angeles. In Los Angeles he and daughter Terry stopped at the Automobile Club, looking for directions to a possible ballpark site he had heard about called Chavez Ravine.[72] He also took another look at Wrigley Field and the Los Angeles Memorial Coliseum. Back in New York he sent Jim Mulvey careful directions to the Chavez Ravine area and asked him to look it over so they could compare notes when Mulvey returned to New York.[73] He said he was on the West Coast to conclude a deal for a Convair 440 and just thought he would check out the site.[74] The forty-four-passenger plane had the seating capacity and range to fly the Dodgers coast to coast (with refueling stops), so that occasioned a new round of questioning in New York.[75]

In early February he upped the ante in an interview with Dick Young, resulting in a story syndicated across the country. New York needed to formulate definite plans for financing and building a stadium within six months, or he would begin negotiations to move elsewhere.[76] In late February O'Malley dropped what Roscoe McGowen of the *New York Times* described as the "bombshell."[77] At the New York baseball writers' annual dinner on February 3, he had sent a note to Philip Wrigley, owner of the both the Chicago Cubs and the Pacific Coast League's Los Angeles Angels.

In the note he asked Wrigley what his price was for the Angels. He wanted $2 million for ballpark and the land, Wrigley wrote on the note, and $1 million for the franchise. O'Malley wrote "Deal" at the bottom of the note and underlined it.[78] It was the same price that Wrigley, a longtime supporter of Major League Baseball for the West Coast, had put on the team in 1954.[79] O'Malley now owned the territorial rights to the Los Angeles market, the market people had been suggesting he had been eyeing for years. The purchase served dual purposes. It gave him entrée into the most desirable market for a move if that became necessary while increasing pressure on New York officials to come up with a reasonable offer.

Los Angeles began to have Major League dreams around 1930. That year's census confirmed it had become the tenth-largest city in the country after its population had more than doubled in the previous decade. Mark Kelly, sports editor of the *Los Angeles Examiner*, had begun writing columns suggesting the city was ready for Major League Baseball.[80] In 1932 the Los Angeles Junior Chamber of Commerce began a campaign for a big-league franchise, pledging to work with San Francisco.[81] Through the next decade it became a mantra of some Angelenos that the city was ready.

In 1941 somebody finally bit—at the wrong time. After extensive discussions with Wrigley, the Pacific Coast League, and the schedule maker, the owners of the St. Louis Browns headed for the American League meetings in Chicago. The Junior Chamber of Commerce had guaranteed them attendance of five hundred thousand a year for five years. They arrived in Chicago on December 7, 1941, and while watching a professional football game heard the announcement of the Japanese attack on Pearl Harbor. They knew immediately their proposal was dead, but presented it to the American League owners the next day. Because of the war it was turned down without serious discussion of the potential issues with travel and scheduling.[82]

The discussion began again in 1946, soon after football's Cleveland Rams moved to Los Angeles. By 1950 the city was the fifth largest in the country. It was not just Brooklyn where the potential of Los Angeles was raised, but in every Major League city where attendance was poor or a ballpark deemed unsatisfactory. In 1945 the baseball world noted that the Pacific Coast League's smallest franchise, Sacramento, had outdrawn both the Cincinnati Reds and the Philadelphia Phillies. The PCL recognized the potential danger to their league and began an ultimately unsuccessful campaign to become a third major league.[83]

Meanwhile, the Los Angeles papers regularly printed articles on how likely West Coast expansion was and when it would be.[84] In 1946 Mark Kelly's successor as the *Examiner*'s sports columnist, Vincent Flaherty, represented movie mogul Louis Mayer in negotiations to buy the St. Louis Cardinals and move them to Los Angeles.[85] The next year oilman Ed Pauley was reported in the bidding for the Cardinals.[86] Flaherty, through his columns and his contacts, was the most consistent mover for Major League Baseball in Los Angeles throughout the 1950s.[87]

The most heavily discussed site for a new Los Angeles ballpark was Chavez Ravine, an area just north of downtown that, by 1953, was mostly owned by the city. Bob Cobb, owner of the Brown Derby restaurants and the Hollywood Stars of the Pacific Coast League, was the first to spot its potential. In 1950 Los Angeles police chief William Parker asked Cobb to set up the kitchen and dining room at the police academy, right on the edge of Chavez Ravine. Cobb fell into the habit of shooting at the police pistol range.[88] Because he needed a ballpark for the Stars, he recognized the potential of the area.[89] He conveyed that to the city and, through his close relationship with Branch Rickey, to the baseball world.[90]

By 1953 Bill Veeck was talking about moving the Browns to Los Angeles.[91] But the other American League owners, upset with Veeck's promotional antics, made it clear the Browns could be moved only by a different owner. Veeck sold to Baltimore interests, and the Browns became the Orioles for the 1954 season.[92]

There were flies in the ointment, however. While Robert Moses was insisting the city could not build a park for the Dodgers, many owners were convinced renting city-owned stadiums was the wave of the future. Thus, baseball owners were dismayed in 1954 when Los Angeles voters did not support a bond issue to build a municipal auditorium, a move interpreted as indicating a lack of commitment to sports. Bill Veeck, reportedly interested in moving the Philadelphia Athletics to Los Angeles, backed off.[93] The next year Los Angeles voters failed to pass a bond issue to build a baseball stadium.[94] Walter O'Malley kept a file of press clippings about the bond issue.[95]

The Athletics would also be mentioned as a possible tenant for Los Angeles when their move talk heated up in 1954.[96] But they went to Kansas City. Three Major League teams had moved without any seeming regard for the population shifts occurring nationwide. The game was still bottled up in the Northeast quadrant of the country.

Some in Los Angeles were not impressed by the second-division résumés of the teams rumored to be considering Los Angeles. They wanted a winner. In 1955 city councilwoman Rosalind Wyman, whose Parks and Recreation Committee was trying to lure Major League Baseball, went to Brooklyn to get an interview with O'Malley.[97] Still focused on Brooklyn, and mindful of the Los Angeles rumors constantly floating around to undermine his quest there, he would not see her.[98] At this point, September 1955, he still clearly preferred to stay in New York. The leverage strategy he had adopted the previous month with the Jersey City games could have been intensified by a public meeting with Wyman, but he passed on that opportunity.

By late 1956 the rumor mill was focused on the Washington Senators. Calvin Griffith had been mightily impressed with Los Angeles's market potential after a September trip and an offer to build him an $11 million stadium and provide $2 million to buy out Wrigley's PCL interests. Ultimately, the Senators' board decided to stay in the nation's capital, saying they were impressed with efforts to keep them there.[99]

Earlier that October O'Malley had visited Los Angeles as the Dodgers flew to their postseason series in Japan. At a press conference he denied any interest in moving to Los Angeles, citing solid attendance and the progress he felt was visible in the approval of the Brooklyn Sports Authority.[100] But he also quietly rounded up daughter Terry, grabbed a cab, and asked to be taken to Chavez Ravine. The cabbie did not know where it was, so they got a gas station map and went up into the hills to see what there was to see.[101] Los Angeles officials then laid on a helicopter trip for him.

Years later Los Angeles County supervisor Kenneth Hahn, one of the city's earliest and most persistent boosters of Major League Baseball, would claim his October meetings with O'Malley produced a commitment to move. In Hahn's version Vincent Flaherty had persuaded him to court Calvin Griffith and the Senators and arranged a dinner at Toots Shor's, New York's marquee sports watering hole, during the 1956 World Series. The meeting went well, but while Hahn was attending a World Series game, he received a note from O'Malley, scribbled on a napkin, asking him not to sign anything with Griffith because O'Malley wanted to bring the Dodgers to Los Angeles. On October 12, according to Hahn, the two met at the Statler Hilton Hotel in Los Angeles, and O'Malley made his promise.[102]

O'Malley's version was different. He sent Hahn the note, but it was to meet him and get a feel for the city and the Chavez Ravine site. He made no commitments.[103] Although O'Malley's description could be shrugged off as part of a campaign to keep things quiet, Hahn's own actions over the next several months were not those of a man who had pocketed a sure thing. In the weeks immediately after O'Malley's supposed commitment, Hahn would continue to pursue the Senators hard. He would make lavish promises to O'Malley when serious talks began a few months later. He would continue to press staff members and negotiators to nail the deal down. He would show frustration as well. Barely a week before the announcement of the Angels purchase, Hahn said O'Malley was using the threat of Los Angeles only as a stalking horse to get what he wanted in Brooklyn.[104]

With the purchase of the Angels franchise, that all changed. Within a week and a half, Los Angeles mayor Norris Poulson was in Vero Beach, leading a delegation including Hahn, members of the city council, and the county's board of supervisors. O'Malley had his private plane meet them in Miami, and they reached Vero Beach in a steady rain. There was a five-hour meeting at Bud Holman's sumptuous "cabin" out in the Florida backcountry.

Poulson emerged from the meeting full of smiles. O'Malley was less fulsome, taking the podium after the mayor, saying, "I'll take the edge off that right now." Both described the talks as throwing out ideas and said the discussion was far too preliminary to make public.[105] Poulson continued to ooze confidence, saying all problems were solvable. Upon his return to Los Angeles, he was quoted as saying, "We've got the Dodgers," but he quickly backed away from that.[106] O'Malley kept his mouth shut.[107]

It would become clear over the next months that the two parties really had not communicated very well. In the words of Jim Murray, then a writer for *Time*, Poulson was "a loud, impulsive man who manages to give the impression of enjoying himself hugely without quite understanding what is going on."[108] It showed. Both sides had tossed ideas into the discussion. O'Malley suggested a number of things, such as a "Milwaukee-style" agreement whereby the city would build the park and lease it to the team. Poulson left the meeting convinced that O'Malley wanted the city to build him a park.[109] But John Leach, the county's assistant chief administrative officer, said O'Malley had wanted to build the stadium himself with the land on a long-term lease from the city.[110] Dick Walsh, the Los Angeles native O'Malley would send out to run the Angels and be his point man in Los Angeles, said the instructions he had been given by O'Malley called for a city-owned stadium.[111]

Alternatively, O'Malley reportedly produced a written summary of what he wanted: two consecutive ninety-nine-year leases on the land at $1 a year, no taxes, the city or county to grade the site so he could build the stadium, plus other demands.[112] Whenever O'Malley raised a possibility or an issue, the city people would say it could be done or the problem could be circumvented. "The meeting was primarily a sparring match," said Poulson. "One of our officials promised O'Malley the moon, and Walter asked for more."[113] As a result the city would spend weeks working out the details of proposals that were not going anywhere, and O'Malley would feel he had been misled. At least part of that was his own fault, for being unclear about what his preferred solution was.

At least things were progressing. Poulson pushed for, and promised, a final offer to O'Malley by a planned spring visit from the Dodgers' owner.[114] By the Monday following the Vero Beach meeting, Poulson was hosting a conference with Hahn and top staff members from both the county and the city. "We're discussing the legal angles, administrative costs and engineering problems," Poulson said.[115] New York sportswriters surveyed by the *Los Angeles Times* noted the differing levels of concern and response.[116] "The Los Angeles case was strengthened if only because six officials took the pains to come all the way to Florida to demonstrate their sincerity to O'Malley. Since the Brooklyn-Chicago deal was announced two weeks ago all that O'Malley has gotten from New York officials is a telegram and a phone call," wrote Dick Young.[117]

Los Angeles officials were also dealing with bouts of public optimism. There were reports the Dodgers would move there for the 1957 season.[118] Then there were reports they would play some exhibition games in 1958.[119] Public expectations were high, and the politicians were under pressure to meet them.

It was not only Los Angeles. For several years city officials had been communicating with their counterparts in San Francisco, recognizing that moving two teams to the West Coast would make more sense for scheduling and travel arrangements.[120] It was recognized by baseball figures and eastern politicians as well. Even though he was still working on Brooklyn at the time, O'Malley addressed the West Coast issue theoretically as early as 1955, saying, "It's unlikely that one club or the other would move. You'll find that the two will move."[121]

Horace Stoneham of the Giants, faced with larger versions of the Dodgers' problems of old ballpark, poor attendance, no parking, and a bad neighborhood reputation, had not pursued a new stadium or other relief as hard as O'Malley, but he had been making some plans. In May 1956 he had said he was "considering moving the New York Giants to Minneapolis."[122]

During spring training in 1957, as O'Malley moved closer to a decision to relocate, he had a confidential talk with Stoneham after a Major League owners meeting in Clearwater, Florida. Stoneham told O'Malley he had decided to move to Minneapolis. O'Malley brought up the idea of moving together. He noted how the rivalry pumped up attendance at both parks and suggested it might be maintained in the West.[123] Although neither was willing to commit, they jointly commissioned a survey by the Doody Company of St. Louis to see how receptive West Coast fans would be to their teams.[124] After the initial positive contacts in Vero Beach, O'Malley asked Poulson how well he knew San Francisco mayor George Christopher. Poulson, who had already sought Christopher's support even before the Vero Beach meeting, said he would arrange something.[125] Meanwhile, Stoneham said he was already in contact with people in San Francisco.[126]

In New York the reporters grasped the import of the purchase of the Los Angeles PCL franchise. O'Malley "holds all the right cards, an invincible hand," wrote *Times* sports columnist Arthur Daley. "The game has reached the put-up-or-shut-up stage."[127] The hard-core Dodger fans got the message. By now there were weekly "Keep the Dodgers in Brooklyn" rallies in front of Borough Hall.[128] The politicians heard the clatter, but did not translate that into any need for cooperation or speed. On March 1, a week after the announcement of the purchase of the Los Angeles territory, Wagner sent O'Malley a telegram saying he was "deeply disturbed" by reports the Dodgers would be moving and again pledged the city's help. A Board of Estimate committee agreed to contact a consulting firm to see if it was interested in doing an engineering and financing study on the Flatbush–Atlantic sites. A week later they met with Madigan & Hyland and said the study might be completed in three months.[129] The contract was not in place until the end of March.[130]

Alternative plans began to appear. Abe Stark, whose "Hit Sign, Win Suit" publicity on Ebbets Field's right-field wall had helped him become president of the city council, proposed building the stadium on a city-owned site known as the Parade Ground just south of Prospect Park in central Brooklyn.[131] Nobody liked the idea. Moses and O'Malley trashed it, as did the Brooklyn Parks Department.[132] Stark was soon saying he was not committed to any particular site.[133]

In mid-April Moses took O'Malley on a tour of the former World's Fair site in Flushing Meadows, Queens. O'Malley had raised the possibility of the site in a meeting at Moses's home earlier in the month.[134] Moses now proposed the city would build the Dodgers a fifty-thousand-seat stadium, costing between $10 and $12 million. Moses, who had previously resisted all efforts to give up Parks Department property, indicated he was feeling pressure from Wagner.[135] The Queens politicians said that was a good idea, drawing a sharp rebuke from Cashmore. O'Malley was mulling other sites in Queens. There was a veterans housing project near the corner of what is now the Long Island Expressway and Queens Boulevard. The project was being abandoned, the property was available, and the site combined highway access to Long Island with a stop for two subway lines and easy access to several more.[136] The two men discussed both projects, and Moses went ahead with drawing up plans for his preferred site. No more was heard about O'Malley's proposed site.

Many Brooklynites were appalled. Cashmore said he was "shocked and surprised" and intimated Moses was being sneaky by not running it past Cashmore in advance. O'Malley was as noncommittal as he had been in Vero Beach a few weeks earlier with the Los Angeles delegation. "If and when this latest reported possibility ever achieves political maturity, I will be pleased to discuss it in detail." The Borough Hall demonstration signs now began to target Queens and Moses.[137] Dodger underlings echoed the "Queens isn't Brooklyn" argument, evidently unaware of O'Malley's April flirtation with Queens and Moses.

In Los Angeles they spent a fair amount of time in the weeks following the Vero Beach meeting trying to figure out how to finance a stadium for the Dodgers.[138] They had taken his "Milwaukee-style" idea as a proposal rather than a talking point. They were, in effect, a captive of their own history. The conventional wisdom was that all the attempts to lure a team to Los Angeles earlier in the decade had foundered on the city's lack of a Major League–quality ballpark and that the solution was for the city to build one.[139]

In early May O'Malley was back in Los Angeles, wearing a "Keep the Dodgers in Brooklyn" button and hoping for a firm offer from the city. He did not get it. The city was starting to hedge. The staff had examined the city and county statutes and concluded that Poulson and Hahn had been overly enthusiastic in what they had offered and in their confidence about overcoming obstacles. O'Malley had also overreached in his term sheet. City attorney Roger Arnebergh had to tell O'Malley the city could not give him 500, or maybe 600, acres in Chavez Ravine as well as certain tax breaks Poulson or Hahn had blithely promised. For example, a pledge that the Coliseum Commission, which had not been represented at the Vero Beach talks, would rent its facilities to the Dodgers for $1 a year could not be honored.[140] In fact, Arnebergh said, negotiations would have to start over.[141] O'Malley made another helicopter tour over Chavez Ravine and concluded the Coliseum might do for exhibition games, but nothing permanent.[142] He remained noncommittal about moving.

In the meetings Los Angeles officials and O'Malley produced what came to be called the Arnebergh Memorandum of terms for negotiations. It was, said Arnebergh, "what Mr. O'Malley indicated in his opinion would be the minimum offer which would be considered by any major league club."[143] The memo proposed:

- The city would put together a parcel of approximately 350 acres in Chavez Ravine and turn it over to the Dodgers.
- The city or county would pay for access roads and superficial paving of the parking lots.
- The property would be kept on the tax rolls.
- The property must be developed with a Major League stadium, but no other deed restrictions would be sought. The stadium must be built by the Dodgers, and the team must move there.
- The Wrigley Field property must be turned over to the city, with a restriction that Major League Baseball could not be played there.
- The Dodgers must build and maintain recreational facilities at adjoining Elysian Park with the details to be determined.
- The Dodgers must create a Knothole Gang program to provide free tickets to juveniles.[144]

Clearly, O'Malley had retreated from his forward position at the Vero Beach meetings. He now was committed to building the stadium himself, giving up Wrigley Field, and paying property taxes. But there were matters to clear up. Poulson made a trip to Washington to clarify the city's title to the Chavez Ravine property. The federal government had conveyed it to the city with the provision it was must be used for a public purpose. In New York Robert Moses was arguing that a privately owned baseball club was not a public purpose. Poulson wanted some assurance the law could be interpreted to allow it.[145] Changes were made to the deed.[146] Hahn wanted more information about the cost of roads around the stadium.[147] Poulson had to get reelected, which he was, and to convince an increasingly fractious city council to include a $2 million provision in the city budget for an open-ended fund to help lure Major League Baseball.[148] The city began condemnation proceedings to buy the parcels it would need around the Chavez Ravine property it already owned.[149] The Coliseum Commission, which was trying to build an enclosed arena for basketball, circuses, and other events, wanted assurances from O'Malley that he had dropped his plans for a domed stadium. O'Malley said Los Angeles's desert-dry summers meant there was no need for a dome.[150]

O'Malley's visit also produced some progress on bringing the Giants to San Francisco. He met with Poulson, Christopher, and Matty Fox of Skiatron. At about nine, according to Poulson, O'Malley called Stoneham in New York. Stoneham, who had guests, could not talk, but called back soon after. O'Malley said Stoneham, who had a ballpark waiting in Minneapolis, was dubious about what kind of deal the Giants could get in San Francisco, so O'Malley suggested Christopher could come to New York and discuss it with him. By May 10 Christopher was talking with Stoneham on his home turf. Actually, it was more O'Malley's home turf, the Hotel Lexington in Manhattan, which O'Malley had helped with financial problems decades earlier. During the discussion the question of terms at a city-owned stadium arose. Christopher said he was unfamiliar with stadium contracts and asked O'Malley for some ideas. O'Malley grabbed a Hotel Lexington envelope and scribbled terms on the back. Christopher and Stoneham both agreed these were acceptable.[151] Christopher announced a preliminary agreement had been reached, but Stoneham said he hoped to stay in New York.[152] Commissioner Ford Frick asked everyone not to talk about possible franchise moves.[153]

Now, Stark came back with another proposal. Ebbets Field could be expanded to fifty thousand seats with five thousand parking spaces. O'Malley was not impressed. "Mr. Stark continues to add confusion to what would have been a simple solution had he given initial support," he said, referring to the Atlantic and Flatbush Avenues site.[154] Dodger fans were getting activated, incorporating as Keep the Dodgers in Brooklyn, Inc.[155] And the Wagner administration put a damper on Moses's Flushing proposal by saying only two specific stadium sites were under official study, the two areas at Atlantic and Flatbush. Nevertheless, the city council threw another site on the table, at Pennsylvania Avenue and the Belt Parkway in far southeast Brooklyn.[156] It was very convenient for cars, but there were no subway stops nearby.

There was also some good news in late May. The National League approved the Dodgers' and the Giants' moves to the West Coast, but only if they moved together.[157] Also, Los Angeles County voters passed a bond issue including funds for some of the street-realignment work around a stadium.[158]

Walter O'Malley was feeling the leverage. The day after the National League's decision, Wagner asked O'Malley for a quick meeting. O'Malley dodged, pleading the "pressure of engagements." One of the engagements was with Norris Poulson, in town to further his city's bid. Los Angeles "tastes blood," Poulson said after the meeting. "I am more encouraged at every stage of developments." Wagner managed to rope O'Malley and Stoneham into a meeting the next Tuesday.[159]

But there was also less promising news for the Dodgers' staying in New York. Getting ready for the Tuesday meeting, Wagner administration officials huddled with Madigan & Hyland executives, who shared some of their preliminary analysis. Looking at the costs and potential revenues of the Long Island Rail Road site (on the north side of Atlantic and Flatbush), they estimated it would take annual income of $2.1 million to cover the costs of upkeep and retiring the bonds that would be used for construction. O'Malley had suggested $500,000 would be the most the Dodgers would be willing to pay. The new estimates were passed to Wagner.[160] The *New York Post* surveyed members of the Board of Estimate and found they were overwhelmingly opposed to subsidizing either the Dodgers or the Giants.[161]

The Tuesday meeting was, as a *Times* headline described it, "A Scoreless Tie." Wagner did not get a firm answer from either man about whether they were staying or going. Neither owner got any firm commitments about what the city would do. Patience was counseled, and O'Malley promised to wait and study the Madigan & Hyland report, said to be due in mid-July.[162]

In mid-June George V. McLaughlin, O'Malley's old mentor in the Brooklyn Trust days and now vice chairman of Moses's Triborough Bridge Authority, came up with a variation of Moses's Flushing Meadows plan. McLaughlin, who unsuccessfully had tried to buy the Giants from Horace Stoneham a week or so earlier, proposed the city build a stadium and parking lots at the Flushing Meadow site while McLaughlin put together a private investor group to raise $5 million and buy an unnamed Major League franchise. His bid for another National League franchise was quickly shot down by league president Warren Giles, and there was another idea that went nowhere.[163]

Later that month O'Malley was in Washington to testify at a hearing of Congressman Emanuel Celler's committee looking into baseball's antitrust exemption. But Celler, a Brooklyn Democrat, was not interested in the Brooklyn owner's positions on that issue. Instead, he questioned O'Malley up, down, and sideways about whether he was going to move the Dodgers to Los Angeles. In slightly different words O'Malley said the same thing he had been saying since the Los Angeles offer had appeared. He did not know what he was going to do, and until the exact parameters of the two cities' offers became clear, he was not going to decide.[164] Celler kept boring in, and O'Malley started dancing. Confronted with "the Arnebergh Memorandum," which O'Malley had brought to the committee, O'Malley characterized it as "an idea" that might apply to any club interested in Los Angeles.[165] Arnebergh had said it might apply to any club, but it was O'Malley's list of minimum conditions.

By mid-July Stoneham was telling the same hearing that he was definitely going to San Francisco.[166] The team's stockholders approved the switch three weeks later.[167] O'Malley was still not committing publicly, but another piece had fallen into place. On July 13 the Dodgers staged Gil Hodges Night in honor of their veteran first baseman. Cashmore and Wagner were introduced in the pregame ceremonies. Both were booed.[168]

In late July, three months after O'Malley's last visit, Los Angeles finally named Chad McClellan as its negotiator. McClellan had been to one professional baseball game in his entire life, but he had an array of business successes and public service. The son of a minister, he had been born in Crow's Landing, a spot on the map of central California, in 1897. His father's work was not lucrative, and his mother was often ill. After Pepperdine College he worked as a salesman and then sales manager for a creamery, before buying a decrepit paint plant at the age of thirty. He built Old Colony Paint and Chemical into a medium-size business and got involved in business community affairs, starting with the Merchants and Manufacturers Association of Los Angeles. The presidency of that organization led him to the National Association of Manufacturers, where he gained notice with his calm arbitration of a factional dispute. By 1953 he was the organization's president. In 1955 President Dwight Eisenhower chose him to be assistant secretary of commerce for international affairs, a post he had left a couple of months before being tapped by Poulson.[169]

McClellan was handed a copy of the Arnebergh Memorandum and asked to craft a deal within those parameters. McClellan set about getting all the details he could find about such matters as acreage, zoning, topography, and deed restrictions. But he found the earlier enthusiastic presentations of local officials had created expectations with O'Malley that were going to be difficult to handle. In addition, unlike in New York, Los Angeles officials were pressing to get things done and were critical he did not go to Brooklyn right away.[170]

On August 5 the final Madigan & Hyland report began to circulate through New York City staff offices. It was even more pessimistic than the figures slipped to Wagner before his June 4 meeting with O'Malley and Stoneham. The project would require $2.5 million in annual payments for bond repayments and maintenance. There was no firm word from the city, but the staff memos were negative or pessimistic.[171]

Within the Los Angeles City Council, Poulson and Wyman were counting noses. They had eight solid votes out of the ten needed. And they had four council members they were sure would never vote to approve any Dodger deal. Their job was to make sure two of the remaining three stuck with the plan.[172]

Three weeks after his appointment McClellan made it to Brooklyn and spent August 21 going over the possible outlines of a deal. McClellan described it as "an exchange of problems."[173] The 500 acres that were discussed in Vero Beach in March had shrunk to 350 acres at the May meeting, but McClellan had to tell O'Malley that there was no way the city could put together more than 307 acres and that a city reservoir on the site could not be moved. McClellan also had to explain that there could be no direct city subsidies to any private-sector project, including a baseball stadium. Indirect help, in the form of road connections, could be provided. He also had to bring up the issue of mineral rights, a hot-button issue in Los Angeles, where oil discoveries in the first half of the century had made ordinary home owners rich. The antis harping on the oil issue had forced the city to include mineral rights in the negotiations.[174]

Sensing a cooling in Los Angeles's ardor, O'Malley made another offer. He offered to buy the land at the Atlantic-Flatbush site and build a stadium, both with his own money. He did say the land would have to be made available at "a common-sense figure."[175] This was the same proposal, among others, he had made previously, but it was treated as a concession by the New York papers, hungry for reassurance. Moses said the Atlantic Avenue site was dead and pushed once again for the Flushing Meadows site.[176]

On September 9 Nelson Rockefeller, his eye on the governor's chair, announced his effort to keep the Dodgers.[177] As it crystallized it called on the city to condemn one of the Atlantic-Flatbush sites for $8 million. A Rockefeller-organized group would then buy the site for $2 million and lease it to the Dodgers, who would build the stadium. The Board of Estimate could not stomach the subsidy of $6 million to cover the price of the land, and when Rockefeller changed the terms to please the board, O'Malley said the offer now priced him out of the proposal.[178]

The ball was completely in Los Angeles's court. After McClellan's August 21 meeting, phone follow-ups, and a trip to Rawlins, Wyoming, where O'Malley was hunting, McClellan won approval from the city council on September 16 for an offer that included "about 300 acres" and a promise of up to $2 million in city investments. In return, O'Malley was to turn over the Wrigley Field property to the city and agree that forty acres of the new ballpark site would be leased to the city for recreational purposes. The Dodgers agreed to spend up to $500,000 on this property to install tennis courts, baseball fields, and other recreational facilities and to maintain them at $60,000 a year for twenty years. At the end of that period the land would revert to the Dodgers. McClellan said O'Malley had not agreed to these terms, but from the conversations McClellan knew most were agreeable to him.[179]

Some were not, and the difficulties quickly became apparent. O'Malley did not like giving up half the mineral rights. He was also concerned at the hostility he perceived from a bloc within the city council that was resisting the agreement. He told McClellan he felt ill-used by New York politicians and did not want to go where he was not wanted.[180] He also insisted on a promise that there would be no amusement tax on tickets and got a letter outside the agreement on that issue.[181] McClellan tried to reassure him, but O'Malley was still noncommittal. "Los Angeles has made me the most concrete offer to date. However, we are still keeping an open mind in New York," O'Malley said after his return from Rawlins.[182] This was after Rockefeller's initial proposal.

And there were still smoke screens. Poulson said he had received feelers from other teams, and "we aren't doing the spade work for Brooklyn alone."[183] Del Webb said he would sell his stake in the Yankees and partner with the Kansas City Athletics owners to bring them to Los Angeles if the Dodgers and the city could not work things out.[184]

The city council was still hung up on the oil issue. Trying to placate the vocal opposition, the city insisted O'Malley make available a parcel within the three hundred acres that could be used for drilling. O'Malley, who had checked with oil industry people, did not feel he was losing anything by giving up the oil rights, but as the opposition mounted and the tone got nasty, he dug in his heels. He demanded half of any profits from the oil and got it. But that raised another stink within the council, which was approaching its final vote. Listening to his council supporters, O'Malley announced that, if there ever were any profits from oil, the Dodgers' share would be donated to youth sports programs.[185] There never were any.

Eventually, on October 7, after a day of sometimes coherent debate, the city council approved the deal.[186] O'Malley had still made no commitment, another factor that had raised questions from the city council members who were challenging the contract. On the eve of the final vote, councilwoman Rosalind Wyman called O'Malley seeking a commitment she could use in the expected debate the next day. He would not give it.[187] As soon as he got word of the favorable vote, though, he announced the move. "Get your wheel barrow and shovel. Will see you at Chavez Ravine," O'Malley telegraphed Poulson.[188]

When exactly Walter O'Malley decided to move is a question whose answer defines loyalties. For the "Hitler, Stalin, and Walter O'Malley" school, it was early, and the entire 1957 season was spent in a cynical attempt to draw every last attendance dollar out of Brooklyn.[189] For the loyal Angeleno, it was very late.[190]

The supposed dates are various. Buzzie Bavasi reported there was a meeting in either the winter of 1956–57 or June 1957 when O'Malley took a poll of top Dodger executives. All but one voted to stay. O'Malley was the one, Bavasi said.[191] Others would place it with the underfunding of the Brooklyn Sports Authority in December 1956 or the purchase of the Angels franchise in February 1957, or, as with Hahn, at the World Series of 1956.[192] Dick Young put it in spring training 1957, after Poulson and the Los Angeles delegation had left. At the daily cocktail hour Young asked O'Malley, off the record, what was the worst thing that could happen to him. "I'll tell you, but you can't write it. The worst thing that could happen would be for New York to come up with an offer good enough to keep us there," Young quoted O'Malley as saying.[193]

Soon after the underfunding of the Brooklyn Sports Authority, O'Malley himself wrote to city councilman Joseph T. Sharkey, saying, "It appears pretty definite that the stadium project is dying a slow death, the result of malnutrition."[194] By late March he was writing Frank Schroth, "My efforts from now on will be quite seriously in the direction of a move."[195] That was the third paragraph of a letter. But by the seventh paragraph he was seeing potential to get Moses interested in the Fort Greene Meat Market project again. "Now you see the inconsistency of the Irish mind," he told Schroth in the last paragraph. "In one paragraph, I am sailing to a distant port and in the last above one, I am still trying to keep an anchor in Brooklyn."[196] He was also subject to a baseball rule, reinforced by Frick in mid-1957, that franchise moves were not to be discussed during the season.

With O'Malley's dithering, his public circumspection, his refusal to commit either way, and his sly answers to questions, it seems obvious to conclude he was playing off the two cities against each other. Los Angeles, in his mind, had started off in 1953 as nothing more than leverage. But as New York officials dawdled the leverage looked more attractive, and when Los Angeles responded promptly and enthusiastically, albeit awkwardly, he began leaning further in that direction. However, there was always hope, backed by his business acumen. The hope was based in lingering sentiment for the city he had grown up in, a sentiment reinforced by the fact that his wife, children, top executives, and many acquaintances did not want the Dodgers to move.[197] In O'Malley's business brain that may not have counted for a great deal, but it counted for something. His abortive examination of a Queens site in April 1957 indicates that indecision still reigned.

The business part of his brain asked him why he would leave the biggest market in the world. It asked him why he would leave a market where he had been the most profitable operator of the past decade. It asked why he would leave the political and business contacts of a lifetime. It asked him if he would really risk his other major business property, the New York Subways Advertising Company. That business had the franchise to sell advertising throughout the city's subways. It was liable to boycott, especially from the city's control of the subways, and he was already receiving indications of possible retribution by the city.[198] As the summer of 1957 wore on, it also asked him about the reliability of these people from Los Angeles who kept reneging on promises and trimming their offer. It also asked, as opposition arose within the city council, if they really wanted him.

His sale of the Ebbets Field property in October 1956 had left him without a firm future or any leverage. He could rely on a city administration that had demonstrated again and again that it really was not all that interested. Or he could keep Ebbets Field open for a few more years and then maybe camp at the Polo Grounds or Yankee Stadium. These, like Moses's offer in Flushing Meadows, or Chavez Ravine, were not in Brooklyn.

He needed one city or the other to make him a definite stadium offer, just to ensure the Dodgers had a place to play when the agreement with Marvin Kratter ran out. New York dithered. Los Angeles's overenthusiastic politicians stumbled again and again. As soon as one of them made an offer he could believe in, he immediately took it.

That returns us to the question of why New York could not work something out in a timely fashion. Undoubtedly, Moses was a major factor. His power was immense, and his opposition began a few days after O'Malley's first contact. It was blunt and communicated to many whom O'Malley counted on for support. O'Malley certainly thought that was where the blame lay.[199] As Robert Caro said, "Not that Moses was solely to blame for the team leaving but that it would have been so easy for him to keep it here."[200]

But Robert Moses was not omnipotent. He would be outmaneuvered on other major projects in the 1950s by savvy operators and community groups.[201] O'Malley clearly understood this was a possibility, and all of his efforts to mobilize his political supporters and raise the level of concern among Dodger fans were aimed in this direction. O'Malley failed in this because he did not perceive where the Dodgers stood in the collective consciousness of New Yorkers. More than a half century later, after decades of bombardment by the committed fans who still had been attending Dodger games, after the rants of New York sportswriters concerned their jobs were disappearing, it is hard for today's observers to think that not every single person in New York was deeply concerned that the Dodgers would leave. It was a delusion shared by even as tough-minded a thinker as Dick Young. Through the summer of 1957, as Young stepped up his rhetoric against O'Malley's "greed," he also railed against the city's politicians and warned them that their halfhearted efforts would lead to their defeat at the polls that fall.[202] Wagner sensed otherwise and, in fact, would not only win reelection by the largest plurality ever, but get 75 percent of the votes in Brooklyn less than a month after O'Malley's announcement.[203] Cashmore, who was a steady Dodger supporter, said he got five letters total about the Dodgers versus five hundred on fluoridation.[204]

The Dodgers had never been a priority for Wagner. He was happy to hold a meeting, promise help, and wring his hands. But when, a few weeks after O'Malley's first attempt at leverage with the announcement of the Jersey City games, he gave his priorities to the city's Planning Commission, he did not mention a stadium for the Dodgers. Instead, the "vital" issues were education, pollution control, public transit, and waterfront development.[205] An examination of letters and telegrams preserved in the Robert Wagner Papers in the New York City Archive shows that correspondents were pretty well split between those who begged him to help the Dodgers and those who told him not to waste taxpayers' dollars subsidizing private enterprise. If anything, the latter were more preponderant.

In fact, it was a priority only for some Brooklyn leaders, and they were undercut by the pact of 1898, when Brooklyn had ceased to be the fourth-largest city in the country and instead became just another borough of New York City. John Cashmore, Brooklyn's borough president, worked hard for a Dodger stadium during this period. But, as with the necessity for a city council majority to request the Brooklyn Sports Authority bill from the legislature or Moses's proposal of the Flushing Meadows site, other boroughs' desires could inhibit unified city response. Even the Brooklyn delegation was not of one mind. Abe Stark, the Brooklyn clothing store owner, was president of the city council when it considered the Brooklyn Sports Authority measure. He voted against it, a move interpreted as a bid for city-wide support in a mayoral race.[206] O'Malley recognized these difficulties. "If the man in Queens won't vote for this to be done in Brooklyn and the man in the Bronx won't vote for it, then Mr. Moses gets disgusted with the whole thing and says let's put them over in Flushing Meadows," he said.[207]

The effort was also hurt by O'Malley's focus on the Atlantic and Flatbush Avenues site. For train and subway connections it was clearly excellent, but for the Long Islanders and other suburbanites who might want to drive, the site required maneuvering crowded city streets for several miles, often at a particularly bad time of day. He consistently brushed aside proposals from other groups, both those outside Brooklyn and those raised by groups from New Lots or Bay Ridge. Early on he dismissed the possibility of expanding Ebbets, but a combination of city help in closing streets and creating parking, plus the use of the Polo Grounds or Yankee Stadium for a year or two, might well have worked.

There is a serious question of whether it was realistic to think that, in that city and time, it was possible to build a downtown ballpark. Robert Wagner, reflecting several years later, did not think so. "The idea of municipalities building stadiums or helping in the building of stadiums was not really politically possible in New York City in 1957," he told author Harvey Frommer.[208] Clearly, Milwaukee, Baltimore, and Kansas City had laid out considerable sums building or expanding ballparks to attract Major League Baseball earlier in the decade. But they were not New York. Aside from its self-image, everything was bigger and more expensive in New York. The seemingly never-ending round of committee meetings and studies that frustrated O'Malley in New York is simply the way big cities work.

And then there was the cost. When O'Malley did his first arithmetic in the early 1950s, he concluded he could not afford the downtown ballpark he wanted. Thus, he turned to the city to help subsidize the cost of putting together the needed acreage. At that point he suggested the subsidy (not what he would have called it) would be $6 million. Through the next several years that figure would move, but never downward. For too many people in the city at that time, the size of that subsidy was simply too large. Given O'Malley reluctance to examine sites in the less expensive parts of the borough, the likelihood of success was reduced.

It is unclear whether O'Malley recognized how some of the people he thought were key supporters were actually in Moses's thrall. Consistently, O'Malley used Frank Schroth and *New York Daily News* publisher M. F. "Jack" Flynn to set up his meetings with Moses and act as intermediary. And, consistently, Flynn's and Schroth's letters to Moses show that although they supported a new stadium for the Dodgers, they regularly deferred to Moses's arguments on specific proposals.[209] Even his old mentor, George McLaughlin, cautioned O'Malley from mid-1953 that Moses was unlikely to respond positively.[210] McLaughlin, with Brooklyn Trust sold, had lost his abiding interest in that borough. He was living in Manhattan and working closely with Moses. His once regular meetings with O'Malley became less frequent.

O'Malley also failed to get New Yorkers to believe he really meant to pay for the stadium himself. In part, that was due to his waffling when the only offer on the table was a city-owned stadium, but it was also that he failed to break through the clutter no matter how many times he tried to distinguish between the city paying for land for the stadium and the team paying the costs of building it. As late as June 1957 Congressman John Rooney, who represented a working-class district in West Brooklyn, said, "Let the Dodgers move to Los Angeles if the alternative is to succumb to an arrogant demand to spend the taxpayers' money to build a stadium for them in Brooklyn."[211]

The Dodger fans must also share some of the blame. Back in 1952, when he finally had firm control of the team, O'Malley noted that low attendance meant the team had less cash, and it also meant it would not have enough potential income to convince bankers that lending for a new stadium was a good idea.[212] Hence, he felt he needed the city to subsidize his land costs. The hard-core fans, those who still complain about the team's relocation today, kept coming, but the less committed fans were not creating profits at the level he needed to build a new stadium.

New Yorkers simply had a hard time believing O'Malley would leave the capital of the world, which was what New York was in the 1950s. Leonard Koppett, then working for the *New York Herald-Tribune*, said the first reaction was total disbelief. "The idea of the Dodgers leaving Brooklyn was inconceivable," he said.[213] "I guarantee you," said Buzzie Bavasi, "if you walked down Montague Street, where our offices were, on Oct. 7 [1957], you wouldn't have found two people who believed we were going to move. They laughed at the idea. No chance."[214] There was, thus, a large capacity for self-delusion with every twist and turn scrutinized for optimistic signs. After Stoneham announced he was moving the Giants, *Times* columnist Arthur Daley was convinced O'Malley had pulled off a coup, getting the National League market in the city all to himself and cementing a decision to stay.[215] In contrast to New York's lack of concern, Los Angeles believed and moved. It was a striver, not the complacent king of the hill.

All that would change with the Dodgers' move. New York politicians, despite the lack of political repercussions in 1957, would become concerned, and a $6 million subsidy to put together a stadium site would not seem so ridiculous. Wagner's administration would build a park in Flushing Meadows that would cost $28.5 million, three to four times the subsidy O'Malley had asked for. In 1970 the administration of John Lindsay, Wagner's successor, would spend $160 million refurbishing Yankee Stadium. Both of these stadiums would be replaced at even higher costs after 2000, with some support from the teams. The City and County of Los Angeles would spend less than $4 million and gain a development that would be on the property-tax rolls fifty years later.

In the aftermath, the New York writers, led by Dick Young, put it all down to O'Malley's "greed." It is clear the Dodgers had been the most profitable team in baseball from 1952 through 1956, the only O'Malley years for which figures are available. In those years the Dodgers earned profits of $1,860,744, a hair ahead of the Milwaukee Braves at $1,857,603. No other National League team came close to this figure. The only American League team over $1 million was the Yankees, at $1,444,339. This was clearly enough income to support the club, but not enough to build a new stadium. It would also not be enough to pay the rent envisioned for a city-owned stadium in the Madigan & Hyland report.

There is an old saying on Wall Street that investors are motivated by fear (of losses) or greed (for more gains). O'Malley's critics clearly saw greed. What they did not appreciate was fear. In many ways O'Malley and the Dodgers were facing the same situation that the American automobile industry faced in the 1950s. In Detroit profits were good, and so it was possible for the American manufacturers to ignore the Volkswagens and the coming Japanese manufacturers, keeping their heads firmly in the sand. O'Malley did not stick his head in the sand. He believed he needed a new stadium to stay competitive, and he probably needed a new television policy as well. In addition, he must have realized that his sale of Ebbets Field, unsuccessful in creating more leverage, had limited his options in New York. On the other hand, the powers that were in New York City clearly dropped the ball.

There was another interpretation. Frank Graham Jr., who had worked for O'Malley through much of the 1950s, said O'Malley had a strong desire to do something no one else had done. O'Malley wanted "to become a pioneer himself. That drove him against the wishes of his family and friends to break ground for the Dodgers in California.[216] It was an interpretation echoed by Braven Dyer, a *Los Angeles Times* reporter and columnist who spent a great deal of time talking to O'Malley in the early days. "I think that Walter O'Malley regards this move as a challenge, a pioneering step which ultimately will establish him as the most progressive executive the game of baseball has ever known."[217]

"They called me carpetbagger," Walter O'Malley told Roger Kahn. "One man wrote I left because I believed the colored, Puerto Ricans and Jews were taking over Brooklyn. Lies. Pejorative Lies. My son, Peter, came home from Penn and said, 'Dad, what are we going to do? The things in the papers are terrible.' They are, Peter, but they will pass and the great ball park I'm going to build in California will stand. That will be remembered—a monument to the O'Malleys."[218]

9

The Laughingstock
of the Country

As Walter O'Malley waved to a crowd greeting him at Los Angeles International Airport on October 23, 1957, he must have thought all his political troubles were over. There he was receiving scrolls from county supervisor Kenneth Hahn and city councilwoman Rosalind Wyman. Flashbulbs popped and cheering fans clapped as he ambled down the steps waving like a Rose Parade queen. Wyman, wrapped in a white coat and sporting a hat with LA on the front, led O'Malley to a microphone set up in front of television cameras.

He had it. He had gotten away from the trap he had felt in Brooklyn. The establishment in Los Angeles had come to him. The Los Angeles newspapers had flocked to the flag. That morning the *Los Angeles Times* had even described the Dodger party's planned route from the airport to their hotel, just in case some readers wanted to follow. Here to greet him were people screaming with joy at the prospect of paying him money to see the Dodgers. They had brought out the Inglewood Boys Band and the Drum City Jive Group. The University of California at Los Angeles (UCLA) had sent the Bruin Belles, and these sixty young ladies were showering O'Malley with chrysanthemum petals like some Roman hero returned from defeating the Germani. Surely, these were only the lead elements. Women pressed forward with cries of joy. Men pushed to shake his hand. City councilman John Ferraro, who barely a decade earlier had been an All-American football lineman at the University of Southern California (USC), found it impossible to force his way through the crowd to the dignitaries' section.[1]

But one other member of the crowd made it. The Los Angeles television audience saw the back of a man whose voice boomed into the microphone. "Mr. O'Malley, greetings from the citizens of Los Angeles. We're glad to have you here. Here's a summons from the people of the Chavez

Ravine." O'Malley kept a smile on his face, but looked down. Wyman's smile wavered to exasperation when "We're glad to have you here" wafted over the airwaves. A man holding a "We want the 'Bums,' not a Bum Deal" sign maneuvered in front of the camera. "What is this?" O'Malley asked. "Walter, just keep walking, I'll tell you later," Wyman said.[2]

O'Malley would not stop worrying for five years. Paradise it was. But Paradise had snakes, snakes filed lawsuits, and lawsuits cost time and money. It cost so much money that at times he was unsure he would make it, even in Paradise.

The political twists and turns of the next few years would go a long way toward undermining the picture of O'Malley as a schemer of Machiavellian proportions. Although he would eventually emerge at the top of the baseball world, with a strong, wealthy franchise in a beautiful team-owned stadium, in the country's second-largest metropolitan area, he would be blindsided politically so many times as to make him seem naive. "Who's the big guy out here? Who do I have to deal with?" O'Malley would ask plaintively.[3] The problem, he discovered, was different from New York. He had figured out eventually that the boss in New York was Robert Moses, and then found he could not outmaneuver him. In Los Angeles he discovered, there were not any bosses. The city council members and county supervisors he had dealt with had made their promises in good faith. Hampered by the vagaries of Los Angeles politics, they just could not deliver.

In those early days, it was near bliss in Los Angeles. There were a thousand people to greet him at the airport and more at the civic parade the next day. O'Malley and Kay rode in a white convertible, with his name emblazoned over the right rear wheel.[4] "There wasn't real euphoria until we had the parade," Wyman recalled. "Parades are a joke in LA," the Los Angeles native said, but "we staged one of the great parades of all time." At least by Los Angeles standards. Wyman shared a car in the parade with a Brooklyn native on the Dodgers named Sandy Koufax. As the parade cruised what Wyman thought were fantastically full streets, Koufax remarked, "We have more people crossing the street in New York than are out for this parade."[5]

O'Malley kept his priorities clear. It was a busy day, filled with courtesy calls on politicians and a large press conference. After the parade Buzzie Bavasi and Fresco Thompson went off to check Wrigley Field and see where the Dodgers would play in 1958. But O'Malley made his way up to the rutted gullies and rocky hills of Chavez Ravine, where he could envision the baseball stadium of his decade-old dream.[6]

The newspapers fawned. They exulted that O'Malley had Los Angeles Dodgers painted on the team plane already. They led off stories with phrases like "Personable Walter O'Malley . . ." The sports editor of the *Herald* headlined his October 24 column, "Give Me a Man Like O'Malley Every Time." And down in the column George Davis gushed, "Nobody coming to town ever made a more favorable impression than this man, who led us out of the baseball wilderness."[7] Vincent Flaherty, the Hearst columnist who had worked so hard to bring Major League Baseball to Los Angeles, wrote, "The Coming of the Dodgers was the pink-diffused dawning of a splendid new era for Los Angeles."[8]

On the following Monday a giant luncheon left Los Angeles agog with its own accomplishment. Although $6 tickets to the luncheon had been on sale only two days the previous week, eleven hundred had been snapped up. Joe E. Brown, the comic actor who was one of Hollywood's true baseball fans and whose son was the general manager of the Pittsburgh Pirates, served as master of ceremonies. The audience was filled with the bright lights of city politics, Hollywood, and the baseball scene. Two local television stations televised the event live for its full two-hour, twenty-minute length.

Branch Rickey, who was in town for hearings as a member of President Dwight Eisenhower's commission on fair hiring practices, was overwhelmed. "You and I have never seen anything like this reception and won't again," he said.[9] That was exactly what Los Angeles wanted to hear—validation. Baseball writer Rube Samuelsen of the suburban *Pasadena Star-News* lashed himself into a fervor of municipal self-congratulation in a dispatch to the *Sporting News*. "Now, surely, even the veriest skeptic must be convinced that major league baseball, a plethora of distractions and counter-attractions to the contrary, can't miss in Los Angeles. Nor can it miss being BIG." A banner strung across the front of the long head table showed a Brooklyn-esque skyline at one end and Los Angeles rendered as a baseball mitt on the other. A bat was propelling a ball from Brooklyn to Los Angeles, and the lettering shrieked, "The Greatest Catch in Baseball."

O'Malley, when introduced, made points with the Los Angeles crowd by immediately going out of his way to recognize Bob Cobb, who had been inadvertently left out during Brown's introductions. Cobb, one of the earliest boosters of Los Angeles as a Major League city and the first to recognize Chavez Ravine's potential as a baseball park, took pains to deny rumors he was a backer of a referendum seeking to overturn the Dodgers' deal with the city.[10]

O'Malley himself turned on the charm, and it worked. One writer compared him to Dale Carnegie, the saint of salesmen who had written *How to Win Friends and Influence People*. "The Walter O'Malley who charmed the baseball fans at International Airport the other night when he made his first public appearance in the city of his choice certainly proved himself to be a far different person than the one we've been reading about recently in stories emanating from New York," wrote Paul Zimmerman of the *Los Angeles Times*. "Unless there has been a case of mistaken identity, this forthright and witty gentleman who stepped off the Los Angeles Dodgers' airplane must have undergone a complete metamorphosis during the half day it took to fly from Gotham to our fair city."

O'Malley was emotional, responding to the positive feelings flowing through the city that first week. "You can feel it at every turn—on the streets, in the cabs, all over the city. People, in welcoming us, make us feel they mean it and we want you to be proud of the day you decided to make the Dodgers the Los Angeles Dodgers."

No doubt O'Malley was also overjoyed that the response was not merely emotional. Although the luncheon was only his fifth day in town (and two of the days had been over a weekend), the team had already taken in 5,000 season ticket requests. Buzzie Bavasi reported he left the luncheon with another 113 stuffed into his pockets.[11] Mayor Norris Poulson passed on the requests that were flooding into his office from the city's glitterati— Jack Warner and Mervyn LeRoy of Warner Bros.; Ben P. Griffith, president of the Water & Power Commission; James L. Beebe of the Chamber of Commerce; James Ruman of 20th Century Fox; and Kent Redwine of the Motion Picture Producers Association. By late November Bavasi was reporting that Los Angeles fans already had bought more season tickets than the team had ever sold in Brooklyn. And, he added, they were paying the full tab up front rather than just making a deposit.[12]

Bavasi was doing more than taking ticket orders that first week. O'Malley had Bavasi and manager Walter Alston along to begin building interest in the coming season. Groups of local officials and newspaper reporters met with both men. Bavasi talked about the team's possible schedule, the number of night games, use of the team plane to fly the team, and the state of the farm system. Alston ran through his lineup and his prospects, neatly putting a little extra emphasis on Los Angeles natives Don Drysdale and Duke Snider.[13] And O'Malley announced he would be moving his family to Los Angeles.[14]

Legal action to overturn the city's agreement with the Dodgers would dominate O'Malley's time and efforts over the next few years, but his immediate problem was where his team would play the 1958 season. He had gotten off the plane ready, if not eager, to use Wrigley Field as the Dodgers' Los Angeles home for the year or two (surely, no more) that it would take to build his stadium.[15] Wrigley Field had come to him when he bought the Los Angeles Angels. It was the jewel of the Pacific Coast League stadiums—a double-decked, cream-colored, red-roofed classic with a distinctive clock tower looming behind the stands a few feet to the first base side of home plate. The stadium had cost William Wrigley Jr. (Philip's father) $1.1 million to build in 1925 at the corner of Forty-Second Place and Avalon Boulevard.[16] The park served as a stadium for Wrigley's Pacific Coast League Angels and a spring training field for his Chicago Cubs. When Wrigley Field opened it was the only park of that name in professional baseball, for Chicago's Wrigley Field, which had debuted in 1914, would remain Cubs Park for another couple of years.

The two Wrigley Fields shared more than name and ownership. Both were designed by Zachary Taylor Davis, who also had designed the original Comiskey Park for the Chicago White Sox. Both had ivy-covered walls, at least in left field. And both were "friendly confines" for hitters. Even more than Chicago's park, Los Angeles's Wrigley Field was a bandbox. Whereas Los Angeles's Wrigley's foul-line distances were fairly respectable, the outfield walls angled slightly toward home plate as they stretched toward center field, rather than away as in most ballparks. That meant the park's power alleys, the angle at which a batter was most likely to hit a ball well, measured a short 345 feet.[17]

Wrigley Field's dimensions made it a natural when the television program *Home Run Derby* was conceived. The program, which was filmed in the late 1950s and appeared on cable television reruns into the 1990s, matched home run hitters such as Mickey Mantle, Willie Mays, and the Dodgers' own Gil Hodges to see who could pop the most balls out of the park. So near Hollywood, Wrigley was also an attractive set for moviemakers and had appeared in the background of many films.

Over the years the park and the clock tower had become well known. Trolley and bus lines ran nearby. It was only three and a half miles southwest of city hall. But now, to O'Malley's eye, Wrigley Field looked an awful lot like Ebbets Field. It could seat 21,500, about two-thirds of Ebbets Field's capacity. The attendance record was 23,497 for an Angels–Hollywood Stars game in 1952, but that included standees. Buzzie Bavasi, after an October tour of Los Angeles, said he thought the capacity could be pushed to 28,000 rather easily, and that would allow attendance of maybe 1.4 million for 1958, but there was also some talk the Los Angeles Memorial Coliseum might be used for some big games.[18] Wrigley had more parking spaces than Ebbets, but still far fewer than would be needed, especially in a city as dependent on the car as Los Angeles. And, O'Malley knew, it carried the tinge of being a "Minor League" ballpark when he was trying to project a totally Major League image.[19] It did not help that Wrigley was on the edge of a neighborhood getting steadily poorer and blacker. O'Malley began doing business out of the twelfth floor of the Statler Hotel in downtown Los Angeles rather than in the clock-tower offices.

The uncertainty was one indication that the move to Los Angeles had not been thought out as thoroughly as it should have been and another blow to the critics who argue O'Malley had it all planned in advance. Angelenos were throwing money at him to buy seats, and he did not know where those seats would be. The ticket department, which had been placed in the Wrigley Field offices, was being overwhelmed with orders, a "bushel" of them, then ticket manager Harold Parrott recalled.[20] Dodger vice president Red Patterson said all of the applications for season tickets had been snapped up. He had been forced to rush more into print and out to the offices distributing them.[21] Another Dodger official told the *Los Angeles Times*, "I don't see how we will be able to accommodate our fans in Wrigley Field."[22] By early November 500,000 tickets had already been sold, bringing more than $1 million in revenue.[23]

On a May 1957 tour O'Malley had rejected the Coliseum as a baseball address.[24] He acknowledged the team might play a few exhibition games there, but said it was unsuitable for permanent use. He also criticized Wrigley Field. Undoubtedly, at that point he was more concerned with saying the things that would get him his own stadium—and keep his options open in Brooklyn—rather than coldly analyzing either site as a real ballpark. But with the certified checks piling up at the corner of Forty-Second and Avalon, the Coliseum and its 102,000 seats was starting to look more and more suitable.

The Coliseum had been conceived and built by the Los Angeles establishment in the 1920s as part of a plan to promote tourism and, more specifically, attract the Olympic Games. It was governed by a nine-person board, whose members were appointed equally by the mayor of Los Angeles, Los

Angeles County's governing Board of Supervisors, and the governor of California. Opened in 1923 at a cost of $800,000, the stadium seated 75,000. When the 1932 Olympics loomed, the capacity was expanded to 104,000 at a cost of an additional $1.1 million. Later adjustments had cut capacity by 2,000 seats. The Coliseum was an oval bowl laid out on an east-west axis, with the playing field sunk well below street level. Its seats banked gradually back from the running track that surrounded the football field at its center. Most customers would take a dank ground-level tunnel through the concrete, emerging over the football field about a third of the way up the banked seats.

Only at the far eastern end was the symmetry of pale-gray concrete broken. There, a series of Grecian columns supported arches, providing a grand entrance from a park facing Figueroa Street, which led directly to downtown Los Angeles, about three miles northeast. Locals called the entrance the peristyle end and used it to orient themselves in the vast sameness of the interior. But as a grand entrance it was basically useless. Because the peristyle reduced the number of available seats, the football field was located at the far western end.

The Coliseum was the center of Los Angeles's sports world. The NFL's Los Angeles Rams played there, as did both the USC Trojan and the UCLA Bruin football teams. Big track meets, high school football games, religious rallies, Fourth of July fireworks shows, and rodeos dotted the Coliseum's schedule of some fifty to sixty events a year.

The idea of using the Coliseum for Major League Baseball had been percolating for nearly a decade. It was the best-known sports facility in a booming city, and its size dwarfed eastern baseball stadiums. The Coliseum's surface area for the football field and track was larger than the entire lot on which Ebbets Field sat.[25] A diagram surfaced in the *Sporting News* in 1947 showing a possible layout for a diamond, and a West Virginia man wrote in, suggesting an alternative configuration.[26] The idea reappeared occasionally thereafter, but never seriously. The proponents all seemed to come from Los Angeles. Onetime Cleveland Indians and St. Louis Browns owner Bill Veeck, commissioned by Philip Wrigley to study Los Angeles as a site for Major League ball, nixed the Coliseum after a 1953 visit. It would cost too much, maybe $2.5 million to $3 million, to make the necessary changes, Veeck said. You would need a new press box, more lighting, better drainage, seats instead of benches, a canopy to cover at least some of the stands, plus some box seats. Then you would have to cut away some of the concrete to make decent foul-line distances. He also did not like the heat, the ban on beer sales, and problems scheduling events with the existing football tenants. Veeck thought it would be a better idea to expand Wrigley Field, which his client just happened to own. He said that for a similar price tag, Wrigley Field in Los Angeles could be pushed close to fifty thousand seats and given adequate parking. The plan was short on specifics.[27]

O'Malley knew the Coliseum had many of the problems of Wrigley Field. It was located in roughly the same neighborhood, about a mile northwest of Wrigley. It had much more parking than Wrigley did, but not anywhere near what was needed for capacity crowds. Both stadiums were famous for the hardheaded acumen of the neighbors who rented their lawns for parking. In November 1957 Bob MacAlwain of Buena Park wrote the *Los Angeles Mirror-News* to complain he had been hit for $3.50 to park on a Coliseum neighbor's lawn during a recent Rams–San Francisco 49ers game. That was the Dodgers' projected price for a box seat.[28]

And the Coliseum had problems all its own. As Veeck and MacAlwain noted, beer sales were banned. MacAlwain and other locals feared what the Coliseum, an airless bowl, would be like on one of the city's one-hundred-degree summer days. Although the Coliseum Commission that oversaw it was eager for more tenants, the existing tenants were numerous and had priority. The Dodgers would have to schedule around the football teams in the fall. The traditional big July 4 fireworks show raised money for charity, and the Dodgers would have to forego that lucrative date.

The city had shared many of O'Malley's assumptions about Wrigley Field, and officials were ill-prepared to deal with an alternative. As word that O'Malley was dissatisfied with Wrigley sifted through the city's networks in late October, the Coliseum Commission floated a field design that clearly reflected more concern with protecting their current tenants than with attracting the Dodgers. It positioned the diamond at the peristyle end.[29] It was an offer begging to be refused. O'Malley centered his remarks on the placement of the playing field, which had home plate in the southeast corner of the stadium. He pointed out that the late-afternoon and early-evening sun would be shining into the batters' eyes as they stood at the plate. Virtually all professional baseball parks located home plate at their southwest corners to avoid this problem. He did not say it as loudly, although it undoubtedly registered higher on his personal decibel scale, but the Coliseum Commission's plan cut sharply into the supply of seats near home plate, the kind of seats for which he could charge higher prices.

The columns and arches of the peristyle end took away two-thirds of the potential seats along the proposed first base foul line.[30]

When the financial terms of the offer were revealed in early December, O'Malley did not like them either. The Coliseum Commission wanted the same 10 percent of the ticket gross paid by the football teams, with the commission keeping all revenue from concessions and parking. Beer sales were still banned, and the existing tenants would have priority on all dates. The diamond must still be at the eastern end, with the skinned part of the infield situated so that it did not impinge on the gridiron. And all costs of alterations must be paid by the Dodgers.[31] Dumbfounded at this offer, O'Malley turned once again to Norris Poulson. Poulson, who had no direct power over the Coliseum Commission, suggested O'Malley start negotiations with another Los Angeles football stadium—the Rose Bowl in nearby Pasadena.[32]

The political infighting in Los Angeles was getting complicated. Members of the Coliseum Commission were already complaining publicly about the pressure being brought on them to give the Dodgers whatever they wanted.[33] Now, the mayor of the Southern California city that had lured the Dodgers was suggesting the team move out of his city into another one. Appearing before the Pasadena Board of Directors (city council), Poulson tried to pass it off as a Southern California–wide issue with the need for everyone to pull together. "We have a great Coliseum in Los Angeles," the mayor straddled, "but I must admit the Rose Bowl can be better adapted to baseball." He told the Pasadenans that ticket sales at Wrigley had already passed the stadium's capacity, which was not true. According to Poulson's statement, the only negative consequence of these sellouts was that O'Malley would be forced to curtail his Knothole Gang program of reduced admissions for children.[34]

O'Malley's first statement about the Rose Bowl tried to keep all of his balls in the air. He said the Rose Bowl seemed suitable, but he would really rather play at the Coliseum. The team could use Wrigley, "but I'd rather start right in at the Coliseum and set some attendance records that would show the rest of the country that what we thought about Los Angeles as a major league city was true." Having smoothly packaged his possibilities with his preferences, and thrown in a dash of civic pride, he then neatly mouse-trapped the Coliseum Commission. "I don't want the Coliseum officials to be whipping boys," he said piously, while putting any onus for failed negotiations on them. (He also threw in a slap at the groups seeking to overturn the city's deal over Chavez Ravine.)[35] "Our problem is how to exist until we can build our new baseball park," he summarized. He even took a desperation trip out to Hollywood Park, the horse racing track about fifteen miles southwest of downtown Los Angeles. It had all the parking he needed and little else, but he felt he could not afford to overlook any possibilities.[36]

Soon, O'Malley was saying more positive things about the Rose Bowl. It did not have a running track, eliminating any conflicts with meets, and putting the field closer to the seats. Its north-south axis also eliminated concerns about the sun hitting batters' eyes.[37] The Rose Bowl sat in the Arroyo Seco ("dry gully" in Spanish) about ten miles northeast of downtown Los Angeles and on the western fringes of Pasadena. Jackie Robinson had grown up just a few hundred yards from the stadium, atop the bluffs on the east side of the arroyo. The Rose Bowl was a slightly older, but very similar, version of the Coliseum. By that time it seated 100,173.

The Rose Bowl had opened in 1922 with 57,000 seats after volunteers raised $272,198 to build the stadium. The Rose Bowl parade, the game, and the bowl itself were all part of a giant marketing campaign for Pasadena and all of Southern California. The theme, explicit at the beginning, was that the climate was so mild, you could grow roses in the middle of winter. The first parade had been in 1890; the first Rose Bowl game in 1902 (Michigan 49, Stanford 0). The theme had become less explicit, but the parade and the game were big business. The bowl had been expanded four times and turned over to Pasadena city management.

Aside from the January 1 bowl game, the stadium hosted a series of smaller events. Its normal terms were even steeper than the Coliseum offer—15 percent of the gross, plus no parking, concessions, or beer sales. But, the newspapers hinted, the Dodgers might be able to negotiate something better. Inevitably, the day O'Malley said the Rose Bowl was now the leading candidate, a group of residents with homes overlooking the arroyo said they had objections to the traffic, noise, and safety problems Dodger tenancy would create.[38]

O'Malley, his eye still firmly on the Coliseum, was dodging arrows from all sides. The next day, Friday, December 13, the Los Angeles Times was calling him "embattled." The previous day the Los Angeles County supervisors had approved the Dodgers' use of the Rose Bowl, but O'Malley had denied to a Chamber of Commerce board luncheon that he was playing the Coliseum off against the Rose Bowl.[39] By the middle of the next week, Pasadena's council approved negotiations with the Dodgers by a six-to-one vote. But at least a couple of the members indicated that nothing further should be read into the motion. They were not committed to a deal, just to negotiations, and if they did not like the contract, they would reject it. Perhaps they had been impressed by the four-hour demonstration organized by Rose Bowl neighbors. The protesters told the council, "Crime problems follow in the wake of big league baseball," "It's sheer gall for major league interests to seek a home in Pasadena," and "Just as sure as night baseball follows day baseball, death follows heavy traffic."[40] Nevertheless, O'Malley was making positive noises about Pasadena, noises tinged with more than a touch of pique at Los Angeles officials. "The warmth I have found in Pasadena, I have found nowhere else," he said.[41]

Six days before Christmas Jim Smith, the president of the Coliseum Commission, came up with a compromise. Smith said he was proposing the new deal only because of the commitments made by both city and county officials to O'Malley in Vero Beach that spring. Smith's proposal set a fairly high basic rent on the stadium, but let the team pay it off by crediting the profits from food and beverage sales against it.[42] Assuming reasonable attendance, it would leave the Dodgers without rent, but it was also likely to leave the team with no profits from concessions. Smith still had the diamond at the east end, and that still bothered O'Malley. "If the Dodgers have to play in the Coliseum's east end, where the sun would shine in the batters' and catchers' eyes, I wouldn't make a deal to play there if it cost me only $1 a year. I don't want another Don Zimmer case."[43] Zimmer, a young infielder of considerable promise, had been badly injured when hit by a pitched ball in 1953. Metal tabs had been inserted in his head. He went on to a journeyman playing career and thirteen years as a Major League manager. Apparently lost in the shuffle was a suggestion by Van Harris, an enterprising contractor from suburban Arcadia, who envisioned a fifty-foot-round hot-air balloon moored strategically over the Coliseum's rim. The balloon could be maneuvered to ensure its shadow shielded batters' eyes from the sun. "It may sound crazy, but it'll work," he told the Coliseum Commission.[44]

O'Malley also had reservations about the financial arrangements. If Dodger attendance was high (his eye was on two million), the Coliseum would actually be getting a huge income just from concession sales. The lost revenue constituted a rent much higher than any other Major League team paid.[45] O'Malley's concerns were irrelevant, for Smith's plan was too much for his fellow commission members. On the Friday before Christmas Smith's trial balloon was rejected.[46] On Christmas Eve a citizens group in Pasadena filed formal notice of intent to sue if the city approved a deal with the Dodgers for the Rose Bowl.[47]

As O'Malley flew back to New York to spend Christmas with Kay, Terry, and Peter, he had much to ponder. His dream stadium faced significant opposition, and the allies who had promised so much in Vero Beach in February were proving much better at chagrin than delivery. He was barely three months from opening day and did not know where he was going to play. All of the possibilities had significant drawbacks, and the one he wanted most seemed unresponsive to either negotiation or the pressure of allies. Even his one ray of sunshine was fading. As uncertainty about where the Dodgers would play grew, ticket orders had slowed to a trickle in December. True, Rin-Tin-Tin, the canine television star, ordered a season box that month.[48] That would have to be O'Malley's Christmas gift.

By New Year's Eve O'Malley was back in Los Angeles with his family. He attended all the Rose Bowl festivities, as well as New Year's Eve parties. He showed up at the *Los Angeles Times*' National Sports Award dinner and heard Bob Hope call his team the Los Angeles Wetbacks, a reference to Mexican immigrants who swam the Rio Grande to enter the United States. Called to the dais, O'Malley kept his remarks short, optimistic, and aimed at selling tickets for the coming season. He glossed over the current problems.[49]

On New Year's Day 1958 the O'Malleys spent the afternoon watching Ohio State beat Oregon 10–7 at the Rose Bowl. They did it in front of 100,173 people, and the local reporters were happy to ask him about his impressions. He duly noted the crowd, the average ticket price ($5.50), and the take (more than $500,000 plus the television contract). He also had to note the event drew forty thousand cars and that the Rose Bowl really was not capable of handling that many. But even a football game had its uses for maneuvering the public debate. "Down deep, I really believe that all the confusion will find a way of working out. I now am actually convinced that the Rose Bowl will prove to be a happy stadium for our West Coast debut," he said.[50]

While O'Malley smirked about the Rose Bowl crowd, his allies were raising the level of pressure on the Coliseum Commission. Poulson insisted the Dodgers had to have the diamond in the west end of the Coliseum. Supervisor Warren Dorn, who represented the Rose Bowl area on the county board of supervisors, tried to blunt the criticism of Poulson for seeking a home for the team outside his own city.[51]

But the Coliseum's established tenants were not showing any flexibility. The athletic directors at both USC and UCLA sent letters to the commission, protesting the use of the west end.[52] They did not want any of the football playing area skinned of grass to make the dirt portions of a baseball infield. They did not want to have to knock down the pitcher's mound or dig up home plate. They did not want to deal with any screens that would protect baseball fans from foul balls but merely interfere with a football fan's view. They did not want to have to negotiate over who would use the Coliseum on September or October Saturdays.

Jim Smith, outgoing president of the commission, noted that O'Malley had never made a formal application to use the Coliseum, nor had he made a firm offer of what he would pay.[53] O'Malley, Smith said, had told him he did not think he could afford to pay more than the 5 percent of the gross the Giants would be paying in San Francisco plus a percentage of the concession profits. Smith was cautiously optimistic.

By the Monday after New Year's, O'Malley and an entourage were motoring up the Arroyo Seco Parkway, the world's first freeway, a route that took him right past Chavez Ravine on his way to inspect the Rose Bowl. For the inspection he took Dick Walsh, a young Los Angeles–born Dodgers vice president who was becoming his point man on local politics and stadium building; Amos Buckley of Allied Maintenance, the company that handled upkeep and construction projects at Ebbets Field; and Emil Praeger, the architect who had been translating O'Malley's stadium ideas into plans for a decade. For any negotiations along came Henry Walsh, O'Malley's brother-in-law and the official club attorney.[54] For leverage O'Malley added National League president Warren Giles to the party. The Pasadena representatives were negotiating, but that was not really what O'Malley wanted. The Rose Bowl was supposed to be a pawn to force the Coliseum Commission's hand. While O'Malley, Praeger, and Dick Walsh measured potential foul lines, Giles dropped into a football stance and began chanting signals for an off-tackle slant.[55] It could only be seen as a commentary on the kind of stadium it was.

Later, it was reported Giles would have required O'Malley to change the name of the team to the Pasadena Dodgers if they had played at the Rose Bowl.[56] And New York sportswriter Dan Daniel, writing in the *Sporting News*, noted that O'Malley's willingness to locate in Pasadena raised questions about his credibility when he had refused to relocate the Dodgers to Moses's proposed Queens stadium.[57] Then, he had argued Queens was not Brooklyn. Now, he would have to argue that Pasadena was Los Angeles.

But in public at that time Giles was not saying anything that would hurt. When O'Malley said time was getting short and they might just have to play at Wrigley Field, Giles nodded and added that other National League clubs would not be happy with limited gates to offset their higher travel costs. Just for good measure Giles reminded one and all that returning to Brooklyn was not completely out of the question.

Pasadena opponents were not impressed. They were still packing city council meetings. And now they began circulating petitions to put their own initiative on the June primary ballot.[58] It would ban the Dodgers from using the Rose Bowl. O'Malley dismissed it as "a civic matter," but the Pasadena newspaper's baseball reporter said, "There were indications he was getting fed up."[59]

O'Malley's attitude could not have been helped by the remarks bubbling to the surface of the Coliseum Commission impasse. Jim Smith said Poulson had tried to get him to stop negotiating with O'Malley while the Dodger president looked at the Rose Bowl. County supervisor Kenny Hahn said, "Somebody has pulled the wool over O'Malley's eyes if he thinks the Rose Bowl is the place to play." Then, just to make it clear who "somebody" might be, he said, "And I'd also like to know why Poulson spearheaded the drive to take the Dodgers to Pasadena. They say he thinks there's less chance of losing the June Chavez Ravine referendum if O'Malley decided on the Rose Bowl, but that's only a smoke screen. I want to know the real reason. I'm not trying to be nasty, but I'm a politician and I know how these things work."[60]

Said Poulson: "I say he's a politician, as he says he is, and a demagogue to boot. Why does not he bring out the minutes of the Coliseum meeting which show that Hahn, and only Hahn, demanded that no concessions be made to O'Malley? It was Hahn who insisted the Dodgers pay the full 10 percent rental fee and that the diamond be located at the east end—two conditions it is impossible for O'Malley to accept. It was after reading the minutes and realizing the Commission was closing the door on O'Malley that I went to Pasadena."[61] The unity these two key O'Malley supporters had shown in Vero Beach ten months earlier was wilting like a Carmen Miranda hat in July.

Matters were not helped January 10 when baseball commissioner Ford Frick went on Red Smith's radio program in New York and bemoaned the possibility Babe Ruth's single-season home run record would be broken in "a cow pasture"—Wrigley Field. If any remark was likely to inflame the sensitivities of the nation's second city, it was something like that coming out of New York. It was quickly pointed out that Frick had been Ruth's ghostwriter as a young man and had a special attachment to the Babe's records. O'Malley distanced himself from the commissioner's remark, suggesting Frick revisit Wrigley and Los Angeles.[62]

Wrigley Field was looming larger and larger. On January 13 Pasadena officials and O'Malley agreed negotiations were going nowhere. The problem was not the layout or even the terms of the contract. The problem was an estimated $750,000 needed to chop out seats to extend the foul lines as well as make other changes. It was just too much. A joint announcement was agreed on, and O'Malley was given a hurried police car ride back down the Arroyo Seco Parkway, past Chavez Ravine, and over to Wrigley Field, where he gave his side of the situation. He said he felt "constrained" to select Wrigley Field for the 1958 season. But he also said he was scheduling a meeting for the next morning to see what could be done about the Coliseum.[63]

That Tuesday morning, January 14, was the first time O'Malley had actually sat down with the commission after two months of jousting at a distance. After the Rose Bowl announcement the previous day, Poulson had quickly written a letter to Burton Chace, the new commission president who had replaced Jim Smith, suggesting O'Malley be offered a deal comparable to the Giants' 5 percent rental in San Francisco. "I'm sorry to say we are the laughing stock of the country and we must redeem ourselves," the mayor wrote.[64]

At the meeting O'Malley rolled out what he called his "Three O'Clock Plan," so named because he said it had come to him at three that morning. "Frankly," he told the commission, "if it hadn't come to me, I doubt if we could have accepted any offer, at this late date, to play in the Coliseum. I say that because time to make physical changes has run out." The plan had the diamond in the west end and home plate in the traditional southwest corner. No current seats would be removed, a feature of several earlier ideas. This would both lower costs considerably and reduce the football tenants' concerns about the removal of some of their best seats. Because this would result in a very short foul line in left field, a movable screen would be placed there to cut down on cheap home runs. Turning to the football teams' arguments, O'Malley suggested that their concern about playing on the skinned part of the infield could be solved by moving the football field a little to the east. He outlined plans to have sod growing and ready to install and smoothly ignored the fact that relocating the football field would move it away from the larger number of seats in the stadium's west end.[65]

O'Malley outlined the Giants' lease terms to the commission: 5 percent of the gross, with a minimum of $125,000 guaranteed to San Francisco. The city would get parking, while the Giants would get all concessions. And, he noted, that deal was better for the Giants than it would be for the Dodgers on a couple of points. The Giants could sell beer at concession stands and would not have to make any changes in Seals Stadium, whereas the Dodgers would have to spend about $200,000 to add lights, a left-field screen, and other improvements at the Coliseum. He was willing to accept similar terms and even offered to pay $50,000 for the right to sell beer, although there was no mention of the minimum $125,000 guaranteed by the Giants. The Dodgers, he said, would assume all the staffing, cleanup, insurance, and baseball-related maintenance costs. Assuming two million in attendance, this would translate to about $200,000 plus parking revenues for the Coliseum Commission.[66]

Then O'Malley pleaded poverty. He noted he was already paying on three stadiums. He had a lease on Ebbets Field for two more years, and that ate $75,000 annually in property taxes, security, and maintenance costs, plus insurance. Roosevelt Stadium in Jersey City also had two more years on its lease, although that set him back only about $18,000. And, he noted, because his deal with Los Angeles for Chavez Ravine had been put on hold by the referendum, he still owned Wrigley Field with its maintenance costs and property taxes. He owed $150,000 a year for the next three seasons to the Pacific Coast League as an indemnity for moving into their Los Angeles territory. He also had had to move the PCL's LA Angels to Spokane and lease them a park there. That move invaded Pioneer League territory, and they had to be paid an indemnity of $40,000. Salaries would come to $500,000; Minor League operations and scouting would take another $750,000. And, lest his numbers seemed vague and snatched from the air, he noted that in 1956 Ebbets Field staffing, cleanup, repairs, supplies, workmen's compensation insurance, ticket printing, and maintenance had cost $587,849.23.[67]

Finally, O'Malley analyzed his ticket revenue. Out of a $1 ticket, he said, 10 cents went to federal taxes, 27.5 cents to the visiting team, 5 cents to the National League, 15 cents for the PCL indemnity, 15 cents had to be set aside for guarantees to the visiting teams that their higher West Coast travel costs would be covered, and 5 cents given to the Coliseum. That left him only 22.5 cents of the dollar before he started paying salaries and other costs. And that was assuming the Coliseum gave him the 5 percent figure he wanted and not the 10 percent they wanted.[68]

Walter O'Malley could make numbers fox-trot. By telling the commissioners that he was going to be "breaking down a dollar ticket," he was playing into their own mind-set, which was focused on the percentage they were going to charge him. But many of the costs he was ticking off were not percentages; they were onetime charges. For the first $1 he was correct, although he had neatly mentioned the PCL indemnity as a percentage charge against the ticket dollar and as something he would have to pay out of his net. However, O'Malley did not plan to charge $1 for any tickets except some promotional items. The cheapest ticket in the house (wherever his house was) was going to be $1.50. The average ticket, it turned out, would go for about $2.69 in 1958. On the average ticket, the numbers would work out very differently.

TABLE 3. Negotiating with the coliseum

	O'Malley's dollar	The avg. ticket[a]	After PCL indemnity[b]
Income	1.00	2.69	2.69
Visitors	0.275	0.275	0.275
National Lg	0.05	0.05	0.05
PCL Indemnity	0.15	0.15	0.00
Fed. Amusement tax	0.10	0.27	0.27
Col. rent (@5)	0.05	0.135	0.135
Vis. guar.[c]	0.15	0.15	0.15
Net	0.225	$1.66	$1.81
Net as % of gross	22.5%	61.7%	67.3%

[a] Los Angeles Times, October 3, 1958. In the article Coliseum general manager Bill Nicholas said the Dodgers' average ticket price after taxes was $2.42. I have added the 10 percent federal tax back in.

[b] The indemnity was structured as 15 percent of the first $1 million in ticket revenue in 1958, 1959, and 1960, and O'Malley already had his first $1 million in the bank for 1958 ticket sales when he made this presentation.

[c] This was a promise by O'Malley to compensate other National League clubs if their visitors' share of the gate was not up to the five-year average at Ebbets Field. Theoretically, this might have cost $100,000 or more. In the event it cost $11,000, or about a half cent a ticket, instead of the 15 cents projected here, although O'Malley could only hope for that little when he made the presentation. Los Angeles Times, December 10, 1958.

If the Coliseum Commission were to keep concession profits, too, which he noted would be about $600,000 at 2.5 million attendance, he would be paying the "highest rent in baseball history." He leaned into his closing. "If it is the function of government to get rich off of private enterprise, then you should get the last dollar out of the Dodgers," he said. "But if it is the function of government to make available a fine public facility for something worth while, then be generous to the Dodgers. Our ball club has a record of the biggest earnings in baseball, and I'm proud of it. What's wrong with making money?"[69] The commissioners, the *Sporting News* noted, "asked a few questions and then recessed to the following day."[70]

Inevitably, it seemed, just as progress was being made, another flank attack materialized. The Coliseum Commission's major project at that time was the construction of the Sports Arena, an 18,000-seat indoor stadium for basketball, hockey, circuses, conventions, and the like. The commission was counting on the additional revenue generated by the Dodgers to allow them to pay off the bonds on the arena much more quickly than originally thought.

The day after O'Malley's first face-to-face meeting with them, the members of the Coliseum Commission joined other Los Angeles officials in jawboning the football tenants about dropping their objections. But as that day's session wore on, the commission received a letter from the two brokerages hired to underwrite the $7.8 million bond issue for the Sports Arena. The letter warned that any action on the part of the commission that alienated the football tenants could have an adverse effect on sales of the bonds. After all, the Dodgers, unlike the football teams, were going to use the Coliseum only for a couple of years. Concession revenue, they noted, had accounted for half of the Coliseum's net income in 1955–56 and 78 percent in 1956–57. Almost lost in the shuffle was a new concession by O'Malley. He would guarantee the commission $200,000 in rent. The commission decided to recess to consider the matter, and Chace asked O'Malley if he was agreeable to leaving the offer on the table while the bond question was worked out. O'Malley raised a small smile, paused, and said, "The bride is impatient."[71]

The football tenants redoubled their efforts to win promises that their Coliseum rental terms would be adjusted. Almost all of the scheduling conflicts were worked out. As the negotiations wore on, the commission began asking more questions. O'Malley, trained for the courtroom, rose each time one was posed. Eventually, Chace asked solicitously, "Wouldn't you be more comfortable seated?" Eyeing the bigger picture, O'Malley said, "That's a sense of feeling I am trying to acquire." He got the first laugh of the day.[72]

By Friday, January 17, four days after the Rose Bowl feint ended, O'Malley and the commissioners had reached a deal. The rent was 5 percent, a figure extended to the football tenants for the two-year length of the Dodger contract. The Dodgers would also get most of the concession revenue, while the football tenants remained shut out. Nine games would be designated in advance as days when the Coliseum would get the food and beverage profits, as well as the traditional 10 percent of the gate. O'Malley neatly played on the commission's desire to reap those profits early. The nine games would be played against some of the less interesting teams of the period—the Cubs, Cardinals, and Pirates. The three series included only one weekend and ran from the end of April into early May, a period before school closed for the summer and parents traditionally became more willing to take the kids to a game.[73]

The other terms, on parking, diamond location, and other issues, would remain as O'Malley had proposed on the fourteenth. Kenny Hahn said the deal could mean as much as $300,000 a year for paying off the Sports Arena bonds.[74] Leaving the Coliseum offices after the final details were set, O'Malley ran into locked doors. "I've been trying to get into this place for months and now I can't get out," he said. He thought it was a passing quip. It would become an anthem for the next four years.[75]

The ticket orders started to pour in again. By the end of January Dodgers business manager Harold Parrott was reporting more than $2 million in ticket orders had been received. Parrott said the best tally in Brooklyn by this point in the off-season was about $600,000.[76] He announced a February 20 cutoff for season ticket sales.[77]

The stream of cash was the major positive, but it stood alone in a sea of financial pressures and an ocean of details that had to be completed by opening day in mid-April. O'Malley had his temporary home and his avid customers, but he had a host of financial worries. He had to pay to move the team's offices and $1,500 apiece to twenty team officials he was bringing west.[78] He still had the costs of the three stadiums and the Pacific Coast League indemnity he had told the Coliseum Commission about. He had the costs of adapting the Coliseum for baseball.

Plus, he had taken on some additional burdens that he was keeping quiet about. There was his agreement to buy out Mrs. Smith's 25 percent interest in the team. And, true to the arguments he had made about competing with the Braves, he had allowed his baseball executives late in 1957 to sharply increase the spending on scouts and bonuses in line with the expected higher revenues in Los Angeles.[79] He had to keep his eye on the main financial ball, his new stadium, and he had to keep saving to pay for that.

While O'Malley flew back to New York to pick up the business threads at that end, the task of transforming the Coliseum began. The public hoo-ha focused on the short distance from home plate to the stands in left field and the screen the Dodgers would build to reduce cheap home runs. But there were thousands of other details.

The Coliseum needed more lighting. What was adequate for football was inadequate for night baseball games. Three light towers had to be erected around the home-plate area. The football press box, which perched at the top of the south rim of the Coliseum, was in an excellent position to see right field. A new press facility would have to be built behind home plate. The left-field screen, and a system for removing it when football took over, would have to be designed and fabricated. A foul ball screen behind home plate was needed, too, with a half-inch-thick shatterproof plastic window for newspaper photographers. Then there were dugouts for the teams, wooden barriers to replace the concrete rim of the playing field in areas where players might crash into it, and a host of smaller items. Cost: more than $200,000, all borne by O'Malley.[80] The contract went to the Del E. Webb Construction Company, owned by one of the Yankees' co-owners.

Then there was the point of the Coliseum—all those seats. Actually, fewer than thought. The football capacity might be more than 100,000, but Parrott recalled taking the portly O'Malley into the Coliseum and sitting him down on the benches in some of the choice locations. When he saw how squeezed his bulk was when surrounded by others, O'Malley agreed to pull every fifth ticket in the choicer sections, a move that pushed capacity down around 92,000.[81]

While the number of seats was being reduced, O'Malley was upping the revenue from them. Originally, the plan had been for 12,485 box seats and 12,300 reserved seats, but when Parrott finally settled on the seating chart, it called for 17,700 box seats at $250 a year and 16,000 reserved seats at $180.[82] That was more box and reserved seats combined than the entire seating capacity of Ebbets Field. Most were a lot farther from the action. The box-seat area extended all the way around the curve of the Coliseum to behind the left-field screen. In the arc behind home plate, customers could pay for a box seat and be as many as fifty-four rows from the bottom. It would never be an intimate park.

The fans were undaunted. The orders rolled in. Some were big names: singers Frank Sinatra and Nat King Cole, actors Gregory Peck and Yul Brynner, comedy team George Burns and Gracie Allen, as well as the comedy nonteam, the recently divorced Jerry Lewis and Dean Martin. Former Dodger first baseman Chuck Connors, soon to be the star of the television hit *The Rifleman*, bought season seats.[83] Some were big corporate customers. United California Bank bought $10,000 in tickets, as did an Alhambra Oldsmobile dealer named Bill Burch, who also provided free Oldsmobiles to players and executives.[84]

For these kinds of customers, the Dodgers were willing to do more than make the spaces wider. The Coliseum seats were hard-backed benches. There were no padding and no individual seats, only numbers branded into the backrests. To increase comfort O'Malley ordered thirty-four thousand seat cushions (blue for box seats, red for reserved) at a cost of another $41,000.[85] The cushioning had the added benefit of covering up the old seat numbers. The decision to pull every fifth box and reserved ticket had been made after the tickets had been printed. Thus, Parrott's ticket people were constantly in the position of explaining to customer Jones that he really did have five seats in a row even though they were numbered 1, 2, 3, 4, 6.[86]

Harold Parrott had joined the Dodgers in late 1943, when Branch Rickey recruited him to be the Dodgers' traveling secretary.[87] The simile most often used for traveling secretaries was nursemaids, for when the club was on the road, that is what its traveling party needed. Traveling secretaries lined up the trains and the hotels. They made all the special arrangements the team, the manager, or players needed on the road, whether it was a doctor, theater tickets, or a bus. They did the same for the newspaper reporters, as well as providing press information and often buying the food and drinks. They also picked up their ball club's share of the receipts after a road series ended.

It was a job that called for a social person who knew baseball and newspapers and had a knack for figures. Harold Parrott was all of that. Born in 1909, he had been something of a Brooklyn child prodigy, entering high school at eleven and leaving St. John's University with a master's degree at twenty-one.[88] He came from a very Catholic, very protective home, and his mother was horrified by some of the associations Parrott acquired as he entered his chosen profession.[89] Jobs were hard to come by in the Depression, but Parrott had been hanging around newspaper offices for several years. One day, maybe more to get rid of him than anything else, the *Brooklyn Eagle*'s managing editor gave him $5 and sent him off to Jamaica Raceway to look at the oral betting system the bookies at the track were then using. Parrott, who said he had never been to a horse track or made a bet before, came back with $17 and a story.[90] Soon after his graduation, he was at work at the *Eagle*'s sports department and building a reputation around the paper as the managing editor's pet.[91]

He covered the Dodgers, as well as the Giants, for a couple of years in the 1930s. He wrote features, served briefly as the sports editor, and eventually was given a column, in part, one contemporary suggested, because he had been the only *Eagle* sports staffer to cross the picket lines during a 1937 strike at the paper.[92] His charm and witty tongue made him a well-known and generally well-liked figure around baseball, and he struck up a friendship with Branch Rickey Jr., then a Minor League executive with the Dodgers. He was especially close to J. G. Taylor Spink, the demanding editor of the *Sporting News*, who bought a good deal of freelance material from Parrott and publicized him at other times, including a front-page story when he was named the Dodgers' traveling secretary.[93]

His youth, his talent, and his name all added up to a series of nicknames, some of which he coined himself. In the 1930s he was Childe Harolde, and his colleagues marveled at how young he was when he won a columnist's berth. He was the Brooklyn Bonfire to *New York American* sportswriter Sid Mercer, who envied his energy. After joining the team and handling publicity as well as the traveling secretary's duties, he became "the Talking Parrott" or "the Flying Parrott." The latter was hung on him during a *Sporting News* story in which the essential information was that Parrott had taken a plane flight, not big news in 1951 but indicative of Parrott's ability to keep his own name as well as the Dodgers' in front of the public.[94]

Parrott's friendship with Branch Rickey Jr. had led to a relationship with Branch Sr. and Parrott's hiring as the Dodgers' traveling secretary. Columnist Tom Meany noted that Parrott's habit of wearing bow ties, as Rickey did, played a part in the hiring. Parrott's relationship with Rickey was complicated. After he left baseball Parrott wrote a book he called *The Lords of Baseball*, which focused on owners and had few good words to say about them, especially O'Malley. The exception was Rickey, whom Parrott continued to regard with a mixture of distaste and awe. The distaste was for Rickey's cheapness. The awe was for his intelligence, grasp of baseball, and fatherly manner.

Parrott did not leave for Pittsburgh with Branch Rickey, although he clearly had a lot of doubts about that decision.[95] He recalled later that he and his wife, Josephine, had chosen to stay in the "friendly Brooklyn surroundings" rather than move to Pittsburgh. But Parrott seemed to feel he had his own rivals within the Rickey men. Preserved in the Branch Rickey

Papers is a memo from Parrott to Rickey dated November 3, 1948, going over the details of the Dodgers' publicity program.[96] Although deferential to Rickey, Parrott was clearly at odds with Arthur Mann, Rickey's alter ego who Parrott thought was interfering in the publicity operation. There was also the money. In his dedication to *The Lords of Baseball*, Parrott notes that he and Josephine admired Rickey for "the love and family warmth he gave us in place of dollars" and then adds his own parenthetical, "Why couldn't it've been both, B. R.?"[97]

As a young sportswriter Parrott had looked to expand his sources of income. During the 1936 World Series he had been both the Giants' Carl Hubbell and the Yankees' Lou Gehrig in ghostwritten newspaper columns.[98] His relationship with Spink generated many assignments, and he also began to write for the *Saturday Evening Post*.

O'Malley's desire to get Parrott into the ticket department was a testimony to Parrott's abilities. Joe Palmer, whose company provided printing and mailing services to the Dodgers in Los Angeles, called Parrott "the brains of the organization."[99] The ticket manager had to take care of a thousand details. He had to accommodate ticket requests from Dodger officials as well as people who knew to come directly to him. He had to know who to turn down, who to put in a reserved seat, and who to ensure got a box near the Dodger dugout. He had to set up the ticket-selling program off-season and in-. He had to control the ticket sellers and the ticket takers. He had to control the vault, for to a ball team tickets are like money. And each night the cash drawer had to balance.

In Los Angeles Parrott would have to perform the ticket manager's ballet called "scaling the house." In its simplest form that meant deciding what each seat would cost. In its advanced form it meant setting the prices for various classes of seats and the boundaries between the classes. It might mean setting flexible boundaries, with the cheap seats starting at row 40 on a slow night and row 60 for a big game. Once those decisions had been made, it had to be communicated clearly to the company printing the tickets and the staff selling them. Brochures had to be printed and tours for potential box holders arranged. These tasks had been hostage to the decision where the Dodgers would play in 1958, although Parrott had made some preliminary estimates of both Wrigley Field, where his office was, and the Rose Bowl. Now he could concentrate on the Coliseum.

The efforts of Parrott and other Dodger officials in Los Angeles were being accomplished without O'Malley's presence. With the Coliseum question wrapped up, a host of other matters were bedeviling the Dodger president. Just eleven days after the Coliseum agreement was announced, Roy Campanella lost control of his rented Chevrolet on an icy road near his Long Island home. The early-morning accident left the former All-Star catcher with no use of his legs and only the barest control of his arms and shoulders. But those results were not fully apparent when O'Malley first heard of the crash early on the morning of January 28. He had returned to New York to clean up some business.

Campanella had always been one of O'Malley's, and the writers', favorite players. He was one of those athletes whose body did not signal his profession. He was of medium height, and more than medium girth, but he carried little fat. He looked like a barrel endowed with the reactions of a Ping-Pong professional. The fireplug body concealed water bug–quick hands and feet. His personality was as open as his figure was misleading. Among the African Americans on the Dodgers, he was the flip side of the coin to Jackie Robinson's militancy. He wanted to like and be liked, and he was.

Jack Lang's phone rang at five thirty that morning. Lang covered the Dodgers for the *Long Island Press*, which was headquartered on the north shore of Long Island, near where O'Malley had grown up and Campanella lived. It was O'Malley from his Amityville home. "Jack," he said, "I just wanted to let you know Campy's had a bad accident." O'Malley called Lang before Bavasi or Fresco Thompson or any other reporters. When Lang asked later why he had gotten the first call, O'Malley said he had just associated the area of the crash with Lang and his paper.[100]

Lang hurried to the hospital. Campanella had gone into surgery at seven that morning. When the operation was over O'Malley joined the surgeon, Dr. Robert Sengstaken, at a press conference. The surgeon said Campanella had a broken neck and a nearly severed spinal cord. The catcher was paralyzed, and it was unclear if he would ever be able to play again, although Sengstaken considered it both unlikely and inadvisable. Asked what he thought of Campanella's chances to play again, O'Malley said, "I'm more concerned with his physical welfare at the moment than whether he can play ball again."[101]

Campanella recalled that, outside of his family, O'Malley was one of his first visitors after the operation. "My mind was still not clear at the time," Campanella recalled in his autobiography. "I couldn't see him but I heard him say: 'Campy, this is Walter O'Malley. Don't worry about a thing. I'll be back when you feel better.'"[102]

Actually, O'Malley would not be back soon, but only when he recovered from his own medical problems. On February 3, only six days after Campanella's accident, O'Malley was walking across a field near Camaguey, Cuba. He had made a quick stop at Vero Beach and then taken off for a few days of hunting guinea hens. At the edge of the field his feet tangled in a barbed-wire fence, and he fell. The sharp pain turned out to be a broken bone in his left ankle, the opposite of one he had broken in Canada a decade earlier.[103]

A quick plane trip back to New York got the ankle in a cast. But as the doctors examined O'Malley, they found what was reported as a polyp on his intestines. It was surgically removed on February 14, but he was not out of Long Island University Hospital for almost a month.[104] O'Malley's brother-in-law Henry Walsh attributed the extended stay to the doctor's concern that O'Malley, an overweight fifty-four-year-old man, was not fully recovered from the operation and from the strain of working at a killing pace over the previous few months.[105]

Campanella and O'Malley were not the only Dodgers with medical troubles that winter and spring. Jim Gentile, Don Zimmer, Johnny Podres, and Duke Snider were all involved in car wrecks, though none was hurt seriously. More serious from O'Malley's point of view, Buzzie Bavasi slipped on the ice outside his Scarsdale home a day before Campanella's accident. He landed on his bottom and broke his tailbone.[106] Bavasi's injury proved more inconvenient than debilitating. He, at least, would make it to Vero Beach that spring. O'Malley would not. After finally being discharged from the hospital in March, a couple of weeks after spring training began, he returned directly to Los Angeles to organize his business for its first season.

One of O'Malley's first moves, while still in the hospital, was to name Bavasi general manager. For the public conception of general manager, Bavasi had filled that role since O'Malley took over the team. He was the one who handled the Dodgers, made the trades, signed the players, oversaw operations such as tickets and publicity, and supervised the team's top farm club. But that was not the same general manager's job defined by other clubs, who put virtually all powers in the general manager's hands and had him, and usually only him, reporting directly to the owner.

Bavasi's new job description, with the title executive vice president and general manager, moved him much closer to that broader definition. Its practical effect was to make Fresco Thompson subordinate to Bavasi. Thompson's job had, in fact, been enlarged. He now oversaw all Minor League operations, including Spokane, and took charge of the scouting operations. But he was also now reporting to Bavasi instead of O'Malley.[107]

With Parrott setting up the ticket plan, O'Malley turned his attention to other matters. He filed papers with the California secretary of state to change the Brooklyn National League Baseball Club, Inc., into the Los Angeles Dodgers, Inc.[108] He announced the Dodgers' Ebbets Field offices would close February 15.[109] He brought players out to stage clinics and do promotional work. Jim Gilliam and Gil Hodges appeared at a ceremony in early February to formally accept the home plate that had been removed from Ebbets Field. Their uniform jerseys bannered "Los Angeles" across the chest.[110]

There was still a feeling of makeshift and borrowed to the team's operations. The Dodgers' offices were spread over three locations. Initially, O'Malley and Bavasi operated from suites in the Statler Hotel downtown. Then they moved into the Metropolitan Federal Savings building across the street with other top officials, then back to offices in the Statler next to the swimming pool. Scouting, marketing, accounting, and the workaday functions of the team moved into the Wrigley Field tower. By mid-February Parrott had taken his ticket operation out of Wrigley and over to the Coliseum.[111]

Fern Hill Colman entered the Coliseum offices in the spring of 1958. She was sent over from a temporary agency to help address envelopes and stuff them. She was promised "rat race overtime for three weeks" and set to work sending celebrities pairs of tickets to a Dodger Father's Day game. At eight o'clock on her third day, O'Malley hove into view. He was "stout as an oversize steam roller," she recalled, "with eyes as sharp and quick as a chipmunk's." O'Malley was fascinated that Colman was an actual native Californian and put her to work digging up names of fellow natives to whom he could send the complimentary pairs of tickets. She, in turn, would sell the Dodger office staff on Gershwin at the Hollywood Bowl and trout fishing at June Lake.[112]

O'Malley was determined not to repeat what he saw as his television mistakes in Brooklyn. In the days right after World War II, when both television and his ownership in the Dodgers were young, he had pushed the Dodgers onto TV over Rickey's objections. Within a few years all the Dodgers' home games were on the tube. It was good money. The postwar boom in attendance was still on, and Ebbets Field could hold only so many people. But a couple of years into the 1950s, his opinion began to turn. Now, just about everybody had a television. His customers were moving to Long Island in droves, and after a long day at work a TV game on the couch could seem a lot more appealing than a drive back into Brooklyn. "When we operated in Brooklyn," he recalled several years later, "we found that our increase in TV revenue was in direct proportion to our decline in attendance. The only difference was, we were losing all the fringe money."[113] The fans were buying their beer from the A&P instead of the Dodgers. "Our people were TV-sated," O'Malley said.[114] Radio, he decided, created an appetite; television satisfied it.

In Los Angeles O'Malley set out to create a radio network. The Dodgers would be on ten stations that blanketed an area from Bakersfield and San Luis Obispo on the north to south of the Mexican border. Another station would serve Las Vegas. The territory covered about sixty thousand square miles—an area bigger than thirty states—and included almost ten million people, all within a six-hour drive of the Coliseum.

In the days immediately after the Coliseum deal, O'Malley announced Eastside Beer, manufacturers of Eastside Old Tap Lager, as a sponsor. O'Malley said he planned to line up additional sponsors in New York. There he had also talked to Al Helfer about whether he wanted to move west with broadcast partners Vin Scully and Jerry Doggett. And, oh, by the way, no games on television.

Two weeks later, with O'Malley in a hospital bed on Long Island, Tareyton cigarettes and Roi-Tan cigars (both products of the American Tobacco Company) joined the sponsor list, and KMPC was announced as the team's flagship station in Los Angeles. Helfer would stay in New York. There would be 190 games, including 36 spring training games, on the radio schedule. "There are no television plans for 1958," O'Malley reiterated.[115]

O'Malley had sold the radio rights for $500,000, about 60 percent of what he had gotten in Brooklyn for both radio and TV in 1957. The lack of television competition for the radio broadcasts was a factor in the price.[116] Spanish-language broadcasts were soon added.[117] By late in February one of the local television stations was announcing it would do a daily fifteen-minute report from Vero Beach on the Dodgers' spring training.[118] But still no televised games.

While O'Malley was recuperating, and Bavasi was off supervising spring training, the other top executives threw themselves into the round of service-club lunches and dinners to promote the team. Across the huge Greater Los Angeles area, no Kiwanis or Rotary, no Holy Name Society or synagogue brotherhood, no Cub Scout pack or animal lodge was too small. Fresco Thompson, with his ready wit, and Red Patterson, with his fund of stories, seemed to live in their cars. Tuck Stainback, a Los Angeles resident who had played briefly in the Majors, was put in charge of group sales. He was working seven fourteen-hour days a week, hitting the service-group circuit and organizing city nights at the Coliseum.[119]

There was no lack of response. The newly Major League Los Angeles chapter of the Baseball Writers' Association of America scheduled a dinner to honor the Dodgers on April 17, the eve of the first game in Los Angeles. The one thousand tickets, at $12.50 each, were sold out without a public announcement being made.[120] More than four hundred people had their checks returned because there was not room.[121]

The schedule also had to be revised. Part of this was inevitable, as the team worked around immovable Coliseum events such as the Fourth of July fireworks show. Part was management listening to the Angelenos talk about the summer heat. The immovable dates wound up creating seven twi-night doubleheaders in the Dodger home schedule. Although these delighted young boys, they had been frowned upon by the league office, and previously permission had been granted only to make up rainouts. This was the first time they had been authorized in advance.

The night-game slate was expanded to forty-two games from the previous thirty-five.[122] Later that season, as a test that would not be adopted permanently, the Dodgers moved three weekend afternoon games to a 4:00 p.m. start, citing the heat and some fans' desire to go to the beach before attending.[123]

The new schedule, which featured the Dodgers at home or in San Francisco for almost the entire first month of the season, sparked talk of attendance records. Within the organization it sparked some jockeying. After doing some early chest-beating himself,[124] O'Malley became concerned that any crowing about attendance records and ticket revenue would inflame the opponents of the Chavez Ravine pact, who were already convinced O'Malley was making too much money.

By early 1958 team officials were becoming less circumspect. Parrott was confidently talking of 80,000 for opening day ("a conservative guess," he said) and 2 million for the season, with perhaps a shot at the single-season record.[125] Allan Roth, the team's statistician, had been asked to dig up figures on baseball's various attendance records. He found the opening-day record was 74,200, as the Boston Red Sox visited the New York Yankees on April 18, 1923, the first game ever played in Yankee Stadium. The National League season attendance mark was Milwaukee's 2,215,404 set the previous year. Cleveland's 1948 team held the overall record, with 2,620,627 people. Parrott was also publicly eyeing the record for any single game, 86,288 for the fifth game of the 1948 World Series in Cleveland and for a single day during the regular season, also in Cleveland, where 84,582 came to a 1954 doubleheader with the Yankees. Speaking with New York reporters in late January, O'Malley downplayed the record-setting talk, saying the only record he was interested in was winning more games than the current world champion Braves.[126] Talking to Los Angeles reporters a week before, he had predicted a "minimum" of 2 million in attendance.[127]

Although O'Malley occasionally downplayed the attendance records in public, he had to be gratified at the results Parrott was reporting. Season ticket sales were cut off at 6,500 seats, almost twice the 3,500-seat level they had considered optimistic when they arrived.[128] Total season attendance of 650,000 was in the bag.[129]

For any records to be set the Coliseum would have to be ready. It was a very wet spring by Los Angeles standards, with fifteen inches of rain (a little more than the annual average) falling between early February and the first week of April.[130] Luckily, the redesign team had chosen to redo the Coliseum's clay-pipe drain system first, finding it clogged with mud and the roots of the playing field's sod. "If this drainage problem had not been accomplished first, this entire construction program would not have been possible," the architects reported to the Dodgers.[131] Other problems had to be solved. Steel manhole covers, out of bounds in football, were on the playing area for baseball. They could not be covered with sod, so a rubber sponge compound, supposedly with the same resiliency as grass, was brought in and glued to the manhole covers. Sod was trucked over from Wrigley Field. The new press box was constructed. The dugouts were dug down. The screen, fences, and light towers went up.

The screen became the subject of loud and occasionally illuminating debate in the baseball world. Soon after the Coliseum deal was settled, the *Sporting News* (advertised as the "Bible of Baseball") quickly interviewed some of the biggest-name left-handers in the National League. Johnny Antonelli of the Giants called it a "farce." Warren Spahn of the Braves (who had rarely pitched in Ebbets Field because of the Dodgers' right-handed power) suggested baseball legislate a minimum distance of 300 feet between home plate and the fences.[132] The Coliseum's left-field screen would be barely 250 feet from home plate. As left-handed pitchers, they were more likely to face right-handed hitters, and right-handed hitters were more likely to hit the ball toward that looming screen.

The Dodgers protested. Manager Walt Alston and first baseman Gil Hodges, the first name usually mentioned as a beneficiary of the short fence, suggested that the screen itself would cut down some home runs and that pitchers would adjust by throwing the ball away from hitters' power. Some other National Leaguers chimed in. But the label of "Chinese" home runs, an image that was supposed to connote cheapness, hung over the debate. The *Sporting News* even featured a Willard Mullin cartoon on one of its covers that spring showing a caricatured coolie called One Flung Wong (One Flung—or pitched—Wrong) hanging over a screenless fence and talking into the ear of a nervous pitcher.[133]

Not all the preparations were the subject of public debate. The details multiplied like smog on a hot afternoon. All those offices needed desks, chairs, safes, and typewriters, which came courtesy of a local bank.[134] Dick Walsh talked the Coliseum into allowing the team to paint some steps in the center-field bleachers a dark green as a background for hitters.[135] ABC Vending Company, which held the Coliseum contract for providing food and beverage concessions, spent $70,000 sprucing up its existing facilities and adding new ones.[136]

The team's office staff was getting settled in. Parrott took a house in Malibu. Grace Therkildsen, known as Miss T. to a generation of Brooklyn baseball writers, moved to Wrigley to remain at the team's switchboard. It was not a hardship to move, the Brooklyn native told LA reporters. She had ten relatives in Southern California these days and only two left in Brooklyn.[137]

10

Now I Learn It's Been Controversial for Years

In Chavez Ravine the winter rains had invoked the annual crop of grass on hillsides and vacant lots. Squatting just north of downtown, visible from city hall, it sat like an emerald begging to be plucked—just as Norris Poulson, Kenny Hahn, and Roz Wyman had described to O'Malley a year earlier. Like everything else in Los Angeles for Walter O'Malley, it was taking on the attributes of a mirage.

Starting with Bob Cobb, he had heard the stories of the pistol range and the Olympics and the Police Academy. He knew less of the political battles, the charges and countercharges of dirty dealing, that had made Chavez Ravine a hot button of Los Angeles politics.

In 1950 the area of Chavez Ravine had been designated for public housing. Internationally renowned architect Richard Neutra was hired to design the project. Among most non-Hispanic Angelenos, the Chavez Ravine area was considered a dump, and there was no doubt trash littered some of the hills. The hill that would become Dodger Stadium was a well-known lovers' parking site, spiced by the perceived threat of the surrounding Mexican American communities of the Ravine. When Neutra visited the area, he found a vibrant community of about eleven hundred families, most of them Mexican American. The families were generally poor, although Crispin Martin, one of the actors who played the Cisco Kid's comic sidekick in the movies and television, lived there. Many of the houses were ramshackle, barely clinging to the slopes. Utilities could be haphazard.[1] It was a close group, and the people who grew up there as children remembered their community fondly. Life centered around the small church and the neighborhood school. Neutra recognized that much of the sense of community that architects and planners were striving so hard to create with urban renewal already existed in the area.

The project—called Elysian Park Heights—went ahead. Congress had voted money in 1949 as part of a plan to build public housing on eleven sites in Southern California. The next year the Los Angeles City Council signed a contract with the Los Angeles Housing Authority (the recipient of the federal money) to build ten thousand housing units for $110 million. The housing authority began work. Landowners were offered cash settlements, most of which were accepted. Almost all the families left, assured that the move was only temporary until the project was built. Their houses were torn down. Neutra walked the hillsides, figuring out where to site the high-rises and planning the spaces between them.

Some people, however, did not like this, or any other, public housing project. Conservatives had denounced public housing as creeping socialism for years. Now, the real estate industry weighed in. The Home Builders Association, the Chamber of Commerce, and, most important, the *Los Angeles Times* joined the movement.[2] Public housing had become the focus of liberal-conservative battling in Los Angeles.

In December 1951 the city council bowed to pressure and reversed itself, adopting a resolution to cancel the city's contract with the housing authority. The housing authority sued and won an April 1952 state supreme court ruling that the contract was valid and that a pending referendum on the issue would be moot. Moot it might be, but the political message was also clear. In June just under 60 percent of Los Angeles voters said they did not want public housing.

Later in 1952 the state senate's Committee on Un-American Activities, the California version of the House of Representatives committee trying to root out Communists in Washington, began to investigate the Los Angeles Housing Authority. Three staff members of the authority failed the litmus test. They all took the Fifth Amendment and refused to answer when asked, "Are you now or have you ever been a member of the Communist Party?"[3] They were fired. In that McCarthyite era the housing authority and all its works were political untouchables.

Senator William Knowland and Vice President Richard Nixon, two influential California Republicans in Washington, were instrumental in pushing a special measure through Congress in 1953 that would allow the city to get out of the contract. But an October U.S. Supreme Court ruling upheld the contract, and the housing authority forged ahead with construction on all but two portions of the housing program.[4] One of the two was Chavez Ravine.

By the 1953 election for Los Angeles's city council and mayor, public housing was the top issue. Incumbent mayor Fletcher Bowron, a centrist Republican supported by unions, the National Association for the Advancement of Colored People, and the League of Women Voters, campaigned on his earlier advocacy of public housing in Chavez Ravine and elsewhere in the city. Norris Poulson, a conservative Republican congressman, was approached to run by a group headed by *Los Angeles Times* publisher Norman Chandler. Poulson protested that the only hot Los Angeles issue he was really familiar with was public housing, which he had opposed in Congress.[5] The delegation said they knew that.

For Poulson, public housing was a senseless waste of public money. He argued that the cost of building the project would require rents that only the middle class could afford. He charged that the housing authority was dominated by "leftists" and that they would show political preference in choosing tenants. He was joined by city councilman John C. Holland, who said "public housing follows the Communist pattern. These are the people who are trying to wreck America."[6]

Bowron supporters charged that Poulson was in the pay of real estate interests. Already, of the eleven sites around the city set aside for public housing, the opposition was focused on Chavez Ravine. They proclaimed Poulson wanted to get it pulled from the list of public housing sites so he could sell it to developers active in his campaign.[7] Poulson acknowledged he had received campaign money from Howard Hughes, but said he was not beholden to real estate interests or any developers.[8]

Other opponents of public housing apparently were. When city councilman Ed Davenport died a few years later, $30,000 in cash was found in his safe-deposit box, and his checking account balance was suspiciously large for a man who had had only a $7,500 annual councilman's salary and lived at the posh Park Wilshire Apartments. His widow said Davenport, whose switch had been crucial in the 1951 vote abrogating the city's contract with the housing authority, had received "gifts of money" from the real estate lobby.[9]

The city's more liberal elements supported public housing. The president of one of the city's most visible unions, a young actor named Ronald Reagan, threw his support behind Bowron.

Poulson won and, with a mandate against public housing, moved quickly through some complicated negotiations with the housing authority and the federal government. The projects Bowron had managed to start would be completed. The others, including Chavez Ravine, would not. The federal government would sell Los Angeles the land it had acquired for public housing and stipulate only that it be used for a "public purpose." The city paid $1,279,000 for the Chavez Ravine property, about $4 million less than the federal government had spent for it.[10]

Four years later bringing up the words *Chavez Ravine* was to pick at scabs that had not quite healed and raised echoes of corruption. The signs were evident even as Poulson, Wyman, and other Dodger supporters were pushing the final contract offer through the city council. And groups that opposed the city's agreement with the Dodgers could count on that reputation to help their cause.

The first taxpayers' suit had been filed in late-September 1957, even before the council had managed to agree on its final offer. But the real blow landed in November and December, when the Citizens Committee to Save Chavez Ravine for the People presented a petition with 70,911 signatures calling for a referendum on the city's deal with the team.[11] On December 1, 1957, Los Angeles city clerk Walter Peterson announced that an initiative to overturn the city's agreement over Chavez Ravine had qualified for the ballot. O'Malley was surprised and dismayed, so dismayed he hinted he might return to New York, a statement he was soon "clarifying."[12] Walter O'Malley, veteran of Tammany Hall, a man who walked through New York City courthouse crowds like a family reunion, was about to discover California politics.

Politically and economically, California burst onto the national consciousness in the late 1840s. The capital was in Monterey in the central part of the state, and it had a potential port on San Francisco Bay. But, especially in its southern areas, California was essentially a backwater province of Mexico where a few New England traders had settled. When the Treaty of Guadalupe-Hidalgo ended the war with Mexico in 1848, California became American territory. Just a few weeks before the treaty was ratified, James Marshall found gold on the American River, northeast of Sacramento, in the northern part of the state. By the summer of 1849 eastern Americans raced across the plains and deserts, sailed on ships around Cape Horn, or trekked across the Central American isthmus in a dash for the goldfields. The state's population exploded to more than 100,000 by the end of 1849.

A few made their money in the goldfields, but the ones who really got rich were those who gave up gold-hunting quickly and settled down in San

Francisco or Sacramento to supply gold seekers. As the gold rush faded, and economic consolidation followed in its wake, four of these merchants emerged to dominate the state and leave their names on the California landscape. Collis P. Huntington and his family left behind Huntington Park, Huntington Beach, and the magnificent Huntington-Hartford Library in Southern California. Charles Crocker had a bank that was one of the state's largest. Mark Hopkins's hotel still sits atop the San Francisco skyline, and the university that Leland Stanford named after his son is one of the best in the country. Their names remain on their projects and their philanthropy, but their power was built on the Southern Pacific Railroad (SPRR).

Eventually, the railroad's power over the state, its miners, and its farmers grew to such a level that novelist Frank Norris would call it "the Octopus" in his 1901 novel. It was an apt name, for the SPRR owned 85 percent of the railroad tracks in the state. And the Southern Pacific's power, used ruthlessly to maximize profits, would provide a major impetus for the strain of Republican politics known as progressivism.

The Southern Pacific oligarchs buttressed their economic power by controlling the state legislature, the governor, and California's major national politicians. Thus, the reformers, led by such figures as Hiram Johnson, moved to introduce a series of measures that soon would be imitated across the country—the initiative, the referendum, and the recall. These reforms allowed Californians to enact legislation without the railroad-dominated legislature and to oust elected officials. They were first enacted in Los Angeles in 1902, receiving statewide approval in 1911. These tools could be used to create a public utilities commission to set the railroad's rates. They could express the electorate's feelings about public housing. They could stop a stadium deal they did not like.

By 1958 the big four were long dead, and their companies had been matched or superseded by other players. The railroads were fading into mundane carriers of cargo rather than symbols of expansion, modernity, national power, and individual greed. But the initiative and the referendum survived, and survived more strongly in the fragmented politics of Southern California. They made it incomparably harder for Poulson, Hahn, and the others to deliver on the promises made a year earlier in Vero Beach.

Los Angeles's growth over the decades, while brilliantly conceived to make a great metropolis out of poor raw material, had resulted in a geographic horror show. The boosters' desire for a port had led to a yo-yo-shaped ganglia extending south of the downtown. State annexation law required that annexed territory be contiguous to the existing city. So the city snapped up a corridor—only four blocks wide in places—connecting it with the harbor lands it wanted around San Pedro. When the city needed greater mass to justify investments in its most critical shortcoming—water—it annexed pieces of virtually empty land around its periphery, including the giant San Fernando Valley.

With the postwar boom in housing, the valley and all the other outlying areas of the city had filled up quickly, much more quickly than the city was able to provide services. Because the city's fifteen city council members were elected by separate districts, the desires and complaints of each member's constituents were far more important to them than the visions of those downtown interests seeking to make Los Angeles a great city.

The downtown interests—concentrated around the *Los Angeles Times*—were the most powerful bloc in the city. The Chandler family, which owned the *Times*, had heavy investments in downtown real estate. They were joined by other property owners, downtown developers and law firms, and the Chamber of Commerce. But this group—white, Protestant, and generally descended from midwestern migrants—was by no means omnipotent. "The *Times* and the business interests simply have not won often enough to let us say that they were the wheels of a machine which functioned behind the screen of non-partisanship," said one academic student of contemporary Los Angeles politics.[13] The countervailing blocs, who most often spoke through city council members, came from the distant districts of the city. San Pedro and the harbor were twenty miles from city hall. The farthest parts of the valley were twenty-five miles.

The city council offered full play to the clashing interests. As mayor Poulson could appoint members of important commissions and begin the budget process, but his other powers were very limited. There was no city manager. The council was asked to decide administrative detail to a level unparalleled in a major American city. Years later O'Malley would tell Roger Kahn he knew of the risks. "We took a chance," he said.[14] But evidence at the time indicates he was surprised. In January 1958 he told *Sports Illustrated*'s Robert Shaplen that Chavez Ravine had "been there since God created the earth and now I learn it's been controversial for years."[15] Discussing the negotiations with the city, he said, "The thing got more and more confusing."[16]

The Chavez Ravine petition had been turned in with considerably more signatures than the 51,767 required to put it on the ballot. But veteran California political figures knew you needed far more signatures because many would be disqualified. Most people were approached to sign at supermarkets, and many were happy to oblige even if they were not registered voters.

Many Angelenos, O'Malley supporters would argue, had been misled by the people asking for their signatures.[17] City councilman Ernest Debs claimed that "many petition circulators . . . have told the public if you want the Dodgers to play ball in L.A., sign here."[18] Actor Buddy Rogers said he had been approached in just such a manner on his way to the Coliseum one night.[19] As was, and is, typical in petition drives in California, circulators had been paid by the signature, a total of about $19,000.[20]

So who was paying for the signatures? Poulson thought some interests were obvious. The community newspapers, especially in outlying areas of the city, still did not like the big downtown dailies and the support they were giving the Dodgers. Just mentioning that the *Times* supported some position was enough to raise the hackles of liberal elements. Television stations did not like O'Malley's strong interest in pay TV and lack of interest in putting his product on one of their channels.[21] And what TV station could resist when the petition backers worked to manufacture a little drama? Just before five o'clock an armored car rolled up before the city clerk's office, where cameras were already primed. A theatrically alert guard jumped out brandishing a shotgun, his eyes pinballing around the scene and a pistol ready on his hip. "A lot of people would give a lot to see that these petitions never reached the city clerk's office," a referendum supporter told an Associated Press reporter.[22]

Although they did not do it publicly at the time, O'Malley and Poulson would later pin the generalship of the antis on two San Diego brothers.[23] John A. "Black Jack" Smith and C. Arnholt Smith had a tuna fleet and canning operation in San Diego that had made them a fortune. John also was in the oil business. They had bought a bank and the San Diego Padres of the Pacific Coast League and that winter had invested $500,000 in the construction of a new stadium. With the inevitable reorganization of the PCL, San Diego would be reduced to a lonely outpost, its three closest PCL rivals—Los Angeles, Hollywood, and San Francisco—pushed out of state by the Dodgers' and Giants' arrival.[24] The Padres would have the lure of Major League Baseball only one hundred miles to the north, and their hometown paper had already assigned a beat writer to the Dodgers. John Smith was "a minor league man who doesn't want major league baseball in Southern California," said O'Malley. "Except for him, there would have been no referendum."[25] When C. Arnholt Smith sent in a check for season boxes, O'Malley grabbed a blue crayon and scribbled a note across the application: "No box seats for this guy—He's against us."[26]

The sports pages of the major Los Angeles newspapers generally treated the sources of a growing round of attacks as a vast mystery, and even the news pages did not begin to discuss the Smiths' participation until well into 1958. Unless voiced in council chambers by Holland or Patrick McGee, the downtown papers detailed the opponents' arguments only when they wanted to refute them. Only a few weeks after the city council and O'Malley had reached agreement, *Los Angeles Times* sports editor Paul Zimmerman used his column to complain that O'Malley—"whose name never has been even remotely connected with a shady deal"—was being "cast in the role of a sharpster."[27] Zimmerman's column was one of the first that asked who was financing the anti-Dodger campaign, although he did not answer his question.

Others, however, had little trouble penetrating the supposed veil of secrecy. *Sports Illustrated*'s Shaplen got an interview with John Smith, and Smith laid out for the record the charges whose source the Los Angeles newspapers were treating as the riddle of the Sphinx. "I know what he's got in mind," Smith said. "He wants to put in motels and bars and restaurants along with baseball. Let's hear him say no."[28] There was talk O'Malley wanted to take over portions of adjoining Elysian Park and build a year-round entertainment center that could make the parking lots more profitable.

Dodger executives were trying to say no. In early February team vice president Fresco Thompson told a sympathetic dinner audience that "contrary to general opinion, which seems to exist in Los Angeles, we are not coming here as carpetbaggers." He denied that O'Malley really had no interest at all in bringing baseball to Los Angeles. O'Malley, he said, was not "planning to build a pre-fabricated ball park in Chavez Ravine, then tear it down in two or three years and dig for oil or uranium."[29]

Oil was the biggest red herring O'Malley had to deal with, one that still pops up in Los Angeles conversations today. As one oil executive told Pasadena baseball writer Rube Samuelsen, "The Dodgers could waive the oil rights and lose nothing."[30] Oil companies had explored over the years and found little. There were a few wells producing in the area, around four to five barrels a day of low-quality crude. But oil rights were a hot issue in California, where suburban bungalows had proved to be sitting atop oil fields in recent decades.[31]

In fact, O'Malley had agreed to waive all mineral rights during his 1957 negotiations with Chad McClellan. The final agreement with the city, however, was more ambivalent. Politically, the city council could not afford to give up on the possibility of oil, so it required the Dodgers to set aside a site in Chavez Ravine for a rig should experts decide it was worth drilling. Oil revenues would come to the city. O'Malley, ever the tough negotiator, got something in return. Because he was obliged to set aside land in case drilling was approved, O'Malley won the concession that half of those earnings would be charged against the Dodgers' obligation to fund youth sports programs. O'Malley won the same half-and-half division for any oil found under Wrigley Field after it was handed over to the city. These were bargaining victories that would come back to haunt him. Theoretically, the Dodgers could have received $1.7 million in oil revenues. In reality, as the experts were predicting, they received nothing.

In early-December 1957 nationally syndicated columnist Drew Pearson dredged up the story of the housing authority, Chavez Ravine, and city councilman Davenport's unexplained wealth and gifts from real estate interests. Although all of Pearson's charges related to events before O'Malley had even begun thinking of Los Angeles, the column was written in a way that implied the Dodgers' hands were soiled as well.[32]

To O'Malley, the attacks seemed to come from every angle. In the down moments of an emotional roller-coaster, he would say, "I want to know why people are against me." In a lighter mood, he would turn it into an ironic bit of humor. It was the winter after the Russians had launched the first satellite into orbit, and America was convulsing over "the space race" and whether we trailed the Communists. At a baseball dinner O'Malley remarked, "It's a good thing I'm not being held responsible for the Sputniks, too."[33]

The opponents had found enough valid signatures, and on December 4 the Los Angeles city clerk said the measure to approve the city's contract would appear on the ballot at the statewide primary election the next June. It would be known as Proposition B.[34] City councilman John Holland, the leader of the anticontract forces, argued strenuously that it ought to be labeled Proposition C, so the proponents could not use a "B for Baseball" tagline.[35] He lost. They did.

Except for swipes such as O'Malley's denial of C. Arnholt Smith's ticket request, he and Poulson decided to take the high road. "The referendum is a democratic process and baseball is a democratic game. We will watch what happens with interest," O'Malley said after the referendum qualified for the ballot. Poulson said he and O'Malley calculated they would win the referendum handily. A poll showed 70 percent of voters supported the Dodgers' deal with the city.[36]

But even caution could get O'Malley in trouble. After his statement about democracy, a reporter asked if this kind of thing would drive him back to Brooklyn. "I haven't given up on LA," he temporized.[37] One New York paper translated that into a headline that implied O'Malley was returning, and the next day he was denying to a Los Angeles audience that he was so flighty. The referendum, he noted, would not come to a vote until mid-season, and so they would stay. This time, he refused to answer "what-if" questions about the referendum.[38]

Over the first half of 1958 the battle for Chavez Ravine would be waged on a number of fronts. Several city councilmen, especially John Holland, ran a campaign against Proposition B in public. Holland seemed to find occasion at almost every city council meeting to raise the issue, find fault with the deal, and denounce it yet again. He was always coming up with alternative uses for the property. Apparently inspired by planning for New York's coming World's Fair, he proposed a world scientific exposition. His proposal had no details about who would attend or pay for the exposition, and Roz Wyman sarcastically asked if the scientists would be housed in pup tents.[39] Holland's bulldog opposition to public spending and Wyman's sarcastic comebacks were indicative of the two pillars of the Chavez Ravine debate in the city council.

John Connell Holland was from the kind of rock-ribbed American stock that had wandered its way across the continent and formed the backbone of Los Angeles—white, Protestant, native born, migrated to Los Angeles, full of the small-town values of the Midwest. Holland's father, William, had been born in Virginia on the eve of the Civil War, moved to Texas, and married Betty Connell there. John was born in Bartlett, Texas (about thirty-five miles northwest of Austin), in 1893. Holland's family kept moving. He spent his high school years in Roswell, New Mexico; returned to Austin for his first year of college; but then moved on to Stanford University. Holland took a prelaw course, gained recognition as a wrestler and debater, and graduated in 1917. With American participation in World War I beginning, Holland joined the Army.[40]

By May 1919, fresh out of the service, Holland settled in the Los Angeles community of Highland Park, just off the future Pasadena Freeway that

O'Malley would use decades later to commute from the Coliseum to the Rose Bowl. Holland married his college sweetheart and opened a neighborhood electrical appliances store. From there his political career was a textbook of small-town Republicanism. He joined the Masons, American Legion, Elks, and Kiwanis. He served on other community organizations. He was a tall man with a ready smile, slightly wavy dark hair over a high forehead, and steel-framed glasses. He neither smoked nor drank, had opposed the expansion of breweries in Los Angeles, and clearly equated beer and baseball.

In 1938, disgusted at the corruption of Los Angeles mayor Frank Shaw's administration, he signed on to the reform campaign that put Fletcher Bowron in the mayor's office. In 1942 Bowron appointed Holland to the Fire Commission, and the next year Holland ran successfully for the city council. For the rest of his career he would win his seat in the primary every time, never having to face a runoff, even when his opposition to the Dodgers flushed out eight opponents in 1959. When he retired in 1967 his twenty-four years on the council constituted the longest term ever.

Over the years he espoused solid Republican values for government. He wanted it small. He wanted it honest. He wanted it frugal. He would start investigations of whether the mayor was co-opting fire department helicopters too often.[41] He gloried in the nickname "Watchdog of the Treasury" and ceremonially passed it on to another council member on his retirement.[42] Unlike Poulson he was more dedicated to these ideas than to any concept of Los Angeles as a great and glorious megalopolis. He described Poulson as a man "with whom I was very friendly until he got in the Dodger deal."[43]

On his retirement Holland said there were three battles he was most proud of. In keeping with his philosophy of limiting government, all the battles had been waged to stop the city from doing something. Twice, he had won. He had played a major role in the struggle against public housing in the early 1950s, and he had stopped the fluoridation of the city's water system in the 1960s. In between he had lost, on Chavez Ravine.[44]

Roz Wyman was not John Holland. She was a short Jewish liberal Democrat and O'Malley's most consistent supporter in Los Angeles politics. "Without Roz Wyman, so help me, there's no Dodger Stadium," said Bavasi long afterward.[45] Rosalind Wiener had been born in Los Angeles, the daughter of two pharmacists, four decades after John Holland. She lived in a neighborhood so established that she went to the high school named after the city, a remnant of the small town Los Angeles had been decades before. Her political talents blossomed at a young age—she recalled being elected president of her sixth grade class. At Los Angeles High she was the first girl to be elected president of the school's house of representatives.[46] Her political interests extended off campus, where she rallied support for Democrat Helen Gahagan Douglas, who lost a bitter Senate election to Richard Nixon in 1950.[47]

Wiener graduated from the University of Southern California with a degree in public administration in 1951 and took a counselor's job with the Laurel Canyon Youth House. But the political bug was strong. Within a year of her graduation, she was elected to the Central Democratic Committee of Los Angeles County and campaigned hard for Adlai Stevenson for president.[48] In 1953 she ran for the city council in a West Los Angeles district that included her parents' duplex, where she still lived.[49] Eight other people stood in that primary, which was nonpartisan, in keeping with Los Angeles's political self-view. But then everyone knew every candidate's party labels anyway.

It was the election that had turned on public housing, and Roz Wiener supported it, for she was no more Norris Poulson than she was John Holland. She had little money. Her campaign headquarters was in her parents' dining room. Wiener walked her district door-to-door from the February start of the campaign through the April primary to the late-May runoff, calling on neighbors and strangers, presenting a well-scrubbed young woman obviously full of vivacity and intelligence, bubbling with energy. She handed out cakes of soap and promised to clean up city hall.[50] Later, she estimated she had rung forty-five hundred doorbells, which was probably a good thing, as she won by only three thousand votes. Poulson's campaign manager endorsed a rival.[51] Wiener had to conspicuously turn down an endorsement from the Communist Party paper.[52] But she did accept some campaign help from Eleanor Roosevelt.[53] Like Poulson, she won in a runoff.

She was quickly the Los Angeles's newspapers' favorite member of the council. It was not that they agreed with her politics. A few months after her election, one of the city's conservative newspapers jumped on her for appointing a field secretary with "a long record of left-wing political associations." The appointee had been an aide to Helen Gahagan Douglas. Wiener, the paper said, was a "leftish Councilwoman."[54] It was that she was too good a story to ignore. She was twenty-two years old and the first woman on the city council since 1915. When council president John Gibson went on vacation that fall, she became the first woman to preside over a Los Angeles City Council meeting.[55] She was pretty and single and had a clever tongue. For the less straitlaced of the newspapers, those that liked their headlines short and snappy, she quickly became Roz.

As a single woman, Wiener's dating habits were a source of interest to the public and the papers. Even in a political profile the *Los Angeles Times* could not help but note she was "an attractive brunette with fine, clear skin." Her clothes that day were a white blouse, royal blue skirt, and plain suede pumps, typically feminine but conservative.[56] "I'm a human, a woman, and I want to go out," she acknowledged, but adding that once she had gone a month without a date, and "I'm not used to that."[57]

When she went to see jazz great Eartha Kitt sing at the Mocambo Club, she was asked if she thought the show was risqué. Kitt was under attack by Poulson and other conservatives for some sexually suggestive songs, such as "Santa Baby, Hurry Down My Chimney Tonight."[58] Wiener had no problem with the lyrics, but perhaps that was because her escort that evening was Eugene Wyman, a young Beverly Hills lawyer. Wyman had been attracted to her at a speech she gave to a Beverly Hills Bar Association luncheon. He found out her next speech was to be at a church in the San Fernando Valley and convinced the pastor to appoint him her escort for the evening. A month later they were at the Mocambo, and by August 1954 they were married. Norris Poulson came to the wedding. Wiener insisted on paying half the costs of the marriage license. The honeymoon was in Honolulu.[59]

Within months of her election Wiener was chairing the council's Parks and Recreation Committee, an outgrowth of her work at the youth center. She acknowledged she liked to fish, but mentioned no other sports, even though her parents' home was about a mile from Gilmore Field, home of the Pacific Coast League's Hollywood Stars. Later, *Los Angeles Herald Examiner* sports columnist Melvin Durslag, a big fan of Wyman's, would say that, at that point, she did not know Mickey Mantle from Mickey Spillane.[60] Her mother, Wyman later said, was a "wild Cub fan," and the Cubs' major farm club played at Wrigley Field.[61]

In 1957, up for reelection, Wyman became a champion of the Dodgers' move to Los Angeles, and shortly after the election she was named to the Coliseum Commission. She established early relations with O'Malley. Harold Parrott recalled he was instructed to make sure she got excellent seats at the Coliseum, and later at Dodger Stadium, and Parrott regarded this as a payment for political support.[62] Wyman's support went beyond the public, for she would send her mother to quietly sit at the back of anti-Dodger meetings and report back on their plans.[63]

For the city's establishment, the debate on Chavez Ravine was a great source of embarrassment. The twists and turns of the debate were drawing attention from around the country. That old saw about Los Angeles being not a city but a collection of disparate suburbs rankled the city's elite. A Major League team, after all, implied a center, the integrated, powerful city they wanted. "Dodgers Get Raw Deal," editorialized the *Los Angeles Mirror News* in prose that echoed the worries of the downtown establishment.[64] "To the rest of the country we must look like prize boobs from the way we've handled the major league baseball situation. We must appear as a community with virtually no idea of what we want. And our indecisiveness certainly tears down the reputation we've been trying to build that we're a cohesive, well-organized metropolitan area."

But Holland, city councilman Patrick McGee, and the other antis were persistent. They did not share the downtown bloc's economic interests or the overweening vision of Los Angeles as a great city that went with it. The downtown interests seemed prepared to overlook their traditional suspicion of the eastern big-city Catholic strain O'Malley represented because he was one of only sixteen team owners who could stamp their city "Major League."

The *Times*, steadily running stories about new groups coming out in favor of Proposition B, let its proprietors' exasperation with the opposition slide into its news stories. "The City Council got in a hassle again yesterday about Chavez Ravine," it reported in mid-May. "Tempers Flare again over Chavez Ravine" was the headline a couple of weeks later.[65] *Again* was a word that appeared again and again in the coverage.

The opponents kept screaming about a secret deal and calling for an investigation. They could not interest Congress, but eventually the state assembly's Interim Committee on Governmental Efficiency and Economy agreed to hold hearings in Los Angeles on the issue. The panel and major witnesses trooped out to Chavez Ravine and had a choice of tour guides—Wyman or McGee—to take them over the hot, dusty hills. Then it was back to the state building downtown for two days of hearings that helped to crystallize the issues behind Proposition B.

The pros reiterated their arguments dating back to the previous fall, many of them enshrined in the contract. The Dodgers' coming would validate Los Angeles as a Major League city. The additional park space would benefit the city. The Dodgers' Knothole Gang program to give free tickets to kids would help with juvenile delinquency. A new stadium would clean up a blighted area, put large hunks of acreage back on the property tax rolls, and add employment.

The antis, always careful to say they did not oppose the Dodgers' coming, only the contract, were much more specific. They said trading the Chavez Ravine property for the Wrigley Field site was inequitable, as Chavez Ravine was worth far more than the city thought. There were better uses for the land, they charged, and O'Malley knew that, which was why he was taking far more acreage than was needed for a stadium. A privately owned stadium would prevent the city from making money by renting out a city-owned stadium to other users. The contract was illegal because of the "public purpose" restriction in the deed. And, of course, there was the oil.

At the hearings, and in subsequent days, at least some of these issues would be dealt with. Others were contemporary judgment calls that would be answered only by time. The oil argument flashed anew. At the hearings John A. Smith offered to pay the city $1,000 an acre plus a 16.67 percent royalty for mineral rights to all the acreage under Chavez Ravine. A couple of days later, when the city council took him up on the offer, Smith began putting conditions on it. He would need more than the one drill site specified in the contract. He would need relief from city ordinances about the removal of derricks. The city council passed a resolution offering the oil rights to anyone who could match or better Smith's offer. No one came forward.[66]

Late on the hearing's first day city councilman Karl Rundberg, who had voted for the contract the previous October, announced he was changing sides, in part because the Dodgers' presence would pull business downtown from his district in the Pacific Palisades on the far western end of the city. Rundberg's switch crystallized the perception that the opposition was coming from the distant parts of the city, parts less likely to benefit directly from the Dodgers' move and stadium construction and areas traditionally suspicious of the downtown elite.[67]

There was also growing anti sentiment in the San Fernando Valley. There, the heavy late-winter rains that had delayed conversion of the Coliseum had caused widespread flooding. On one rainy day that spring, two-thirds (sixty-four) of the city schools in the San Fernando Valley had to close because of flooding. No schools elsewhere in the city had to shut. Opponents reminded residents that the city had not gotten around to providing promised flood-control channels and sewers while spending money to woo the Dodgers.[68]

Hotel owners, movie theater operators, developers who worked in outlying communities, and newspapers serving distant parts of the Los Angeles area had been notable in supporting the antis' movement.[69] These interests were also the ones who focused on what other uses O'Malley might make of the land—suggesting hotels, shopping facilities, and other developments.[70] This led to questions about whether the Dodgers really needed 300 acres to build a stadium. They noted that Disneyland, the recently opened jewel of Southern California entertainment, used only 225 acres.[71] In his testimony at the hearings O'Malley noted that the ballpark itself would take 75 acres, plus the land for the extensive parking lots Los Angeles's driving habits would make necessary and the 40 acres that would go back to the city as park space.[72] Even opponents conceded that much of the acreage was so hilly it could not be developed.[73] But O'Malley never rejected categorically the argument that the space could be used for other development, leaving him open to suspicion. He never pledged not to develop any excess acreage, and, in later years, he rejected suggestions that limitations were appropriate.[74] He also never developed any of the land except for a gas station complex within the stadium, an idea that went back to his first stadium plans in Brooklyn.

While these arguments were fading, the antis were also raising concerns that cut to the heart of the issue. The Dodgers' contract, Holland told the hearing, "deprives the city of the only large parcel of publicly owned land near the Civic Center available for future expansion of public services." The procontract forces did not deal with that argument, and the antis soon undermined it.

Questioned about who else wanted the land, Holland said he had had an offer of $30 million for the property, but could not disclose the bidder. Wyman challenged him to reveal enough to judge the validity of the offer. Holland returned to the witness stand and said the offer had come from Maytor H. McKinley, president of Utter-McKinley Mortuary, a large Los Angeles burial services firm. Having undercut his own point about the land being useful for a public purpose, Holland then finished himself off by saying he would never agree to sell the land for a cemetery anyway.[75]

The cemetery offer was just part of a larger debate about what the Chavez Ravine land and the Wrigley Field site were worth. Gibson and Wyman trotted out Charles Detoy, a former president of the Los Angeles Chamber of Commerce. Detoy noted the city had received no reasonable offers for the land since buying it from the federal government three years earlier. "The property has no market value today. If I was to put it before any of my clients as a potential [investment] property I would be doing them a disservice. The city is fortunate to be getting someone to develop this problem property."[76]

Aside from the cemetery, the antis were able to come up with no specific rebuttal to Detoy. But any glance at the map of downtown Los Angeles would confirm Holland's basic point: whether for public purposes or private, the Chavez Ravine site was the largest tract of open land adjacent to downtown Los Angeles. At some point, to some one, it would be highly attractive. Aside from O'Malley's offer of Wrigley Field in trade, though, nothing was on the table. Poulson would write later that Walt Disney had turned down Chavez Ravine as a site for Disneyland.[77] Especially for those interested in raising the profile of their city, the Dodger bird in the hand was worth far more than any future potential the Chavez Ravine site had.

And what was the Wrigley Field property worth? The official city appraisal was $2.5 million. Holland and McGee argued that figure was far too high and demanded retired admiral Cushing Phillips, president of the Municipal Board of Public Works, report to the council on its real value. Phillips put it at $4.25 million, saying the city would have many uses for the stadium and it would be hard to replace.[78] He projected amateur baseball, high school sports, and other events could use the facility. Nobody made the simpler argument that, in effect, the city would be paying $1,279,000 (the money given to the federal government for Chavez Ravine) for Wrigley Field, below even the lower estimates of that property's assessed value.

It is also interesting to note that, as in New York, O'Malley had become fixated on one site. When the assembly commission came to town, O'Malley told them, "I don't know of any other suitable site in Los Angeles."[79] In hindsight it seems clear that, as with the Atlantic Avenue property in New York, he had the best site in mind. But could Chavez Ravine be the only site? The opposition came forward with no concrete suggestions.

That left the ultimate argument. Why shouldn't the city hang on to this land, build the Dodgers a stadium, and lease it to them? If this land was such a good stadium site, ripe for development, why shouldn't the city take those profits for itself?

The relevant model at that time was San Francisco. San Francisco had agreed to build the Giants a park and rent it to them for $125,000 or 5 percent of the gross annually, whichever was larger.[80] The opponents of Los Angeles's deal with the Dodgers, although describing themselves as conservatives who opposed government ownership of business, regularly held this up as a model for what Los Angeles should be doing.

O'Malley's supporters tried to argue that San Francisco had made itself a bad deal by taking on the risks of a municipally owned facility. The city would have to maintain the facility and stage enough other events to pay off the bonds. "It boils down to whether you want the city to go into business or whether you sell property to a private enterprise," Chad McClellan told the state assembly committee.[81] McClellan raised a subtler point about municipal ownership. Because Chavez Ravine would become O'Malley's property, he would have to pay property taxes on it—which various people estimated at $300,000 to $350,000 a year.[82] A municipally owned stadium would not pay taxes. Thus, the cash difference to the city would be not only what it cost them to operate the stadium, but what the city had to forego in property taxes.

Three decades later Dean Baim, an economist at Pepperdine University, set out to determine how much stadium and arena deals were costing cities. He looked at the fourteen venues where he could get data. Some of these stadiums dated back to the 1930s, and the study covered costs and incomes to their cities through 1986. He found that only one stadium had contributed steady, positive income to its city. The others ranged from the loss of less than $1 million at Buffalo's War Memorial Stadium to New Orleans's deficit of $70.4 million on the Superdome. The one positive stadium deal was Los Angeles's trade of the Chavez Ravine land, which grossed the city $5.9 million over the period, mostly from property taxes.[83]

Counterattacking on the issues was just one of O'Malley's tactics, for after first dismissing the antis, he began to take them very seriously indeed. Late in 1957, as the signatures were being certified, O'Malley and Poulson were taking the high road publicly.[84] They were also taking the high road privately because their polls indicated two-thirds of voters approved of the city's contract.[85] In late April O'Malley was still complacent, telling a Los Angeles Food Brokers Club audience that he would leave the campaign to the city's "able public servants" and letting Roz Wyman give the food brokers the hard sell on Proposition B.[86] O'Malley was focused on finding a place to play, getting the team moved, and solving his financial worries.

Clearly, the antis were reading similar polls. When, in late-December 1957, a city council committee set the referendum vote for June, the Citizens Committee to Save Chavez Ravine for the People opposed a vote. They wanted the city to abrogate the contract.[87] But by May, with the Dodgers mired in last place, the team's private polls indicated only 37 percent of Los Angeles city voters approved of the contract.[88] O'Malley swung into gear.

There was not much he could do about what he thought was his biggest problem—the team's poor play—except to push the blame toward the anti–Proposition B camp. "Uncertainty about their future worries our players, most of whose families are in the East. It has caused a mass stage fright."[89] Nor could he do much about the downtown-suburbs split, the ghosts of Chavez Ravine, or the uncompleted storm drains.

What he could do was create a stew from his old Tammany skills and the media savvy of his new friends in Los Angeles. Tammany meant blending politicians and the business establishment with everyday folks. Norris Poulson, always with an eye on how this would affect his city's image, staged a Dodger Week and urged Angelenos to support it "in every way possible in recognition of its status as our newest civic enterprise."[90] O'Malley could ensure that Mrs. James B. Fredericks, chairwoman of the Women's Committee for Yes on Baseball, could throw out the first ball at a Dodger home game.[91] He could tell a businessmen's luncheon that the Knothole Gang program to let kids in free would operate every day instead of eight to ten times, as originally announced.[92]

He could leap on the tiniest opportunity to build support. In early May O'Malley received a letter from Dan Teola, a salesman for Acme Visible Records, suggesting the Dodgers could use Acme's wonderful system of cards and folders to keep track of personnel. Different colored stock for batters and pitchers, Teola pitched. O'Malley, undoubtedly deluged with such letters as the prominent new business in town, turned this one over to team statistician Allan Roth with the scribbled note: "At least write and thank this VOTER—WOM."[93]

In late April O'Malley caved in on television, announcing that the Dodgers' road games at San Francisco would be televised in Los Angeles, starting with a three-game series May 9 to 11. O'Malley said his change of heart was due to "sincere requests from the fans, including many shut-ins and baseball-minded Los Angeles city officials."[94] That the "baseball-minded Los Angeles city officials" were concerned about losing an election would seem to go without saying. Disingenuously, O'Malley told one Los Angeles audience that the broadcasts had not happened earlier because of the lack of sponsors, but the same sponsors who had paid for radio quickly stepped forward for the television games as well.[95] Reportedly, he was also concerned about offending the Giants' Horace Stoneham. Stoneham, like O'Malley, was strongly interested in pay television and had elected not to televise any Giants games in San Francisco. Stoneham was concerned O'Malley's move would increase pressure on him to televise the Giants' road games, especially those in Los Angeles.[96]

Hollywood was a great gift to O'Malley, for its support was almost unanimous, and it provided a raft of people whose opinions would always get exposure. As the pro–Proposition B campaign swung into gear, he could get actor Joe E. Brown to complain the Dodgers' political efforts did not have the funds the antis did.[97] He could count on luminaries such as television host Art Linkletter to make jokes funny enough to make the papers, but sharp enough to make a point of how the Dodgers felt they were being treated. "I understand Walter O'Malley's building an ulcer-shaped swimming pool here," Linkletter told a dinner.[98]

Plus, there was always the reliable support of the downtown establishment. On the Friday before the vote O'Malley called Richard Moore, president of KTTV, the television station owned by the Chandlers, to talk about last-minute tactics. Moore came up with the idea of a telethon (a Dodgerthon, it was called) for that Sunday, two days before the election.[99] The telethon was five hours of unabashed support for Proposition B. KTTV had cameras at the airport for a live telecast of the team's return from a (dismal) road trip. Hollywood notables such as Jack Benny, George Burns, Danny Thomas, Bill Frawley, Debbie Reynolds, Dean Martin, and Jerry Lewis flashed their smiles and said a few words. Ronald Reagan lashed out at the measure's opponents, calling their arguments "dishonest." Joe E. Brown announced for the first time that all blind and deaf people who wished to attend Dodger games would be admitted free.

O'Malley appeared and did himself proud. *Sports Illustrated*, which wanted to be sarcastic, wound up treading a softer line. "Waving his big fat cigar, he turned on the O'Malley charm. He gave his viewers warmth and dignity and, using a blackboard and pointer, he gave them O'Malley-style facts," the magazine reported. O'Malley "created an image of a gentle, kindly, fatherly type who wanted nothing in this world (at the moment) but 300 acres of city property to build happiness and parking space for all."[100] The *Los Angeles Times*, whose sympathies were committed, called him the "star performer."[101] The *Times* used the third page of its first section for pictures of the stars and O'Malley.[102]

Although such coverage could help, it could also be a two-edged sword. The major downtown newspapers kept up a steady stream of news stories about one group or another throwing their support behind Proposition B. The *Times*, for instance, averaged such a story every three days in the three weeks before the vote.[103] When O'Malley appeared in public at some innocuous event, such as a Humanitarian of the Year banquet for Joe E. Brown, they could run a picture of him presenting the plaque and beaming benevolently.[104] But the constant run of stories slanted to one side of an issue could also remind readers of their suspicions of O'Malley's downtown allies.

Deprived of a decent team, the sportswriters turned to almost slavish portraits of O'Malley, painting him as a devoted baseball fan who lived simply by "the O'Malley code despite the fact that he has been a top executive for years in a number of million-dollar enterprises."[105] On the editorial pages the *Los Angeles Times* ran two pro–Proposition B cartoons in the eight days before the June 3 vote.[106] It used its lead Sunday editorial two days before the vote to push the measure, call the opponents "simply crackpot," and frame the vote as a question of Los Angeles patriotism. "Do you, a citizen-voter, want Los Angeles to be a great city, with common interests and the civic unity which gives a great city character; or are you content to let it continue its degeneration into a geographical bundle of self-centered sections each fighting with the other for the lion's share of the revenues and improvements that belong to all?"[107]

As the last days of the campaign approached, O'Malley stepped up his activities. He was sniping at his opponents—"two Councilmen and one minor league owner"[108]—and getting much more involved in defending Proposition B. Although he was happy to have all the Hollywood people expressing their support, he wanted to answer questions personally and publicly. He undoubtedly felt he could make his points better himself, and his personal appearances put a human face on the arguments, which in many cases had raised doubts about his character. He was no longer the faceless, behind-the-scenes manipulator but a man who smoked cigars, made jokes, and answered questions with seeming clarity.

He was also getting help from outside Los Angeles. On May 22 National League president Warren Giles said, "If the vote on the city's Chavez Ravine contract is refuted by the citizens of Los Angeles, it will be my personal recommendation to our league that we take immediate steps to study ways and means of relocating the franchise in another city."[109] Publicly, O'Malley expressed concern about Giles's statement and said he would have to meet with him. A day later Giles was suggesting Houston, Toronto, or Minneapolis–St. Paul as possible sites, and baseball commissioner Ford Frick was saying he did not want to get involved but that Los Angeles could face a "terrific problem" if Proposition B lost.

Given his place in baseball's upper councils, it seems highly unlikely O'Malley was surprised by these remarks. Furthermore, the suspicion must linger that he orchestrated them, for they suited his purposes perfectly.[110] The threat he needed had been voiced, but voiced in such a way that it allowed him to reiterate his desire to stay in Los Angeles. He could cite "the location, the weather, the fans and the attendance records." But he could then throw his hands in the air and argue that if six of eight National League owners voted to move the franchise, he would be helpless. He could say, "I pledge to try to keep major league baseball here" and leave supporters and opponents to parse how hard he would try.[111]

The next day, May 28, Holland threw another smoke bomb. Surrounded by television cameras, he flourished a copy of a draft press release he had obtained from the files of the Celler Committee in Washington. The draft press release was dated May 2, 1957, and prepared by Los Angeles city attorney Roger Arnebergh and Los Angeles County counsel Harold W. Kennedy. The draft dealt with the legality of using the Chavez Ravine land for a baseball stadium, which Arnebergh and Kennedy both supported. Across the top of the draft O'Malley had scrawled, "Vetoed in toto." This, said Holland, was "incredible" proof that O'Malley was "actually participating in the operation of our city and county government."[112]

Once Arnebergh, Kennedy, and O'Malley recovered their wits that afternoon, they tried to explain. They pointed out that a virtually identical press release had been issued on May 6. The only substantive change in the text was the deletion of the name of the Brooklyn Dodgers and the substitution of "National League Baseball." O'Malley acknowledged he had vetoed the original wording, claiming it was because at that time he was talking about getting National League baseball to Los Angeles, not specifically about moving the Brooklyn Dodgers there.[113] Although this statement may have caused a few chuckles in New York City, it was accepted in Los Angeles, mostly because it did explain the change in the wording. More important, it made it clear that O'Malley was not vetoing Los Angeles officials' actions, but quibbling about wording.

May 28 was also the beginning of a round of radio and television appearances by O'Malley to rally support for the measure in the last five days before the vote. He was on Bill Brundige's sports show that Thursday evening, answering questions. Sunday was the five-hour Dodgerthon, with O'Malley answering more questions. Monday night another locally owned television station staged a two-hour debate, and again O'Malley rather than a Hollywood figure or some other local face had the final word on Proposition B. After Wyman and Los Angeles sports announcer Tom Harmon traded barbs with Holland and McGee, O'Malley stepped to the microphone for the summation and returned to the high road. "I know the Dodgers' case will be tried by the fairest jury in the land and I want to tell you all that I'm willing to abide by the decision the voters make. There's not going to be any bitterness. I'm not going to be angry with anyone, and I know that whichever side loses, the losers will measure up to the situation."[114] Still, Rube Samuelsen noted an air of "tenseness" surrounded O'Malley in the final days before the election.[115]

Tuesday, June 3, found the Dodgers playing an evening game at the Coliseum against the Cincinnati Reds. O'Malley, still in suit and tie, held one of the new small transistor radios to his ear, trying to get election results.[116] The first night's results were encouraging, but it would not be certain until later Wednesday that Proposition B had been approved. The *Los Angeles Times* rejoiced in the victory. "The City Is Finding Itself" was the headline over a self-congratulatory editorial. "The vote is an answer to the deriding critics of Los Angeles who have characterized it as a group of villages in search of itself."[117]

O'Malley chose to ignore the relatively slim margin—24,293 votes out of 666,577 cast, with the Dodgers winning 51.8 percent of the vote. Lighting a victory cigar with Buzzie Bavasi, he talked about how construction could begin within a month, "if there are no road blocks such as problems of proper clearance or delays due to litigation." The new stadium could be open by July 1, 1959, he predicted. How about a name for the stadium? he was asked. "Heavens, no. The child has just been legitimized," he said.[118]

O'Malley knew there were still those questioning the legitimacy. Councilman Holland and his wife visited the Registrar of Voters office late on June 4 to check on security provisions for the votes, "particularly those registering a vote for Proposition B." Holland would not confirm he was planning to ask for a recount. "Gangsters or others might get in and change the election results," the *Times* reported Holland had told a guard.[119]

O'Malley acknowledged to *Examiner* reporter Bud Furillo that he expected even further legal entanglements.[120] There were, after all, still three taxpayer lawsuits pending.[121] Nevertheless, he was telling reporters construction could start as early as July 5.[122]

Johnny Podres, the team's veteran lefthander, said the poll victory helped the team relax and win a 3–0 victory on Wednesday. "I know I felt different out there," he said.[123]

11

In Court

The referendum victory could wipe away only so many problems—especially on the field. The great Dodgers of the past decade were declining. Jackie Robinson had retired two years earlier, and Roy Campanella's career had ended in January's car crash. Pee Wee Reese, Carl Erskine, and Carl Furillo were wearing Dodger uniforms but playing out the string. It was not quite apparent yet, but Don Newcombe's playing career had been destroyed by alcohol. Gil Hodges and Duke Snider were distracted by the bizarre proportions of the Los Angeles Memorial Coliseum. Hodges was trying to pop everything over that neighborly screen down the left-field line. Snider, who had lived by popping balls over the short right-field wall in Brooklyn, was looking at a right-field fence 440 feet away in the power alley. Then, he hurt his powerful throwing arm in a childish bet to see if he could throw a ball out of the Coliseum.

Years later Dodgers executives would say that after the 1957 season, Walter O'Malley had leaned on players such as Reese and Erskine to delay their retirements. He felt the Dodgers would need marquee names to help market the team to an audience largely unfamiliar with Major League Baseball.[1] In the event, Buzzie Bavasi said, the city was so enthusiastic that the big names made little difference, and keeping those players delayed the development of the next generation.[2]

The players were having trouble adjusting to Southern California. Wives were struggling with housing, in part because team officials did not have lists of furnished apartments that were available without a lease, another example of how poorly planned the move had been. Even when his wife rented a place, manager Walter Alston had trouble finding it at the end of the first road trip. He had no idea how the city was laid out.[3] "It was very traumatic," said Carl Furillo. "Los Angeles just didn't feel right. All everybody did was talk about Hollywood. Everybody wanted to meet movie stars or see who was in the stands. Nobody had his mind on the game."[4]

Wives, led by Brooklyn native Joan Hodges, were reluctant to come to California. When Hodges did move, she soon went home, leaving morale worse.[5] Dick Young of the *New York Daily News*, who stayed with the team until the June referendum, was always happy to note homesickness and unhappiness among team members that spring.[6] O'Malley would later blame much of the poor performance on the anxieties of the move. "Their families were back East, they were worried over their kids, there was a referendum that threatened to run us out of town and there was generally a feeling of tenseness and uncertainty," he said.[7] Bavasi said that until Proposition B passed, he was advising his subordinates such as Al Campanis, Fresco Thompson, and broadcaster Jerry Doggett not to buy homes in California.[8]

They lost the opener in San Francisco on April 15, 8–0. Three days later they edged the Giants 6–5 in their home opener at the Coliseum, but then dropped two in a row to the San Franciscans and two of three to the lowly Chicago Cubs. They kept losing. On the morning of the referendum vote, they were 17-26 and in last place, ten games behind the Giants.

At the Coliseum it did not matter. The customers came. On opening day there were 78,672 paying fans, breaking the Major League record for opening day, or for any day game, for that matter. It doubled the Brooklyn single-game attendance record (37,512 in 1947). They mingled with Jimmy Stewart and Edward G. Robinson, Groucho Marx and Tennessee Ernie Ford, Nat "King" Cole and Alfred Hitchcock ("taking up a seat and a half in Section 9"). Both candidates for California governor showed up, as did two hundred reporters. Cigar in hand, O'Malley wore a "Dodger Blue" flower in the lapel of his brown suit, while Kay and Terry were dressed entirely in blue. Kay obligingly carried a prominent copy of a yearbook and scorecard, for she regularly kept score. Including free passes, police, and vendors, there were more than 80,000 people in the park.[9]

It was just the beginning. By July 3 attendance was more than 1 million, despite losing about 10,000 fans that night because seats had been roped off for the traditional July 4 fireworks show the next night.[10] After losing the July 4 date to fireworks, the Dodgers passed their 1957 attendance level in Brooklyn on July 5. They overtook the Brooklyn season record, set in 1947, on September 24. For the first time since 1945, the Dodgers beat the Yankees in attendance. All these milestones came despite a terrible performance from the players. The Dodgers' first ten home games drew average crowds of 39,721. The last ten averaged 16,558, still higher than the per-game average for the last six years in Brooklyn. The late-season fade held the year's attendance to 1,845,556, short of O'Malley's goal of 2 million fans.

Many of these new fans could not see well, for the Coliseum was as ill-suited to viewing a game as it was to playing it. Dodger pitcher Ed Roebuck tabbed it the "Grand Canyon with seats."[11] Even behind home plate a fan in the top rows was 700 feet from the plate. A customer who bought a seat beyond the right-field fence was 560 feet from home plate—if he sat in the first row.[12]

O'Malley did not sit 700, or even 560, feet from home plate, but the owner's box was not what he was used to in Brooklyn. "I always sat behind home plate at Ebbets Field, but not as publicly as this. It's like an isolation booth," he said, referring to the game-show variety where the audience could watch a contestant ponder. O'Malley's box was a wooden platform with a bright-green canopy behind home plate. It sat eight (nine uncomfortably, O'Malley said) with a Plexiglas window set into the screen in front of it. O'Malley said the frequency of foul balls left him "shell-shocked." On opening day he had sat in a regular box behind the Dodger dugout but found it was too far from the press and team officials clustering behind home. So part of the photographers' setup was converted for the use of O'Malley and his guests.[13]

Los Angeles Times reporter Jeane Hoffman, who spent an evening with O'Malley in the box early that year, reported he was "the Dodgers most fervid rooter. He yelps continually during a game, urging the players on with such comments as 'Holy cats, get IN there . . . Don't try to KILL it, just DUMP it . . . Let's all HIT.'"[14]

O'Malley had plenty of company. Going to the Coliseum to see the team that had stamped Los Angeles "Major League" was clearly the thing to do in the city that summer. The stadium might be a topless Dutch oven, with seats stretching forever from home plate, but it was Angelenos' validation of their city. And, in straining to see what was going on at that plate so far away, the fans found the man who was to personalize and personify the Dodger team for this and the next three generations of Dodger fans.

In Brooklyn Vin Scully had started as Red Barber's understudy. Then, he had been a young man working in the shadow of Barber and Mel Allen with the Yankees and Russ Hodges with the Giants. In Los Angeles he was a phenomenon. A couple of decades later, after three World Series wins and exposure to Hall of Famers Snider, Reese, Koufax, Drysdale, Sutton, and Alston, Dodger fans would overwhelmingly select Scully as the most memorable person in team history.

It was a conjunction of talent, preparation, and technology. The talent was something Scully and his mentors had nurtured since he decided at a young age to be a radio announcer. The preparation was the years of listening to others and then working with Barber. The technology was the transistor radio.

The cheap, portable transistorized radio, barely as big as a person's hand, was new and ideally suited to be taken to the beach, hidden in a pocket at school, or lugged to some high row in the Coliseum, where Don Drysdale looked like a praying mantis unwinding to strike. The Dodgers were soon stocking transistor radios at souvenir stands to supply fans who had forgotten theirs.

Scully was there, his rich baritone flowing out into the best radio market in the country. With its growing suburbs, dispersed job base, and miles of freeways, Los Angeles was the commuting capital of the world. Stuck in their cars, people listened to their radios more in Los Angeles than any other major city, and the preferred program quickly became a Dodger game. "'Everybody' is probably not a mathematically precise description of the number of people who listen to Scully's broadcasts, but it is close enough," wrote *Sports Illustrated*'s Robert Creamer.[15] Radio, as O'Malley had realized, whetted the listeners' appetite for baseball. And nobody could slip a commercial into play-by-play and make it sound like a casual comment better than Scully. "Craig looked a little bit like Robin Roberts on that last batter, and that reminds me, Roberts and the Phillies will be here this weekend . . ."

Vincent Edward Scully was born in New York City on November 29, 1927. His neighborhood, the Washington Heights area at the far northern tip of Manhattan, was not too far from O'Malley's Bronx homeland. Also like O'Malley, he grew up a Giants fan, making the pilgrimage to the Polo Grounds to watch his boyhood hero, Mel Ott.[16] It was clear from an early age that Scully had a fantastic ear for accent, rhythm, and tone. His father died when he was eight, and his mother took Scully with her on a trip back to Ireland, a trip from which the red-haired Scully returned with a brogue it took him months to lose.[17]

In eighth grade, Scully remembered, Sister Virginia Maria asked his class to write essays on what they wanted to be when they grew up. Scully said he wanted to be a radio announcer. Instead of telling him of the long odds, the nun set him off on a program of reading aloud to prepare him. At Fordham Prep the Jesuit fathers reinforced the program with debate, oratory, and dramatics. Scully recalled that when he showed up to represent the high school at an oratorical competition, his mentor was horrified Scully had only brown shoes. He scoured the rectory to come up with a pair of black shoes that fitted.[18] His education and lifelong reading would enable him to steal a line from T. S. Eliot in the middle of play-by-play or quote Shakespeare between pitches.

While training his voice and his mind for a life of talking, Scully was also doing practical work in his chosen field. Left-handed all the way, he spent hours in the street at stickball and broadcast the games as he went. He said the constant reiteration of outs, men on base, and count made him a more alert outfielder. When he got home from school, he would take a glass of milk and a plate of crackers and crawl under the family's large table-mounted radio. From there he imitated Ted Husing and Red Barber, his heroes behind the mike.[19] He would later say he felt he had a great advantage over these pioneers because he was of the first generation that grew up listening to radio. Thus, he knew that when something big happened, he did not want to hear the announcer; he wanted to hear the crowd scream. A quick description followed by the uninterrupted roar of the crowd would be his lifelong practice.[20]

From Fordham Prep, where he played on the baseball team, Scully went to Fordham University, graduating in 1949 after a short stint in the postwar Navy. At Fordham he continued to play on the baseball team (good field, fair hit) but became more and more involved in the campus radio station, WFUV, a small FM outlet where he did Ram football, basketball, and baseball games.[21]

As graduation approached Scully sent out letters to radio stations throughout the country, seeking a job. The only offer was for summer replacement work at WTOP in Washington DC. It was not permanent, but WTOP was a big station and part of the CBS Radio Network. He spent the summer filling in for vacationers, reading sports and news, and pronouncing the station's call letters at all the appropriate times. He did well enough to be offered a job that was due to come open in early 1950.[22]

But he returned to New York that fall without work. On the strength of the CBS connection, he dropped in at network headquarters. He was told there was not an opening just then, but maybe he should meet Red Barber, who oversaw CBS sports programming in the off-season. Catching Barber as he was about to leave, Scully had a few minutes of conversation and left hoping against hope he had made some kind of impression.[23] Evidently, he had. A few weeks later Chicago newspaperman Warren Brown, who was scheduled to broadcast that week's big college football game, North Carolina–Notre Dame in New York City, came down ill. Barber quickly moved his young Dodger broadcasting colleague Ernie Harwell over to that game. But then he had to come up with an announcer for the Maryland–Boston University game Harwell had been slated for. What about that kid from Fordham? he asked.[24]

Scully returned home that day to his mother's excited report that Red Skelton had called. After figuring out it was the other Red, Scully returned the call and got his assignment.[25] He had heard from some college buddies that there would be a dance after the Fordham–Boston College game in Boston the day of his broadcast debut, so Scully dressed for the dance. When he got to Fenway Park, the site of his game, he found he had miscalculated. He should have worn the long johns. There was no radio booth for him at Fenway, just a microphone and a long cord on a cold, windy day. Dressed in a light suit and topcoat, Scully kept (barely) warm by moving up and down the stadium roof with the ball. In those days CBS Radio staffed a number of college games every Saturday. Mostly, they stayed with the featured game and turned to the other games only for quick summary updates. But the format was flexible, and that afternoon the featured North Carolina–Notre Dame game turned out dull, while Maryland–Boston University was the tightest game of the afternoon. After a series of more frequent updates, Barber turned the broadcast over to Scully, who wound up doing play-by-play rather than summaries.[26]

Too frozen to dance, and totally unsure of how he had done, Scully returned to his hotel room and burrowed into bed for twenty-four hours, fearful of pneumonia. On Monday he returned to New York and checked in at CBS, as he had been told to, half fearful he would be flayed for his performance. Instead, he was congratulated. After Barber found out about the conditions under which Scully had done the broadcast (and not mentioned either during the broadcast or to Barber afterward), he shot up in Barber's estimation. A few weeks later Barber had him do the Harvard-Yale game.[27] And at the turn of the year, when Harwell moved from the Dodgers' to the Giants' announcing team, Barber asked Scully if he wanted to join the Dodgers for the 1950 season.

Scully's early years with his hero were at times difficult. "He sometimes treated me like a little boy," Scully later said.[28] Barber was a perfectionist and occasionally quick with cutting remarks. Scully's style was more casual and conversational than Barber's. But Scully persevered and grew, always giving Barber credit for the quality and the concern of his teaching.

His relationship with O'Malley was better from the beginning. After the 1950 season Scully was very impressed that the news he was coming back for 1951 was delivered by O'Malley personally and not by letter or an underling.[29] When Barber left the Dodgers after the 1953 season, O'Malley was willing to leave Scully in the lead chair. Scully, meanwhile, would admit later that he never really felt comfortable operating in the shadow of Barber and Allen in New York. "I really don't think the real me began to emerge truly until I got here to California. I think until that time I was still somewhat frightened, doing ballgames with a white knuckle."[30]

Scully developed a close relationship with the O'Malley family. He would later describe Walter O'Malley as "like a father to me" and Peter as "like a brother."[31] When O'Malley and his family continued around the world after the 1956 Japan trip, Scully accompanied the family. Scully—twenty-eight years old, attractive, a devout Catholic with an excellent future—seemed a good match for Terry, then twenty-three. But that did not work out. On the eve of the move to Los Angeles, Scully married Joan Crawford, a New York model.[32]

In the early years O'Malley often counseled Scully to be "positive" on the air.[33] But Scully, while perfectly happy to sell the product, stuck to Barber's objective style, which Barber, Scully, and O'Malley all felt was necessary in the sophisticated New York market. But during the winter of the move, Scully and O'Malley talked about whether Scully should adopt the rooting style more popular with midwestern announcers (and generally used by the broadcasters for the Pacific Coast League Angels and Stars). They decided against it, and Scully later said that given the nationwide sources of Los Angeles's population, that was a good idea. Too many people in town were still rooting for the Cubs or the Cardinals.[34]

Scully also had the touch for converting liabilities into strengths. Conscious that he would inevitably make mistaken references to Brooklyn, he and partner Jerry Doggett set up a pool on the air during spring training games that first year. Each time one of them referred to the Brooklyn Dodgers, he had to put $1 in a kitty. The money was used to buy baseball equipment for a needy kid. It was the kind of openness that made a great impression on fans, a number of whom began to send in their dollars for the kitty.[35]

Unlike O'Malley, Bavasi, and the other public faces of the team, Scully was young and notably not "New Yorkish." He was tall and skinny, with a shock of red hair that was almost a pompadour and a quick grin. Although he never lost a couple of New Yorkisms (AH-renge for the Californian's o-renge), he did not sound eastern. Scully's main job was to introduce the team, and the Major League game, to Los Angeles. Although the city had its share of people who knew the game, the phenomenon of the team was attracting a wider and less sophisticated audience. Scully had the knack of teaching the nuances of the game by making his audience see situations through the eyes of the manager and players. With a runner on first and a left-handed hitter up, he had run through the variables a manager would keep in his mind for the decision on whether to hold the runner—the speed of the runner, whether the batter was a pull hitter, how good the pitcher's move to first was. Many Southern California Little Leaguers would learn more from Scully than their coaches. "It would be impossible to overestimate his worth to the team," summed up *Los Angeles Times* columnist Jim Murray.[36]

While Los Angeles was falling in love with Scully and the Dodgers, the brand of baseball played in the Coliseum and the supposed naïveté of Los Angeles fans and newspapers were being lampooned throughout the rest of the country, fanned by a cadre of New York writers clearly still upset at the move. The first few games at the Coliseum saw a flurry of home runs fly over the left-field screen. Press box Solomons immediately began to differentiate between "Chinese" or "legit."[37] The Coliseum became "O'Malley's Chinese Theater." Baseball became a game called "Screen-O." The comments ran from "mockery of big league baseball" (the *New York Daily News*) and "turns big league baseball into handball" (*New York Post*) to "It's a magnificent park—for football" (*New York Herald-Tribune*) and "Good baseball is sacrificed for gold" (*New York Mirror*).[38]

Sports Illustrated weighed in with the headline "Every Sixth Hit a Homer!" and editorialized that the Coliseum "threatens to make a travesty of the game." After nine games the magazine decided that "puny right-hand hitters will bash more home runs than ever before in their lives."[39] It produced a cartoon theoretically focused on the home run controversy, but showing how the New York media had come to see the team. It portrayed a toga-wearing, cigar-puffing O'Malley as David, about to sling a stone over a chain-link fence at a towering statue of Babe Ruth. Of course, it was a hitter like Gil Hodges who was most likely to hit the home runs, not O'Malley, but his image had merged so much with that of the team that he was being portrayed doing things he literally could not do. And, as would be seen three years later with Roger Maris, any threat to Ruth was automatically portrayed in a negative light.

The *Sporting News* was the lone voice from east of the Rockies suggesting that the Coliseum and its screen were not the end of Western civilization. It editorialized that it was too early to judge and did a piece on the origins of the term *Chinese home run*, which it traced to descriptions of balls hit down the lines at the Polo Grounds in New York.[40] The St. Louis–based weekly did not drop the issue, either. At the end of the season the paper's Cliff Kachline found that, although the Coliseum did lead the league in home runs, the Dodgers and their opponents fell 14 short of the Ebbets Field home run record.[41]

Significantly, the 193 home runs hit in 1958 would be the highest total of the four years the team played in the Coliseum. As Alston and Hodges had suggested before the season started, the players quickly began to adjust. In the early games the reaction was to pitch inside, as beanballs whizzed by the batters' heads. But the pattern quickly became to pitch right-handed hitters outside, making it much more difficult for them to pull the ball. By the Dodgers' tenth home game, Pittsburgh Pirates manager Danny Murtaugh had already figured out this strategy.[42] When the Milwaukee Braves made a West Coast road trip in June, a survey found more than two-thirds of their hitters thought San Francisco's Seals Stadium was a better home run park because of a steady wind blowing out to left field.[43]

But the Coliseum was only one topic for the New York writers. The columns of New York papers, and the *Sporting News* articles from the New York writers that spring and summer, were full of shots at the Dodgers, Los Angeles, Los Angeles baseball writers, and, of course, O'Malley. It was such an obsession that New York Yankees general manager George Weiss, who had hoped to capitalize on being the only Major League Baseball team in town, complained that the Dodgers were getting more coverage in New York papers than his team.[44]

Although O'Malley was the favorite target for spite, he was not alone. One New York reporter told National League president Warren Giles, "You have to have a team in New York." Giles sarcastically replied, "Who says you HAVE to have a team in New York?" The reporter turned that into a headline that twisted his reply into "Giles Says Who Needs New York?" while ignoring Giles's additional thought that it would do the league good to have a team back in the city.[45]

The chorus had amplified in spring training, when several New York writers quit following the team, ostensibly because of unfair treatment. (It would seem likely their newspapers had realized that readers' interest in a team three thousand miles away would flag.) Some reporters detailed to readers, presumably fascinated readers, their "mistreatment" at the hands of the Dodgers. There was no more press bus to shuttle them between hotel and ballpark, the stories complained. Instead, the club had hired a couple of cars to handle the Los Angeles press contingent, which, with fewer newspapers, was smaller than the New York group. "The difference in cost between two cars and one bus would have been so small. Instead, the club was so small," wrote Dick Young.[46]

Young was the leader of the chorus. His "Clubhouse Confidential" columns in the *Sporting News* were filled with digs. He quoted players complaining about the smog, repeated jokes about the freeways, and noted the crackpot orators in Pershing Square across from the hotel used by most visiting teams. He pointed out items as petty as reversed captions in the Dodger yearbook. He criticized the lights and the public address system and the winds. He retailed a joke suggesting O'Malley be given "drop-dead pills." He suggested the Dodgers' front office had no interest in winning because they were making too much money.

He slammed the Los Angeles writers covering the Dodgers, suggesting the crowds were as big as they were because that was the only way people could find out what was really happening. He ridiculed one Los Angeles writer who had printed some praise from Alston for a dinner the Los Angeles writers had thrown for the manager and traveling secretary Lee Scott. And amid all these shots, he wrote, "Isn't it a little beneath a man of his stature for Walter O'Malley to run down New York and Brooklyn at every opportunity . . . ?"[47]

Young's writing had always had an edge, but it became more and more like advocacy. Leonard Koppett, a longtime New York sportswriter, said most of the New York sportswriters slacked off over time. "They didn't make a federal case out of it the way Dick did."[48] As the referendum issue had come to a close, Los Angeles reporters discovered a "New York writer" was feeding questions to O'Malley's opponents during the closing referendum debates.[49] Because Young was the only New York reporter covering the battle day to day, it seems clear he was the New York writer. Young had crossed from being a reporter to being a player.

All this was immensely irritating to the Los Angeles writers. The New York writers were questioning their competence and their balance, while demonstrating some balance problems of their own. One Dick Young article strongly praised Harold Parrott for organizing the pulling of every fifth seat at the Coliseum while not acknowledging that the man who approved the move was O'Malley, a man consistently being portrayed as interested in nothing but money.[50] Arthur Daley, the *New York Times*'s Pulitzer Prize–winning sports columnist, did a piece for the *Times*'s Sunday magazine, which carried the subhead "Having been lured West by handsome grubstakes, New York's departed ball clubs still face the question of whether Los Angeles and San Francisco are really 'big league.'" In it Daley neatly deflected the criticisms aimed at Horace Stoneham, while accepting all the anti-O'Malley arguments. The Giants' Candlestick Point ballpark would be protected from the wind and the cold, he said. More important, it would be city owned, which he reported was a much better deal for San Francisco than Los Angeles's offer to O'Malley.[51]

The Los Angeles writers were defensive. They, too, knew that the Coliseum was a poor place to play baseball, but reacted when the New Yorkers criticized anything, much less suggested their city was not "big league." After all, the arrival of the Dodgers was supposed to confirm their ascension, not raise questions about it. Connecticut native Jim Murray, then a staffer for *Time-Life* and soon to be a columnist for the *Los Angeles Times*, noted that some unnamed executives in the Dodger organization also rubbed local writers the wrong way with their assumptions that everything New York was better.[52] O'Malley, whom Murray would later describe as part of his "crowd," was not included in this criticism.

And the hardboiled New York writers could be sensitive, too. Dick Young suggested Los Angeles "writers, like many other Angelenos, should drop the defense-mechanism when referring to non-Californians. The words 'Easterner,' and 'New Yorker,' are employed by them in the same way that 'Jew' was used by Adolph Hitler."[53]

O'Malley's fears of further legal entanglements for his stadium were confirmed all too quickly. On Wednesday, June 4, with the win for Proposition B confirmed, O'Malley was talking of construction work within a month. On Friday, June 6, the courtroom tussles began in earnest. Superior court judge Kenneth Newell issued a preliminary injunction blocking the city from transferring the Chavez Ravine land to the Dodgers.[54] It was a move that O'Malley must have expected, notes Neil Sullivan, whose *The Dodgers Move West* is the definitive study of the legal and public policy issues surrounding O'Malley's battles to build his stadium in both New York and Los Angeles.[55] Newell's decision to grant the injunction was based on questions about whether the Dodgers constituted a "public purpose" under the Federal Housing Act, the issue that had dogged O'Malley's steps in New York.

The injunction had been sought by Phill Silver and Julius Reuben, attorneys representing taxpayers who had filed suits to stop the deal. The two, especially Silver, would lead the courtroom fight over the next two years. Silver constantly had to distinguish himself from Phil Silvers, the comic who was then starring as Sergeant Ernie Bilko in the popular television show.[56] The Dodger suits would be the first of several high-profile, often lonely, legal battles for Silver. In later years his suits would eventually force reapportionment of the state legislature, and he would wind up a top aide to Los Angeles mayor Sam Yorty. He unsuccessfully ran for the state assembly, the city council, the board of education, and judgeships at both the municipal and the superior court levels.[57]

Born the son of a factory worker in Lynn, Massachusetts, Silver worked his way through college making tintype photographs. Eventually, he migrated to Los Angeles, attended law school, and set up practice in Hollywood. A short, pudgy man with close-cropped hair and beveled rimless glasses, Silver was fifty-one in 1958, living in a duplex near Wilshire Boulevard with his third wife.[58]

The lawsuits raised a number of issues, but the key one was highly similar to the argument Robert Moses relied on in New York. In New York Moses had said he could not use the city's powers to put together a plot of land for O'Malley's stadium because federal law said those powers could be used only for a "public purpose." A baseball team was not a public purpose, Moses said. Now, Phill Silver was saying the same thing. The deed that had transferred the core of the Chavez Ravine land from the federal government to the city after the public housing failure had said the land must be used for a "public purpose," and the Dodgers were not one, Silver argued. This time, as Sullivan noted, the issue would be decided in court.

The trial started June 20 in the downtown courtroom of Judge Arnold Praeger (no relation to O'Malley's engineer-architect). As Sullivan notes, the trial was unusual because there were few issues of fact involved. It would focus on whether the provisions of the city council's contract with the Dodgers conformed to law. The referendum had asked voters if they thought the contract was a good deal for the city. Silver's and Reuben's suits asked if the contract was legal. The resulting trial focused on narrow and often arcane legal issues.[59]

By the time the trial began O'Malley had left town. He had flown to New York on June 11, telling reporters he was going to get a medical checkup and attend to some business matters.[60] There were, that summer, rumors circulating about O'Malley's health. Late that month Dick Young noted in the *Sporting News* that rumors held O'Malley was "a lot sicker than they say," but concluding that he looked healthy. "The Dodger prexy has gained weight, if anything. He is also glaringly devoid of the humility which invariably saturates people who are 'a lot sicker, etc . . .'"[61] O'Malley spent four weeks in the East, returning July 9. Four days later he was reported ill.[62]

Although O'Malley may not have been deathly ill, he was also clearly not well. His February broken ankle, the discovery of the intestinal polyp, and the operation to remove it had caused him to miss spring training for the first time since he had been an owner. He had barely returned to the team for opening day in mid-April, and within a few weeks it had become apparent to him that he would have to drop his sideline role and throw himself into the referendum fight. Through May and into early June he had been consumed by the issue, driving himself hard. He was fifty-four years old, overweight, living in hotel rooms, and facing the biggest financial risk of his life. The strain had to be tremendous.

Before he left in June O'Malley conferred with his lawyers over the battles with Silver and Reuben. O'Malley had a good sense of his strengths and weaknesses. He gave Buzzie Bavasi virtual autonomy in the baseball decisions. But when it came to legal issues, he was fully ready to get involved in planning strategy. He made one last attempt to put a stake through the heart of the oil issue. On June 13 O'Malley sent a letter to Poulson, relinquishing all oil rights in Chavez Ravine.[63] The letter was couched as a public relations exercise. The Dodgers are "in the baseball, not the oil, business," O'Malley said in the letter. The rights were being abandoned because the Dodgers wished to help the Parks and Recreation Department create opportunities for kids.[64] But it was sound legal strategy. The transfer of the Chavez Ravine land was a onetime occurrence, but if oil were found the language negotiated in 1957 would have the city giving the Dodgers money for at least twenty years. From the debate leading up to the referendum, O'Malley knew that one of his opponents' arguments would be that the city-Dodger pact had given the team illegal control over how city money would be spent. That issue could still arise because of the contract provisions allowing the Dodgers to decide how to spend the city's $2 million pledge to help prepare the Chavez Ravine land and to decide how to develop the forty acres of city parkland. But renouncing the oil rights removed a third instance and helped remove an issue that had clouded the stadium deal from the beginning.

Not immediately, however. John Holland continued to try to roll back the deal in the city council, arguing that O'Malley's repudiation of the Chavez Ravine oil rights should force the renegotiation of the entire contract with the team. He lost again.[65]

Silver, Reuben, and the attorneys for the Dodgers and the city spent a week arguing the case to Praeger. Silver and Reuben concentrated on the public purpose clause and the city's delegation of spending control to the Dodgers, but managed to bring up virtually every argument that had been raised by opponents in city council or during the Proposition B campaign. Praeger, poking vigorously with his questions, frustrated Silver and Reuben by keeping the case focused on narrow legal issues. He did not care if one of them argued such-and-such provision was a bad idea; he wanted them to focus on whether the deal was legal. When the city and Dodger attorneys took over, Praeger's questions bored in on the provisions allowing the Dodgers to decide exactly how to spend city money and whether the city could close public streets for the benefit of a private corporation. He also raised the public purpose issue.[66]

Praeger announced his decision July 14, striking down the contract. It was illegal, he ruled, for the city to transfer land formerly designated for public housing (a public purpose) to the Dodgers (a private corporation). It was illegal for the city to pledge to spend public money to acquire more land in the area to be given to the Dodgers, to close streets for the benefit of a private corporation, to delegate to the club decisions on exactly how to spend public money provided for grading, and how to spend the money for parks raised by any oil revenues. "The manner of expenditure of public money is in the nature of a public trust and cannot be delegated to others," Praeger wrote.[67] On the public purpose issue, he said the city council had exceeded its authority. "If the city can use public funds to acquire property for the purpose of conveying it to a ball club for a ball park, to be operated as a private enterprise for private profit, then the city may use public funds for the purpose of selling it for use for a private bowling alley, a private golf course, a steel mill, a hotel or any other private purpose."[68]

The Dodgers and the city were surprised. Three decades later Los Angeles city attorney Roger Arnebergh would tell Sullivan the decision was "flat wrong."[69] Arnebergh was out of town when the decision was announced, but his deputy who had argued the case, Bourke Jones, indicated some kind of appeal would be made.

O'Malley had barely returned from a weekend resting at Lake Arrowhead, a Southern California mountain resort. At a hastily assembled press conference, he also talked of appeal and expressed confidence it would all come out in the end. "I remain an optimist," he said. "This is just another hurdle which we will have to take in stride. What hurts is the delay. Our timetable is out the window and I'm afraid San Francisco will have its new stadium first."[70]

The first decision to be made was how to use the appeals process. The regular appeals process was available, but the city and the Dodgers worried that it would be time-consuming. Arnebergh calculated an appeal could not be completed before 1960. With construction time tacked on after that (and the unspoken thought that any California decision might be appealed to the U.S. Supreme Court), it looked unlikely the Dodgers could have their stadium until late in the 1962 season.[71] Instead, Arnebergh told Sullivan, the Dodger-city team made the decision to seek a writ of prohibition from the California Supreme Court. If granted, the writ would prohibit enforcement of Praeger's decision and, in effect, overturn it.[72]

While O'Malley was involved in the talks about legal strategy, he was also up to his ample hips in what-ifs and maybes. Praeger's decision had reporters asking what would happen if the Dodgers' contract with the city was invalidated. The questions came in two parts: Where else might he build a stadium (either in Los Angeles or elsewhere)? And after O'Malley said he thought he would win the legal battle eventually, where would the Dodgers play the 1960 season, after their two-year deal with the Coliseum ran out?

The questions began coming the afternoon of Praeger's decision. In line with his commitment to the appeals process, O'Malley first had to deny he would seek to rework his contract with the city. "It would not be good tactics to discuss another contract with the city while this one is involved in litigation," he said.[73] Then he refused to answer a variant question about whether he would pay rent to the city if it built the stadium in Chavez Ravine for him.[74]

What about other sites? the reporters asked. O'Malley first reinforced his commitment to appeal by saying, "I'm a stubborn man, but we were offered the Chavez site, accepted it and came out with the intention of building a modern park on it." Then, as he had during the referendum debate or the closing months in New York, he blinkered his eyes to the other sites. "We have had many other parcels of land offered us, but we have never inspected any of them. I want to make it very clear, moreover, that we have not gone shopping for any alternate site."[75]

That did not stop columnists from speculating. The *Los Angeles Times*'s Al Wolf suggested a plot of land on the west side of the Coliseum property.[76] Others brought up the site of Universal Studios in the San Fernando Valley and a six-hundred-acre parcel at the Dominguez junction, about halfway between Los Angeles and Long Beach. The racetrack at Hollywood Park and Wrigley Field were resurrected as possibilities.[77] Wrigley Field was also a prime candidate for what might happen after the Coliseum contract ran out. But O'Malley ruled out its use even on an interim basis.[78] There were provisions in the Coliseum contract allowing for additional years, but the rent would be much higher, with the percentage increasing to match that of the football tenants and the concession revenues being lost.

Praeger's decision, especially in light of National League president Warren Giles's remarks that O'Malley had orchestrated during the referendum campaign barely two months earlier, inevitably raised the possibility that the Dodgers might leave. While the Los Angeles newspapers danced around that question, the *New York Times* dealt with it near the top of its story and noted "Club Is Expected to Stay on Coast" in its headline.[79]

The visiting club at the Coliseum that day was the Cincinnati Reds, and reporters grabbed general manager Gabe Paul, who added a dash of reality to the idea the Dodgers would move on. "As for the possibility of the Dodgers being forcibly taken out of Los Angeles by the National League, it is technically possible but never would be done against Mr. O'Malley's wishes," Paul said. "It would be presumptuous to tell him what to do with his property."[80]

O'Malley's construction plans were clearly shot. The July 5 start of grading he had mentioned in the wake of the referendum victory was ten days in the past, and now there were more roadblocks. "Our timetable is completely out the window," he said.[81] With fans still bringing their money to the Coliseum, *Time* said Los Angeles was the "Garden of Eden and the Black Hole of Calcutta rolled into one" for O'Malley.

Speaking to the Optimists Club a couple of weeks later, O'Malley was clearly keeping up his own optimism, pledging an appeal.[82] By mid-August he was talking plans again. "I had hoped to get a bulldozer up in the ravine last month to begin shoving a pile of dirt around, even if it was simply pushing the same pile back and forth," he wryly told a Rotary Club lunch. February 1959 was his new target to start grading.[83] He appealed to the Rotarians for their continued support, despite the team's "shoddy" performance. Los Angeles fans were already getting past unbridled acceptance. Andy Vitalich hung Walter Alston in effigy at his San Pedro gas station.[84]

Another blow came in late September, as the Dodger-city legal team prepared for its October hearing before the California Supreme Court. Los Angeles County took $1.35 million of the money it had pledged for roadwork around Chavez Ravine and agreed to spend it on projects spread around the five supervisors' districts. "They may be in the courts for years and meanwhile we need the roads in other sections of the county," said supervisor Frank Bonelli, who proposed the move.[85]

On October 15 the California Supreme Court granted the city and the Dodgers a temporary writ of prohibition and set a hearing on a final decision for November 6.[86] In November they postponed, pushing any decision until early 1959 at best.[87] By then O'Malley was on an African hunting trip, but not before saying, "People have been shooting at me all of the past baseball season. Now, it's hunting season and it's going to be O'Malley's turn."[88]

Actually, O'Malley said later, he was hiding. He said he would have gone to the South Pole to get away while the court deliberated. "I didn't want to be in the position of commenting on something up before the high court. It's unethical."[89] Given the fact that he simply could have told reporters he would not comment on a matter before the court, it would seem likely he had other reasons for the trip. The most likely was further recuperation from the strains of the spring and summer. He was back by mid-November.

In January he got his decision. The state supreme court unanimously ruled in favor of the contract and made it clear they looked at the contract in an entirely different way than Praeger had. "In considering whether the contract made by the city has a proper public purpose, we must view the contract as a whole," wrote Chief Justice Phil S. Gibson in the court's opinion. "The fact that some of the provisions may be of benefit only to the baseball club is immaterial, provided the city receive benefits which serve a legitimate public purpose."[90] The judges did not comment on whether the benefits were equal, but Gibson's opinion did note that the contract's provisions did not represent an abuse of the city's discretionary powers, which could have triggered court action. Significantly for O'Malley's role in planning strategy, Gibson's opinion did take favorable note of the decision to renounce any oil revenues, an issue Praeger had excluded from consideration because it had occurred after the contract was signed.

O'Malley heard about the decision as he drove down the freeway that morning. By the time a press conference was assembled that afternoon, he was bubbling. Groundbreaking for the new stadium, he said, would happen within thirty days. It would be open for the 1960 season, although it might have only thirty-two thousand of its seats at that point, with more being added as time went on.[91] O'Malley said he had been so confident of the decision that he had written his response to it the day before it was announced.[92]

By the next day reality had set in again. Roger Arnebergh said O'Malley had been "extremely optimistic," noting it would take a minimum of sixty days to clean up the paperwork and get the city-Dodger contract signed. Only then could the Dodgers begin the process of submitting documents to the City Planning Commission, applying to modify the property's zoning, and petitioning to vacate streets.[93] County supervisor Frank Bonelli predicted the stadium would not open until 1964, as opponents would keep throwing up roadblocks. O'Malley was still hopeful of opening day 1960, but his architect, Emil Praeger, said that if he got all the approvals by July 1, he could work the crews at a "more leisurely and economical pace" and be ready for opening day 1961.[94]

More important, Phill Silver said he would appeal, a move O'Malley surely could have anticipated.[95] The process slogged on, as Silver continued to raise issues. In February and again in April, the top California court rejected Silver's pleas for a rehearing and then to overturn the earlier decision. The latter was the last gasp in state courts, but Silver indicated he was willing to continue his appeals to the U.S. Supreme Court if someone was willing to pay the costs.[96] Because the Supreme Court did not even come back into session until October, the process could stretch for months more. The April decision at least cleared the way for the city and the Dodgers to sign a contract. It was affirmed by the city council in late May, despite more attempted delays by Holland, and signed June 3, the first anniversary of the referendum victory and twenty months after the city council first approved its terms.[97]

O'Malley, eternally optimistic in public, was predicting a July 1, 1959, groundbreaking and the partial opening in 1960. Barely three weeks later, on the eve of O'Malley's proposed July 1 groundbreaking, Silver appealed to the U.S. Supreme Court without saying where he had gotten the money.[98]

O'Malley had taken on another task that spring. Since Roy Campanella's auto accident in early 1958, O'Malley had been looking for a way to help Campanella financially. He had kept him on the payroll as a coach and scout at $25,000 a year.[99]

A couple of months after the accident, talk surfaced in New York of a benefit game for Campanella, but the idea never got off the ground there. O'Malley went to work. He talked to Yankee owner Del Webb, who, interested in having his construction company build the Chavez Ravine stadium, was willing to do a benefit game. But Yankee general manager George Weiss and manager Casey Stengel were lukewarm. Then, at a dinner for Stengel after the 1958 season, Stengel praised Campanella strongly. O'Malley, in the audience with Webb, urged the Yankee owner to persuade Stengel while he was in the rhetorical afterglow. It worked. When the schedules came out, the Yankees said the only day they could play was May 7, when they had two days off between Kansas City, the westernmost stop in the American League, and the start of a home stand in New York. That posed a problem because the Dodgers were scheduled to play in San Francisco that afternoon, and Major League rules forbade a team from playing games in two different cities in the same day. O'Malley talked baseball commissioner Ford Frick and Giles into waiving that rule, persuaded player representative Carl Erskine and the team to agree, and reserved the Coliseum for that date.[100]

In Los Angeles the response was overwhelming. The Dodgers sold more than 80,000 tickets by the day of the game. When the last 10,000 seats went on sale the afternoon of the game, the two ticket windows were overwhelmed by a crowd estimated at 20,000 to 30,000 people. O'Malley opened another ten ticket windows, but police later reported about 15,000 ticketless people in a near riot outside the stadium during the game. One group did break down a perimeter fence, and some standees filled the empty space behind the right-field fence.[101] The announced crowd came to 93,103, the largest crowd ever to see a baseball game up to that time.[102] Inside, after the fifth inning, the lights were turned off, and public address announcer John Ramsey urged the crowd to make a "birthday cake" for Campanella with lighters, matches, and candles. "I've never seen anything like it," said Campanella.

O'Malley would never say how much Campanella received from the game. He refused to call it a "benefit" game, saying instead it was simply to honor Campanella. "Whatever a father does for a son, so to speak, is something between them. No one wants any public credit for such things," he said. Each team received $87,500 as its share of gate receipts, and Bavasi said the

Yankees gave nothing to Campanella.[103] Campanella would later tell *Ebony* magazine he received between $70,000 and $75,000.[104]

Campanella was not the only former employee O'Malley would support after their career. After the deaths of both Fresco Thompson and clubhouse man Babe Hamberger, their families would receive money for years.[105] In 1967, a dozen years after Sandy Amorós's catch preserved the Dodgers' 1955 World Series victory, O'Malley would put the thirty-seven-year-old outfielder back on the roster, and pay him for a month, so he could qualify for his pension.[106]

The Campanella game wrapped O'Malley, the Dodgers, and the City of the Angels in a cloud of civic virtue. But, as with all the early times in Los Angeles, the virtuous cloud evaporated within a couple of days. Television presented a morality play in which O'Malley was the bad guy. It was a public relations disaster that haunted him and the team decades later. And, like so many of O'Malley's problems, it was the difference between civic leaders' promises and delivery that would leap up to bite him.

When Chavez Ravine seemed destined for public housing in 1951, the Los Angeles Housing Authority had started the eminent-domain process to take control of the land. Settlements had been reached with most of the property owners. People had moved. Of the eleven hundred families living in the area when it was designated for public housing, only about twenty still clung to their homes by early 1959, although squatters had moved into the area.[107]

Most of the twenty were in disputes with the city over the value of their property. The housing authority had placed the offered amounts in escrow accounts in 1953. After the political fight the city bought the land from the housing authority in 1955, but because there was no pressing use for the land, the city lost interest in cleaning up the disagreements. The residents, technically squatters on public property, remained in their homes.

The troubled history of Chavez Ravine burst back into Los Angeles's consciousness the evening of Friday, May 8. That morning television cameras and a television helicopter had accompanied sheriff's deputies who were enforcing the city's writs of possession against the remaining residents of the area. On the news programs that evening, pictures of deputies carrying screaming, kicking women from frame houses assaulted the viewers. The pictures showed bulldozers knocking down the houses, while those evicted watched in anger and shock from the lawn. The announcers told viewers these were the Arechigas, a close Mexican American family who had lived there for thirty-six years. Seventy-two-year-old Manuel Arechiga, his wife, two daughters, one son-in-law, and five grandchildren had lived in two houses on three lots. In a touch of irony the television reporters loved, son-in-law Mike Angustian was a gardener for the City of Los Angeles.[108]

On Saturday the Arechigas took the drama to another level by setting up tents amid the ruins of the houses. They were refusing to move. The pictures touched off sympathy around the city. City councilmen who had fought the Dodgers kicked in $100 apiece. Roz Wyman added $50. Councilman Holland and his supporters leaped on the story, posing more questions. Jim Donnell, a resident of suburban Sun Valley, towed in a trailer and parked it nearby for the Arechigas to live in. Television reporters played and replayed the tape, the pictures showing poor Mexican American people being evicted from longtime family homes to make way for a stadium owned by a rich arriviste, an arriviste whose acquisition of the land had acquired a scent of impropriety after all the questions asked by opponents.

Over the next few days words placed the pictures in an altogether different context. City attorney Arnebergh started that first afternoon, noting that the superior court, acting at the request of the housing authority, had set the value of the Arechigas' property at $10,050 in 1953. That money, less $11 in fees, was available to them anytime they wanted to pick it up from the escrow account. After the voters rejected public housing later in 1953, the Arechigas filed suit to get back their house but lost. However, they did not file an appeal to the $10,050 assessment, an oversight that weakened their legal position later. Arnebergh said the Arechigas had been given multiple court orders to vacate the property over the years. The latest had been delivered March 9, giving them thirty days, and warning them the sheriff's deputies could arrive anytime after April 9.

The pictures continued. The family was colorful, keeping chickens, turkeys, goats, and dogs. One daughter, Aurora Vargas, one of whose husbands had been killed in military service, evoked more sympathy, especially when she became "semi-hysterical" on Sunday, May 10. The family asked the ambulance attendants to take her to a hospital, but they would agree to take her only to the psychiatric ward at County General Hospital. Family members would not sign the papers, saying, "She's not crazy."[109] A doctor later arrived and gave her a sedative.

The emotion dragged on. Newspaper reporters quoted elderly neighbors claiming the Arechigas had been coached by activists and television cameramen to gesture threateningly at the cameras. Under oath at a city council meeting, one neighbor denied that the quotations attributed to her were accurate, but the reporter who had written the story immediately took the stand to contradict her. Clete Roberts, a television personality who had been one of the most active in promoting the Arechigas' case, also felt compelled to deny any coaching. Then, on Wednesday, May 13, the *Los Angeles Mirror News*, an afternoon paper later absorbed by the *Times*, reported that Arechiga family members owned eleven homes around Southern California, several of which were rented to nonfamily members for income. Suddenly, people who looked poor and victimized appeared merely stubborn. The resistance seemed less a matter of principle when another daughter, Mrs. Angustian, said they had an appraisal at $17,000 for their properties, which they had been willing to accept. But now, she said, they wanted $30,000. By Thursday Donnell showed up to evict the Arechigas from his trailer. City councilman Edward Roybal, in negotiations lasting late into the evening, persuaded the Arechigas to leave the property in return for a letter from Arnebergh saying the move did not compromise their legal position. Roybal used a newspaper reporter's walkie-talkie to contact Arnebergh, who said he would be happy to write such a letter. The Arechigas eventually pulled out the following Tuesday, eleven days after the sheriff's deputies first appeared on the scene.

Poulson and *Los Angeles Times* editorialists blasted the television stations for turning the eviction into a cartoon morality play. Poulson called the television reporters "actors."[110] The *Times* was only too happy to agree, but noted that the eviction was an act "an easygoing government had put off for at least six years."[111] Years later Kenneth Hahn would tell Neil Sullivan that the evictions had been badly handled politically.[112] And, the *Times* noted in another editorial, "The damage done by the television 'coverage' of the Chavez Ravine incident is hard to measure. How many people who look and listen but only read while they run will ever be cured of the opinion that the Arechiga clan was turned out of doors without decency or fair warning?"[113]

It was a question the *Times* itself would fail to recognize. Decades afterward, the *Times* would often cover an annual get-together of former Chavez Ravine residents. Mrs. Vargas, other Arechigas, or former residents would be quoted about the destruction of the community. The death of the community would be contrasted with Dodger Stadium standing on their hills and gullies. The enduring visibility of the stadium would entwine O'Malley's name indelibly with the destruction of the community, even though 1,080 of the community's 1,100 families had been evicted by government agencies years before O'Malley even thought of Los Angeles. The 20 families the city finally got around to evicting in O'Malley's name were remembered and the emotional pictures tied irrevocably to the image of Dodger Stadium.[114] The reality was that the families were gone and Dodger Stadium was there. The intervening trail of responsibility was lost.

While embattled on the public relations front, O'Malley was increasingly confident about the legal picture, despite Silver's Supreme Court appeal. He had already started slogging through the city permitting process. He was ready to schedule a grand-opening ceremony and willing to guarantee refunds to the city for grading work if the Supreme Court ruled against the contract.[115] He settled on September 17, 1959, and decided on a public extravaganza.

O'Malley invited fans to come, bring their own shovels, and take away some souvenir dirt.[116] An estimated three to five thousand showed up, driving their cars up dirt roads, walking up paths, and clustering on a flat area that had been scraped out roughly where the playing field would be. "An unbelievable traffic jam," said *Herald Examiner* sports editor George Davis, already worrying about auto congestion when the stadium opened.[117] Scully acted as emcee, introducing the dignitaries and then the team, with the starters running out to areas of the dirt where their fielding positions would be. The Dodgers provided souvenir boxes so the fans could carry their souvenir dirt home. O'Malley circled the crowd with his own camera, taking pictures of the dignitaries, the scene, and the ceremony. He was also besieged with autograph requests. At a signal giant earthmovers appeared over the crest of the hill and, pushing tons of dirt before them, roared down the hill toward the crowd.[118] O'Malley was in heaven. The team had passed two million in Coliseum attendance the night before, and now his stadium was finally under way.

On October 19 the U.S. Supreme Court sped up the process enormously. They declined to hear Silver's appeal, giving no reason. O'Malley, pleased but properly chastened after nearly two and a half years of fighting for what he thought he had been promised in February 1957, said he hoped there would be no more "political" delays. Delay, he said, had already added $3 million to the projected cost of the stadium.[119] He hoped the ballpark would be ready for opening day 1961, with maybe some games late in 1960.[120]

That $3 million increase was a little bit easier to accept because the team's financial picture kept looking better. The dismal team had cooled enthusiasm down to merely excellent attendance levels by the end of 1958. But that was enough to generate steep profits. Working from figures supplied to the Coliseum Commission, the *Los Angeles Times* calculated the team's 1958 ticket sales gross had come to $4,465,548. That figure did not include concessions profits, which were calculated at $268,102; novelty sales, estimated at well over $200,000; or radio and television revenues, at least another $500,000.[121] From their share of road attendance, the team would have picked up another $320,000. A total income of $6 million seems a reasonable estimate.

To be sure, some of O'Malley's costs were also higher than they had been in Brooklyn. He was still paying rent or taxes or upkeep on Ebbets Field, Roosevelt Stadium in Jersey City, and Wrigley Field in Los Angeles. He had paid about $13,500 to put up and take down the Coliseum screen nine times. He had paid $150,000 of his indemnity to the Pacific Coast League. He had paid $200,000 to make improvements in the Coliseum. His team was taking much longer and more expensive plane flights every time it went on the road. His guarantee to other National League teams that he would cover their additional travel costs if they did not do better in Los Angeles than Brooklyn cost him $11,000. But five of the seven teams did earn more in Los Angeles than they had in Brooklyn. For the Braves it was $45,625 more, for the Cardinals nearly $40,000.[122]

The best part of the gravy was the novelties, for the Coliseum took no cut, and they could be sold outside the Coliseum as well as in it. O'Malley was lucky to find the man who would make the Dodgers the leading team in novelty sales for the next two decades. Danny Goodman was not just a guy to crank out caps and key chains, but one who was always looking for a fresh opportunity to transfer money from the customer's pocket to O'Malley's cash register. That first year in the Coliseum individual fans rose in the stands to play a six-note bugle call that had elicited the cry of "Charge" at University of Southern California football games for years. The crowd was happy to respond. Goodman went out and found a manufacturer to make footlong brass trumpets. They sold for $1 and came with instructions for playing those six notes.[123]

Goodman was quick on his feet because he had spent almost four decades in the entertainment business before he had even joined the Dodgers. He had worked in burlesque houses and ballparks since the 1920s, forsaking an education and becoming famous for his attacks on the English language. Goodman was "an off-the-field syntactical equivalent of Yogi Berra," said *Times* columnist Murray. "I may not be the best talker, or the best educated man in this room, but at least I'm illiterate," Goodman responded.[124]

Over time Goodman came to accept the entertainment industry's belief that all publicity was good, and the impact of the stories he told reporters was far more important than the accuracy of the details. At different times, he told different reporters that he had dropped out of school and started working when he was eleven, or twelve, or fourteen, or seventeen.[125] Born in Milwaukee on May 17, 1912, Goodman had lost his father at the age of eleven. He was already a paper boy but became a vendor for the Jacobs Brothers, who served burlesque houses, theaters, and the American Association's Borchert Field. Within a few years he was a full-time employee.

When Goodman was in his teens the Jacobs Brothers were already sending him to handle their various operations around the country. In the late 1920s he was in Baltimore, running the Jacobs' concession operation for Jack Dunn's International League Orioles. By the early 1930s he had been moved to Newark of the same league, where he worked for George Weiss. But he handled any assignment—racetrack, theater, or stadium—that the Jacobs Brothers needed.

In 1934 the Jacobs Brothers moved all their top operators to Detroit for the World Series. Goodman was given charge of the outfield bleachers and was doing a tremendous business in pies. The business picked up even more in the seventh game. After St. Louis outfielder Joe Medwick slid hard into Detroit third baseman Marv Owen in the sixth inning, the Tiger fans, already upset the home team was losing badly, showered Medwick with food and trash when he took the field. Eventually, baseball commissioner Kenesaw Mountain Landis would make his well-known decision ordering Medwick out of the game. He also made a less well-known decision, ordering Goodman to stop selling pies.[126]

Goodman learned all the tricks. In those days vendors turned in their unsold merchandise at the end of the game and were refunded what they had paid the concessionaire. As part of his education Goodman found that cola salesmen filled empty bottles with coffee and turned them back. Ice cream vendors put wood blocks in empty cartons. One hot dog vendor painted his forefinger with iodine, slipped it into the bun, let the customer see it, and then pulled the reddened finger back. When the customer complained there was no frankfurter, the vendor suggested the customer had dropped it.[127] One day the Jewish Goodman caught the unmistakable fragrance of kosher hot dogs, which Jacobs Brothers did not sell. He found a vendor who was bringing his own supplies to the park.[128]

Soon, he started making up tricks of his own. In Reading, Pennsylvania, he found customers would not pay a nickel to rent seat cushions. So he had the seats hosed down.[129] He claimed to be the first to sell hats and pennants.[130] Chuck Stevens, who played for the Pacific Coast League Hollywood Stars, said Goodman came up with the idea of dragging the infield between innings during the years Jack Salveson pitched for the Stars. Salveson, a fast worker with excellent control, tended to pitch short games, and Goodman needed the extra time to sell food and souvenirs.[131]

Jacobs Brothers moved Danny Goodman to Hollywood for the 1939 baseball season and the opening of Gilmore Field. It was a match made in heaven. A number of real Hollywood stars (Gary Cooper, George Raft, Robert Taylor, Cecil B. DeMille, Barbara Stanwyck, Bing Crosby, and William Powell, among others) owned stock in the team.[132] Bob Cobb, owner of the Brown Derby restaurants, was the principal owner and convinced Goodman to expand the Gilmore menu to a higher class of food. Soon, Goodman said, they were back to hot dogs and hamburgers because that is what Raft and the others wanted when they showed up.[133] "We've experimented with dozens of chef's specials, but they've all been a flop in the pan," Goodman explained.[134]

Gilmore Field became known as a place where starlets could get their pictures taken, and Danny Goodman was only too happy to pose them, holding the newest of his souvenirs. He could also get entertainment industry friends to pitch in. When he introduced the toy trumpets to the Coliseum, he brought jazz trumpet great Ziggy Elman to ham it up with the merchandise.[135]

When the Dodgers moved West, Goodman's position became uncertain. He had already turned down the Jacobs Brothers' offers to run Major League concessions elsewhere.[136] Both the Stars and the Los Angeles Angels, two of his major responsibilities, would be moving. Goodman also oversaw the Jacobs' operations elsewhere on the West Coast, which included several race courses in the San Francisco area and most PCL ballparks.[137] But the Jacobs

Brothers (by then known as Sportservice, Inc.) had no anchor to keep him in Los Angeles, and he had come to enjoy the Hollywood life thoroughly.

Danny Goodman lived in Beverly Hills 90210 before it became famous. He was an early riser who was usually in the office before six. He spent his morning on the phone, having meetings and setting up business. He would have a long lunch at a very public restaurant or club, always ready to talk, tell stories, and buy drinks for reporters. He would take a midafternoon nap, go to the ballpark or another public dinner, and be in bed by ten or so.[138]

Goodman was a guy always willing to buy a drink, give a gift, or do a favor, especially for a reporter or somebody from the movies or television. Through the 1950s he was the only nonentertainment industry figure who had been the subject of a Friars' Club roast, an honor he received in 1953.[139] Ronald Reagan acted as "roastmaster," with Jack Benny, Phil Silvers, George Burns, Chico Marx, and others pitching in. Goodman was also honored with similar dinners by the Leukemia Foundation of California and the Westwood Shrine Club.[140] He did a lot of volunteer work, serving on the Friars' board of directors for thirty-two years and organizing benefit dinners for other clubs.[141] He also helped organize dinners for Ty Cobb, Stan Musial, Casey Stengel, Maury Wills, Vin Scully, Lefty O'Doul, Leo Durocher, Sandy Koufax, and a host of Hollywood types and other celebrities. "You want celebrities for this event?" he asked one group. "I'll get you celebrities you never even heard of."[142]

The Dodgers arrived with a front-office crew from Brooklyn and the Coliseum's concessions contract locked up by rival ABC Vending Company, which had handled the Coliseum for years.[143] Bob Hunter, who covered the Dodgers for the *Los Angeles Examiner*, later told how he kept urging O'Malley to meet Goodman. Eventually, Hunter picked up the phone in O'Malley's Statler Hotel office and made the call himself, shoving the phone into O'Malley's hand. It was a shove O'Malley would never regret. Goodman served as vice president of advertising for twenty-five years, handling novelties and selling the ads for the yearbook and programs. Hunter said later O'Malley told him, "That was a great thing you did that day."[144]

Goodman was always looking for new ideas. He said he first saw bobblehead dolls when a Japanese manufacturer brought them to him in 1958.[145] They became a staple, with the Dodgers one of the first teams to adopt them. He came out with plastic bats in 1958 as well, and his supplier had to go to double shifts by the item's second month.[146] When the Dodgers opened in the Coliseum, Goodman offered a dozen brands of hats, from Tyroleans with a feather to sun visors. The roofless Coliseum, baking in the Southern California sun, proved an excellent place to sell woven-straw coolie hats ($1.50), and Goodman gave them a larger and larger role in the merchandise mix. Even O'Malley bought one, but refused to have his picture taken wearing it.[147]

With two months left in the 1958 season, Goodman's novelty operations had contributed more than $200,000 to the team's profits.[148] By the end of the season, Goodman reported, Dodger fans had bought more souvenirs than all other Major League teams combined.[149] And that was just at the ballpark. He had also persuaded Sears and local department store chains to carry the Dodger merchandise.[150] With a year's experience Goodman rolled out an even more lavish array for the Coliseum's fifteen novelty booths in 1959. There were twelve hat styles and thirty-three other items, from bolo ties to pillowcases to complete child-size uniforms.[151] There were aprons emblazoned with "To Heck with Housework, let's go to the ball game."[152]

But selling souvenirs was not always a sure thing. Even the bugles did not work out. They shattered when dropped by kids, and adults had a distressing tendency to expect them to work well. O'Malley made him discontinue the line.[153]

If O'Malley was naive about Los Angeles politics and lucky with Danny Goodman, his luck got even better in 1959. Half the Dodgers' season ticket holders canceled after the dismal 1958 season.[154] The political, public relations, and financial troubles surrounding his new stadium were multiplying. He needed a little luck, and he got it. The team that had looked old, uncertain, undermanned, and scared in 1958 won a pennant and a World Series the following year. The turnaround was part inevitable and part unbelievable.

The 1959 Dodgers were a team in transition. The old Brooklyn stars were fading. The players who would help the Dodgers dominate the early 1960s were only beginning to arrive. Widely picked to finish in the second division, and 15–1 in Las Vegas, it was a team that caught lightning in a bottle.[155]

Partially, the predictions were wrong because the Dodgers were not as bad a team as they had looked in 1958. The dislocation of the move, the political uncertainties of the team's status, the odd configuration of the Coliseum, and the bright lights of Hollywood all played a role in the team's 1958 performance. In 1959, with more players settled in Southern California, the referendum if not the court cases behind them, and the Coliseum and Sunset Strip clubs now known quantities, the team regained its focus.[156]

The restructuring of the team began during the 1958 season. Don New-combe was traded. Pee Wee Reese stuck out the year, but then announced he would move to the coaching lines. During the off-season Bavasi made only one major trade, sending the disappointing Gino Cimoli to the Cardinals for their disappointing Wally Moon, an outfielder who had won the Rookie of the Year Award in 1954, but done little since.

As 1959 opened Moon added significant juice to the attack. Veterans such as Gil Hodges and Jim Gilliam bounced back. Duke Snider responded to the shortening of the ridiculously long fences in the Coliseum's right field. Young catcher John Roseboro matured. Don Demeter had a solid rookie season. Charlie Neal had a career year at second base. The pitching staff, led by Don Drysdale, had learned to pitch in the Coliseum. The only hole was at shortstop, where Don Zimmer, one of the few players who had done well in 1958, slumped terribly.

The team started the season well enough, briefly holding first place in late April, but by June they had fallen into the second division. Erskine retired but Roger Craig returned from the Minors in sensational fashion, and with the arrival of another young hurler, Los Angeles product Larry Sherry, the club started to rebound. In a desperate move caused by Zimmer's ineffectiveness, Bavasi called up Maury Wills, a shortstop who had been bouncing around the farm system for nearly a decade. Just that spring Bavasi had let him go to camp with Detroit in the hope the Tigers would buy his contract. In another bit of luck, they did not. Wills provided a spark the team needed. By mid-July the team had a solid hold on second place.

The crucial weeks started September 18, the day after the stadium groundbreaking ceremony, as the Dodgers and Walter and Kay O'Malley left on a road trip that would consume the rest of their regular season. The first stop was Seals Stadium, with three games against the league-leading San Francisco Giants, two games ahead of the Dodgers and Braves. That Friday night it rained, raising the tension for a Saturday doubleheader. Kay put a short-stemmed red rose in her lapel, and Evit Bavasi began knitting a white sweater.[157] But it was the aged rookie Wills who led the team. Wills had been fielding well for three and a half months. Now, he began to hit. He got seven hits in the three games, and the Dodger pitching staff held the Giants to six runs. By Sunday evening the Dodgers had taken over first place. Kay O'Malley would wear a rose every day for the rest of the year, as she and Walter trailed the team through St. Louis and Chicago.

On September 26, the last Saturday of the season, the rose looked wilted. The Dodgers were crushed by the Cubs 12–1, while Spahn pitched the Braves into a tie and the Giants pulled within a game. On Sunday, the final day, the Braves won again, but Craig staved off the Cubs and the veterans put together seven runs. The teams finished in a tie and headed for a best-of-three playoff. O'Malley was "bubbling excitedly."[158]

Statistically, it was hard to find dominant performances by any of the Dodgers. None made the *Sporting News*' Major League All-Star team. Don Drysdale was the only category leader in a major statistic—strikeouts. They did not have a top-five performer in any of the offensive categories. Nobody had a hundred RBIs. Nobody had more than twenty-five home runs. The team did lead the league in fielding, as the Brooklyn veterans blended their experience and poise with some young arms and quick feet.

It was a short trip from Chicago to Milwaukee for the start of the play-offs Monday. The winner would face the American League champion Chicago White Sox. The Braves took an early lead in the first game, but Sherry relieved in the second inning and finished the game. Roseboro's sixth-inning home run proved the winning margin. That evening both teams flew seventeen hundred miles to Los Angeles for the second game.

By now a Los Angeles florist was providing Kay and all of the ladies in O'Malley's box with their "lucky" red roses. Evit Bavasi kept knitting her white sweater until her hands shook too much in the late innings.[159] The Braves took a 5–2 lead into the bottom of the ninth of the second game, but Burdette tired and a sacrifice fly from Brooklyn hero Carl Furillo tied the score. "I look at the ball, and I see dollar signs instead of stitches," the veteran said.[160] In the twelfth inning Furillo hit a twisting ground ball that Milwaukee substitute shortstop Felix Mantilla fielded but threw away as Hodges scored the pennant-winning run. Said Scully, "We go to Chicago," and closed his mouth to let the home crowd's noise tell the story.

As Scully spoke, Wyman recalled, horns began to blare around the city. "It was the first time my city finally came together," she said.[161] In O'Malley's box there was much coming together, with O'Malleys and Walshes and Bavasis and LeRoys and Parrotts hugging and kissing while the loudspeakers played the gimmick hit of the summer—"Angeltown." Within a few hours the Dodger party was back on a United Airlines charter, flying toward Bill Veeck and the Chicago White Sox. Three thousand Angelenos cheered the departing team.[162]

While the team and the O'Malleys tried to rest in Chicago during the off day, Wednesday, Dodger officials dealt with the mechanics of preparing for Los Angeles's first World Series game the coming Sunday. By noon on Thursday, October 1, Harold Parrott announced the last seventeen thousand seats for the three games scheduled for the Coliseum had been sold. They had gone to people who had camped out overnight.[163] After Friday night's USC football victory over Ohio State, a crew swarmed over the field, reinstalling the left-field screen, the foul screens, and the other baseball necessities. It took eight hours and cost $3,500.[164]

Parrott's ticket news was the best thing O'Malley heard that Thursday. His tired team absorbed an 11–0 thrashing at the hands of the White Sox, a team with a justified reputation for light hitting. But, as they had all season, the Dodgers rebounded in the second game, Friday. Pinch hitter Chuck Essegian tied the game with a seventh inning homer, and Charlie Neal put it away with a two-run homer later in that inning. Larry Sherry, beginning his Series heroics, saved the game.

Saturday was another day of limited rest, as the team and the O'Malleys traveled back to Los Angeles. For Los Angeles's first World Series game, O'Malley's pagoda (shaded and glass enclosed) had been expanded. O'Malley had been forced to pay USC for five hundred tickets for the Friday-night football game because the larger personal box had taken over the seats.[165] As Game Three started on Sunday, October 4, it held forty personal guests—from Governor and Mrs. Pat Brown through Henry Kaiser and the Mervyn LeRoys (she brought a five-inch television set, a definite novelty in 1959). Kaiser had orchids flown in from Hawaii, but Kay insisted on her good-luck red roses for all the ladies in the party.[166] President Eisenhower turned down an invitation, even though he was vacationing in nearby Palm Springs.[167]

He missed a great game. Drysdale huffed and puffed through seven innings, giving up nine hits and four walks, but not one run. Dick Donovan of the White Sox was even better, surrendering only one hit until the seventh inning, when the Dodgers put together a single, two walks, and a pinch single by Furillo to take a 2–0 lead. Drysdale looked shaky in the eighth, but Alston brought in Sherry to gain his second save, 3–1.

In the fourth game an early Dodger 4–0 lead was squandered by Craig, with the White Sox tying it up in the seventh. Sherry replaced Craig, and a homer by Hodges gave the Dodgers a victory and a 3-1 Series lead. The fifth game was another pitching gem, as Chicago's Bob Shaw, with relief help from Billy Pierce and Donovan and a spectacular catch by outfielder Jim Rivera, shut down the Dodgers 1–0.

After the fifth game, O'Malley invited every Dodger employee, from his board members to the ticket takers, to fly to Chicago for the rest of the World Series, with everything at his expense. More than a hundred accepted the offer.[168]

The sixth game was almost anticlimactic. A Duke Snider homer gave the Dodgers a 2–0 lead in the third, and a six-run fourth, anchored by a Wally Moon homer, sank the White Sox. Johnny Podres faltered in the bottom of the fourth, but Sherry, despite fatigue, came on and threw five and two-thirds innings of shutout relief. He won the game, the Series MVP award, and the Chevrolet Corvette that went with it in those days. It was duly noted that both Sherry and Essegian had attended Fairfax High School in Los Angeles. O'Malley declined invitations to go into the dressing room, saying it was the players' victory and their time for the limelight.[169]

For the Dodger party and "several hundred friends," it was a steak, champagne, and caviar party at the Chicago Conrad Hilton, lasting well into the evening. O'Malley grabbed a trumpet from a band member and tooted a few bars. When his fifty-sixth birthday rolled around at midnight, there was a new round of toasts for the owner of the champions on the field and at the box office.[170]

Not all the Dodger staff were there. Even before the team had returned to Chicago for the sixth game, Thompson, Parrott, and Goodman had been taken to the hospital with exhaustion or ulcers or combinations of the above. Bavasi had collapsed getting out of a cab and been confined to his hotel bed in Los Angeles.[171] O'Malley was driving the troops to establish the Dodgers' image in their new city with their new fans. It was working. Back in Los Angeles the day after the World Series win, 5,000 fans, including Wyman and Poulson, met the team at the airport, and O'Malley won another birthday cheer.[172]

O'Malley was on a roll. His team had won the World Series. The final Supreme Court decision, of which he was becoming more confident, would come out in less than two weeks. And now that the World Series was over, he and Kay could glory in their first grandson, John Joseph Seidler, born August 12.

While O'Malley rejoiced in his triumphs, it was attendance that was the talk of the World Series. The third, fourth, and fifth games in the Coliseum each drew more than 92,000 people, each day slightly higher and each setting a new record. After throwing out the first ball before 92,394 people at the third game, Brooklyn Hall of Famer Zack Wheat said, "Tell you something! Never saw anything like this in Brooklyn."[173] And even all those tickets could not satisfy Los Angeles's desire to attend the World Series. Scalpers were getting $120 for $10 box seats and $35 for the $4 reserved seats.[174] Treasury Department agents, concerned with collecting Washington's 10 percent amusement tax, arrested several scalpers.[175] Every single way you sliced the World Series money—players' share, Commissioner's Office share, television receipts—it was a record.[176] In fact, the attendance for the Dodgers' three home World Series games exceeded total attendance for thirty-seven of the fifty-five previous World Series.

It was the cap on a second year of strong attendance performance. After two years in the Coliseum, the Dodgers held the Major League single-game attendance records for any game, a World Series game, a day game, and an opening-day game. They held the National League records for a night game and a doubleheader.[177] And all these crowds were smaller than that for the Campanella benefit game. The Dodgers had edged past 2 million fans in 1959 and finally beaten the Braves to lead the National League in attendance for the first time since 1952, the Braves' last year in Boston.

Profits were accruing. After the 1958 season the *Los Angeles Times* tried to analyze the Dodgers' finances and came up with revenues of $4.4 million.[178] In early 1960 *Sports Illustrated* presented a lengthy deconstruction that concluded that O'Malley had made a $3.3 million profit in 1959.[179] Both of these stories had problems. The 1958 figures were based on numbers obtained from the Coliseum Commission and covered only ticket sales and some concessions. There was no attempt to estimate the team's expenses or an overall profit. The *Sports Illustrated* story was much more exhaustive, but neglected the major element of federal taxes, which were then running at about the 50 percent level for successful corporations. O'Malley contended that, in fact, his profit for 1959 was $764,114.19.[180] Of course, O'Malley also noted that one of the elements the story had neglected to include was spring training expenses. He did not mention that spring training expenses were generally covered by sales of excess players, an offsetting income element the story also neglected.[181] Pulling together all of the financial information made public, and doing a fair amount of extrapolating, it would appear the Dodgers' after-tax profit in those years came to about $2.1 million—$650,000 for 1958 and $1,426,000 for 1959. These amounts would be put toward the eventual cost of Dodger Stadium.[182]

12

A Monument to the O'Malleys

With a pennant, a profit, and a grandson, Walter O'Malley was finally beginning to settle into Los Angeles. Until August 1958 O'Malley had lived in
a suite at the Statler Hotel, while Kay remained on Long Island. After his
medical problems in February and March 1958, he spent several weeks
recuperating in Amityville, missing spring training for the first time since
buying into the team.[1] Amityville was still home, where family surrounded
him comfortably. Peter could visit him from Penn, where he was still an
undergraduate. O'Malley remained there until taking a fishing trip a few
days before the season opened, when he rejoined the team for an exhibition game in Las Vegas.[2]

With the frantic action of the 1958 referendum campaign, he was almost
better off leading a bachelor existence, concentrating on his business. In
July 1958, fresh from a trip east that was supposed to help him recover
from the campaign, he became ill. With his discomfort exacerbated by the
heat, he took some advice and spent a weekend in Lake Arrowhead.[3] Lake
Arrowhead, a mile high in the San Bernardino Mountains about seventy-five
miles east of Los Angeles, looks more like western Colorado than Southern California. With its pine trees, 784-acre lake, and cooler climate, it was
clearly more to O'Malley's taste than the regular ninety-degree-plus days
of Los Angeles in July.

By August he had rented a house there.[4] It was supposedly just for the
hot months, but the lease kept extending. By the next spring he was buying
a sailboat, naming it the *Kay-O'* and setting it afloat on the lake.[5] Clearly, it
felt more like a home than the suite he continued to maintain at the Statler.

His clothes remained generally dark and conservative—aside from a willingness to don strange hats as long as his picture was not taken wearing
them. Business wear was business wear—dark suits, white shirts, respect-

able ties, even though colleagues noticed he had trouble matching coat and trousers.[6] His casual wear began to branch out. Bolo ties appeared, worn with striped shirts. Golf shirts were worn buttoned to the neck. Business or casual, there tended to be a little cigar ash down the front, usually from Anthony and Cleopatras with a filterless plastic holder. He appeared to have gained a few more pounds. Branch Rickey, in the fall of 1959, said O'Malley had become "huge and fat," adding that O'Malley felt somehow this was protection against the abdominal troubles that had flared up a couple of times.[7] *Jowly* was a word newspaper reporters used more and more, along with *gravelly* for his voice. When he found time to cook, it was dishes he liked, such as boiled tripe with onion sauce.

Terry, twenty-five years old in the spring of 1958 and social, settled into Southern California more quickly. She had all the charm of her father and none of his capacity to intimidate. She had spent much of her time since graduating from the College of New Rochelle working for the Dodgers. For several years she had been on the staff at the Dodger summer boys camp at Vero Beach. She had helped in the office, taught the boys to dance and swim, and was the sole female presence at the camp. She got a dorm wing to herself and slept in the bed Pee Wee Reese used during spring training.[8]

In Los Angeles she still worked for her father, but now, she said, she was "cooped up in the Statler Hotel with Dad, taking his phone calls, answering 20–30 letters a day." She dodged a reporter's question that first spring about dating any of the Dodgers, but conceded she had "no young friends out here." Typically of Terry, she confidently said, "I'm not worried about meeting new people."

She did not need to be. By August 1958 she was engaged to Roland Seidler Jr., a young stockbroker. In early October the couple was married in a ceremony as Irish as O'Malley could make it. The church was St. Therese in Alhambra, in keeping with his daughter's name. His personal touch was a green boutonniere. The reception band kept playing "When Irish Eyes Are Smiling," and the roster of priests was a litany of Dublin. Father William Hennessy, the O'Malleys' parish priest in Amityville, said the wedding mass. Fathers Columban Fitzgerald of St. Therese's and Patrick Gallagher of New York helped James Francis Cardinal McIntyre, archbishop of Los Angeles, perform the wedding ceremony.[9]

The cardinal's presence at Terry's wedding was indicative of O'Malley's quick emergence as one of the most prominent Roman Catholics in the city.

The two men, both native New Yorkers with strong backgrounds in finance, appeared to hit it off. McIntyre was already famous with his staff for prefacing discussions of how things should be done with, "Back in New York . . ."[10] He and O'Malley shared an uncanny ability to remember numbers, a love for baseball, and a strong desire to build things. McIntyre, a protégé of New York's Francis Cardinal Spellman, could use the church grapevine to get a quick read on the new man in town. The fact that O'Malley was wealthy and generous to Catholic charities undoubtedly was transmitted quickly.

O'Malley, like many Catholics of his generation, was a devout, and undemonstrative, believer. The afternoon the Dodgers beat the Braves to clinch the 1959 pennant, with a hundred World Series details hanging over his head and a plane to catch to Chicago, he, Kay, and board member Sylvan Oestreicher stopped at St. Vincent's Church to say a prayer of thanks and take a moment of contemplation.[11] "Many people have their own way of giving thanks," he said. "Many once a week. It's largely a matter of personal training and belief." Because of his own background, the commitment did not extend to the Catholic school system. Both Peter and Terry were educated in secular schools, and only Terry's children would return to the Catholic school system. Seidler had been educated at Loyola High School, a Jesuit prep school, in Los Angeles.

In the early days in Los Angeles, O'Malley latched on to movie stars as a way to sell his team and, even more important, reach voters before the Proposition B voting. The lure of Hollywood had done so much to put Los Angeles on the map and attract dreamers from across the country that the city was a star-besotted town. The *Los Angeles Times* routinely reported movie star marriages, arrests, and even dates (but only with heads of state or royalty) on the front page.

Hollywood had its genuine baseball fans, but its culture was never to be adverse to publicity, and the Dodgers were the hottest thing in town. Bing Crosby, Nat "King" Cole, Dick Powell, and Joe E. Brown all worked prominently in the campaign for Proposition B. O'Malley was happy to have them on the telethons, in the box seats at the Coliseum, and participating in the annual Hollywood Stars game (a promotion picked up from the PCL Hollywood Stars). But most of these were mere acquaintances, people caught in a mutually beneficial publicity arrangement. Cronies such as Henry Ughetta remained on the team's board and in the owner's box. When the Dodgers hosted the 1959 All-Star Game, it was the old New York crowd—Bud Holman, Dearie and Jim Mulvey, and Sylvan Oestreicher—who joined the O'Malleys.

The exception was Mervyn LeRoy. LeRoy had grown up in San Francisco, and, like O'Malley, his father had been in the dry goods business. Whereas O'Malley's father had been cut down in the late 1920s, LeRoy's had been brought to his knees by the 1906 San Francisco earthquake. LeRoy left high school early, wound up on the stage, and worked his way into being one of the most powerful men in the film colony. He had directed *Little Caesar* and *Little Women* and produced *The Wizard of Oz*. He had introduced Ronald Reagan to Nancy Davis and made friendships with baseball fans such as Joe E. Brown and Danny Kaye. He had a taste for money-wise friends. Like his father, who had been president of the Emeryville horse-racing track near Oakland, LeRoy admired the ponies. He had been president of the Hollywood Park racetrack since the 1940s. In heavily Jewish Hollywood, LeRoy was also Catholic, the president of two prominent Catholic charities. And, he was, like O'Malley, "somewhat square myself."[12]

By the end of the 1959 season the relationship between the O'Malleys and the LeRoys was firm. The LeRoys were the only people from outside the "Dodger family" in the owner's box during the playoffs and World Series, and LeRoy was the only person outside the organization to receive a World Series ring.[13]

But Mervyn LeRoy was not going to get O'Malley's stadium built. Although pennants, profits, and being a grandfather were all wonderful, the stadium remained at the center of O'Malley's dreams. Unfortunately for O'Malley, the dreams were not that widely shared.

For the next eighteen months, the construction so optimistically begun on the eve of the Supreme Court decision would proceed in fits and starts. At every step where the club had to deal with the city—plan approvals, zoning changes, land sales, closing escrow—delays occurred. There was business unfinished by the local officials who had promised so much. There was the continued obstructionism of the opponents. And the fear that the opponents placed in city and county officials made them try to pick every nit themselves before the opponents got there.

The Supreme Court announced it would not hear Phill Silver's appeal on Monday, October 19, 1959. By Wednesday morning O'Malley had Dick Walsh deliver stadium plans to the city to support a request for necessary zoning changes on the Chavez Ravine land. Immediately, there were problems. The plans were not as specific as city councilman Ransom Callicott, chairman of the council's planning committee, wanted. Callicott also noted the plan included a number of commercial enterprises—a gas station, a car wash, and several restaurants—that had not been anticipated. Callicott, who had been a consistent Dodger supporter on all the earlier votes, indicated he was troubled by these unexpected additions. The contract called for the Dodgers to build a stadium and necessary or obvious buildings (such as adjacent souvenir stands) to go with it, not for other commercial ventures.[14]

With O'Malley's opponents smirking, "I told you so," the council asked the Dodgers for more detailed drawings and plans. O'Malley said he would submit them to clear up "confusion" about the Dodgers' intentions, for which he took responsibility.[15] Within a few days more exact maps came back. The car wash was gone. The restaurants—a fast food outlet, an outdoor luau-type arrangement, and a sit-down restaurant—had been moved inside the stadium structure. The gas station was still there. O'Malley said it had been requested by city planners, as there were no others in the immediate area.[16]

O'Malley never explained the change in public. He told the council the Dodgers would not "repudiate" the first map, but he did acknowledge the map had confused the issue. He said Dick Walsh knew of the contents of the map when he submitted it.[17] But whether it was a trial balloon submitted and then withdrawn under fire or a mistake in the Dodger offices was never made clear. Critics such as Dick Young would maintain for decades that O'Malley's move was nothing but a grab for Southern California real estate, but nothing beyond the stadium, its parking lots, and the gas station were built on the site.[18]

The changed plans won the zoning approval requested, but not before another uncomfortable afternoon in city council chambers. After the council dithered through several procedural issues, O'Malley rose to say that the referendum and the lawsuits had already pushed the stadium back so far that the cost had risen by $3 million. The delays were also forcing him to return to the Coliseum for at least one more year at a much higher rent. Plus, the higher price tag meant the Dodgers would have to take out a bank loan, and banks would require clear zoning before they would. "I cannot afford to have this drag on," he concluded. The council voted approval.[19]

Work picked up. But by early 1960 it was clear that yet another of the city's casual procedures was about to cause problems. As with the Arechigas and their neighbors, this was a fistful of property owners whom the city had not dealt with as promised. They owned homes, and one small store, that had not been included in the Los Angeles Housing Authority's land. They should have been bought as part of the city's 1957 deal with the Dodgers. The city had started eminent-domain proceedings but dropped them.[20] There had been some desultory bargaining, but that had stalled. The city did not want to budge too far from the pre-Dodger assessed value, and the home owners knew that with the bulldozers tearing up the hill above them, their properties had skyrocketed in value.

Caught between the city's casual attitude and his timetable, O'Malley bit his tongue and paid. There were a dozen lots involved. All the property owners had hired the same attorney and promised that none would break ranks. The dozen lots had been assessed at $82,850 during the eminent-domain proceedings. O'Malley paid $494,400. Almost a third of that—$150,000—went to Francis Scott, who owned the key lot as far as O'Malley was concerned. Scott's house was in a ravine behind what is now the third base stands. It was already surrounded by graded dirt walls twenty feet above its roof. It would eventually be buried one hundred feet under the parking lot surface, and O'Malley's graders were waiting to start that work. The city had offered $6,000 for the home in the early 1950s. Scott's father, and then he, had held out for more, eventually forcing the bid up to $9,000. But, Scott conceded, he would have settled for $20,000 a couple of years earlier.[21]

By the time escrow closed on these houses, O'Malley was forced to concede the stadium would not be ready for opening day 1961. For another month he held out hope for July 1961, but then agreed it would take at least until opening day 1962.[22] "I can't tell you when we can open the park. It depends on how long are the delays that may be caused by our dedicated opponents," he told an Associated Press News Executives Council meeting in late April. Asked if the Dodgers could learn anything from the problems popping up all over at the newly opened Candlestick Park in San Francisco, he said, "The way things are going, we will have more than ample time."[23]

He did. As every Dodger-related piece of paper entered the city council, John Holland and his supporters found a way to delay. When the question of closing city streets in the Chavez Ravine area arose in August 1959, everybody in the council except Holland treated it as pro forma. Holland voted no. The lack of a unanimous vote automatically forced a second reading and a delay of another couple of weeks.[24] In May 1960 it was approval of a tract map for the stadium.[25] In June it was an appropriation to buy a former elementary school site on the property from the school district.[26] In July O'Malley's supporters on the council were finally able to get an escrow on the exchange of Chavez Ravine for Wrigley Field set up and approved.[27] In August the city granted a conditional-use permit for the property, which would automatically turn into a building permit ten days later unless an appeal was filed. With fifteen minutes left in the appeal period, Silver filed one.[28] A little more than a week later the appeal was overturned, but August had been lost to construction as well.[29] In October the Dodgers and the city finally swapped land titles.[30] In December the council gave approval to the final tract map, with Holland voting doggedly against each of the four necessary motions. The key vote was eighteen to one, Holland's remaining supporters having thrown in the towel.[31]

It was the October 1960 swap of land titles that had really allowed construction to get going. For the previous year grading had been going on whenever the city permit process allowed. Now actual construction could begin. Now, the contractors could begin building forms and creating the precast concrete pieces that would make up most of the stadium.

Even as construction progressed through 1961 and into early 1962, however, there were further difficulties with the city. A stadium had not been built in Los Angeles since Wrigley Field in the 1920s, noted Fresco Thompson, and nobody in the city inspector's office had any experience with a stadium project. With the knowledge that Holland and other opponents were looking for issues to jump on, the inspectors had to be very thorough. They insisted a sewer line be increased in size because a zoo might be built in neighboring Elysian Park. (It was not.) They required that each car be given a separate parking slot so people could leave easily during games (the two major arenas where the city had a voice, the Coliseum and the Hollywood Bowl, both allowed the operators to park cars bumper to bumper). "We had almost as many city officials swarming over the park as we did contractors' workmen. You couldn't tell 'em without a scorecard," Thompson said.[32]

Then there was the phantom road. As construction progressed, said Chad McClellan, a road that crossed the stadium area had to be rebuilt. There was only one alternate route. McClellan argued that the alternate road was enough for existing traffic volume, and even if it was not, a temporary simple graded roadbed would have sufficed. Instead, the city required the Dodgers to build a finished road, complete with curbs and streetlights. The road was used for 109 days before being torn up. It cost the Dodgers $59,742.[33]

Sums like this were just one of the reasons the cost of the stadium kept rising. O'Malley had come to Los Angeles planning for a $10 million ballpark to open for the 1959 season. He was now looking at $16 million for a ballpark that would open in 1962. As he had said to the city council several times, the costs of the stadium now required a bank loan, and banks were uneasy at the resistance the project was receiving at every step.

O'Malley had arrived in Los Angeles fairly confident of his finances. He had received $3 million for selling Ebbets Field to Marvin Kratter in 1956. He got $1 million from selling the ballpark in Montreal. He had made close to $2 million in profits over the previous seven seasons of Brooklyn Dodger ownership.[34] Later, it was reported that O'Malley had $4 million in cash when the Dodgers reached Los Angeles.[35]

That $4 million to $6 million or so looked pretty good in the face of a $10 million stadium. O'Malley figured he could borrow the rest, and the profits of the first two seasons in Los Angeles could have improved the picture enormously if delays had not kept forcing up the price of his stadium and his legal costs.[36] At $15 million, the late-1959 estimate, the picture looked poorer.[37] The cost was up to $16 million by the next year and would be pegged at $18 million when it opened.[38] Some of these costs were money already spent, and some were money that never would be spent. When Dodger publicity chief Red Patterson broke it down for reporters in early 1960, the then $16 million price tag included a $3 million tab for Wrigley Field and the Angels' PCL franchise. It included $350,000 spent fixing up the Coliseum and the $450,000 indemnity paid to the Pacific Coast League. It included $1.7 million for the erection and maintenance of the forty-acre youth and recreation park on the property.[39] Although all of these things (except the youth and recreation park, which has never been built) were costs O'Malley had to pay to move his team to Los Angeles, they were not actual stadium costs. Still, borrowing would be necessary, hence O'Malley's concern to get clear title to the land and approved building permits from the city council to reassure potential lenders. O'Malley's financial situation was raising echoes of Brooklyn. He was making money, but not enough to finance his dream stadium. There was pressure from both the income and the cost lines of the financial ledgers.

On the revenue side, attendance rose in 1960 with the usual post–World Series bounce. It was up 9 percent to 2,253,887, breaking the National League record. In 1961 it fell to 1,804,250, still over 400,000 customers more than San Francisco, which finished second in attendance. Milwaukee, the cause of so much handwringing just a few years before, finished fifth, 700,000 behind the Dodgers. It was the third year in a row the Dodgers had drawn more than 20 percent of the league's fans.

Still, it was not what O'Malley wanted. The Dodgers in those years typically drew up budgets based on 1.8 million, 2 million, 2.25 million, and 2.5 million fans. The lowest figure was about the worst they wanted to do. The Dodgers netted about $1 million less in 1961 than they had in 1960. "We're not hurting seriously, but the loss of a million dollars in any business is no drop in the bucket, especially when you've got a construction project going that's costing you $16 million," O'Malley said.[40]

The cost-side problems, while probably short-term, were more distressing. The lawsuits and municipal bungling had pushed the team back into the Coliseum, at first for just the 1960 season and then for 1961 as well. From the beginning it was clear the Dodgers were not going to get the terms O'Malley had won for the first two years. The Coliseum Commission was more sophisticated and had seen how the original contract worked to O'Malley's benefit. The other tenants were still irritated at the Dodgers' deal. The commission had the Sports Arena bonds to pay off, and they knew there was no point in building a long-term relationship with a short-term tenant. O'Malley attempted to get the existing deal extended, but the Coliseum held firm to the terms the non-Dodger tenants had paid before 1958— 10 percent of the gross plus all concession and parking revenues. The net effect for 1960 was close to $1 million in additional costs to the Dodgers.[41]

At times the financial risks seemed overwhelming to O'Malley, despite the strong attendance. Buzzie Bavasi, who shared an office with O'Malley, could hear the concern in phone conversations that drifted over the low partitions separating them. Once in those early years he found O'Malley slumped in his chair, head in hands, sure he was not going to be able to stay in business and build his stadium. "He was very subdued," Bavasi said. "I had never seen him so concerned before." Bavasi offered to help out financially with family money, but O'Malley turned him down.[42]

Added to the amounts he was paying for land parcels the city had promised him for free, his profits were being pinched at a time he needed them the most. O'Malley cut back on the budget Bavasi had been given to sign amateur prospects. Bavasi explained it by saying the pipeline was full and he didn't want too many prospects who were the same age.[43]

The profits and the potential were enough to keep O'Malley going, but he spent much time in 1959 and 1960 worrying how he would finance the ballpark that seemed to get more expensive every day. He talked to banks, but found them hesitant because of the political turmoil and the lack of title to the stadium land. Even with clear title, a stadium was unattractive collateral because it would be hard to find alternative uses. (The banking community's memory of the city's years of failing to interest a buyer in Chavez Ravine before O'Malley was fresh.) Bankers' unfamiliarity with lending to a large sports organization, where revenues could vary greatly with the team's fortunes on the field, did not help either.[44] Nor did the talk in baseball circles in late 1960 of placing an American League team in Los Angeles, cutting into the Dodgers' market.[45]

Finally, as 1960 turned to the new year, he struck the deal that would finance his stadium. Union Oil, a large regional chain of gasoline stations, had replaced Eastside Brewery as the team's major radio and television sponsor after the 1959 season. The company was so pleased with the response in 1960 that it agreed to help provide financing for O'Malley's stadium.[46] Union Oil would also get the gasoline station located in the parking lot and the right to the only non–Dodger advertising spot in the stadium, a round sign atop the message board above the left-field pavilion.

Work on the stadium site had started with the grading, a job that eventually involved eight million cubic yards of earth. Little of the work was in Chavez Ravine, despite the popular name. Chavez Ravine still runs up the hillsides just south of the ballpark site, along a road now called Stadium Way. The bulldozers began on a 720-foot ridge variously called Lookout Mountain or Goat Hill, which overlooks Chavez Ravine (to the south) and Sulphur Gulch (to the north, the area where the playing field sits).[47] The ridge was a shallow U, almost in the shape of a boomerang, with the middle of the convex side pointed just west of downtown Los Angeles and the open side facing generally north.

Below the ridge the land was split by gullies and interrupted by small hills. The terrain was broken further because dirt scooped out to form the neighboring Pasadena Freeway in the late 1930s, and the nearby Hollywood Freeway in the late 1940s and early 1950s, had been dumped in large mounds on the site. The plan was to trim the top of the ridge to 624 feet and sculpt the boomerang.[48] The inside of the boomerang would be shaped ready for the precast concrete forms of the stadium; the outside would be terraced for parking lots. The loose dirt created and the mounds left over from freeway construction would be pushed into the gullies to create level ground for the surrounding parking areas.

The stadium itself would be built into the hillside, something O'Malley had already done on a small scale at Holman Stadium in Vero Beach. Using the hillside as support reduced the cost and made it easier to build the stands using cantilevered construction, an idea O'Malley had made a centerpiece of all the designs dating back to Brooklyn. Cantilevers, giant versions of the horizontal brackets that support wall-mounted bookshelves, replaced pillars for supporting the decks of a stadium. No pillars meant no obstructed views, but the cantilevers also meant that upper decks had to be set back at least a bit from the first deck. As a result, patrons would have unobstructed views, but, in all but the lowest deck, their seats would be much farther from the action than comparable seats in older ballparks with pillars.[49]

Maximizing use of the hill would also allow most people to park on the same level as their seats. The parking terraces could be shaped and marked so that fans could park their cars and walk to their seats with a climb of no more than a few feet. This would allow fewer interconnections between decks. The stadium would be built with two small elevators and limited internal staircases. None of the large ramps, stairs, or escalators that connected the decks of other stadiums would be used.

Furthermore, because the design and execution were being overseen by Emil Praeger, the stadium would be heavy on precast concrete forms, a system that provided both increased strength and ease of maintenance. Much of what would later be the playing field and the outfield seating pavilion areas would be a giant plant for casting and curing twenty-three thousand shapes of concrete reinforced with steel bars. The largest would be fifty-six feet by thirty-five feet and weigh thirty-eight tons apiece.

O'Malley arrived in Los Angeles with the Norman Bel Geddes–Emil Praeger plans in his pocket. Many of the ideas, such as the cantilevered, pillar-less construction, would not change. But others would be adapted, both because conditions were different, as with the availability of the Chavez Ravine hillside, and because new ideas were incorporated.

The first version of the Chavez Ravine plan, shown in an artist's rendering in the 1958 team yearbook, portrayed an exterior design roughly similar to the ballpark built a decade later in Kansas City. Each of the four decks was a bit smaller than the one below it. The ends of each deck were curved, with the bottom of one deck lining up with the top of the one below and creating the appearance of a smooth sweep from top to bottom. The effect was like arms encircling the stadium from behind home plate and embracing the fans. This worked well with another idea O'Malley retained from the Brooklyn plans. The decks would all be slightly curved so that each seat was oriented toward the pitcher's mound, rather than building a more rectangular structure with the seats looking straight ahead, an orientation more appropriate for football. There were pavilions beyond the outfield, attached to the lowest deck.

In all versions each deck would extend downward from a concourse at its top, where concession stands, souvenir booths, and restrooms would be located. In early designs it was pledged that no fan would have to descend more than ten feet to their seat, a pledge later broken with regard to the top deck.

The capacity was tagged at 52,000. But soon after the referendum win in June 1958, O'Malley was up walking the Chavez Ravine hills with New York Yankees owner Del Webb, who was interested in the construction contract for his firm. The Dodgers had recently concluded a three-game home stand with the Milwaukee Braves in which the smallest crowd had been 54,639. O'Malley emerged from the jaunt talking of maybe 65,000 seats.[50]

Capacity would be a moving target for the next three years. Seven months after his walk with Webb, O'Malley was talking 52,000 again, saying, "I would like to somehow recapture the friendly feeling of Ebbets Field. We'll lose the intimacy if we go too big."[51] But soon after he was saying the stadium could be as large as 70,000 seats.[52]

O'Malley and Praeger were also keeping alive the idea of the dome. In February 1959 Praeger discussed a ten-acre, two-and-a-half-inch-thick dome to be made of translucent material ribbed with concrete and steel. It would cost $2.5 million to $3 million. O'Malley acknowledged there was not much chance of a rainout in Los Angeles, but said the potential to use the stadium for industrial shows, conventions, or exhibitions might make it worthwhile in five or ten years.[53] The dome still fascinated O'Malley, who said he would have built one if the Dodgers had moved to the Texas heat or the Montreal cold. "The strange thing is I landed in the one place in the world where you don't need a dome," he said. "I would have invested in a dome."[54]

By late 1959 the design had changed again. The outfield pavilions had disappeared, and each of the four decks had been extended to curve around slightly into fair territory and then stop. The ends of each deck were now flush with each other.[55] O'Malley said the capacity of this design was 56,000, although it could be expanded.[56]

The final version of the stadium first surfaced in late 1960. In this version, the fourth deck was cut back to extend only partway toward first and third bases, rather than all the way down around the foul poles. The pavilions in left and right fields also reappeared. Capacity was still tagged at 56,000, but O'Malley said the design and foundation work had been done that could push capacity as high as 80,000.[57] Possibilities included building the fourth deck out farther or extending some or all of the lower decks farther into the outfield.

To this day the Dodgers maintain that the capacity of the stadium is 56,000, even when you ask them for an exact figure.[58] Sid Ziff of the *Los Angeles Times* once reported that the stadium contained exactly 55,792 seats, but the Dodgers will not confirm that.[59] After the 1963 Series, when they reported ticket sales to the commissioner's office, they said they had sold 57,206 tickets for both Game Three and Game Four.[60] Some extra seats had been added at the front edge of the lower deck for these games.

The construction contract for the stadium was a plum, and the Yankees' Webb had been the high-profile candidate from the beginning. His company had built several large structures in Los Angeles, and his business interests brought him regularly to the city, where he would consult with O'Malley about the stadium. But when the time came to award the contract, the Dodgers gave the job to Vinnell Constructors, a company from suburban Pasadena that had won the bidding for the first grading work in 1959. In his book *Veeck—as in Wreck*, onetime White Sox owner Bill Veeck reported Webb was very confident he would win the contract and had lost by overbidding the job by $6 million.[61] Although a $6 million overbid on a contract of about $8 to $10 million seems unlikely, and Veeck had a strong dislike of Webb, the Vinnell bid was clearly superior. The *Sporting News* reported Webb had recommended the Vinnell firm, in part because it had its equipment on the site already. The report said Webb would remain as a consultant to the project.[62] The contract was signed in August 1960, soon after the city finally issued a building permit.[63]

Dick Walsh was promoted to vice president of stadium construction and operations two days after Vinnell signed the contract.[64] He had been O'Malley's point man on the stadium for two years already, but now the thirty-four-year-old Walsh was being given day-to-day responsibility for the stadium. He was O'Malley's detail guy.

Born in South Bend, Indiana, in 1926, Walsh moved with his family to Los Angeles in 1938. He graduated from Los Angeles High School in 1943, just a few years before Rosalind Wyman. He had been the third baseman on the all-city team that spring and was offered a tryout with the Cincinnati Reds. But with World War II on, Walsh went into the Army. A year later he was a lieutenant, serving in the Philippines, before joining the occupation forces in Japan. He did not leave the Army until 1948. He tried to resume his baseball career at a tryout camp in Anaheim early that year held by the Dodgers, but five years in the Army had cut into his speed. Wid Matthews, the Rickey veteran running the tryout camp, was impressed nonetheless. He called Walsh aside, told him he had no future as a ballplayer, but asked if he had any interest in a career in the business side of the game. Walsh said yes, and a few months later Matthews called with an offer to be assistant general manager of the Fort Worth Cats.[65]

Assistant general manager was a very splendid title for a twenty-two-year-old gofer. Walsh sold hot dogs, took tickets, cleaned the ballpark, and lit gasoline to dry the playing field after a rain. After a year in Fort Worth, Walsh spent 1949 and 1950 in Danville, Illinois, as business manager, essentially the same responsibilities as in Fort Worth, although he was in charge. After the 1950 season he recommended the Dodgers sell the Danville team, which they did, and Walsh moved to Brooklyn as an assistant farm director under Fresco Thompson.[66]

As an assistant farm director Walsh won little notice, although the one time he entered the news indicated the workaholic thoroughness that would make him invaluable to O'Malley in building the stadium. In late 1952 teams circulated lists of their Minor League rosters in preparation for the annual winter meetings. At those meetings teams had the opportunity to pluck players from each other. Walsh took home the lists, which contained thousands of player names. He studied them, comparing the lists to the Dodgers' files on players seen by their scouts and Minor League managers. He noticed the Yankees had not protected a young pitcher named Don Bessent, who had had two excellent seasons before missing 1952 for back surgery. Walsh checked, found Bessent had recovered from the surgery, and recommended the Dodgers draft him.[67] Bessent would spend several years in the Majors, winning eight games for the 1955 Dodger World Series champions.

Walsh began to move up when he took over as temporary traveling secretary during the Dodgers' trip to Japan after the 1956 season. O'Malley noticed the exact and farsighted arrangements and that his occupation duty in Japan had given Walsh the opportunity to learn some Japanese.[68]

A few months later, after buying the Minor League Los Angeles Angels, O'Malley made Walsh the president of that team.[69] Beginning that year the

Los Angeles boy was O'Malley's liaison with the city's political leaders. Now, that job would be formalized with the new title.

Dick Walsh—crew-cut, square jawed—was a ferociously organized man. Branch Rickey, canvassing possible candidates for his Continental League in the fall of 1959, noted that Walsh was "a tireless worker, very able, a lot of initiative."[70] He was a "great detail guy," said Tom Seeberg, then a young front-office employee and later an executive with the Dodgers, Cincinnati Reds, and California Angels.[71] He also had a sly sense of humor. When asked why he had been chosen to oversee the stadium project, he said, "I was the only one in the Dodger organization who studied drafting at John Burroughs Junior High."[72]

But, noted Rickey, Walsh was "completely without any touch of sentiment. The word compassion has never been in his vocabulary."[73] In later years, when he was general manager of the California Angels, the players he negotiated with on salaries would dub him "the smiling python."[74] The *Los Angeles Times*'s Jim Murray called him "a tough, taciturn guy who went through life as if he were flushing machine-gun nests."[75] For dealing with the city and with contractors over the stadium, this was a valuable attitude. "I was the buffer between outsiders and Walter O'Malley, and general manager Buzzie Bavasi. They were the yes men. If the answer had to be no, the appointment would be with me," Walsh said.[76]

Walsh, by temperament and ambition, became consumed by the job. "There's no wind, little fog, and no swamps—but I go over those plans a thousand times, looking for some unsuspected little bug that may throw the whole thing out of kilter. You know, like corridors that run nowhere, or rooms you can't get into without going outside the building," he said.[77]

If the cantilevered design and the precast concrete reflected Emil Praeger, it was all the smaller parts of the design that made this project O'Malley's stadium. O'Malley and his team would bring hundreds of new ideas to this ballpark. Some ideas were large. Some were small. Some were borrowed— from sources as widely scattered as Japan, Madison Avenue, and racetracks. But all were part of O'Malley's general philosophy of trying to make a ball game a pleasant experience for the fan, whether the home team won or not. "Why should we treat baseball fans like cattle? I came to the conclusion years ago that we in baseball were losing our audience and weren't doing a damn thing about it," he said.[78] "Race tracks are way ahead of us in imagination, planning, showmanship."[79] In Los Angeles, he quickly realized, people were not as fanatical about professional sports as New Yorkers. There was a greater emphasis on doing things yourself rather than watching others, and with Southern California's weather the opportunities for doing so were much greater. O'Malley said later he wanted the stadium to be perfect to chase away customers' memories of the Coliseum.[80]

Peter O'Malley said his father was influenced greatly by Disneyland, the new Southern California tourist attraction, which had opened in 1955. After his first visit, Peter recalled, O'Malley came home and said, "You just have to see that place—the presentation of it, the restrooms, the food. He realized the standard had been set by Disneyland."[81]

O'Malley did not want to be way behind anybody, especially in attracting fans. Take color. Madison Avenue had cottoned to the symbolism and uses of color many years before. Industrial engineers had found its uses for subconsciously guiding the eye and making connections. O'Malley would code his whole ballpark in color. Each of the four main decks would have different-colored seats, and correspondingly colored signs would guide the fan there.[82] Tickets would be the same color as the seats they were for. In the parking lots the baseball-shaped signs marking the various areas would be color-coded to the appropriate deck, a visual clue to help people avoid climbing the Dodger Stadium ridge.

As with the parking plan some of O'Malley's innovations were designed into the stadium. The Dodgers would claim 70 percent of the stadium's seats were in the arc from first base to third base behind home plate, as O'Malley had been hoping with the original Bel Geddes–Praeger design in Brooklyn.[83] Using an idea O'Malley had picked up on the 1956 trip to Japan, the Dodgers would build an arc of seats at the same level as the dugouts and between them, giving a select group of fans the same angle on the game as both managers.[84] The dugout seats would also allow the team to boast of seven front rows (the four main decks, the dugout seats, the small deck that spread from the press box just below the third deck, and the outfield pavilions). This was a significant change from the Coliseum, with its single front row.

Dodger Stadium would cater to those who were willing to pay more. There would be deluxe boxes with food service. There would be a large stadium club at the same level as the press box, but far down the right-field line. With a $250 membership on top of a $265 season box seat, a customer could dine on swordfish or rack of lamb served on china while watching the Dodgers.[85]

But the hot dog set would be served as well. The 47,964 seats ordered from the American Seating Company of Grand Rapids, Michigan, would range between nineteen and twenty-two inches in width. The standard stadium seat of the time was seventeen to eighteen inches wide, the company said.[86] There would be forty-eight bathrooms, with twenty-six being set aside for men after studies of the fan base.[87] Two thousand pairs of seats, dubbed love seats, would be fitted with retractable armrests between them. "This was Walter's idea. He's all for compatibility," said Dick Walsh.[88] Spaces for wheelchairs were designed at the playing-field edge of each deck's concourse, right behind the top row of seats.[89] There was a map of stadium access routes and the parking lot design on the back of each ticket.[90] The main benefit for the average fan, however, would be that ticket prices would be maintained at the same level as the Coliseum. In fact, they would be maintained at the Coliseum level into the mid-1970s.

For the players O'Malley and Praeger dreamed up the idea of building the outfield fences out of plywood, far more forgiving to outfielders in pursuit of a fly ball than concrete.[91] For women performers in the fashion show and other pregame events, the design team provided a separate dressing area.[92] For the media, which overwhelmingly meant newspaper reporters in those days, the press box would contain showers, large workspaces, and a small restaurant. It was also where visiting-club officials, scouts, and other baseball people could eat for free, giving the reporters access to people with knowledge and stories.

O'Malley even insisted on just the right kinds of dirt. H. Chandler Van Wicklen worked for the A. E. Schmidt Company, the firm charged with providing the playing-field dirt for Dodger Stadium. Van Wicklen said O'Malley specified three different kinds of dirt—one for the foundation layer, another for the pitchers' mound, and a third for the infield and the exposed areas around home plate. For the latter he demanded a particular shade of red because he wanted to ensure it showed up well on television. The company had to go to a remote canyon near Lone Pine, in the desert almost two hundred miles north of Los Angeles, to find the right mix.[93] O'Malley fed the grass with an underground sprinkler system that delivered not only water but also fertilizer and nutrients.[94]

Once the fans were in the stands, they would find a large scoreboard above the right-field pavilion that would display the lineups as well as the score, count, time of day, and umpires. Above the left-field pavilion was another innovation—a message board. O'Malley said it would allow the Dodgers to post statistical notes and other interesting material.[95] It would also permit the Dodgers to recognize visiting groups, lead cheers, and plug upcoming events.

Aside from the round Union Oil sign perched atop the message board, the plugs for upcoming events and Dodger souvenirs would be the only advertising in the stadium. O'Malley would eschew several sources of revenue and keep prices low in an effort to maintain an aura about the ballpark as a pristine place to take the family for wholesome entertainment. O'Malley planned to reinforce that almost rural feel of the ballpark with extensive landscaping, indulging in another of his passions with color-coordinated displays of flowers.[96] For a while he even considered trying to coordinate the flowers with the colors of the various decks.[97]

Not all the ideas got in. The wire mesh used for the infamous left-field screen in the Coliseum was moved to make a green backdrop in center field at Dodger Stadium. But it proved impossible to stabilize the screening mesh, and a substitute material had to be found.[98] There was the idea for a forty-foot waterfall behind the fence in center field. When a Dodger hit a home run, the water would shoot up like a fountain while colored lights played over it. O'Malley claimed he would issue an umbrella with every bleacher ticket.[99] When the city required a water-retention basin during construction, O'Malley talked about landscaping it as a permanent lake on-site.[100] There was talk of building the stadium in the shape of the city seal, or orienting it so fans could see both the mountains surrounding Los Angeles and the city skyline, an idea with geographic difficulties.[101]

He looked at a number of systems, modeled on Disneyland, for transporting people from the distant sections of the parking lots to the stadium. In the 1958 team yearbook they were called "mule trains" and featured a drawing of a nineteenth-century locomotive pulling tram cars. By early 1961 the drawings showed blunt-nosed open-air cars with a driver's seat in the front row.[102] In the months before the stadium opened, O'Malley was in talks with Lockheed Corporation about providing a monorail system to move the fans.[103] None was built, presumably because of cost and the terraced design of the parking lots.

And then there was the stadium's name. Generally, when asked the question, O'Malley would be coy, especially when the questioner suggested that "O'Malley" be part of the name.[104] The newspapers received letters suggesting naming it after worthy citizens or calling it "Los Angeles Civic Stadium."[105] The fledgling Los Angeles Angels of the American League, who would play in the new stadium beginning in 1962, asked O'Malley not to call it Dodger Stadium because that name would make it difficult for the Angels to create a clear, separate identity.[106] In the end the name Dodger Stadium was presented as a product of inertia. The plans and architectural drawings had carried the name for years, and the Dodgers would simply go ahead and use it, the team said.[107] Unspoken was that in a marketing sense, Dodger Stadium was the most sensible name. It tied the location to the product. Three decades later sports teams and cities would begin to sell stadium naming rights to businesses willing to pay millions of dollars for the advertising the repeated use of the name would generate. O'Malley was keeping that advertising value for his own business, and the Angels' reaction showed they appreciated that fact. In their four years in the stadium the Angels would consistently call the park Chavez Ravine.

In the spring of 1960 Candlestick Park opened in San Francisco, and the Dodgers began to learn all kinds of negative lessons quickly. Some were gleefully learned, as the Dodgers' political opponents had held up Candlestick as the model for Los Angeles during the 1958 referendum campaign. Some lessons were cautionary, because they raised fears in Los Angeles fans that the Dodgers had not thought they would encounter. After Candlestick opened club officials and team brochures would talk about the lack of wind up in Chavez Ravine, although they would mention a nice breeze.[108]

The *Los Angeles Times* happily spent May 1960 reporting on Candlestick's inoperable heating system, the steep climb from the parking lot that become known as Cardiac Hill after several incidents, the pickpockets Candlestick attracted, and, of course, the winds.[109] O'Malley, Praeger, and Vinnell officials made several trips to scout out possibilities, and the Dodgers would institute a parking-control operation after watching the postgame exit from the San Francisco park, which did not have one. Dodger Stadium became the first stadium built with traffic signals inside the park.[110]

O'Malley's trips to Candlestick were only one part of his almost obsessive involvement in the park. Each time the stadium was redesigned, he would commission a new scale model. The model would start in his office and then migrate out to public display in bank lobbies and the Los Angeles County Fair. He would interrupt vacations and the spring sojourn in Vero Beach for visits to the stadium site. When visitors came to town he would take them up himself, pointing out all the wonders and, as construction progressed, driving a car through the stadium's concourses to show features.[111] O'Malley himself would drive up to Chavez Ravine almost every day, often on his own. He would walk the site, kicking the tires, worrying about details, dreaming.[112]

After the unexpected World Series victory of 1959, the 1960 and 1961 Dodger teams proved disappointments. The team stumbled to fourth place in 1960 and then rebounded to second place in 1961, still a letdown for a team many picked to win the pennant. After the successes of the early Dodger Stadium years, Fresco Thompson explained that Bavasi and he had built a team emphasizing speed and pitching for the new stadium, which was supposed to open in 1959 or 1960. Instead, that team had been forced to play in the Coliseum, a ballpark that rewarded power.[113] Although there may be some truth to that, it was also clear that Bavasi and manager Walt Alston were sorting through the young talent, while phasing out the last of the Brooklyn stars.

O'Malley was feeling confident enough to buy his first house in Southern California. He had toyed with the idea of living at his new stadium. He had a building at the top of the stadium, used originally as a public restaurant and later as a gift shop, reinforced so an apartment could be built on top. But Kay vetoed that idea.[114] Through 1959 and 1960 O'Malley continued to spend considerable time in Lake Arrowhead, staying in a hotel suite while in Los Angeles. In the summer of 1961 he finally moved to buy a house on North Shore Drive in Lake Arrowhead for a reported $75,000. It was an A-frame house with three staggered levels inside, about a hundred yards from the edge of the lake. It had brick, wood, five bedrooms, and three baths. The living room had a striking view of the lake and the boathouse and landing that went with it. O'Malley also bought the lot just south of the house. Later, he would pick up the lot on the other side. He was putting down roots. Typically, he put a bumper sticker on the wall next to the freezer. "Keep Arrowhead green. Bring money," it said.[115]

When he could avoid dealing with the authorities, O'Malley's main real estate venture proceeded smoothly for much of 1961.[116] Seats were ordered. Work on designing usher and usherette uniforms was begun.[117] Detailed drawings were being passed out to Dodger staffers by March so they could comment on the design of their work spaces.[118]

The continuing fly in the ointment was the delay in finished access roads. The government still had not put the contracts out to bid by April 1961.[119] This was feeding into the latest concerns raised by the stadium deal's dedicated opponents—the specter of massive traffic jams.[120] The specter was not diminished, as stadium opponents continued to delay the approval of roads.[121] The situation became more complicated when Norris Poulson lost a bitter reelection bid for mayor on May 31. He was replaced by Sam Yorty. Yorty had generally remained silent on the stadium itself, turning new trash regulations into the centerpiece of his campaign. But he lambasted Poulson over a broad portfolio of issues and consciously appealed to the distant districts of the city against the downtown interests who had supported the Dodgers.[122] Many Dodger opponents had signed on to the Yorty campaign, including Phill Silver, who would become a Yorty administration official later in the decade. With the newspapers still clearly in the Dodgers' camp, Yorty chose not to use the various access-road design and construction issues to hold up the stadium even further. By August O'Malley could tell a Kiwanis Club luncheon at the Biltmore Hotel that Yorty had pledged not to "sabotage any legislation vital to completion of the park and its access roads."[123] But that did not mean the Yorty camp was converting. The next month Yorty's chief of staff, Joe Quinn, engaged in a sharp exchange with the manager of the city traffic department over postgame traffic, with Quinn arguing that neither the Pasadena Freeway nor Sunset Boulevard would be adequate.[124]

While the politicians squabbled, the stadium had become a tourist destination. Visitors had been driving onto the property since the grand-opening ceremonies, and by August 1961 the buses of Tanner Tours rolled through the site every day.[125] The target date for completion was still February 1, barely five months away. O'Malley remained tightly focused on the project. The week the 1961 season opened O'Malley chose to report that construction had seen its biggest week of progress so far.[126] When Lew Fonseca, a former player who had become director of motion pictures for both leagues, came to town to make an instructional film, O'Malley grabbed him to film the construction.[127]

As the 1961 season ended the smooth pace picked up. Then, in late September, a 125-ton derrick hoisting precast concrete pieces into place collapsed. It broke one worker's leg and smashed thirty-five seat units, the precast concrete pieces that would hold anywhere from a few to several dozen seats. Walsh estimated the delay at two to three weeks but noted they had been ahead of schedule. Much of the delay was caused by the necessity for recasting the seat units and then giving them time to dry. The accident was attributed to a structural defect in the crane. The next day the arm of a 45-ton mobile crane buckled while trying to remove some damaged sections and dropped its load onto the front edge of the second deck. It caused less damage but more muttering.[128]

The pace started to resume in October. Deliveries of the seats began.[129] Work started on the access roads in November, and, as the rainy season approached, the Dodgers announced that "provision has been made in the time schedule for some delays caused by weather."[130] Walsh said the stadium was still ahead of schedule.[131]

By early-January 1962, however, the Angels were worried. Heavier than usual rains in November and December had slowed the pace again. The team paid the city for another year's option on Wrigley Field, where they had played in their inaugural 1961 season. O'Malley denied the Dodgers had a similar arrangement with the Coliseum. "We absolutely will not play another game there. We have burned our bridges behind us," he said.[132]

Still, O'Malley was concerned. Early-January rains washed away the topsoil of the playing field, meticulously prepared and waiting for sod. It would take ten days to dry out before that work could be redone. The unpaved parking-lot areas needed to dry out as well. After touring the site with Walsh, the engineers, and staff, he decided to change the order in which parking lots would be paved to ensure at least some would be ready by opening day. He also made his first concession to the Dodgers' yearlong mantra that all would be ready. "We may not have the refinements April 10, but the roads, seats, diamond, rest rooms and concession stands will be there. So will the parking and the teams."[133]

A few days later O'Malley and *Los Angeles Herald Examiner* sports columnist Melvin Durslag took a helicopter tour of the site. "Walter called his inspection trip to Chavez Ravine routine, but you had the feeling he was searching quietly for reassurance," Durslag wrote. County supervisor Warren Dorn had recently made the same tour and announced there was no way the stadium would be ready. O'Malley, thoroughly fed up with all the local officials, suggested Dorn was grandstanding. Construction on the stadium itself remained nearly three weeks ahead of schedule. They were also ahead on the parking lots, and 40 percent of the seats were installed. "You can't very well expect better performance." And if it's not ready? asked Durslag. "I would wind up in the hospital with my condition not at all trivial," O'Malley said. "But I'm certain we're going to make it on schedule." After the flight landed Durslag and O'Malley walked to the edge of the infield. "With the pride and fascination of a tenement dweller who has grown his first geranium, O'Malley sifted the dirt with his hand," Durslag reported.[134]

Jack Young of Vinnell Constructors could rattle off the reassuring statistics as quickly as O'Malley (all storm drains in, 30 percent of parking lots paved, the volcanic cinder base under the playing field being laid).[135] But he also asked O'Malley for uniformed security guards at the site. "I'll finish it on time if you keep the people out of here," he told O'Malley.[136]

Then it really started to rain. By late January the rains had added $400,000 to the stadium's price tag.[137] In early February work stopped both on the stadium and on the access roads. Water covered the infield and washed away topsoil again. The *Herald Examiner* called it "the worst storm here in a number of years." The additional cost was now tabbed at $500,000. There were more reports the Dodgers were looking at alternatives, including moving the opening series or two to their opponents' cities. There were more denials by O'Malley. The playing field presented a major problem. The second generation of topsoil, and the first 150 square feet of sod, had been washed away. Now, the playing field would take at least another ten days to dry out and then more time as it was reconditioned and prepared for sod. O'Malley was becoming an expert on coming rainstorms, reporting more were predicted for late February and late March.[138]

Ten days later O'Malley hired two helicopters to hover over the playing field to help it dry out.[139] By February 23 Los Angeles had seen seventeen inches of rain that month alone. A normal November-to-March rainy season in the city is twelve to fifteen inches. The helicopter did not work well enough. The next day a jet engine removed from an Air Force F-84 fighter was mounted on a truck and driven around the field, shooting out a three-hundred-foot blast of heat.[140] The additional price tag was now up to $600,000, as O'Malley headed back to Vero Beach on February 24 to watch spring training for a week to ten days. Optimistically, he was reporting that the "big headache" for opening day was the entrance to the stadium off the Pasadena Freeway, not anything on the stadium site itself.[141]

O'Malley was also bemoaning the fact that he had missed a financing trick. In Houston, where the expansion Colt .45s franchise was planning the Astrodome, team president Roy Hofheinz had figured out he could get a federal subsidy if he built a bomb shelter in the basement. O'Malley said it would have been easy to add such a thing to Dodger Stadium.[142]

In early March Walsh admitted much of the parking-lot paving had been ripped up because the most recent rains had created bumps and dips. But, he said, the stadium would open on time. Some work crews were working seven days a week.[143] On Wednesday, March 7, O'Malley flew back to Los Angeles with Praeger and immediately drove up to the construction site, where the stadium lights were being tested for the first time. "I thought it was a thrilling sight," O'Malley said.[144] Not everything he found in Los Angeles was thrilling. Nursing a toothache, he and Praeger toured the stadium and had their fears the city would not finish the Pasadena Freeway connection confirmed.[145] By Sunday, March 11, he was on his way back to Florida for a couple of weeks.

When he returned to Los Angeles he faced a mild political storm over the Dodgers' refusal to provide city council members with free tickets. The *Herald Examiner* reported Mayor Yorty's office had asked for two tickets to opening day and been told to send in $7 and the Dodgers would see what they could do. Roger Arnebergh, the city's attorney and O'Malley ally in the court fights, said he had been told he would have to pay. Without allowing the paper to use their names, several council members who had supported the Dodgers complained about the treatment, using the phrase "double-cross." Perhaps O'Malley was taking revenge for all his troubles with the city. Roz Wyman had already bought season tickets.[146]

Although he did not admit it publicly at the time, O'Malley was fed up. "One of the biggest mistakes I made when I came West was taking western politicians at their word. I had been informed that a western politician was a hearty, candid fellow whose handshake was his bond. I learned otherwise," he said years later. "I didn't expect a double-cross."[147]

The stadium project staggered into its final days, shedding pieces that would not be completed. The auxiliary scoreboards were not ready. The restaurant aimed at the general public would not open on time. The finally sodded grass of the playing field was turning brown all over the place. Plugs were being moved from the sod-growing area out beyond the parking lots, but the Dodgers acknowledged the turf would be rough for a while.[148] The message board was still being wired. The right-field pavilion barely made it, too.

O'Malley's focus on the project was intense, with his engineering experience coming out as he surveyed the details. Touring the Dodger dugout during the last week of construction, he decided the players' bench should be pulled out a couple of inches farther from the rear wall to allow a backrest.[149]

The turf would be more than rough. With multiple replantings and waterlogged ground, it came in thin and pale. After a suggestion from Mervyn LeRoy, O'Malley used the Hollywood expedient and had it dyed. Most of the turf was a very bright green by the eve of opening day, except for the parts that the dye had turned yellow. That was just one of the projects that ran through that final week. The stadium lights stayed on all night, glowing above the Los Angeles skyline and visible for miles. O'Malley was there constantly. "Here's the gent again," said one plasterer. "We've seen more of him than we have our own boss." Asked how he was on the day of the dedication ceremony, the eve of opening day, O'Malley clipped off, "Just fine. Really wonderful. Haven't slept in a week."[150]

O'Malley, of course, could not just be an engineer or construction supervisor. He had to be the owner, carrying out all the public duties designed to build sentiment for the team and the stadium. In early December the city and the Dodgers had announced a "civic celebration" to dedicate Dodger Stadium in April. The event was planned as a nineteen-day fiesta, from April 1 through the Angels' opening game at the stadium. O'Malley said he hoped the event turned into an annual weeklong celebration, kicking off the baseball season. For the Dodgers there would be an "elaborate dedicatory luncheon" outside the stadium on April 9, the day before the opening game. O'Malley appeared at the announcement press conference wearing the cap of the American League expansion team the Los Angeles Angels, with its distinctive halo around the crown. The Angels would be his tenant. Angels president Bob Reynolds wore a Dodger cap. Of more comment in Los Angeles, Mayor Sam Yorty and his defeated rival, Norris Poulson, appeared on the same podium, shook hands, and were nice to each other. Chad McClellan was named chairman of the dedication committee. Even John Holland showed up, saying he was a baseball fan.[151]

The traffic issue would not go away. City traffic commissioner Edward J. Crowley advised fans to start early on April 10. The Automobile Club of Southern California distributed a special map, warning that all the freeway connections would not be completed and suggesting alternate routes. *Los Angeles Times* columnist Braven Dyer slyly suggested O'Malley work out a plan to dismiss the crowd alphabetically or by cities.[152] The Pasadena Freeway connection had even O'Malley supporters such as Wyman worried about traffic.[153] O'Malley suggested the stadium would empty in an hour. City traffic engineer S. S. "Sam" Taylor said that was virtually impossible.[154] Police chief William Parker predicted it would take two hours for all the cars to get in and a similar amount of time for the parking lots to empty.[155] O'Malley decided that with a guaranteed sellout, the debut game could be televised on KTTV, Channel 11. A rival station, KTLA, Channel 5, owned by the Angels' Gene Autry and Bob Reynolds, announced it would have its helicopters up, televising the traffic problems.[156]

The serious festivities began Monday, April 9, with speeches at city hall, a parade up to Dodger Stadium, a $5 box lunch, and what was advertised as an intrasquad game by the Dodgers. The events fell a little short of the advertising. On the steps of city hall Ford Frick spoke, his voice cracking as he refuted those who said baseball was dying. Then it was National League president Warren Giles and then a local dignitary who modestly predicted the stadium would become "a symbol of peace for this world." The Dodgers, arrayed in uniform in the front row, fidgeted like a group of first graders. When O'Malley finally got to the podium, in the middle of what would prove to be a six-hour ceremony, he told the audience that, if they had not known it already, they now appreciated that other things besides baseball were long and drawn out.[157] *Los Angeles Times* columnist Sid Ziff noted the organizers did not take the hint. "The committee wouldn't budge an inch and went ahead with more folderol," he wrote.[158] The committee did present O'Malley with copies of some important city documents, and O'Malley trotted out his jabbing humor to say he thought they might be more subpoenas.[159]

Cardinal McIntyre gave the invocation, a Protestant clergyman gave a benediction, and a rabbi was invited.[160] So was Albert Chavez, born in Chavez Ravine and a grand-nephew of the Julian Chavez who had left his name on the area.[161] The organizers did not have enough fried chicken lunches and wound up reimbursing people.[162] Given the condition of the playing field, O'Malley agreed to cancel the intrasquad game. The batting practice disappeared when the batting cage could not be found. The crowd groaned. The Dodgers did stage an infield drill, but people were already leaving.[163]

That night O'Malley entertained at a "family" cocktail party in the Stadium Club, with press, VIPs, and others involved in the project along for a preview of the facilities. The stadium lights were on, and guests could watch the beginnings of a feverish night of activity.[164] The patchy dye job on the grass was being fixed, and on opening day the balls used for batting practice would come back from the outfield tinted green.[165] The wiring of the message board was being finished. Painters, plasterers, welders, and carpenters were everywhere.[166]

On the morning of opening day the message board triumphantly flashed its first message—WLCMSX DDGZA FNSA—but it was working properly by game time.[167] Because it was an afternoon game, the in-game information included stock market closing averages, a practice soon discontinued.[168]

On the day itself the 52,564 paying fans arrived early, and, inevitably, not everything worked. With fans packing around the still-closed gates, the ticket takers took the wrappings off the turnstiles—and moths flew out.[169] One elevator failed and the other was erratic. Frank Sinatra, Jimmy Stewart, and Jack Warner got tired of the forty-minute wait for the elevator and skipped the Stadium Club. This was probably a good idea, as the Stadium Club line was more than a block long. The kitchen was not finished, so the food was catered and served buffet style.[170] Approached by a woman asking how she could get a drink, O'Malley said, "If I knew, I would have one myself."[171]

The fans wandered around, ignoring the color scheme. One fan got into an argument with an usher who wanted him on his own level in his own seat. The fan said he wanted to wander. Dick Walsh said let him go.[172] One *Times* reporter said half the seats were empty when the first pitch was thrown because the fans were still wandering and gawking.[173] A noticeable bare patch showed up in the right-field pavilion where a ticket foul-up had prevented the sale of seats.[174] The Cincinnati Reds' team bus got caught in a line of fans' cars on the approaches to the stadium, and the driver was forced to pay $4 to park.

O'Malley was still entertaining, with all the spaces in his twenty-four-seat private section in the press box crowded with friends and allies.[175] But he also wandered the crowd during the game, posing for photographers on the edge of the field during the fourth inning. Perhaps indicative of O'Malley's pique with the local politicians, Norris Poulson was not in the owner's box. He got a seat in the dugout boxes.[176] Kay O'Malley threw out the ceremonial first pitch.[177]

Johnny Podres's first pitch to Eddie Kasko was a ball. The Dodgers lost 6–3. Under teasing from *Times* columnist Jim Murray, a curiously prophetic Buzzie Bavasi noted that early-season losses could come back to haunt you at the end of the season. But that conversation quickly changed, as did almost all conversations at the ballpark that day, into comments on Walter O'Malley's new stadium. "Beautiful ballpark," said Murray. "Lots of bugs in it yet," said Bavasi. "I know," said Murray. "I got some in my beer."[178] The consensus was much more along the lines of Murray's first remark. Podres, the losing pitcher, echoed the other players, saying, "This ballpark knocks your eyes out."[179] Commissioner Ford Frick caught more of the stadium's importance to the business of the game. "Baseball has never had anything like this. It marks the beginning of a new era."[180]

The traffic fears proved to be unfounded, with the park emptying within forty-five minutes of game's end.[181] "The game was OK," wrote Murray, "but the traffic jam was strictly bush league. . . . I hope the chief has a better line on the Mafia than he has on traffic."[182] O'Malley fired a blast at city officials for the warnings. Police chief William Parker responded that things were eased because 75 percent of the fans had left before the ninth inning to avoid the traffic.[183]

Walter O'Malley must have been on an emotional moon mission that day. He was physically drained. He knew in his heart he had built a paradigm shift of a stadium, a stadium that would be imitated both well and poorly over the next decade. He also knew how much work remained to finish it. "Dodger Stadium is the culmination of a personal dream I've had ever since I became a part of baseball's executive family," O'Malley wrote a few days before the stadium opened.[184] He now had his "monument to the O'Malleys."

13

Loose Ends

The "monument to the O'Malleys" was not monumental in its details yet. From the embarrassing to the merely delayed, Walter O'Malley would spend the next four years cleaning up both his stadium and the residue of his agreements with local officials. Amid the general approbation locally, the problems that seem to plague all opening days cropped up. Signs featured directions such as "louge" and "feild." Some of the turnstiles had been installed backward, and each entering ticket holder was recorded as a minus one. One patron wandered into O'Malley's office to borrow the phone.[1] By the fifth game problems had developed in the parking system.[2] But the detail that would catch everyone's eye and go down in Dodger Stadium lore was the lack of drinking fountains.

Three days after the stadium opened, *Los Angeles Times* columnist Sid Ziff reported that his personal investigation still had not found a drinking fountain in the stadium. Dodgers public relations people said they did not know if the stadium had any.[3] It turns out there were three, one in each team's dugout and one in O'Malley's office.[4] Two days later Ziff reported one of his readers had been told to get her drink from the tap water in the bathrooms.[5] The newspapers ran pictures of enterprising boys selling water on the approaches to the stadium.[6] Adults tied in their complaint with gripes about the price of beer (forty or forty-five cents for a six-ounce cup in the general sections, but seventy-five cents for the same in the Stadium Club).[7]

The immediate assumption was that the "greedy" O'Malley had deliberately left the drinking fountains out to sell more beer and soda.[8] The city's health department ordered the installation of an "adequate" number of water fountains.[9] Two more or less official stories emerged over time. The first was that, as Ziff's reader had been told, drinking water was available in the restrooms, with paper cups provided.[10] But when the controversy arose the city said drinking facilities had to be a certain distance from any toilets or urinals. O'Malley would later lament he had wanted to color-code the paper cups to the different levels of the stadium. The second version was that it had simply been overlooked.[11] In June Bavasi presented Ziff with a gold charm bracelet featuring miniature drinking fountains with a note, "Have a drink on me."[12]

Other things had been overlooked as well. There were no electrical outlets in the clubhouses and no steps from the dugouts to the field level.[13] When 124 sweepers reported for work at 6:00 a.m. after a night game, there were only five brooms available, but all had to be paid.[14]

The county's inability to finish the approaches from the adjoining Pasadena Freeway to the stadium also continued to cause problems, especially when attendance was very heavy.[15] They were completed in August.[16]

There were also problems with educating the fans, and the staff, that Dodger Stadium's unique design forced people to approach the park differently. Whether it was the local Wrigley Field or whatever other ballparks fans had been to, the standard approach was to arrive behind home plate and be directed from there. But this stadium's multiple levels and its construction into a hillside made this impossible. Only the small top deck, which was general admission seating, could be approached from behind home plate. Entrances to all the other levels were down the foul lines, and the bottom-deck entrances were at the far wings of the stadium, past the foul poles. In addition, the various terraced levels of the parking lot, which theoretically fed people into the proper levels, all looked a great deal alike to the eye unfamiliar with the layout. Internally, there were two small elevators and one set of stairs to take people from one level to another. Opening day, these were jammed to gridlock, as people, many of them on the top deck, tried to find their seats. Undertrained staff did not help. The *Herald Examiner* printed a letter from "B. L. B., a disgusted fan," who wrote: "Why doesn't Walter O'Malley spend a little time (and money) educating his ushers, ticket takers and parking attendants?" B. L. B. said he had been sent to three different levels and five different seat locations.[17]

Some of the employees were not too happy. They complained they were required to park as far from the stadium as possible and had to pay to do so, that the team would not allow a lunch wagon onto the grounds, that they could not use the elevator to haul trash between levels, and they were required to get on their hands and knees to scrub the seating tiers.[18]

Other ideas were dropped. The stadium had opened with a system of tokens rather than printed tickets for general admission. But the team found that fans, and scalpers, were hoarding them to be used when the Giants came to town. They were gone after the 1962 season.[19] O'Malley had wanted to put a sit-down restaurant on every level, but dropped the idea after resistance from the company that ran the Stadium Club.[20]

In early May a water main burst under the right-field pavilion. The dugouts and dugout seats were three feet deep, and parts of the outfield and infield were ankle deep.[21] Fortunately, the Dodgers were in St. Louis. When the Yankees came to play the Angels in early June, the New York writers took the opportunity to complain about the elevators and a consequent postgame wait to get to their bus. They voted Dodger Stadium "the worst press box in the American League."[22]

What the Dodgers were trying to keep quiet was that it was probably the worst infield in either league.[23] It was a combination of the late rain, California's normal heat and aridity, groundskeepers unfamiliar with same, and the red clay that had been brought in to make the field look good on television. That particular clay hardened very well. Outfielder Gordon Windhorn called it "a $20 million stadium with a 10-cent field."[24] Groundskeepers, used to the soils and rainfall patterns of the Midwest and East, thought the best way to take care of the infield was with liberal doses of water. In California's dry heat, that was like preparing an adobe brick. Even three years later the Milwaukee Braves' Joe Torre would say, "Ask the groundskeeper to fill in the holes around first base. He can fill them with cement so they'll be like the rest of the infield."[25]

The late rain had ensured that the grass never really took hold. With the Angels and the Dodgers alternating home stands, off days for the field were few, but it was resodded during the All-Star break.[26] After the season the infield was completely rebuilt, but the hard ground would persist for decades.[27]

Much of this was inevitable. O'Malley outlined a "typical" fan letter to Ziff. "Dear sir: We congratulate you on a perfectly beautiful stadium. We're so proud of it and we're so happy with it. But,—" the writer starts. "And then," shuddered O'Malley, "the writer of the letter will go on to state some very valid complaints."[28] Answering a complaint letter from comedian Milton Berle, O'Malley wrote, "We opened a new park which was not completed, with elevators that were not running properly, with a traffic program that left much to be desired, and with an entirely green staffing crew."[29] He kept promising the team would deal with the problems, and, eventually, it did.

It was a whirlwind season for Walter O'Malley. He was finally in his stadium. The team Buzzie Bavasi and Fresco Thompson put on the field was not Branch Rickey's. The blame and the plaudits would all be O'Malley's, and he was looking to build an image for long-term success. Winning was even more important than normal. It began even before spring training. "I want to reward the fans with a pennant this season, and everything has been geared toward that goal," he told reporters on the Dodger plane to Vero Beach. "This is the year to win the pennant. I expect nothing less."[30] After the opening-day loss, the team played well, but trailed the sizzling Giants into June. On June 8 they won a thirteen-inning game against the newborn Houston Colt .45s and moved into first place, as the Giants endured a six-game losing streak. Except for a blip in early July, the Dodgers held first place throughout the summer, and, even with a devastating injury to Sandy Koufax in mid-July, expectations rose in the stands, the dugout, and Walter O'Malley's glass-walled office overlooking left field.

On September 23 the Dodgers led the Giants by four games with seven left to play. The Giants won five of their games, the Dodgers only one. Bob Hunter of the *Los Angeles Herald Examiner*, who had excellent sources throughout the Dodger organization, reported that "shortly" before the regular season ended, O'Malley called Alston, his coaches, and veteran Duke Snider into this office. "If you blow it, every man gets cut, and I'll do it myself. I'll review the whole payroll. I have a big investment and can't afford to lose this thing," Hunter quoted O'Malley saying.[31] The losing week left the teams with identical regular-season records. In the final playoff game the Dodgers then did blow it, losing a two-run ninth-inning lead, the game, and the season.

After the game the team locked the clubhouse door for an hour.[32] "How the hell would you feel if you all just blew $12,000," outfielder Wally Moon told the gathered reporters.[33] O'Malley skipped the postgame "party."[34] The closed clubhouse and newspaper reports of the next few days teemed with stories of Alston's failure to make moves and how it would have been better if coach Leo Durocher had been the manager.[35]

Reports differ on O'Malley's reaction. *Herald Examiner* columnist Melvin Durslag reported he "stormed out of town to hunt bighorn sheep in Wyoming."[36] Others reported the defeat "left O'Malley stunned, Bavasi actually ill and the players blaming everyone but themselves."[37] O'Malley's equilibrium was not helped by the necessity to refund $2.4 million paid for World Series tickets.[38]

There were other versions. O'Malley called the embattled Alston still in his office hours after the game and told him, "Go home, Walt. Get a rest and everything will be all right."[39] Alston, strongly supported by Bavasi, would stay another fourteen seasons.

The high-demand expectations, the flashing anger, and then a calm and often generous response were a pattern visible over many Dodger seasons. In this case O'Malley paid the players for the three-game playoff series even though it was not mandatory.[40] He also paid for different groups of sixty front-office people to fly to San Francisco for the first two games of the World Series.[41]

After his Wyoming hunting trip O'Malley returned to stadium projects deferred. As with the orchids he had grown in Amityville for years, and the plants and trees he had designed and installed at Dodgertown, he had big plans for the landscaping of Dodger Stadium. The winter after the disappointing 1962 season, he began to put them into effect.

O'Malley talked of $1 million spent on five thousand trees, a million plants, and other landscaping.[42] One slope behind the parking lots visible from the stands was designated Poppy Hill for California golden poppies and another Lupine Hill for the blue and purple plants.[43] Elsewhere, there would be red bougainvillea, plumbago, petunias, larkspur, paintbrush, wild pansies, palms, willows, eucalyptus, olive trees, bird of paradise plants, and Johnny-jump-ups, plus thirty-two miles of sprinkler pipes.[44]

Despite winning a landscape architecture award for his forward thinking, it did not all work, at least at first. Much of the poppies and lupine came up as scrub.[45] It would take several years for the flowers to really seed and the hillsides to be regularly covered in color.[46] By 1969 there were fifteen men regularly working on the landscaping, and the budget was $200,000 annually.[47] The landscaping remained a particular point of pride for O'Malley. He touted the work to NBC for its national "Game of the Week" and got them to have Curt Gowdy point it out on the air.[48]

The other major project for the first winter was the installation of escalators to minimize the problems of people moving between seat levels. The escalators were to be built into the hillside outside the stadium proper and would allow one of the elevators to be dedicated to Stadium Club members and the other held for emergencies.[49] Contracts were awarded in early 1963 with a promise they would be operating by June.[50] In late June the $250,000 improvement was opened.[51]

As with the Pasadena Freeway connections that were not done when the stadium opened, other pieces of uncompleted business with the city and county would jump up to bite O'Malley in the next few years. As the stadium neared completion, the city's semiautonomous Parks and Recreation Commission began to dither over another provision of the contract with the Dodgers. It called for the Dodgers to take forty of the three hundred acres the city had deeded to them, spend up to $500,000 developing a recreational facility on it, and pay the city $60,000 annually for twenty years to maintain it. At the end of twenty years and $1.7 million, the parcel would revert to the Dodgers.

Now, the commission began suggesting that it was not such a great place for a park and that O'Malley should just turn over the $1.7 million total to the city for use in other neighborhoods.[52] O'Malley, who was strapped by the cost of completing the stadium and content to spread these payments out over two decades, said no. For three more years, as O'Malley paid the $60,000 annual fee, the parks commission and the city wrangled with each other while the Dodgers graded the site and then waited for a decision.[53]

The city could not decide whether to vest title to the land in the commission or the Board of Public Works.[54] The city attorney and his deputy could not agree on when the twenty-year contract had gone into effect.[55] The commission charged that the Dodgers had used the grading process to dump dirt from stadium construction onto the recreational site in harmful ways.[56] The Dodgers' contention that they had spent $288,000 on grading and that this amount should be credited against the $500,000 investment was questioned, investigated, and eventually ratified.[57]

Finally, in late 1964, O'Malley and the city worked out a deal. O'Malley would keep the forty-acre site, pay the city the $212,000 remainder of the promised investment, and keep up the annual $60,000 payment.[58] The city would eventually build baseball diamonds and other facilities across the street from the north edge of the stadium property.

The land set aside for the recreation area was a particular irritation to O'Malley because it dovetailed with another issue that always sent his blood pressure up—taxes. And, to him, it was another example of Los Angeles officials not keeping their word.

In his 1957 negotiations with Chad McClellan, O'Malley had questioned what his property taxes would be. McClellan checked with the Los Angeles County Assessor's Office and came up with figures between $300,000 and $350,000.[59] O'Malley, who said he had paid $55,000 a year for Ebbets Field, was not happy, but accepted.[60] The Dodgers paid $8,000 a year while the stadium was built. But with it almost completed, the property taxes shot up to $470,000.[61] In late 1962 Philip Watson was elected county assessor. Watson was a young man with ambition and firm ideas about how the assessor's office should be run.[62] A few months into his term, he said the Dodgers' property taxes were likely to double, to around $900,000 annually.[63]

O'Malley began the process of appeals, but the process left him "explosively irate," and Al Wolf of the *Los Angeles Times* reported he was talking of selling Dodger Stadium.[64] O'Malley quickly denied that idea. But he was using the press and his contacts to make his arguments. Bob Hunter, the *Herald Examiner*'s Dodger beat reporter, and Melvin Durslag, its sports columnist, were shoveling out words supporting O'Malley's arguments. He noted that both the size and the uncertainty of the tax bill were making it hard for him to find the long-term financing he needed to pay off the stadium's construction loans. After talking with him Hunter noted Horace Stoneham was making lease payments of only $102,000 to the City of San Francisco for Candlestick Park.[65] Comparable properties, such as the Hollywood Park and Santa Anita racetracks, were not being reassessed upward.[66] Durslag quoted O'Malley that of the eleven privately owned ballparks in the Major Leagues, the Yankees' $168,000 was the highest property tax levied. And the total for the eleven was less than the projected figure for the Dodgers.[67] It was particularly irritating that the Dodgers were being assessed for the forty-acre recreational parcel owned by the city that the Dodgers were supposed to develop and, in twenty years, get back.

Durslag also was the person to whom McClellan came when he wanted to support O'Malley's version of the assessor's estimates and their role in the city's agreement with the Dodgers. "I am red-faced. I have lived in this area for 51 years and this is the first time I have been made to be ashamed of my home town. . . . [T]he Dodgers have been deceived," he told Durslag. He noted that during the 1958 referendum on the city's contract with the Dodgers, both sides had accepted and used a $345,000 figure for the Dodgers' likely property-tax contribution.[68]

At a late hearing O'Malley noted that the assessor's figure valued the stadium and land at $32 million. He sarcastically offered to sell it to anyone willing to pay that much. When a foundation came forward with a purchase-leaseback offer a week later, he backed out.[69] But he also noted that deed restrictions, which limited the land's use to a baseball stadium and a limited number of nonbaseball events each year, made it useless to anyone but a baseball team, severely limiting the property's salability.

It was yet another lesson in Los Angeles politics for O'Malley. The city administration had turned. Sam Yorty, the new mayor, was much less sympathetic to the Dodgers than Poulson had been. Watson was a new player who accepted some of the arguments about the inequity of the trade of Chavez Ravine for Wrigley Field that were still being made by city councilman John Holland and others.[70] And a lot of people were irritated at the money the Dodgers were making off the new stadium. Watson, and supporters such as county supervisors Kenneth Hahn and John Anson Ford, argued that an estimate was not a promise and that the value of the property had increased enormously now that it had been developed and begun to produce profits.[71]

The Dodgers were turned down on appeal, leaving them with a bill for $705,000.[72] They would appeal their assessment virtually every year that decade and lose every time.[73]

14

The Most Powerful
Man in Baseball

There is a story about a meeting of baseball's owners. A new topic makes it to the top of the agenda. Philip Wrigley, owner of the Chicago Cubs, turns to Walter O'Malley and says, "Well, Walter, what do I think on this issue?"[1] It's a tale that has the ring of both myth and truth. People who know Phil Wrigley have a hard time seeing him being so deferential, but they acknowledge that other owners looked first to O'Malley, reflecting the sport's leadership in the Dodger owner's three decades of activity.[2]

The idea was crystallized by Bill Veeck, in exile from team ownership in the early 1960s. "O'Malley is the most powerful man in baseball," Veeck wrote in an article with an elaborate diagram of how owners, the commissioner, the league presidents, and other powers interacted.[3] It was a combination of "native intelligence, Irish charm and extremely agile tongue," Veeck said. Veeck, who saw O'Malley's influence, mostly malign, behind every bush, was not alone. Writers probing the question of O'Malley's omnipotence would find those, mostly anonymous, who agreed with Veeck. Others doubted. In private baseball commissioner Ford Frick dismissed O'Malley's influence, putting the "most powerful" crown on the Pirates' John Galbreath, as did National League president Warren Giles.[4] Many observers, especially in the media, simply accepted Veeck's assertion as fact.[5]

O'Malley was not impressed with the accolade. His usual response was to note all the sport's decisions that had gone against him. There would have been no limits on bonuses for amateur talent, he noted, and no amateur draft, no expansion in 1969, no divisional playoffs, minimal municipal involvement in stadium building, and no lockouts of the players.[6] O'Malley also said things echoed by people throughout the business. He was one of the few owners who made his living through baseball. He did not manufacture gum or brew beer or sell stocks and bonds. He paid attention to his business full-time, and the other owners recognized that.[7] In 1951, when he was less than a year into control of the Dodgers, the National League's owners elected him to the sport's executive council as their league representative. At that time the council consisted of an owners representative from each league, the two league presidents, and the commissioner and was the commissioner's first line of advice on baseball issues. O'Malley would remain on the council until near his death, serving with three commissioners, two National League and three American League presidents, six other National League ownership representatives, and fifteen from the American League.[8]

There was no doubt that he got his way more than most, whether it was through better ideas, cleverer arguments, or the power of his personality. In 1976 the owners were considering the rules governing expansion. As the owners left an early meeting, reporters in the hallways started throwing questions at M. Donald Grant of the New York Mets. "As Grant began responding to questions, a gravelly voice was heard from the rear of the group: 'Donald, the agreement was not to speak to the reporters until after our final meeting.' Grant seemed to cower, apologized to the press, and walked away," wrote Ross Newhan of the *Los Angeles Times*. The gravelly voice belonged to O'Malley.[9] Bowie Kuhn, who benefited greatly from O'Malley's support at reelection time, and was often portrayed as O'Malley's "puppet," nevertheless could describe him as sometimes "selfish, narrowminded and devious."[10]

Invited into one meeting of the council, Yankees executive Michael Burke found O'Malley, "a shrewd, clever, bullying man," running the meeting, while a "guileless" Commissioner Eckert looked on.[11] William O. DeWitt, an executive with several Major League teams, described an owners meeting where O'Malley waited until Wrigley left the room and then raised the question of the lack of lights at Wrigley Field. O'Malley felt it was a league problem, hurting attendance with the lack of night games. The discussion progressed, and by the time Wrigley returned he was confronted by the group. Now, however, someone besides O'Malley was leading the charge. Wrigley refused.[12] "When O'Malley is on our side on any issue during a meeting, I tell our fellows to let him carry the ball, just sit back and let him do the talking, we just ride along," said one executive.[13] Leonard Koppett, who became the first newspaper reporter to cover baseball as a business, felt O'Malley was focused on what was good for Walter, but, he said, "Walter achieved his power within the baseball community basically by being right."[14]

O'Malley was "the husky voice everyone hears," said Warren Giles, the National League president from 1951 to 1969. "His style was to sit back and absorb, letting others rant and rave, so that when he finally spoke, as one observer put it, he made 'the definitive declaration.'"[15] The idea O'Malley brought to a head might well have been planted in earlier conversations with people who tended to agree with him—the Phillies' Robert Carpenter, the Pirates' John Galbreath, and league president Warren Giles. He would have regular conversations with these and other owners, perhaps stroking them, as Irving Rudd heard one day in 1953. O'Malley was on the phone with Lou Perini, then principal owner of the Boston Braves. Perini wanted to move to Milwaukee and was soliciting O'Malley's support. O'Malley dripped superlatives over his potential ally: "Lou, that is why you are so brave and brilliant. That is why you are a pioneer."[16] Peter Bavasi, Buzzie's son, joined O'Malley at the owners' table in 1978, when Peter became president of the Toronto Blue Jays. The executives sat at a large U-shaped table, with each league occupying one of the long legs and the commissioner and league presidents across the bottom of the U. O'Malley would sit in the middle of the National League line, never raising his voice or pounding the table. "Most of what he needed to be done was done before the meeting," Bavasi said. "He never forced anything down anybody's throat, nor did he help the Dodgers at the expense of the league. It was all logical argument," he said.[17]

Or it could be a threat. When the House of Representatives discussed a bill to limit the ways owners could use their investments in baseball teams to limit taxes, O'Malley was quick to pick up the shillelagh. "Washington wants a team, but now you're making it more difficult to buy one. The atmosphere for putting a team in Washington is not being encouraged by these proposals," he snapped.[18]

Other executives noted that any manipulative manner was complemented by the ideas and the commonsense approach that had impressed them in 1951. O'Malley saw himself as a "stand-patter," whose Irish conservatism made him warm slowly to new ideas.[19] Others saw him as visionary, citing his work on television contracts, pensions for players and office staff, negotiations with umpires, and recognizing and gaining markets and market share. "Walter O'Malley has been baseball's man of vision and ideas from the start, and he's still going strong," wrote one columnist in 1968.[20] He had also learned not to come on too strong. Ted Turner had heard all the "O'Malley runs baseball stories" when he bought the Atlanta Braves in 1976. After some exposure, Turner said, "I haven't personally seen it. I haven't heard him make a promise or a proposal that I couldn't go along with or that I felt wasn't in the best interests of the game. I think it's true he has a lot of influence on the other owners and on the commissioner but I think they look up to him out of respect for his experience and success. He certainly has never tried to force anything on me."[21]

O'Malley's influence, or lack of it, would be played out over a number of issues in the years after he moved to Los Angeles. The first was stimulated by his decision to move the Dodgers to Los Angeles. The shift of the Dodgers and Giants to the West Coast had only skimmed the top of demographic change in North America. The West and South were growing; most of the Northeast and northern Midwest were stagnating. The moves of the Boston Braves to Milwaukee, the St. Louis Browns to Baltimore, and the Philadelphia Athletics to Kansas City in the mid-1950s had recognized that some cities in the old circuits were not capable of supporting two teams anymore. But there was more to be had. Kansas City, after all, is closer to Boston than Los Angeles. Baseball's owners and officials had a hard time figuring out how to grab the baton.

As early as 1948 the Braves' Lou Perini was talking about two twelve-team leagues.[22] In 1950 soon-to-be-commissioner Ford Frick was talking about a third eight-team league.[23] By 1952 Philip Wrigley of the Cubs was talking about four major leagues.[24] Frick's and Wrigley's suggestions were wrapped up in more than the demographic change. The Pacific Coast League was making an abortive bid for Major League status aided by West Coast legislators in Washington.[25] Congressman Emanuel Celler was holding hearings on baseball's antitrust exemption and asking questions about its relationships with the Minor Leagues and its plans for expansion.

Talk of expansion receded as the PCL's bid failed and the threat from Celler faded. By 1955 National League president Warren Giles said, "There is no sentiment for a ten-club league at this time."[26] Still, the demographics were there to tempt any club with financial difficulties, a temptation reinforced when the Dodgers and Giants moved.

The dominoes began to topple predictably enough. Sensitive to charges he had "lost" the Dodgers, New York City mayor Robert Wagner started an effort to get National League baseball back even before O'Malley's final announcement.[27] By November he had appointed a panel headed by William Shea, a prominent New York lawyer.[28] Shea and his colleagues—former postmaster general James Farley, Bernard Gimbel of the department store family, and Clinton Blume, a real estate operator—spent the next year trying to lure one of the less profitable National League franchises to town. They created an alliance with Robert Moses, now committed to building a stadium on the Flushing Meadows site he had offered O'Malley. By the spring of 1958, having talked at length to the Cincinnati Reds, the Pittsburgh Pirates, and the Philadelphia Phillies, Shea told the mayor that tactic was not making any progress.[29] He began casting about for leverage.

By November 1958 Shea was in contact with Branch Rickey, eased out the door by the Pirates and, as usual, full of ideas.[30] In May Rickey had suggested a third major league and outlined some ideas of how it could be built up without infringing on Major League teams' control of current players.[31] Now Shea, with Rickey remaining behind a curtain, announced the mayor's committee would seek to form such a league.[32] Shea and Rickey began to assemble what they would call the Continental League. With Rickey's experience they knew they needed ownership groups with the capital to acquire players and a ballpark, set up a minor league system, and organize a front office.

In July 1959 the league was announced.[33] Only five franchises had committed to contributing $50,000 to the league, but it was a group calculated to make the Majors take notice. The New York franchise was led by Joan Payson, a former minority owner of the Giants and heiress to the Whitney fortune. Her brother owned the *New York Herald Tribune* and was ambassador to Great Britain. It also included Dwight Davis Jr., son of the founder of tennis's Davis Cup, and George Herbert Walker of the merchant banking firm of Brown Brothers Harriman.[34] The Houston franchise was fronted by former Houston mayor Roy Hofheinz, but the real money was Craig Cullinan, heir to the Texaco fortune, and Bud Adams and R. E. "Bob" Smith, two wealthy oilmen. In Minneapolis it was merchant banker Wheelock Whitney and representatives of the Dayton family (Target stores), Pillsbury, Hamms Brewing, and the *Minneapolis Star-Tribune*. In Toronto it was Jack Kent Cooke, with wide media interests. Denver's management did not have that kind of money, but it was headed by Rickey protégé Bob Howsam. More important, Howsam's father-in-law and partner was Edwin Johnson, a recent Colorado governor and a three-term U.S. senator with many contacts in Washington.[35]

Although the Continental League would never get off the ground, it accomplished several things. It coalesced several highly qualified and attractive ownership groups and educated them about dealing with the Majors. In the process it identified these groups to the Majors as potential viable owner-ship groups for expansion franchises. It also scared the Majors on two fronts.

First, Johnson used his contacts to lobby hard for a bill that would have made it easier for the Continental League to acquire players. Introduced by Tennessee senator Estes Kefauver in early 1959, the bill would have limited each Major League team to eighty players under contract.[36] In later ver-sions it would have allowed the Continental League to draft players from Major League farm clubs who had signed after the passage of the bill. As the Continental League entered its death spiral in the summer of 1960, the bill died, but for a time it concerned the owners greatly.[37]

Second was the Billy Cannon parallel. Cannon was the 1959 Heisman Trophy winner from Louisiana State University. He was drafted by the Los Angeles Rams of the National Football League and agreed to a contract for $10,000. Then the Houston Oilers of the fledgling American Football League stepped in with a contract for $110,000 in early 1960. The Oilers' major owner was Bud Adams, one of the partners in Houston's Continen-tal League group. Although the Continental League promised to respect Major League contracts and the reserve system, the Cannon parallel clearly indicated there would be expensive competition for future talent, while the Majors were already concerned about the escalation of payments to bonus babies.

The Continental League reinvigorated the Majors' expansion talk, but added little coherence, at least in the beginning. O'Malley proposed that both leagues expand to nine teams and begin interleague play.[38] The idea never gained any traction, even within the National League. Expansion to ten teams and the third league were also reconsidered. Although Frick sug-gested the third league again, he resisted Rickey's appeals to take the lead in making the Continental League that third league.[39]

The question that loomed over all the expansion talk was the desire of the National League to get back into New York and the American League's reciprocal interest in Los Angeles now that the Dodgers had proven the market. Even before the Dodgers moved, the Yankees were asserting a right to block the National League's return.[40] Frick consistently rejected the Yan-kees' assertion, but also championed rules that made both New York and Los Angeles available for expansion.[41]

O'Malley was more ambivalent. At times he offered to leave Los Angeles open to the American League.[42] At others he opposed.[43] His critics, such as Del Webb and Bill Veeck, believe he deeply opposed any intrusion and acquiesced only at the bitter end.[44] There is no doubt he had problems reconciling his personal interest in monopolizing Southern California with his league's interest in having a presence in what was still the nation's largest market and leading media center. But he acquiesced much sooner than the bitter end, and he gained both personal and league advantages as he did so.

Ultimately, O'Malley understood expansion was a struggle for markets and that the price of the National League's return to New York was the American League's entrance into Los Angeles. The question for him and the National League was how much to expand and what cities to grab and to do all these things before the American League moved. In July 1960, with O'Malley leading the expansion committee, the National League said it would expand to ten teams for the 1962 season, with or without the Continental League. He was immediately named chair of the committee to oversee the expansion process.[45] He said they were willing to talk to the American League about joint expansion, but would add teams on their own if necessary.[46]

It was the last bugle call for Rickey's dream. His ownership groups were straining to apply for the expansion franchises. Shea's crusade for leverage had worked. In early August the Continental League announced it was folding in return for an agreement that the expansion franchises would be chosen from its members.[47] O'Malley was meeting with the various Continental League ownership groups, but it was clear his interest was focused on New York and Houston. The Dallas–Fort Worth group came calling September 7 and came away feeling positive.[48] Alarmed, some American League executives began to pressure Del Webb to speed up the American League process before the National League snapped up the best markets.[49] It did not work.

On Sunday, October 9, as Webb's Yankees fell into a tie with the Pittsburgh Pirates after four games of the World Series, George Kirksey of the Houston group ran into Webb at the Waldorf-Astoria in New York. Webb questioned him about the Houston commitment to the American League. Kirksey said he told Webb he favored the American League, but Craig Cullinan, who was the big-money man, leaned toward the National. Webb called together the American League Expansion Committee to press for a commitment on Houston on the morning of the tenth.[50]

O'Malley quickly outflanked him, with Giles announcing the next day that the Houston group had applied for membership in the National

League, joining New York, which had applied October 1.[51] A week later Giles announced that New York and Houston had been accepted as members, to begin play in 1962.[52] The National League had wrapped up the two most attractive markets available.

Outmaneuvered, Webb and his colleagues were clearly in reactive mode and riddled with divisions.[53] Ten days after the National League coup, Webb announced his league would add two teams, but would get a jump on the Nationals by having them begin play in 1961. They would also outexpand the NL by adding two more teams by 1964 and maybe do it by 1962. The *New York Times*'s Arthur Daley accurately summed it up as "needless impetuosity," noting this timetable gave the new owners barely four months to put together a management team, players, a ticketing and sales group, and a minor league system.[54] The league owners also allowed the Washington Senators to move to Minneapolis–St. Paul, opening up the Washington DC market. Although not committing to any cities, Webb hinted strongly that Los Angeles would be one of the chosen.[55] In private he also conceded to Rickey that the American League would not follow through on its August promise to choose its expansion ownership groups from the Continental League roster.[56] In public Rickey displayed his rhetorical thunder. "This is not expansion. The dictionary definition of perfidy had now been confirmed."[57]

On November 17 the American League announced one of the expansion teams would go into Washington DC, hoping to head off any political backlash from the exodus of Griffith's Senators. As for the other they would try to get baseball rules amended to allow them into Los Angeles. O'Malley then took a shot at getting the second American League team to be placed in Toronto rather than Los Angeles, a ploy that swung no weight with Webb.[58]

Walter O'Malley had done his best for his league. Now was the time to make the best bargain he could for himself. He had been dropping hints about his terms since the summer. He noted he had invested $16 million in building Dodger Stadium, paying indemnities to the Pacific Coast League and other costs, and he wanted some of that back.[59] He also argued that any American League expansion into Los Angeles should not take place until Dodger Stadium was completed in 1962.[60] Frick was soon echoing O'Malley. He again dismissed the Yankees' arguments that they were the sole owners of the New York territory, noting they had shared it with the National League for decades. In fact, both the Giants' and the Dodgers' franchises had predated the Yankees by nearly twenty years. And he backed up the

Dodgers' arguments that they should be compensated for the expenses of opening up a new territory to Major League Baseball. He noted the $450,000 indemnity to the Pacific Coast League and the $150,000 spent on making the Coliseum into something usable for baseball. He did not mention the $3 million spent to buy the Angels' PCL franchise, but he did say of the American League, "They want to pay nothing, to do nothing. I won't stand for it."[61]

Two days later former Detroit Tigers slugger Hank Greenberg, consistently reported as the leading contender for the Los Angeles franchise, said he was dropping out. American League president Joe Cronin said it was because of Frick's comments.[62] Bill Veeck, a friend and sometime partner of Greenberg, said the straw that broke Greenberg's back was the American League's plan for franchise fees and stocking the new team. But, he said, Greenberg's desire for the franchise had already been undermined by Frick's insistence that Greenberg compensate O'Malley somehow and agree that his team could not play in the Coliseum.[63]

Use of the Coliseum was complicated. O'Malley argued that there were not enough open dates to accommodate a second team. As he had discovered in his negotiations two years earlier, weekends late in the baseball season were reserved for the NFL's Rams and the college football squads of USC and UCLA. A July 4 fireworks show made that date unavailable, and other dates were reserved for religious rallies and long-standing tenants. Greenberg met with Coliseum officials in early November, asking for a two-year contract with an option for two more. The commission's baseball committee would not approve that contract, but did offer one year at the same terms as the Dodgers. Greenberg submitted a list of proposed dates, but the committee did not take up the details. They did approve a contract with the Dodgers for 1961 with dates specified.[64] The issue of adequate dates was still up in the air when Greenberg backed out.

Newspaper speculation about ownership turned to Kenyon Brown, Gene Autry, and Gene Klein.[65] Both Brown and Autry owned television stations and other businesses. Autry had been drawn into the talks by Greenberg, who was trying to line up a radio station for his team. Autry was interested because the Dodgers had dropped his station, KMPC, after the 1959 season. The station's signal power had to be lowered at 8:00 p.m. each evening, and Walter O'Malley, in his new retreat at Lake Arrowhead, could not hear the games.[66] The Dodgers moved to station KFI. Klein was an executive with National Theatres & Television, which operated Fox movie theaters on the West Coast, and also owned the Volvo distributorship for the western United States.

With the American League bid in trouble, Webb flew to Los Angeles for a meeting with O'Malley, who then journeyed to New York for a conference with Webb, Frick, and the two league presidents. Before the meeting O'Malley outlined what he said were his terms: no American League expansion for 1961, and not in the Coliseum; ultimate stadium location at least fifteen miles from Dodger Stadium; owners "genuinely interested in baseball and not just temporary publicity seekers" (a provision that would give O'Malley veto power over anybody he did not like); and some undefined payments to the Dodgers for pioneering the territory.[67] Charles O. Finley, the Chicago insurance man soon to buy the Kansas City Athletics, and Williams Cousins, director of a Chicago research firm, were also mentioned as possible owners of the AL franchise.[68]

At the New York meeting the American League said it could go along with O'Malley's terms as long as there was expansion to nine teams for 1961 with interleague play. The New York and Los Angeles expansion franchises would join their leagues in 1962.[69] O'Malley had proposed the nine teams with interleague play years earlier, only to have his National League colleagues shoot it down. Again, it died quickly, as O'Malley still could not sell it to his fellow owners.[70]

By the time American League owners met in early December, the suitors had been reduced to Finley and the Autry group. Kenyon Brown had been downgraded as a partner because of unspecified objections from O'Malley, Veeck said.[71] The *Los Angeles Times* noted Brown's television station had opposed the Dodgers' contract with the city during the Proposition B fight.[72] Autry and his radio station partner, Bob Reynolds, spent the morning of December 6 in O'Malley's suite, working out terms. The next day, a day Autry joked would live in infamy, his group was awarded the Los Angeles franchise in a vote of six to two.[73] "The action of the American League in acceding to many of Walter O'Malley's wishes is an indication of the respect our circuit has for the man," Yankees co-owner Dan Topping said, with tongue perhaps moving toward cheek.[74]

The terms would go a long way toward easing O'Malley's concerns about paying for Dodger Stadium. The Angels would play the 1961 season in Wrigley Field, rather than the Coliseum. Then they would become O'Malley's tenant at Dodger Stadium for at least four years, with an option for three more. The rent would be 7.5 percent of revenue, with a minimum of $200,000. Concession revenue and maintenance costs would be split. Parking revenue would be O'Malley's. The Angels would also pay $350,000 to cover O'Malley's investment in Pacific Coast League indemnities and legal costs in Los Angeles.[75] Autry would later estimate the Angels were worth $750,000 a year to the Dodgers, even after the initial payments.[76] In addition, noted Bavasi, "it would have been a terrible public relations blunder if we hadn't" accepted the Angels.[77]

The American League, still in reactive mode, did the Angels no favors. After receiving the franchise on December 7, the expansion draft was held December 14, giving the Angels barely a week to find a general manager and a manager and gather enough information to choose their players intelligently. The collection of castoffs, prospects, and retreads cost $2.1 million, and the mechanics of the draft were bungled in the process.[78] "Baseball rushed into expansion," Walter O'Malley said. "We are not—and are not now—ready for it. A big mistake has been made."[79]

Since the end of World War II Major League owners had been trying to curb their willingness to fall in love with eighteen-year-olds with strong arms and fast legs and to pay them steadily higher bonuses to sign with their clubs. They had made rules to limit bonuses in the late 1940s, but dropped them as ineffective.[80] In 1952 they instituted a more stringent law that mandated that players signed for more than a minimum bonus figure must be kept on the Major League roster for two years.[81] For every Al Kaline, who quickly prospered, or Sandy Koufax, another Hall of Famer who took several seasons longer to develop than he would have with Minor League time, there were a dozen Bob Powells.[82] That rule was dropped at the winter meetings in Colorado Springs in 1957.

The open market that took over was made for Walter O'Malley. The night before the rule was revoked, Bavasi, Fresco Thompson, and other top advisers gathered in O'Malley's room to urge him to take advantage. In the midst of preparing for the first season in Los Angeles and despite the other financial commitments in those early years, O'Malley agreed to major expenditures for new talent.[83] In 1958 alone the figure was $800,000 for ninety-eight players, a group that included Frank Howard, Ron Fairly, Willie Davis, and others who would fuel the successes of the 1960s Dodgers.[84] "Los Angeles has signed more good players than anyone in baseball," said Pirates general manager Joe L. Brown. "They spend more money than anyone else and do it with intelligence. . . . It isn't just spending money. The

Dodgers have good management both on and off the field."[85] The Dodgers spent another $900,000 in 1959 and $425,000 in 1960, but then cut back because the rising costs of his delayed stadium were making O'Malley more concerned about cash flow.[86]

Other owners, lacking the ability or the willingness to spend money on bonuses and scouts as the Dodgers did, were up in arms.[87] Branch Rickey called bonuses "the silliest thing in baseball."[88] Baseball's lawyers cautioned that a draft might jeopardize baseball's antitrust exemption and began to work with their Washington lobbyist on a bill that would allow a draft process such as professional football and basketball were using. Because neither of those sports had an antitrust exemption, it was feared Congress might use the occasion to put baseball in the same category.[89] O'Malley, saying that "we may be equipped to pay, but we don't want to," favored a return to the kind of spending limits in force during the 1950s. But instead of keeping bonus players on the Major League roster, he wanted to fund stricter enforcement by the Commissioner's Office to limit under-the-table payments, scouting contracts for players' fathers, and similar skullduggery.[90] He was not persuasive. "We have done very well at the box office," he said, "but the spice in baseball is still outmaneuvering the other guy on the field. This will become increasingly hard for the Dodgers with new legislation which will prevent us from getting the help we can afford."[91] The Majors began a draft of amateur players in 1965, when the Oakland Athletics' first choice was Rick Monday, the kind of Southern California–bred player the Dodgers had routinely rounded up just a few years earlier.

The limits on bonuses and the creation of a draft touched on one of Walter O'Malley's hot buttons. As with many things he did not like, such as revenue sharing, these measures were "socialism."[92] "Under any profit-sharing plan in sports, the responsibility is placed on the most industrious operators. The others count on them to be carried. I see no reason why the vultures should sit back, waiting for a morsel to drop. If they were placed on their own, they would make a stronger effort to produce more," he argued, neatly avoiding the differences in size and prosperity of local markets.[93]

In August 1964 Ford Frick confirmed what people had been assuming—he would not seek reelection as commissioner when his term ended a year later. The announcement set off a yearlong chase to find his successor.

In his image as baseball's most powerful man, many have assumed or asserted the Dodger owner played a large role in the selection of General

William Eckert. Michael Burke, then a Yankees executive, said that O'Malley "had plucked him out of Air Force Blue and made him commissioner."[94] Soon after Frick's announcement O'Malley did suggest that before selecting a replacement, the owners sit down and figure out what they wanted in a commissioner.[95] They did not, and when the search committee was selected, it was John Fetzer of the Detroit Tigers and John Galbreath of the Pittsburgh Pirates who were named.[96] Eckert, as it happens, had taken off his blue uniform to enter private business several years earlier.

Veteran baseball writer Jerome Holtzman, in his book on the commissioners, makes no mention of an O'Malley role, quoting executives as pointing to Fetzer as the man who promoted a man quickly dubbed "the Unknown Soldier."[97] Eckert said he had first been approached by Fetzer and Galbreath.[98] O'Malley had consistently pushed for someone with experience in baseball, and Eckert was none of that.[99] Eckert's name had not appeared on an initial list of dozens of possible candidates or on the short list of sixteen.[100]

George Vass, a baseball writer for the *Chicago Daily News*, managed to position himself to overhear most of an October meeting on selecting the commissioner—a meeting that cut the list to seven, still without Eckert's name appearing.[101] In his article on Vass's scoop, *Sports Illustrated* writer William Furlong reported, "If there was any coherence or continuity to the meeting, it was in the canny maneuvers of Walter O'Malley." Furlong reported a "suspicion" and a "theory" among baseball men that O'Malley was delaying the decision, hoping for a stalemate that would allow him to bring forward his (unnamed) candidate.[102] When Eckert, unfamiliar to virtually everyone, emerged a couple of weeks later, it seemed to match the theory.

Eckert had gone from West Point to the Air Force. During World War II he had built a reputation as a strong manager of logistics. He filled important administrative jobs in the Air Force in the postwar years, before retiring in 1961 to work in private business. In his initial press conference he said he had not been to a Major League game in several years and clearly did not realize the Los Angeles Dodgers had once been in Brooklyn. The owners backed him up with Lee MacPhail on baseball issues, but their hope Eckert would give them a strong presence in Washington DC proved ephemeral. Eckert had been an "inside" man, and his capital contacts were at the Pentagon rather than Congress.[103]

O'Malley had hoped a new commissioner would help him with his plan for a much more centralized administration for the game. The idea went back at least as far as Happy Chandler, but had languished with the two leagues' perpetual inability to agree on things.[104] Chandler had proposed one office to govern both the Majors and the Minors. In 1963 O'Malley helped develop a plan that went even further. It envisioned a commissioner with four deputies, one each for the two Major Leagues, one for the Minors, and one for relations with the players. Umpires would be trained uniformly and assigned from the same pool rather than the contemporary practice of two separate groups.[105] Again, the idea languished, although most of these ideas would be adopted in the decades after O'Malley's death.

In early 1964 O'Malley was named to the Major League Television Council.[106] The new body was headed by the Detroit Tigers' John Fetzer, who owned a number of television stations around the Midwest, and had been pushed by the American League. Because the New York Yankees had their own national television contract and attendant revenues with CBS, television policy was even more a problem for the American League, but it was a growing problem for both circuits.[107]

Now, it appeared, was the time to act. Congress had passed the Sports Broadcasting Act of 1961, which allowed sports leagues freedom from antitrust laws to negotiate with television networks. The National Football League showed the possibilities with a two-year contract worth $28 million with CBS that tripled their payments. Last, the Yankees' contract with CBS would end after the 1965 season, freeing up all Major League games to be put into one package.

Major League Baseball did not have a television policy. There had been "Games of the Week" from all three major networks off and on since 1953. But all of these broadcasts had been circumscribed by blackouts in home cities, or cities of the visiting team, or Minor League markets. The scene was a hodgepodge of rules and exclusions built on the Majors' radio broadcasting experiences and the Minor Leagues' strident arguments that televised Major League games were cutting into their attendance, arguments echoed in Congress by representatives of those areas. In fact, O'Malley had sought to smooth the way for a true national television package a decade before the committee was formed. In 1955 he unsuccessfully tried to find accommodation with the Minor Leagues with a plan under which revenue from the telecasts would be shared, but the Minors resisted.[108] O'Malley's interest in a national package and a clear policy continued.

Fetzer came up with the committee's first major proposal, a Monday-night "Game of the Week."[109] Because many Minor and Major League clubs used Mondays to travel, the conflicts would be minimal. For the networks it was a night with few sports programming opportunities. That August O'Malley flew to New York for the committee's presentation to the networks, but the response was cool.[110] Critics suggested baseball had not given the networks enough time to study the proposal and take the temperature of possible sponsors.[111] Just six years later ABC would launch *Monday Night Football*, which would become a huge success, but that was after NFL commissioner Pete Rozelle built up the idea for several years by scheduling Monday-night games and selling them in small packages to prove the concept and the audience.

With the Monday-night game relegated to Fetzer's desk drawer, the committee looked to a national contract for the traditional weekend games. For 1965 they struck a two-year deal worth $12 million with ABC for a Saturday-afternoon game. The contract was limited to eighteen clubs because of the Yankees' deal with CBS and the Philadelphia Phillies' contractual obligations, but it contained a revolutionary step for Major League Baseball. The eighteen clubs would share revenue from the contract equally.[112] O'Malley's aversion to "socialism" apparently did not extend to national television contracts, as he perceived the value of a flagship broadcast to sell the sport nationally.

For ABC the contract was not a success. Whereas the network had the only national game, the owners had not limited local broadcasts. "The reason that football gets the big TV money is that it does not compete with itself," said Roone Arledge, ABC's vice president in charge of sports.[113] In addition, the network wanted more flexibility in choosing which games to broadcast. At the end of the season ABC dropped the contract for 1966.[114]

The vacuum was filled quickly, as NBC signed a three-year $30 million contract after negotiations that took O'Malley and his colleagues until well past midnight at the Edgewater Beach Hotel in Chicago. The relationship would continue for twenty-four years. For NBC the "Game of the Week" contract was acceptable because it could now include the Yankees, and it gave them much more control over what games could be selected. Other days besides Saturdays could be scheduled, and teams would be encouraged by Major League Baseball to stay away from NBC's time slots.[115] But a more important development was that the committee had learned how to package. NBC was not particularly interested in doing a "Game of the Week." Ratings were not strong for afternoons when the outside attractions of summer called. The committee insisted, however, that if a network wanted the coveted World Series and All-Star Game rights, they would have to do a "Game of the Week" as well.[116] Some questioned whether the committee used this reasoning as an excuse. *New York Times* columnist Leonard Koppett echoed Major League Baseball Players Association concerns that the World Series price tag had been lowered because part of those revenues would go to the players' pension plan, while "Game of the Week" revenues stayed with the clubs.[117]

"Game of the Week" ratings jumped nearly 60 percent for 1966, a leap attributed to color telecasts, flexible scheduling that allowed targeting games in the close National League pennant race, the inclusion of the Yankees, and more cooperation from clubs about their local telecasts.[118] By 1968 blackouts would be reduced to the home cities of the "Game of the Week" participants, and those cities would receive a backup game.[119]

O'Malley's role within the National League was never clearer than when new owners of the Milwaukee Braves got antsy. The Braves' box-office success after moving from Boston to Milwaukee in 1953 had given O'Malley ammunition for his stadium arguments in Brooklyn. But attendance there had faltered, as the team's performance declined in the early 1960s. The American League's move into Minneapolis–St. Paul had cut into the Braves' market in northern Wisconsin. O'Malley also thought out-of-town ownership hurt.[120] In 1962 owner Lou Perini, who had never moved his residence from Boston, sold controlling interest in the team to a Chicago group headed by William Bartholomay.[121] The group tried to finance part of their purchase with stock sales to Braves fans, but only 11 percent of the shares offered were taken up.[122] Conversations between the new owners and a franchise-fishing expedition from Atlanta at the 1963 All-Star Game began a series of stories that the Braves would move south.[123]

Braves management denied the stories, but kept talking to the persistent Atlanta group. By mid-1964 the Braves were saying they were not "necessarily" going to Atlanta, and Milwaukee was threatening to sue.[124] When the Braves' board did vote to move, on October 21, the city did sue.[125] Frick, as was his wont, declared the move a league matter, leaving it up to O'Malley and his colleagues. As always O'Malley was sympathetic to an owner's desire to move, but he recognized reality as well. Reality was the Braves' contract to play at Milwaukee County Stadium through 1965. So, on November 7, the league owners gave Bartholomay's group permission to move to Atlanta for the 1966 season.

It was a lame-duck year at County Stadium in 1965, but an active one in the courts. Milwaukee County sued, won in local courts, but then lost on appeal. Baseball was without sympathetic characters in the drama, and executives worried about its image.[126] O'Malley drily said, "If I had been a public relations man for the National League or the Braves, I would have played my cards a little differently."[127] As Eckert took over the Commissioner's Office in the winter of 1965–66, he was being urged to block the move. In appointing Eckert the owners had insisted that a "baseball man" act as his right-hand man and had hired Lee MacPhail, Larry's son and a longtime baseball executive in his own right. MacPhail also urged Eckert to take action, but, with an "ultimatum" from O'Malley and National League president Warren Giles, the new commissioner chose to do nothing.[128] Even with the Braves in Atlanta, the legal battles dragged through 1966. O'Malley participated in meetings, trying to settle the suit, but the threat, the headlines, and the embarrassing testimony did not end until, after several unsuccessful appeals all the way to the Supreme Court, Milwaukee County decided there was no more point.[129]

The American League was having its parallel drama, as Charles Finley sought to move his Kansas City Athletics to Oakland. That drama would have broader consequences for baseball management. If the Braves' move to Atlanta showed O'Malley's power within the National League, the expansion of 1969 showed its limits.

Charles O. Finley, unsuccessful in his bid for the Los Angeles American League expansion franchise in 1960, managed to buy the Kansas City Athletics from Arnold Johnson's estate late that year. As was his wont, Finley was soon battling with the city over a new stadium and with his fellow owners over a host of issues. He threatened to move his team to Oakland, which was building a new sports complex, but was stymied by a lease with the city and the disapproval of his fellow owners. When the lease ran out and he threatened to sue the other owners, they allowed him to move.[130] "Oakland will find it's the luckiest city since Hiroshima," said Missouri senator Stuart Symington.[131] With Kansas City threatening its own suit, the American League owners promised the city an expansion team for 1969 and offered one to Seattle as well, after a telegram from Senator Warren Magnuson of Washington stirred them to commit.[132] O'Malley, who was hunting in Africa, was surprised by the American League's precipitate decision to expand.[133] Even worse, so were all the other National League owners. In April baseball's executive council, including O'Malley, American League president Joe Cronin, and Gabe Paul of the American League's Cleveland Indians, had agreed on a vague plan for future expansion. Expansion was termed "inevitable, but not an immediate requirement," and they agreed to develop a set of standards for cities, stadiums, and ownership groups.[134] Seven months later the American League had presented a fait accompli.

Up to that point O'Malley had been resolutely opposed to expansion. He thought the 1961–62 growth still had not been absorbed. "When they voted 10 teams, they knew eventually we'd have to go to 12 and by that time everybody may be fed up with the ridiculous problems that will be caused," he said in early 1962, even before the New York Mets and Houston Colt .45s began to display their early incompetence.[135] "One of the biggest mistakes I ever made was to vote to approve that expansion," he said in a deposition for the City of Milwaukee's suit against the Braves.[136] If there had to be expansion, he wanted to create a third eight-team league, but, like his nine-team league proposal of the late 1950s, this went nowhere with his colleagues.[137]

Now, he was resigned. The National League would have to follow like dominoes, he said.[138] National League president Warren Giles said his league would go along, "in the interest of baseball as a whole, and in the interest of not having a fight."[139] In the wake of their own acquiescence to Bartholomay and the Braves, they certainly could not take the high ground in public. In addition, O'Malley had to be irritated at the American League's invasion of the San Francisco Bay Area, which could only weaken the Giants. And a solid Giant franchise, as a rival for the Dodgers, was important to O'Malley.

The rush for the two National League expansion franchises began even before the league's owners had collected their wits. With the first vague guidelines, expansion could take place as late as 1972. That did not stop Buffalo, Dallas–Fort Worth, Denver, Milwaukee, Montreal, San Diego, and Toronto from putting in applications.[140] In April 1968 the National League appointed its expansion committee, and, as usual, O'Malley was on it.[141] Momentum was clearly on the side of keeping up with the American League. By the time expansion was approved April 19, the National League owners had already conceded it would have to be for the coming year.[142] The cities were still to be chosen, although Toronto and Denver had fallen off the list.

San Diego was seen as a foregone conclusion, mostly because of O'Malley's firm support. He was paying for loyalty. By the late 1960s, Buzzie Bavasi said, he could see the writing on the wall. He had held the same job for almost two decades, but in a family-owned corporation he could not go much higher and he could see Peter O'Malley being groomed to be the team's president. He was resentful that he had been underpaid. There were, however, compensations. He discussed his future with O'Malley, who told him to go out and identify the expansion group he would like to be associated with and O'Malley would see that the city and ownership group would be accepted. After trips to Montreal, where he had been the Royals' general manager in the late 1940s, and Seattle, Bavasi settled on San Diego, where he was able to overcome O'Malley's antipathy to the major owner, C. Arnholt Smith. Smith's brother "Black Jack" Smith had been one of O'Malley's most difficult opponents in the 1958 election battle over the Dodgers' contract with the Los Angeles City Council.[143] Some writers also speculated O'Malley was interested in a San Diego franchise because it would make it harder for the Angels to draw from the South.[144] Peter Bavasi, Buzzie's son and later a top executive in Cleveland and Toronto, noted the move both helped a loyal employee and gave O'Malley access to another vote in the National League and baseball-wide meetings.[145] San Diego also had a Major League–quality stadium, built for the football Chargers but also as a lure to baseball.

A similar concern killed the Dallas–Fort Worth bid, despite its clear position as the most attractive market on the list, an opportunity O'Malley had seen several years earlier.[146] Roy Hofheinz's Houston club enjoyed considerable radio and television income from north-central Texas and did not want to give it up.[147] Hofheinz failed to appreciate the possibilities of an intrastate rivalry, an opportunity that would be realized nearly fifty years later when Houston joined Dallas–Fort Worth in the American League's Western Division.

Milwaukee still carried the stigma of the lawsuits. Publicly, that was dismissed as an issue, but observers felt the feelings lingered. Buffalo was considered the front runner after San Diego, but the team would have to spend three years in War Memorial Stadium before a new domed park could be built.[148] Montreal came from the outside, and only after a promise to greatly expand a local amateur park for the first two years and build a domed stadium by 1971.[149] Walter O'Malley's familiarity with the city from its long years as a Dodger farm club undoubtedly helped.[150] He had not been able to stop expansion, but he had tailored the results.

The expansion episode heightened the tensions between the two leagues. For O'Malley, the American League's lunge at expansion to avoid legal problems in Kansas City showed their usual lack of planning. "I don't know how much thinking the American League did before it voted to expand," he said as he ticked off the issues. The Americans' proposed two-division setup would probably create an additional round of playoffs within that league, so what, O'Malley asked, would happen to the World Series? He noted that the American League with twelve teams and the National League with ten would mean that the Americans would get more of the national television revenues and a greater share of the picks in the amateur draft. And, he asked, what about the players' association? Would they be willing to have their share of the World Series and All-Star Game money divided over an additional fifty or one hundred players?[151] These things would have to be negotiated under deadline pressure created by the American League's move rather than thought out thoroughly in advance.

Yankees general manager Lee MacPhail, done with his stint as Commissioner Eckert's "baseball man," was not impressed. The National League "moves with the speed of the tortoise and the adaptation to change of the dinosaur," he said. Still, he acknowledged he did not really understand why the AL owners had voted to let Finley move and that the Seattle situation, without a Major League–quality ballpark or adequately financed ownership, was "a blueprint for future trouble."[152]

The comments were symptomatic of the league's feelings about their relative status. The resentment was fueled by O'Malley's often dismissive remarks about American League owners and their ideas. There was the time he was tired of a proposal from Baltimore Orioles owner Jerry Hoffberger, the chairman of National Brewery. "Hey, leave it alone, Jerry, I haven't got time for beer salesmen today." Or when he stripped down an argument from the perpetually underfunded Bob Short of the Texas Rangers: "When you can buy the chips, you play. When you can't, don't."[153]

Beginning with Branch Rickey's signing of Jackie Robinson, the National League had clearly moved into the dominant position, a position papered over by the success of the New York Yankees. Chasing the Dodgers, National League teams had moved much more quickly to sign African American talent, and as the 1950s turned to the 1960s the Nationals dominated the All-Star Game, having won seventeen of the last twenty-two by 1967. They were in the middle of a 22-1 run from 1962 through 1982. The results had shown up at the box office. National League teams drew 58 percent of Major League attendance in the first six years after the leagues went to ten teams. The attendance imbalance was in great part due to the National League's more successful tactics in seizing markets, with the Dodgers' and Giants' pioneering of the West Coast and the league grabbing the better markets in the early-1960s expansions.

The National League was particularly incensed that the Americans had allowed Charlie Finley to move into the San Francisco Giants' territory, rightly foreseeing that the move would turn a prosperous franchise into two marginal ones.[154] The American League felt Ford Frick had been too much a National Leaguer and favored his old circuit.[155] And the Yankee dynasty of the 1950s and early 1960s had faded with the dismissal of manager Casey Stengel and general manager George Weiss in 1960 and the subsequent drying up of the farm system. When Del Webb and Dan Topping sold control of the team to CBS in 1964, the league lost Webb's leadership and had drifted since then. In some ways that was a good thing. Hank Greenberg noted that American League meetings were punctuated by Webb's trip to the hallways to tell New York reporters what was going on and thus curry favor. The National League, Greenberg noted, kept its collective mouth shut.[156]

As the inferior member the American League was much more willing to advocate changes, whether it was the designated hitter, interleague play, night World Series games, or the other topics of the times. The more successful National League, as befitted O'Malley's personality, wanted to be sure, to think things over, and to study before making a move.

A group of mostly American League owners, dubbed the "Young Turks," decided to force the issue. According to Mike Burke, one of the Turks, he and Dick Meyer of the St. Louis Cardinals engineered the ouster of Eckert in December 1968.[157] *Sports Illustrated* reported that Eckert's ouster "means that the reign of Walter O'Malley as the high priest of the game has ended."[158]

The Young Turks were poised for the next step. Immediately, Milt Richman of United Press International (UPI) put Burke at the head of the list to replace Eckert, reporting that Burke would be confirmed within two or three days.[159] He was not. Instead, other names began to surface. Joe Brown, general manager of the Pirates; Hank Greenberg, then out of baseball; Chub Feeney, vice president of the Giants; Dan Devine, general manager of the Cardinals; Joe Cronin, president of the American League; Lee MacPhail, general manager of the Yankees; Robert Cannon, a Milwaukee attorney who had done some work for the players' association; and Buzzie Bavasi, settling into his role as president of the expansion San Diego Padres, were all named.[160] So was O'Malley, although Jerome Holtzman said O'Malley's early candidate was Cannon.[161]

Two weeks after Eckert's beheading, the owners gathered at Chicago's O'Hare Inn. It turned into a thirteen-hour marathon, ending at five in the morning after nineteen ballots and no decision. It was clear each league had its candidate. The National League's Feeney came closest to the nine votes he needed from each league, gaining all twelve from his own league and five from the American. The American League's initial candidate was Burke, who peaked at eight votes, six from his own league. The American League subsequently moved to MacPhail and then Montreal Expos executive John McHale. None came close. The moguls adjourned, agreeing to reconvene in thirty or forty days.[162]

The analysis was quick. "The obstinacy of the Lords of Baseball in making all decisions along league lines is the tipoff to their weakness," wrote Dick Young.[163] Leonard Koppett echoed, "The overriding problem is the intransigence of the club owners in dealing with each other."[164] But then comes Milt Richman, Burke's John the Baptist, who summed up the problem as O'Malley "seems determined that no new Commissioner of Baseball will be elected without his personal seal of approval."[165]

When the owners met again February 4 in Bal Harbour, Florida, the names floating around included only one addition, Phil Piton, an executive with the National Association, which governed Minor League Baseball.[166] The result, however, was different. The American League, led by the Cleveland Indians' Gabe Paul, resurrected Burke. The National League, especially O'Malley, championed Feeney. There was discussion, which went nowhere, and then O'Malley got the meeting to return to one of his pet projects, the consolidation of various baseball functions into the Commissioner's Office, doing away with league presidents, and unifying such functions as overseeing umpires. It was agreed that this plan should get first priority before a commissioner was elected. Paul, O'Malley, Feeney, Burke, Lee MacPhail, and four others were appointed to a committee to recommend the means of implementing such a plan. Committee members from each league caucused and then rejoined to formulate the final version. When the full committee returned to the overall meeting, it recommended Bowie Kuhn to head the committee and act as interim commissioner for a year. Kuhn, a longtime lawyer for the National League, was well known and instantly received unanimous approval.[167] As heads of the committee, O'Malley and Paul conveyed the news to him.

To the people who did not agree with him, O'Malley had become the bogeyman, all-powerful and appearing everywhere. It would become an article of faith that Bowie Kuhn was O'Malley's choice and remained under his thumb thereafter. But an examination of the press reports of the time and the reminiscences of those involved paints a more obscure picture.

Both Kuhn and Burke said the first person to approach Kuhn about the commissionership was Burke, who did not like O'Malley and was not likely to follow his lead.[168] Lee MacPhail said he and Gabe Paul first brought up Kuhn's name in the American League caucus and won acceptance there before they presented it to the National Leaguers.[169] Others, none of whom were present, pinned Kuhn onto O'Malley's lapel.[170] Whether O'Malley controlled, influenced, or participated, there was a National League man with a foot in the door, and his plan for centralized administration of the game was back on the table.

A number of baseball men feel that O'Malley's influence increased with Kuhn as commissioner.[171] He knew Kuhn's hot buttons about the integrity of the game. They shared law backgrounds. O'Malley was no longer the younger parvenu, but baseball's acknowledged elder statesman, a man any commissioner would turn to. But O'Malley still did not win every argument. He may have been the most powerful man in the game, but his power was never absolute.

When Ted Turner joined his first meeting as an owner, he was asked to say a few words. "I'm glad to be here because I love competition," the America's Cup captain said. "There's nothing like being on the ocean, with the strong winds blowing, and the wind in your face and not knowing your destiny." Said O'Malley: "Son, you came to the right place."[172]

15

A Totally Different Person

With all the time and effort Walter O'Malley put into his baseball-wide activity, he never forgot that the core of his wealth, his influence, and the security for his family came from the performance of the Dodgers, both on and off the field. The debut of Dodger Stadium had been a huge success, but the season had been soured by the team's late-September collapse and loss in a playoff series with San Francisco. O'Malley was "enraged," in Buzzie Bavasi's words, and sought to fire manager Walter Alston. But Bavasi threatened to resign if he did so, and the owner backed off, ever mindful of letting the baseball people run the baseball operation.[1]

As the winter progressed into 1963, O'Malley turned to the tactic he had used since the early years in Brooklyn—alternating optimism and threats through the newspapers. "We must win," he said in February. "If Alston does the job, he stays. If he doesn't do the job, he's out."[2] He called the manager in for a talk during a rocky spring training and filled the papers with quotes designed to build pressure on the team.[3] Columnist Melvin Durslag wrote it was the first time he had seen O'Malley show "nerves" since he had been in Los Angeles.[4] After a Freeway Series exhibition game against the Angels, O'Malley and his black Cadillac pulled up beside a couple wandering the Dodger Stadium parking lots. They had forgotten where they had parked. O'Malley offered to help and told them he was cruising around the stadium just trying to blow off some steam.[5] His state of mind could not have been helped when the home opener drew 33,578, a third off the previous worst attendance for an opener in Los Angeles.

Much of the exhortations were newspaper talk, designed to stimulate interest and keep the team in the customers' minds. Alston, Bavasi, and the players knew they could ignore most of it, but not all.[6] The team played poorly through the early going, hurt by sloppy fielding. John Griffin, the

Dodgers' clubhouse man and beloved team clown, died of a heart attack in the Forbes Field dressing room in early May.[7] Alston rushed to the dressing room and then back to the dugout to finish the game. The Dodgers left Pittsburgh for St. Louis with a record of 12-14. The bus taking them to the airport was old, and when the Pirates passed them in a new air-conditioned bus, remarks began to float up from the backseats. Why was a second-division team better treated than the biggest attendance draw in the Major Leagues? Traveling secretary Lee Scott, responsible for the bus rentals, suggested they would get better treatment if they won some games. And the tone and volume of the remarks escalated. Alston, troubled by the pressure, the team's performance, and Griffin's death, had hit his limit. He stood up and ordered everyone to shut up, and then he sat down and steamed for twenty minutes in the silence. Finally, he ordered the bus driver to pull to the side of the road. He stood at the front, told the players to quit complaining and start playing, and if anybody had a problem with that, he would meet them outside the bus. The fifty-one-year-old Alston was famous for his strength, and none of the players took up the challenge.[8] The next day Koufax beat the Cardinals 11-1, and the team went 15-6 for the rest of the month.

Not all the tensions had gone away. The hitting was spotty, the fielding was weak, but the pitching was dominant. In late August, with the Giants closing the gap to five and a half games and the Cardinals close behind them, Bavasi felt it necessary to hold a meeting with players and coaches (notably Leo Durocher), warning them not to second-guess Alston.[9] The Dodgers then won three of four from the Giants at Dodger Stadium, reversing the playoff results of the previous year. In mid-September, when the Cardinals closed to one back, the Dodgers swept a three-game series in St. Louis and then maintained their lead to the end.

As the World Series approached, the pressure for World Series tickets grew. Dodger Stadium might be the second-biggest park in the Majors, but it had nearly forty thousand fewer seats than the Coliseum. One female employee received an offer of a mink stole if she could deliver a bloc of tickets. O'Malley, asked if he would give her a stole as a reward, said it was too hot for furs in Southern California.[10] Scalpers were getting $200 a ticket for $12 seats.[11]

As the Series approached, old nemesis Dick Young surfaced with the prediction that the Dodgers would be World Series losers. "Walter O'Malley can console himself with the fact that he'll have enough money to pay his increased taxes."[12] For Dodger fans the results were worth scalper prices. Their team won four straight, outscoring the Yankees twelve runs to four over the course of the Series. Because the bulk of receipts for the first four games of a Series go to the players, the Dodgers received only $169,591.08, not as much as the increase in their property taxes. In 1959, after a six-game Series, they had received just under twice that much.[13]

In later years O'Malley would describe the sweep as his greatest thrill in baseball.[14] It was now clearly his team (assembled by Bavasi), not Branch Rickey's. It was his organization. It was his ballpark, and he was going to be able to pay for it. It was all the sweeter because the victim had been the Yankees and, by extension, New York. Frank Finch of the *Los Angeles Times* said he had gotten a big charge "from the look of dismay, consternation and disbelief—at one and the same time—on the face of a New York Dodger-hater after the second game of the World Series," a clear reference to Dick Young.[15]

All the success seems to have softened some of O'Malley's edges. Brooklyn employees—Parrott, Rudd, Graham—resented a sharp tongue and a tight wallet. Los Angeles employees talked of a positive team atmosphere in which their contributions were appreciated. "Walter O'Malley in Brooklyn and Walter O'Malley in Los Angeles was a totally different person," said Bavasi. "With success, Dodger Stadium, and more World Series victories, the buccaneer in O'Malley subsided somewhat," said Roger Kahn.[16] He still needled, and expected the hard work, but he seemed to appreciate it more.[17] He also knew the image he had been given and could joke about it. In 1969 O'Malley opened the "Dodger Cafeteria" at his new golf course near Dodgertown. It was open to the public, and *Herald Examiner* columnist Melvin Durslag complimented O'Malley on the forty people outside trying to get in. Replied O'Malley: "You're so vulgar. All you think about is money."

In Brooklyn O'Malley's standard lunch was at Room 40 in the Hotel Bossert with his political cronies. In Dodger Stadium a room off the kitchen in the press box was dubbed Room 40, but the companions were the team's top staff members. Fred Claire, who started in the public relations department in 1969 and worked his way up to general manager over three decades, remembers four tables with four chairs. O'Malley's seat, in the corner to the right as you entered the room, was reserved, but the others were open. The conversation could be the events of the day, but it could also be a forum to discuss a problem or float an idea.[18] It was much like the lunches

John Smith had orchestrated at Pfizer two decades earlier. The meals often ran two hours, Bavasi said. If the Dodgers were home for a night game, O'Malley, Bavasi, Fresco Thompson, and maybe someone else would have dinner in Room 40 as well.[19] Claire would remain with the team for two decades after Walter O'Malley's death, but said nobody sat in the chair reserved for O'Malley again.[20]

O'Malley's involvement in the team was spreading. In Brooklyn he had done the contracts, the radio-television work, the marketing, and the overwhelming project of a new stadium. In Los Angeles the monument to the O'Malleys led him into stadium operations, concessions, and ticketing, all of which had previously been in Bavasi's orbit. It was not as if Bavasi was pushed aside, though. "'Boss' was the wrong word. He was more like an associate," Bavasi said.[21] In some cases issues were even put to a vote of senior staff. When O'Malley lost he would grumble but go along.[22] "I sort of sit around as a trouble-shooter," said O'Malley. "When they want me, they call on me. My principal function is to keep all the loose ends tied together."[23]

Bavasi, for example, had a budget to work with but enormous amounts of autonomy. As he had with Jackie Robinson, Bavasi felt he could ignore broad hints a player should be traded. He could keep Walter Alston in the manager's chair even though he wasn't O'Malley's kind of attention-grabbing leader. He said he never consulted with O'Malley on baseball matters unless they had strong financial implications, such as the Koufax-Drysdale holdout. Matters that crossed jurisdictions within the Dodger organization were usually thrashed out at the lunches.

The downside was the pay. O'Malley never paid himself more than $50,000 a year, Bavasi said, less than similar positions in corporate America and far less than the Dodgers could afford.[24] Other employees were paid similarly. Bavasi never made more than $40,000 and never had a contract. When Bavasi entered the ownership ranks, and saw the Dodgers' financial reports at league meetings, he said O'Malley felt compelled to approach Bavasi and apologize for the salary he had paid him over the years. Bavasi said he had pointed at four World Series rings and said that was his reward.[25]

A few days after Claire joined the team, O'Malley popped in his office door to show him a cartoon. The cartoon featured an office with "CEO" on the door and a sign that said, "Please disturb," Claire recalled. "It was the way he wanted to operate."[26] Tom Seeberg, who worked for several organizations over four decades in the game, said the strength of O'Malley's management was that "everybody knew what their role was all the time," something not true on other teams. The work atmosphere was very positive, he said. O'Malley was very family-oriented, always asking about spouses and children. At the end of the season the Dodger staff and spouses would go to a retreat in northern San Diego County for several days of organizational meetings and group activities. "It was both work and family, very O'Malley," he said.[27]

O'Malley's focus on people was a core of his management philosophy. As a young executive, Buzzie Bavasi's son Peter was talking with O'Malley. "Peter," the younger Bavasi recalled him saying, "there are only two kinds of problems—problems you can't solve, and people problems."[28] With all that O'Malley had not lost his penchant for a little pointed conversation. In 1978 the Dodgers set a record for season attendance with 3,347,845 people passing through the turnstiles, the first team to break the 3 million level. Claire showed up at his office the next morning and was summoned to O'Malley's. Expecting a raise and congratulations, Claire was asked why he had not fudged the figures by adding the number of people who had bought tickets, but did not show up. The team could have reported 3.5 million, and nobody would ever break that record, O'Malley told Claire. Immediately, Claire promised they would break the record in 1979. On the drive home that evening Claire realized he had gotten the raise, and the praise, but had also been led to promise to do even better the next year.[29] The Dodgers would not actually get to 3.5 million until 1982, three years after O'Malley's death, but still another record.

Bump Holman, Bud's son and the Dodgers' team pilot for most of the 1950s, said that at his regular meals with O'Malley, they would always talk hunting, or flying, or business, because the Dodgers' owner knew Bump had no interest in baseball. O'Malley was always "very inquisitive about what I was doing," and he remembered what he had been told. Holman said he found O'Malley constantly widening his mind with whatever special knowledge was held by the people he talked to.[30]

O'Malley remained especially concerned with public relations and marketing. He would have Bavasi remind executives that they should be willing speakers at baseball banquets, Cub Scout father-son nights, and similar functions.[31] He kept a stock of Dodger Stadium postcards on his desk and handwrote answers to all the letters he received from fans.[32] With the Dodgers' arrival in Los Angeles, he had his executives work out a code system for odd plays such as strikeouts on fouled-off two-strike bunts and published the code in the scorecard.[33] It was designed for new fans and just happened to stimulate scorecard sales. As J. G. Taylor Spink, editor and publisher of the *Sporting News*, wrote, O'Malley "has come to be regarded as the 'Professor' in the science of successful and aggressive operation."[34]

The emphasis on promotions he had established in Brooklyn continued. By the seventh game at the Coliseum, the first of the "community nights" was held, celebrating Riverside, a suburb sixty miles east of Los Angeles.[35] Without Irving Rudd, there were fewer of the spontaneous, offbeat promotions such as Music Appreciation Night, but the pace was more relentless. Seeberg, in the public relations and promotions department from 1958 to 1968, said O'Malley rarely came up with his own ideas for promotions, but encouraged creative discussions at the Room 40 lunches.[36] The Dodgers adopted Hollywood Stars Night from the Pacific Coast League's Hollywood Stars, and baseball fans could see the likes of Mickey Rooney, Nat "King" Cole, Danny Thomas, and Donald O'Connor in a pregame match.[37] They created a pregame show of "baseball skills," such as a relay throw from center field to the plate and a home-run hitting contest.[38] They brought in baseball clown Jackie Price for an exhibition and started an annual fashion show "for the ladies."[39] The community nights added ethnic groups, such as Chinatown, to the geographical ones.[40] There were Boy Scouts and Girls Scouts and Little Leaguers. Eventually, there would be an annual Nuns Day, where the Dodgers treated hundreds of Catholic nuns to a ball game and its cuisine.[41] It became a favorite of O'Malley's. By the mid-1960s they were joining a promotion pioneered by other teams, with Bat Night. It was their first giveaway night, with kids receiving a Hillerich & Bradsby Little Leaguer bat. It was a sellout, with the Dodgers telling people to stay away an hour before the game's scheduled start.[42] The number of giveaway nights would grow, although the bats would disappear because the kids could not resist pounding them on seats, railings, siblings, and friends.

O'Malley used his own box, both for family and for business purposes, which often mingled, as he could present a softer front to his colleagues from the corporate world. His box contained his own hot dog grill, and he made sure draft beer, Popsicles, banana ice cream bars, and Crackerjacks were available.[43] Vin Scully's broadcast, and later television coverage, was piped in.

A large part of O'Malley's management success was his willingness to focus on details. Claire remembered the day O'Malley was walking the concourse for a weekday afternoon game billed as a "Businessman's Special." He spotted a customer reading the *Wall Street Journal* while waiting for the game to start. He immediately called Claire to get a picture for use in future advertising of such games.[44] Bavasi told the story of Jim Powell, a top executive with Lucky Lager Beer, who had sixteen box seats. Even though the Dodgers had sponsorships with other brewers, O'Malley made sure the concession stands near Powell's boxes had cases of Lucky Lager so Powell's guests would be served his product. It was keeping a prospective sponsor happy.[45]

Leonard Koppett, the first journalist to take on the sports business as a full-time job, delved into the skills and practices that he thought made O'Malley a top executive. He listed them as:

- An appropriate background.
- A stress on stability in positions of authority.
- Hiring on ability, not reputation.
- Building a team based on internal talent from the farm system.
- Making trades only to fill specific, short-term needs
- Paying enormous attention to low visibility chores such as scouting, ticket promotion and budgeting.
- Working at it full time.
- Staying out of the limelight and keeping the focus on what his customers are interested in—the players.[46]

His flexibility and deal-making skills were nowhere better demonstrated than in his purchase of a new team airplane in the early 1960s. The team-owned Convair 440 could not make cross-country flights without refueling. As a result the Dodgers often took charters. By 1960, however, the team's charter bill with United Airlines was up to $125,000 (just under $1 million in 2013 dollars).[47] On December 23, 1960, at his office in Vero Beach, Bump Holman got a call from O'Malley, who wanted to talk to him about airplanes. Holman said, sure, right after Christmas. O'Malley said, "No, now."[48]

When Holman got to Los Angeles, O'Malley told him he was concerned about the cost of charters and also did not want his valuable ballplayers flying on a plane with only two engines. Holman's recommendation was a Lockheed Electra, but said Lockheed would not sell them to corporate customers because they thought the plane was too difficult to maintain. His second recommendation was a Douglas DC-6B. Holman told O'Malley he thought he could buy one for around $1 million and sell the Convair for between

$300,000 and $400,000. O'Malley told Holman to get all the instruments he wanted for the cockpit and to make sure the cabin was configured with first-class seats, five card tables, and four bunk beds. He was prepared to pay the expected $650,000 or so.

Holman flew to Copenhagen and struck a deal with SAS to buy a DC-6B for $390,000 and then sold the Convair to Avianca Airlines of Colombia for $700,000.[49] So O'Malley had his new plane and a potential $300,000 in profit. Now, however, O'Malley said, wait a minute. He put SAS on hold while Holman was sent looking for an Electra, with an estimated cost of $1.6 million to $1.8 million. The only Electra available was owned by General Motors, which had been using it to test the airplane engines GM manufactured. O'Malley insisted the GM plane be in Los Angeles for inspection the next day. Holman tracked down the GM executive at a party and got him to agree to bring the plane in. The next day Holman went into the control cabin while O'Malley sat in the back with the GM executive. When Holman came out O'Malley asked what the cockpit needed. Holman mentioned a couple of things that came to about $20,000. O'Malley then turned to the General Motors representative and offered $1.8 million for the plane, with the upgrades Holman mentioned, plus the plane being brought up to full Federal Aviation Administration (FAA) compliance and updates. Stunned, the executive agreed, and, stunned, Holman said he had not thought it possible to buy such a plane in under a year. Because the Electra could not be delivered before late 1961, O'Malley passed on the SAS DC-6B and instead bought one from Western Airlines for $300,000, saving another $100,000.[50]

Holman said O'Malley essentially got the Electra for free by the time he rolled together the proceeds from the sale of the Convair, a profit from the eventual sale of the DC-6B, and the money General Motors spent upgrading the Electra, which would serve as the Dodgers' plane for a decade. As Holman noted, "In all these deals, the buyers or sellers would show up with thick stacks of documents" (his hands were positioned six inches apart). "Walter would draw up a one-page contract and they'd all sign it." O'Malley never quibbled about costs, Holman said. The flights featured steak dinners and trays of sandwiches for snacks. There was beer and alcohol. The veterans would make the rookies serve the food. "He was the most thorough man I ever saw about everything," Holman said. He delegated very quickly, with very specific instructions, and then left subordinates to follow through. If they did not get it done, he would come back to find out why. And, Holman said, he always listened to subordinates with technical expertise.

Overwhelmingly, O'Malley took pride in the reputation the Dodger organization had developed, the picture Spink had painted in the *Sporting News*. The steaks on team flights were just one aspect of wanting both the outside world and employees to feel they were part of the best organization in baseball.

The Dodgers were the first team to set up a pension plan for full-time employees. Players were already covered by their own pension plan. The team contributed an amount equal to 15 percent of the annual salaries of staff employees, and eligibility would be based on historical as well as future service. O'Malley called the affected staff into a meeting room at Dodgertown at spring training of 1961 and said, "I want you to know we are proud of the job you all have been doing. We think we have the finest organization in baseball."[51] Medical and insurance plans followed.[52] "The pay was not great, but the benefits and the perks were very good," said Seeberg.

As with Bavasi's move to San Diego, O'Malley would not stand in the way of an employee improving his position by leaving the team. Seeberg spent seven years working for Red Patterson in promotions and public relations and a year as the general manager at the Santa Barbara Minor League club. When the Cincinnati Reds offered him their top publicity job, he was encouraged to go. Nearly a decade later Gene Autry approached Patterson with an offer to be the Angels' president. Again, he had O'Malley's blessing, despite Patterson's twenty-year record of excellent work.

Dodger employees were rarely fired, and when they were they were not flayed in public or shot down in finding their next job. In Roger Kahn's *Boys of Summer*, he tells of O'Malley forcing Buzzie Bavasi out to make way for O'Malley's son, Peter, and then ordering a heartbroken Fresco Thompson, Bavasi's successor, to go to Albuquerque and fire Peter Bavasi, Buzzie's son, as general manager there. To steel himself to fire a young man he had known since babyhood, Thompson drank a bottle of whiskey. The hangover exposed symptoms of cancer, and Thompson died painfully a few months later, a death Kahn implicitly hangs on O'Malley.[53]

Both the Bavasis disputed the story, and Buzzie said Kahn, who wrote parts of *The Boys of Summer* at Bavasi's home, had called to apologize.[54] As mentioned earlier Buzzie said O'Malley told Buzzie to find the expansion franchise he wanted to be involved in and O'Malley would ensure that franchise was approved. As Bavasi's dream approached reality, Bavasi said he met with O'Malley to talk about how many Dodger personnel Bavasi would be allowed to hire, a standard procedure in baseball. Peter Bavasi was so obvious a hire for Buzzie that it was assumed rather than discussed, but it was agreed that because Albuquerque was the top Dodger farm club, and because the San Diego organization was not established enough to need Peter yet, he would finish out the season working for the Dodgers, which he did. Thompson's visit to Albuquerque was part of the general manager's standard tour of farm clubs, and although he had a good deal to drink, his cancer was already far advanced.

O'Malley fully supported Red Patterson in taking care of the newspapers, still the major source of publicity for any baseball team. There were lunches and free liquor in the press box. The team paid travel costs for the writers in those days and gave them presents such as television sets at Christmas. "The whole atmosphere, the whole Dodger family, was first class," recalled John Hall, a reporter and later a columnist for the *Los Angeles Times*. Spring training was "like going to a resort," he said. "They were kind of a model organization."[55]

O'Malley would also work to keep bad news out of the papers. In the early 1960s O'Malley became concerned that the John Collins problems were resurfacing in the ticket department. He hired a former military officer named John Burns to audit the department, and Burns turned up evidence that led to Harold Parrott's firing. Parrott had been providing choice tickets to favored customers such as hotels and pocketing a gratuity for the service. Bavasi said the day after Parrott was let go, an executive from the Statler Hotel arrived at the ticket office with a $900 check to cover three hundred tickets at $3 apiece, plus three $100 bills for Parrott.[56] "It was a similar story to Jack Collins in the Fifties," said Bavasi. It was not technically illegal, but O'Malley wanted clean transactions with his customers. Parrott protested his innocence and later wrote a book that painted an unrelentingly negative portrait of O'Malley, while claiming he had been railroaded by Burns.[57] O'Malley had the public relations department put out some vague information about a car accident and granting Parrott a leave of absence.[58] In November Parrott quietly joined the Angels in a lesser role.[59] O'Malley would refrain from telling the tale even when Parrott's book excoriated him.

The departure of Allan Roth a year later was treated even more circumspectly. In early September the *Los Angeles Herald Examiner*'s Bob Hunter noted that Roth was not on the Dodgers' current road trip.[60] The next day the Dodgers told Hunter Roth had resigned after eighteen seasons because he did not like the travel.[61] Actually, Roth had been let go a month earlier, after pushing one of O'Malley's hot buttons. O'Malley did not like anything negative in the papers, said Frank Graham Jr. of the public relations department in the Brooklyn days. "To be guarded against at all costs was an 'incident,' O'Malley believed, especially one that might be triggered by interracial sex."[62] The married Roth, said Bavasi, had developed a relationship with an African American woman who accompanied him on road trips. In Philadelphia, on the previous road trip, he had gotten into a screaming match with her in the corridor outside his hotel room. This qualified as an "incident," and Roth was fired.[63]

Despite the elbows thrown in the expansion process, the Angels-Dodgers relationship started smoothly enough. In the week between the Angels' winning the franchise and their expansion draft, O'Malley ordered Dodger personnel to be available to the Angels even over the intervening weekend. Bavasi had the Dodgers turn over their scouting reports on American League prospects to the Angels. With new general manager Fred Haney, recently manager of the Milwaukee Braves, and Casey Stengel, just fired by the Yankees and angry about it, the Angels got good advice and drafted young players, many from the Yankees, who would help them immensely in their early years. Even though the Dodgers owned the rights to the name "Los Angeles Angels" from their purchase of the Pacific Coast League team in 1957, O'Malley did not dun the Angels for payment.[64] O'Malley showed up on the Angels' opening day, blew some foam off his stein, and estimated a team could make $80,000 a year selling beer with 2 million in attendance. At the Coliseum he still could not sell beer.[65]

The honeymoon was short-lived. The Angels struggled through their first year at Wrigley Field, drawing barely 600,000 fans, while the Dodgers pulled in 1.8 million in the Coliseum. Angel partisans complained O'Malley had excluded them from the Coliseum to cut their crowds, but the Angels never drew a crowd as big as Wrigley's listed capacity of 21,009.[66] Their biggest crowd was 19,930 against the Yankees on August 22, and the nine Wrigley Field games against the Yankees provided 28 percent of the Angels' home attendance. In fact, even when they moved to 56,000-seat Dodger Stadium in 1962, the Angels would draw only eight crowds more than 19,000 in their four years there, none in 1964 or 1965.

Autry had seen the problem from the very beginning. Operating in O'Malley's ballpark, the Angels would never be able to develop their own identity. "We've been a step-child of the Dodgers and always will be as long as we stay there," said Autry.[67] "We had no future in Dodger Stadium," he summed up.[68] Said his partner, Bob Reynolds, "We play in a park that advertises Union Oil, and one of our sponsors is Standard Oil. We are cast under the Dodgers shadow as long as we remain in Chavez Ravine."[69] O'Malley had recognized the issue even before Autry and Reynolds got involved. In his negotiating points for allowing the American League into Los Angeles, he had insisted that the future stadium he assumed the expansion team would build had to be at least fifteen miles from Dodger Stadium. In the following four years in Dodger Stadium, the Angels were never happy tenants, and the Dodgers were never gracious landlords. The Dodgers did not drive the Angels out, but the Dodgers extracted their pound of American League flesh nickel by nickel from Gene Autry.

Lines began to be drawn. The Angels insisted on calling the ballpark Chavez Ravine, even though Dodger Stadium is not located in the ravine itself. That was not just semantics but a necessary marketing strategy to distinguish the Angels' brand. Similarly, they banned Dodger Stadium employees from listening to Dodger road games on transistor radios while working Angel home games.[70]

Then things started to get petty. The Angels put up an announcement on the message board, saying the Dodgers ran the concession stands, so if you have complaints, go to them.[71] The Angels on the fly scheduled a pregame sportscasters-versus-sportswriters promotion barely three weeks before a similar Dodger promotion that had been advertised since before the season. Bavasi was "teed off, but good," especially after paying $1,500 for uniforms.[72] The teams agreed to a preseason Freeway Series, and, said Irv Kaze, the Angels' first publicity director, "we took the series like the World Series and Super Bowl rolled into one."[73] The Angels won regularly, and Kaze entered the Dodger Stadium press box to announce that "the city champions come to town Tuesday night."[74]

The Dodgers got their shots in, and their nickels out, more quietly. The instrument was the contract Autry had signed and the man who enforced it, Dick Walsh, O'Malley's lieutenant in building the stadium and now its manager.[75] Walsh, whom Autry would later hire as his general manager, was a single-minded man. He made sure the Angels paid for half of stadium maintenance costs. That included half the toilet paper, even though 75 percent of the people who entered the stadium for those four years came to see the Dodgers. It included half the cost of resurfacing and restriping the parking lot, even though the O'Malley kept all the parking revenues. It included half the cost of washing the Dodger Stadium office windows, even though the only Angel offices in the building had no windows. The Angels' ticket offices were confined to the bowels of the stadium, and advance ticket customers had to walk past the groundskeepers' manure pile.[76] It included half the cost of watering O'Malley's beloved trees and flowers. And it just seemed to happen that when the field had to be dug up for repairs or maintenance, it was when the Angels were at home.[77]

The Angels' muttering indicated these things were irritants, but the overriding issue was the need to create their own identity and the ballpark they felt they needed to do it. The team's first year was barely half over, the Dodger Stadium irritants had not arisen, and already the Angels were examining the possibilities. "We've had at least five communities approach us, seeking to have us move there or build us a park. Nothing definite has been discussed. We note that the population is drifting East, and we think in time we should have our own park to establish our own identity," said Autry.[78]

The Angels would continue to receive feelers, and to do their own research, after they moved into Dodger Stadium.[79] Autry concluded he could never build his own stadium and would have to work with a city.[80] As the deadline approached for them to give notice that they would be leaving after the initial four years, they did so.[81] They also mentioned that O'Malley's battle with Los Angeles County over property taxes made them worried the Dodgers would have to raise the rent.[82]

Eventually, Autry's friendship with Walt Disney led him to Anaheim, where the Angels struck a deal to move into a city-owned stadium beginning with the 1966 season.[83] Six weeks later the Dodgers canceled the Freeway Series.[84] A few years later the Angels would also drop out of using the Dodgers' Electra aircraft for road trips, opting to move to chartered jets.[85] After their last road trip the previous season, the Dodgers had sent them a bill for $25,000 after Angels players trashed the plane.[86]

The Angels' lease, and the attendance records, had gone a long way toward removing O'Malley's biggest worry—the debt from building Dodger Stadium. By 1965 he told one confidant he had only $11 million to repay. A year later he said it was down to $8 million from the $26 million he had borrowed to build and complete Dodger Stadium.[87] In 1969 he said it would be paid off "in a couple of years."[88] While being cagey about net, gross, and taxes paid, O'Malley generally indicated the team sold about fourteen thousand season tickets each year, and the after-tax profits were generally around $2 million annually.[89] The assessor's report the Dodgers had prepared for their battle with the Los Angeles County Assessor's Office indicated total income of $12.3 million in 1962 and $11.4 million in 1963.[90]

The Dodgers had led the league in attendance every year from 1959 through 1966, setting a new National League record in 1960 and a new Major League Baseball record in 1962. That record would hold until the Dodgers set a higher mark in both 1977 and again in 1978. But revenues were not purely from baseball. There was an annual winter recreational vehicle show.[91] There were sports-car races, a ski-jump competition, Harlem Globetrotters basketball, a Cantinflas show, and boxing.[92] There was only one night of boxing, as veteran fighter Davey Moore died of brain injuries three days later.[93] O'Malley's standard rent seemed to be 5 percent of the gross plus all parking and concessions income.[94]

There was a flurry of discussion with the Los Angeles Rams about moving to the stadium and a rumor the San Diego Chargers were interested as well.[95] The most historic event was a concert by the Beatles on August 28, 1966. The screaming of the heavily young, female audience was so loud the group felt no one could hear the music and there was no point in doing any more live concerts. They fulfilled a commitment at Candlestick Park a few days later, but thereafter became a studio band.[96]

Other financial ideas did not work out. In California O'Malley clung to his hopes for pay television. Matty Fox and Skiatron had been unable to get its system up and running in either San Francisco or Los Angeles. Startup dates were promised, but the deadlines were never met.[97] Still, the promise remained. Skiatron reportedly had signed a deal to pay the Giants $37.5 million over fifteen years for their pay-television rights.[98] O'Malley said he was "very interested," but still had no contract.[99]

O'Malley was clearly more than "very interested." As Skiatron's promise faded, he was meeting with the Los Angeles Rams as well as drive-in theater owners to see if they could put together a pay-television network.[100] In August 1963 a new player surfaced—Subscription Television, Inc. (STI)—a combination of the remains of Skiatron with Pat Weaver, who had headed NBC in the 1950s. The Associated Press reported both the Giants and the Dodgers had signed contracts with the new company, but both teams refused to comment.[101] The situation got messier when the California Department of Corporation and the federal Securities and Exchange Commission began investigating the premature release of information about STI's stock offering.[102] The premature talk had reportedly taken place at a San Francisco meeting of the Bohemian Club, of which O'Malley was a member. Eventually, the $20 million offer was allowed to proceed.[103]

STI began to ramp up for broadcasting on July 1, 1964, but was having trouble getting houses wired. It pushed the start date back to mid-July.[104] Another shadow fell over the project when Matty Fox died of a heart attack on June 2.[105] When it started only twenty-five hundred houses in West Los Angeles were ready to go, but the Dodgers were receiving $1.50 for each game watched.[106]

The system worked through the end of the season, but then came up against its final nemesis. The movie theater owners organized, calling themselves the California Crusade for Free Television. They altruistically sponsored an initiative on the November 1964 ballot to ban pay-TV. It won with almost two-thirds of the vote.[107] The California Supreme Court ruled the initiative was unconstitutional, but STI had already filed for bankruptcy.[108]

Some of his other initiatives worked out better. Dating back to Brooklyn, O'Malley was friends with Dr. Clifford Brownell, chairman of the Physical Education Department at Columbia University. O'Malley had suggested to Brownell that there was a need for a program to train executives for professional sports. "For the most part, people filling sports and recreation administrative jobs have not been trained by education to do so, but have learned their particular job by trial and error."[109] One spring in Vero Beach, Brownell took a protégé named James Mason to talk over the idea with O'Malley. The idea clicked with Mason, but for a decade he had no way to implement it. By 1966 Mason was a professor at Ohio University, and his boss was interested in a master's degree program in sports management. Mason got back in touch with O'Malley and found he was still enthusiastic. "Many of his ideas were put to use in planning the curriculum for this new program," Mason said. The Ohio University program would be the seed from which sprang similar sports management programs around the country.

O'Malley's interest in promoting international baseball, and especially in a relationship with Japan, did not die after the Dodgers' 1956 postseason trip. The Yomiuri Giants, Japanese baseball's dominant team, responded to repeated invitations, sending a promising young battery to Vero Beach in 1957 and bringing the entire roster in 1961.[110] O'Malley would roll out the little touches, printing the mess-hall menus in both languages and scouring Los Angeles music stores for a record of the Japanese national anthem to be played during the Giants' games in Vero Beach.[111] He used his contacts to help Dodgers player Lee Walls set up baseball clinics in Japan after the 1963 season.[112]

It was not only Japan. The Dodgers would play three exhibition games in Mexico in the spring of 1964.[113] But Japan remained at the top of his thinking, even during a spat. In September 1965 Bob Hunter of the *Herald Examiner* wrote a story saying an unnamed Japanese team had made a $500,000 offer for Don Drysdale.[114] O'Malley, who knew nothing of any offer, sent an angry note to his main Japanese contact, Sotaro Suzuki of the Giants.[115] It quickly produced an apology from Matsutaro Shoriki, president of the Giants, and soon thereafter an invitation from Shoriki for the Dodgers to tour Japan again.[116]

After another successful tour, the Japanese government presented O'Malley with the Order of the Sacred Treasure, Third Class, in recognition of his efforts to promote friendship between the two countries.[117] The Giants would return with full squads in 1967, 1971, and 1975 and with lesser groups in many other years. Peter O'Malley would make promoting international baseball one of the cornerstones of his ownership, diversifying from Japan, but never losing the connection. When the Dodgers signed the first major Japanese star, Hideo Nomo, in 1995, Peter would credit the relationships the team had built up over the years.[118]

Not everything about the Japan trip had gone as planned, and overall the off-season from 1966 to 1967 was one of the low points of O'Malley's ownership. The first problem dated back to the previous spring.

The Japanese offer to Drysdale, although withdrawn, apparently opened his eyes to his market value. He knew his fellow pitcher Sandy Koufax was even more valuable. The pair had won 45 percent of the team's games over the previous four seasons, and one or the other had won the Cy Young Award for the game's best pitcher in three of those years. As the 1966 season approached the *Herald Examiner* reported that the pair wanted three-year contracts at $200,000 a year for Koufax and $150,000 annually for Drysdale.[119] Actually, they had asked for $1 million over three years to be split equally.[120] The amounts and the partnership were unprecedented, and the term was unusually long for a baseball contract. They also asked Bavasi to deal with their lawyer. O'Malley noted that "it is not our club's policy to grant contracts of more than a year's duration" and then made it clear the negotiations were Bavasi's to handle.[121] That was normal policy. O'Malley and Bavasi agreed on an overall budget for player salaries, and Bavasi worked out the details with individual players.[122]

O'Malley refrained from criticizing the players or getting involved in the negotiations for much of March. "I wish the boys well. They are entitled to everything they can get out of Buzzie Bavasi. Their only problem is what Buzzie can get out of me."[123] Bavasi made an offer that he described as more than any two players on a team had ever made.[124] This was later described as $110,000 for Koufax and $85,000 for Drysdale, both for one year.[125] The duo's attorney said his clients were studying "a multitude of offers in and out of the country."[126] O'Malley suggested the team would "get by" if they did not sign.[127]

On St. Patrick's Day, while O'Malley held his annual party at Vero Beach, Koufax and Drysdale signed a contract to star in a movie called *Warning Shot*. Drysdale was to play a television commentator, a role he would later fill in real life, while Koufax was to be a detective sergeant, a role he would never fill.[128] Cameras were scheduled to roll April 4. O'Malley was clearly getting a little frayed around the edges. The *Herald Examiner* published a story that O'Malley had called Drysdale, and O'Malley exploded about leaks to the press.[129] Both sides traded stories about who had instigated whatever phone calls there were.[130] Drysdale announced that he was negotiating with Screen Gems about a part in a television series to be called "Iron Horse," about "a fellow who inherits a train." The contract would be for seven years.[131]

At last, with spring training winding down, Bavasi raised his offer, then raised it again, and the pair signed. The last meeting was between Bavasi and J. William Hayes, the pair's lawyer, who said the final offer came after he threatened to challenge the legality of baseball's reserve clause in court.[132] Koufax received $120,000 and Drysdale $105,000, according to newspaper estimates.[133] The amounts, the joint effort, the use of an agent, and the threat to the reserve clause were all straws in the wind noted by Marvin Miller, then touring spring training camps to persuade players to hire him as executive director of the Major League Baseball Players Association.[134]

Another consequence of the holdout was that the Dodgers agreed neither Koufax nor Drysdale would have to go on the 1966 postseason trip to Japan. The problem that popped up was another Dodger star who did not want to go.

Maury Wills had been the ignition for the Dodgers' offense for the past seven seasons, setting stolen base records and putting speed back into a game that had been dominated by home run hitters since the end of World War II. Wills also had other ambitions. He played the banjo well enough to win club dates and other off-season work, and he wanted to advance that career. After begging off the team plane to Hawaii with ear trouble, he joined up for the first four games in Japan and then disappeared.[135] He had asked O'Malley for permission to leave to have a doctor look at his knee and had been denied.[136] O'Malley, who saw the trip as an adventure in personal diplomacy, a feeling backed by strong support from the U.S. State Department and the Lyndon Johnson administration, felt compelled to offer a personal apology to Japanese premier Sato Eisaku.[137] Bavasi described O'Malley as "very depressed."[138]

Despite his expressed desire to have his knee looked at, Wills did not proceed to Los Angeles, holing up in Hawaii to jam with Don Ho at the latter's night club. He said he needed to unwind before returning and facing whatever consequences there might be.[139] Bavasi soft-pedaled the situation, saying, "Maury Wills' leg comes first with us."[140] O'Malley was not willing to soft-pedal. For the first time in his career with the Dodgers, Bavasi was ordered to trade a player.[141] On December 1 Wills was shipped to the Pirates for Bob Bailey and Gene Michael. In public O'Malley said it was just business, not punishment.[142] In fact, the Dodgers would trade to get Wills back three years later.

Overall, it was a bad winter. Two days before the Wills deal, Bavasi traded Tommy Davis, the National League batting champion in 1962 and 1963 and the Dodgers' only .300 hitter in 1966. But the real blow had fallen in mid-November, while O'Malley was on an African hunting trip. Sandy Koufax announced his retirement. Koufax said he was quitting because he feared permanent damage to his left elbow from traumatic arthritis. "I've had a few too many shots and taken a few too many pills," he said. "It got to the point where I was told I could do permanent damage."[143] Both O'Malley and Bavasi left the door wide open in case Koufax wanted to return. But he did not. From the Baltimore Orioles' World Series sweep of the Dodgers in October, through Japan, Wills, and Koufax, it was a bad winter for O'Malley. And there was more to come. The Dodgers would have two of the worst years of the Walter O'Malley era in 1967 and 1968.[144] In early 1967 the winter woes would be topped off by the Dodgers' first home rainout in ten years in Los Angeles.[145]

There were those who felt the Dodgers' commitment to integration tapered off under Walter O'Malley.[146] But a look at the production of the Dodger farm system in the late 1950s, 1960s, and early 1970s belies that. Tommy Davis, Willie Davis, Willie Crawford, Von Joshua, Dave Stewart, and Dave Lopes all came up and made substantial contributions. The Dodgers had great hopes for Earl Robinson, Nate Oliver, and Glenn Burke, although none established himself. Jim Gilliam became one of the first African American coaches, but there were no black faces in the management ranks. The Dodgers were also slow to move into Latin America until they acquired Manny Mota in 1969 and used his substantial contacts in the Dominican Republic to build a strong base.

Racism was definitely a factor in Vero Beach, and O'Malley would make a number of moves over the years to convert the spring training base he enjoyed so much into a place his African American players could enjoy as well. From its beginnings under Branch Rickey, Dodgertown was a refuge from the surrounding Jim Crow South. But it was also a bit of a trap. White players could leave the campus to get a drink, see a movie, or get a haircut, but that was more difficult for the blacks.[147]

At times, Jim Crow could even threaten to breach the gates of Dodgertown. Bavasi told a story of 1951, when he got a loud complaint from Vero Beach's mayor about the number of African American players. Bavasi said he had traveling secretary Lee Scott go to a nearby racetrack and obtain $20,000 in $2 bills. He then had Kay O'Malley and his own wife, Evit, stamp "Brooklyn Dodgers" on the bills, which were then distributed to players, wives, and camp staff on a Friday. On Monday Bavasi said he got a call from the mayor, saying his point had been made.[148] The amount of money made available in a period when O'Malley was nagging Bavasi about the costs of spring training seems high, especially when he was negotiating with the city for an extended lease. But Larry Reisman, editor of the *Vero Beach Press-Journal* some five decades later, said he had tried to check the story with older residents and came away convinced Bavasi's basic story was correct, but perhaps took place in a different year or with smaller amounts of money.[149]

Still, as late as 1971, African American players were complaining that if they wanted to play golf, eat at a restaurant, or go to a movie in Vero Beach, they could not.[150] That year Willie Crawford was refused service at a Vero Beach cocktail lounge.[151] Although O'Malley was too much of a conservative to attack Jim Crow directly, it was part of his management philosophy to keep his employees as happy as possible.

Thus, he made the changes within Dodgertown. In 1962 the Dodgers defied a local ordinance by taking down the segregated-seating signs at Holman Stadium.[152] He installed a movie theater that showed first-run films. The team rented three cars each spring that were made available to the African American players so they could go the dozen miles to Fort Pierce to play golf or get a haircut.[153] But he was cautious because his hold over Dodgertown was being challenged by the Federal Aviation Administration and was ultimately entangled in local politics. The FAA noted that title to the old naval base had been turned over to the city with the proviso that the property be used to generate money that could be used to support aviation. The proceeds of the single spring training game the Dodgers paid were not much, and the little money it did generate was not being used for airport development and promotion.[154] The city worked out a deal with the FAA to make up any difference in 1962, but the discussions surrounding it soon progressed into talks about the Dodgers buying the property. In 1965 O'Malley struck a deal to buy 113 acres of Dodgertown from the city for $133,087.50.[155] He soon bought another 180 acres northwest of the property.[156]

Within months of the first purchase he began construction of a nine-hole golf course on his new property. By the spring of 1966 he was fighting the flu while taking a golf-cart tour of his new course.[157] On March 8 the First Annual Walter O'Malley International Golf Tournament, a far more grandiose name than event, kicked off, with the Dodgers' black players included.[158] He was soon planning an eighteen-hole course called Dodger Pines on the additional acreage he had purchased.[159] When it opened it would include a restaurant open to all.[160]

Housing was another issue. The barracks from the naval air station had been designed to last through a war of a few years. By the mid-1960s the buildings were more than twenty years old, and showing it, even though O'Malley had used a barracks room himself since 1948. The second-floor rooms all came with a bucket to catch the rain. After Peter O'Malley took over as Dodgertown's manager, each room was provided with its own can of bug spray, a move regarded as an upgrade.[161] The housing was a favorite target for Los Angeles sportswriters every spring. "The décor shows what can be done with plywood and a blank mind," wrote LA Times columnist Jim Murray. "They tell me this place used to be a barracks for the Navy. Up until now, I didn't know the Confederacy had a navy."[162] The established white players could afford their own housing off the base, but the black players could not, and the newspapers were happy with the price (free) in the barracks. O'Malley began planning improved housing, discussing design with the Holiday Inn chain.[163]

As a joke he also started a "grassroots" movement to save the barracks. Drawing a parallel to the anti–Vietnam War protests sweeping the country, he claimed, "It was like a San Francisco demonstration a year ago. Guys were saying, 'Who is O'Malley to displace us from our homes?'"[164] The complex finally opened in 1972, described as "a motel, albeit a very nice one."[165]

There was definitely an effort to promote a family atmosphere at Dodgertown. Walter and Kay stood in the line in the cafeteria just like everyone else.[166] Walter would drink with all comers, but frequent guest Jim Murray said, "I saw O'Malley tipsy at a few St. Patrick's parties but never saw him what you might call drunk. Walter O'Malley was always in control of Walter O'Malley."[167] He would play cards, often poker, with the newspaper reporters, avoiding high stakes in deference to their salaries and because he was more interested in the process than the win.[168] As one *Los Angeles Times* reporter said, "O'Malley loves poker. As in life, he doesn't play his cards. He gauges the people, and bets accordingly."[169]

One opponent came away with the suspicion that O'Malley did not always play to win, but to keep his playmates happy. "He sat there at the table covered with green felt in a blue shirt with a collar that had seen better days and a string tie, and he called every raise, and sometimes he said he had won and sometimes he said he had lost. We saw the time he threw away three aces and said he was beaten when the young reporter who had been losing money said he had two pair."[170]

Kindness could appear in other ways. There was the corporate-image giving that almost every organization does—to children's groups and organizations that fought diseases or aided some distressed group. These were announced in press releases.[171] But others happened without trumpets. In 1978 O'Malley invited former pitcher Carl Erskine and his family back for the twentieth anniversary of the Dodgers' first game in Los Angeles, a game Erskine had started. Erskine's son Jimmy had Down syndrome. When O'Malley asked what they would like to eat, Jimmy said, "Hot dog." O'Malley had to ask what Jimmy had said, and the boy popped up with "Two of them." O'Malley and Jimmy retired to the hot dog grill at the back of O'Malley's box, while Jimmy gave orders about ketchup and mustard and O'Malley missed the opening pitches.[172]

As with Campanella and Fresco Thompson's widow, O'Malley stepped in to help Bobby Maduro. Maduro's family had been quite wealthy, owning the Minor League team in Havana, among other ventures. With the coming of Fidel Castro's revolution, the Maduro family holdings were confiscated. Maduro arrived in the United States broke. O'Malley paid him $1,000 a month for a couple of years until he got back on his feet.[173]

16

Peter

Walter O'Malley turned sixty-five in late 1968. Despite two poor recent years on the field, the Los Angeles Dodgers were recognized as the model for a sport franchise. The time was coming to pass the torch, and he had been planning the ceremony for more than a decade.

His son, Peter, had been groomed systematically and willingly for the post of running the Dodgers. Born in late 1937, Peter had gone to elementary school at Froebel Academy in Brooklyn, graduating just a few months after Walter took control of the Dodgers. He was the class outstanding athlete. He went to high school at La Salle Military Academy, a Catholic prep school about eight miles east of the Amityville house. There, he played football, basketball, and baseball, where his tall frame led him to the pitcher's mound and first base. He kept an autographed picture of Jackie Robinson in his room.[1] His real interest was on the water, where both Peter and his sister, Terry, were avid sailors, winning trophies in various classes of boats, mostly on the Great South Bay of Long Island, where an inlet lapped at the back of the Amityville house.[2]

It was the spring of his freshman year at La Salle that he first became involved in the business side of the game. His father set him up with a booth at Vero Beach, selling rosters to fans who came to see the workouts. His mother bought the first one. He sold a hundred.[3] At sixteen Peter became a counselor for the Dodgertown Boys Camp held every summer at Dodgertown, specializing in rifle instruction.[4]

Peter followed his father to Penn, majoring in business law and heading up the Phi Gamma Delta fraternity chapter. At least one summer was spent touring Dodger farm clubs from Montreal to Great Falls, Montana. "I've just spent the greatest two weeks of my life studying the Dodgers' farm operation," he said.[5]

In February 1961 Walter was off to Philadelphia to see Peter graduate from the Wharton School.[6] Quickly thereafter, Peter was flying to Vero Beach for his first important assignment, handling all the details of the Yomiuri Giants' spring training visit.[7] Then he spent the summer touring Dodger farm teams.

By October he was back in Vero Beach, where he would run Dodgertown for the next three years. In those years that meant dealing with the city over the lease and the problems with the Federal Aviation Administration. It meant the continuing problems with the deteriorating naval barracks and the host of other issues that went with it. It meant selling advertising for game programs and overseeing a kitchen that served fifteen hundred meals daily. He won the plaudits of the newspaper people for some of the improvements on the old barracks, but they still could make suggestions. "If Peter will place the leg of the chair in the bucket, pack the base with several sticks of dynamite, light the unraveled bamboo and walk away briskly, he will have fulfilled a personal request concerning my quarters," wrote *Herald Examiner* columnist Melvin Durslag.[8]

In early 1965 Peter was named president and general manager in Spokane, the Dodgers' top farm team. It was a very similar routine on a larger scale, and the younger O'Malley did it for two years, taking dates to the top of Mount Spokane. It was not for the view, he said, but because you could pick up radio station KFI, the Dodgers' 50,000-watt clear-channel station for the big club's games.[9] In early 1966 he succeeded his uncle Henry Walsh as corporate secretary and member of the Dodgers' board of directors.[10]

The next year, with Dick Walsh leaving to become commissioner of the North American Soccer League, Peter was promoted to director of stadium operations at Dodger Stadium. The monument to the O'Malleys was now his daily charge. And the goal was making things smooth for two million guests a year—from parking through seating, concessions, maintenance, ushers, souvenirs, scoreboards, and organ music, it all fell under his title.

It was the kind of education Walter wanted for his son. Obviously echoing his father, Peter said, "Very few club owners try to be the baseball brains these days. The successful ones hire baseball men to run that end of it. This is what we have always believed and is the reason we have men like Buzzie Bavasi, Fresco Thompson and Al Campanis running it. This is a pretty big operation, you know. We own our own park, our own airplane, our own training camp and three minor league franchises. Our ticketing, accounting and novelties departments are the biggest in baseball."[11]

Late in 1968 Peter was named executive vice president.[12] Walter said he had intended to step completely aside after his sixty-fifth birthday in October, but the departure of Bavasi for San Diego and the death of Fresco Thompson, Bavasi's replacement, led him to postpone the full move for a year.[13] Peter became president, with Walter moving to chairman of the board, in early 1970.[14]

Baseball people found Peter thoughtful and considerate. He was more deliberate than his father and far more reserved. Walter would try to charm you. Peter would be polite. "Peter is very much like his father philosophically but very different in style and approach. His father operated off one of the great charm supplies I've ever seen. He used wit and whimsy in dealing with people whereas Peter is more restrained, more businesslike. In some ways, Peter is easier to work with. Walter had his pixie side. He enjoyed the oral fencing. He loved to play around with a problem. Peter goes straight at things," said Bowie Kuhn.

Peter's dry humor would come out occasionally, as during one St. Patrick's Day party at Vero Beach when everyone was asked to hug the person sitting next to them. "This is now the Yankees got into trouble," he said. It was just a few days after Yankee pitchers Mike Kekich and Fritz Peterson announced they were swapping wives, children, and dogs.[15]

And he was not above a practical joke, sending then Dodger coach Tommy Lasorda a letter, which contained only page 2 of an apparently longer missive. Page 2 read:

"and the very serious consequences involved. I'm sure
you will agree, Tom, that I had no alternative but to give
them the information that they requested. I certainly
hope this will in no way affect our friendship.
Sincerely,
Peter

Lasorda, in Houston with the team, called Peter in a near panic, only to be told Peter would not be available for some time. When he finally reached Peter at home after the game, the young president just laughed.[16]

In 1971 Peter married Annette Zacho, daughter of the chief surgeon of the Finsen Institute in Copenhagen. She had been educated at various artistic schools in Europe and was working as the costume supervisor and designer for the Copenhagen Royal Theater.[17] An indication of the circles they ran in was they had met at a party at the home of Danish opera tenor Lauritz Melchior.[18]

Peter's coronation reflected three years of steadily increasing responsibility, as Walter handed over more and more of the daily duties to his son. Walter was never far away, always available for advice, and deeply involved in baseball matters at the national level. But, Walter said, "this leaves the old man with more time to play golf."[19]

Indeed, late in life golf had become O'Malley's prime hobby. The design and building of the two golf courses in Vero Beach had stimulated his interest, and he became a regular player. He designed one hole there with two fairways and rough down the middle.[20] "He couldn't play a lick, but he loved it," said Phil Collier, a reporter for the *San Diego Union-Tribune* who covered the Dodgers for their first decade in Los Angeles.[21] He would try to play every day at Vero Beach, and players he enjoyed—Willie Davis, Ron Fairly, Lou Johnson, Jim Lefebvre, and Tommy Lasorda, for example—often played with him. He also played with Peter, other executives, business associates, reporters, and whoever else showed up at spring training.

O'Malley liked to make a little bet and liked to win it. Because it was his course, he could make up the rules and often did so flexibly. He enjoyed a bit of cheating and loved to be called on it, laughingly changed the course rules to suit himself and pocketing a bet or two.[22] Fairly challenged O'Malley to a round one year but found he would be paired with the groundskeeper, while O'Malley got the club professional.[23] O'Malley carefully tracked the tee shots of Jim Mulvey, his co-owner and frequent golf partner and betting victim. When he had a good read on Mulvey's likely landing zone, he put a trap there.[24]

Fishing, which had occupied so much of his time when he lived in Amityville, did not survive the trip to the West Coast, especially after the construction of the Vero Beach golf courses. Vero Beach and Dodger Stadium absorbed his interest in growing things, although he continued to have hothouses for orchids in both Los Angeles and Vero Beach.[25]

His remaining hobby was hunting. He had been shooting in the fall near Rawlins, Wyoming, for a number of years, but his first serious trip came at the end of the 1958 season, when he went to Tanganyika, looking to shoot an elephant.[26] Two days after the 1963 World Series sweep, he and Peter were back in Africa, in Bechuanaland, where the death toll included a near-record sable antelope (Walter), an elephant (Peter), two leopards, a lion, a water buffalo, a gemsbok, and "a wide variety of other antelopes." Peter also collected a number of insects for the Los Angeles County Museum.[27] The next summer Walter was off to northern Norway to shoot a polar bear.[28] The lion's head wound up on the wall of his office, while the polar bear greeted patrons of the Stadium Club.

There was another African trip, this time to Mozambique in 1967, and a tiger hunt in India the next year.[29] In 1969 it was Africa again. O'Malley also extended his interests to dining on his shooting, partnering with some of his Los Angeles hunting cronies, one of whom owned a restaurant specializing in wild game.[30] After Peter's marriage, with a wife who said, "I don't think I could shoot," Peter took down his trophy heads and gave up shooting.[31] With Walter's advancing age and health problems, the hunting trips came to an end.

Not all his new free time as chairman was devoted to play. He had been asked to sit on the boards of Union Bancorp., Knudsen Creamery, and KFI, the Dodgers' radio outlet. He became a trustee of the Leisure World Foundation, the nonprofit arm of various retirement communities around the United States.[32]

His major new activity was more philanthropic. The University of Pennsylvania had sought to cultivate him as a donor for several years, a role he avoided until agreeing to be chairman of the Capital Campaign Committee for Southern California in 1964. Early the following year he was heading a team to represent the university on the CBS *Alumni Fun* show, which pitted teams of graduates against each other in a College Bowl–like format. O'Malley joined Marietta Peabody Tree, the U.S. representative to the United Nations Commission on Human Rights, and Pete Martin, a nationally known writer. They won several rounds of competition before meeting the University of Michigan in the finals.[33]

By the next year he was representing alumni on the school's board of trustees. He would serve there eight years before becoming an emeritus trustee. He started his serious donations to the university right after the 1965 season with a $20,000 check from the Dodgers.[34] By 1971 he was over $50,000, and in the late 1970s he would pledge an additional $100,000, which Peter would pay off in 1985.[35] He was also using his persuasive skills on alumni and other donors. After O'Malley appealed to California cement manufacturer Garner Beckett, Penn's director of alumni relations described the sales pitch as "the greatest I have ever seen."[36]

O'Malley's appearance on *Alumni Fun* was not his only television moment. O'Malley was active in the Bohemian Club, a San Francisco–based club of VIPs. One summer he recruited former Dodger Chuck Connors, by then a star of television westerns, to perform "Casey at the Bat" for the Bohemians. Connors had performed it several times at Vero Beach during his Dodger career. Connors agreed to do it if O'Malley would make a cameo appearance on his current show, *Branded*. O'Malley agreed, and in August 1965 he spent a day on the set to play Doc O'Malley, a country doctor who treats a gunshot wound for Connors. He had a couple of lines, hammed it up a bit, and donated his $300 check to the Motion Picture Relief Fund. It was the minimum, and Connors said that was right because that's all the Dodgers ever paid him.[37]

O'Malley's routine was strenuous through the 1960s. He got up at six, was at his Dodger Stadium desk at nine, and, if there was a night game, stayed until late in the evening. "I notice that when the president of the Dodgers comes to work at 9 a.m., the rest of the staff tends to do the same," he said.[38] He did not need more than a few hours of sleep and would stay up late reading an eclectic mix of tomes, issues of *National Geographic*, Damon Runyon, and murder mysteries, especially those starring Nero Wolfe, a detective of enormous girth, gourmet tastes, and an orchid fetish.[39] His reading left him with a wide range of facts at hand, from the best way of controlling gophers to Mayan figurines that resembled baseball players.[40]

His weight was up, the jowls were prominent, the suits were conservative, although he retained the military school habit of putting a bright shine on his shoes. In spring training his dress got quirkier, reflecting the liberation he felt at Vero Beach. In 1966 he sported a Twins cap (to celebrate the previous year's World Series win) and a Tokyo Giants jacket.[41] The next season, after the Baltimore Orioles swept the Dodgers in the World Series, O'Malley's cap featured a black band sent to him by Orioles' owner Jerry Hoffberger.[42] The cigar was ever present, usually an Antonio y Cleopatra, but sometimes a Bock. It was a pointer, a wand, a punctuation mark whenever he was speaking.

For all who came in contact with her, Kay O'Malley was the great humanizer of her husband. She was unfailingly polite, gracious, and a reminder to everyone of the softer side of her often intimidating husband. The Dodgers' plane, in its various configurations, was named the *Kay O'*, and O'Malley took his 1955 World Series ring and had it turned into a charm with a gold heart on top and "You Gotta Have Heart," the title of Kay's favorite song, engraved on it. "Kay spent a lifetime making people feel that Walter must be okay to have a wife such as her," wrote Walter's nemesis, Dick Young.[43]

In Los Angeles she was an active fan who kept her own scorecard for every game, even those she listened to on the radio. And she made more road trips than Walter, using the New York trips to see old friends. She was deeply involved with Terry's ten children and, a decade later, Peter's two.[44] She served on the board of the Los Angeles Orphanage Guild, was a founding member of the Music Center, and was a sponsor of the Civic Light Opera, all activities that led to her being named *Los Angeles Times*'s Woman of the Year in 1971.[45]

In her new city she had learned to drive and to love the flexibility it gave her. Bump Holman, who had helped her learn to drive, called her "Barney Oldfield," after the early-twentieth-century race car driver.[46] There were daily drives to Sierra Madre to see the Seidler grandkids (they called her Kay-Kay) and trips to various outer suburbs to see friends or take out-of-town visitors to the tourist attractions. There was the main house in the Hancock Park neighborhood a bit west of downtown Los Angeles, as well as the Lake Arrowhead house, where she could retreat on a summer day. "God has been very good to me. I have lived a full life. That's due to my husband, of course," she told one interviewer. "My life is my church, my family, my friends, and baseball."[47]

His Catholicism was also a big part of O'Malley's life, although he made few public mentions of it. His first act on getting out of bed was to light a cigarette, but his second was to get on his knees to say his morning prayers.[48] Sunday mass was always part of the schedule. Whereas Kay was active in the Mary and Joseph League, Walter showed his devotion in other ways. There was the annual Nuns Day at Dodger Stadium and favors such as using the Dodger plane to fly forty-four priests to Notre Dame for the 1958 Fighting Irish game against Army.[49] He could also reflect his views in public speeches, as when he told the National Association of Counties that it was "too bad" there was no prayer in the public schools."[50]

He struck up a relationship with James Francis McIntyre, the archbishop of Los Angeles, with whom he shared much. McIntyre was New York Irish who had wanted to become a priest but needed to secure his family's financial future first. He went to work in banking and finance, made the money, and then entered the seminary. As a priest the training he had received on

Wall Street led him quickly to one of the country's fastest-growing regions, where the need for new parish churches and schools called for a fund-raiser who knew how to spend judiciously. O'Malley, who was a regular donor, found McIntyre was also a baseball fan who had met Babe Ruth and could recite statistics from the 1930s.[51]

The O'Malleys did not live up to their means, but they definitely lived well. The houses were large and in expensive neighborhoods. Extended hunting trips to Africa and India were not cheap. The family income could be extended by using team assets for food, drink, and entertainment. And some of their travel could be done on the corporate plane. It could also be used for the kind of gesture that employees who felt underpaid noted. One spring O'Malley was hosting a large party when the vermouth ran out. The group was at Bud Holman's hunting lodge in the boondocks, forty miles from Vero Beach. A call was made, and the martini ingredient was flown in.[52]

Peter's training would prove to be a fine investment. His eternal emphasis, reflecting the jobs he held on the way up, was marketing and customer service.[53] Peter loved promotions. He started autograph signings every Sunday. There were giveaways several nights every week. Helmet Day became Helmet Weekend. The results were impressive. The Dodgers set new Major League single-season attendance records in 1977 and 1978, when they were the first team to surpass 3 million. They did it again in 1982, setting a record that stood for eleven years. The Dodgers remained the model franchise as people looked around baseball.[54] But possibly in reaction to his father's dominance, or because of his own low-key and less imaginative style, Peter would never have the kind of influence in baseball's upper circles that his father had.

17

Marvin Miller and
Andy Messersmith

One issue loomed over all others as Walter O'Malley moved from president to chairman of the Dodgers. While Peter was left to run the team, Walter continued to serve on the Major League Baseball Executive Council and to deal with the owners' most crucial issue—its relationship with the Major League Baseball Players Association. In the owners' councils, O'Malley would play a moderating role, seeking accommodation with the players. But the practices on his own team would play a major role in the rise of the union and the breaking of the reserve clause.

O'Malley's first brush with what would become union matters had come in 1953, and it had not gone well. At that time the players had a loose system of representation, with each team choosing a player representative and those players choosing a league representative. The two league representatives would deal with the owners and commissioner on baseball-wide matters. In 1953 the players made proposals for increases in the minimum salary and improvements in the pension plan.[1] In addition, they hired a lawyer, J. Norman Lewis, to give them advice, a move resented by owners and some players.[2] Giving in to his pixieish side, O'Malley suggested that if there was going to be any increase in the minimum, the players ought to agree to a maximum as well. "This is not the time for the players to tamper with the subject," he said condescendingly.[3]

As the summer went on confusion set in. In late September the executive council met with Lewis and player representatives Allie Reynolds of the American League and Ralph Kiner of the National League. They discussed possible improvements in the pension plan and agreed to look into new ways of organizing and funding it. As the winter meetings approached, Frick invited the players to meet with him about the pension, but then balked when they showed up with Lewis. Frick said he wanted to talk with

the player representatives because the owners were going to consider a resolution at their meeting to get rid of the pension plan entirely. Moreover, he
said, Reynolds, Kiner, and Lewis had approved this resolution at the late-
September meeting.[4] That started a furor. Kiner and Reynolds denied they
had approved any such thing.[5] Frick said the players' proposal was a huge
increase, and the highly pro-owner *Sporting News* turned his statement
into the screaming headline "$7,580,000 Cost Hike Threatens Pension."[6]

The tensions dissipated only when Walter O'Malley took one for the
team. O'Malley had been an author of the late-September resolution, and
he said the proper wording had gotten lost in the process of having lawyers
write the final version. The original resolution called for a committee of
one owner from each league to study ways of improving the plan. According to O'Malley, the original wording had included a preamble saying that
if a way to improve the current plan could be found and implemented
immediately, then the existing plan would be terminated. This was the
version Kiner, Reynolds, and Lewis had agreed to. However, the version
the owners voted to adopt called for "terminating the major league baseball players annuity and insurance plan" due to "excessive demands of the
player representatives and their attorney." In reality, there was no intention
to get rid of the pension plan, O'Malley said.[7] As convoluted as that explanation sounded, the pension plan did survive. So did the players' skepti-
cism. A few months later they formed the Major League Baseball Players
Association, adopted by-laws and a constitution, and hired Lewis as an
adviser for $30,000 a year.[8]

A decade later the players were still focused almost exclusively on the
pension, but the rising tide of national television contracts moved them to
find a full-time executive director. The new generation of players was also
more inclined to question other ways in which they were treated.

Owners and general managers tended to take a patriarchal, condescending
attitude toward players. There were differences of age, education, experience, and wealth. There were the handful of players on every team who did
not know how to manage their money or their appetites. They had to be
loaned money, bailed out of jail, or provided with lawyers. The players, in
general, came and went. The executives and the owners stayed on.

When Koufax and Drysdale staged their joint holdout in 1966, Bavasi
and O'Malley consistently referred to them as "boys," as in "they're good
boys."[9] Koufax was thirty and Drysdale twenty-nine. They knew how to

manage their money and their lives, but they were still physically talented "boys" in the eyes of the front office.

Bavasi, as with other general managers, would tell the players that it was bad practice to tell reporters what was going on during salary negotiations. Then the player would see details known only to himself and Bavasi show up in the newspapers. When Koufax retired Drysdale dated the left hander's disenchantment to early 1964. Koufax was reported asking for a $90,000 salary, when he had actually asked for $70,000. Although the Dodger official quoted in the story was Bavasi, Koufax thought O'Malley was behind it.[10] That same spring Frank Howard exploded when his contract details showed up in the papers.[11]

It was not as if Bavasi was unique among general managers. In fact, he was generally very well liked by the players for a host of small generosities. He did bail the childish out of jail or other troubles. He would give a player $50 or $100 and tell him to go out and have a good time. He gave veterans such as Don Zimmer and Gil Hodges their choice of what teams to go to as their careers wound down.

Bavasi had certainly grown into a baseball force of his own, a name consistently dropped when league presidencies or the Commissioner's Office was open. "Bavasi was one of baseball's free spirits," said Bowie Kuhn. "He had a catlike ability to spring over, around, and under our rules. He knew where all the bodies were buried, and more often than not, who had put them there."[12]

What was unique was Bavasi's brazenness. Bavasi prided himself on his manipulative abilities. In salary negotiations he liked the fake-contract trick. He would have a contract for Player X made up, leave it on top of his desk, and then have himself called out of his office while talking with Player Y. Player X was chosen because he was better than Player Y, and the phony salary was chosen because it was less than Player Y was asking for. The idea, which Bavasi said worked all the time, was that Player Y would recalculate based on the phony figure and accept something in the range Bavasi was offering.

In May 1967, just as Marvin Miller was settling into his new job as executive director of the players association, *Sports Illustrated* began a four-part series under Bavasi's byline. It was full of stories of his triumphs over the years and included extensive material on salary negotiations and other ways of manipulating players, including the fake-contract trick and the names of players in other scams. "As far as I'm concerned, anything goes at salary time," Bavasi wrote.[13] Miller had the series copied and sent to every team's player representative, encouraging them to make sure all the players saw it.[14]

Marvin Miller was not what baseball was used to, and the owners were not at all prepared for what he was.[15] Miller was a bit short, with limited use of his right shoulder due to an injury during birth. He was an intellectual liberal with a career as a union economist and negotiator. He was Jewish. And he had a trim black mustache that seemed to scream "con man" to a baseball world that universally eschewed facial hair. "I'm a prime subject for characterization," he conceded. "My clothes, for example, range from nondescript to below average. I've never owned a monogrammed shirt. I take the subway to work. If my mustache makes me look like some kind of slicker, I can't shave it off. I had it when I married my wife 35 years ago and she refuses to live with an unfamiliar face."[16]

To the owners Miller quickly became a bogeyman. He kept objecting to their practices, pointing out their violations of their own rules, and arguing for a bigger piece of the pie. He won a basic agreement to cover the player-owner relationship and then used it to begin filing numerous grievances over the quality of hotels, buses, and locker rooms; the delayed payment of meal money; or the rules governing the transfer of players back to the Minors.

The owners, stuck in the "boy" mode of player treatment, calculated all these changes were Miller's ideas. "He speaks only for a few rabble-rousers and greedy ball players," said Paul Richards, then an executive vice president of the Braves.[17] It took them years to realize that Miller was not so much leading the players by the nose as educating them on the possibilities. When he started the players association was focused almost completely on the pension, and Miller's first big victory in the players' eyes was making gains there. But, soon, his steady winning record on the small irritations of life on the road gave him immense credibility.

He encouraged the players to attend bargaining sessions and then explained to them the owners' tactics. He made sure they saw owners' and executives' disparaging remarks about them. As with the Bavasi articles in *Sports Illustrated*, he made sure they saw how they were being manipulated.

He was met in the baseball press with resentment and derision based on their close relationship with owners. Bob Hunter of the *Los Angeles Herald Examiner*, the dean of Los Angeles baseball writers during the 1960s and 1970s, started off feeling Miller was an "imposter." But, Hunter said, over the years of dealing with him, and watching him win, you came to an appreciation, especially as a newsman. "He had the facts, and he never lied to you."[18]

Marvin Miller developed a strong relationship with O'Malley. One spring in the late 1960s, Miller got complaints from Dodger players about souvenir glasses sold at concession stands. The glasses had the players' images frosted on, but the players were not getting a cut of the profit. When Miller went to talk, O'Malley twirled his cigar and pointed out the standard player contract allowed them to use player images for promotional purposes. Miller countered that the player had the right to control his own image and that the glasses were a profit-making venture, not publicity. As he related the story, Miller clearly was recalling the cut-and-thrust between two New York boys. "I enjoyed our whole relationship," he said. O'Malley conceded nothing in the conversation, but did stop selling the glasses.[19] "He is the one baseball owner I respect," Miller said. "O'Malley is a hard, realistic businessman who is part of this century and who does not pretend baseball is something it isn't."[20]

In the years the players association was establishing itself, O'Malley was not always supportive or realistic. When some players questioned the national television contract that forced NBC to continue the "Game of the Week" package, some players felt that was a ploy for moving money out of the All-Star Game and World Series part of the package, which provided money for the pension program, into the "Game of the Week" part, which provided them with no benefits. O'Malley suggested that Miller was the cause of the agitation.[21] He brushed off an early proposal for collecting union dues.[22]

But early on he also appreciated the benefits of what a union could offer. There was one place to go to talk over a problem and to find a resolution that the union would be willing to enforce.[23] When baseball won the new television package, Miller asked to see the financial details, as the players' pension plan was financed from these revenues. The other owners balked, arguing it was their money and the funds for the pension plan were their largesse. O'Malley acknowledged the players would need to see the details, and when the owners finally agreed to a payroll check-off system for association dues, O'Malley got Miller to the side and told him that if there were any problems working out the details with Bowie Kuhn, then the National League's attorney and not yet the commissioner, Miller should give him a call. There were difficulties. Miller called. Kuhn called back "as nice as pie," said Miller.

O'Malley also developed a positive relationship with the most militant of the Dodgers' player representatives—relief pitcher Mike Marshall. Marshall had become the Dodgers' player representative within months of joining the team in 1974.[24] He had long been a committed and outspoken union member. He was a man of iconoclastic beliefs, somewhere beyond the edges of both the Right and the Left; no one could quite figure out which. Marvin Miller encouraged his outbursts during negotiating sessions with the owners because he made Miller look exceptionally moderate. Marshall described his role as "outrageous point man" who was "amazed that so many people took me seriously."[25]

He did take his role as player representative seriously, but said he never had to file a grievance while he was with the Dodgers. He would bring an issue to the attention of Al Campanis or Walter O'Malley, and it would be solved.[26] For example, the Dodgers stopped ordering players to make personal appearances after a Marshall complaint.

Eventually, Marshall and O'Malley developed what amounted to a friendship. Marshall was well educated, working on his PhD. Some days O'Malley would have a message left in Marshall's locker, asking him to drop by. The conversation would range over a wide area, Marshall said. Sometimes the topics could be baseball related, as when Marshall proposed the owners pay a fixed percentage of income to the players association, which would then parcel it out along a bell-shaped curve. O'Malley liked the idea, and they spent a long time discussing it. Marshall felt a similar and later salary-structure proposal from Ray Grebey, the owners' negotiator, came to the bargaining table through O'Malley.

Other times the topics could be more personal, such as Marshall's studies in graduate school or his plans after his playing career. Marshall also developed a friendship with Kay O'Malley. In the spring of 1979, with Kay very sick and O'Malley feeling his mortality, he asked Marshall to drop by for a last talk. "He just wanted to chat, say goodbye," Marshall said.

Marshall was an exception, for O'Malley generally kept his distance from the players. "I always thought he regarded them as obstreperous children, fiscally irresponsible, functionally illiterate and as ineducable and temperamental as horses. He trusted his underlings [Thompson and Bavasi] to keep them in line," wrote Jim Murray.[27] At the Vero Beach St. Patrick's Day parties, players were not invited, except to show off musical skills. Those parties were not for the "boys." They were for "adults"—office and stadium staff, managers, coaches, scouts, visiting baseball people, business associates, Vero Beach residents, and friends and spouses of same. With the completion of Dodgertown's golf courses, O'Malley added a tournament to the day's festivities, and players were allowed to participate.

John Gaherin was the experienced labor negotiator hired by the owners and given the thankless task of educating them about the realities of labor unions and the laws designed to protect them. To him, O'Malley was the man he wished the other owners would listen to more often.[28] For many of the owners, their baseball team was a side business, a toy that gave them the adult perks of a boyhood passion. Successful, rich, they saw themselves as benevolent nobles paying boys immense amounts of money to play a game they were not talented enough to play themselves. Gussie Busch, owner of the Cardinals, and Bob Howsam, president of the Reds, were personally affronted at the way Miller and the player representatives questioned their policies and proposed changes.[29] They often saw confrontations as manliness issues that had to be resisted at all costs.

O'Malley, as always, was a businessman. He wanted his players happy and focused on winning. When strike talk threatened spring training in 1969, he offered to fly players to Vero Beach and let them use the Dodger golf course for free until the issue was settled. They could use Vero Beach High School for workouts, he suggested.[30] When he saw a spring training strike in 1972 heading toward opening day, his mind turned to a simple calculation. If the season were to be delayed a further eight days, he would save about $30,000 in player salaries. At the same time, he would lose close to $600,000 in revenue.[31] He did whine about the increased cost, but, as Miller phrased it, "O'Malley could see the train coming and knew when to move."[32]

The 1972 strike was a pivotal year for O'Malley. As the issues coalesced Miller said he was surprised to find the Dodger owner was not as realistic as at other times. "I got this condescendingly tut-tut, there-there business" from O'Malley, he said.[33] To Miller the issues presented that year were a relatively minor increase in pension benefits, much of which could be financed by the fund's surplus.[34] To the likes of Busch and Howsam, the issue was not the pension funds, but whether the players would listen to Marvin Miller or to them.

To the players this was not a real question. Miller had already won their trust through six years of small but steady victories over the owners. Unlike general managers in salary negotiations, he told the truth. Miller said years later that he himself was surprised at the players' militancy that year. He counseled against a strike. He drafted a statement backing down. The players pushed him into it.[35]

It took O'Malley a while to perceive the players' unity and militancy, partly because the Dodgers' player representative, Wes Parker, was one of the players least sympathetic to the union. Once O'Malley did catch on, and the strike began to approach opening day, he began to appreciate the potential financial costs of a strike. By the end he was concerned about what the strike revealed about his team. Three other Dodger players joined Parker in voting against the strike, out of only ten players total nationwide. O'Malley asked Miller who the four were. Miller said he did not know and would not tell O'Malley if he did. Miller asked why O'Malley wanted to know. "I don't want dissenters on my club opposing their teammates," Miller quoted O'Malley as saying. By the end of the 1972 season, Parker and the three others were gone.[36]

O'Malley's health contributed to a weaker voice on labor issues during these years. During the 1970 negotiations O'Malley had to send Peter to an owners meeting because he was still recovering from an abdominal operation.[37] In 1972 O'Malley spent the first ten days of the strike at the Mayo Clinic, as Kay underwent gallbladder surgery.[38] When the owners tried a lockout during spring training of 1976, O'Malley was in the hotel where negotiations were taking place, but, according to Miller, never left his room. "You knew he was there," Miller said with a smile.[39] And, soon, everyone else did too. When Bowie Kuhn announced the lockout would be ended and spring training camps would open, enraging the hard-line owners, the accepted wisdom was that O'Malley had told him to do so.[40]

If Kuhn was listening, it is not clear the other owners were paying as much attention. Peter Bavasi, who entered the owners' councils in the mid-1970s, said O'Malley's declining health contributed to his declining influence.[41] Longtime sportswriter Harold Rosenthal felt the distractions of his own and Kay's health were "worth ten lawyers and a couple of arbitrators to the Players Association."[42] Although O'Malley could still play an important role in helping Gaherin convince the other owners to accept salary arbitration, the challenges to his leadership were growing.[43]

The 1972 strike also changed perceptions among the players. Although the financial stakes had been small, it affirmed they could win if they remained united. Now, they could move on to the central issue—the reserve clause. But first Miller had to deal with what he thought was a losing tactic and a distraction.

The reserve clause, in some form, had existed since the 1870s. By the 1970s the standard player contract contained a clause that said if a player had not signed a new contract by March 11, the team could renew his old one for a year. This "reserved" his services for the team. The owners' position was that the renewal incorporated the entire contract, including the provision about renewal, making it in essence eternal. Miller's position was that one year meant one year, and he felt he was well backed by a series of labor-law rulings.[44]

One player, on his own, decided to do something about it. In 1969 outfielder Curt Flood had been traded from the St. Louis Cardinals to the Philadelphia Phillies. He did not want to go from the top of the league to the bottom. And, with the civil rights movement in full flower, the African American Flood did not want to be treated as property. He sued, seeking an injunction against the reserve clause and using words such as *slavery*. He asked the court to remove baseball's exemption from the antitrust laws, which allowed the owners to act as a cartel to limit players' freedom. The exemption from the antitrust laws was a half century old by then, and the Supreme Court had reaffirmed the exemption in the early 1950s.

Flood went to the players association for support, which it gave, despite Miller's conviction Flood would lose. But Miller was also concerned that poor representation might result in a verdict that would put the association in a weaker position.[45] So Miller had the association hire former Supreme Court justice Arthur Goldberg to argue Flood's case. Kuhn felt it necessary to send his choice for baseball's lawyer to be vetted by O'Malley.[46] In the end Miller was right. When the Supreme Court's decision was handed down in June 1972, they stayed with precedent, upholding the antitrust exemption while noting it made little legal sense and throwing any potential change into the laps of Congress.

Miller was now free to turn to his preferred tactic for overthrowing the reserve clause. And he was to do it in a changing psychological environment for the players. Although Flood's suit had been a legal dead end, it was an inspiration to the players, who knew Flood was throwing away a lucrative career. Just two years later a more mundane inspiration came to the players from Charlie Finley and Jim "Catfish" Hunter.

Finley owned the Oakland Athletics, was a thorn in the side of Bowie Kuhn (and many others), and was running a highly successful franchise on a shoestring.[47] Hunter was his All-Star pitcher. Finley and Hunter agreed on a $100,000 contract for 1974, and Finley agreed to pay half of that amount into an annuity that would mature for Hunter after his career was over. Finley then failed to make the annuity payments. As the 1974 World Series began, Hunter's agent revealed the pitcher would file a grievance seeking free agency because Finley had failed to fulfill the contract. On December 16 of that year the arbitrator ruled in Hunter's favor, and barely two weeks later he signed a five-year contract with the Yankees worth around $3.75 million.[48] Although Hunter's situation had no legal ramifications for other players, the financial possibilities of free agency were now clear.

Miller had been working on his tactic for three years at this point. From previous experience with labor contract law, he was confident an arbitrator would accept the association's argument that "one year" in the reserve clause meant just that. What he needed was a player who would be willing to refuse to sign a new contract, play a season with a contract renewed under the reserve clause, and then take his case to the arbitrator.

Every year beginning in 1972 at least one player began the year with a renewed contract. Through 1974 none of them made it to arbitration. The owners simply threw piles of money at the player as the deadline approached. In 1972 it was Cardinals catcher Ted Simmons who asked for $30,000. In the end he got a two-year contract for $40,000 and $45,000.[49] In 1973 Stan Bahnsen, Dick Billings, Mike Andrews, Rick Reichardt, and Jerry Kenney all started the season with renewed contracts. Kenney was released. The others signed. In 1974 it was two big names—Sparky Lyle and Bobby Tolan. Lyle signed in September. Tolan went all the way to scheduling a December arbitration hearing.[50] Just as Hunter was being declared a free agent, Tolan signed when other owners leaned very hard on Buzzie Bavasi, Tolan's boss in San Diego.[51] The grievance was withdrawn soon thereafter.[52] In talking to reporters, and in arguing in court, the owners consistently stuck to the line that the ever-renewing one-year provision of the reserve clause was perfectly legal. But their actions, as with Simmons, indicated they knew otherwise.

As early as the 1890s John Ward, a dominant player of the era who became a lawyer, sought to challenge the reserve clause. But the owners recognized his intent and dodged court.[53] In 1910 the *Washington Post* could note that the clause was unenforceable because it lacked the basic legal principle of "mutuality," where a contract should offer something to both parties.[54]

When John Gaherin first read the reserve clause, his immediate interpretation was the same as Marvin Miller's. Later, talking to Lou Carroll, a retired attorney known in baseball circles as "the Wise Man," he asked about the players association bringing it up in court or arbitration. "Don't ever let them try that renewal clause," Carroll advised.[55] In one of his business law classes at the University of Pennsylvania, Peter O'Malley had been told the reserve clause would not hold up in court.[56]

The tactics could not work forever, and O'Malley and the Dodgers were at the center of the denouement. The player at the front was Andy Messersmith. Messersmith came with some history that was not appreciated at the time. He had attended the University of California. Jocks such as Messersmith were not as likely to demonstrate or campaign as the campus radicals, but he had been exposed to the ideas percolating through Berkeley in the 1960s. He had endured the normal indignities of the Minor League system. And when he reached the Majors and had some success, he ran smack into the nasty realities of Major League contract negotiations.

After an excellent season in 1969 with the Angels, Messersmith had slumped in 1970. He went into contract talks with general manager Dick Walsh, who had trained under Buzzie Bavasi with the Dodgers. Walsh, however, had little of the charm or the gift for small favors that made Bavasi a player favorite. When Messersmith balked at Walsh's offer, the "Smiling Python" said he had had detectives watching Messersmith on the road and was prepared to share the results with Mrs. Messersmith.[57] The pitcher was outraged and demanded to be traded. Two years later he was.

Messersmith had outstanding seasons in 1973 and 1974. He wanted a raise from the $90,000 he had made in 1974. Somewhere early in the negotiation process, Dodger general manager Al Campanis said something personal that infuriated Messersmith, and he refused to talk to him anymore. The talks moved to the desk of Peter O'Malley, and Messersmith added a demand for a no-trade clause. He had grown up in Southern California and preferred to stay there. Also, he did not want to be at the mercy of Campanis. Peter O'Malley said the Dodgers did not give no-trade clauses. And there it stood. "I never went into this for the glory and betterment of the Players Association. Al Campanis had stirred my anger, and it became a pride issue. When I get stubborn, I get very stubborn," Messersmith said. As the 1975 season progressed, and the five other renewed players signed or were released, Messersmith began to have regular talks with Miller and began to see the broader perspective.[58] The Dodgers' offer was up to $540,000 over three years, but they still were not willing to give a no-trade clause and were being lobbied by National League president Chub Feeney and others to hold fast. Messersmith had also become close with Mike Marshall, who had joined the Dodgers in 1974. At first the bond was pitching, but as Messersmith's free-agency move advanced, Marshall's other roles began to increase.[59]

On October 15, 1975, Messersmith filed a grievance asking to be declared a free agent.[60] Two days before Christmas the arbitration panel freed Messersmith from the reserve clause. The owners fired the neutral arbitrator. Despite a basic agreement that said the arbitration process was binding, they then sued in federal district court (where they lost), took it to the U.S. District Court of Appeals (where they lost again), and then locked the players out of spring training for a while.[61] On March 22 O'Malley stood up before an owners meeting and told his colleagues the Dodgers would not be bidding on any free agents. The message to be received was that they should not either.[62] Miller immediately threatened a grievance charging conspiracy.[63] O'Malley's message did not get through to new owners willing to spend money to win. Messersmith soon signed a three-year $1 million contract with the Atlanta Braves.[64]

That is the standard story of the death of the reserve clause, but it misses an important wrinkle as far as Walter O'Malley was concerned. Messersmith was clearly a talent that any baseball team would want, but legally he was just another player. In fact, there was another player. Dave McNally had fashioned a stellar career with the Baltimore Orioles. But as his performance faded, he was traded to the Montreal Expos. He did not sign a 1975 contract, but did pitch through the first two months of the season, before retiring in June.[65] Because of his contract situation, Miller recognized McNally had the same legal potential as Messersmith, and he found McNally was willing to play the role.[66] McNally was disturbed by some promises he felt the Expos had not kept, and he resented the way he and other young players had been treated over the years.[67] McNally filed his grievance the same time as Messersmith.[68]

McNally was done as a player. He knew it. The Expos knew it. But in November Expos general manager John McHale showed up in McNally's hometown of Billings, Montana. He said he just happened to be passing through a town few but the residents visit in the winter months. He offered McNally a two-year contract. It was clear to McNally that the offer was in effect a bribe to undermine his grievance, and he declined to sign.

In the end Walter O'Malley left it up to the arbitrator. Charles Korr, in his history of the players association, argues that O'Malley understood the risk of going to arbitration with Messersmith and decided to take it.[69] Bowie Kuhn, in his memoirs, says O'Malley was willing to head off the grievance by granting the no-trade clause, but that the owners' player-relations committee talked him out of it.[70] Miller believes that O'Malley's influence was so strong he could have ignored the player-relations committee had he chosen to do so.[71]

To look at it from O'Malley's viewpoint, McNally's participation, and his rejection of McHale's offer, made it a different game. He might have been able to change Messersmith's mind with a no-trade clause, but he could not influence McNally, who had no interest in staying in baseball as a manager, coach, scout, or anything else. Even assuming O'Malley could have bought out Messersmith, McNally was going to break the reserve clause. So, from O'Malley's perspective, there was no need to break a team policy on no-trade clauses.

There is also the possibility Walter O'Malley knew re-signing Messersmith would not be a good deal from a purely baseball perspective. In the early months of 1975, as Messersmith sorted through offers on a new contract, a story began to circulate, attributed to "two scouts," who said Messersmith's shoulder was shot. Miller, hearing the rumors and thinking they were another attempt by the owners to minimize the financial impact of free agency, called Al Campanis. The Dodger general manager said Messersmith, who made forty starts in 1975 without missing a turn and won nineteen games for a mediocre team, was just fine. The team had never asked him to have a physical, Campanis told Miller.[72]

Mike Marshall told a different story. As he became closer to Messersmith, they began to talk about Marshall's theories of pitching mechanics. Marshall was completing his doctorate in kinesiology at Michigan State University. After the 1974 season Messersmith went with Marshall to the laboratory in Lansing for X-rays and other tests. The results led Marshall to tell Messersmith the end was near and he should be looking for that last big contract.[73] Marshall said he never mentioned the tests to the Dodgers, but Messersmith's career after free agency never approached the quality of his earlier years.

O'Malley's last muscle-flexing in baseball's ownerdom came in the wake of the Messersmith decision. The loss of the reserve clause enraged traditionalist owners such as Gussie Busch, and it spurred Charlie Finley to make another rational economic decision that flew in the face of Bowie Kuhn's vision of the game and the commissioner's powers.

Charlie Finley of the Oakland Athletics cottoned to the new world faster than his brethren. Virtually all of the stars of his 1972–74 World Series winners refused to sign 1976 contracts. They would get a lot more money out of either Finley or some other team. Finley did not want to pay the higher prices and knew he would get nothing in return for free agents. So he started to deal. Reggie Jackson and Ken Holtzman were traded just before opening day. Finley then got on the phone to other American League general managers. On June 14, with the trading deadline of the time looming, Finley sold Joe Rudi and Rollie Fingers to the Boston Red Sox for $1 million apiece and Vida Blue to the Yankees for $1.5 million.

The sales did not take place in a political vacuum. Kuhn and Finley had already clashed over various Finley antics, and O'Malley had had to save Kuhn's job over a recent tiff. In 1975 Kuhn had been due for reelection at an owners meeting in Milwaukee. Each league needed a 75 percent vote (nine of twelve owners) for reelection. The National League (12–0) was no problem, but when Gussie Busch of the Cardinals asked for acclamation, Charlie Finley cut him short. The Oakland owner said he had four anti-Kuhn votes in the American League. They were Finley, who had fought with Kuhn over, among other matters, Finley's treatment of Mike Andrews during the 1973 World Series; the Yankees' George Steinbrenner, whom Kuhn had suspended after a conviction for illegal campaign contributions; the Baltimore Orioles' Jerry Hoffberger, who felt Kuhn was just one more cause of the owners continuing to lose fights to the union; and Brad Corbett, new owner of the Texas Rangers. The meetings broke up for the day, and Kuhn retired to an uncertain evening.

At six the next morning he got a call from O'Malley, telling him not to worry. The Dodgers' owner had figured out that Corbett's vote was based on advice from Bob Short, the Rangers' previous owner, who had clashed with Kuhn over the commissioner's unsuccessful attempt to keep Short from moving his Washington Senators to Dallas–Fort Worth, where they had become the Rangers. O'Malley tracked down Corbett at a Florida hotel, discussed the situation with him, and persuaded him to support Kuhn.[74]

Now, a year later, Kuhn did not like Finley's sales and sought the advice of the executive council, which split, with O'Malley, Edmund Fitzgerald of the Milwaukee Brewers, and John Fetzer of the Detroit Tigers arguing for cancellation, while the two league presidents suggested letting the matter pass untouched. "You must not allow this to happen. You have to turn it down," O'Malley was quoted as saying.[75] Kuhn's and O'Malley's critics interpreted this quotation as an order to Kuhn, whereas it could easily be interpreted as the forceful conclusion to an argument. In the event the argument was persuasive or the order was heard. In his announcement of the cancellation, Kuhn said he was concerned that major pieces of the Athletics, who had just won five consecutive division titles, including three World Series, were being sold off for cash, with A's fans left holding the bag.[76]

Charlie Finley called Kuhn "the village idiot" and sued him for $10 million. O'Malley spent considerable time on the stand during the trial, mostly being disingenuous. Asked by Finley's attorney if he had ever recommended specific actions to Kuhn, O'Malley said, "I've been careful over the years with Commissioner Kuhn not to recommend anything. He's not the kind of commissioner you can tell what to do." However, after twenty-five years on the executive council, he knew its role was to give advice and make recommendations to the commissioner. The court came down on Kuhn's side, saying that baseball's rules clearly gave Kuhn the authority to block the sales.

O'Malley was showing his personal conservatism and the more general inability of Kuhn and the owners to recognize the reality, and the potential, of the free-agent era. Finley understood it immediately, but it took the other owners years to catch on to the tactic of selling or trading players on the verge of free agency to get something in return. It would also take a decade for them to realize that a player who won a salary decision in arbitration could be released if the team felt that player was simply not worth what the arbitrator had awarded.

There remained the much more important question of what system could replace the reserve clause, as both the player-relations committee and the players association tried to formulate a position. In their intransigence the owners decided to lock the players out of spring training to gain leverage in their negotiations. That worked only until mid-March, when O'Malley persuaded Kuhn to open the camps. He knew Miller held all the cards in designing any new system and he might as well start making money.[77]

Miller knew his victory had been so complete, he would need to give something back. He also understood the basic economics of scarcity. If every player was a free agent every year, the market would be flooded and prices kept down. Again, it was Charlie Finley who understood the new world and proposed just such a thing. Miller said he held his breath. Fortunately for the players, Finley's reputation was such that none of the other owners joined him. Eventually, Miller, Gaherin, and their groups fashioned an agreement that would give clubs control over the first six years of a Major League career.

The owners still could not accept the new world. Their response was to fire Gaherin, the man who had been giving them good advice for years. Instead, they hired Ray Grebey, who would do no better. But before Grebey got going he was sent to see Walter O'Malley. O'Malley showed Grebey his secret cache of now-forbidden cigars and then proceeded to lay out the personality type, finances, and tendencies of every other owner. "He was one hundred percent right one hundred percent of the time," Grebey said later.[78]

18

Bottom of the Ninth

The lack of energy and focus that at times inhibited Walter O'Malley's participation in the battle with the Major League Baseball Players Association was a sign the engine was running down. For much of his adult life, O'Malley had been battling medical problems, especially in his intestinal system, although the details released to the public were incomplete and vague. In early 1958 an operation to remove an intestinal polyp kept him in the hospital for a month. That situation was probably complicated by the broken ankle that had brought him to the hospital in the first place and by overwork attendant to setting up the Dodgers in Los Angeles.[1] In late 1959 Branch Rickey said O'Malley had "become huge and fat and does not apparently care too much because he thinks that this is some kind of protection against his abdominal ailment which has on one or two occasions given him considerable concern."[2]

Within a few years he was having an annual checkup at the Mayo Clinic in Rochester MN, a habit that was passed to Peter and eventually made a benefit for other top executives.[3] After their deaths the clinic would name its student-faculty lounge in honor of Walter and Kay, who had become donors as well as patients.[4] In early 1964 what was originally described as hernia surgery kept him in the hospital for ten days afterward.[5] He missed the first month of the season that year but was soon off to Norway to hunt polar bears.

In the summer of 1967 Alan Bussey of the Penn fund-raising staff wrote home from Vero Beach that O'Malley had been "quite ill" for the entire week Bussey was in Los Angeles. The next spring he was hit twice by viruses.[6]

As O'Malley passed the daily management to Peter and settled into the role of chairman, the illnesses became more frequent. In 1970 it was more abdominal surgery, which kept him from his first game until late May.[7] "I feel great," he said then. "The only thing hurting is my golf game."[8]

If O'Malley was not going to the Mayo Clinic for his own problems, it was for Kay's. At Vero Beach in 1972, she suffered a gallbladder attack that required surgery.[9] By mid-April he was begging out of a Penn trustees meeting because he had been out of his office for two months, and Kay, finally back in Los Angeles, was facing a long convalescence.[10] The convalescence did not go smoothly, and she had returned to the clinic by late May.[11] Two years later, it was more of the same, with O'Malley expressing reluctance to get involved with a Penn fund-raising campaign because of "his need to be attentive to her."[12] This may be what O'Malley was referring to when he wrote another Penn official that October that he had been out of the office for two months "as a result of a ridiculous surgical experience," but there was no further explanation.[13]

O'Malley was trying to slow down, to get as far away as possible from the daily grind of running the team. Peter was doing most of it, and his marketing efforts were allowing the Dodgers to set attendance records year after year. But he did not know everything, and Dad could get irritated. Jim McConnell of the suburban *Pomona Progress-Bulletin* was at Vero Beach in 1977 interviewing O'Malley when a Holman Stadium security official came up with a problem. Walter said he should talk to Peter. The official said he had and that Peter did not know what to do. Walter rattled off the answer, then added, "God damn it. I'm trying to get out of this. Tell Peter and tell him that's how we do it."[14]

There was a lot of *we* in O'Malley's talks in those years. The message he liked to deliver, and clearly the one in which he took the most pride, was the reputation of the Dodger organization and the methods that had earned that reputation. He talked to everybody at Dodgertown, knowing the names of even the part-timers and going out of his way to make them feel important. "There was no stuffiness about the guy, at all," McConnell said.

By 1977 the surgical experiences had gone from ridiculous to serious. Late in the season of that year, O'Malley had what was described as "major surgery" at the Mayo Clinic.[15] The following February it was more abdominal surgery, and the previous year's surgery was now specified as "chest surgery."[16] He was released from the clinic, but a few days later, while flying from Los Angeles to Vero Beach for spring training, he developed a high fever, and the plane was diverted to Rochester.[17] It was now reported that the early-February abdominal surgery had revealed a "diseased artery," which had required treatment.[18] In an interview later that year, O'Malley told Associated Press reporter Jim Cour that the 1977 operation had been on his lungs, while the February surgery had been for an aneurism on his aorta. The "fever" that had redirected the *Kay O'* to Rochester had actually been a blood infection.[19] However, when he saw reporters at the end of spring training, he said, "I feel so damn good right now, the golf course better watch out." *Los Angeles Times* reporter Ross Newhan said that "in appearance, spirit and voice," O'Malley seemed to have bounced back well from the surgery.[20]

But the surgeries had also taken a toll. He was no longer "Whalebelly," a nickname Leo Durocher had hung on him. His jowls had almost disappeared, and he complained to *Los Angeles Times* reporter Penelope McMillan that he couldn't gain weight and his clothes didn't fit.[21]

That fall O'Malley checked into Queen of Angels Hospital in Los Angeles with numbness in his legs.[22] He had been there ten days when he asked doctors to let him remain a while longer. A spokeswoman for the hospital said there had been "real improvement," and the numbness had been caused by a "temporary decrease of blood through his spinal cord." She said O'Malley had told his doctors he wanted to stay until he could get around on his own.[23]

By early 1979 O'Malley was back at the Mayo Clinic after experiencing dizziness while riding his golf cart at Vero Beach. He stayed a week, but was back for himself in April, June, and July.[24]

His life those months was wrapped around his health and that of Kay, who was fading as well. Terry said her mother had a series of strokes and became housebound. "She couldn't go [to Dodger games], so he didn't go. Some nights, I'd bring some of the grandchildren in to see them and I can sort of see the two of them just listening to the radio, listening to the ball games on the radio, sitting together sort of holding hands, you know, like they were youngsters in love."[25]

That last spring in Vero Beach, O'Malley seemed to sense it would be his last. After Kay was wheeled into the dining room each morning, he would make sure she was properly fed.[26] When Marvin Miller, in his annual tour of the spring training camps, stopped at Vero Beach, O'Malley, as usual, invited him to drop by his house for a visit. The Dodger owner, who had a full-time attendant, came out for the meeting in a bathrobe and with a "voice so husky you could hardly understand him." They chatted for an hour on light topics, and Miller came to see that O'Malley, who had always enjoyed fencing with Miller, was saying good-bye.[27]

On July 12, while Walter was still at the Mayo Clinic, Kay Hanson O'Malley died of yet another stroke.[28] Four weeks to the day later, Walter O'Malley died of congestive heart failure at the Mayo Clinic.[29] He was seventy-five.

As Sandy Koufax said, "There was nothing about him that was not sort of exceptional. Some people liked him and some people didn't, but I don't think anybody felt nothing at all."[30] And the obituaries showed it.

Red Smith: "The inescapable fact was that O'Malley, making large profits in Brooklyn, took Brooklyn's team away to make even bigger profits. You didn't have to be a Dodger fan to be affected by the move. . . . O'Malley was the first to say out loud that it was all business—a business that he owned and could operate as he chose, and the community the team had pretended to represent for almost seventy years had no voice in the matter at all. From that day on, some of the fun of baseball was lost."[31]

John Fetzer: "His passing in many ways leaves the ship without a rudder."[32]

Dick Young: "The thing to remember about Walter O'Malley is this: he was making a fortune in Brooklyn but chose to make a real estate killing in Los Angeles."[33]

Jerry Izenberg: "For all the power he wielded and all the toes on which he trod, the man they called The O'Malley may have been the most visionary force in all of baseball."[34]

Jim Murray: "He brought the game kicking and screaming into the 20th Century."[35]

Tom Knight, in a letter to the editor of the *Sporting News*: "The Sporting News obituary of Walter O'Malley failed to mention the utter contempt the man had for the baseball fans of Brooklyn. O'Malley could thank the fans of Brooklyn for anything he achieved. Brooklyn lined his pockets with money for 15 years before the ingrate pulled one of the best franchises in baseball to Los Angeles where he could acquire his millions. Since he talked the Giants into moving with him, O'Malley was responsible for the largest city in the country being deprived of National League baseball for four seasons. No one bothered to mention that!"[36]

Terry Seidler: "He was a great dad. He was very loving. He and my mother just had a great marriage."[37]

19

Postgame

At some point in our lives as fans, probably when we are in our late teens or early twenties, it finally hits home that baseball is a business. We had heard our father or a more cynical friend say it. But it did not resonate until our favorite player was not offered a contract extension or the team raised parking prices yet again. The reality always comes as a bit of a shock because we came to baseball as a love affair, and the owners sell the game to us relentlessly as a romance that is both timeless and exciting. It's fathers and sons, the first glimpse of the emerald grass, and "Take Me Out to the Ball Game." It's linking last year's home run hero to the trail of Pablo Sandoval, Joe Carter, Kirk Gibson, Bill Mazeroski, Gabby Hartnett, and Babe Ruth. Every team has a home run hero. Your father, who took you to your first game, had one. If he is recent, you can watch the video. If older, you can listen to the tale.

As a businessman, what Walter O'Malley did is completely justified. He moved his plant to a better market. He prospered there.

Most companies have products that are completely independent of where they are made. We will buy Bonzo's Beans whether they are boiled down the block or in Bhutan. But the relationship of a baseball team with its customers is completely different. Its foundation is emotion. And that emotion is reinforced by the owner with his advertising, his public relations machine, and his announcers.

A few years ago I was part of a discussion about who we root for. It obviously wasn't owners, whom we tolerated or despised to varying degrees. It obviously wasn't players. In the free-agent era, they were gone tomorrow if not today. It wasn't the game itself, because Texas Rangers fans could watch the Astros, or the Corpus Christi Hooks, or the University of Texas Longhorns, or high school baseball, and appreciate the game just as much.

Ultimately, we decided we rooted for "shirts," the jerseys of our favorite team. "Shirts" was shorthand for a community. Being a fan of whatever team gave us an emotional attachment to others with similar loyalties. Even if we had seen the game on TV, or listened on the radio, we could join in the communal scream of joy or gasp of disappointment at the ballpark. We could relive those emotions as we pored over the box score the next morning. We could take those emotions to school or work or the barbershop the next day and replay them, analyzing what happened, and why, pointing out things the others had not seen, reexperiencing the hope, joy, and defeats of a very long season.

That is not Bonzo's Beans; it is an emotion. Like all emotions, it can be ephemeral. It thrives on loyalty and repetition. If one side of the emotional partnership is not loyal, why should fans be?

Saying that Walter O'Malley had the property rights to move his team is true. Saying he had ample economic justification and could see little responsiveness among the New York politicians is true. But that is to ignore the emotional bond he had worked so hard to build. Brooklyn fans were loyal enough to make the team profitable, but not loyal enough and numerous enough to generate the profits or political pressure to build a new stadium. And there is where they parted. Above all, Walter O'Malley wanted to build his monument to the O'Malleys.

And for every outraged Brooklyn fan, there was a Los Angeles fan who could appreciate that his set of shirts had an owner who worked very hard to ensure his business gave the fan what he wanted. O'Malley would take in a lot of money, but he would not spend it on himself. He did not live the lifestyle his business could have afforded him. He spent it ensuring his players were given an environment conducive to good performance. Although New York writers such as Dick Young would permanently attach greedy as O'Malley's first name, he would not raise ticket prices at Dodger Stadium for fifteen years. His stadium, his monument to the O'Malleys, would not be covered in advertising. Only one sign, for the oil company that had solidified his financing of the stadium, would grace the park. He would not develop the real estate Young claimed was the reason he moved. In business parlance he was not a "profit maximizer," at least in the short term. Walter O'Malley almost always thought long term.

Young was also consistent in his belief that the Dodgers' move to Los Angeles was without risk. After more than fifty years of success at Dodger Stadium, it is easy to believe that. But any examination of O'Malley's adventures from the moment he stepped off the plane in October 1958 until the Supreme Court refused to review the last taxpayers' lawsuit could not sustain the idea that the venture was without risks.

Bill Madden, who followed Young at the *Daily News*, would describe the move as a "calculated and monumental undertaking."[1] Monumental it was, but the clear lack of planning the Los Angeles Dodger organization demonstrated in its opening months cannot support the word *calculated*. They did not know where they would play or where they would live. O'Malley showed no grasp of things such as initiatives and referendums, which any competent political observer of the Los Angeles scene could have warned him about.

You will see it repeated again and again that O'Malley persuaded Horace Stoneham to leave New York.[2] He did persuade Stoneham to go to San Francisco, but Stoneham had already made the decision to leave New York for Minneapolis. O'Malley only changed the destination. Similarly, you will hear it said O'Malley wanted New York City to build him a ballpark. O'Malley was not only willing to build himself a ballpark, but also willing to pay property taxes on it. What he wanted was the city to subsidize his purchase of the land, an expensive-enough proposition, although cheaper than the cost of Shea Stadium.

Ultimately, Walter O'Malley wanted to build a stadium. And he did.

Source Acknowledgments

Portions of chapter 2 appeared in earlier form as "A History of Dodger Ownership," *National Pastime* 13 (1993): 34–42.

Portions of chapter 5 appeared in earlier form as "Two Out of Three Ain't Bad: Branch Rickey, Walter O'Malley, and the Man in the Middle of the Dodger Owners' Partnership," *Nine: A Journal of Baseball History and Culture* 14, no. 1 (2005): 41–46.

Portions of chapters 4 and 5 appeared in earlier form as "Walter O'Malley," "Branch Rickey," "John L. Smith," and "Ownership Issues in Brooklyn," in *The Team That Changed Baseball and America: The 1947 Brooklyn Dodgers* (Lincoln: University of Nebraska Press, 2012), 279–83, 15–21, 284–86, 333–36, respectively.

Portions of chapter 11 appeared in earlier form as "The King of Coolie Hats," *National Pastime* (1999): 24–27.

Notes

ABBREVIATIONS

BOD   Minutes of the Boards of Directors of the Brooklyn National League Baseball Club or the Ebbets-McKeever Exhibition Company, Rickey Papers

Celler I   *Organized Baseball: Hearings before the Subcommittee on Study of Monopoly Power of the Committee on the Judiciary, House of Representatives, 1952* (Representative Emanuel Celler was the chair of the subcommittee)

Celler II   *Organized Baseball: Hearings before the Subcommittee on Study of Monopoly Power of the Committee on the Judiciary, House of Representatives, 1957*

LAHE   This actually covers two Hearst newspapers in Los Angeles, the *Herald Express* and the *Herald Examiner* (the change took place in 1962)

LAT   *Los Angeles Times*

NYT   *New York Times*

SN   *Sporting News*

INTRODUCTION

1. Golenbock, *Bums*, 448.
2. Timothy Snyder, "Hitler vs. Stalin: Who Killed More," *New York Review of Books*, Mar. 10, 2011.
3. Frommer, *New York City Baseball*, 10.
4. Riess, *City Games*, 236.
5. Claire with Springer, *Fred Claire*, 57.
6. *Los Angeles Times, New York Times*, and *New York Daily News*, Aug. 10, 1979; SN, Aug. 25, 1979, 12.
7. Kahn, *The Era*, 261n.
8. Kahn, "Bums' Rush Turns into a Big Bonanza," 28.
9. D'Antonio, *Forever Blue*, 3.
10. M. Miller, *Whole Different Ball Game*, 209.

1. Dan Parker column, *New York Mirror*, Jan. 15, 1951; or *LAT*, May 21, 1972.
2. Thomas listed his parents' birth in Ireland on both the 1880 and the 1900 census forms. His death certificate (Brooklyn Death Cert. 1473 from 1918) listed his mother's maiden name as Margaret Collins, also a native of Ireland. But, indicative of the genealogical difficulties, Thomas's wife's death certificate (Bronx death certificate 11635 for 1940) said *her* mother's maiden name was Margaret Collins, an Irish native. Either we have the coincidence of a married couple both of whose mothers had the same name, or we have some confusion among the descendants. Thomas and Georgiana's daughter Kathryn was the informant for Georgiana's death certificate. No informant is listed on Thomas's.
3. K. Miller, *Emigrants and Exiles*, 71 (85 percent of Catholic Mayo residents were illiterate in 1841), 297 (90 percent of Mayo emigrants were Irish speakers). See also *The Great Famine, 1845–1849* in Co. Mayo, Ireland, at www.mayohistory.com/famine.htm for the 90 percent figure.
4. Werner, *Tammany Hall*; Weiss, *Charles Francis Murphy*; O. Allen, *Tiger*; Eisenstein and Rosenberg, *Stripe of Tammany's Tiger*; Erie, *Rainbow's End*; Slayton, *Empire Statesman*. The latter is especially valuable because Smith grew up in the same neighborhood in the years between Thomas and Edwin O'Malley.
5. The family website, http://www.walteromalley.com/biog_short_page1.php?lang=eng, claims fourteen pregnancies with eleven survivors, but the handwriting on the 1900 census page clearly says nineteen.
6. Spero, *Labor Movement*, 59.
7. Libby, "O'Malley," 46.
8. *New York Mirror*, Jan. 15, 1951; *LAHE*, Apr. 16, 1958.
9. *LAT*, May 21, 1972.
10. Libby, in "O'Malley," has O'Malley saying that both an uncle and an aunt were born in San Francisco, but the sisters born immediately before and after Joseph appear in the census as born in New York City.
11. Michael Svanevik and Shirley Burgett, "GG Park's Expo Experience," *San Francisco Examiner*, Aug. 5, 2002.
12. *LAT*, May 21, 1972.
13. He did not appear in the San Francisco city directories of 1891 or 1893.
14. Walsh and Magnum, *Labor Struggle*, 48–49.
15. Baxter, *Labor and Politics*, 59.
16. Homberger, *Historical Atlas*, 106–7.
17. *Brooklyn Eagle*, Apr. 12, 1953; *SN*, Apr. 22, 1953, 30.
18. Manhattan birth certificate 370854, dated July 7, 1883.
19. http://www.walteromalley.com/biog_ref_page6.php.
20. Libby, "O'Malley," 46.
21. I am grateful to Roger Repohl, administrator of St. Augustine's Parish, for digging out this record and helping me understand it.

22. Kahn, *The Era*, 262.

23. Alma's obituary in NYT, June 4, 1940, said she and Edwin had been married thirty-seven years, putting the marriage in late 1902 or early 1903.

24. The 1910 census, taken Apr. 20, found Edwin still in the Bronx. The family's website (www.walteromalley.com) says the family moved to Queens when O'Malley was seven, or from Oct. 1910 to Oct. 1911.

25. Article dated Dec. 7, 1907, from an unnamed newspaper contained in a packet titled "History of Hollis, Borough of Queens, New York City, N.Y.," compiled by Robert C. Friedrich of the Long Island Division of the Queens Borough Public Library, Nov. 1993.

26. *Brooklyn Eagle*, July 30, 1915, Apr. 12, 1953; NYT, Apr. 12, 1953; *Amityville Record*, Apr. 16, 1953.

27. An undated issue of *Jamaica Jinjer* featuring an article titled "Historical Sketch of Hollis–Queens Village," which also appeared in the "History of Hollis" packet from the Queens Borough Public Library; see note 25.

28. *Dictionary of American Biography* (1964), s.v. "John Francis Hylan," supp. II, 11:330; Bullock, "Hylan," 444; NYT, Jan. 12, 1936.

29. Connable and Silberfarb, *Tigers of Tammany*, 260.

30. Bullock, "Hylan."

31. *Dictionary of American Biography*, s.v. "John Francis Hylan."

32. Garrett, *The La Guardia Years*, 137.

33. See Weiss, *Charles Francis Murphy*; and Slayton *Empire Statesman*. Also, one of the many controversies of Edwin O'Malley's tenure concerned the replacement of one of his deputies who was a Murphy/Smith man with one loyal to Hylan. See daily stories in NYT from July 30 through Aug. 3, 1922.

34. *Brooklyn Eagle*, Oct. 17, 1919; NYT, Oct. 19, 1919.

35. *Brooklyn Eagle*, Nov. 29, 1919; NYT, Dec. 2, 3, 4, 1919.

36. *New York State Joint Legislative Committee*, 255–56.

37. *New York State Joint Legislative Committee*, 10.

38. *Brooklyn Standard-Union*, Aug. 24, 1921. For the sake of "expediency" and on orders from Hylan, O'Malley restored the permits a day later. *Brooklyn Daily Eagle*, Aug. 25, 1921.

39. NYT, Feb. 3, 1920.

40. NYT, June 27, 1921.

41. NYT, Sept. 1, 1921. See also *New York American*, *Brooklyn Eagle*, *Brooklyn Standard-Union*, and *Brooklyn Times*, all same date.

42. NYT, Sept. 1, 1921. See also *New York American*, *Brooklyn Eagle*, *Brooklyn Standard-Union*, and *Brooklyn Times*, all same date.

43. *New York Catholic News*, Aug. 4, 1956.

44. *Sports Illustrated*, Mar. 24, 1958, 64.

45. Two slightly different versions of the baseball card story are *Sports Illustrated*, Mar. 24, 1958, 64; and *New York Post*, Nov. 5, 1950.

46. *Long Island Press*, Nov. 19, 1950.

47. *New York Catholic News*, Aug. 4, 1956.

48. Worden to Culver Military Academy, July 13, 1920. See also O'Malley application to Culver, signed by Edwin O'Malley, July 9, 1920, Culver Academy Archives.

49. Edwin O'Malley to Culver Military Academy, July 19, 1920, Culver Academy Archives.

50. *Long Island Press*, Nov. 19, 1950.

51. *Brooklyn Eagle*, Oct. 19, 1919. Height and weight are from his Culver Military Academy application nine months later.

52. Edwin O'Malley to Culver, July 19, 1920. The exams certified that Walter had mastered all the basic material mandated by the state of New York for high school students. Most tests were taken during the senior year of high school, when the students would have been seventeen or eighteen.

53. Referral forms from Vosburgh and F. D. Asche and a letter from Worden to Culver, Culver Academy files.

54. Martin, "Martin Calls on O'Malley," 4.

55. Martin, "Martin Calls on O'Malley," 4. See also *LAT*, May 21, 1972; and *New York Catholic News*, Aug. 4, 1956.

56. Culver's athletic program was based on the West Point model. A student was expected to be participating in some sport at all times. Each company formed teams for whichever sports were in season, and the best company players were chosen for the varsity clubs.

57. *Roll Call* (1922), 118, Culver Military Academy yearbook, Culver Academy Archives.

58. Letter to Edwin O'Malley, Apr. 4, 1922, Culver Academy Archives.

59. *Vedette*, Apr. 8, 1922, "Green Megaphone" column.

60. Letter to Edwin O'Malley, Apr. 4, 1922, Culver Academy Archives.

61. Walter O'Malley to Colonel H. G. Glascock, June 15, 1922, Culver Academy Archives.

62. Walter O'Malley to Major F. L. Hunt, June 25, 1922, Culver Academy Archives.

63. It was often reported that this feat was unprecedented, but a university press release dated Apr. 6, 1925, O'Malley file, University of Pennsylvania Archives, says O'Malley's election was the third time this was accomplished.

64. Bob Hunter, "O'Malley: Mr. Midas with a Smile," *SN*, Oct. 6, 1962, 3.

65. Martin, "Martin Calls on O'Malley."

66. *Pennsylvanian*, Mar. 6, 8 (editorial), 1924.

67. *Pennsylvanian*, Mar. 17, 20, May 20, 1924.

68. *Pennsylvanian*, Sept. 28, 1925.

69. Kavanagh and Macht, *Uncle Robbie*, 161; Goldstein, *Superstars and Screwballs*, 159.

70. University of Pennsylvania yearbook (1926), University of Pennsylvania Archives.

71. *Pennsylvanian*, Mar. 12, May 23, 1924. For motto, see University of Pennsylvania yearbook (1926), University of Pennsylvania Archives.

72. University of Pennsylvania yearbook (1926), University of Pennsylvania Archives.

73. University of Pennsylvania yearbook (1926), University of Pennsylvania Archives.

74. Martin, "Martin Calls on O'Malley."

75. *Time*, Apr. 28, 1958, 64.

76. Martin, "Martin Calls on O'Malley."

77. University of Pennsylvania yearbook (1926), 114, University of Pennsylvania Archives.

78. University of Pennsylvania press release, Mar. 12, 1926, O'Malley file, University of Pennsylvania Archives.

79. *LAT*, Aug. 10, 1979.

80. Transcript, Walter Francis O'Malley, University of Pennsylvania Archives.

81. Durslag, "Visit with O'Malley," 31. See also *LAT*, May 21, 1972; *LAHE*, Apr. 16, 1958; Gross, "Artful O'Malley," 48; and Kahn, "Exported to Brooklyn."

82. Unfortunately, the University of Pennsylvania Archives do not contain course descriptions, so exactly which aspects of psychology O'Malley studied is not clear. More than a third of his units were in psychology courses, and two-thirds of the units for which he was given "distinguished" marks were in psychology.

83. See Martin, "Martin Calls on O'Malley," for "average circumstances"; and Gene Ward's column in the *New York Daily News*, Jan. 12, 1968, for "hod carrier."

84. *LAT*, May 21, 1972.

85. *LAT*, May 21, 1972.

86. University of Pennsylvania yearbook (1926), University of Pennsylvania Archives.

87. Martin, "Martin Calls on O'Malley."

88. *Pennsylvania Gazette* (University of Pennsylvania alumni magazine), Nov. 5, 1926.

89. *LAT*, May 21, 1972.

90. *LAT*, May 21, 1972. See also Gross, "Artful O'Malley"; and *SN*, Sept. 8, 1955, 13.

91. Boucher, *20,000 Years of Fashion*, esp. 401.

92. The stock market crash story is preferred by the family. See http://www.walteromalley.com/biog_short_page1.php?lang=eng. It is repeated in Kowet, "The Forty-Niner," 60.

93. Edwin seemed to recover quickly. The 1930 census would show him as the owner of the Belvedere Hotel, 319 West Forty-Eighth Street, where he, Alma, and Walter were living as Walter finished law school at Fordham. The hotel was valued at $25,000.

94. The date of O'Malley's hiring is actually a bit of a conjecture and might well have come earlier. The *Board of Transportation of the City of New York Proceedings* for June 26, 1928, indicates that O'Malley was given a raise on May 1,

1928. The proceedings for 1927, which presumably would have recorded his hiring, were not available, but an examination of other years indicates raises were normally given on the hiring anniversary. The proceedings do make it clear that O'Malley was not hired in 1928 or in 1926 in the period after he graduated from Penn.

95. *Board of Transportation of the City of New York Proceedings*, Oct. 1, 1929. O'Malley was by then making $180 a week or $2,160 a year, although he later recalled the figure as $3,019 annually. *LAT*, Aug. 10, 1979.

96. *NYT*, Oct. 26, 1929. See also *Board of Transportation of the City of New York Proceedings, 1929*, letter of Nov. 26, 1929, 2332.

97. Gross, "Artful O'Malley"; *Long Island Press*, Nov. 19, 1950.

98. Arch Murray, *New York Post*, Nov. 5, 1950; *SN*, Sept. 28, 1955, 13.

99. Gross, "Artful O'Malley."

100. *LAT*, June 4, 1978.

101. Kahn, "Exported to Brooklyn."

102. *LAHE*, Apr. 16, 1958.

103. *Time*, Apr. 28, 1958.

104. *NYT*, May 16, 1931. The bar exam had actually been given three times between the end of O'Malley's last year at Fordham and the occasion he passed. Whether O'Malley didn't take those exams or didn't pass them is not clear. Only a bit more than a third of those who took these tests passed. See *NYT*, May 14, Aug. 23, 1930, Jan. 5, 1931. O'Malley may also have been so involved in his other ventures that he did not feel he had time to prepare himself well enough.

105. Gross, "Artful O'Malley."

106. *NYT*, Mar. 16, 1933.

107. Martin, "Martin Calls on O'Malley."

108. Several stories about the O'Malleys say Walter and Kay were neighbors in Brooklyn as young people as well as in Amityville, but the listings for Edwin O'Malley and Peter Hanson in city phone books and directories do not show this. Perhaps this is because after the marriage, Walter and Kay did take an apartment very close to her parents' residence.

109. *NYT*, Dec. 14, 1927. Other sources, including his *NYT* obituary, Apr. 16, 1965, put the date in the year 1878, but I have chosen to go with the 1877 date because it was exact (Sept. 30, 1877), while the others referred only to a year.

110. *NYT*, Dec. 14, 1927.

111. *LAT*, Dec. 20, 1971.

112. Some sources describe her as unable to speak (see *Time*, Apr. 28, 1958), but the *Los Angeles Times* profile of Dec. 20, 1971, describes an interview with her in which she can converse in a whisper.

113. *Time*, Apr. 28, 1958.

114. U.S. Department of Labor, Immigration Service, list of U.S. citizens arriving in New York on the ss *Veendam* from Bermuda on Nov. 18, 1930. Held in National Archives, made available through Ancestry.com.

115. Kahn, "Exported to Brooklyn." See also Gross, "Artful O'Malley."

116. Investors bought the bonds. Their money was used to build, and the rents or lease payments on the buildings paid off the bond owners.

117. Gross, "Artful O'Malley." Reporters' summaries of O'Malley's descriptions of these corporations and instruments are uniformly vague. This is the clearest. See also *NYT*, Apr. 8, 9, 1933.

118. None of the coverage in the *New York Times* or the *New York Evening Journal* (the daily papers that paid the most attention to the issue) made any mention of O'Malley. Admittedly, there was not a great deal of coverage. The Bill Jackets—files on individual pieces of legislation—for the authorizing laws also contain no mention of O'Malley. The Bill Jacket for Bill Nos. 2273 and 2383 of Apr. 4, 1933, also contain dozens of letters to Governor Herbert Lehman and others with interest in the bills. None of them are from O'Malley or mention him. One is from Milbank, Tweed, a major Manhattan law firm. The Bill Jackets are held at the New York Public Library.

119. This story is told several places, but most completely in the *New York Post*, Nov. 5, 1950.

120. *NYT*, Dec. 27, 1925, Jan. 3, 1926, Feb. 25, 1965, Dec. 8, 1967.

121. *NYT*, Dec. 22, 23, 24, 27, 28, 1925, Jan. 3, 1926.

122. *NYT*, Feb. 20, Oct. 20, 21, 1927.

123. *NYT*, Mar. 30, 1927.

124. *NYT*, Nov. 18, 1927.

125. *NYT*, Jan. 15, 1926.

126. Garrett, *The La Guardia Years*, 99.

127. Parrott, *The Lords of Baseball*, 20.

128. Shapiro, *The Last Good Season*, 25.

129. O'Malley listing in *Who's Who in America*, 1954–55 edition.

130. Gross, "Artful O'Malley"; Kahn, *Memories of Summer*, 212.

131. Gross, "Artful O'Malley."

132. Parrott, *The Lords of Baseball*, 20.

133. Gross, "Artful O'Malley"; Kahn, "Exported to Brooklyn"; *LAT*, May 21, 1972.

134. Kowet, "The Forty-Niner," 61.

135. B. Bavasi, interview with the author, Aug. 30, 1994.

136. Kahn, *The Era*, 262.

137. Kahn, *The Era*, 30.

138. Gross, "Artful O'Malley."

139. *Long Island Press*, Jan. 9, 1953.

140. Oates, "Visit with O'Malley," 37 (emphasis added).

141. O'Malley file, University of Pennsylvania Archives.

142. O'Malley files, Culver Academy Archives and University of Pennsylvania Archives.

143. *NYT*, Oct. 14, 1950. See also *Kingsbury*, 13.

144. *Kingsbury*, 105.

145. Michelson, *Charlie O.*, 23.

146. *NYT*, Oct. 29, 1939.

147. Barnewall to Rickey, Nov. 2, 1942, Rickey Papers.

2. FROM GOWANUS TO MONTAGUE STREET

1. For simplicity's sake, I have called the team the Dodgers in this chapter even though for much of this period, Dodgers was just one of many nicknames for the team. These nicknames were almost always assigned by newspapers, and such nicknames were not incorporated into the team's formal names until much later. The Dodgers nickname was not formalized until 1932, after a long period when the team had been known as the Robins (after manager Wilbert Robinson). In addition to Dodgers, earlier versions had been known as the Superbas and Bridegrooms, as well as the fuller and original Trolley Dodgers, a nickname applied generally to Brooklynites of the late 1800s because it was said the proliferation of trolley lines in the borough forced them into dodging the cars.

2. For a fuller account of the Dodgers' early ownership and economics, see McCue, "History of Dodger Ownership," 34.

3. Solomon, *Where They Ain't*, 139; Peterson, *Man Who Invented Baseball*, 53.

4. Many sources report that Ebbets started by printing and selling scorecards. But his first wife, Minnie, dismissed that as a canard, saying he was the team's bookkeeper. *New York Daily News*, Sept. 28, 1941.

5. *Sporting Life*, Jan. 8, 1898, 1. Ebbets's reputation was such that he drew up schedules for other organizations around Brooklyn. *New York Clipper*, Apr. 16, 1892, 89.

6. Lieb, *Baseball as I Have Known It*, has both the laundress and the car-ownership anecdotes, 268.

7. L. Allen, *Giants and Dodgers*, 127–28.

8. Ebbets to Herrmann, May 12, 1912, Herrmann Papers.

9. Ebbets to Herrmann, May 12, 1912, Herrmann Papers.

10. *Sporting Life*, Sept. 7, 1912, 5.

11. Background on the McKeevers is mostly drawn from obituaries. Edward's, *NYT*, Apr. 30, 1925; Steve's, *NYT*, Mar. 7, 1938, and *SN*, Mar. 10, 1938, 7. See also *Brooklyn Eagle*, Apr. 9, 1913; and *SN*, Nov. 21, 1935.

12. *NYT*, Sept. 6, 1892; *SN*, Nov. 16, 1944, 8.

13. Hynd, *Giants of the Polo Grounds*, 182–83.

14. See Fitzgerald, *Story of the Brooklyn Dodgers*, 26, for the lack of a press box; and *Sporting Life*, May 11, 1912, on the consultation.

15. Allan Sangree in *New York American*, Apr. 6, 1913, quoted in Goldstein, *Superstars and Screwballs*, 101.

16. *SN*, May 14, 1925, 2.

17. Ed McKeever's will is described in the *NYT*, May 9, 1925, and *SN*, May 14, 1925, 2. The "rat" quote is in Graham, *The Brooklyn Dodgers*, 116.

18. Rickey to Hobbs, Rickey Papers. There was no public reporting of such an offer at the time. After the Federal League competition had pushed his costs up, Ebbets said he and the McKeevers were willing to sell the team for $2 million, but no takers appeared. See *NYT*, Oct. 11, 12, 1916.

19. *New York Daily News*, Sept. 28, 1941; *SN*, Nov. 16, 1944, 8.

20. *NYT*, May 1, 1925.

21. *NYT*, May 1, 1925.

22. *NYT*, Jan. 10, 1928.

23. *NYT*, Feb. 25, 1928.

24. Tom Meany and Bill McCullough, "Once a Dodger," in *Story of the Brooklyn Dodgers*, edited by Fitzgerald, 30–31.

25. Holmes, *The Dodgers*, 26.

26. Creamer, *Stengel*, 182.

27. The figure of $600,000 is in Holmes, *Dodger Daze and Knights*, 80. The suit was reported in *SN*, Dec. 24, 1931, 7. The farmers' story is in Meany and McCullough, "Once a Dodger," in *Story of the Brooklyn Dodgers*, edited by Fitzgerald, 39. Stengel's complaint is in his *Casey at the Bat* (with Paxton), 152.

28. Meany, *The Magnificent Yankees*, 30.

29. Burr, "That Picturesque Magnate," 303.

30. Taylor, "Borough Defender," 20.

31. Parrott, *The Lords of Baseball*, 99.

32. A. Mann, "MacPhail Story," *Sport*, 76.

33. For example, see *Brooklyn Eagle*, June 25, 1936.

34. "Brooklyn and Queens."

35. "Record of Loan Transactions," Mann Papers. Mann compiled the record, which extended from 1925 to 1941 when he worked as Branch Rickey's assistant later in the 1940s. The size of the mortgage is mentioned in A. Mann, "MacPhail Story," 76.

36. Celler I, 1600.

37. Kahn, *The Boys of Summer*, 427.

38. *SN*, May 28, 1966, 14.

39. There are many variations of this story. Later in life, after a complete break in his relationships with Rickey, MacPhail would vehemently deny any role by Rickey in MacPhail's advance, but the record would seem to contradict that. See Graham, *The Brooklyn Dodgers*, 150; R. Barber, *1947*, 9; and A. Mann, *Baseball Confidential*, 153. See also A. Mann, "MacPhail Story," 42; MacPhail to Irv Goodman, managing editor of *Sport*, Mar. 12, 1956, Rickey Papers; and Holland, "The Great MacPhail."

40. In addition to the *Sport* and *Sports Illustrated* profiles cited above, see also Warfield, *Roaring Redhead*.

41. Durocher with Linn, *Nice Guys Finish Last*, 97.

42. Taylor, "Borough Defender," 41.

43. Warfield, *Roaring Redhead*, 62.

44. MacPhail, *My 9 Innings*, 12.

45. Newspapers did not report the club was out of debt to the bank until 1942 (*SN*, Mar. 5, 1942, 11), but the accounting of loans and repayments contained in the Mann Papers and created when Mann worked for the team showed the bank had been repaid by July 16, 1941.

46. *SN*, Oct. 1, 1942, 5.

47. William J. Gibson, memo to Rickey, Nov. 7, 1942, Rickey Papers.

48. Celler I, 1601.

49. Parrott, *The Lords of Baseball*, 112.

50. *SN*, Aug. 20, 1942, 1.

51. McGrew, memo to Rickey, Oct. 30, 1942, Rickey Papers.

52. Kahn, *Good Enough to Dream*, 56.

53. *SN*, Oct. 1, 1942, 5; Aug. 20, 1942, 13; Parrott, *The Lords of Baseball*, 117.

54. Drebinger, "The Rise of Rickey," 341.

55. *New York Herald-Tribune*, Aug. 31, 1941. The section on Rickey draws heavily on Murray Polner's *Branch Rickey: A Biography*, Lee Lowenfish's *Baseball's Ferocious Gentleman*, and profiles such as Dick Farrington, "Branch Rickey, Defending Farms, Says Stark Necessity Forced System," *SN*, Dec. 1, 1932; Chamberlain, "Brains, Baseball, and Rickey"; Rice, "Profiles: Thoughts on Baseball"; Holland, "Rickey and the Game," 38; Fitzgerald, "*Sport*'s Hall of Fame"; and *Current Biography, 1945*, 497.

56. *SN*, Nov. 5, 1942, 14.

57. Kiner with Gergen, *Kiner's Korner*, 23.

58. *SN*, Oct. 29, 1942, 13; Rice, "Profiles: Thoughts on Baseball," 34.

59. Broeg, *Redbirds*, 131.

60. Quoted in *SN*, Nov. 5, 1942, 8.

61. Both the letter to Robinson, dated Feb. 21, 1964, and the receipt for the check are in the Rickey Papers.

62. See Rickey to MacPhail, Aug. 22, 1941, and telegram to Fred Saigh, July 14, 1951, Rickey Papers.

63. The anti-Catholic remarks are in Falkner, *Long Time Coming*, 106. The quotes about the purchaser are in Rickey to Hobbs, Nov. 29, 1944, 5, Rickey Papers.

64. Sanders, "American Baseball Dream," 39.

65. *SN*, May 18, 1949, 38.

66. *SN*, Nov. 5, 1942, 8, quoting Smith's column in the *Philadelphia Record*.

67. *NYT*, Feb. 12, 1943.

68. The matches anecdote is in Chamberlain, "Brains, Baseball, and Rickey;" the fingers and noses is in Dexter, "Brooklyn's Sturdy Branch," 17; Mrs. Rickey's quote is in Rice, "Profiles: Thoughts on Baseball," May 27, 1950, 32.

69. *SN*, Dec. 1, 1932, 3.

70. Drebinger, "The Rise of Rickey," 382.

71. Farrington, "Branch Rickey, Defending Farms," 3.

72. Woodward, "In the Rickey Manner," 20.

73. Although most of these innovations are widely attributed to Rickey, the batting tee is in Young, "Rickey's Tee Party," 6, a story that also notes failures with other attempts to cure hitters of overstriding.
74. Chamberlain, "Brains, Baseball, and Rickey," 350.
75. *SN*, Dec. 25, 1965, 14.
76. *Sports Illustrated*, Mar. 7, 1955, 59.
77. *New York Post*, Dec. 20, 1944; *SN*, Aug. 27, 1947, 14.
78. Rickey to Bricker, Dec. 31, 1945, Rickey Papers.
79. Drebinger, "The Rise of Rickey," 341.
80. Breadon to Rickey, June 20, 1942, and Rickey to Breadon, Sept. 26, 1942, Rickey Papers.
81. *SN*, Mar. 5, 1966, 30.
82. *SN*, Mar. 5, 1966, 30.
83. R. Barber, *1947*, 9.
84. D. Walker Wear to Rickey, June 30, 1937, Rickey Papers.

3. UNDER NEW MANAGEMENT

1. *NYT*, Feb. 26, 1942.
2. A number of Dodger histories have reported that O'Malley replaced Wendell Willkie as the team's lawyer. This is, at best, a long stretch. Some of the Dodgers' legal work had been done by Louis Carroll, a partner in the firm of Miller, Boston & Owen, which added Willkie as a name partner in April 1941 soon after Willkie's loss to Franklin D. Roosevelt in the 1940 presidential election. The firm then became Willkie, Owen, Otis & Bailly, with Carroll still doing the team's legal work. Carroll, a man widely respected in baseball circles, also did legal work for the National League and the Commissioner's Office. It was these latter connections where Rickey saw possible conflicts, as he had clashed with Commissioner Landis during Rickey's St. Louis years. There is no evidence that Willkie himself did any work for the Dodgers or any other baseball entity. Most of the team's routine legal work was handled by a Brooklyn firm, Gray & Tomlin. William Gibson to Rickey, Nov. 7, 1942, Rickey Papers.
3. Rickey to Roscoe Hobbs, Nov. 29, 1944, Rickey Papers
4. *Long Island Press*, Nov. 19, 1950; Kahn, *The Boys of Summer*, 427.
5. *LAHE*, Apr. 4, 1964.
6. *NYT*, Aug. 8, 9, 13, 1940.
7. What is referred to here and in all other references as Dodger stock is actually stock in two separate corporations, the Brooklyn National League Baseball Club, Inc., and the Ebbets-McKeever Exhibition Co., Inc. (which owned the Ebbets Field real estate). However, shares in these two companies were always held and sold in tandem. If you bought 10 percent of one, you were also buying 10 percent of the other, and thus they are treated as one unit.
8. *NYT*, Feb. 2, 9, 15, 16, 1944. Rickey to Lieutenant (JG) T. M. Jones, U.S. Naval Reserves, Feb. 29, 1944, Rickey Papers. On June 15, 1948, in testimony in a

hearing on settlement of the Ebbets estate, Joseph Gilleaudeau (Ebbets's son-in-law who represented the heirs on the Dodgers' board) testified that they had agreed to sell the Ebbets stock to Meyer before he backed out. Testimony is in Mann Papers.

9. *NYT*, Mar. 2, 1944.
10. Rickey to Hobbs, Nov. 29, 1944, Rickey Papers.
11. Rickey to Hobbs, Nov. 29, 1944, Rickey Papers.
12. Rickey to Lou Wentz, Mar. 25, 1944, and Rickey to Hobbs, Nov. 29, 1944, Rickey Papers.
13. Rickey's loan agreement is dated Sept. 15, 1944, and the transaction date is recorded in a letter from O'Malley to all the partners, Nov. 29, 1944, Rickey Papers.
14. *Brooklyn Eagle*, Nov. 1, 1944; *NYT*, Nov. 2, 1944; *SN*, Nov. 9, 1944, 1, 10.
15. Unpublished manuscript, "How to Buy a Ball Club for Peanuts," 608–9, Mann Papers.
16. *SN*, Jan. 11, 1945, 1.
17. *NYT*, Feb. 9, 1945.
18. Rickey to Hobbs, Nov. 29, 1944, Rickey Papers.
19. Rickey to Hobbs, Nov. 29, 1944, Rickey Papers.
20. O'Malley to Rickey, May 3, 1945, and "Memorandum: Stock Purchase, May 4, 1945," Rickey Papers.
21. *Brooklyn Eagle*, Aug. 14, 1945; *NYT*, Aug. 14, 1945; *SN*, Aug. 16, 1945.
22. Draft Memorandum re Ball Club, May 3, 1945, Rickey Papers.
23. Meany, *The Artful Dodgers*, 6.
24. "Memorandum of Agreement, entered into as of the 21st day of September 1945, between John L. Smith, Walter F. O'Malley and Branch Rickey," Rickey Papers.
25. "Memorandum for Messrs. O'Malley, Smith and Rickey," Sept. 25, 1948, and an undated "Memorandum re Stock Purchase," Rickey Papers.
26. *NYT*, July 11, 1950. Other obituaries: *SN*, July 19, 1950, 20; *Brooklyn Eagle*, July 10, 1950.
27. Much of this profile is based on Mines, *Pfizer: An Informal History*; Roden-gen, *The Legend of Pfizer*; "Some Enduring Impressions of Pfizer Leadership"; "Corporations: Penicillin Grows in Brooklyn," 75–77; "Looping the Loops," *SN*, June 26, 1946, 1; and "Kingpin of Penicillin Recalls Miracle Drug's Early History," *Brooklyn Eagle*, June 30, 1946.
28. *Long Island Press*, Dec. 2, 1950. What was seen was a photocopy in the University of Pennsylvania Archives. The month and year are clear, but the date is a best guess.
29. Mary M. Thacher, librarian, Stonington Historical Society, to Lee Lowenfish, May 22, 1997. My thanks to Dr. Lowenfish for providing a copy of the letter.
30. *NYT*, June 24, 1942.

4. LEARNING THE BUSINESS

1. Olean matter is in Brooklyn Board of Directors minutes beginning Oct. 22, 1945; Fort Worth matter begins in Brooklyn BoD minutes, Jan. 2, 1945; negotiating with the contractors is in Brooklyn BoD minutes, June 11, 1946; the union issues are in BoD, Sept. 16, 1946, and *Brooklyn Eagle*, Aug. 13, 1950; the franchise tax issue first surfaced in the Brooklyn BoD minutes, Jan. 2, 1945. There are technically two companies, the Brooklyn National League Baseball Club and the Ebbets-McKeever Exhibition Company, which owned Ebbets Field and the property it sat on. Because the board meetings of the two companies generally took place back-to-back and the firms had identical boards, the meetings of the two are both referred to simply as BoD.

2. BoD, Jan. 21, 1948.

3. William J. Gibson to Rickey, Nov. 7, 1942, Rickey Papers.

4. *SN*, Dec. 18, 1946, 1.

5. BoD, June 21, 1950.

6. Mann to Max Kase, Oct. 25, 1957, Mann Papers.

7. Mann to Rickey, July 1, 1948, Mann to Kase, Oct. 25, 1957, Mann Papers. In the 1948 memo, Mann said Yurkovsky's principal was a Pat McCall.

8. *SN*, Aug. 18, 1948, 17.

9. Durocher, *Nice Guys Finish Last*, 184.

10. *SN*, Nov. 17, 1948, 16.

11. Mann to Kase, Oct. 25, 1957, Mann Papers.

12. *SN*, Nov. 17, 1948, 16.

13. *Sports Illustrated*, Feb. 26, 1962, 4.

14. Holland, "Visit with the Artful Dodger," 56; Kahn, *The Boys of Summer*, 427–28.

15. Walker and Bellamy, *Center Field Shot*, 12.

16. *SN*, Nov. 7, 1951, 18.

17. *SN*, Nov. 13, 1946, 10.

18. *NYT*, Nov. 8, 1946, 33; *Broadcasting*, Nov. 11, 1946, 79.

19. *NYT*, Mar. 1, 1947.

20. Dollar amount is *SN*, Feb. 18, 1948, 5. The 1947 World Series revenues are in *Baseball Guide and Record Book, 1948*, 114.

21. BoD minutes. See also R. Barber, *The Broadcasters*, 168.

22. BoD, Oct. 22, 1946.

23. *SN*, Dec. 15, 1948, 1.

24. Mann to Rickey, Dec. 13, 1946, Mann Papers.

25. BoD, Oct. 16, 1947.

26. For Rickey, see *SN*, Dec. 8, 1948, 16; and May 10, 1950, 4. For O'Malley, see *Broadcasting*, Mar. 5, 1951, 24.

27. BoD, Sept. 16, 1946.

28. BoD, June 26, 1947, June 21, 1950.

29. *NYT*, Feb. 25, 1948.

30. *NYT*. Feb. 25, 1948; Dec. 6, 1947.

31. BoD, June 21, 1950.

32. BoD, Oct. 22, 1945. This was not O'Malley's first meeting of the board of directors, but the first after he, Rickey, and Smith assumed control.

33. Ebbets, "Why I Am Building a Baseball Stadium."

34. See "Book Value of Capital Stock," June 30, 1950, Rickey Papers, for the maintenance outlays. The net profit is in Celler I, 1600.

35. Donald E. Beach to Mann, Oct. 17, 1949, Mann Papers. Beach was the Dodgers' chief financial officer.

36. BoD, Nov. 8, 1945, June 11, Oct. 17, 1946.

37. BoD, Mar. 7, 1949.

38. The *Sporting News Guide* for 1946 lists capacity at 35,000. In the 1947 and 1948 guides, it fell to 34,000, while in 1950 the guide reported 32,111 seats. For the 1947 World Series, the official forms filed with the Commissioner's Office and signed by both the Dodgers and the Yankees show 33,098 total attendance for Game 3, 33,433 for Game 4, and 34,379 for Game 5.

39. R. Barber, *1947*, 293–94.

40. *SN*, Feb. 12, 1947, 24.

41. BoD, Nov. 8, 1945, June 11, 1946.

42. BoD, Dec. 7, 1947, Jan. 31, Feb. 21, 1948. Why these same problems did not apply to staging baseball games was not addressed.

43. BoD, Jan. 7, 1948.

44. BoD, Feb. 21, 1948.

45. BoD, Oct. 22, 1946.

46. Praeger would go on to design both Holman Stadium in Vero Beach as well as Dodger Stadium in Los Angeles and Shea Stadium in New York. His earlier credits included chief engineer of the Henry Hudson Bridge connecting the Bronx and Manhattan and for the New York City Department of Parks and Recreation. He worked for Robert Moses on these projects. In the Navy during World War II, he had designed an artificial harbor for use on the beaches immediately after the Normandy invasion.

47. Minutes, annual stockholders meeting, Sept. 10, 1947, Rickey Papers.

48. Langill, *Dodger Stadium*, 9. Langill is the Dodgers' team archivist. Praeger would eventually design Dodger Stadium.

49. BoD, Dec. 21, 1947.

50. BoD, Jan. 21, 1948.

51. BoD, Feb. 21, 1948.

52. J. Robinson, *Baseball Has Done It*, 40–43.

53. A. Mann, *Branch Rickey*, 213–14.

54. R. Barber and Creamer, *Rhubarb*, 265–73.

55. R. Barber, *1947*, 248.

56. *SN*, Dec. 21, 1949, 6.

57. *LAT*, Apr. 14, 1958. Rickey biographer Murray Polner (*Branch Rickey: A Biography*, 147) tells the same story, but in an interview with Jim Kreuz, Polner made clear his source was O'Malley. Kreuz, "Tom Greenwade," 98. My thanks to Mr. Kreuz for providing Brooklyn Dodger internal documents from Greenwade's papers about this issue and for telling me about Polner's source for the story.

58. Hal Middlesworth column, *Oklahoma City Oklahoman*, June 3, 1947, unpaginated copy found in the Rickey Papers.

59. Jim Kreuz, who was researching the Greenwade-Garcia story, said Buzzie Bavasi told him O'Malley's claim was made up, although O'Malley may have gone to Mexico on vacation at that time. E-mail communication from Kreuz, Sept. 7, 2007. His communication from Bavasi came after Bavasi read Kreuz's article cited in note 57.

60. *NYT*, Oct. 1, 1947, Jan. 12, 1949. The Rickey Papers do contain a copy of an Aug. 23, 1947, contract with the Memphis Red Sox to purchase Dan Bankhead for $15,000.

61. *SN*, May 16, 1946, 10; May 23, 1946, 2.

62. *SN*, May 9, 1946, 4.

63. *SN*, May 23, 1946, 1.

64. Marshall, *Baseball's Pivotal Era*, 54.

65. *SN*, June 15, 1949, 12. See also Marshall, *Baseball's Pivotal Era*, 231.

66. Eskenazi, *The Lip*, 203–5.

67. Rev. Vincent Powell to George C. Wildermuth, Feb. 26, 1947, and Rev. Charles E. Bermingham to Branch Rickey, Mar. 5, 1947, Rickey Papers. See also *NYT* (and other New York papers), Mar. 1, 1947.

68. *SN*, Apr. 23, 1947, 37.

69. Parrott, *The Lords of Baseball*, 203–4.

70. Eskenazi, *The Lip*, 214.

71. R. Barber, *1947*, 97.

72. Lowenfish, *Branch Rickey*, 410.

73. Durocher with Linn, *Nice Guys Finish Last*, 193–95.

74. *LAT*, June 1, 1961.

75. *New York Daily News*, Mar. 10, 1947. See also *SN*, Mar. 19, 1947, 5.

76. *Brooklyn Eagle*, Mar. 3, 1947.

77. *NYT*, Mar. 16, 1947.

78. Chandler with Trimble. *Heroes, Plain Folks, and Skunks*, 186–91.

79. *SN*, Apr. 2, 1947, 1. See also R. Barber, *1947*, 72.

80. Chandler, *Heroes, Plain Folks, and Skunks*, 213.

81. Marshall, *Baseball's Pivotal Era*, 18–20, 38–40.

82. *SN*, Mar. 12, 1947, 17, for a contemporary view. The Rickey and Robinson biographies treat the issue in depth.

83. Durocher with Linn, *Nice Guys Finish Last*, 202. For similar reaction from the New York press, see *New York Daily Mirror*, Mar. 16, 1947.

84. A. Mann, *Baseball Confidential*, 95.

85. *NYT*, Mar. 25, 1947.

86. A. Mann, *Baseball Confidential*, 98–99.

87. A. Mann, *Baseball Confidential*, 100.

88. A. Mann, *Baseball Confidential*, 101.

89. A. Mann, *Baseball Confidential*, 104–5.

90. A. Mann, *Baseball Confidential*, 101–2.

91. A. Mann, *Baseball Confidential*, 111–12.

92. A. Mann, *Baseball Confidential*, 113–14.

93. Chandler, *Heroes, Plain Folks, and Skunks*, 213.

94. A. Mann, *Baseball Confidential*, 113–14.

95. *NYT*, Apr. 10, 1947; *SN*, Apr. 16, 1947.

96. Tom Meany column, *PM* (New York), Apr. 10, 1947.

97. *NYT*, Apr. 10, 1947.

98. *SN*, Apr. 16, 1947, 4, 8. See also editorial, "The Commissioner Gets Tough," 4.

99. *NYT*, Apr. 14, 1949.

100. BoD, Mar. 7, 1949.

101. John L. Flynn to O'Malley, Apr. 19, 1949, Rickey Papers.

102. O'Malley to Flynn, Apr. 22, 1949, Rickey Papers.

103. Polner, *Branch Rickey: A Biography*, 217. Polner provides no source for the quote.

104. *SN*, Oct. 13, 1948, 8.

105. *SN*, Mar. 31, 1948, 27.

106. Seating arrangement pamphlet for the Feb. 6, 1949, New York Baseball Writers Association annual dinner, Chandler Papers.

107. The version in the Rickey Papers is full of editing changes and was apparently never made public.

108. Polner, *Branch Rickey: A Biography*, 128–29.

109. Parrott, *The Lords of Baseball*, 142, argues that Rickey had been trapped by his overblown rhetoric into looking more like a religious hard-liner than he was. He notes a dinner at which Mrs. Rickey asks Parrott to order her a cocktail because Rickey is afraid someone will see and comment. She notes she and her husband have quit going to the racetrack for similar reasons.

110. Red Smith interview, Nov. 13, 1979, Oral History Collection, University of Kentucky.

111. *SN*, June 2, 1948.

112. *SN*, Sept. 29, 1948.

113. Leonard Cohen columns in *New York Post*, Apr. 14, Apr. 25, 1948; *Brooklyn Eagle*, Apr. 25, 1948; *PM*, Apr. 29, 1948; *SN*, May 5, 1948, 30.

114. *SN*, June 30, 1948, 6.

115. Rickey to O'Malley, June 22, 1948, Rickey Papers. See also memorandum, June 22, 1948, Rickey Papers, where he outlines what he wants O'Malley to say on a number of issues.

116. *Brooklyn Eagle*, Nov. 26, 1948.

117. Ughetta's obituary, *NYT*, Sept. 17, 1967. See also *NYT*, Jan. 8, Feb. 22, Apr. 23, 1953; and *Brooklyn Eagle*, June 21, 1953, Sept. 9, 1954.

118. *Brooklyn Eagle*, Apr. 30, 1950.

119. BoD, Sept. 10, 1947. Ughetta joined the boards of both the Brooklyn National League Baseball Club and the Ebbets-McKeever Exhibition Company on that date.

120. *Brooklyn Eagle*, June 1, 1952.

121. Parrott, *The Lords of Baseball*, 20–21.

122. *NYT*, July 20, 26, 1938; Aug. 29, 31, 1939; Aug. 6, 23, 1940; Feb. 14, May 4, 1941; Apr. 28, Aug. 8, 1942.

123. O'Malley to Rickey, Aug. 30, 1948, Rickey Papers.

124. *Brooklyn Eagle*, Aug. 11, 1947.

125. *LAT*, Mar. 5, 1978.

126. *NYT*, Dec. 27, 1936; Feb. 14, 28, 1937; Mar. 4, 1939.

127. L. Barber, *Lylah*, 170–71.

128. Polner, *Branch Rickey: A Biography*, 153–54.

129. *NYT*, July 18, 1948.

130. Powers, "Don't Get Me Wrong," 83.

131. Mines, *Pfizer: An Informal History*, 19.

132. *SN*, Mar. 10, 1948, 6. For the same sentiment ("If I ran my company as Rickey runs the Dodgers, I'd go broke"), see *SN*, July 26, 1950, 2.

133. BoD, Feb. 2, 1949.

134. BoD, Mar. 7, 1949.

135. R. Barber, *The Broadcasters*, 183.

136. R. Barber, *The Broadcasters*, 184–85.

137. Polner, *Branch Rickey: A Biography*, 219.

138. "President's Report to the Stockholders Brooklyn National League Baseball Club, Inc.," Oct. 23, 1950, Rickey Papers.

139. Rickey to Mickey McConnell, Fresco Thompson, and Branch Rickey Jr., Aug. 16, 1949, Rickey Papers.

140. BoD, Oct. 15, 1947.

141. *SN*, May 25, 1949, 33.

142. BoD, June 6, Aug. 25, Nov. 7, 1949.

143. *Brooklyn Eagle*, Apr. 7, 1947.

144. BoD, Sept. 10, 1947.

145. McCue, "Half-Century of Springs," 9–12.

146. B. Bavasi, interview with the author, Aug. 30, 1994.

147. BoD, Oct. 15, Dec. 19, 1947.

148. Polner, *Branch Rickey: A Biography*, 134.

149. Rice, "Profiles: Thoughts on Baseball," pt. 1, 36–38, for the overall average costs. Rickey's "President's Report" of Oct. 23, 1950, includes some more detailed figures.

150. BoD, Sept. 16, 1946.

151. BoD, Feb. 19, 1947.

152. BoD, Dec. 6, 7, 1947. In an internal memo of Apr. 6, 1948, Rickey Papers, Rickey said, "I agree with Mr. John Smith that the charges for the maintenance of our park are amazingly high."

153. BoD, Mar. 7, 1949.

154. *SN*, July 14, 1948, 8; Joe Trimble column, *New York Daily News*, Nov. 19, 1947.

155. *NYT*, Dec. 6, 1947, for the CYO position; Polner, *Branch Rickey: A Biography*, 211, for O'Malley's attendance fears.

156. BoD, Dec. 6, 1947. In later years Rickey would claim to interviewer Davis J. Walsh that he had the full support of both O'Malley and Smith on the Durocher issue, but that seems to be undercut by the contemporary evidence. Undated transcript of Rickey-Walsh interview in Rickey Papers, 13. From context, it is clear the interview took place in the mid-1950s.

157. "Confidential #1," Apr. 2, 1948, Rickey Papers.

158. Durocher with Linn, *Nice Guys Finish Last*, 228. Durocher said he wanted Campanella to catch and Hodges to play first, while Rickey wanted Campanella at St. Paul (ostensibly to integrate the American Association) and Hodges behind the plate. Actually, it seems clear Rickey wanted Bruce Edwards, who had had an excellent 1947 campaign, at catcher. Edwards suffered injuries, however, and Campanella was eventually called up later in the spring. If Durocher's roster suggestions included getting rid of Edwards, that might explain Rickey's reference to a potential loss of $250,000.

159. Another sidelight on Rickey's business management skills is in O'Toole, *Branch Rickey in Pittsburgh*, 49, where the author notes that it was only after a full year with the Pirates that Rickey realized how precarious their financial position was. He was shocked when he sought a loan to expand the team's spring training facilities and the bank turned him down because of the size of the team's debt.

160. Rickey to Mel (Jones), July 1, 1945, Rickey Papers. BoD, Mar. 23, 1945, indicates an AAFC franchise was also made available.

161. "Memo To: Branch Rickey, Re: Brooklyn Football Dodgers," Nov. 17, 1947, Rickey Papers.

162. *SN*, Jan. 7, 1948, 6.

163. BoD, Dec. 19, 1947.

164. BoD, Dec. 21, 1947. This is the minutes of the Brooklyn National League Baseball Club.

165. BoD, Dec. 21, 1947. As was common practice the meeting of the Baseball Club was immediately followed by a meeting of the Ebbets-McKeever Exhibition Company, where the compromise was reached.

166. "Memorandum of Agreement, between Mr. Dan Topping, representing the New York Yankees, Inc., and Mr. Branch Rickey, representing the Brooklyn National League Baseball Club, Inc., made on Thursday, January 20th, 1949," Rickey Papers. See also Smith to Rickey, Nov. 10, 1949, Rickey Papers.

167. Addie, "Did Dodgers Lose Flag on Gridiron?," 19. The consistent weak spot in the Boys of Summer lineup of the early 1950s was left field, a spot that Noren or Jethroe could have filled.

168. *New York Daily Mirror*, Aug. 19, 1949.

169. The 1948 figure is in A. Mann, *Branch Rickey*, 275. The 1949 figures are in Mann to Rickey, Dec. 6, 1949, Rickey Papers.

170. BoD, Jan. 24, 1950.

171. "Book Value of Capital Stock," June 30, 1950. However, at that point, the books on the company's 1950 fiscal year, which began Oct. 1, 1949, or the middle of the football season, had not closed. BoD, Dec. 7, 1949, indicates an expected football loss of $341,330, but it is not clear how that relates to the other figures.

172. Celler I, 1600.

173. "Notes: Annual Meeting of the Stockholders, Ebbets-McKeever Exhibition Company, Inc., October 23, 1950," Rickey Papers. This appears to be a semi-formal transcript of the meeting rather than the official minutes.

5. BUYING OUT RICKEY

1. The terms are stated in a letter from Joseph Gilleaudeau, a Dodger board member, to Rickey, Oct. 28, 1942, copy in the Rickey Papers. Also in the Rickey Papers is an Oct. 27, 1942, memo from "G.H.W." to Rickey analyzing the terms. G.H.W. is undoubtedly George H. Williams, a former U.S. senator from Missouri and a friend of Rickey's who sometimes acted as his lawyer, as he did in the Chandler-MacPhail-Durocher-Rickey imbroglio in 1947. Many newspaper and magazine articles and books over the years have reported Rickey also received 10 percent of the sale price of player contracts. There is no evidence of that in Rickey's contract. However, because player sales were often the last thing accounted for in the Dodgers' books, income from the sales often reflected the size of the team's profit.

2. BoD, July 9, 1945.

3. BoD, Nov. 8, 1945.

4. Rickey's profit-sharing total is calculated from a sheet labeled "Consolidated Report, Period Covered 1945, 1946, 1947, 1948, 1949," Rickey Papers. This sheet is undated but was part of a package Rickey prepared as he left the team in November 1950, when the books on the 1950 season were not closed. The sheet shows accumulated net profits of $2,290,170.73 for the five-year period. The highest-paid player's salary is an estimate based on a chart of 1949 team executive and player salaries kept by team statistician Allan Roth and currently in the Roth Papers as part of the collection of the Society for American Baseball Research. The chart shows Pee Wee Reese, at $23,500, as the highest salaried player on the team, with manager Burt Shotton at $35,000. Because salaries across baseball were rising in the postwar attendance boom, it can be assumed Reese's 1949 salary was his highest during the period.

5. *LAT*, Apr. 14, 1958.

6. This is computed based on the profit amounts reported to the Celler Committee and included in Celler I. These figures are about $70,000 higher than the figure Rickey reported to the board and cited in note 4. The profits for 1945 to 1949 were used for the calculation, as they give a fuller picture of how much Rickey made during the team's most profitable years during his presidency. Before 1945 World War II limited profits, and the 1950 figure was actually a small loss due to the football fiasco. The Dodgers were criticized by Celler for including the football losses and hiding baseball profits behind the losses.

7. BoD, June 11, 1946.

8. Carroll to Rickey, June 16, 1947, Rickey Papers. Carroll cites the board resolution as occurring Nov. 8, 1946, but this conflicts with the copy of the minutes in the Rickey Papers, clearly marked 1945. Whichever made the mistake, it is moot for the sake of this narrative.

9. Rickey to Board, Sept. 24, 1948, Rickey Papers.

10. Lowenfish, *Branch Rickey*, 64.

11. Leonard Koppett, interview with the author, July 25, 2001.

12. Veeck with Linn, "Walter O'Malley," 80, for O'Malley; Veeck with Linn, *The Hustler's Handbook*, 39, for Rickey.

13. Polner, *Branch Rickey: A Biography*, 222.

14. BoD, Aug. 25, 1949. Barber got the loan from the team.

15. Kahn, *Games We Used to Play*, 70.

16. Parrott, *The Lords of Baseball*, 20–21.

17. Lowenfish, "Two Titans and the Mystery Man," 178n57.

18. R. Barber, *1947*, 85, for the devious-man quote. Polner, *Branch Rickey: A Biography*, 215, has the remark to Rex Bowen.

19. *LAT*, Apr. 10, 1962.

20. Shaplen, "O'Malley and the Angels," 62–70.

21. Plaut, *Chasing October*, 18.

22. Rickey Papers.

23. *NYT*, Feb. 22, Mar. 10, 16, 17, 23, Apr. 4, 12, 1950; *SN*, Mar. 29, 1950, 33; Apr. 5, 1950, 6; April 12, 1950, 31; April 19, 1950, 12. O'Malley made most of the public comments, but Rickey had a long-standing relationship with New York Republican governor Tom Dewey.

24. *SN*, Nov. 24, 1948, 18. The "reliable source" cited is probably Mann.

25. Mann to M. I. Yurkovsky, Oct. 3, 1949, Mann Papers.

26. The report on Yurkovsky is dated Aug. 2, 1949, and is in the Rickey Papers.

27. "Meeting of the Board of Directors, Brooklyn National League Baseball Club, Inc. and Ebbets-McKeever Exhibition Company, Inc., 4:00 o'clock in the afternoon, June 21st, 1950," 20, Rickey Papers. Despite the title, this is not the formal minutes of the meeting but what appear to be transcribed notes with a sense that many things are being quoted verbatim.

28. Mann's accounting to Yurkovsky in the letter of Oct. 3, 1949, put the value of all Dodger assets at more than $6.5 million.

29. R. Barber, *1947*, 84.

30. Thompson with Rice, *Every Diamond Doesn't Sparkle*, 111.

31. Parrott, *The Lords of Baseball*, 28–29; R. Barber, *The Broadcasters*, 168–69. A few years earlier, however, there is a note from Rickey to himself dated Aug. 7, 1946, in his papers that shows how he financed his life. It reports he owes "the bank" (presumably Brooklyn Trust) $650,000 for a loan with his stock in the team as collateral. This is stock he had paid just under $350,000 for over the previous eighteen months.

32. Marshall, *Baseball's Pivotal Era*, 200.

33. *SN*, July 26, 1950, 3.

34. Board to Rickey, Sept. 1, 1950, Rickey Papers.

35. O'Malley to Rickey telegram, Sept. 1, 1950, Rickey Papers.

36. Rickey to O'Malley telegram, Sept. 2, 1950, Rickey Papers.

37. O'Malley to Rickey telegram, Sept. 1, 1950, Rickey Papers.

38. BoD, Sept. 19, 1950.

39. A. Mann, *Branch Rickey*, 283.

40. A. Mann, *Branch Rickey*, 283. For Zeckendorf's short version, see Zeckendorf with McCreary, *Zeckendorf*, 140. There is also some discussion of the negotiations in the *Daily News* and other New York papers, Sept. 24, 1950. Zeckendorf revealed more details in *SN*, Oct. 4, 1950, 2.

41. A. Mann, *Branch Rickey*, 283. The name of the buyer might have come as a surprise, but O'Malley certainly knew Rickey's general plan.

42. *New York Daily News*, Sept. 24, 1950.

43. Kahn, *The Era*, 264–67; J. Mann, "King of the Jungle," 116.

44. *SN*, Oct. 4, 1950, 2.

45. All the New York papers were asking the Rickey-to-Pittsburgh, general manager–and-manager questions. The two who reported the Smith stock-sale possibility were the *New York Mirror*, Sept. 24, 1950; and *New York World Telegram Sun*, Sept. 25, 1950.

46. *NYT*, Sept. 25, 1950; *New York Post*, Sept. 25, 1950; *New York Mirror*, Sept. 25, 1950.

47. *SN*, Oct. 4, 1950, 4.

48. *New York Journal-American*, Sept. 26, 1950.

49. Polner, *Branch Rickey: A Biography*, 220.

50. Every New York paper I have seen carried a story on Oct. 25. I have seen the *Brooklyn Eagle*, *New York Times*, *New York Mirror*, and *New York Herald-Tribune*.

51. *SN*, Nov. 15, 1950, 5.

52. The contract is in the Rickey Papers. It called for the same annual $100,000 for five years as general manager and $50,000 annually for five additional years as an

adviser. The difference was in the size of the expense account, $12,000 a year in Pittsburgh.

53. *New York Herald-Tribune*, Oct. 27, 1950.

54. *New York Herald-Tribune*, Oct. 27, 1950.

55. *NYT*, Oct. 27, 1950. Despite O'Malley's multiple complaints over the years about paying Zeckendorf $50,000, it seems clear he convinced Rickey to pay half the amount. That explains why the formal documents refer to Rickey receiving $1,025,000. Arthur Mann's calculation in *Branch Rickey: American in Action*, 285, implies this solution.

56. *NYT*, Oct. 27, 1950.

57. O'Malley to Rickey, Nov. 1, 1950, Rickey Papers.

58. Mary Louise Smith to Rickey, Nov. 20, 1950, Rickey Papers.

59. Arthur Mann reported the calculation for Rickey's 25 percent went as follows. Rickey received $975,000 after paying Zeckendorf's fee. Of that, just under $350,000 was the original purchase price, leaving the capital gains at approximately $600,000, a quarter of which went to taxes. As she was not selling, Mrs. Smith would not be subject to a capital gains tax, but the principal on which the estate tax would be based had increased. A. Mann, *Branch Rickey*, 285.

60. O'Malley to Rickey, Nov. 24, 1950, Rickey Papers.

61. *LAT*, Aug. 10, 1979.

62. In fact, O'Malley paid off Rickey by the end of 1955. Henry J. Walsh to Rickey, Nov. 16, 1955; Rickey Power of Attorney, Dec. 14, 1955, Rickey Papers.

63. *Brooklyn Eagle*, Oct. 26, 1950; *NYT*, Oct. 24, 1951. In subsequent discussions this ruling was also affirmed by the commissioner, Ford Frick. Frick to Rickey, Feb. 16, 1953, Rickey Papers.

64. Rickey to Board of Directors, Oct. 26, 1950, Rickey Papers.

65. Rickey to Board of Directors, Oct. 26, 1950, Rickey Papers.

66. "Book Value of Capital Stock," June 30, 1950, Rickey Papers. A. Mann, *Branch Rickey*, 284, lists some different figures for these statistics, but he does not cite a source and they are in the same ballpark.

67. "Cash on Hand—October 26, 1950," Rickey Papers.

68. Kahn, *The Boys of Summer*.

69. Graham Jr., *A Farewell to Heroes*, 234. See also Bavasi with Strege, *Off the Record*, 39. At the age of nearly eighty, after four successful decades as a general manager and team executive, Bavasi still called him Mr. Rickey, too. Bavasi, interviews with the author, July 23, Aug. 30, Nov. 9, 1994.

6. RUNNING THE TEAM

1. Voigt, *American Baseball*, 88.

2. *SN*, Nov. 1, 1950, 3.

3. The fish tank is in Rampersad, *Jackie Robinson: A Biography*, 233; the elk head is in *SN*, Mar. 7, 1951, 7; and the portrait switch is *SN*, Dec. 6, 1950, 32.

4. *SN*, Mar. 7, 1951, 7.

5. *SN*, Nov. 1, 1950, 3. New York papers of Nov. 2 and 3, 1950, carried much the same criticisms in the stories about Bavasi and Thompson's ascensions. See also *SN*, Mar. 7, 1951, 7. Despite O'Malley's rhetoric, the Dodgers would continue to sell players since the farm system Rickey had created kept producing more than the Dodgers could use. Fresco Thompson estimated the Dodgers' Minor League clubs produced about a dozen major leaguers a year in that era, far more than the parent club could absorb. *SN*, Feb. 28, 1951, 5.

6. Polner, *Branch Rickey: A Biography*, 226–27.

7. Substantially identical letters to the four men from Rickey dated Sept. 27, 1950, are in the Rickey Papers.

8. A. Mann, *Branch Rickey*, 287–90. See also Polner, *Branch Rickey: A Biography*, 226.

9. Praeger, *Echoing Green*, 183.

10. *New York Mirror*, Jan. 15, 1951.

11. This was not direct action on the part of either Rickey or O'Malley. Rickey offered jobs to the Catholics Bavasi and Parrot, for example, but both stayed. O'Malley offered jobs to Protestants Branch Rickey Jr. and George Sisler, who left, and Red Barber, who stayed.

12. Kahn, *The Era*, 328.

13. Golenbock, *Bums*, 263. Actually, few of O'Malley's top executives over the years had Irish surnames. His general managers over three decades were Bavasi, a French-Italian mix, and Al Campanis, of Greek descent. The first "O'Malley man" on the club's board of directors was Henry Ughetta, an Italian.

14. Thompson with Rice, *Every Diamond Doesn't Sparkle*, 120; Rudd and Fischler, *Sporting Life*, 133–34.

15. Beech to Rickey, Jan. 23, 1951, Rickey Papers.

16. Interclub communication, O'Malley to Beech, Jan. 23, 1951, Rickey Papers. In his letter to Rickey, Beech characterized this note as "nasty," but, while abrupt, Beech's "nasty" characterization seems a product of the O'Malley versus Rickey camps' tension around the office. The text reads: "Dear Don. Confirming our conversation, I have other plans for your department, and I would appreciate having you turn over your work to Miss Duignan for the time being. There is a possibility, if you desire, that other employment in the organization might be found for you, and I would like you to explore the possibilities with Messers. Bavasi and Thompson. Should nothing develop along those lines you know from our talk that you may expect to be continued on our payroll for the next two months, unless you find employment elsewhere in the meantime. Yours truly, Walter F. O'Malley."

17. Rickey to Beech, Mar. 2, 1951, Rickey Papers.

18. *SN*, Nov. 8, 1950, 4. Home attendance was 1,633,747 in 1949 and 1,185,896 in 1950.

19. *New York Mirror*, Jan. 15, 1951.

20. *SN*, Dec. 6, 1950, 15.

21. *SN*, Jan. 3, 1951, 10.

22. *SN*, Mar. 7, 1951, 7.

23. *SN*, May 7, 1952, 14.

24. Young, "Dick Young, Baseball Writer," 29–30.

25. *SN*, May 7, 1952, 13.

26. Kahn, *The Boys of Summer*, 100–101. Bavasi denied he was given this charge. B. Bavasi interview, Aug. 30, 1994.

27. Kahn, *October Men*, 259.

28. *SN*, Jan. 11, 1956, 6.

29. *SN*, Jan. 31, 1951, 4.

30. B. Bavasi interview, Nov. 9, 1994.

31. *SN*, Mar. 21, 1951, 24.

32. *SN*, Jan. 11, 1956, 6, gives the *NYT* circulation and fall 1938 dates. Bavasi's autobiography says he had no job between graduation and asking Frick for the recommendation in the spring of 1939. Bavasi with Strege, *Off the Record*, 9–10.

33. B. Bavasi with Strege, *Off the Record*, 14.

34. "Bauasi" is in *SN*, Mar. 5, 1942, 8. "Bervasi" is in *SN*, Feb. 18, 1943, 8. Parrott's piece appeared in *SN*, Oct. 28, 1943, 11. His military service appeared in *SN*, Jan. 31, 1951, 4, where he said he served with the Eightieth Division, the *LAT*, Apr. 14, 1958; where he said he served with the Eighty-Eighth Division; and in Oliphant, *Praying for Gil Hodges*, 56, where he told Oliphant he had served with the 350th Mountain Division.

35. *SN*, Jan. 11, 1956, 6.

36. Tygiel, *Baseball's Great Experiment*, 146.

37. Madden, "Nashua, N.H., Was Safe Haven," *Boston Globe*, Mar. 28, 1997.

38. Lanctot, *Campy*, 136–37.

39. *SN*, Mar. 12, 1958, 11.

40. *SN*, June 27, 1951, 12.

41. B. Bavasi interview, Aug. 30, 1994.

42. *SN*, Mar. 7, 1951, 7.

43. B. Bavasi interview, Aug. 30, 1994.

44. *SN*, Apr. 11, 1951, 23.

45. *SN*, Sept. 26, 1951, 21.

46. *SN*, May 7, 1952, 13.

47. *SN*, June 4, 1952, 12.

48. Stephan, "Roth's True Discovery of Sabermetrics," 89.

49. The papers are housed with the archives of the Society for American Baseball Research at Case Western Reserve University, Cleveland OH.

50. "O'Malley's Alley," in *Dodgers 1952 Yearbook* (Brooklyn: Brooklyn Dodgers, 1952), 4.

51. *NYT*, July 24, 25, 31, 1951; *SN*, Aug. 8, 1951, 1.

52. In his autobiography Frank Graham Jr. says Irving Rudd planned Music Depreciation Night with O'Malley (*A Farewell to Heroes*, 268). Rudd, however, did not join the promotions department until late 1951 (Rudd and Fis-

chler, *Sporting Life*, 69, 134). Also, *SN*, Jan. 30, 1952, 9, is the first time Rudd is described as a team employee.

53. *SN*, Oct. 3, 1951, 25.

54. *New York World-Telegram*, Aug. 22, 1951.

55. *SN*, Feb. 1, 1950, 1.

56. Cannon, "Jackie Robinson's Precious Gift," 144.

57. Frommer, *Rickey and Robinson*, 176.

58. Lanctot, *Campy*, 176–77.

59. Lacy, *Fighting for Fairness*, 121.

60. Frommer, *Rickey and Robinson*, 177, has Campanella describing Rickey telling him and Robinson, "I have stuck my neck out of the windows for you fellows. Please don't let them chop it off." Frank Graham Jr. tells of Robinson agreeing to racist treatment in Miami as a favor to Dodger PR man Irving Rudd, whom Robinson liked (*A Farewell to Heroes*, 272).

61. Graham Jr., *A Farewell to Heroes*, 272–73.

62. *SN*, Apr. 4, 1951, 14.

63. *SN*, May 9, 1951, 3. See also *NYT*, May 2, 3, 1951.

64. *SN*, Dec. 10, 1952, 3.

65. *SN*, Sept. 15, 1954, 7.

66. *LAT*, Jan. 8, 1997.

67. *SN*, Feb. 23, 1955, 18.

68. Text of undated Rickey speech in Mann Papers.

69. Rampersad, *Jackie Robinson: A Biography*, 304.

70. Rampersad, *Jackie Robinson: A Biography*, 305.

71. *New York Daily News*, Dec. 14, 1956.

72. B. Bavasi interview, Aug. 30, 1994.

73. The text appears in Rowan with Robinson, *Wait till Next Year*, 282. A somewhat different version of the text and Robinson's response are in Kahn, *The Era*, 333.

74. *SN*, Dec. 19, 1956, 3.

75. *SN*, Jan. 16, 1957, 3.

76. *Newark Star-Ledger*, May 9, 1958.

77. *LAT*, Dec. 14, 1959.

78. Rowan with Robinson, *Wait till Next Year*, 255–62, 269, 282, 332–33.

79. J. Robinson, *Baseball Has Done It*, 160.

80. *LAT*, Mar. 22, 1964.

81. *LAT*, June 5, 1972.

82. *SN*, July 1, 1972, 24, and Mar. 31, 1997, Jackie Robinson fiftieth anniversary commemorative section, 2.

83. *SN*, Dec. 27, 1950, 6.

84. *NYT*, Mar. 13, June 15, 1951.

85. The best discussion of Chandler's career in baseball is Marshall's *Baseball's Pivotal Era*. Marshall was the curator of the Happy Chandler Papers at the University of Kentucky Library, and the book is built around Chandler. In

private conversation Marshall told me he had not been able to figure out how O'Malley voted.

86. *SN*, Dec. 20, 1950, 1; Mar. 7, 1951, 7.

87. *SN*, Dec. 20, 1950, 3.

88. *NYT*, Mar. 13, 1951; *SN*, Mar. 21, 1951, 6.

89. *Sunday Compass*, May 27, 1951.

90. William DeWitt interview by William Marshall, Oral History Collection, 130. This interview is connected to the university's holdings of Chandler's papers. In two different places historian David Q. Voigt asserts that Chandler said O'Malley had organized his ouster. In "They Shaped the Game," 18, the assertion comes without a source note. In *American Baseball*, 128, he attributes his information to a two-part series Chandler wrote with John Underwood for *Sports Illustrated*. "How I Jumped from Clean Politics into Dirty Baseball" ran on Apr. 26 and May 3, 1971. The only mention of O'Malley I can find in these articles (p. 76 on Apr. 26) refers to his plans to move the Dodgers to Los Angeles several years later. As contemporary articles did, Chandler identified his core opponents as Del Webb and Dan Topping of the Yankees, Lou Perini of the Braves, and Fred Saigh of the Cardinals.

91. *SN*, July 4, 1951, 3.

92. *SN*, July 4, 1951, 3.

93. The Executive Council at that time also included American League president Will Harridge and owners Tom Yawkey of the Red Sox and Warren Giles, an executive with the Reds.

94. *SN*, July 25, 1951, 7.

95. *NYT*, Sept. 21, 1951.

96. *SN*, May 7, 1952, 13.

97. *Vero Beach (FL) Press-Journal*, Feb. 22, 1951; Rosenfeld, *Great Chase*, 180.

98. Rosenfeld, *Great Chase*, 200; R. Robinson, *Home Run Heard 'round the World*, 205.

99. *NYT*, Oct. 4, 1951.

100. Rosenfeld, *Great Chase*, 236. See also Snider with Gilbert, *The Duke of Flatbush*, 112.

101. Meany, *The Artful Dodgers*, 7–8.

102. Thompson with Rice, *Every Diamond Doesn't Sparkle*, 113.

103. *SN*, Apr. 19, 1950, 6.

104. Collins to Rickey, "My duties as Business Manager and Purchasing Agent . . . ," memo with handwritten "1942," in the Rickey Papers. Rickey asked all department heads to send him a memo summarizing their duties when he joined the team, and this is clearly one of those memos.

105. *NYT*, *New York Daily News*, *New York Mirror*, and *Brooklyn Eagle* of Feb. 2 and Feb. 3 covered the story, and the details are drawn from them. The exact figure of the loss is from *NYT*, June 25, 1952.

106. A. P. Kitchin to Chandler, June 20, 1947, with a cover letter from Chandler assistant Walter Mulbry to Rickey, July 11, 1947, Rickey Papers.

107. *NYT*, May 7, 1952, on the arrest and June 25, 1952, on the lack of indictment.

108. *SN*, Mar. 26, 1952, 16.

109. Jack Lang, interview with the author, Sept. 12, 1996.

110. "Memorandum dictated by Mr. Rickey is his wuite [*sic*] in the Commodore Hotel, Friday, November 6, 1959 . . . ," Rickey Papers.

111. *SN*, Feb. 18, 1953, 2.

112. Frommer, *Rickey and Robinson*, 175, says O'Malley refused to schedule exhibition games with the Pirates because of Rickey. Actually, the Pirates trained in California in 1951 and 1952 and in Havana in 1953. In 1954 they moved to Fort Pierce, Florida, becoming the closest team to Vero Beach. The Dodgers began playing them that spring.

113. B. Bavasi interview, Aug. 30, 1994.

114. *SN*, Feb. 24, 1954, 9.

115. Undated Dodgers press release, late 1954 or early 1955, Roth Papers. See also *SN*, Aug. 25, 1954, 34.

116. *Vero Beach (FL) Press-Journal*, Mar. 29, 1951.

117. *Vero Beach (FL) Press-Journal*, Jan. 31, 1952.

118. *SN*, Mar. 12, 1952, 9.

119. The seated capacity was variously reported as 4,200 (*SN*, Sept. 10, 1952, 23), 4,500 (Nov. 5, 1952, 24), and "nearly 5,000" (Oct. 29, 1952, 24). Attendance often went over 5,000 because of the berm seating.

120. *SN*, Sept. 10, 1952, 23.

121. *SN*, Oct. 29, 1953, 24.

122. *Vero Beach (FL) Press-Journal*, Oct. 30, 1952.

123. *SN*, Nov. 5, 1952, 13; Feb. 4, 1953, 6; Mar. 18, 1953, 17.

124. *SN*, Mar. 4, 1953, 23.

125. *SN*, Mar. 7, 1956, 17.

126. *SN*, Jan. 2, 1974, 18.

127. *SN*, Jan. 27, 1954, 24.

128. *SN*, Nov. 4, 1953, 9.

129. Bump Holman, interview with the author, Feb. 7, 2000. Holman, Bud's son, said he taught O'Malley to drive during his visits to Vero Beach in the 1950s.

130. *SN*, Mar. 9, 1955, 26.

131. *SN*, Oct. 27, 1954, 8.

132. Lang interview, Sept. 12, 1996.

133. Kahn, *Memories of Summer*, 89.

134. *SN*, Oct. 8, 1952, 26.

135. *SN*, Oct. 1, 1952, 30.

136. *SN*, Jan. 7, 1953, 15.

137. *SN*, Jan. 11, 1945, 12.

138. For one example of Dearie exercising horses, see *SN*, Apr. 2, 1936, 4. See also her *NYT* obituary, Nov. 25, 1968, 47.

139. *SN*, Jan. 11, 1945, 12.

140. *NYT*, Dec. 4, 1973, 48.

141. For example, see *SN*, June 18, 1936, 3, which includes the Mungo discipline, and Dec. 23, 1937, 1.

142. *SN*, Nov. 26, 1936, 2.

143. *SN*, July 23, 1942, 1.

144. Berg, *Goldwyn: A Biography*, 371; *SN*, July 22, 1943, 13, for Jim Mulvey's role. Dearie Mulvey's role is in Bak, *Lou Gehrig*, 174.

145. *SN*, July 2, 1936, 5.

146. *NYT*, Feb. 15, 1944, 21.

147. BoD, Nov. 8, 1945.

148. *SN*, Nov. 9, 1944, 1; *NYT*, Aug. 14, 1945; *PM*, Aug. 14, 1945. (The *SN* and *PM* reporter was Tom Meany, who often seemed to have a pipeline to Mulvey.) The Rickey Papers also contain an undated "confidential memo," which appears to be notes for a press conference after the purchase of the Ed McKeever shares. It indicates that questions about McLaughlin's participation in ownership were anticipated. This issue was raised obliquely in the Ebbets bloc purchase as well. The response was always the same. The bank's fiduciary duty to get the Ebbets heirs the best deal possible precluded any bank official from buying the stock.

149. BoD, June 11, 1946. Mulvey was also voted off the board of the Brooklyn National League Baseball Club, whose annual meeting was held on the same day.

150. BoD, Sept. 16, 1946.

151. BoD, Sept. 10, 1947. News of the stenographer did not appear until the BoD meeting of Sept. 23.

152. BoD, May 3, 1948. The papers also contain a document entitled "Notes, Annual Stockholders, Brooklyn Natl League Baseball Club, Inc., May 3, 1948," which appears to be a partial transcript of the meeting.

153. See Tom Meany in *SN*, July 7, 1948, 7; Dan Parker of the *New York Mirror*, Oct. 26, 1951; and Arch Murray of the *New York Post* (in *SN*), Feb. 28, 1951, 12.

154. BoD, July 18, 1947.

155. Memorandum of conversation, June 5, 1947, Louisville KY, Rickey Papers.

156. BoD, Sept. 10, 1947.

157. Notes, annual meeting of the stockholders, Ebbets-McKeever Exhibition Company, Oct. 23, 1950, Rickey Papers.

158. Parrott, *The Lords of Baseball*, 226.

159. In addition to the sources cited above, see Memorandum of Impressions Stockholders Meeting, May 3, 1948, for Rickey strategizing with his partners over how to deal with Mulvey.

160. *SN*, June 16, 1946, 4.

161. Meany in *SN*, July 7, 1948, 7.

162. *SN*, Feb. 28, 1951, 12.

163. *SN*, Nov. 29, 1950, 24; Oct. 31, 1951, 17.

164. *SN*, Oct. 1, 1952, 9.

165. *SN*, Oct. 28, 1959, 7; Parrott, *The Lords of Baseball*, 32–33.

166. Parrott, dedication to *The Lords of Baseball*.

167. Parrott, *The Lords of Baseball*, 146.

168. Parrott, *The Lords of Baseball*, 32.

169. Parrott, *The Lords of Baseball*, 34.

170. Graham Jr., *A Farewell to Heroes*, 268.

171. Rudd and Fischler, *Sporting Life*, 141.

172. B. Bavasi interview, Aug. 30, 1994.

173. R. Barber and Creamer, *Rhubarb*, 284–86.

174. R. Barber and Creamer, *Rhubarb*, 284–85.

175. R. Barber and Creamer, *Rhubarb*, 279.

176. L. Barber, *Lylah*, 171.

177. R. Barber and Creamer, *Rhubarb*, 286–89.

178. R. Barber and Creamer, *Rhubarb*, 282.

179. Graham Jr., *A Farewell to Heroes*, 234.

180. *LAT*, Aug. 19, 1999.

181. *SN*, Apr. 8, 1972, 42.

182. The first quote is from "Walter in Wonderland," 58. The second is from Murray, *Jim Murray*, 53.

183. *LAHE*, Feb. 2, 1967.

184. Conlan and Creamer, *Jocko*, 145–46.

185. *New York World Telegram and Sun*, Apr. 29, 1957.

186. *LAT*, June 18, 1959.

187. Kahn, *Good Enough to Dream*, 70.

188. Graham Jr., *A Farewell to Heroes*, 234. As Graham notes, he felt O'Malley was highly conscious that Graham's father was a columnist for the *New York Journal-American*.

189. *SN*, Mar. 3, 1954, 8.

190. John Burton, interview with the author, May 9, 2001.

191. Shapiro, *Last Good Season*, 21.

192. Lang interview, Sept. 12, 1996.

193. *New York Daily News*, Jan. 19, 1955.

194. *SN*, May 25, 1955, 6; June 1, 1955, 25.

195. *SN*, May 16, 1954, 6.

196. *SN*, Oct. 14, 1953, 16.

197. *SN*, Oct. 24, 1951, 17; Oct. 1, 1952, 9; Graham Jr., *A Farewell to Heroes*, 265–68.

198. *SN*, Aug. 19, 1953, 7.

199. *SN*, Oct. 21, 1953, 9.

200. Parrott, *The Lords of Baseball*, 36–37.

201. Kahn, *Era*, 316–17.

202. Graham Jr., *A Farewell to Heroes*, 264–66.

203. Bavasi with Strege, *Off the Record*, 52–53.

204. Bavasi with Strege, *Off the Record*, 55. Graham describes Bavasi asking in such a way that Reese knew what the expected answer was. Graham Jr., *A Farewell to Heroes*, 266.

205. Bavasi with Strege, *Off the Record*, 54.

206. Polner, *Branch Rickey: A Biography*, 234.

207. *NYT*, Mar. 17, 19, 1953; Flaherty, "Miracle Move of the Dodgers," 9.

208. Golenbock, *Bums*, 436.

209. Koufax with Linn, *Koufax*, 64–72.

210. *SN*, Mar. 3, 1954, 26.

211. Bavasi and Strege, *Off the Record*, 72–73. Here and elsewhere Bavasi tells of supposedly trying to hide Clemente by limiting his playing time and starting him only against right-handed pitchers. Research indicates that was not the case. See Thornley, "Clemente's Entry," 61–71.

212. *SN*, Dec. 1, 1954, 4.

213. *SN*, May 25, 1955, 11.

214. *LAT*, Mar. 10, 1967.

215. B. Bavasi interview, Aug. 30, 1994.

216. Oliphant, *Praying for Gil Hodges*, 59. With slight variations, he told the same story to Shapiro for *Last Good Season*, 170–71.

217. *LAT*, Feb. 19, 2005. Markusen, *Roberto Clemente*, 32–33, and Wagenheim, *Clemente!*, 35, both claim there was a racial quota in effect, but provide no evidence. Wagenheim's claim that the Dodgers' five blacks in 1954 were never allowed to play at the same time is demonstrably untrue. See Thornley, "Clemente's Entry."

218. Lanctot, *Campy*, 304–19.

219. *NYT*, May 28, July 6, 1955; *SN*, June 8, 1955, 9; July 27, 1955, 37.

220. *SN*, Feb. 22, 1956, 28.

221. *LAHE*, Nov. 20, 1957.

222. Wolpin, *Bums No More!*, 60.

223. *SN*, Sept. 21, 1955, 7.

224. *SN*, Sept. 28, 1955, 9.

225. In another example of O'Malley's tin ear, Sandy Amoros was celebrating his game-saving catch of a drive by Yogi Berra during the clubhouse party. O'Malley, making his rounds, approached, gripped his shoulders, and asked, "Where's that $100 you owe me?," a reference to a spring training fine. Wolpin, *Bums No More!*, 116.

226. Bavasi with Strege, *Off the Record*, 66.

227. *SN*, Oct. 12, 1955, 9.

228. *SN*, Oct. 19, 1955, 9.

229. See O'Malley's testimony in *Finley v. Kuhn* on Jan. 11, 1977, transcript 1623-5.

230. *SN*, Apr. 8, 1953, 20.

231. Henry J. Walsh to Rickey, Nov. 16, 1955; "Power of Attorney" signed by Branch Rickey, Dec. 14, 1955; Branch Rickey Ledger, with Rickey Statement of Assets, Mar. 5, 1952, Jan. 31, 1960, Rickey Papers.

232. *SN*, Jan. 4, 1956, 1.

233. *SN*, June 25, 1952, 14.

234. *SN*, Apr. 30, 1952, 14.

235. *SN*, June 25, 1952, 6.

236. *Sunday Compass*, May 27, 1951.

237. *SN*, May 18, 1955, 23.

238. *SN*, Nov. 10, 1954, 8.

239. I found the document containing this proposal in the archives of the *Sporting News* with a stamp date of Oct. 1956. It is captioned "National Baseball Day." It has the appearance of an article marked up for use in the newspaper, but it did not appear. Much of the verbiage also clearly was written by someone at Stephen Fitzgerald & Co. It is pretty clear the proposal died in the Commissioner's Office after the Fitzgerald report.

240. *Newsweek*, Apr. 23, 1956, 84.

241. *NYT*, May 21, 2010.

242. John Burton interview, May 9, 2001.

243. *SN*, Feb. 20, 1952, 33.

244. *SN*, Apr. 23, 1952, 19.

245. *SN*, Aug. 29, 1956, 13; Sept. 5, 1956, 15.

246. *LAT*, Oct. 5, Oct. 17, 1956, 26.

247. *SN*, Oct. 17, 1956, 22.

248. Celler II, 358.

249. Obojski, *Japanese Baseball Power*, 56.

250. *SN*, July 16, 1952, 1; Aug. 27, 1952, 1; Sept. 10, 1952, 4.

251. Obojski, *Japanese Baseball Power*, 50–55.

252. *Dodger Yearbook, 1957* (Brooklyn: Brooklyn Dodgers, 1957), 38–39.

253. *SN*, Nov. 21, 1956, 6; Dec. 5, 1956, 10; Dec. 26, 1956, 11.

254. Bump Holman interview, Feb. 7, 2000.

255. Bump Holman interview, Feb. 7, 2000.

256. United Press International story datelined San Diego, Jan. 4, 1957, clip from an anonymous newspaper in the Roth Papers.

257. Bump Holman interview, Feb. 7, 2000.

258. "Press Box Pickups," Apr. 25, 1961, Roth Papers.

259. B. Bavasi interview, Aug. 30, 1994.

260. *LAHE*, Mar. 15, 1964.

261. *SN*, Jan. 27, 1954, 12, which reported the offer as $5 million and *SN*, Aug. 14, 1965, which reported it as $6 million. See also Kiner with Gergen, *Kiner's Korner*, 18.

7. A NEW STADIUM—ECONOMICS

1. *SN*, Aug. 13, 1952, 10.

2. Holmes, *Dodger Daze and Knights*, 11.

3. I have avoided making comparisons to 1957 because the belief the Dodgers would leave Brooklyn was clearly affecting attendance that year. If I had, the comparisons would have looked worse.

4. UPI, "Baseball Situation in New York Is Mired in Unhealthy State, Says Bums' Prexy," *Wichita Eagle*, Dec. 6, 1954, O'Malley file, Culver Academy Archives.

5. *SN*, Aug. 10, 1955, 5.

6. "Press Box Pickups," July 19, 1956, Roth Papers.

7. You could have walked up and bought a ticket to Games 2 and 3 as well. The Polo Grounds was only a subway ride from Brooklyn.

8. *NYT*, Sept. 27, 1956.

9. Golenbock, *Bums*, 434.

10. *Brooklyn Eagle*, Sept. 4, 1941; *SN*, Sept. 10, 1947, 20. O'Malley considered this in 1951 as well: *SN*, Sept. 19, 1951, 1.

11. Wilfrid Sheed, "The Field, the Fans, and the Bums," *Brooklyn Bridge*, Sept. 1, 1995, 59–65.

12. "Stank" is in Oliphant, *Praying for Gil Hodges*, 12. "Fetid troughs" is in Kahn, *Games We Used to Play*, 170.

13. R. Barber with Creamer, *Rhubarb*, 290. The rusting girders is in Maury Allen's column in the *New York Post*, Aug. 10, 1979.

14. Quoted in the documentary *The Brooklyn Dodgers: The Original America's Team*.

15. Frommer, *New York City Baseball*, 3.

16. Golenbock, *Bums*, 433.

17. Rudd and Fischler, *Sporting Life*, 137.

18. Kahn, *The Era*, 327.

19. Bavasi with Strege, *Off the Record*, 77. Dodger publicity man Irving Rudd echoed Bavasi, saying O'Malley's concerns were serious, but economic rather than racial. See Rubin, "Brooklyn Dodgers and Ebbets Field," 167.

20. Rubin, "Brooklyn Dodgers and Ebbets Field," 167.

21. Schroth, *"Eagle" and Brooklyn*, 257. Schroth was a member of the family that owned the *Eagle*.

22. Thompson with Rice, *Every Diamond Doesn't Sparkle*, 145.

23. "Brooklyn: Waves from Manhattan Break," 126–34.

24. "Walter in Wonderland," 59; Shaplen, "O'Malley and the Angels," 64; Durslag, "Visit with O'Malley," 104.

25. Fetter, *Taking on the Yankees*, 201–3.

26. Lieb, *The Boston Red Sox*, 207–8.

27. John Collins to Rickey, n.d., beginning "My duties as a Business Manager and Purchasing Agent are as follows," 5, Rickey Papers. Although undated, this is clearly one of the reports Rickey requested from department heads when he joined the team.

28. Hamill, "Brooklyn: The Sane Alternative."

29. Willensky, *When Brooklyn Was the World*, 218.

30. Walker and Bellamy, *Center Field Shot*, 324–31.

31. A. Mann, "Baseball's Astounding Blueprint," 10.

32. Coughlan, "Baseball," 57.

33. Flaherty, "Miracle Move of the Dodgers," 3.

34. *SN*, Mar. 14, 1956, 25.

35. *Wall Street Journal*, Oct. 31, 1957.

36. *SN*, Sept. 7, 1955, 12; *NYT*, Sept. 18, 1955.

37. *SN*, Jan. 4, 1956, 1.

38. Celler II, 354–63. Very roughly, this income was the equivalent of 350,000 to 400,000 in paid attendance. The average Dodger ticket sold at $1.77 in 1955 (calculated from *the 1955 Sporting News Dope Book*, 43). Add a guesstimate of parking and concessions revenue and subtract the portion of the $888,270 due to radio rather than television, and I come up with this range.

39. *New York Herald-Tribune*, Mar. 4, 1952.

40. *New York World-Telegram and Sun*, Jan. 28, 1953.

41. Ted Leitzell of Zenith Radio Corporation to O'Malley, Jan. 29, 1953, National Baseball Hall of Fame and Museum Archives.

42. Celler II, 1874–75. Although O'Malley's reaction may be accurate, the 2.4 million figure seems very high. In 1953, to pick a year in the era O'Malley is talking about, there were about 25 million television sets in the entire country. To have 10 percent of them tuned to one program in one city, albeit the country's largest, seems unlikely.

43. *NYT*, Jan. 9, 1978.

44. *Wall Street Journal* and *LAT*, May 5, 1955.

45. Shapiro, *Last Good Season*, 132–33.

46. *LAT*, May 31, 1957.

47. *Chicago Daily Tribune*, June 1, 1957.

48. *LAT*, June 10, 1957.

49. *SN*, July 10, 1957, 24. The Dodgers would have gotten only 25 cents of that price, after taxes and a share for the visiting team.

50. *LAT*, June 6, 1957.

51. *LAT*, June 9, 1957. This was a Leonard Koppett story that had run a day or two earlier in the *New York Post*.

8. A NEW STADIUM—POLITICS

1. BoD, Oct. 22, 1946. The board minutes refer to Cedar Place, but that street had been renamed for Steven McKeever after the former owner's death in 1938.

2. *New York Herald-Tribune*, Mar. 16, 1948.

3. *Brooklyn Eagle*, Mar. 16, 1948

4. *NYT*, Mar. 16, 1948.

5. http://flyawaysimulation.com/news/3322/huge-aviation-of-1930s-k-7- and -bel-geddes-4/.

6. *SN*, Aug. 13, 1952, 1.

7. *NYT*, Mar. 6, 1952.

8. Meany, "Baseball's Answer to TV," 60–62.

9. Kahn, *The Era*, 311–12.

10. O'Malley to Schroth, June 17, 1953, http://www.walteromalley.com/docu _detail.php?gallery=1&set=1&pageNum=1&docuID=13.

11. O'Malley to Moses, June 18, 1953, http://www.walteromalley.com/docudetail .php?gallery=1&set=1&pageNum=1&docuID=15.

12. O'Malley to McLaughlin, June 18, 1953, http://www.walteromalley.com/docu _detail.php?gallery=1&set=1&pageNum=1&docuID=16.

13. Caro, *The Power Broker*, 9. My portrait of Moses outside the O'Malley interactions, which Caro did not discuss, is drawn heavily from Caro's outstanding work.

14. Caro, *The Power Broker*, 85.

15. Caro, *The Power Broker*, 5, 86.

16. Caro, *The Power Broker*, 133.

17. Moscow, *What Have You Done for Me Lately?*, 195–96.

18. Moses to O'Malley, June 22, 1953, http://www.walteromalley.com/docu _detail.php?gallery=1&set=1&pageNum=2&docuID=18.

19. *NYT*, Apr. 29, 1954. A full text of the speech is in the Moses Papers.

20. Moses to George Spargo, Sept. 9, 1954, Moses Papers.

21. *NYT*, Feb. 19, 1939, Oct. 10, 1973.

22. I have not been able to find a direct record of this meeting, but O'Malley summarized these ideas in a letter to Moses, Oct. 28, 1953, Moses Papers.

23. O'Malley to Moses, Oct. 28, 1953, Moses Papers.

24. Moses to William Lebwohl, Sept. 15, 1953; Moses to Spargo, Sept. 15, 1953, Moses Papers.

25. Moses to Brooklyn borough president John Cashmore, Sept. 24, 1953, Moses Papers.

26. Moses to O'Malley, Sept. 28, 1953, Moses Papers.

27. Schroth to Moses, Oct. 8, 1953, Moses Papers.

28. Schroth to Moses, Oct. 15, 1953, Moses Papers.

29. Moses to Schroth, Oct. 16, 1953, Moses Papers.

30. O'Malley to Moses, Oct. 19, 1953, Moses Papers.

31. Moses to O'Malley, Oct. 20, 1953, Moses Papers.

32. Moses to Spargo, Oct. 26, 1953, Moses Papers.

33. O'Malley to Moses, Oct. 28, 1953, Moses Papers.

34. O'Malley to Moses, Dec. 17, 1953, http://www.walteromalley.com/docu _detail.php?gallery=1&set=2&pageNum=1&docuID=25.

35. *NYT*, Mar. 22, 1951, editorial page. See also Moscow, *What Have You Done for Me Lately?*, 210–11.

36. For example, see Caro, *Power Broker*, 1011.

37. O'Malley to Schroth, Feb. 11, 1954, http://www.walteromalley.com/docu _detail.php?gallery=1&set=2&pageNum=1&docuID=26.

38. Moses to Schroth, Mar. 10, 1954, Moses Papers.

39. Shapiro, *Last Good Season*, 42.

40. O'Malley to Moses, Aug. 17, 1954, Moses Papers.

41. Moses to O'Malley, Aug. 18, 1954, Moses Papers.

42. See Moses to Walter Rothschild, May 6, 1955, Moses Papers, for yet another unsuccessful attempt by O'Malley supporters to win over Moses.

43. *Brooklyn Eagle*, Dec. 11, 1953, for the news story and Dec. 13, 1953, for the editorial.

44. For example, see Jimmy Powers's column in the *New York Daily News*, Jan. 19, 1955, or Dan Daniel in *SN*, May 25, 1955, 17.

45. *New York Herald-Tribune*, Aug. 16, 1955.

46. For example, see *New York Journal-American* and *NYT*, Aug. 18, 1955.

47. *New York World-Telegram and Sun*, Aug. 18, 1955.

48. *New York Daily News*, Aug. 20, 1955.

49. *NYT*, Aug. 29, 1955. For Moses's attitude on the Fort Greene site survey, see Moses to George V. McLaughlin, Aug. 22, 1955; for his attitude toward the wider survey, see Moses to Cashman, Aug. 26, 1955, Moses Papers.

50. *SN*, Oct. 12, 1955, 10. Daniel was not alone. Oscar Ruhl reported that "opposition by Robert Moses . . . has been eliminated." *SN*, Nov. 9, 1955, 13.

51. *SN*, June 22, 1955, 2.

52. Edison, New Jersey, is in *New York World Telegram and Sun*, Aug. 18, 1955; Queens, specifically the old World's Fair site in Flushing, is in *New York Daily News*, Aug. 19, 1955; Sheepshead Bay, specifically the Luna Park amusement park, is in *New York World Telegram and Sun*, Aug. 20, 1955; Bay Ridge is in *New York World Telegram and Sun*, Oct. 24, 1955; the Nassau and Suffolk Counties offers are in *New York Post*, Aug. 25, 1955.

53. Richardson to Moses, Aug. 22, 1955; Moses to Richardson, Sept. 1, 1955, Moses Papers.

54. Moses to Cashmore, Oct. 17, 1955, Moses Papers.

55. *NYT*, Feb. 6, 1956.

56. *NYT*, Feb. 7, 1956.

57. *NYT*, Feb. 7, 24, 1956.

58. *NYT*, Feb. 29, 1956.

59. *NYT*, Feb. 22, 1956.

60. *NYT*, Mar. 12, 1956.

61. *NYT*, Apr. 22, 1956.

62. *SN*, May 16, 1956, 6.

63. *NYT*, July 25, 1956. Interestingly, O'Malley had nominated the three who were chosen, Chester A. Allen of the Kings County Trust Company and the Brooklyn Chamber of Commerce, Robert Blum of Abraham & Strauss, and Charles Mylod, a highly successful real estate executive. They had been among ten nominees from O'Malley, and he had provided biographies of the three chosen, apparently at Wagner's request. See Peter Campbell Brown (the city's attorney) to Wagner, June 27, 1956; O'Malley to Brown, July 5, 1956, Wagner Papers. Moses's assessment: "Mylod is slow, ponderous, believes successful businessmen can ipso facto solve all public problems, is actually a babe in the woods in City government, but no fool. Bob Blum is wonderful fellow but lacks force. Allen is nothing." Moses to Jack Flynn, Nov. 7, 1956, Moses Papers.

64. John J. Theobald (deputy mayor) to Assemblyman John Di Leonardo, Sept. 20, 1956, Wagner Papers.

65. *NYT*, Oct. 31, 1956. See also *New York World-Telegram and Sun* and *New York Daily News*, Oct. 31, 1956.

66. Celler II, 1860.

67. "A Planning Study for the Area Bounded by Vanderbilt Avenue, DeKalb Avenue, Sterling Place and Bond Street in the Borough of Brooklyn, New York, New York," by Clarke and Rapuano, Nov. 20, 1956; John McGrath (lawyer) to Cashmore, Nov. 21, 1956; Charles F. Noyes to Cashmore, Nov. 21, 1956, Wagner Papers. See also *NYT*, Nov. 29, 1956.

68. *NYT*, Dec. 5, 1956.

69. Moses to Wagner, Dec. 7, 1956, Moses Papers.

70. *NYT*, Dec. 24, 29, 1956.

71. *SN*, Jan. 9, 1957, 1.

72. Jim Murray column, *LAT*, Feb. 20, 1961.

73. O'Malley to Mulvey, Jan. 8, 1957, http://www.walteromalley.com/docu_detail .php?gallery=1&set=12&pageNum=1&docuID=76.

74. *SN*, Jan. 16, 1957, 15.

75. *NYT*, Jan. 5, 1957.

76. *LAT*, Feb. 12, 1957; *Chicago Daily Tribune*, Feb. 12, 1957.

77. *NYT*, Feb. 22, 1957.

78. Flaherty, "Miracle Move of the Dodgers," 3.

79. On the sale, see *NYT* and *LAT*, Feb. 22, 1957. For Wrigley's attitude and the price setting, see *LAT*, Feb. 5, 1954.

80. *LAT*, Apr. 14, 1958.

81. *LAT*, Aug. 25, 1932.

82. *LAT*, Dec. 10, 1941; *SN*, Dec. 4, 1957, 5.

83. McCue, "Open Status Delusions," 288–304.

84. For example, see *LAT*, Mar. 5, 1935, Dec. 6, 1956, June 12, 1947, and Dec. 3, 1948.

85. *SN*, Oct. 16, 1946, 1.

86. *SN*, July 30, 1947, 5. This is the major donor for Pauley Pavilion, the UCLA basketball arena.

87. *SN*, Feb. 22, 1961, 15.

88. The police academy had actually been built around the pistol range, which had been created when Los Angeles hosted the 1932 Olympics. *LAT*, July 15, 1995.

89. *LAT*, June 7, 1957.

90. Cobb to Rickey, Apr. 28, May 1, 1954; and "Report of Mayor's Committee on Chavez Ravine and Rose Hill Public Housing Areas," undated but from a cover letter, about May 5, 1954, Rickey Papers.

91. *LAT*, Aug. 20, 1953.

92. *NYT*, Sept. 26, 30, 1953.

93. *SN*, July 14, 1954, 19; Mehl, *The Kansas City Athletics*, 46.

94. *LAT*, June 2, 1955.

95. Langill, *Dodger Stadium*, 9. Langill is the Dodgers' team archivist.

96. *SN*, Oct. 6, 1954, 1.

97. The Los Angeles City Council passed a resolution Aug. 22, 1955, inviting O'Malley and Horace Stoneham for a meeting about moving to the city and a look at the city's facilities. The resolution said Councilwoman Wyman would be in New York on Sept. 22 and would try for a meeting with O'Malley then.

98. Meany, *The Artful Dodgers*, 13; *NYT*, Aug. 23, 1955.

99. *Washington Post*, Oct. 6, 15, 17, 20, 1956.

100. *LAT*, Oct. 12, 1956. That month O'Malley received a note from Vincent Flaherty outlining terms that Hahn would offer the Dodgers to relocate. O'Malley said he was "not interested," as he was optimistic about the Brooklyn Sports Authority at that point. http://www.walteromalley.com/docu_detail.php ?gallery=1&set=11&pageNum=1&docuID=66.

101. *LAT*, June 4, 1978.

102. Hahn made these assertions in a brochure produced by his supervisorial office called *Dodgers, from Brooklyn to Los Angeles: The Story of How the Dodgers Came West*. The brochure is undated, but refers to the Dodgers' thirtieth anniversary in Los Angeles, which was in 1988, so was clearly produced more than three decades after the events in question. Hahn was running for reelection in 1988. Hahn gave similar testimony, although in language not quite so direct, in the 1982 suit the Los Angeles Raiders brought against the National Football League. Hahn's wording of O'Malley's quote was "I will come down here but I will deny it to the press."

103. *LAT*, June 4, 1978.

104. *LAT*, Feb. 13, 1957.

105. *LAT*, Mar. 7, 1957.

106. *LAT*, Mar. 10, 1957.

107. *LAT*, Mar. 8, 1957.

108. "Walter in Wonderland," 60. *Time* did not use bylines at that time, but Jim Murray claimed authorship in his autobiography.

109. Poulson, "Untold Story," 14.

110. "Leach Explains County Had No Part in Accord," *LAT*, Aug. 25, 1963. This was a special section examining the city's and county's negotiations with the Dodgers. I have identified the individual articles by headlines.

111. Sullivan, *The Dodgers Move West*, 98.

112. "Walter in Wonderland," 60.

113. "Walter in Wonderland," 60.

114. *LAT*, Mar. 7, 1957.

115. *LAT*, Mar. 12, 1957.

116. *LAT*, Mar. 7, 1957.

117. *LAT*, Mar. 8, 1957; Meany, *The Artful Dodgers*, 18.

118. *LAT*, Feb. 23, 1957.

119. *LAT*, Feb. 23, 1957.

120. For example, see *SN*, Oct. 14, 1953, 27; and *LAT*, Aug. 10, Sept. 22, 1954.

121. *NYT*, Aug. 20, 1955.

122. *Minneapolis Tribune*, May 20, 1956. See also *SN*, May 30, 1956, 1.

123. "File Memorandum re Giants, Los Angeles, Etc.," March 23, 1957, http://www.walteromalley.com/docu_detail.php?gallery=1&set=13&docuID=101&pageNum=1.

124. *SN*, Aug. 3, 1960, 36.

125. Poulson, "Untold Story," 17.

126. *SN*, Mar. 6, 1957.

127. *NYT*, Feb. 25, 1957. For further examples, see *SN*, Mar. 6, 1957, 13; and Mar. 20, 1957, 12.

128. McCullough, *Brooklyn*, 179.

129. Minutes of the Meeting of the Sports Center Committee of the Board of Estimates, Mar. 5, 1957, and memorandum of the subsequent meeting with Madigan & Hyland, Mar. 11, 1957, Wagner Papers.

130. *NYT*, Mar. 27, 1957.

131. *NYT*, Mar. 25, 1957.

132. *NYT*, Mar. 26, 28, 1957.

133. *NYT*, Mar. 29, 1957.

134. O'Malley memo on Apr. 11, 1957, conversation with Moses, http://www.walteromalley.com/docu_detail.php?gallery=1&set=14&pageNum=1&docuID=106.

135. *NYT*, Apr. 19, 1957.

136. Henry D. Fetter, "The Queens Dodgers," *NYT*, op-ed, Aug. 14, 2005.

137. Cohen, *Dodgers!*, 124.

138. *LAT*, Mar. 12, 1957; *NYT*, Mar. 22, 1957.

139. This was a constant theme, but as an example see an editorial in *LAT*, Oct. 13, 1954, and a news analysis in *LAT*, Oct. 15, 1954. Veeck, in seeking to move both the Browns and the Athletics to Los Angeles, had cited this reason and urged the commission that controlled the Los Angeles Memorial Coliseum to take over Wrigley Field and upgrade it. *LAT*, Feb. 9, 1954.

140. "'Sick about Whole Deal' Says Gibson," *LAT*, Aug. 25, 1963.

141. "Arnebergh Explains His '57 Memorandum," *LAT*, Aug. 25, 1963.

142. *LAT*, May 3, 1957.

143. "Arnebergh Explains His '57 Memorandum," *LAT*, Aug. 25, 1963.

144. "Arnebergh Explains His '57 Memorandum," *LAT*, Aug. 25, 1963.

145. "McClellan Tells 'Full Truth' of Dodgers' Coming to L.A.," *LAT*, Aug. 25, 1963.

146. *LAT*, June 12, 1957.

147. *LAT*, May 29, 1957.

148. *LAT*, June 13, 19, 1957.

149. *NYT*, June 13, 1957.

150. *LAT*, July 18, 1957.

151. Poulson, "Untold Story," 17; Holland, "Visit with the Artful Dodger," 58.

152. *LAT*, May 12, 1957.

153. *Chicago Daily Tribune*, May 11, 1957.

154. *NYT*, May 17, 1957.

155. *SN*, May 22, 1957, 27.

156. *NYT*, May 23, 1957.

157. *LAT*, May 29, 1957.

158. *LAT*, May 30, 1957.

159. *NYT*, May 30, 1957.

160. Robert G. McCullough to James Felt, May 31, 1957, with attached memo, Wagner Papers.

161. *LAT*, June 1, 1957.

162. *NYT*, June 5, 1957.

163. McLaughlin to Stoneham, June 11, 1957, and Stoneham to McLaughlin, June 6, 1957, for Stoneham's refusal of the offer; McLaughlin to Wagner, June 13, 1957, for his Flushing Meadows plan, Wagner Papers. Giles's response is in *New York Daily News*, July 9, 1957.

164. *NYT*, June 22, 1957. O'Malley's testimony is produced in full in Celler II, 1850–86.

165. Celler II, 1853.

166. *LAT*, July 17, 1957.

167. *LAT* and *Wall Street Journal*, Aug. 7, 1957.

168. *LAT*, July 14, 1957.

169. *LAT*, July 27, 1957; "Background of Chad McClellan," *LAT*, Aug. 25, 1963. See also *Current Biography, 1954*; *NYT*, Aug. 4, 1979; *LAT*, Aug. 2, 1979; "Now McClellan Heads NAM," 34; and "Management: No Magic Wand," 102.

170. "McClellan Tells 'Full Truth' of Dodgers' Coming to L.A.," *LAT*, Aug. 25, 1963.

171. Madigan-Hyland, "Brooklyn Stadium and Related Developments," Aug. 5, 1957, Wagner Papers; James Felt to Adolph Klein, Aug. 9, 1957, Wagner Papers. See also *New York Daily News*, Aug. 6, 1957; *NYT*, Aug. 6, 7, 1957; and *SN*, Aug. 14, 1957, 18.

172. Poulson, "Untold Story."

173. *LAT*, Aug. 27, 1957.

174. "McClellan Tells 'Full Truth' of Dodgers' Coming to L.A.," *LAT*, Aug. 25, 1963.

175. *NYT*, Aug. 27, 1957.

176. Moses to Peter Campbell Brown, Aug. 28, 1957, Wagner Papers.

177. *NYT*, Sept. 11, 1957.

178. *NYT*, Sept. 19, 20, 21, 1957.

179. "McClellan Tells 'Full Truth' of Dodgers' Coming to L.A.," *LAT*, Aug. 25, 1963.

180. "McClellan Tells 'Full Truth' of Dodgers' Coming to L.A.," *LAT*, Aug. 25, 1963.

181. O'Malley to Horace Stoneham, Jan. 27, 1971. Notes on this letter have been supplied to me courtesy of Dr. Robert Garratt, who is working on a biography of Stoneham.

182. *LAT*, Sept. 12, 1957.

183. *LAT*, Sept. 4, 1957.

184. *LAT*, Sept. 25, 1957.

185. *LAT*, Sept. 25, 1957.

186. *LAT*, Oct. 8, 1957.

187. Quoted in the documentary *The Brooklyn Dodgers: The Original America's Team*.

188. *SN*, Oct. 16, 1957, 3.

189. Cohane, "Baseball's Strangest Story," 58. For a slightly different take, see McGee, *Greatest Ballpark Ever*, 240. McGee even argues that O'Malley deliberately badmouthed Ebbets Field in 1956 to depress attendance and make his case for city help even stronger.

190. Roz Wyman quoted in *The Brooklyn Dodgers: The Original America's Team*.

191. E-mail, Bavasi to Paul Hirsch, Oct. 20, 2003, for the winter 1956–57 date. Speech to the San Diego chapter of the Society for American Baseball Research, Oct. 20, 2001, for the June date. My thanks to Hirsch for a copy of the e-mail.

192. *Dodgers, from Brooklyn to Los Angeles: The Story of How the Dodgers Came West*, campaign brochure for Ernest Hahn (1988), author's holdings.

193. *New York Daily News*, Dec. 23, 1957.

194. O'Malley to Sharkey, Jan. 17, 1957, http://www.walteromalley.com/docu _detail.php?gallery=1&set=12&pageNum=1&docuID=79.

195. O'Malley to Schroth, Mar. 31, 1957, http://www.walteromalley.com/docu _detail.php?gallery=1&set=14&pageNum=1&docuID=103.

196. O'Malley to Schroth, Mar. 31, 1957, http://www.walteromalley.com/docu _detail.php?gallery=1&set=14&pageNum=1&docuID=103.

197. *NYT*, Oct. 14, 1957.

198. O'Malley to Schroth, Mar. 11, 1957, http://www.walteromalley.com/docu _detail.php?gallery=1&set=13&pageNum=1&docuID=98.

199. Kahn, *The Boys of Summer*, 429.

200. Caro quoted in *The Brooklyn Dodgers: The Original America's Team*.

201. For example, see Doig, *Metropolitan Transportation Politics*; and Krieg, *Robert Moses*.

202. *LAT*, June 9, 1957.

203. Wagner's analysis is in *NYT*, May 30, 1957. The election statistics are in Jackson, *Encyclopedia of New York City*, 740; and *NYT*, Nov. 6, 1957.

204. *SN*, May 1, 1957, 16.

205. *NYT*, Sept. 16, 1955.

206. *New York World-Telegram and Sun*, Feb. 20, 1957.

207. Celler II, 1860–81.

208. Frommer, *New York City Baseball*, 15.

209. For example, see Schroth to Moses, Oct. 19, 1953; and Flynn to Moses, Aug. 17, 1955, Moses Papers.

210. McLaughlin to O'Malley, June 22, 1953, http://www.walteromalley.com/docu _detail.php?gallery=1&set=1&pageNum=1&docuID=17.

211. *NYT*, June 4, 1957.

212. *SN*, Aug. 13, 1952, 1.

213. Leonard Koppett interview, July 25, 2001.

214. *LAT*, Oct. 8, 2007.

215. *NYT*, Aug. 23, 1957.

216. Kahn, *The Era*, 298.

217. *LAT*, June 9, 1957.

218. Kahn, *The Boys of Summer*, 429–30.

9. THE LAUGHINGSTOCK OF THE COUNTRY

1. *LAT* and *LAHE*, Oct. 24, 1957. See also *The Brooklyn Dodgers: The Original America's Team*, pt. 5, "The Last Trolley." In early 1962 the Hearst Corporation shuffled its Los Angeles newspapers, folding the morning *Examiner* into the afternoon *Herald Express* and calling the result the *Herald Examiner*. The abbreviation *LAHE* applies to both versions.

2. *Brooklyn Dodgers*, pt. 5, "The Last Trolley."

3. "Walter in Wonderland," 58.

4. *Brooklyn Dodgers*, pt. 5, "The Last Trolley."

5. *Brooklyn Dodgers*, pt. 5, "The Last Trolley."

6. *LAT*, Oct. 25, 1957.

7. *LAT* and *LAHE*, Oct. 24, 1957.

8. *LAHE*, Oct. 24, 1957.

9. *SN*, Nov. 6, 1957, 5.

10. *SN*, Nov. 6, 1957, 5.

11. *SN*, Nov. 6, 1957, 5.

12. *NYT*, Nov. 23, 1957.

13. *SN*, Nov. 5, 1957, 5.

14. *SN*, Nov. 6, 1957, 5.

15. *LAHE*, Oct. 24, 1957; *LAT*, Oct. 10, 1957.

16. Ziff, "Relates Colorful Past of Wrigley Field Baseball," 1; Ritter, *Lost Ballparks*, 197–203.

17. Ritter, *Lost Ballparks*; Benson, *Ballparks of North America*, 209–10.

18. *LAT*, Oct. 4, 1957.

19. Bavasi with Strege, *Off the Record*, 86.

20. Parrott, *The Lords of Baseball*, 241.

21. *LAT*, Oct. 26, 1957.

22. *LAT*, Nov. 9, 1957.

23. *SN*, Nov. 20, 1957, 1; *NYT*, Nov. 23, 1957.

24. *LAT*, May 3, 1957.

25. Benson, *Ballparks of North America*, 212.

26. *SN*, July 30, 1947, 5; Aug. 13, 1947, 37.

27. *SN*, Dec. 9, 1953, 25.

28. *SN*, Nov. 27, 1957, 11.

29. *LAT*, Oct. 26, 1957.

30. *LAT*, Dec. 12, 1957.

31. *LAT*, Dec. 5, 1957.

32. *LAHE*, Sept. 24, 1961.

33. *LAT*, Dec. 5, 1957.

34. *SN*, Dec. 18, 1957, 9.

35. *LAT*, Dec. 10, 1957.

36. *SN*, Dec. 18, 1957, 9.

37. *LAT*, Dec. 12, 1957.

38. *LAT*, Dec. 12, 1957.

39. *LAT*, Dec. 13, 1957.

40. *LAT*, Dec. 18, 1957; *SN*, Dec. 25, 1957, 3.

41. *SN*, Jan. 1, 1958, 4.

42. *LAT*, Dec. 20, 1957.

43. *SN*, Jan. 1, 1958, 4.

44. *LAT*, Jan. 3, 1958.

45. *SN*, Jan. 15, 1958, 8.

46. *LAT*, Dec. 21, 1957.

47. *LAT*, Dec. 25, 1957.

48. *SN*, Jan. 1, 1958, 4.

49. *SN*, Jan. 8, 1958, 13.

50. *SN*, Jan. 8, 1958, 8.

51. *SN*, Jan. 1, 1958, 4.

52. *LAT*, Jan. 3, 1958.

53. *LAT*, Jan. 3, 1958.

54. *LAT*, Jan. 6, 1958.

55. Shaplen, "O'Malley and the Angels," 63.

56. *LAT*, Mar. 19, 1963.

57. *SN*, Dec. 25, 1957, 4.

58. *LAT*, Jan. 8, 1958.

59. *SN*, Jan. 15, 1958, 8.

60. *SN*, Jan. 15, 1958, 8.

61. *SN*, Jan. 15, 1958, 8.

62. *SN*, Jan. 15, 1958, 8.

63. *SN*, Jan. 22, 1958, 5.

64. *SN*, Jan. 22, 1958, 5. See also Shaplen, "O'Malley and the Angels"; and *LAT*, Jan. 14, 1958.

65. *SN*, Jan. 22, 1958, 5.

66. *SN*, Jan. 22, 1958, 5; *LAT*, Jan. 15, 1958.

67. *SN*, Jan. 22, 1958, 5; *LAT*, Jan. 15, 1958; Shaplen, "O'Malley and the Angels."

68. *SN*, Jan. 22, 1958, 5; *LAT*, Jan. 15, 1958.

69. *LAT*, Jan. 15, 1958.

70. *SN*, Jan. 22, 1958, 5.

71. *SN*, Jan. 22, 1958, 5; *LAT*, Jan. 16, 1958.

72. *SN*, Jan. 22, 1958, 5; *LAT*, Jan. 16, 1958.

73. In the event this proved a poor tactic. The 1958 team played so poorly that attendance sagged badly late in the season.

74. *LAT*, Jan. 18, 1958.

75. *SN*, Jan. 29, 1958, 6.

76. *SN*, Feb. 5, 1958, 12.

77. *SN*, Feb. 12, 1958, 9.

78. Undated AP dispatch in O'Malley file, National Baseball Hall of Fame and Museum, marked Mar. 1958.

79. Cope, "How the Dodgers Are Building a Dynasty," 50.

80. *LAT*, Jan. 31, 1958; *SN*, Feb. 5, 1958, 12.

81. Parrott, *The Lords of Baseball*, 242.

82. *LAT*, Feb. 9, 1958.

83. *LAT*, Feb. 9, 1958.

84. Parrott, *The Lords of Baseball*, 245.

85. *SN*, Feb. 12, 1958, 9.

86. Parrott, *The Lords of Baseball*, 242.

87. *The "Sporting News" Official Baseball Guide, 1988 Edition*, 305.

88. *SN*, Jan. 6, 1944, 1.

89. Parrott, *The Lords of Baseball*, 83.

90. *SN*, Jan. 6, 1944, 1. In *The Lords of Baseball*, 71, Parrott says he was given $50 and returned with $62.

91. *SN*, Jan. 6, 1944, 1.

92. Silber, *Press Box Red*, 166–67.

93. *SN*, Jan. 6, 1944, 1.

94. *SN*, Sept. 26, 1951, 21.

95. Parrott, *The Lords of Baseball*, 255–56.

96. Parrott to Rickey, Nov. 3, 1948, Rickey Papers.

97. Parrott, dedication to *The Lords of Baseball*.

98. Parrott, *The Lords of Baseball*, 165.

99. Joe Palmer, interview with the author, May 20, 1995.

100. Jack Lang interview, Sept. 12, 1996.

101. Campanella, *It's Good to Be Alive*, 200–201.

102. Campanella, *It's Good to Be Alive*, 212.

103. *LAHE*, Feb. 6, 1957; *LAT*, Feb. 7, 1958.

104. *LAT*, Feb. 15, Mar. 19, 1958.

105. *SN*, Mar. 12, 1958, 31.

106. *LAT*, Jan. 28, 1958.

107. *SN*, Mar. 12, 1958, 11; *Los Angeles Dodgers 1958 Yearbook*, 3.

108. *LAT*, Feb. 8, 1958.

109. *SN*, Feb. 5, 1958, 12.

110. *LAT*, Feb. 9, 1958. The Dodgers had not worn Brooklyn on their road jerseys since 1945, but would wear Los Angeles through the 1970 season. In 1999 they would return to Los Angeles for the road jerseys. The home jerseys used Dodgers, as they had since 1938. Okkonen, *Baseball Uniforms of the 20th Century*.

111. *SN*, Feb. 19, 1958, 26.

112. *LAT*, Sept. 2, 1979.

113. Durslag, "How to Become a Baseball Billionaire," 17.

114. Johnson, *Super Spectator*, 29.

115. *LAT*, Feb. 13, 1958.

116. *SN*, Mar. 19, 1958, 16.

117. *LAT*. Apr. 17, 1958.

118. *LAT*, Feb. 22, 1958.

119. *LAT*, Apr. 13, 1958.

120. *SN*, Feb. 19, 1958, 26.

121. *SN*, Mar. 12, 1958, 11.

122. *LAT*, Jan. 19, 1958.

123. *SN*, Aug. 27, 1958, 9.

124. *SN*, Feb. 5, 1958, 4.

125. *SN*, Feb. 5, 1958, 1; Feb. 19, 1958, 26.

126. *SN*, Feb. 5, 1958, 4.

127. *SN*, Jan. 29, 1958, 5.

128. *SN*, Mar. 26, 1958, 8.

129. *SN*, Feb. 19, 1958, 26.

130. *SN*, Apr. 23, 1958, 15.

131. "Weather vs. Construction," Bennett & Bennett, Architects, Apr. 10, 1958, Roth Papers.

132. *SN*, Jan. 29, 1958, 5.

133. *SN*, Mar. 5, 1958, 1.

134. Parrott, *The Lords of Baseball*, 245.

135. *LAT*, Feb. 14, 1958.

136. *SN*, Feb. 12, 1958, 9.

137. *LAT*, Dec. 15, 1957.

10. IT'S BEEN CONTROVERSIAL FOR YEARS

1. Hines, "Housing, Baseball, and Creeping Socialism," 130–33. See also Normark, *Chavez Ravine, 1949*.

2. Normark, *Chavez Ravine, 1949*, 137.

3. Normark, *Chavez Ravine, 1949*, 138.

4. Normark, *Chavez Ravine, 1949*, 139–40.

5. Poulson, "Who Would Ever Have Dreamed?," 158.

6. Hines, "Housing, Baseball, and Creeping Socialism," 138.

7. Poulson, "Who Would Ever Have Dreamed?," 179.

8. Poulson, "Who Would Ever Have Dreamed?," 168.

9. Drew Pearson, "Helping the Dodgers Get to Los Angeles," *Riverside (CA) Daily Enterprise*, Dec. 4, 1957.

10. Hines, "Housing, Baseball, and Creeping Socialism," 140.

11. *LAT*, Dec. 5, 1957.

12. *NYT*, Dec. 7, 1957.

13. Carney, "Decentralized Politics of Los Angeles," 111. I am also grateful for Dr. Carney's insights into Los Angeles politics over a long and pleasant lunch, Apr. 26, 2000. Other written sources for this section are M. Fogelson, *The Fragmented Metropolis*; Gottlieb and Wolt, *Thinking Big*; and Bollens and Geyer, *Yorty*.

14. Kahn, *Season in the Sun*, 51.

15. Shaplen, "O'Malley and the Angels," 62.

16. "Walter in Wonderland," 60.

17. *LAT*, Dec. 5, 1957.

18. *LAT*, Jan. 17, 1958.

19. Cohane, "Baseball's Strangest Story," 50.

20. "Walter in Wonderland," 63.

21. Poulson, "Who Would Ever Have Dreamed?," 345–46.

22. *Chicago Tribune*, Nov. 15, 1957.

23. Poulson, "Who Would Ever Have Dreamed?," 348–49.

24. The Dodgers moved the Los Angeles Angels to Spokane, Washington, and the Giants moved the San Francisco Seals to Phoenix, Arizona. The Hollywood Stars took their Pittsburgh Pirates affiliation to Salt Lake City, Utah.

25. *LAT*, May 27, 1958.

26. Parrott, *The Lords of Baseball*, 3. Ralph Kiner, who was general manager of the Padres at that time, said C. Arnholt tried to restrain his brother, but without success. John, C. Arnholt told Kiner, was a "wild man." Ralph Kiner, interview with the author, July 26, 1997.

27. *LAT*, Oct. 9, 1957.

28. Shaplen, "O'Malley and the Angels," 65.

29. *SN*, Feb. 19, 1958, 33.

30. *SN*, Apr. 30, 1958, 28.

31. In fact, the first successful oil well in the Los Angeles area was drilled by Edward Doheny about two miles southwest of Chavez Ravine in 1892, a well long abandoned by the 1950s. Doheny later was a major figure in the Teapot Dome scandal in the 1920s.

32. Pearson, "Helping the Dodgers Get to Los Angeles."

33. Shaplen, "O'Malley and the Angels," 69.

34. *LAT*, Dec. 5, 1957.

35. *SN*, Apr. 23, 1958, 15.

36. Poulson, "Who Would Ever Have Dreamed?," 348.

37. *LAT*, Dec. 6, 1957.

38. *LAT*, Dec. 7, 1957.

39. *LAT*, Jan. 14, 1958.

40. Biographical form filled out by Holland in the Los Angeles Public Library's Local History Collection. See also Biographical Reference Library of Los Angeles City Hall, Sept. 15, 1961.

41. *LAT*, Dec. 12, 1963.

42. *LAT*, Dec. 1, 1966, Mar. 12, 1970; *Valley News*, June 30, 1967.

43. *LAT*, June 26, 1967.

44. *LAT*, June 26, 1967, Oct. 30, 1966.

45. B. Bavasi interview, Aug. 30, 1994.

46. *LAT*, May 28, 1953. See also undated clipping from *LAHE* in Roz Wyman clip file, Los Angeles Public Library, *Herald Examiner* clippings collection.

47. Berges, "Rosalind Wyman," 74.

48. Undated clipping from *LAHE* in Wyman clip file, Los Angeles Public Library, *Herald Examiner* clippings collection. See also Berges, "Rosalind Wyman," 74.

49. Berges, "Rosalind Wyman," 86.

50. Ainsworth, *Maverick Mayor*, 181.

51. Associated Press, Sept. 14, 1953.

52. Unidentified paper in Los Angeles Public Library, *Herald Examiner* Wyman clippings file, dated May 27, 1953.

53. *LAT*, June 10, 1999.

54. Unidentified paper in Wyman clip file, Los Angeles Public Library, *Herald Examiner* clippings collection, dated Nov. 2, 1953.

55. *Los Angeles News*, Oct. 23, 1953.

56. *LAT*, May 28, 1953.

57. Associated Press, Sept. 14, 1953.

58. *Los Angeles Mirror*, Nov. 19, 1953.

59. *LAHE*, Aug. 30, 31, 1954; *Los Angeles News*, Aug. 30, 1954.

60. *LAHE*, June 2, 1965.

61. *Brooklyn Dodgers*, pt. 5, "The Last Trolley."

62. Parrott, *The Lords of Baseball*, 12.

63. *Brooklyn Dodgers*, pt. 5, "The Last Trolley."

64. *Los Angeles Mirror News*, Dec. 19, 1957.

65. *LAT*, May 15, 27, 1958.

66. *LAT*, May 20, 1958, Sept. 15, 1959. On Sept. 14, 1959, the city's oil administrator told the city council he had notified twenty-three oil companies about the availability of the Chavez Ravine oil rights and none had been willing to bid. Holland and McGee told the *Times* their concerns had not been the existence of oil profits, but how they would be distributed.

67. *LAT*, May 16, 17, 1958. Rundberg, among other things, had a running feud with Carlton Williams, the *Los Angeles Times* reporter assigned to cover city hall and convey the Chandlers' desires to the council.

68. Nadeau, *Los Angeles*, 278–79.

69. *SN*, Apr. 2, 1958, 11.

70. *SN*, Apr. 2, 1958, 20.

71. *SN*, Oct. 30, 1957, 15.

72. *LAHE*, May 15, 1958. He was a bit more detailed a few days later. See "The Complete Text of the Dodger Prexy's Statement," *LAT*, May 27, 1958.

73. *SN*, Apr. 2, 1958, 20.

74. Durslag, "Visit with O'Malley," 105.

75. *LAT*, May 17, 1958.

76. *LAT*, May 18, 1958.

77. Henderson, "Los Angeles and the Dodger War," 282. There is at least one hint that some private developers were aware of the site's potential, although none came forward at the time. See Keane, *Fritz B. Burns*, 185.

78. *LAT*, May 24, 1958.

79. *LAHE*, May 15, 1958.

80. *SN*, Aug. 28, 1957, 3.

81. *LAT*, May 16, 1958.

82. *LAT*, May 16, 1958.

83. Baim, *Sports Stadiums as "Wise Investments."* See esp. tables on 7 and 26.

84. *LAT*, Jan. 19, 1958. O'Malley: "I'll be happy to discuss the situation with anybody, but as for getting up on a soapbox and stumping for it, I'm not going to do it."

85. *LAT*, June 5, 1958.

86. George Davis column, *LAHE*, Apr. 30, 1958.

87. *LAT*, Dec. 28, 31, 1957.

88. *LAT*, June 5, 1958.

89. *LAHE*, May 15, 1958.

90. *SN*, Apr. 23, 1958, 15.

91. *LAT*, May 5, 1958.

92. *LAT*, May 13, 1958.

93. Roth Papers.

94. *LAT*, Apr. 28, 1959; *SN*, May 7, 1958, 9.

95. *LAT*, Apr. 30, 1958.

96. Cohane, "Baseball's Strangest Story," 56.

97. *LAT*, Apr. 12, 1958.

98. *SN*, Apr. 23, 1958, 15.

99. Gottlieb and Wolt, *Thinking Big*, 269.

100. *Sports Illustrated*, June 16, 1958, 22.

101. *LAT*, June 2, 1958.

102. *LAT*, June 2, 1958.

103. *LAT*, May 15, 19, 20, 21, 23, 27, 29, 1958.

104. *LAT*, May 19 or June 1, 1958, where he is showing a Dodger yearbook to a child from the Kiwanis Crippled Children's Fund, beneficiaries of a Dodger game six weeks in the future.

105. Sam Balter, "O'Malley Man of Courage," *Los Angeles Examiner*, Apr. 14, 1958.

106. *LAT*, May 26, June 2, 1958.

107. *LAT*, June 1, 1958.

108. *LAT*, May 27, 1958.

109. *LAT*, May 23, 1958.

110. Poulson, "Who Would Ever Have Dreamed?," 350n, says he called Giles to get the ball rolling.

111. *LAT*, May 27, 1958.

112. *LAT*, May 28, 1958.

113. *LAT*, May 28, 1958.

114. *LAT*, June 3, 1958.

115. *SN*, June 4, 1958, 16.

116. *LAT*, June 4, 1958.

117. *LAT*, June 5, 1958.

118. *LAT*, June 5, 1958; *SN*, June 11, 1958, 6.

119. *LAT*, June 6, 1958.

120. *LAHE*, June 4, 1958.

121. *LAT*, June 5, 1958.

122. *LAT*, June 5, 1958.

123. *LAT*, June 5, 1958.

11. IN COURT

1. Thompson with Rice, *Every Diamond Doesn't Sparkle*, 154–55.

2. B. Bavasi interview, Aug. 30, 1994. See also Melvin Durslag's "Walt Alston," 64.

3. *LAT*, Apr. 20, 1958.

4. Westcott, "Carl Furillo," 230.

5. Parrott, *The Lords of Baseball*, 248.

6. Dick Young, "Clubhouse Confidential" column, *SN*, Apr. 30, May 14, 1958.

7. Durslag, "Visit with O'Malley," 105. Bavasi later expressed a similar sentiment. See Alston and Burick, *Alston and the Dodgers*, 66–67.

8. B. Bavasi interview, Aug. 30, 1994.

9. *LAT*, Apr. 19, 1958.

10. *LAT*, July 4, 1958.

11. Parrott, *The Lords of Baseball*, 3.

12. Cohen, *Dodgers!*, 126.

13. *LAT*, June 10, 1958.

14. *LAT*, June 10, 1958.

15. Creamer, "The Transistor Kid," 96.

16. King, "Vin Scully," 14.

17. King, "Vin Scully," 14.
18. *LAT*, June 7, 1958. Scully told the story of the nun many times, and it is generally reported as happening when he was eight years old. However, this is the one version that he wrote himself, and because it also makes more sense to write an essay in eighth grade rather than third, I have chosen this version.
19. *SN*, Aug. 3, 1955, 15; C. Smith, *The Storytellers*, 54.
20. *SN*, Aug. 3, 1955, 15.
21. Dodger press release, Jan. 4, 1950, Roth Papers.
22. Dodger press release, Jan. 4, 1950, Roth Papers.
23. Dodger press release, Jan. 4, 1950, Roth Papers.
24. *SN*, Oct. 14, 1953, 21.
25. *SN*, Oct. 14, 1953, 21.
26. *SN*, Aug. 3, 1955, 15. See also Creamer, "The Transistor Kid," 9.
27. *SN*, Aug. 3, 1955, 15. See also Creamer, "The Transistor Kid," 9.
28. Creamer, "The Transistor Kid," 9.
29. Scully interviewed on radio station KLAC, Oct. 3, 2011. Transcript available at http://www.am570radio.com/player/?station=klac-am&program_name =podcast&program_id=petrosmoney.xml&mid=21460722.
30. Langill, "Voice of the Dodgers," 9.
31. *USA Today*, Jan. 8, 1997.
32. *LAT*, Feb. 22, 1958.
33. Kahn, *Games We Used to Play*, 11.
34. Creamer, "The Transistor Kid," 9.
35. *SN*, Mar. 26, 1958, 23.
36. *LAT*, Sept. 4, 1961.
37. *LAT*, Apr. 20, 1958.
38. *SN*, Apr. 30, 1958, 2 (for Chinese Theater) and 10 for others.
39. Terrell, "Every Sixth Hit a Homer!," 11.
40. *SN*, Apr. 30, 8, 10, 12, May 7, 1958, 3.
41. *SN*, Oct. 8, 1958, 24.
42. *SN*, May 7, 1958, 24.
43. Bitker, *Original San Francisco Giants*, 38.
44. *SN*, May 14, 1958, 12.
45. *SN*, Jan. 24, 1970, 33; Feb. 24, 1979, 42.
46. *LAT*, Mar. 25, 1958.
47. The columns cited ran from Apr. 16 to Sept. 3. The quoted item appeared May 7.
48. Leonard Koppett interview, Feb. 25, 2002.
49. *LAT*, June 11, 1958.
50. *SN*, Apr. 30, 1958, 2.
51. Daley, "Will the Dodger-Giant Gold Rush Pan Out?," 34. See also Cohane, "Baseball's Strangest Story," 50. Wrote Cohane: "Fortunately for Stoneham, a smart, realistic native San Franciscan, Charles Leonard Harney, is in the pic-

ture. Harney, a top-drawer contractor, happened to own 80 acres ideal for a ball park on Candlestick Point."

52. *Time*, Apr. 28, 1958, 64. It was a thought Murray repeated in his autobiography, *Jim Murray*. See also Snyder, *Lady in the Locker Room*, 26.

53. *SN*, May 21, 1958, 16.

54. *LAT*, June 7, 1958.

55. Sullivan, *The Dodgers Move West*.

56. Silvers chose the Bilko name after Steve Bilko, a Pacific Coast League slugger who had played for the Los Angeles Angels for three years before the Dodgers arrived.

57. *LAT*, June 8, 1975.

58. Undated AP story contained in *Sporting News* files, stamped Aug. 1958.

59. Sullivan, *Dodgers Move West*, 164–65.

60. *LAT*, June 12, 1958.

61. *SN*, June 25, 1958, 16.

62. *LAT*, July 14, 1958.

63. *LAT*, June 20, 1958.

64. *SN*, June 25, 1958, 6.

65. *LAT*, June 21, 1958.

66. *LAT*, June 25, 1958.

67. *LAT*, July 15, 1958; *NYT*, July 15, 1958.

68. *LAT*, July 15, 1958.

69. Sullivan, *Dodgers Move West*, 169.

70. *SN*, July 23, 1958, 10.

71. *LAT*, Sept. 7, 1958.

72. Sullivan, *Dodgers Move West*, 171.

73. *SN*, July 23, 1958, 10.

74. *LAT*, July 15, 1958.

75. *SN*, July 23, 1958, 10.

76. *LAT*, July 15, 1958.

77. *SN*, July 23, 1958, 10.

78. *SN*, July 23, 1958, 10.

79. *NYT*, July 15, 1958.

80. *SN*, July 23, 1958, 10.

81. *Time*, July 28, 1958, 55.

82. *LAT*, July 31, 1958.

83. *LAT*, Aug. 16, 1958.

84. *LAT*, July 30, 1958.

85. *LAT*, Sept. 24, 1958.

86. *LAT*, Oct. 16, 1958.

87. *LAT*, Nov. 7, 1958.

88. *SN*, Oct. 29, 1958, 22.

89. *LAT*, Jan. 16, 1959.

90. *LAT*, Jan. 14, 1959.

91. *LAT*, Jan. 14, 1959.

92. *LAT*, Jan. 16, 1959.

93. *SN*, Jan. 21, 1959, 15.

94. *LAT*, Jan. 28, 1959.

95. *LAT*, Jan. 14, 1959.

96. *LAT*, Feb. 12, Apr. 22, 1959.

97. *LAT*, May 29, June 4, 1959.

98. *LAT*, July 1, 1959.

99. *SN*, Aug. 5, 1959, 12.

100. *LAT*, May 6, 7, 1959.

101. *LAT*, May 8, 1959; Los Angeles Dodgers Press Box Notes, May 7, 1959, Roth Papers; *SN*, May 20, 1959, 5.

102. In 2008 the Dodgers returned to the Coliseum for an exhibition game against the Boston Red Sox and reported attendance of 115,000.

103. Bavasi with Strege, *Off the Record*, 86.

104. *SN*, Aug. 5, 1959, 12. The finances of the game remain somewhat murky. The *Los Angeles Times* reported June 13 that the game had "netted" $174,000, indicating that was the figure after all expenses had been paid. That jibes fairly closely with Bavasi's later recollection that the Dodgers' share was $87,500 (half of $175,000). The *Sporting News* reported May 20, 1959, 5, that Campy had received $55,000, while Bavasi said it was $50,000. Campanella himself, as noted, gave a higher figure, but all three of these figures are consistent with the idea that the Yankees contributed no cash.

105. B. Bavasi interview, Aug. 30, 1994, for Thompson; Babe Hamberger, *SN*, Dec. 9, 1978, 33.

106. *LAT*, May 13, 1967; *SN*, May 20, 1967, 29.

107. Hines, "Housing, Baseball, and Creeping Socialism," 141.

108. *LAT*, May 9–16, 18, 19, 1959.

109. *LAT*, May 11, 1959.

110. *LAT*, May 14, 1959.

111. *LAT*, May 13, 1959, editorial page.

112. Sullivan, *Dodgers Move West*, 181.

113. *LAT*, May 15, 1959, editorial page.

114. For example, see *LAT*, June 4, 1978, or July 11, 1999.

115. *LAT*, Sept. 15, 1959.

116. *LAT*, Sept. 16, 1959.

117. *LAHE*, Sept. 18, 1959.

118. *LAT*, Sept. 18, 1959; *SN*, Sept. 23, 1959, 4.

119. *LAT*, Oct. 20, 1959; *SN*, Oct. 28, 1959, 19.

120. *LAHE*, Oct. 19, 1959.

121. *LAT*, Oct. 3, 1958. Novelty sales are from *SN*, Aug. 6, 1958, 8.

122. *LAT*, Dec. 10, 1958.

123. *SN*, Mar. 25, 1959, 12.

124. *LAT*, Aug. 29, 1971.

125. Bob Hunter in *SN*, Oct. 27, 1962, 9; Ned Cronin in *Los Angeles Daily News*, Sept. 4, 1947; Vincent Flaherty column from *Los Angeles Examiner* in *Sporting News* files, marked Feb. 1956; Frank Finch in *SN*, May 14, 1958, 13. Goodman also reported that he went to work for the Stars in 1937, 1938, and 1939 in different interviews, but because all the interviews tied his start to the opening of Gilmore Field, it seems safe to place it in 1939, the year the park did open.

126. *SN*, Oct. 27, 1962, 9.

127. *Los Angeles Daily News*, Apr. 4, 1951.

128. *SN*, May 14, 1958, 13.

129. *Los Angeles Daily News*, Sept. 4, 1947; *SN*, Oct. 27, 1962, 9.

130. *Los Angeles Major League Baseball News*, Apr. 15, 1963 (saying he started in 1940 in Hollywood), and *LAT*, Aug. 29, 1971 (where he says it was 1931 in Newark).

131. Chuck Stevens, interview with the author, May 17, 1997. See also *Los Angeles Major League Baseball News*, Apr. 15, 1963; and *LAT*, Aug. 29, 1971. This claim is open to question. Jon Light's *Cultural Encyclopedia of Baseball*, 308, says the custom of dragging the infield was invented by the Cincinnati Reds between 1949 and 1951. Cincinnati general manager Gabe Paul is quoted as saying the custom led to greater concession sales. Interestingly, Salveson pitched for the Stars from 1949 to 1951, the same time period. Stevens played for the Stars from 1948 to 1954.

132. Beverage, *Hollywood Stars*, 99.

133. *LAT*, July 11, 1957.

134. *LAT*, Aug. 29, 1971.

135. *SN*, Aug. 26, 1959, 15.

136. *Los Angeles Daily News*, Sept. 4, 1947.

137. Vincent Flaherty column dated Feb. 1956; *LAT*, Oct. 24, 1957.

138. *LAT*, Aug. 29, 1971.

139. *SN*, May 14, 1958, 13.

140. *SN*, May 14, 1958, 13.

141. *SN*, May 14, 1958, 13. See also *LAT*, June 17, 1983.

142. *LAT*, Aug. 29, 1971.

143. *LAT*, Feb. 6, 1958.

144. *SN*, Oct. 27, 1962, 9.

145. *LAT*, Aug. 29, 1971. The article claims the Dodgers were the first to sell bobbing head dolls in the United States, but fourteen teams, including three in the Pacific Coast League, were selling them a year before the Dodgers. See T. Hunter, *Bobbing Head Dolls*, 12. These dolls were generic Dodgers, not the replicas of real players that became such a hot collectible several decades later.

146. *LAT*, May 30, 1958.

147. After the first nine home games, Goodman said he had sold five thousand coolie hats. *LAT*, Apr. 29, 1958.

148. *SN*, Aug. 6, 1958, 8.

149. *SN*, Jan. 14, 1959, 13.

150. *LAT*, Apr. 7, 1960.

151. *LAT*, Mar. 10, 1959; *SN*, Mar. 25, 1959, 12.

152. *LAT*, Aug. 26, 1963.

153. *LAT*, May 11, 1971.

154. Parrott, *The Lords of Baseball*, 251.

155. *LAT*, Feb. 8, 1959.

156. *LAHE*, June 17, 1962.

157. *LAT*, Sept. 30, 1959.

158. *LAT*, Sept. 28, 1959.

159. *LAT*, Sept. 30, 1959.

160. *Time*, Oct. 5, 1959, 80.

161. *Brooklyn Dodgers*, pt. 5, "The Last Trolley."

162. *LAT*, Sept. 30, 1959.

163. *LAT*, Oct. 2, 1959.

164. *Chicago Daily Tribune*, Oct. 4, 1957.

165. *SN*, Oct. 14, 1959, 20

166. *LAT*, Oct. 5, 6, 1959.

167. *SN*, Oct. 14, 1959, 20.

168. *SN*, Oct. 14, 1959, 25.

169. *SN*, Oct. 14, 1959, 26.

170. *LAT*, Oct. 9, 1959. In a book written twenty years later, Harold Rosenthal of the *New York Herald-Tribune* recalled that O'Malley cut off the party at 10:30, but Veeck kept his going until after midnight to show up the Dodger owner. Rosenthal, *10 Best Years of Baseball*, 3. Rosenthal also thought the party was in Los Angeles.

171. *LAT*, Oct. 6, 1959; *SN*, Oct. 14, 1959, 7.

172. *SN*, Oct. 21, 1959, 8

173. *The "Sporting News" Baseball Register*, 21.

174. *LAT*, Oct. 5, 1959.

175. *SN*, Oct. 14, 1959, 26.

176. *SN*, Oct. 21, 1959, 16.

177. The Cleveland Indians still held the Major League record for a night game and a doubleheader.

178. *LAT*, Oct. 3, 1958.

179. Murray, "The $3,300,000 Smile," 54.

180. *LAHE*, *LAT*, and *Los Angeles Mirror News*, Mar. 16, 1960.

181. B. Bavasi interview, Aug. 30, 1994.

182. These estimates were put together using official attendance figures, including discount tickets not counted in official figures but available in the Roth Papers, ticket price figures provided by the Coliseum Commission, and cost and income estimates from the following stories: *SN*, May 7, 1958, 1; Aug. 6, 1958, 8; Oct. 15, 1958, 6; Oct. 14, 1959, 23; *LAT*, May 6, Oct. 3, Dec. 10, 1958, Oct. 2, 1959;

Associated Press, Mar. 3, 1958; *Sports Illustrated*, Feb. 29, 1960; and Thompson with Rice, *Every Diamond Doesn't Sparkle*.

12. A MONUMENT TO THE O'MALLEYS

1. *LAT*, Mar. 19, 1958.
2. *LAT*, Apr. 15, 1958.
3. *LAT*, July 14, 1958.
4. *LAT*, Aug. 26, 1958.
5. *LAT*, Mar. 6, 1959.
6. Snyder, *Lady in the Locker Room*, 64.
7. Memorandum, Nov. 6, 1959, Rickey Papers.
8. *LAT*, Apr. 14, 1958.
9. *LAT*, Oct. 6, 1958; *SN*, Oct. 15, 1958, 9.
10. Weber, *His Eminence of Los Angeles*, 1:225, 235, 271.
11. *LAT*, Sept. 30, 1959.
12. LeRoy as told to Kleiner, *Mervyn LeRoy: Take One*, 53.
13. *LAHE*, Jan. 30, 1962.
14. *LAT*, Oct. 22, 1959.
15. *LAT*, Oct. 24, 1959.
16. *LAT*, Nov. 5, 1959.
17. *LAT*, Nov. 5, 1959.
18. *SN*, Aug. 25, 1979, 2.
19. *LAT*, Nov. 6, 1959. A few days later *New York Times* sports columnist Arthur Daley would portray this as the council caving in as O'Malley cried wolf. He noted the team's attendance and asked, "O'Malley walk out on such a windfall? He ain't that crazy." Daley, evidently unfamiliar with the continuing battle, did not recognize that the 9–5 vote in favor of the zoning changes reflected the consistent split on Dodger issues during that time period. Nobody's mind had been changed either by the opponents' or by O'Malley's rhetoric. *NYT*, Nov. 11, 1959.
20. Sullivan, *The Dodgers Move West*, 175.
21. *LAT*, Feb. 12, 13, 19, 1960; *LAHE*, Feb. 11, 12, 18, 1960.
22. *LAT*, Feb. 12, Apr. 26, 1960.
23. *LAT*, Apr. 26, 1960.
24. *SN*, Sept. 2, 1959, 20.
25. *LAT*, May 26, 1960; *LAHE*, May 26, 1960.
26. *LAHE*, June 22, 1960.
27. *LAT*, July 2, 1960.
28. *LAHE*, Aug. 5, 1960; *LAT*, Aug. 16, 1960.
29. *LAT*, Aug. 24, 1960.
30. *LAHE*, Oct. 26, 1960.
31. *LAT*, Dec. 23, 1960.
32. Thompson with Rice, *Every Diamond Doesn't Sparkle*, 197.

33. *LAT*, Aug. 25, 1963.

34. Celler II, 2032, shows an after-tax profit of $1,860,744 for the years 1952 through 1956. Adding 1951 and 1957 probably pushed the team's net over $2 million, although pieces of that could well have gone to pay off the purchase of Rickey's shares.

35. *LAHE*, Sept. 24, 1961.

36. *LAHE*, Sept. 24, 1961, reports O'Malley accumulated more than $4 million in cash in his first four seasons in Los Angeles.

37. *LAT*, Dec. 16, 1959.

38. *LAT*, Apr. 26, 1960; *SN*, Feb. 21, 1962, 22. Defining the cost of the stadium is somewhat subjective. O'Malley's current heirs describe the cost as $22 million, although it is unclear exactly what that covers. In 1965, while in a dispute with the Los Angeles County assessor, the Dodgers paid for a third-party appraisal. In the report the assessor totaled up stadium construction contract costs of just over $19 million, a figure that did include cost overruns, but did not include the land or postopening improvements.

39. *LAT*, Feb. 12, 1960.

40. *SN*, Sept. 20, 1961, 14.

41. *LAT*, Jan. 14, 1960. The net effect takes some calculation. In 1958 the Dodgers owed the Coliseum Commission $288,000, which was 5 percent of the gross plus the concession profits from the nine designated games. The commission owed the Dodgers $268,000 for the concession profits from the remaining games on the schedule. In net terms the Dodgers paid $20,000 to the commission. In 1959 the net figures were almost reversed, with the Dodgers owing the commission $319,000 for the 5 percent plus the nine games' concessions, while the commission owed them $338,000 for the remaining concession profits. In net terms the commission paid the Dodgers $19,000. For two years the Dodgers effectively paid no rent, but had to forego any concession profits while paying for modifications, cleanup, and maintenance and pocketing all souvenir profits. The Coliseum received just over $600,000 (plus parking fees) that they could apply to the Sports Arena. In 1960 the Dodgers paid 10 percent of the gross, which meant they would owe the Coliseum $565,000. O'Malley did get the commission to pick up more of the maintenance costs, which had the effect of cutting the tab down around $525,000, but there now were no concession profits coming back to the team. Because attendance in 1960 was almost 10 percent higher than in 1959, it would seem likely the Dodgers would have earned at least the $338,000 concessions profit of 1959 had the terms remained the same. *LAT*, Oct. 3, 1958, Oct. 2, 1959. Finally, the *Examiner* (Nov. 2, 1960) estimated the Dodger games garnered the Coliseum $350,000 a year in parking revenues.

42. B. Bavasi interview, Aug. 30, 1994.

43. *LAT*, Mar. 23, 1961.

44. *LAHE*, Nov. 4, 1960.

45. *LAT*, Nov. 5, 1960.

46. The exact mechanism Union Oil used remains unclear. In the *Chicago Sun-Times*, May 15, 1962, Jerry Holtzman, substituting for the Dick Hackenberg column, reported that the oil company had agreed to advance $10 million in advertising payments for radio and TV broadcasts over the next eight years. This is the clearest explanation of the deal I have found, but there are variants. Oates, "Visit with O'Malley," 35, reported the payoff period was twelve years. In his *Herald Express* column of Nov. 4, 1960, Melvin Durslag reported O'Malley had a bank loan of $9 million. This does not appear to be true. Either O'Malley told him he was close to a loan at that point, which is a possibility, and Durslag took it the rest of the way, or Durslag was describing a short-term line of credit rather than long-term financing for the stadium, or the banks provided the up-front cash against a guarantee by Union Oil, which might well be a more exact description of the deal. However, all this is speculation. Union Oil's surviving documents use phrases such as the company "helped finance" Dodger Stadium, but representatives says its records do not indicate the exact mechanism.
47. *LAT*, Dec. 16, 1959; "Meanwhile, at Chavez Ravine," 48.
48. *LAHE*, Apr. 28, 1961.
49. The use of cantilevers was actually a trend that O'Malley and Praeger took to its logical conclusion. Cantilevers had been creeping into stadium construction for decades. When the first of the classic ballparks were created in the first dozen years of the century, the forward edge of upper decks in parks such as Tiger Stadium (Detroit) or Shibe Park (Philadelphia) had been directly over the first deck, with the front edge directly supported by pillars or slightly cantilevered (the supports set back only a few feet). By the time of the opening of County Stadium in Milwaukee (1953), the only baseball park built between Yankee Stadium (1923) and Dodger Stadium, cantilevered construction had advanced so that the front edge of the second deck was about a third of the way back from the front of the bottom deck. The first pillars were set a bit back from the front of the second deck, or about two-thirds back from the front of the bottom deck. In Dodger Stadium the second-deck setback was increased farther, and there were no pillars between any seats and the field. For a discussion, see Borton, "Stadium Design Is a Challenge," 48. Borton's firm designed County Stadium.
50. *LAT*, June 13, 1958; *SN*, June 25, 1958, 11.
51. *LAT*, Jan. 16, 1959.
52. *SN*, Jan. 28, 1959, 5.
53. *LAT*, Feb. 28, 1959.
54. *LAT*, Feb. 4, 1962.
55. *LAT*, Oct. 20, 1959; *1960 Dodger Yearbook*, 3.
56. *LAT*, Dec. 9, 1959.
57. *LAT*, Dec. 9, 1959. See also Dodgers brochure *What's Ahead for Dodger Fans*, Roth Papers. In the Roth Papers a memo from Dick Walsh dated Mar. 22, 1961, said Praeger had completed "what we believe to be the final set of architectural plans for the Chavez Ravine stadium."

58. This is probably because their final planning documents with the city called for 16,000 parking spaces and a ratio of 3.5 attendees for a game. The 16,000 figure is as roundly suspicious as the 56,000.

59. *LAT*, July 17, 1962.

60. World Series Attendance and Receipts Reports, Oct. 5 and Oct. 6, 1963.

61. Veeck with Linn, *Veeck—as in Wreck*, 362.

62. *SN*, Apr. 20, 1960.

63. *LAT*, Aug. 26, 1960.

64. *LAT*, Aug. 27, 1960.

65. *SN*, Aug. 7, 1957, 35; *LAT*, Apr. 14, 1958.

66. *SN*, Aug. 7, 1957, 35; *LAT*, Apr. 14, 1958.

67. *SN*, Dec. 31, 1952, 14.

68. *Miami Herald*, Mar. 29, 1969.

69. *LAT*, Mar. 29, 1957.

70. Rickey memorandum dated Nov. 6, 1959, Rickey Papers.

71. Tom Seeberg, interview with the author, Jan. 31, 1995.

72. *LAHE*, Apr. 8, 1962.

73. Rickey memo, Nov. 6, 1959, Rickey Papers.

74. *SN*, Mar. 6, 1971, 44

75. *Miami Herald*, Mar. 29, 1969.

76. *LAT*, Jan. 27, 1971.

77. *LAT*, Oct. 4, 1960.

78. "Walter in Wonderland."

79. Shaplen, "O'Malley and the Angels."

80. Oates, "Visit with O'Malley."

81. Helyar, *Lords of the Realm*, 60.

82. *SN*, June 11, 1958, 7.

83. *What's Ahead for Dodger Fans*, team brochure, 1961, Roth Papers.

84. *Riverside (CA) Daily Enterprise*, Jan. 23, 1962.

85. *LAHE*, Feb. 28, 1962.

86. *SN*, Nov. 29, 1961, 15.

87. *LAHE*, Apr. 1, 1962.

88. *LAHE*, Mar. 22, 1962.

89. *LAT*, Sept. 4, 1963.

90. *LAT*, Mar. 12, 1961.

91. *LAHE*, Mar. 30, 1962.

92. *LAHE*, Feb. 27, 1962.

93. Chandler Van Wicklen, interview with the author, Mar. 19, 1998.

94. *LAHE*, Feb. 27, 1962.

95. *LAT*, Feb. 7, 1962.

96. *Dodgers 1958 Yearbook*.

97. *LAT*, Mar. 30, 1958.

98. *LAHE*, Sept. 16, 1961; *LAT*, Apr. 10, 1962.

99. *LAT*, Oct. 4, 1960.

100. *LAT*, Mar. 12, 1961.

101. *LAHE*, Apr. 5, 1961; *Dodgers 1958 Yearbook*.

102. *What's Ahead for Dodger Fans*, team brochure, Roth Papers.

103. *LAHE*, Oct. 5, 25, 1961, Feb. 24, 1962.

104. *SN*, June 11, 1958, 6.

105. *LAHE*, Apr. 30, 1961.

106. *LAT*, Nov. 11, 1961.

107. *SN*, Nov. 22, 1961, 9. In the Sept. 27, 1952, Collier's article where the domed stadium plan was first revealed in detail, the drawings did refer to it as Dodger Stadium.

108. *What's Ahead for Dodger Fans*, team brochure, Roth Papers.

109. *LAT*, May 12, 17, 19, 26, 1960.

110. *LAT*, Apr. 11, 1962.

111. Baseball commissioner Ford Frick, *SN*, Mar. 4, 1959, 13; National League president Warren Giles, *LAT*, Dec. 16, 1959; Yankees general manager George Weiss, *LAHE*, July 7, 1961; *SN* editor and publisher J. G. Taylor Spink along with Frick and American League president Joe Cronin and Minnesota Twins owner Calvin Griffith, *SN*, May 16, 1961, 6; and Giles again, *LAT*, Feb. 6, 1962.

112. Chandler Van Wicklen interview, Mar. 19, 1998.

113. *SN*, Oct. 27, 1962, 14. See also *SN*, Feb. 14, 1962, 7.

114. *LAT*, June 6, 1996.

115. Durslag, "Visit with O'Malley," 31. See also records at San Bernardino County Assessor's Office.

116. *LAHE*, Jan. 22, 1961; *LAT*, Jan. 23, 1961.

117. Staff meeting notes, Jan. 17, 1961, Roth Papers.

118. Memo, Allan Roth to Dick Walsh, Mar. 22, 1961, Roth Papers.

119. *LAHE*, Apr. 8, 1961.

120. *LAT*, Oct. 26, 1959; *LAHE*, May 26, 1960.

121. *LAT*, June 16, 1961; *LAHE*, June 16, 1961.

122. Yorty apparently understood the difference between the Dodgers and the downtown interests well. Yorty's most thoughtful biographers feel city councilman Patrick McGee's defeat in the mayoral primary in 1961 was due to his opposition to the Dodgers, while Yorty's dark-horse victory over Poulson that year grew from Yorty's unceasing condemnation of the "downtown machine" and his characterization of Poulson as its tool. Bollens and Geyer, *Yorty*, 116–35.

123. *LAT*, Aug. 3, 1961.

124. *LAT*, Sept. 21, 1961.

125. *LAT*, Aug. 23, 1961.

126. *SN*, Apr. 12, 1961, 14.

127. *LAT*, Sept. 5, 1961.

128. *LAT*, Sept. 27, 1961; *LAHE*, Sept. 27, 1961; *LAT*, Sept. 28, 1961; *SN*, Oct. 11, 1961, 25. The Los Angeles papers and *SN* gave different locations for where

the first accident occurred. One death had occurred early in the construction project when an embankment caved in and crushed a worker against a boulder. *LAHE*, May 8, 1961.

129. *LAHE*, Nov. 9, 1961; *LAT*, Nov. 22, 1961.

130. *LAT*, Nov. 21, 1961.

131. *LAT*, Nov. 22, 1961.

132. *LAHE*, Jan. 5, 1962.

133. *LAHE*, Jan. 5, 1962; *LAHE*, Feb. 11, 1962.

134. *LAHE*, Jan. 8, 1962.

135. *LAT*, Jan. 11, 1962.

136. *LAHE*, Jan. 18, 1962.

137. *LAHE*, Jan. 28, 1962.

138. *LAT*, Feb. 11, 1962; *LAHE*, Feb. 11, 1962; *SN*, Feb. 21, 1962, 22.

139. *LAHE*, Feb. 22, 1962.

140. *LAT*, Feb. 23, 1962.

141. *LAHE*, Feb. 25, 1962.

142. *LAHE*, Feb. 27, 1962.

143. *LAT*, Mar. 4, 1962; *LAHE*, Mar. 4, 1962.

144. *LAHE*, Mar. 8, 1962.

145. *LAT*, Mar. 9, 1962.

146. *LAHE*, Mar. 27, 1962.

147. *LAT*, Feb. 18, 1969.

148. *LAT*, Apr. 8, 1962.

149. Bingham, "Boom Goes Baseball," 21.

150. Bingham, "Boom Goes Baseball," 21.

151. *LAHE*, Dec. 12, 1961; *LAT*, Dec. 12, 1961; *SN*, Dec. 27, 1961, 15.

152. *LAT*, Feb. 11, 1962.

153. *LAT*, Mar. 4, 1962.

154. *NYT*, Apr. 1, 1962.

155. *LAT*, Apr. 10, 1962.

156. *LAT*, Apr. 8, 1962.

157. Bingham, "Boom Goes Baseball," 21.

158. *LAT*, Apr. 10, 1962.

159. *LAT*, Apr. 10, 1962.

160. *LAHE*, Mar. 7, 1962.

161. *LAT*, Apr. 8, 1962.

162. *SN*, Apr. 18, 1962, 31.

163. Bingham, "Boom Goes Baseball," 21.

164. *SN*, Apr. 18, 1962, 17.

165. *LAT*, Apr. 11, 1962.

166. *Sport*, Aug. 1962, 48.

167. Bingham, "Boom Goes Baseball," 23.

168. Plaut, *Chasing October*, 43.

169. *LAT*, Apr. 11, 1962.

170. Bingham, "Boom Goes Baseball," 23. See also *LAT*, Apr. 11, 1962.

171. *LAT*, Apr. 11, 1962.

172. *LAT*, Apr. 11, 12, 1962.

173. *LAT*, Apr. 11, 1962.

174. *SN*, Apr. 18, 1962, 17.

175. *SN*, Apr. 18, 1962, 17.

176. *LAT*, Apr. 11, 1962. In a somewhat prophetic comment on the dugout boxes, Poulson said he really would have preferred something a little higher.

177. *LAT*, Apr. 11, 1962.

178. *LAT*, Apr. 11, 1962.

179. *LAT*, Apr. 10, 1962.

180. *LAT*, Apr. 10, 1962.

181. *SN*, Apr. 18, 1962, 17.

182. *LAT*, Apr. 11, 1962.

183. *LAT*, Apr. 12, 1962.

184. *LAHE*, Apr. 8, 1962.

13. LOOSE ENDS

1. *LAHE*, Apr. 12, 1962.

2. *LAT*, Apr. 16, 1962.

3. *LAT*, Apr. 13, 1962.

4. *LAHE*, Apr. 19, 1962.

5. *LAT*, Apr. 15, 1962.

6. *LAHE*, Apr. 19, 1962; *LAT*, Apr. 20, 1962.

7. *LAHE*, Apr. 18, 1962.

8. For example, Jim Murray's column, *LAT*, Apr. 19, 1962.

9. *LAT*, Apr. 18, 1962.

10. *LAHE*, Apr. 17, 1962; *LAT*, Apr. 18, 1962.

11. Sportscaster Gil Stratton, interview with the author, Jan. 17, 2000, with Stratton recounting a conversation with O'Malley.

12. *LAT*, June 14, 1962.

13. See Langill, *Dodger Stadium*, 22, on the electricity; and Ray, *Grand Huckster*, 315, on the steps.

14. *LAT*, Apr. 26, 1962.

15. *LAT*, July 29, 1962.

16. *LAHE*, July 16, 1962.

17. *LAHE*, Apr. 18, 1962.

18. *LAHE*, Apr. 23, 1962; *LAT*, Apr. 24, 1962.

19. Langill, *Dodger Stadium*, 25.

20. *LAT*, Dec. 12, 1962.

21. *LAT*, May 13, 1962; *LAHE*, May 14, 1962.

22. *LAHE*, June 3, 1962.

23. *LAT*, July 12, 13, 1962.

24. *LAHE*, July 15, 1962.

25. *LAHE*, July 24, 1965.

26. *LAT*, July 5, 1962.

27. *LAHE*, Oct. 23, 1962.

28. *LAT*, Aug. 5, 1962.

29. O'Malley to Berle, June 8, 1962, http://www.walteromalley.com/docu_detail
.php?gallery=2&set=5&docuID=146&pageNum=1.

30. *LAHE*, Feb. 25, 1962.

31. *LAHE*, Oct. 13, 1962.

32. *LAT*, Oct. 4, 1962, reported the gap as fifty-six minutes. The *LAHE*, Oct. 4, 1962,
said fifty-eight minutes.

33. *LAT*, Oct. 4, 1962.

34. Roseboro with Libby, *Glory Days*, 205.

35. Roseboro, *Glory Days*, 205; *LAT*, Oct. 4, 1962.

36. *LAHE*, Feb. 20, 1963.

37. *SN*, Oct. 20, 1962, 12.

38. *LAT*, Mar. 14, 1963.

39. Finch, *Los Angeles Dodgers*, 42. A similar quote was reported in a UPI story that
appeared in the *San Francisco Examiner*, Oct. 4, 1962.

40. *LAHE*, Nov. 1, 1962.

41. *LAT*, Oct. 5, 1962.

42. *SN*, Dec. 8, 1962. The tab would later be raised to $1.4 million (*LAHE*, Feb. 22,
1963) or $1.5 million (Langill, *Dodger Stadium*, 22).

43. *LAT*, Dec. 9, 1962.

44. *Sports Illustrated*, Dec. 24, 1962, 11; *LAHE*, Feb. 22, 1963.

45. *LAHE*, Feb. 22, 1963; *LAT*, Feb. 4, 1964.

46. *LAT*, Apr. 26, 1969.

47. The budget figure is in *LAHE*, June 14, 1966, and the size of the landscaping
staff is in *LAT*, Apr. 26, 1969. *Los Angeles Baseball News*, Apr. 15, 1965, reported
the staff was seventeen people.

48. Johnson, *Super Spectator*, 206–7.

49. *LAT*, Dec. 9, 1962.

50. *LAHE*, Feb. 17, 1963; *LAT*, Apr. 4, 1963.

51. *SN*, July 13, 1963, 16; July 20, 1963, 2.

52. *LAHE*, May 3, 1962.

53. *LAT*, June 2, 5, 1964; *LAHE*, June 4, 5, 1964.

54. *LAHE*, June 28, 1964; *LAT*, June 9, July 20, 1964

55. *LAT*, June 5, 1964. City attorney Roger Arnebergh said it should be dated from
June 3, 1959, when the Dodgers signed the contract with the city. His deputy
Bourke Jones said it should be dated from the day the stadium was completed.

56. *LAHE*, June 4, 1964.

57. *LAHE*, June 1, 1964; *LAT*, June 5, Aug. 28, 1964.

58. *LAT*, Oct. 23, 1964.

59. *LAHE*, Aug. 2, 1963. The numbers varied because even O'Malley was not sure of the stadium's capacity at that point and because the assessor's office set the valuation, but not the actual tax rates, which were the sum of annual assessments from various school, water, utilities, and other districts.

60. *LAHE*, June 17, 1963.

61. *LAHE*, Apr. 14, 1963.

62. *LAT*, Dec. 6, 1964.

63. *LAHE*, May 23, 1963.

64. *LAT*, July 2, 1963.

65. *LAHE*, July 3, 1963.

66. *LAHE*, July 15, 1963.

67. *LAHE*, June 17, 1963. Watson said the Yankees actually paid $225,000 in property taxes in the most recent year plus the 5 percent entertainment tax O'Malley had complained about in Brooklyn.

68. *LAHE*, Aug. 2, 1963.

69. *LAHE*, July 25, Aug. 1, 1963; *LAT*, Aug. 1, 1963.

70. *LAT*, Aug. 25, 1963.

71. *LAT*, Aug. 25, 1963. The *Times* produced a special section that day including a long statement by McClellan and responses from all the other players in both the city (pro-Dodgers) and the county (less committed).

72. *LAT* and *LAHE*, Sept. 5, 1963.

73. *LAHE*, Aug. 2, 1964, Mar. 4, 1965, Mar. 22, 1967; *LAT*, Mar. 5, 1965.

14. THE MOST POWERFUL MAN IN BASEBALL

1. Sands and Gammons, *Coming Apart at the Seams*, 24.

2. B. Bavasi interview, Aug. 30, 1994.

3. Veeck, "The Baseball Establishment," 45. He had taken a similar theme earlier while promoting his book *Veeck—as in Wreck*. See Veeck with Linn, "Walter O'Malley," 80.

4. "Memorandum of conversation with Ford Frick at Dorset Hotel, Monday afternoon, 2:30 p.m., November 23, 1959" and "November 24, 1959, Just completed a conversation with Mr. Warren Giles," Rickey Papers.

5. *LAT*, Mar. 19, 1965; *LAHE*, Apr. 17, 1965; *New York Daily News*, Jan. 12, 1968; *LAT*, Jan. 19, 1977.

6. O'Malley noted such decisions many times. They are best pulled together in *LAT*, Feb. 18, 1969.

7. Again, this idea was circulated many times and is best summarized in *LAT*, Jan. 19, 1977.

8. The leagues added an alternate owner representative for each league in 1952, expanding to two representatives apiece in 1972 and four each in 1978. All representatives are counted in this tally. O'Malley was the only man to be on the council each year during the period.

9. *LAT*, Jan. 19, 1977.

10. Kuhn, *Hardball*, 23.

11. Burke, *Outrageous Good Fortune*, 277.

12. William O. DeWitt interview, Oral History Collection, University of Kentucky. DeWitt's anecdote is undated, but certainly dates to the early 1960s. While DeWitt was a baseball executive from the 1920s until 1981, it was only from 1961 to 1966 that he was in the National League.

13. *New York Daily News*, Dec. 23, 1957.

14. Koppett interview, Feb. 9, 2002.

15. *LAT*, Aug. 10, 1979.

16. Golenbock, *Bums*, 436.

17. P. Bavasi, interview with the author, Nov. 15, 2001.

18. *SN*, Oct. 4, 1975, 6; *LAT*, Oct. 19, 1975.

19. *Detroit Free Press*, Dec. 8, 1968.

20. *New York Daily News*, Jan. 12, 1968.

21. *LAT*, Jan. 19, 1977.

22. *SN*, Aug. 18, 1948, 1.

23. *NYT*, May 3, 1950.

24. *SN*, Mar. 5, 1952, 1.

25. McCue, "Open Status Delusions," 288.

26. *NYT*, Jan. 30, 1955.

27. *NYT*, Sept. 27, 1957.

28. *NYT*, Nov. 30, 1957.

29. *NYT*, May 30, 1958. See also Shea to William R. Peer, Apr. 30, 1958, Wagner Papers.

30. Rickey to Robert Howsam, Nov. 6, 1958, Rickey Papers.

31. *SN*, May 21, 1958.

32. *NYT*, Nov. 14, 1958.

33. *SN*, July 29, 1957, 7; *NYT*, Aug. 2, 1959.

34. Walker was also the brother-in-law of Senator Prescott Bush (R-CT) and thus uncle to his namesake George Herbert Walker Bush, forty-first president of the United States.

35. *SN*, Aug. 5, 1959, 7.

36. *SN*, Feb. 11, 1959, 16.

37. *SN*, July 6, 1960, 8.

38. *SN*, Nov. 11, 1959, 8.

39. "Memorandum dictated by Branch Rickey re meeting with Commissioner Ford Frick at his office, starting at 10 a.m.," Oct. 12, 1959, and "Memorandum of conversation with Ford Frick at Dorset Hotel, Monday afternoon, 2:30 p.m., November 23, 1959," Rickey Papers.

40. *NYT*, July 26, 1957.

41. *SN*, Jan. 15, 1958, 1; *NYT*, Jan. 4, 1958.

42. *NYT*, Jan. 26, 1958; *LAT*, July 19, 1959.

43. *LAT*, July 9, 1960.

44. "Tuesday, October, 25, 1960—11:40 a.m.," Rickey Papers; Veeck with Linn, *Veeck—as in Wreck*, 360.

45. *LAT*, July 19, 1960.

46. *LAT*, July 20, 1960.

47. *LAT*, Aug. 3, 1960.

48. *SN*, Sept. 21, 1960, 15.

49. *SN*, Sept. 21, 1960, 15.

50. Shapiro, *Bottom of the Ninth*, 240–41.

51. *SN*, Oct. 19, 1960, 4.

52. *LAT*, Oct. 18, 1960.

53. "Tuesday, October, 25, 1960—11:40 a.m.," Rickey Papers.

54. *LAT*, Oct. 28, 1960.

55. *LAT*, Oct. 27, 1960.

56. "Tuesday, October, 25, 1960—11:40 a.m.," Rickey Papers.

57. Terrell, "Damndest Mess Baseball Has Ever Seen," 16.

58. "November 23, 1960. Hank Greenberg called me at about 10:02 a.m. . . . ," Rickey Papers.

59. *LAT*, Aug. 7, 1960.

60. *SN*, Oct. 19, 1960, 4.

61. *LAT*, Nov. 16, 1960.

62. *LAT*, Nov. 18, 1960.

63. Veeck with Linn, "Walter O'Malley," 81. See also "November 23, 1960. Hank Greenberg called me at about 10:02 a.m. . . . ," Rickey Papers, where Greenberg blamed it all on the player draft limitations and costs.

64. *LAT*, Nov. 4, 1960.

65. *LAT*, Nov. 19, 1960.

66. Autry with Herskowitz, *Back in the Saddle Again*, 146. Autry misreports that KMPC carried the Dodgers for three years. Actually, it was two. See *SN*, Dec. 2, 1959, 11.

67. *LAHE*, Nov. 21, 1960; *LAT*, Nov. 22, 1960.

68. *LAT*, Nov. 23, 1960.

69. *LAT*, Nov. 23, 1960.

70. *LAT*, Nov. 24, 1960; *NYT*, Dec. 6, 1960.

71. Veeck with Linn, *Veeck—as in Wreck*, 365.

72. *LAT*, Dec. 7, 1960; *LAHE*, Dec. 8, 1960.

73. The Day of Infamy joke is in Autry with Herskowitz, *Back in the Saddle*, 149. The 6–2 vote is in Veeck with Linn, *Veeck—as in Wreck*, 369.

74. *LAHE*, Dec. 8, 1960. *Sports Illustrated*, Dec. 19, 1960, 16, attributed this same quotation to Ford Frick, which would make it more understandable.

75. *LAHE*, Jan. 22, 1961; Newhan, *Anaheim Angels*, 80.

76. *LAT*, Feb. 20, 1963.

77. B. Bavasi interview, Nov. 9. 1994.

78. McCue and Thompson, "Mis-management 101," 42–45.
79. *LAHE*, Apr. 16, 1961.
80. *SN*, Aug. 24, 1949, 11; Dec. 30, 1950, 7. The best discussion of the various bonus rules is in Brent Kelley's *Baseball's Biggest Blunder*.
81. *SN*, Nov. 12, 1952, 1; Dec. 10, 1952, 5.
82. Powell appeared twice over three years as a pinch runner for the White Sox. He scored once.
83. Cope, "How the Dodgers Are Building a Dynasty."
84. *SN*, Oct. 1, 1958, 48.
85. *LAT*, Mar. 23, 1961.
86. *LAHE*, June 29, 1961.
87. *SN*, Aug. 10, 1963, 1.
88. *SN*, Nov. 10, 1962, 7.
89. *SN*, July 5, 1961, 5; Aug. 22, 1964, 2.
90. *SN*, Dec. 22, 1962, 1.
91. *LAHE*, Sept. 16, 1965.
92. *LAHE*, Sept. 16, 1965.
93. *LAHE*, Sept. 19, 1966.
94. Burke, *Outrageous Good Fortune*, 279.
95. *LAHE*, Aug. 12, 1964.
96. *SN*, Apr. 10, 1965, 6.
97. Holtzman, *Commissioners*, 121–32.
98. *NYT*, Nov. 18, 1965.
99. *LAT*, July 23, 1965. At one point O'Malley was rumored to be pushing *Washington Post* sports editor Shirley Povich for the job. *LAHE*, Mar. 20, 1965.
100. *SN*, Feb. 6, 1965, 1; Aug. 7, 1965, 5.
101. Furlong, "Uninvited Guest," 62.
102. Furlong, "Uninvited Guest," 62.
103. Holtzman, *Commissioners*, 121–32.
104. *SN*, July 31, 1946, 1, where Chandler proposes one central office for organized baseball.
105. SN, Aug. 17, 7, Aug. 24, 1963, 18.
106. *SN*, Feb. 8, 1964, 1.
107. Walker and Bellamy, *Center Field Shot*. Much of my discussion of the general baseball-television picture draws on this excellent work.
108. *NYT*, Nov. 29, 1955.
109. *SN*, Mar. 14, 1964, 5.
110. Walker and Bellamy, *Center Field Shot*, 113. For O'Malley's presence, see *LAT*, Aug. 23, 1964.
111. Walker and Bellamy, *Center Field Shot*, 114.
112. *SN*, Dec. 26, 1964, 17.
113. *SN*, Sept. 11, 1965, 7.
114. *SN*, Oct. 23, 1965, 16.

115. *SN*, Oct. 30, 1965, 8.

116. Walker and Bellamy, *Center Field Shot*, 121–23.

117. *NYT*, June 5, 1966.

118. *SN*, Jan. 7, 1967, 42.

119. *SN*, Apr. 6, 1968, 11.

120. *LAHE*, June 4, 1965.

121. *SN*, Nov. 24, 1962, 27.

122. *SN*, Feb. 2, 1963, 1; Apr. 20, 1963, 27.

123. *SN*, Sept. 21, 1963, 5.

124. *SN*, July 18, 1964, 9.

125. *SN*, Nov. 7, 1964, 7.

126. *SN*, editorial, Nov. 21, 1964, 16.

127. *SN*, June 19, 1965, 17.

128. MacPhail, *My 9 Innings*, 99.

129. *SN*, Apr. 30, 1966, 5; Feb. 11, 1967, 26.

130. *SN*, Nov. 4, 1967, 33.

131. Parrott, *The Lords of Baseball*, 5.

132. *LAT*, Nov. 14, 1967.

133. *Denver Post*, Nov. 12, 1967.

134. *SN*, Apr. 15, 1967, 6.

135. *LAT*, Feb. 4, 1962.

136. *LAHE*, Mar. 22, 1966.

137. *LAHE*, Feb. 1, 1966; *Denver Post*, Nov. 12, 1967.

138. *LAT*, Nov. 16, 1967.

139. *LAT*, Nov. 14, 1967.

140. *SN*, Dec. 2, 1967, 29.

141. *SN*, Apr. 13, 1968, 42.

142. *LAT*, Apr. 20, 1968.

143. B. Bavasi interview, Aug. 30, 1994.

144. Jerry Izenberg column from the *Newark Star-Ledger*, simply dated July 1968, in the O'Malley file, National Baseball Hall of Fame and Museum.

145. P. Bavasi interview, Nov. 15, 2001.

146. *LAT*, Feb. 4, 1962.

147. *SN*, Dec. 9, 1967, 45. See also Ray, *Grand Huckster*, 423.

148. *SN*, June 8, 1968, 5.

149. *NYT*, May 28, 1968.

150. Brown, *Baseball's Fabulous Montreal Royals*, 6.

151. *LAT*, Nov. 16, 1967.

152. MacPhail, *My 9 Innings*, 111.

153. Helyar, *Lords of the Realm*, 190–91.

154. *SN*, Oct. 12, 1968, 14.

155. Kuhn, *Hardball*, 32.

156. Greenberg, *Story of My Life*, 215.

157. Burke, *Outrageous Good Fortune*, 280–81.

158. Leggett, "Court Martial for a General," 24.

159. *LAT*, Dec. 12, 1968.

160. *LAT*, Dec. 11, 20, 1968; *LAHE*, Dec. 15, 1968.

161. *LAHE*, Dec. 7, 1968; Holtzman, *Commissioners*, 33.

162. *SN*, Jan. 4, 1969, 41.

163. *SN*, Jan. 4, 1969, 14.

164. *SN*, Jan. 18, 1969, 26.

165. *LAHE*, Jan. 30, 1969.

166. *SN*, Feb. 1, 1969, 27.

167. *NYT*, Feb. 5, 1969.

168. See Burke, *Outrageous Good Fortune*, 283; and Kuhn, *Hardball*, 33, although the details of place and manner differ.

169. MacPhail, *My 9 Innings*, 113.

170. Helyar, *Lords of the Realm*, 93; M. Miller, *Whole Different Ball Game*, 102.

171. B. Bavasi interview, Nov. 9, 1994; Holtzman interview, June 18, 2001.

172. Helyar, *Lords of the Realm*, 180.

15. A TOTALLY DIFFERENT PERSON

1. B. Bavasi interview, Aug. 30, 1994.

2. *LAHE*, Feb. 10, 1963.

3. *LAHE*, May 23, 1963; *SN*, Apr. 6, 1963, 28.

4. *LAHE*, Apr. 15, 1963.

5. *LAT*, Apr. 8, 1963.

6. *LAT*, Feb. 19, 1963; *LAHE*, Mar. 23, 1963.

7. *LAHE*, May 4, 1963.

8. Leggett, "Dodgers in a Dogfight," 9–12.

9. *LAHE*, Aug. 28, 1963.

10. *LAHE*, Sept. 27, 1963.

11. *LAHE*, Oct. 1, 1963.

12. *New York Daily News*, Sept. 4, 1963.

13. World Series Attendance and Receipts Reports, 1965, from the Office of the Commissioner of Baseball. The Dodgers' 1959 receipts were calculated as $335,140.61 by Allan Roth and are in his papers at the Case Western Reserve University Library, Cleveland OH.

14. *LAT*, Mar. 2, 1977.

15. *SN*, Jan. 4, 1964, 34.

16. Roger Kahn, "A Dodger Generation, Always in Season," *LAT*, Oct. 19, 1988.

17. B. Bavasi interview, Aug. 30, 1994.

18. Fred Claire, interview with the author, July 22, 2011.

19. *LAT*, June 12, 1963.

20. Claire with Springer, *Fred Claire*, 56.

21. B. Bavasi interview, Aug. 30, 1994.

22. *LAT*, July 31, 1968.

23. *Philadelphia Daily News*, May 2, 1968.

24. O'Malley gave the same figure. *SN*, April 1, 1972, 26.

25. B. Bavasi interviews, July 23, Aug. 30, 1994.

26. Fred Claire interview, July 22, 2011.

27. Tom Seeberg interview, Jan. 31, 1995.

28. P. Bavasi interview, Nov. 15, 2001.

29. Claire with Springer, *Fred Claire*, 57–58.

30. Bump Holman interview, Feb. 7, 2000.

31. Staff Meeting Notes, Jan. 17, 1961, Roth Papers.

32. *LAT*, Feb. 18, 1969.

33. *LAT*, June 26, 1960.

34. *SN*, Dec. 6, 1961, 1.

35. "Press Box Pickups," Apr. 22, 1958, Roth Papers.

36. Tom Seeberg interview, Jan. 31, 1995.

37. *LAT*, July 27, 1960.

38. Press release, June 16, 1959, Roth Papers.

39. *LAT*, June 3, 12, 1960.

40. *LAHE*, Apr. 8, 1962.

41. "Press Box Pickups," Aug. 1, 1962, Roth Papers. The sisters received their seats, free hot dogs, peanuts, soda, copies of the team yearbook, and a scorecard. *LAHE*, Aug. 3, 1962.

42. *LAHE*, July 27, 1966.

43. *LAHE*, Feb. 12, 1967.

44. Fred Claire interview, July 22, 2011.

45. B. Bavasi interview, Aug. 30, 1994.

46. *SN*, Apr. 29, 1978, 4.

47. *LAT*, Aug. 2, 1960.

48. Holman's story over the next several paragraphs is drawn from an interview in his Vero Beach office, Feb. 7, 2000.

49. *LAT*, Feb. 4, 1961.

50. *LAT*, Feb. 15, 1961.

51. *SN*, Mar. 22, 1961, 9.

52. Tom Seeberg interview, Jan. 31, 1995.

53. Kahn, *The Boys of Summer*, 434–35.

54. B. Bavasi interviews, Aug. 30, Nov. 9, 1994; P. Bavasi interview, Nov. 15, 2001.

55. John Hall, interview with the author, Feb. 13, 1995.

56. B. Bavasi interview, Aug. 30, 1994.

57. Parrott, *The Lords of Baseball*, 257–58.

58. *LAT*, Aug. 8, 1963.

59. *SN*, Nov. 23, 1963, 7.

60. *LAHE*, Sept. 2, 1964.

61. *LAHE*, Sept. 3, 1964.

62. Graham Jr., *A Farewell to Heroes*, 253.

63. B. Bavasi interview, Aug. 30, 1994.

64. *LAHE*, Dec. 8, 1960.

65. *LAHE*, Apr. 28, 1961.

66. R. Smith, "O'Malley in a Manger," 120. This column was written in May 1961. Capacity of 21,009 is in *LAHE*, Apr. 27, 1961, while the *Sporting News Guide* for 1961 lists capacity as 20,457.

67. *LAT*, Apr. 13, 1964.

68. Autry with Herskowitz, *Back in the Saddle Again*, 156.

69. Newhan, *Anaheim Angels*, 78–79.

70. *LAHE*, Sept. 2, 1962.

71. *LAHE*, Aug. 4, 1963.

72. *LAT*, May 15, 1961.

73. Irv Kaze, interview with the author, May 30, 1994.

74. *LAHE*, Apr. 15, 1962.

75. B. Bavasi interview, Nov. 9, 1994, said O'Malley himself knew little of the details of contract enforcement.

76. Newhan, *Anaheim Angels*, 80–81.

77. *LAHE*, Sept. 10, 1963, Apr. 14, 1965.

78. *LAT*, July 9, 1961.

79. *SN*, Feb. 16, 1963, 8; *LAT*, Feb. 20, 1963.

80. *LAT*, Aug. 9, 1963.

81. *LAHE*, Sept. 12, 1963; *LAT*, Sept. 27, 1963.

82. *LAT*, Aug. 25, 1963.

83. *LAT*, June 30, 1964.

84. *LAHE*, Aug. 27, 1964.

85. *LAHE*, Jan. 14, 1968.

86. Bump Holman interview, Feb. 7, 2000. Holman was the Dodgers' pilot.

87. Edmund A. Carlson to Robert P. Roche, Feb. 26, 1965, and Robert F. Longley (director of alumni relations for the University of Pennsylvania) to Roche et al., O'Malley file, University of Pennsylvania Archives.

88. *LAT*, Feb. 18, 1969.

89. For example, see *LAHE*, Jan. 18, 1962; *SN*, Apr. 20, 1963, 1; *LAT*, Aug. 25, 1963; *SN*, Sept. 14, 1963, 1; *LAHE*, Feb. 3, 1966; *Baseball Digest*, May 1969, 35.

90. James G. Thomas, M.A.I., "Appraisal of Dodger Stadium Property and Recreation Site," Feb. 5, 1965. Thomas was manager of the Appraisal Department of Coldwell, Banker & Co. These figures need some context. For most categories Thomas used—ticket sales, concessions revenue, and parking revenue—only the income was presented, not the costs. There are no player and staff salaries, benefits, debt payments, maintenance or supplies costs, or similar expenses included. This is very much a gross income figure, not a profit figure. However, souvenir and novelty income is presented on a net basis. The figures include both the Dodgers and the Angels figures, and the Dodgers' share of the Angels

income is based on the publicly announced terms of the contract with the assumptions that all Angels novelty income was retained by that team and that Stadium Club revenue, which was presented as a lump sum for both teams, was treated to the 50 percent rule applied to concessions.

91. *LAHE*, Oct. 20, 1966.

92. *LAT*, Mar. 4, Sept. 1, 1963, Feb. 2, 1964, Nov. 5, 1965, Mar. 22, 1963; *LAHE*, Sept. 21, 1965.

93. *LAHE*, Mar. 25, 1963.

94. *LAHE*, Feb. 6, 1963. For the Cantinflas concert, it was a flat $7,500 plus parking and concessions. *LAT*, Nov. 5, 1965.

95. *LAHE*, June 1, 1963, June 22, Nov. 5, 1965; *LAT*, Oct. 31, 1963, Jan. 17, 1964.

96. Langill, *Dodger Stadium*, 37. My beautiful and talented wife, Mary Colleen Kenney, was one of the screamers.

97. *SN*, Sept. 24, 1958, 8; *LAT*, Feb. 6, Apr. 7, 1959. Skiatron even asked the city of Los Angeles to revoke the pay television franchises it had given them because political opposition had arisen in the city. *SN*, Feb. 18, 1959, 15.

98. *LAT*, Apr. 1, 1958. When Skiatron ran out of cash, Stoneham released it from the contract. Durslag, "The Dodgers, the Giants, and Pay-TV," 24.

99. *LAT*, Feb. 6, 1959.

100. *LAHE*, Nov. 9, 1961, Jan. 28, 1963.

101. *LAHE*, Aug. 15, 1963.

102. *LAT*, Aug. 24, 1963.

103. *SN*, Jan. 4, 1964, 10.

104. *LAHE*, July 9, 1964.

105. *SN*, June 20, 1964, 38.

106. *SN*, Aug. 1, 1964, 2.

107. *LAT*, Nov. 5, 1964.

108. *SN*, Apr. 10, 1965, 30; Mar. 19, 1966, 33.

109. *SN*, Mar. 4, 1967, 36.

110. *SN*, Feb. 27, 1957, 23; *LAT*, Sept. 21, 1960.

111. Undated Dodger press release, Roth Papers. See also *LAT* and *LAHE*, Mar. 12, 1961.

112. *LAT*, Apr. 5, 1963.

113. *SN*, Feb. 29, 1964, 10.

114. *LAHE*, Sept. 9, 1965.

115. *LAHE*, Sept. 17, 1965.

116. *LAHE*, Sept. 20, 1965; *LAT*, Apr. 24, 1966.

117. *LAHE*, Nov. 15, 1966.

118. *Baseball America*, Dec. 25, 1995, 12.

119. *LAHE*, Feb. 22, 1966.

120. Koufax with Linn, *Koufax*, 285.

121. *LAT*, Feb. 23, 1966.

122. B. Bavasi interview, Aug. 30, 1994.

123. *LAHE*, Feb. 24, 1966.

124. *LAT* and *LAHE*, Feb. 25, 1966.

125. *LAHE*, Mar. 24, 1966.

126. *LAHE*, Mar. 3, 1966.

127. *LAHE*, Mar. 10, 1966.

128. *LAT*, Mar. 18, 1966.

129. *LAHE*, Mar. 23, 1966.

130. *LAHE*, Mar. 24, 1966. See also Koufax, *Koufax*, 288.

131. *LAT*, Mar. 25, 1966.

132. *LAHE*, Mar. 31, 1966.

133. *LAT*, Mar. 31, 1966. In the *Herald Examiner*, the same day, Koufax's salary was estimated at $132,500.

134. Marvin Miller, interview with the author, Apr. 18, 2001.

135. *LAHE*, Oct. 22, 28, 1966.

136. *LAHE*, Oct. 29, 1966.

137. *LAT*, Nov. 3, 1966.

138. *LAHE*, Oct. 30, 1966.

139. *LAHE*, Nov. 11, 1966.

140. *LAT*, Nov. 15, 1966.

141. B. Bavasi interview, Nov. 30, 1994.

142. *LAHE*, Dec. 2, 1966.

143. *LAT*, Nov. 19, 1966.

144. The year 1967's .451 winning percentage was the worst, with 1968's .469 the third worst. The 1958 season, at .461, was the second worst.

145. *SN*, May 6, 1967, 6.

146. Burk, *Much More than a Game*, 132.

147. Snyder, *Lady in the Locker Room*, 92.

148. B. Bavasi interview, Aug. 30, 1994.

149. Larry Reisman, interview with the author, Jan. 11, 2000. Reisman noted the paper had not printed anything about it at the time. The timing of Bavasi's story is also suspect because Harold Parrott was the Dodger traveling secretary in 1951, not Lee Scott.

150. Roseboro with Libby, *Glory Days*, 110–14. See also *LAHE*, Feb. 19, 1961; and *SN*, Mar. 20, 1971, 46.

151. *LAT*, Mar. 5, 1971.

152. *SN*, Apr. 11, 1962, 18.

153. *LAT*, Mar. 4, 1972.

154. McCue, "Half-Century of Springs," 9.

155. *Vero Beach (FL) Press-Journal*, Mar. 18, 1965.

156. *Vero Beach (FL) Press-Journal*, July 29, 1965.

157. *LAHE*, Feb. 28, 1966.

158. *LAHE*, Mar. 5, 1966; *SN*, Mar. 19, 1966, 12.

159. *SN*, Dec. 30, 1967, 31.

160. *Vero Beach (FL) Press-Journal*, 50th Anniversary Spring Training Edition, Feb. 1998.

161. *LAT*, Feb. 26, 1962.

162. *LAT*, Mar. 28, 1962.

163. *LAHE*, Feb. 20, 1969.

164. *LAHE*, Feb. 29, 1969, Mar. 8, 1970.

165. *LAT*, Feb. 27, 1972.

166. Thompson with Rice, *Every Diamond Doesn't Sparkle*, 130.

167. Murray, *Jim Murray*, 57.

168. Chester L. Smith, sports editor of the *Pittsburgh Press*, in his column, Feb. 24, 1957.

169. *LAT*, June 4, 1978.

170. *LAT*, Apr. 1, 1969.

171. For examples from one season, the Ken Hubbs Foundation, *LAT*, May 5, 1964; the Kiwanis Crippled Children's Fund, *LAT*, July 24, 1964; U.S. Olympic Committee, *LAT*, Aug. 16, 1964.

172. Erskine, *Tales from the Dodger Dugout*, 180.

173. Thompson, *Every Diamond Doesn't Sparkle*, 118.

16. PETER

1. *New York Post*, Sept. 4, 1955.

2. *Brooklyn Eagle*, Aug. 7, 1952, Apr. 16, 1953, Sept. 24, 1954.

3. *Brooklyn Eagle*, Feb. 29, 1952.

4. *SN*, June 29, 1955, 7.

5. *LAT*, July 23, 1960.

6. *SN*, Feb. 15, 1961, 14.

7. *SN*, Mar. 28, 1962, 13; *LAT*, Mar. 14, 1967.

8. *LAHE*, Feb. 22, 26, 1962.

9. *LAHE*, Dec. 5, 1968.

10. *LAT*, Feb. 12, 1966.

11. *LAT*, Mar. 14, 1967.

12. *LAT*, Dec. 19, 1968.

13. *LAHE*, Dec. 5, 1968.

14. *SN*, Mar. 28, 1970, 9.

15. *SN*, Mar. 21, 1973, 15.

16. *SN*, Aug. 25, 1973, 5.

17. *LAHE*, Apr. 27, 1971; *LAT*, Apr. 28, 1971.

18. *LAT*, Apr. 7, 1972.

19. *LAT*, Apr. 7, 1972.

20. *LAHE*, July 1, 1969.

21. Phil Collier, interview with the author, May 16, 1998.

22. B. Bavasi interview, Aug. 30, 1994.

23. *LAT*, Mar. 9, 1968.

24. *LAT*, May 7, 1967. For another Mulvey-O'Malley golf confrontation, see Holland, "Visit with the Artful Dodger," 24.

25. Holland, "Visit with the Artful Dodger," 24.

26. Bump Holman interview, Feb. 7, 2000, on the Wyoming trips; *LAT*, Sept. 28, 1958 and *SN*, Oct. 22, 1958, 10, on the 1958 Africa trip.

27. *LAT*, Nov. 20, 1963; *LAHE*, Nov. 22, 1963, Feb. 5, 1964.

28. *LAT*, June 9, 1964.

29. *LAT*, Nov. 21, 1967; *LAHE*, Oct. 30, 1968.

30. *LAT*, Feb. 11, 1968.

31. *LAT*, Apr. 7, 1972.

32. O'Malley to William L. Day, national chairman, University of Pennsylvania Development Program, June 17, 1965, O'Malley file, University of Pennsylvania Archives.

33. *Philadelphia Bulletin*, Jan. 29, Feb. 14, 1965; O'Malley file, University of Pennsylvania Archives.

34. Photocopy of canceled check dated Oct. 26, 1965, in O'Malley file, University of Pennsylvania Archives.

35. University of Pennsylvania press release, Jan. 14, 1971, and Sheldon Hackney to Peter O'Malley, Oct. 7, 1985, O'Malley file, University of Pennsylvania Archives.

36. Longley, director of alumni relations, to Roche, E. Craig Sweeten, and H. Craig Watkins, June 16, 1966, O'Malley file, University of Pennsylvania Archives.

37. *LAHE*, Aug. 19, 1965; *LAT*, Aug. 20, 1965.

38. Roger Kahn, "A Dodger Generation, Always in Season," *LAT*, Oct. 19, 1988.

39. *LAT*, June 4, 1978.

40. Holland, "Visit with the Artful Dodger," 56.

41. *LAHE*, Mar. 19, 1966.

42. *LAHE*, Feb. 28, 1967.

43. *SN*, Aug. 4, 1979, 29.

44. *SN*, June 15, 1968, 26.

45. *LAT*, Dec. 20, 1971.

46. Bump Holman interview, Feb. 7, 2000.

47. Bump Holman interview, Feb. 7, 2000.

48. Shapiro, *Last Good Season*, 21.

49. Bump Holman interview, Feb. 7, 2000. Holman, who piloted the plane, said the Army victory led to overindulgence by the priests, who trashed the plane's interior.

50. *LAHE*, Feb. 20, 1964.

51. Weber, *His Eminence of Los Angeles*, esp. 1:271. "Walter Frank [*sic*] O'Malley C-26," a summary document dated July 10, 1975, in the O'Malley file, University of Pennsylvania Archives, lists his philanthropic interests (through the Walter F. O'Malley Foundation) as "Roman Catholic church support and church-related institutions."

52. *LAHE*, Mar. 22, 1966.

53. *LAT*, Jan. 26, 1975.

54. Merwin, "Most Valuable Executive in Either League," 129. See also Levering and Moskowitz, *100 Best Companies*; and Roy J. Harris Jr., "Forkball for Dodgers: Costs Up, Gate Off," *Wall Street Journal*, Sept. 4, 1990.

17. MARVIN MILLER AND ANDY MESSERSMITH

1. *SN*, May 27, 1953, 1; July 22, 7, 1953.

2. *SN*, Sept. 2, 1953, 1; *Brooklyn Eagle*, Aug. 28, 1953.

3. *SN*, Sept. 9, 1953, 4.

4. *NYT*, Dec. 3, 1953.

5. *LAT*, Dec. 7, 1953; *NYT*, Dec. 9, 1953.

6. *SN*, Dec. 9, 1953, 1.

7. *NYT*, Dec. 11, 1953; *New York Herald-Tribune*, Dec. 11, 1953; *SN*, Dec. 16, 1953, 16.

8. *NYT*, July 13, 1954.

9. For example, see *LAHE*, Feb. 24, 28, 1966.

10. *LAHE*, Feb. 28, 1964; *LAT*, Nov. 23, 1966.

11. *LAT*, Mar. 13, 1964.

12. Kuhn, *Hardball*, 71.

13. *Sports Illustrated*, May 15, 22, 29, June 5, 1967. The quoted material and the salary negotiation stories are in the May 22 chapter, beginning on p. 44.

14. Korr, *End of Baseball*, 61–65.

15. Most of this section is drawn from M. Miller, *Whole Different Ball Game*.

16. *SN*, June 3, 1972, 21.

17. *SN*, Feb. 15, 1969, 33.

18. Korr, *End of Baseball*, 45.

19. Marvin Miller interview, Apr. 18, 2001. Miller said he never felt any anti-Semitism from O'Malley, although that has been implied elsewhere. See Helyar, *Lords of the Realm*, 38.

20. *LAT*, Mar. 27, 1973.

21. Korr, *End of Baseball*, 48.

22. Korr, *End of Baseball*, 49.

23. B. Bavasi interview, Aug. 30, 1994. See also Korr, *End of Baseball*, 115.

24. *LAT*, Apr. 30, 1975.

25. Korr, *End of Baseball*, 148.

26. Mike Marshall, interview with the author, June 30, 2006.

27. Murray, *Jim Murray*, 56.

28. Korr, *End of Baseball*, 147.

29. *SN*, Apr. 1, 1972, 25.

30. *LAHE*, Feb. 22, 1969.

31. *LAT*, Aug. 12, 1972.

32. *SN*, Aug. 1, 1972, 26; M. Miller, *Whole Different Ball Game*, 377.

33. Marvin Miller interview, Apr. 18, 2001.

34. M. Miller, *Whole Different Ball Game*, 203.

35. Helyar, *Lords of the Realm*, 114.

36. Helyar, *Lords of the Realm*, 209. Miller identified the four as Parker, "two veteran stars who were managerial candidates," and a "utility catcher." The latter is clearly Duke Sims, waived on Aug. 4. The others could be Hoyt Wilhelm, released July 21; Maury Wills, released Oct. 24; or Jim Lefebvre, released Nov. 27.

37. *LAT*, May 15, 1970.

38. *LAT*, Apr. 29, 1972.

39. Marvin Miller interview, Apr. 18, 2001.

40. M. Miller, *Whole Different Ball Game*, 264; MacPhail, *My 9 Innings*, 163.

41. P. Bavasi interview, Nov. 15, 2001.

42. Rosenthal, *10 Best Years of Baseball*, 11.

43. Korr, *End of Baseball*, 130.

44. Marvin Miller interview, Apr. 18, 2001.

45. Marvin Miller interview, Apr. 18, 2001.

46. Helyar, *Lords of the Realm*, 105

47. Clark, *Champagne and Baloney*; Green and Launius, *Charlie Finley*; Libby, *Charlie O. and the Angry A's*; Michelson, *Charlie O.*

48. J. Hunter with Keteyian, *Catfish*, 150.

49. Ted Simmons, interview with the author, July 15, 2000.

50. *SN*, Nov. 9, 1974, 47.

51. Korr, *End of Baseball*, 141.

52. *LAT*, Jan. 14, 1975.

53. Di Salvatore, *Clever Base-Ballist*, 364–65.

54. Morris, *Game of Inches*, 185.

55. Helyar, *Lords of the Realm*, 35.

56. Claire with Springer, *Fred Claire*, 137.

57. *SN*, Dec. 16, 1972, 16.

58. Helyar, *Lords of the Realm*, 153–55.

59. *SN*, July 6, 1974, 9.

60. *LAT*, Oct. 16, 1975.

61. *LAT*, Feb. 4, Mar. 11, 1976.

62. *Chicago Sun-Times*, June 21, 1976.

63. *LAT*, Mar. 25, 1976.

64. *LAT*, Apr. 11, 1976.

65. *LAT*, June 10, 1975.

66. Marvin Miller interview, Apr. 18, 2001.

67. "Dave McNally," 764.

68. *LAT*, Oct. 16, 1975.

69. Korr, *End of Baseball*, 149.

70. Kuhn, *Hardball*, 158.

71. M. Miller, *Whole Different Ball Game*, 244.

72. M. Miller, *Whole Different Ball Game*, 252–53.

73. Mike Marshall interview, June 30, 2006.

74. Kuhn, *Hardball*, 146–50.

75. Helyar, *Lords of the Realm*, 193.

76. Kuhn, *Hardball*, 177–78.

77. Helyar, *Lords of the Realm*, 175.

78. Helyar, *Lords of the Realm*, 219.

18. BOTTOM OF THE NINTH

1. *NYT*, Feb. 15, 1958; *LAT*, Mar. 19, 1958.

2. Rickey, "Memorandum," Nov. 6, 1959, Rickey Papers.

3. *LAHE*, Sept. 20, 1962.

4. Press release from the Mayo Clinic dated Oct. 30, 1980, O'Malley file, National Baseball Hall of Fame and Museum.

5. *LAHE*, Apr. 18, 19, 20, May 3, 1964.

6. *SN*, Mar. 30, 1968, 8.

7. *LAT*, Apr. 25, 1970.

8. *LAT*, May 22, 1970.

9. *LAT*, Mar. 29, 1972.

10. O'Malley to John P. Butler, Apr. 19, 1972, O'Malley file, University of Pennsylvania Archives.

11. *LAT*, May 28, 1972.

12. Burt Williams, Memo to Record of interview with O'Malley, May 9, 1974, O'Malley file, University of Pennsylvania Archives.

13. O'Malley to E. Craig Sweeten, Oct. 21, 1974, O'Malley file, University of Pennsylvania Archives.

14. Jim McConnell, interview with the author, July 26, 2012.

15. *SN*, Sept. 10, 1977, 23.

16. *LAHE*, Feb. 7, 1978; *SN*, Feb. 18, 1978, 63.

17. *LAHE*, Feb. 24, 1978.

18. *LAHE*, Feb. 26, 1978.

19. Clip dated May 21, 1978, O'Malley file, National Baseball Hall of Fame and Museum. The paper's name was not recorded, but the story is from the Associated Press.

20. *LAT*, Mar. 26, 1978.

21. LAT, June 4, 1978.

22. *LAHE*, Sept. 28, 1978.

23. *LAHE*, Oct. 5, 1978.

24. *LAT*, Mar. 3, Apr. 5, June 13, 1979; *SN*, July 7, 1979, 36.

25. Quoted in the video *Brooklyn Dodgers*, pt. 5, "The Last Trolley."

26. *Baltimore News-American*, Aug. 10, 1979.

27. Marvin Miller interview, Apr. 18, 2001.

28. *LAT*, July 14, 1979.

29. *LAT*, Aug. 10, 1979.

30. *LAT*, Aug. 10, 1979.

31. *NYT*, Aug. 13, 1979.

32. *Binghamton Press*, Aug. 10, 1979.

33. *SN*, Aug. 25, 1979, 2.

34. *New York Post*, Aug. 10, 1979.

35. *Washington Post*, Aug. 10, 1979.

36. *SN*, Sept. 8, 1979, 4. Knight later headed the Brooklyn Dodgers Hall of Fame.

37. Quoted in the video *Brooklyn Dodgers*, pt. 5, "The Last Trolley."

19. POSTGAME

1. *New York Daily News*, Aug. 10, 1979.

2. Letters to the editor, *SN*, Sept. 8, 1979, 4.

Bibliography

ARCHIVES AND WEBSITES

Chandler, Happy. Papers. University of Kentucky Library, Lexington.

Friedrich, Robert C., comp. "History of Hollis, Borough of Queens, New York City, New York." Long Island Division of the Queens Borough Public Library, Nov. 1993. This is a packet of newspaper clippings and other materials.

Goodman, Danny. File. *Sporting News*, St. Louis MO.

Herrmann, August "Garry." Papers. National Baseball Hall of Fame and Museum, Cooperstown NY.

Los Angeles Herald Examiner. Clippings collection. Los Angeles Public Library.

Los Angeles Public Library's Local History Collection. California Vertical File.

Mann, Arthur. Papers. Manuscripts Division, Library of Congress, Washington DC.

Moses, Robert. Papers. Manuscripts and Archives Division, New York Public Library.

National Baseball Hall of Fame and Museum. Archives. Cooperstown NY.

O'Malley, Walter. File. Archives, Alumni Office, Culver Academy, Culver IN.

———. National Baseball Hall of Fame, Cooperstown NY.

———. *Sporting News*, St. Louis MO.

———. University of Pennsylvania Archives, Philadelphia.

Oral History Collection. University of Kentucky Library, Lexington.

Poulson, Norris. "Who Would Ever Have Dreamed?" Transcript in Oral History Program, University of California at Los Angeles, 1967.

Rickey, Branch. Papers. Manuscripts Division, Library of Congress, Washington DC.

Roth, Allan. Papers. Western Reserve University, Cleveland OH.

Wagner, Robert. Papers. New York City Municipal Archives.

World Series Attendance and Receipts Reports. Archives, National Baseball Hall of Fame, Cooperstown NY.

www.baseball-reference.com.

www.retrosheet.org.

www.walteromalley.com, maintained by the O'Malley family.

Addie, Bob. "Did Dodgers Lose Flag on Gridiron?" *Baseball Digest* (Nov. 1950).

Ainsworth, Ed. *Maverick Mayor: A Biography of Sam Yorty, Mayor of Los Angeles.* Garden City NY: Doubleday, 1966.

Allen, Lee. *The Giants and the Dodgers.* New York: G. P. Putnam's Sons, 1964.

Allen, Oliver E. *The Tiger: The Rise and Fall of Tammany Hall.* Reading MA: Addison-Wesley, 1993.

Alston, Walt, and Si Burick. *Alston and the Dodgers.* Garden City NY: Doubleday, 1966.

Autry, Gene, with Mickey Herskowitz. *Back in the Saddle Again.* Garden City NY: Doubleday, 1978.

Baim, Dean V. *Sports Stadiums as "Wise Investments": An Evaluation.* Chicago: Heartland Institute, 1990.

Bak, Richard. *Lou Gehrig: An American Classic.* Dallas: Taylor, 1995.

Barber, Lylah. *Lylah.* Chapel Hill NC: Algonquin Books of Chapel Hill, 1985.

Barber, Red. *The Broadcasters.* New York: Dial Press, 1970.

————. *1947: When All Hell Broke Loose in Baseball.* New York: Doubleday, 1982.

Barber, Red, and Robert Creamer. *Rhubarb in the Catbird Seat.* Garden City NY: Doubleday, 1968.

Bavasi, Buzzie, with John Strege. *Off the Record.* Chicago: Contemporary Books, 1987.

Baxter, Vern K. *Labor and Politics in the U.S. Postal Service.* New York: Plenum Press, 1994.

Benson, Michael. *Ballparks of North America.* Jefferson NC: McFarland, 1989.

Berg, A. Scott. *Goldwyn: A Biography.* New York: Alfred A. Knopf, 1989.

Berges, Marshall. "Rosalind Wyman." *Los Angeles Times Home Magazine*, Dec. 10, 1978.

Beverage, Richard. *Hollywood Stars: Baseball in Movieland, 1926–1957.* Placentia CA: Deacon Press, 1984.

Bingham, Walter. "Boom Goes Baseball." *Sports Illustrated*, Apr. 23, 1962.

Bitker, Steve. *The Original San Francisco Giants: The Giants of '58.* Champaign IL: Sports Publishing, 1998.

Bollens, John C., and Grant B. Geyer. *Yorty: The Politics of a Constant Candidate.* Pacific Palisades CA: Palisades, 1973.

Borton, Homer T. "Stadium Design Is a Challenge." *Consulting Engineer* (Aug. 1956).

Boucher, François. *20,000 Years of Fashion: The History of Costume and Personal Adornment.* New York: Harry N. Abrams, 1966.

Broeg, Bob. *Redbirds: A Century of Cardinals' Baseball.* Marceline MO: Walsworth, 1992.

"Brooklyn: Waves from Manhattan Break over City in a City." *Business Week*, Oct. 3, 1953.

Brooklyn and Los Angeles Dodger yearbooks, 1947– 2013. Author's collection.

Brooklyn and Los Angeles Dodger press and media guides, 1950–2013. Author's collection.

"Brooklyn and Queens." *Fortune,* July 1939.

The Brooklyn Dodgers: The Original America's Team. Video. Arts Alliance America, 1996.

Brown, William. *Baseball's Fabulous Montreal Royals.* Montreal: Robert Davies, 1996.

Bullock, William. "Hylan." *American Mercury,* Apr. 1924.

Burk, Robert F. *Much More than a Game: Players, Owners, and American Baseball since 1921.* Chapel Hill: University of North Carolina Press, 2001.

Burke, Michael. *Outrageous Good Fortune.* Boston: Little, Brown, 1984.

Burr, Harold C. "That Picturesque Magnate—Stephen McKeever." *Baseball Magazine,* May 1932, 303.

Butler, Jack. "Boss Man of the Brooklyn Dodgers." *New York Catholic News,* Aug. 4, 1956.

Campanella, Roy. *It's Good to Be Alive.* Boston: Little, Brown, 1959.

Cannon, Jimmy. "Jackie Robinson's Precious Gift." In *The Dodgers Reader,* edited by Dan Riley. Boston: Houghton Mifflin, 1992.

Carney, Francis. "The Decentralized Politics of Los Angeles." *Annals of the American Academy of Political and Social Science* 353 (May 1964).

Caro, Robert. *The Power Broker.* New York: Alfred A. Knopf, 1974.

Chamberlain, John. "Brains, Baseball, and Branch Rickey." *Harper's,* Apr. 1948.

Chandler, Happy, with Vance Trimble. *Heroes, Plain Folks, and Skunks: The Life and Times of Happy Chandler.* Chicago: Bonus Books, 1989.

Chandler, Happy, with John Underwood. "How I Jumped from Clean Politics into Dirty Baseball." *Sports Illustrated,* April 26 and May 3, 1971.

Claire, Fred, with Steve Springer. *Fred Claire: My 30 Years in Dodger Blue.* Champaign IL: Sports Publishing, 2004.

Clark, Tom. *Champagne and Baloney: The Rise and Fall of Finley's A's.* New York: Harper and Row, 1976.

Cohane, Tim. "The West Coast Produces Baseball's Strangest Story." *Look,* Aug. 19, 1958.

Cohen, Stanley. *Dodgers! The First 100 Years.* New York: Birch Lane Press, 1990.

Conlan, Jocko, and Robert Creamer. *Jocko.* Philadelphia: J. B. Lippincott, 1967.

Connable, Alfred, and Edward Silberfarb. *Tigers of Tammany.* New York: Holt, Rinehart, and Winston, 1967.

Cope, Myron. "How the Dodgers Are Building a Dynasty." *Sport,* July 1961.

"Corporations: Penicillin Grows in Brooklyn." *Time,* May 20, 1946.

Coughlan, Robert. "Baseball: Nine Men, a Diamond, and $10 Million." *Sports Illustrated,* Feb. 27, 1956.

Creamer, Robert. *Stengel.* New York: Simon and Schuster, 1984.

———. "The Transistor Kid." *Sports Illustrated,* May 4, 1964.

Current Biography, 1954: Who's Who in California. Los Angeles: John M. Moore, 1958.

Current Biography Yearbook. New York: H. W. Wilson, 1945.

Daley, Arthur. "Will the Dodger-Giant Gold Rush Pan Out?" *New York Times Magazine,* May 11, 1958.

D'Antonio, Michael. *Forever Blue.* New York: Riverhead Books, 2009.

"Dave McNally." In *Baseball: The Biographical Encyclopedia*. New York: Total / Sports Illustrated, 2000.

Dexter, Charles. "Brooklyn's Sturdy Branch." *Collier's*, Sept. 15, 1945.

Di Salvatore, Bryan. *A Clever Base-Ballist: The Life and Times of John Montgomery Ward*. New York: Pantheon Books, 1999.

Doig, Jameson W. *Metropolitan Transportation Politics and the New York Region*. New York: Columbia University Press, 1966.

Drebinger, John. "The Rise of Rickey." *Baseball Magazine*, Jan. 1943.

Durocher, Leo, with Ed Linn. *Nice Guys Finish Last*. New York: Simon and Schuster, 1975.

Durslag, Melvin. "The Dodgers, the Giants, and Pay-TV." *TV Guide*, Nov. 11, 1963.

———. "How to Become a Baseball Billionaire." *TV Guide*, Apr. 5, 1975, 17.

———. "A Visit with Walter O'Malley." *Saturday Evening Post*, May 14, 1960.

———. "Walt Alston . . . Manager with a Hair Shirt." *Look*, July 30, 1963.

Ebbets, Charles H. "Why I Am Building a Baseball Stadium." *Frank Leslie's Weekly*, Apr. 4, 1912.

Eisenstein, Louis, and Elliot Rosenberg. *A Stripe of Tammany's Tiger*. New York: Robert Speller and Sons, 1966.

Erie, Steven P. *Rainbow's End: Irish-Americans and the Dilemmas of Urban Machine Politics, 1840–1985*. Berkeley: University of California Press, 1988.

Erskine, Carl. *Carl Erskine's Tales from the Dodger Dugout*. Champaign IL: Sports Publishing, 2000.

Eskenazi, Gerald. *The Lip*. New York: William Morrow, 1993.

Falkner, David. *Long Time Coming: The Life of Jackie Robinson, from Baseball to Birmingham*. New York: Simon and Schuster, 1995.

Fetter, Henry D. *Taking on the Yankees: Winning and Losing in the Business of Base-'ball, 1903–2003*. New York: W. W. Norton, 2003.

Finch, Frank. *The Los Angeles Dodgers: The First Twenty Years*. Virginia Beach: Jordan, 1977.

Fitzgerald, Ed. "*Sport*'s Hall of Fame: Branch Rickey, Baseball Innovator." *Sport*, May 1962.

———, ed. *The Story of the Brooklyn Dodgers*. New York: Bantam Books, 1949.

Flaherty, Vincent X. "The Miracle Move of the Dodgers: From Flatbush to Fantasia." In *Baseball Register*. St. Louis: C. C. Spink and Sons, 1960.

Fogelson, Robert M. *The Fragmented Metropolis*. Cambridge MA: Harvard University Press, 1967.

Frommer, Harvey. *New York City Baseball: The Last Golden Age, 1947–1957*. New York: Macmillan, 1980.

———. *Rickey and Robinson*. New York: Macmillan, 1982.

Furlong, William. "An Uninvited Guest Spills Baseball's Beans." *Sports Illustrated*, Nov. 1, 1965.

Garrett, Charles. *The La Guardia Years*. New Brunswick NJ: Rutgers University Press, 1961.

Goldstein, Richard. *Superstars and Screwballs: 100 Years of Brooklyn Baseball*. New York: Dutton, 1993.

Golenbock, Peter. *Bums: An Oral History of the Brooklyn Dodgers*. New York: G. P. Putnam's Sons, 1984.

Gottlieb, Robert, and Irene Wolt. *Thinking Big: The Story of the "Los Angeles Times," Its Publishers, and Their Influence on Southern California*. New York: G. P. Putnam's Sons, 1977.

Graham, Frank. *The Brooklyn Dodgers*. New York: G. P. Putnam's Sons, 1948.

Graham, Frank, Jr. *A Farewell to Heroes*. New York: Viking Press, 1981.

Green, G. Michael, and Roger D. Launius. *Charlie Finley: The Outrageous Story of Baseball's Super Showman*. New York: Walker, 2010.

Greenberg, Hank. *The Story of My Life*. New York: Times Books, 1989.

Gross, Milton. "The Artful O'Malley and the Dodgers." *True*, May 1954.

Hamill, Pete. "Brooklyn: The Sane Alternative." *New York Magazine*, July 14, 1969.

Helyar, John. *Lords of the Realm: The Real History of Baseball*. New York: Villard Books, 1994.

Henderson, Cary S. "Los Angeles and the Dodger War, 1957–1962." *Southern California Quarterly* 42 (Fall 1980).

Hines, Thomas E. "Housing, Baseball, and Creeping Socialism: The Battle of Chavez Ravine, Los Angeles, 1949–1959." *Journal of Urban History* 8, no. 2 (1982).

Holland, Gerald. "The Great MacPhail." *Sports Illustrated*, Aug. 17, 24, 31, 1959.

———. "Mr. Rickey and the Game." *Sports Illustrated*, Mar. 7, 1955.

———. "A Visit with the Artful Dodger." *Saturday Evening Post*, July 13, 1968.

Holmes, Tommy. *Dodger Daze and Knights*. New York: David McKay, 1953.

———. *The Dodgers*. New York: Macmillan, 1975.

Holtzman, Jerome. *The Commissioners: Baseball's Midlife Crisis*. New York: Total Sports, 1998.

Homberger, Eric. *The Historical Atlas of New York City*. New York: Henry Holt, 1994.

Hunter, Jim "Catfish," with Armen Keteyian. *Catfish: My Life in Baseball*. New York: McGraw-Hill, 1988.

Hunter, Tim. *Bobbing Head Dolls, 1960–2000*. Iola WI: Krause, 1999.

Hynd, Noel. *The Giants of the Polo Grounds*. New York: Doubleday, 1988.

Jackson, Kenneth, ed. *The Encyclopedia of New York City*. New Haven CT: Yale University Press, 1995.

Johnson, William O., Jr. *Super Spectator and the Electric Lilliputians*. Boston: Little, Brown, 1971.

Kahn, Roger. *The Boys of Summer*. New York: Harper and Row, 1972.

———. "Bums' Rush Turns into a Big Bonanza." In *The "Sporting News" 1983 Baseball Yearbook*. St. Louis: Sporting News, 1983.

———. *The Era: 1947–1957, When the Yankees, the Giants, and the Dodgers Ruled the World*. New York: Ticknor and Fields, 1993.

———. "Exported to Brooklyn." *New York Herald Tribune Sunday Magazine*, Apr. 11, 1954.

———. *Games We Used to Play*. New York: Ticknor and Fields, 1992.

———. *Good Enough to Dream*. New York: Doubleday, 1985.

———. *Memories of Summer*. New York: Hyperion, 1997.

———. *October Men*. New York: Harcourt, 2003.

———. *A Season in the Sun*. New York: Harper and Row, 1977.

Kavanagh, Jack, and Norman Macht. *Uncle Robbie*. Cleveland OH: Society for American Baseball Research, 1999.

Keane, James Thomas. *Fritz B. Burns and the Development of Los Angeles*. Los Angeles: Thomas and Dorothy Leavey Center for the Study of Los Angeles and the Historical Society of Southern California, 2001.

Kelley, Brent. *Baseball's Biggest Blunder: The Bonus Rule of 1953–1957*. Lanham MD: Scarecrow Press, 1997.

Kiner, Ralph, with Joe Gergen. *Kiner's Korner: At Bat and on the Air—My 40 Years in Baseball*. New York: Arbor House, 1987.

King, Gregory. "Vin Scully: The Voice of Summer." *Lefthander Magazine* (May–June 1992).

Kingsbury: A Venture in Teamwork. New York: Todd and Brown, 1946.

Korr, Charles P. *The End of Baseball as We Knew It: The Players Union, 1960–1981*. Urbana: University of Illinois Press, 2002.

Koufax, Sandy, with Ed Linn. *Koufax*. New York: Viking Press, 1966.

Kowet, Don. "The Forty-Niner." In *The Rich Who Own Sports*. New York: Random House, 1977.

Kreuz, Jim. "Tom Greenwade and His '007' Assignment." In vol. 27 of *The National Pastime: A Review of Baseball History*. Cleveland OH: Society for American Baseball Research, 2007.

Krieg, Joann P., ed. *Robert Moses: Single Minded Genius*. Interlaken NY: Heart of the Lakes, 1989.

Kuhn, Bowie. *Hardball: The Education of a Baseball Commissioner*. New York: Times Books, 1987.

Lacy, Sam. *Fighting for Fairness: The Life Story of a Hall of Fame Sportswriter*. Centreville MD: Tidewater, 1998.

Lanctot, Neil. *Campy: The Two Lives of Roy Campanella*. New York: Simon and Schuster, 2011.

Langill, Mark. "Dodgers in a Dogfight." *Sports Illustrated*, Sept. 2, 1963.

———. *Dodger Stadium*. Charleston SC: Arcadia, 2004.

———. "The Voice of the Dodgers." In *1999 Los Angeles Dodgers Commemorative Yearbook*. Los Angeles: Los Angeles Dodgers, 1999.

Leggett, William. "Court Martial for a General." *Sports Illustrated*, Dec. 16, 1968, 24.

———. "Dodgers in a Dogfight." *Sports Illustrated*, Sept. 2, 1963.

LeRoy, Mervyn, as told to Dick Kleiner. *Mervyn LeRoy: Take One*. New York: Hawthorn Books, 1974.

Levering, Robert, and Milton Moskowitz. *The 100 Best Companies to Work for in America*. Reading MA: Addison-Wesley, 1984.

Libby, Bill. *Charlie O. and the Angry A's: The Low and Inside Story of Charlie O. Finley and Baseball's Most Colorful Team*. Garden City NY: Doubleday, 1975.

———. "O'Malley: Looking Back on the First 10." *Los Angeles Magazine*, Sept. 1967.

Lieb, Frederick G. *Baseball as I Have Known It*. New York: Coward, McCann, and Geohegan, 1977.

———. *The Boston Red Sox*. New York: G. P. Putnam's Sons, 1947.

Light, Jon. *Cultural Encyclopedia of Baseball*. Jefferson NC: McFarland, 1997.

Lowenfish, Lee. *Branch Rickey: Baseball's Ferocious Gentleman*. Lincoln: University of Nebraska Press, 2007.

———. "Two Titans and the Mystery Man: Branch Rickey, Walter O'Malley, and John L. Smith as Brooklyn Dodgers Partners, 1944–1950." In *Jackie Robinson: Race, Sports, and the American Dream*, edited by Joseph Dorinson and Joram Warmund. Armonk NY: M. E. Sharpe, 1998.

MacPhail, Lee. *My 9 Innings*. Westport CT: Meckler Books, 1989.

"Management: No Magic Wand." *Time*, Dec. 14, 1953.

Mann, Arthur. *Baseball Confidential: The Secret History of the War among Chandler, Durocher, MacPhail, and Rickey*. New York: David McKay, 1951.

———. "Baseball's Astounding Blueprint." *Sport*, Sept. 1955.

———. *Branch Rickey: American in Action*. Boston: Houghton Mifflin, 1957.

———. "The Larry MacPhail Story, Part One." *Sport*, Apr. 1956.

Mann, Jack. "The King of the Jungle." *Sports Illustrated*, Apr. 18, 1966.

Markusen, Bruce. *Roberto Clemente: The Great One*. Champaign IL: Sports Publishing, 1998.

Marshall, William. *Baseball's Pivotal Era, 1945–1951*. Lexington: University Press of Kentucky, 1999.

Martin, Pete. "Pete Martin Calls on Walter O'Malley." *Philadelphia Sunday Bulletin Magazine*, May 2, 1965.

McCue, Andy. "A Half-Century of Springs: Vero Beach and the Dodgers." In *Road Trips: A Trunkload of Great Articles from Two Decades of Convention Journals*, edited by Jim Charlton. Cleveland OH: Society for American Baseball Research, 2004.

———. "A History of Dodger Ownership." In vol. 13 of *The National Pastime: A Review of Baseball History*. Cleveland OH: Society for American Baseball Research, 1993.

———. "Open Status Delusions: The PCL Attempt to Resist Major League Baseball." *Nine: A Journal of Baseball History and Social Policy Perspectives* 5, no. 2 (1997).

McCue, Andy, and Eric Thompson. "Mis-management 101: The American League Expansion of 1961." In *The National Pastime, Endless Seasons: Baseball in Southern California*. Phoenix: Society for American Baseball Research, 2011.

McCullough, David W. *Brooklyn . . . and How It Got That Way*. New York: Doubleday, 1983.

McGee, Bob. *The Greatest Ballpark Ever: Ebbets Field and the Story of the Brooklyn Dodgers*. New Brunswick NJ: Rutgers University Press, 2005.

"Meanwhile, at Chavez Ravine." *Sport*, Aug. 1962 .

Meany, Tom. *The Artful Dodgers*. New York: A. S. Barnes, 1953.

———. "Baseball's Answer to TV." *Collier's*, Sept. 27, 1952.

———. *The Magnificent Yankees*. New York: Grosset and Dunlap, 1957.

Mehl, Ernest. *The Kansas City Athletics*. New York: Henry Holt, 1956.

Merwin, John. "The Most Valuable Executive in Either League." *Forbes*, Apr. 12, 1982.

Michelson, Herb. *Charlie O*. Indianapolis: Bobbs-Merrill, 1975.

Miller, Kerby A. *Emigrants and Exiles: Ireland and the Irish Exodus to North America*. New York: Oxford University Press, 1985.

Miller, Marvin. *A Whole Different Ball Game: The Sport and Business of Baseball*. New York: Birch Lane Press, 1991.

Mines, Samuel. *Pfizer: An Informal History*. New York: Pfizer, 1979.

Morris, Peter. *A Game of Inches: The Game behind the Scenes*. Chicago: Ivan R. Dee, 2006.

Moscow, Warren. *What Have You Done for Me Lately? The Ins and Outs of New York Politics*. Englewood Cliffs NJ: Prentice Hall, 1967.

Murray, Jim. *Jim Murray: The Autobiography of the Pulitzer Prize Winning Sports Columnist*. New York: Macmillan, 1993.

———. "The $3,300,000 Smile." *Sports Illustrated*, Feb. 29, 1960.

Nadeau, Remi. *Los Angeles: From Mission to Modern City*. New York: Longmans, Green, 1960.

Newhan, Ross. *The Anaheim Angels: A Complete History*. New York: Hyperion, 2000.

New York State Joint Legislative Committee to Investigate the Affairs of the City of New York, 1921–1922. Albany: J. B. Lyon, 1922.

Normark, Don. *Chavez Ravine, 1949*. San Francisco: Chronicle Books, 1999.

"Now McClellan Heads NAM." *Business Week*, Dec. 5, 1953.

Oates, Bob. "A Visit with Walter O'Malley." *Baseball Digest* (May 1969).

Obojski, Robert. *The Rise of Japanese Baseball Power*. Radnor PA: Chilton Book, 1975.

Okkonen, Marc. *Baseball Uniforms of the 20th Century*. New York: Sterling, 1991.

Oliphant. Thomas. *Praying for Gil Hodges: A Memoir of the 1955 World Series and One Family's Love of the Brooklyn Dodgers*. New York: St. Martin's Press, 2005.

"O'Malley, Walter." In *Who's Who in America, 1954–55*. Chicago: A. N. Marquis, 1955.

"O'Malley's Alley." *Dodgers 1952 Yearbook*. Brooklyn: Brooklyn Dodgers, 1952.

O'Toole, Andrew. *Branch Rickey in Pittsburgh*. Jefferson NC: McFarland, 2000.

Parrott, Harold. *The Lords of Baseball*. New York: Praeger, 1976.

Peterson, Harold. *The Man Who Invented Baseball*. New York: Charles Scribner's Sons, 1973.

Plaut, David. *Chasing October: The Dodgers-Giants Pennant Race of 1962*. South Bend IN: Diamond, 1994.

Polner, Murray. *Branch Rickey: A Biography*. New York: Atheneum, 1982.

Poulson, Norris. "The Untold Story of Chavez Ravine." *Los Angeles Magazine*, Apr. 1962.

Powers, Jimmy. "Don't Get Me Wrong: I LOVE Branch Rickey." *Sport Magazine*, Dec. 1948.

Praeger, Joshua. *The Echoing Green: The Untold Story of Bobby Thomson, Ralph Branca, and the Shot Heard 'round the World*. New York: Pantheon Books, 2006.

Rampersad, Arnold. *Jackie Robinson: A Biography*. New York: Alfred A. Knopf, 1997.

Ray, Edgar W. *The Grand Huckster: Houston's Judge Roy Hofheinz, Genius of the Astrodome*. Memphis TN: Memphis State University Press, 1980.

Rice, Robert. "Profiles: Thoughts on Baseball." Pts. 1 and 2. *New Yorker*, May 27, 1950; June 30, 1950.

Riess, Steven A. *City Games: The Evolution of American Urban Society and the Rise of Sports*. Urbana: University of Illinois Press, 1989.

Ritter, Lawrence. *Lost Ballparks*. New York: Viking, 1992.

Robinson, Jackie. *Baseball Has Done It*. Edited by Charles Dexter. Philadelphia: J. B. Lippincott, 1964.

Robinson, Ray. *The Home Run Heard 'round the World: The Dramatic Story of the 1951 Giants-Dodgers Pennant Race*. New York: HarperCollins, 1991.

Rodengen, Jeffrey L. *The Legend of Pfizer*. Fort Lauderdale FL: Write Stuff Syndicate, 1999.

Roseboro, John, with Bill Libby. *Glory Days with the Dodgers and Other Days with Others*. New York: Atheneum, 1978.

Rosenfeld, Harvey. *The Great Chase: The Dodgers-Giants Pennant Race of 1951*. Jefferson NC: McFarland, 1992.

Rosenthal, Harold. *The 10 Best Years of Baseball: An Informal History of the Fifties*. Chicago: Contemporary Books, 1979.

Rowan, Carl T., with Jackie Robinson. *Wait till Next Year: The Story of Jackie Robinson*. New York: Random House, 1960.

Rubin, James. "The Brooklyn Dodgers and Ebbets Field: Their Departure." In *Brooklyn USA: The Fourth Largest City in America*, edited by Ruth Seiden Miller. New York: Brooklyn College Press, 1979.

Rudd, Irving, and Stan Fischler. *The Sporting Life: The Duke and Jackie, Pee Wee, Razor Phil, Ali, Mushky Jackson, and Me*. New York: St. Martin's Press, 1990.

Sanders, Charles J. "In Search of the Great American Baseball Dream." *Baseball Digest* (Feb. 1985).

Sands, Jack, and Peter Gammons. *Coming Apart at the Seams: How Baseball Owners, Players, and Television Executives Have Led Our National Pastime to the Brink of Disaster*. New York: Macmillan, 1993.

Schroth, Raymond A., SJ. *The "Eagle" and Brooklyn: A Community Newspaper, 1841–1955*. Westport CT: Greenwood Press, 1974.

Shapiro, Michael. *Bottom of the Ninth*. New York: Times Books, 2009.

————. *The Last Good Season: Brooklyn, the Dodgers, and Their Final Pennant Race Together*. New York: Bantam Doubleday Dell, 2003.

Shaplen, Robert. "O'Malley and the Angels." *Sports Illustrated*, Mar. 24, 1958.

Sheed, Wilfrid. "The Field, the Fans, and the Bums." *Brooklyn Bridge*, Sept. 1, 1995.

Silber, Irwin. *Press Box Red: The Story of Lester Rodney, the Communist Who Helped Break the Color Line*. Philadelphia: Temple University Press, 2003.

Slayton, Robert A. *Empire Statesman: The Rise and Redemption of Al Smith*. New York: Free Press, 2001.

Smith, Curt. *The Storytellers*. New York: Macmillan, 1995.

Smith, Red. "O'Malley in a Manger." In *The Best of Red Smith*. New York: Franklin Watts, 1963.

Snider, Duke, with Bill Gilbert. *The Duke of Flatbush*. New York: Kensington, 1988.

Snyder, Flo Thomasian. *Lady in the Locker Room: Madcap Memories of the Early L.A. Dodgers*. Palm Springs CA: Desert, 2008.

Solomon, Burt. *Where They Ain't*. New York: Free Press, 1999.

"Some Enduring Impressions of Pfizer Leadership." *Pfizer Scene* (Feb. 1962): 11–15.

Spero, Sterling Denhard. *The Labor Movement in a Government Industry*. New York: Macmillan, 1927.

Sporting News Baseball Guides, Dope Books, and *Registers*, 1941–79. The *Guides* and *Registers* came out annually during those years. The *Dope Books* appeared most years.

Stengel, Casey, as told to Harry T. Paxton. *Casey at the Bat: The Story of My Life*. New York: Random House, 1962.

Stephan, David. "Allan Roth's True Discovery of Sabermetrics Revealed." In *Grandstand Baseball Annual, 1994*, edited by Joseph Wayman. Downey CA: Joseph N. Wayman, 1994.

Sullivan, Neil. *The Dodgers Move West*. New York: Oxford University Press, 1987.

Taylor, Robert Lewis. "Borough Defender." *New Yorker*, July 12, 1941.

Terrell, Roy. "The Damndest Mess Baseball Has Ever Seen." *Sports Illustrated*, Dec. 19, 1960.

————. "Every Sixth Hit a Homer!" *Sports Illustrated*, May 5, 1958.

Thompson, Fresco, with Cy Rice. *Every Diamond Doesn't Sparkle: Behind the Scenes with the Dodgers*. New York: David McKay, 1964.

Thornley, Stew. "Clemente's Entry into Organized Baseball: Hidden in Montreal?" In vol. 26 of *The National Pastime: A Review of Baseball History*. Cleveland OH: Society for American Baseball Research, 2006.

Tygiel, Jules. *Baseball's Great Experiment: Jackie Robinson and His Legacy*. New York: Oxford University Press, 1983.

Veeck, Bill. "The Baseball Establishment." *Esquire*, Aug. 1964.

Veeck, Bill, with Ed Linn. *The Huster's Handbook*. New York: G. P. Putnam's, 1965.

————. *Veeck—as in Wreck*. New York: G. P. Putnam's, 1962.

————. "Walter O'Malley: Boss of Baseball." *Look*, July 3, 1962.

Voigt, David Quentin. *American Baseball*. Vol. 3, *From Postwar Expansion to the Electronic Age*. University Park: Pennsylvania State University Press, 1983.

———. "They Shaped the Game: Nine Innovators of Major League Baseball." *Baseball History* (Spring 1986).

Wagenheim, Kal. *Clemente!* New York: Praeger, 1973.

Walker, James R., and Robert V. Bellamy Jr. *Center Field Shot: A History of Baseball on Television*. Lincoln: University of Nebraska Press, 2008.

Walsh, John, and Garth Magnum. *Labor Struggle in the Post Office*. Armonk NY: M. E. Sharpe, 1992.

"Walter in Wonderland." *Time*, Apr. 28, 1958.

Warfield, Don. *The Roaring Redhead: Larry MacPhail, Baseball's Great Innovator*. South Bend IN: Diamond, 1987.

Weber, Msgr. Francis J. *His Eminence of Los Angeles: James Francis Cardinal McIntyre*. 2 vols. Mission Hills CA: St. Francis Historical Society, 1997.

Weiss, Nancy Joan. *Charles Francis Murphy, 1858–1924: Respectability and Responsibility in Tammany Politics*. Northampton MA: Smith College, 1968.

Werner, M. R. *Tammany Hall*. New York: Doubleday, Doran, 1928.

Westcott, Rich. "Carl Furillo: The Man with the Golden Arm." In *Diamond Greats*. Westport CT: Meckler Books, 1988.

Willensky, Elliot. *When Brooklyn Was the World, 1920–1957*. New York: Harmony Books, 1986.

Wolpin, Stewart. *Bums No More! The Championship Season of the 1955 Brooklyn Dodgers*. New York: St. Martin's Press, 1995.

Woodward, Stanley. "In the Rickey Manner." *Baseball Digest* (July 1950).

Young, Dick. "Dick Young, Baseball Writer, *Daily News*, New York." In *Baseball Is Their Business*, edited by Harold Rosenthal. New York: Random House, 1952.

———. "Rickey's Tee Party." *Baseball Digest* (June 1948).

Zeckendorf, William, with Edward McCreary. *Zeckendorf: The Autobiography of William Zeckendorf*. New York: Holt, Rinehart, and Winston, 1970.

Ziff, Sid. "Relates Colorful Past of Wrigley Field Baseball." *Los Angeles Major League Baseball News*, Apr. 30, 1961.

Index

Mayer, Louis, 142

Mayo, County (Ireland), 1

Mayo Clinic (Rochester MN), 342, 351, 352, 354

Mays, Willie, 165

McClellan, Chad, 151–52, 153, 199, 208, 253, 271, 280–81

McConnell, Jim, 352

McDonald, Eugene, 126

McGee, Patrick, 198, 204, 207, 213, 406n66, 418n122

McGowen, Roscoe, 113, 114, 140

McGrew, Ted, 37

McHale, John, 304, 346

McIntyre, James Francis, 248–49, 272, 333–34

McKeen, John, 49, 51

McKeever, Ed, 28–29, 29–30, 369n18

McKeever, Steve, 28–29, 30, 32, 103, 369n18

McKeever heirs (stock shares), 30, 31, 33, 36–37, 43, 45, 47–48, 103, 388n148

McKinley, Maytor H., 206

McLaughlin, George V., 122, 150; McKeever shares role, 103, 104, 388n148; O'Malley and, 21–23, 25, 65, 129, 132, 136, 158; role in Dodgers franchise, 33, 37, 43–44, 45, 47, 52, 57

McLaughlin, Hugh, 29

McNally, Dave, 346

Meany, Tom, 65, 98, 105, 182

Medwick, Joe, 238

Melchior, Lauritz, 330

Messersmith, Andy, 345–47, 346–47

Mexican League, 58–59, 64

Meyer, Dick, 303

Meyer, Max, 45, 103, 371n8

Miami (FL) spring training, 100

Michael, Gene, 323

Miller, Marvin, xiii, xv, 322, 337–40, 341–47, 349–50, 353, 434n19

Minor Leagues, 40, 286, 296–98. *See also* farm clubs

Mitchel, John Purroy, 9, 130

MLB (Major League Baseball). *See* Major League Baseball (MLB)

Monday, Rick, 294

Montreal farm club, 70, 84, 89

Moon, Wally, 242, 245, 278

Moore, Davey, 319

Moore, Richard, 210

mortgage bond legislation, 21, 367n116, 367n118

Moscow, Warren, 131–32

Moses, Robert, 22, 129–40, 146–47, 156, 158, 225, 287, 395n63

Moskowitz, Belle, 22, 130

Mota, Manny, 324

Mullin, Willard, 190

Mulvey, James A. "Jim," 31–33, 36–37, 41, 45, 47, 79, 102–5, 112, 117, 140, 250, 330

Mulvey, Marie "Dearie" (née McKeever), 31, 37, 45, 47, 79, 102–5, 117, 250

Mungo, Van Lingle, 103

Murphy, Charles Francis, 9, 10

Murphy, Frank, 61, 63

Murray, Jim, 76, 108, 144, 221, 224, 238, 261, 273–74, 325–26, 340, 354

Murtaugh, Danny, 222

Musial, Stan, 240

Music Appreciation Night, 92, 384n52

Mylod, Charles, 395n63

National Baseball Day, 115, 391n239

National League (NL): Brooklyn Dodgers in, 26; council, 97, 284, 422n8; Dodger ownership issues, 31; expansion, 286–87, 288–93, 300–303; O'Malley's role in, 298–99; West Coast expansion approval, 150

NBC network, 55, 297–98

Neal, Charlie, 242, 244

Netherlands Plaza Hotel (Cincinnati), 93

Neutra, Richard, 191–92

Raft, George, 60, 239

Rampersad, Arnold, 94

Ramsey, John, 232

Reagan, Nancy (née Davis), 250

Reagan, Ronald, 193, 210, 240, 250

recreational facility (Dodger Stadium), 148, 153, 254, 280

Reds (Cincinnati), 34, 273, 412n131

Redwine, Kent, 164

Reese, Pee Wee, 106, 107, 111, 214, 242, 379n4, 389n204

Reeves, John, 85

referendums (Los Angeles), 195, 199–200, 204–13

Reichardt, Rick, 344

Reisman, Larry, 324

reporters: in Los Angeles, 163, 198, 210–11; in New York, 136–37, 138, 146, 159–60, 221–24, 395n50; O'Malley and, 90–91, 102, 315–16

reserve clause, 58–59, 64, 322, 342–47

Reuben, Julius, 225–26, 227–28

Reynolds, Allie, 335–36

Reynolds, Bob, 271, 292, 316–17

Reynolds, Debbie, 210

Richards, Paul, 338

Richardson, Charles M., 138

Richman, Milt, 303, 304

Rickenbacker, Eddie, 116

Rickey, Elizabeth, 69

Rickey, Jane (née Moulton), 38, 39, 75, 82

Rickey, Wesley Branch: baseball innovations, 40–41, 371n73; on bonuses, 294; as Cardinals' manager, 39–41; characteristics, 37–38; Continental League work, 287–89, 288, 289, 290; contract with Dodgers, 74–75, 379n1, 379n4, 380n8, 381n52; criticism of, 65, 87, 376n109; on Dick Walsh, 261; as Dodgers' general manager, 41–42, 43–44, 53–54, 98–99; Durocher situation, 60–64, 378n158; early years, 38–39; financial situation, 381n31;

integration and, 57–58, 92, 94, 385n60; leaving the Dodgers, 77–83, 85–86; on Los Angeles' welcome, 163; MacPhail and, 33, 34, 36, 369n39; management style, 75, 76, 378n159; on O'Malley, 25, 42, 248, 351; owners partnership (Smith-O'Malley), 44–48, 67–73, 76–77, 378n156, 387n112; with the Pirates, 111, 112; relationship with Parrott, 182–83

Rickey, Wesley Branch, Jr., 85, 182

Riley Drilling Company, 18

Rin-Tin-Tin (canine TV star), 172

Rivera, Jim, 245

road issues (Los Angeles), 148, 266–67, 268–69

Roberts, Clete, 235

Robinson, Earl, 323

Robinson, Edward G., 215

Robinson, Jackie, 98; birthplace, 170; integration, 57, 61, 82, 89; racism, 70, 385n60; radio program, 106; relationship with O'Malley, 92–95; relationship with Rickey, 38

Robinson, Rachel, 94, 95

Robinson, Wilbert, 30, 31

Rockefeller, Nelson, 38, 152–53

Roebuck, Ed, 216

Roettger, Harold, 85

Rogers, Buddy, 197

Room 40 (Dodger Stadium), 308–9

Rooney, John, 158

Rooney, Mickey, 311

Roosevelt, Eleanor, 202

Roosevelt Stadium (NJ), 137

Roseboro, John, 242, 243

Rose Bowl stadium (Pasadena), 169–71, 172, 173–75

Rosenthal, Harold, 76, 81, 121, 122, 342

roster limits, 111–12, 293

Roth, Allan, 40, 85, 86, 91, 109, 115, 188–89, 209, 315–16, 379n4

Rothschild, Walter, 136

Yankee Stadium, 121, 159, 189
Yawkey, Tom, 44, 124, 386n93
yearbooks, 91
Yorty, Sam, 225, 267, 270, 271, 282, 418n122
Young, Arthur, 99
Young, Dick: 1963 World Series prediction, 307–8; on baseball owners, 304; on Bavasi, 88; on Dodgers' move, 140, 145, 154, 215; on Kay O'Malley, 333; on O'Malley, 94, 122, 156, 159, 226, 251, 354, 356–57; Rickey's stock, 80; on Shotton, 87; writing style, 223–24

Young, Jack, 268–69
"Young Turks," 303
Yurkovsky, Michael, 54, 77

Zeckendorf, William, 78, 79, 80, 135, 381n40, 382n55
Ziff, Sid, 95, 259, 272, 275–76, 277
Zimmer, Don, 171, 185, 242, 337
Zimmerman, Paul, 164, 198